FOURTH EDITION

In Search of Ourselves

An Introduction to Physical Anthropology

Frank E. Poirier
Ohio State University

William A. Stini
University of Arizona

Kathy B. Wreden
University of Arizona

Prentice Hall, Englewood Cliffs, New Jersey 07632

Library of Congress Cataloging-in-Publication Data

Poirier, Frank E.
    In search of ourselves : an introduction to physical anthropology
    Frank E. Poirier, Kathy B. Wreden, Univ. of Arizona. -- 4th ed.
        p.   cm.
    Includes bibliographies and index.
    ISBN 0-13-455783-2
    1. Physical anthropology.   I. Stini, William A.   II. Wreden,
Kathy B.   III. Title.
    GN60.P64   1990
    573--dc19   88-37569
                                                                    CIP

Editorial/production supervision: Marina Harrison
Cover design: Linda J. Den Heyer Rosa
Manufacturing buyer: Ed O'Dougherty

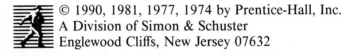
Printed in the United States of America
10 9 8 7 6 5 4 3 2 1

ISBN 0-13-455783-2

Prentice-Hall International (UK) Limited, *London*
Prentice-Hall of Australia Pty. Limited, *Sydney*
Prentice-Hall Canada Inc., *Toronto*
Prentice-Hall Hispanoamericana, S.A., *Mexico*
Prentice-Hall of India Private Limited, *New Delhi*
Prentice-Hall of Japan, Inc., *Tokyo*
Simon & Schuster Asia Pte. Ltd., *Singapore*
Editora Prentice-Hall do Brasil, Ltda., *Rio de Janeiro*

Contents

7 *Population Biology in Evolutionary Perspective*   97

8 *The Behavior of Prosimians and Monkeys*   114

13   *The Fossilization Process and Dating Methods*   227

14   *Early Primate Evolution*   239

21   *The Appearance of Homo Sapiens Sapiens*   405

22   *Human Growth and Development*   430

23 *The Biology of Human Diversity*   458

24 *How Biological Anthropologists Measure Human Variation*   478

25 *Human Skin: The First Line of Defense*   495

26 *Ancient Enemies: Disease and the Immune System*   514

27 *High Altitude Adaptation: An Example of Strong and Persistent Stress*   537

Preface

The first edition of this book appeared in 1974. Somewhat analagous to a living organism, this book has undergone a number of changes in an attempt to stay abreast of modern developments and continuing discoveries. This is the first edition of *In Search of Ourselves* with the publishing firm of Prentice Hall. This is the also the first edition to feature two new co-authors, Dr. W. Stini and K. Wreden. Their work includes the chapters on genetics and human biology.

This book is about human life: its past and present conditions. The book was written for the instructor and the student who have an interest in understanding how biology and culture interface. Human evolution results from a reciprocal relationship between biology and culture. What follows is a biological explanation of how humanity came to inhabit this Earth and why humanity is represented today in a diversity of sizes, shapes and pigments. Our perspective on human development is the scientific perspective, whose theoretical framework is evolutionary biology. We will discuss the basic principles of evolutionary theory and the biological relationship that humans share with other members of the Animal Kingdom. We will demonstrate that humans have, for survival, evolved a biocultural existence without direct parallels in the animal world. By understanding this fact, we can easily see that our existence as humans has been biotic, social, psychological and cultural.

An unhealthy intellectual arrogance has been created by our scientific successes, our ability to conquer many diseases and many natural frontiers—including that of outer space. Although humans are subjected to the same biological laws as any other living creature, humans alone have the ability to destroy life on this planet and to destroy the planet itself. A better understanding of the processes that led to our appearance, perhaps as early as six million years, and our continued survival, can help to replace some of this arrogance and lead to a greater appreciation of the fragility of human survival. How we exploit the planet Earth will determine whether we, the other animals and the plants, and the planet Earth, itself, will survive. We need to attain a new humility based on an expanding knowledge of the complexity of life, of which we are but one small part.

Kierkegaard once stated that life can only be understood backward, but that it must be lived forward. However, life can only be lived forward with knowledge and an appreciation of our past and present conditions. The late biologist Thomas Henry Huxley noted that "The question of all questions for mankind—the problem which underlies all others and which is more deeply interesting than any other—is the ascertainment of the place Man occupies in nature and his relations to the universe of things."

The biological experiment that humans represent is one in which the ability to adapt has continually expanded until it has become our principle adaptation. As the first and only known species that is conscious of its own evolution and in certain respects, influential in its ongoing nature, we occupy a unique position among the millions of species that have inhabited Planet Earth. Understanding the processes of evolution required many years of observation and experimentation that necessarily was based on the simplest and most straight-forward examples. In order to develop a genetical theory of evolution, it was essential to isolate certain traits determined by single genetic loci in relatively simple organisms through observation, experimental manipulation and mathematical modelling. It then became possible to test the validity of hypotheses concerning the path by which gene frequencies will change under the circumstances of selection, migration, mutation and random genetic drift. The simplified models that were used to gain an understanding of how evolution worked were very useful and often served to identify more sophisticated questions. The explosion of knowledge bearing on the molecular basis of inheritance has led to greater emphasis on the minutiae of these processes and has forced acknowledgment of the complexity of the mechanisms underlying evolutionary change. While the first half of the twentieth century was marked by an increased understanding of the rules of inheritance and evolutionary change, the second half of this century has been a time of increasing attention to the *exceptions* to those rules. Because of this shift of emphasis, the uniqueness of human biology is becoming especially significant, not only for what it reveals about ourselves, but also for what it can tell us about the fundamental characteristics of biological evolution.

Evolution is a process that reflects the interplay between the genetic determinants of a species' characteristics and the environment to which the species must adapt. Because humans have increasingly gained control over large segments of their environment, we have in many respects become a self-domesticated species. The corollary of self-domestication is that we have increasingly influenced our own evolution. By relaxing the constraints of natural selection through the development of culture, humans have been able to preserve aspects of variation that might otherwise have been lost. By increasing the world's human population to more than 5 billion, we have been able to maintain ever more variability. By controlling reproduction to conform to societal norms, we have unconsciously imposed selective pressures largely independent of environmental ones.

As the subtlety and complexity of the molecular bases of evolution and adaptation become better understood, the challenging problems presented by the unique pattern of adaptation characterizing humans will become increasingly relevant. Therefore, we think that the coming decades will be a time of ever increasing interest in the origins and adaptations of our species. This book is an effort to integrate the historical and processual approaches to human evolution in a manner appropriate to form the background for exploration of the questions that will engage biological and social scientists into the 21st century.

Many new ideas were taken into consideration to produce this new edition. User suggestions based on previously published editions inspired rewriting and reorganization. The continuing explosion of knowledge in anthropology and related fields makes it virtually impossible for one author to adequately synthesize all the new information. The knowledge explosion in such disciplines as genetics, molecular genetics and biotechnology has had an enormous impact on our understanding of ourselves. We have a clearer understanding of our genetic makeup, for example. Technological breakthroughs in many areas have had an impact upon physical anthropology and other branches of evolutionary biology. This is very noticeable, for example, in a clearer understanding of our evolutionary relationship to the other primates, especially the great apes.

Discoveries of human fossil remains from Africa, Asia, Europe and elsewhere continue to fascinate the scientist and lay person alike. New discoveries necessitate a fresh look at previous interpretations. The fossil record is like an iceberg, all we see is the tip and there is so much yet below the surface. Paleoanthropology is a vibrant field that is continually adjusting, reassessing and fine-tuning its theories. The process is never ending. It is highly unlikely that the major current theories concerning human evolution will need to be totally altered. However, there is a continual need, necessitated by new fossil discoveries and supported by new technologies, to reanalyze previously-discovered specimens and to reassess previously-analyzed data. Some individuals may find this rather frustrating; however, the true strength of the scientific endeavor is that it allows alteration or rejection of theories if new information requires that such be done.

Users of previous editions of this book will recognize many changes. For example, a considerable amount of rewriting and reorganization reflects the current state of knowledge in human biology. The objective of this edition is the same as the three previous editions, that is, to provide a comprehensive review of human evolution and diversity for students with little or no background in anthropology or biology. The attempt to integrate biology, behavior, and culture is of key importance as we look at human evolution, nonhuman primate behavor, and human diversity. We hope that the readers will enjoy this introduction to physical anthropology as much as we have enjoyed writing it.

A number of features in this book enhance its readability and usability for students. For example, we have incorporated a diversity of viewpoints. In such a dynamic research field as human biology there is room for a diversity of opinion. In a true learning situation, students should be helped to form their own opinions based on the current evidence. We hope enough evidence for major conflicting viewpoints has been presented for students to begin this process.

Other features of this book which will enhance learning include extensive bibliographies for each chapter, separate introductions and conclusions for each chapter, boldfacing important words and concepts when they are first introduced and defining these terms in an extensive glossary, the judicious use

Acknowledgments

Few people can write a book or teach a course without the help of others. We wish to acknowledge the help of those many undergraduate students and graduate teaching assistants who, during our combined years of teaching, have taken the time and effort to comment on our teaching and to provide constructive criticism. We are grateful to the adopters of previous editions as well as the reviewers of the drafts of the present edition for their insightful comments and suggestions.

An author's family is always involved, directly or indirectly, in the writing of a book. Sincere thanks are due to Darlene, Alyson and Sevanne Poirier for their understanding and to Ruth Stini for her continuing encouragement.

As is perhaps true of many who have researched a topic for many years and who have had the good fortune of being able to present this research to interested audiences, it soon becomes difficult to differentiate your own ideas from those which you have read and which rightfully belong to others. The task of the synthesizer, to take the ideas which many have labored to produce and attempt and to put them into some comprehensive format, is a fascinating challenge. If we have succeeded in doing this, our debt lies with so many who have worked hard to produce the original ideas and data. We trust that we have repaid our debt for many enjoyable hours by acknowledging these sources. If we have erred even once in this process, we hope we may be forgiven by the researcher whose work is discussed. We have always tried to acknowledge our debt to the research of others. To paraphrase a line from Tennyson's *Ulysses:* This work is part of all we have read, of all those we have had the good fortune of knowing, and of all we have been privileged to see.

We wish to thank Ms. Nancy Roberts, Ms. Marina Harrison and Mr. Robert Thorenson of Prentice Hall for their help and patience.

F.E. Poirier, Columbus, Ohio.
W.A. Stini, Tucson, Arizona
K.B. Wreden, Tucson, Arizona

The Nature of Physical Anthropology

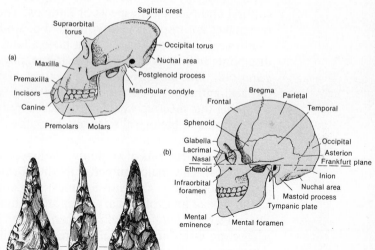

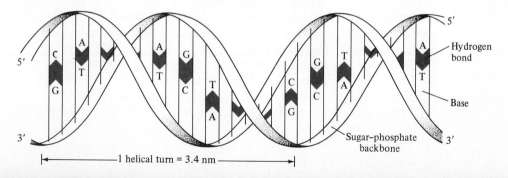

DNA DOUBLE HELIX

1 helical turn = 3.4 nm

An anthropologist is a student of humans. The discipline of anthropology is concerned with all aspects of the human endeavor: social behavior and organization, technology, and our evolutionary past. Anthropology is one of the few remaining holistic disciplines. Some disciplines study one aspect of the human condition, such as economics or religion, but anthropology considers the findings of all research that pertain to humans specifically and to primates generally.

Anthropologists who study human cultures are usually called *cultural* (or *sociocultural* or *social*) *anthropologists.* Anthropologists who study the technological remnants (the artifacts, or objects, made or modified by humans) of past cultures are called *archaeologists,* or *prehistorians.* Anthropologists who study human biological variation and primate evolution are *physical* (or *biological*) anthropologists. This book deals with the research of the latter.

Researchers in all the anthropological subfields agree that culture is the unifying concept of anthropology. As will be noted when we discuss the fossil evidence for human evolution, biology and culture have been intertwined for at least 2 million years. Humans are unique animals who have a culture, so anthropologists must realize the importance of understanding both the cultural and biological aspects of humans. The biocultural research perspective makes anthropology a unique field of study.

Physical anthropology does not have a long history as a separate scientific discipline. In fact, as a separate discipline, physical anthropology is about 100 years old. The first professional meeting of researchers calling themselves physical anthropologists was held in 1930. Even at this time, however, most attending this meeting were anatomists. Physical anthropology's roots are in the natural and biological sciences. Therefore, one finds physical anthropologists teaching and conducting research not only in departments of anthropology, but in departments of anatomy, zoology, biology, and other closely related disciplines. The major impetus to the formation of the field of physical anthropology, as is the case for most fields of biological research, was the acceptance of an evolutionary perspective, first presented in modern form in Darwin's book *On the Origin of Species* (see Chapter 2).

Twentieth-century physical anthropology underwent two distinct phases of development, distinguished by their outlook, technique, and subject matter. From the late 1800s until approximately 1950, physical anthropology was dominated by a concern with measuring and describing the form of the human body. The major endeavors fell into two large categories called **osteometry** (measurement of bone) and **anthropometry** (comparison of human body measurements). While both concerns are still pursued by modern physical anthropologists, today's researchers are more concerned with the functional meaning of such measurements.

Formation of racial taxonomies was a second major focus of early twentieth-century physical anthropologists (Stockings, 1988). Living populations were placed into any one of a number (varying from five to many) of so-called racial types. Many early attempts at classifying human populations were blatantly racist and supported the status quo, colonialism, and restrictive immigration. Early attempts at establishing racial typologies proceeded without any genetic foundation, and much of this so-called scientific research and its resultant data, which causes many modern physical anthropologists great embarassment, has been disavowed.

A number of factors led to the development of modern physical anthropology, the inception of which was approximately in the year 1950. In 1951, Dr. S. L. Washburn delivered a speech titled "The New Physical Anthropology," which provided a major catalyst for change. Washburn suggested a realignment of priorities. He suggested more field work and a more experimental research approach grounded in evolutionary theory. Beginning in the 1950s, physical anthropology metamorphosed from a collecting to an experimental stage. Much of the "new" physical anthropology is a new approach to evolutionary studies. This process was greatly assisted by the assimilation of data and theory from population genetics, by new geological dating techniques, and by computerization of data for easy, rapid access, among other developments.

Although very important human fossil remains were recovered prior to 1940, few such remains were accepted as evidence of human ancestors. A major advance in the recovery and description of the fossil evidence for human evolution began in the late 1950s (see Chapters 17–21). Fossil evidence, comparative anatomy, and comparative genetic studies upheld the view that humans are closely related to the Old World primates and most closely related to the chimpanzees (see Chapter 12). A third area of major concern to the modern physical anthropologist is understanding the origins and significance of modern human diversity. As we will discuss in Chapters 23–27, physical anthropologists have spent considerable time and effort identifying the components of human diversity and trying to understand the evolutionary significance of this diversity. A fourth area of concern for physical anthropologists is the comparative study of the behavior of the other primates, notably the monkeys and apes. Because humans are primates, we can learn a good deal about ourselves today as well as about our evolutionary past by studying monkeys and apes (see Chapters 8 and 9).

Modern physical anthropology is concerned with both applied and theoretical interests. This book deals more with the theoretical interests of physical anthropology—for example, primate evolution, human biological diversity, and primate behavior. However, applied interests are also addressed in such topics as nutrition and human ecology. In the larger sense, most physical anthropological research can be called applied. For example, understanding how monkeys and apes react in certain situations may help us understand how humans would react in similar situations. An understanding of how or why certain early members of the human family became extinct has implications for modern society. If it is true that we learn from the past, or that the present and future are only comprehensible in the context of the past, then much of physical anthropological research is applicable to modern problems. The simple knowledge that all humanity traces its roots back to Africa about 5 or 6 million years ago argues strongly for the proposition that all modern human populations share a long and common evolutionary heritage. Accepting this fact could help remove some prejudices in today's world. At the very least, it should make us wonder why more effort does not go into documenting similarities among humans from different parts of the world.

Research in physical anthropology requires a background in a number of related sciences, such as biology, genetics, geology, paleontology, chemistry, zoology, physiology, anatomy, and psychology. Physical anthropology is partially a composite of these sciences; it is a research area that attracts all those interested in human evolution. To illustrate this point, let us look at the kinds of knowledge required to conduct research on some of the topics discussed in this book. Although incomplete, this list is illustrative of the breadth of interest of physical anthropology. To conduct research in primate behavior, the investigator must know not only about primates and their behavior, but also about botany and the principles of ecology and comparative behavior. The paleoanthropologist, the researcher who studies primate fossils, needs a knowledge of paleontology, geology, and comparative anatomy, among other subjects. Research on human variability requires knowledge of population genetics, ecology, nutrition, and physiology.

BIBLIOGRAPHY

CLARK, W. L. 1958. Reorientations in physical anthropology. In *The Scope of Physical Anthropology and Its Place in Academic Studies,* D. Roberts and F. Weiner, eds., pp. 1–6. Oxford: Church Army Press.

SLOTKIN, J. 1965. *Readings in Early Anthropology.* New York: Wenner-Gren Foundation.

SPENCER, F., ed. 1986. *Ecce Homo: An Annotate Bibliographic History of Physical Anthropology.* Westport, Conn.: Greenwood Press.

STOCKINGS, B., ed. 1988. *Bones, Bodies, Behavior.* Madison, Wis.: University of Wisconsin Press.

WASHBURN, S. 1951. The new physical anthropology. *Transactions of New York Academy of Science* 13: 298.

Chapter

2

Explanations of Organic Change

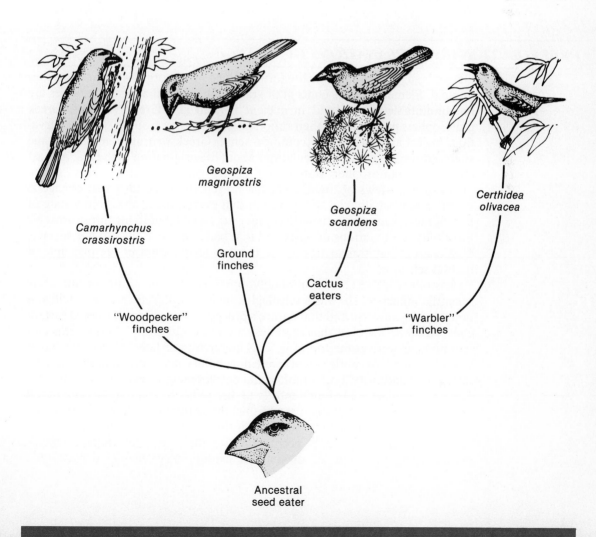

Camarhynchus
crassirostris

"Woodpecker"
finches

Geospiza
magnirostris

Ground
finches

Geospiza
scandens

Cactus
eaters

Certhidea
olivacea

"Warbler"
finches

Ancestral
seed eater

As is true for most pioneers, Darwin's intellectual journey was partially charted by his predecessors and his contemporaries. The proponents of the biblical version of creation argued vociferously against the notion that life forms change over time, the concept now called evolution. The biblical account of life stated that the Earth was of comparatively recent origin and that God created life. There was no time available for change in the biblical account. A prime requisite for evolution is an extended time span.

There were explanations of organic change prior to that suggested by Charles Darwin. French naturalist Jean Baptiste de Lamarck offered an explanation—which was shown to be incorrect—that is referred to as the inheritance of acquired traits. In addition to the geological foundation provided by Lyell's work, Darwin was also influenced by the writings of T.R. Malthus. The best known of Darwin's works, On The Origin of Species, *is important for accounting how the evolutionary process works. Darwin's principal contribution to modern evolutionary theory was his insistence that the process of natural selection was the key to understanding how evolution occurred.*

PREEVOLUTIONARY EXPLANATIONS OF CHANGE

Darwin's suggestion that one life form evolved into another was not altogether original. Elements of the concept of gradual change—that is, that species are not immutable—are found in ancient Persian and Greek writings. Greek philosophers proceeded in their rationale from *a priori* grounds, from observation, logical arguments, and common sense. Greek writings dating from the sixth century B.C. contain speculations about life originating in the sea. At least one Greek philosopher stated that **fossils** were animal remains. Greek philosophers' views of organic change ranged from the idea that change is merely a sensory illusion to the notion that everything is always in a state of flux. Some writings from the fifth century B.C. argued that living things arose by fortuitous combinations of parts and that bad combinations did not survive. This concept has similarities to the modern formulation of the principle of natural selection.

Aristotle (388–322 B.C.) probably provided the most important early scientific influence. He was a **teleologist;** he argued that there was intelligent design in the universe and that nature's processes were directed toward certain ends. Aristotle believed that there was a natural hierarchy of organisms and that humans were at the top of it. This hierarchy was later labeled the "great chain of being." Aristotle's views were nonevolutionary, and in many ways his intellectual authority long inhibited the development of evolutionary theory. Medieval scholars contributed mostly to disciplines of metaphysics and moral philosophy, and some of them established the notion that life was immutable. The world was thought to be static from the moment of creation.

Many other intellectual speculations on the nature of organic change preceded the development of modern evolutionary theory. Berosus, the

Chaldean priest of Babylon, wrote in a history of Assyrian and Babylonian civilizations that "there resided creatures in which were combined the lines of every species." The early Greek philosopher Thales wrote: "Nothing comes into being out of nothing, and nothing passes away into nothing." The Chinese mystic Lao Tzu suggested in approximately 504 B.C. that the survival of the fittest is the basic theme in nature. He wrote that "nature is unkind" and that "it treats creation like sacrificial straw-dogs." The Roman Marcus Aurelius wrote that "nature, which governs the whole, will soon change old things thou seest, and out of their substances will make other things, and again other things from the substance of them, in order that the world may be ever new." More recently, the eighteenth-century German philosopher Immanuel Kant wrote about a "mechanism of nature that may yet enable us to arrive at one explanation of life . . . strengthening the suspicion that species have an actual kinship due to descent from a common parent." This is very close to a modern-day evolutionary explanation.

JEAN BAPTISTE DE LAMARCK

Jean Baptiste de Lamarck, a French naturalist who lived from 1744 until 1829, proposed a systematic theory of change as an explanation of biological diversity. Lamarck accepted the nonevolutionary Aristotelian idea that organisms could be ranked in a progressive series, with humans at the apex. He argued that change resulted from some inner-directed drive for perfection.

Lamarck argued that an organism acquired new traits by using or not using different body parts, and that newly acquired behavioral or anatomical traits could be transmitted to one's offspring. Lamarck suggested that once a trait was acquired, it could be passed to subsequent generations. His explanation is known as the *theory of the inheritance of acquired characteristics.*

Lamarck's contribution to evolutionary theory lies in his proposal that life is dynamic and that there is a mechanism in nature that promotes ongoing change. Lamarck's proposed mechanism of change is incorrect, however, for acquired traits are not passed to one's offspring. For example, cutting off the tails of rats for untold generations still fails to produce a generation of tailless rats. Parents pass only genetically inherited traits to their offspring. Because rats continue to be born with tails, the gene for the appearance of a tail is maintained within the population, despite the fact that the tail was surgically removed. In other words, the genotype (the rat's genetic structure) is not altered, even though the phenotype (the outward appearance) is. (The concepts of genotype and phenotype are discussed fully in Chapter 5.) Although the details of Lamarck's scheme are inaccurate, his emphasis on change stimulated others who would ultimately explain the biological change he proposed.

Lamarck emphasized the relationship between an organism and the environment. It is this context in which evolution occurs. Although Lamarck may have offered an inaccurate explanation for the mechanism of organic change, he played an important role in establishing the intellectual climate that allowed Darwin's ideas to be accepted. Larmarck's mechanism of change focused on anatomical changes in individuals, whereas modern evolutionary theory focuses on populations.

THE GEOLOGICAL FRAMEWORK

An important element for evolutionary theory, an expanded time frame, was provided by geologists. During the seventeenth century, it was known that older rock layers were covered by more recent rock layers. The fact that an orderly arrangement of layers, or strata, reflects relative age is the *rule of superposition.*

In approximately 1800, Georges Cuvier and Alexandre Brogniart, two French scientists who were working in the fossil beds surrounding Paris, discovered that particular fossils were restricted to a certain layer, and that fossils changed in an orderly fashion from one layer to another. Comparing these fossils to living forms, they found that fossils from higher layers were more similar to modern forms than fossils from lower layers. With this observation of biological change in life forms over time, coupled with the observation that the more recent fossils most closely resembled modern forms, you might imagine that nineteenth-century geologists would hit upon the idea of evolution. However, they were unable to satisfactorily explain why fossils in earlier and later layers differed.

Prior to the contributions of such geologists as James Hutton and Charles Lyell, scientists suggested that the world was approximately 4,000 years old. The biblical scholar James Ussher (1581–1659), using the ages of each of the named generations recorded in the Bible, arrived at a date of 4004 B.C. for the creation of the earth. Reverend J. Lightfoot later added that "heaven and earth . . . were created all together in the same instant, . . . and man was created by the Trinity on October 23, 4004 B.C., at nine o'clock in the morning."

Long periods of time are often necessary for evolutionary change; the theological limit of 6,000 years for creation was quite constraining and was presented as strong evidence in contradiction of the concept of evolutionary change. The establishment of a suitable time frame was left to geologists, many of whom adhered to biblical scripture for their interpretations.

One of the best known geologists was the aforementioned Georges Cuvier, a young contemporary of Lamarck. Cuvier's scheme, known as **catastrophism,** claimed that various geological layers were deposited as a result of a series of cataclysms that periodically overwhelmed the earth and totally destroyed life. New life appeared through a series of successive creations after each cataclysm. Each successive appearance of new life exhibited an advance in complexity and superiority of organization over its predecessors. Cuvier's belief that the last great cataclysm was the biblical flood meant that human remains should not be discovered in previous layers. Cuvier's contribution is important because it tries to account for changes of form. Although he recognized that geological change occurred, Cuvier did not recognize that natural forces could account for differences in ancestral and descendant populations.

Cuvier's concept of catastrophism provided little comfort for the budding group of scientists whose intent was to prove that life was much older than biblical accounts and that recent life forms resulted from millennia of previous change. Lyell provided the necessary time frame with which evolutionists could work. However, even his projections of the earth's age were far short of those provided by modern geologists.

Lyell rejected Cuvier's idea of catastrophism, offering instead the principle of **uniformitarianism,** an idea first introduced by James Hutton in 1785 and further developed by Lyell in his book *Principles of Geology,* published in 1830. The principle of uniformitarianism states that, given enough time, the same geological agents that operate in the present could have been used to explain changes in the past geological history of the earth. While Lyell's work provided the basis of a geological time span for constructing an evolutionary scheme, he was disturbed by the inclusion of humans in that scheme. He accepted the fact that some organisms became extinct and were replaced by others, but he was uncertain of the mechanism. Because the uniformitarian view could not explain why new life forms developed, Lyell's critics adopted an alternative view—divine creation.

In the early decades of the eighteenth century, scientists resorted to contending that miracles, which they admitted being unable to comprehend, accounted for natural phenomena. Unable to explain geological processes, many accepted Cuvier's explanation of catastrophism. Coupled with catastrophism was the belief in the divine creation of new life. How else, these scientists reasoned, could one account for the new life forms that followed the mass destruction espoused by Cuvier?

For those who accepted it, the idea of catastrophism and divine creation seemed to explain everything about the neatly stratified rocks and the origin of new life. The interrelationship of catastrophism and creationism was presented by the British cleric William Paley in his 1802 book *Natural Theology.* Paley argued that all living forms had a design; there was, therefore, a need for a designer. Paley contended that God had designed all of life's adaptations. Even Lyell, the geologist whose works had profound effects on Darwin, turned to miracles or to church doctrine to explain the appearance of new life. Lyell argued that the earth had always had living things on it, and he turned to the Bible to explain human origins.

Prior to Darwin's *On the Origin of Species,* there were two leading theories: (1) that life's inexorable ascent argued for preordained directionality and (2) that humans mark the ideal measure of perfection.

CHARLES DARWIN: THE FOUNDATIONS
OF MODERN EVOLUTIONARY THEORY

Darwin was born in England in 1809. During his lifetime, one commonly held view on the origin of life was that life resulted from divine creation and that, once created, life was immutable. Darwin himself seems to have sympathized with this view until the time of his famous voyage as an unpaid naturalist aboard the HMS *Beagle.* Darwin's journey aboard the *Beagle,* which began in 1831, covered 5 years and more than 40,000 miles.

Partially as a result of reading Lyell's *The Principles of Geology,* Darwin began to assess the effects of weather through time on the face of the earth. Darwin came to his understanding of organic change partly from reading Thomas R. Malthus's *An Essay on the Principles of Population.*

In his *An Essay on the Principles of Population,* published in 1798, Malthus (1766–1834) noted that population size increases faster than the food supply. If left unrestrained, the size of the human population would double every 25 years, but the food supply could not keep pace. Malthus reasoned that chronic starvation operates as a check on population growth. He also noted that multiplication in nature is balanced through the struggle for existence. Humans, however, have to apply artificial restraint to constrain population growth.

It was from Malthus's ideas that Darwin saw how selection in nature could be explained. In the struggle for survival, those individuals with the most favorable traits would be more likely to survive, while those with the least favorable traits would die off in greater numbers. Darwin realized that Malthus's ideas might hold the key to understanding organic change and diversification in natural animal populations. Malthus argued that reproductive potential vastly exceeds the reproductive capacity necessary to maintain constant population sizes. This argument raised two related questions: (1) Why should reproductive potential exceed the capacity necessary to maintain constant population sizes? and (2) What mechanism could account for the fact that some individuals in a population survive and reproduce, while others die or do not reproduce as effectively? Darwin realized that those individuals who survived were often better adapted than those who did not. Furthermore, whatever traits increased an organism's ability to produce fertile offspring would be retained, while traits that decreased fertility would eventually be removed from (that is, selected out of) the population.

While in South America, Darwin found fossils of extinct animals that looked, except for their size, like forms still living in the area. He wondered whether the fossils were ancestral to the living populations. Darwin also noted a number of geological changes that had occurred over time. However, it was during his stay in the Galapagos Islands, located some 500 to 700 miles west of Ecuador in the equatorial Pacific Ocean, that Darwin began to realize that populations are not static and that they change in response to environmental pressures. He noted that the plants and animals of South America were similar to those he saw in the Galapagos Islands. Darwin also noted variations in the islands' inhabitants. He was struck by the differences among the tortoises. He was forced to ask what mechanisms might account for the variations that he was observing.

The best example of the variations observed by Darwin is the size and shape differences in the beaks of the Galapagos finches. This variation reflected, and presumably arose in response to, different feeding strategies. While the Galapagos finches are related to finches on the South American mainland, there are variations among island populations. If life was static and immutable, as many argued during Darwin's time, then beak size should not vary. If life were unchanging, as theologians and many scientists argued, then there should be no differences in such characteristics as beak size and feather color among birds inhabiting different Galapagos Islands or between Galapagos birds and birds inhabiting the mainland.

The Galapagos finches illustrate the effect of geographical isolation on population variation. Finches are common birds with a wide geographical distribution. They are basically seed eaters whose short, stout beaks provide an efficient feeding mechanism. The surprisingly wide variety of beak sizes and shapes among Galapagos finches is related to their feeding on a variety of foods (Figure 2-1). The first finches to inhabit the Galapagos apparently rapidly increased in number due to a lack of both natural enemies and competitors for food. Increasing population size soon outstripped the main food supply, forcing individual finches to seek alternative foods (Figure 2-2). Finding less competition for these alternative foods, subpopulations continued to feed on less restricted sources. Modifications of beak size and shape to allow for maximum exploitation of particular food niches appeared within each subpopulation. Those finches that had the appropriately modified beaks were best able to exploit the specific food sources and thus survived to reproduce in greater numbers. The difference in reproductive rates is called **differential reproduction.**

Despite the importance of Darwin's finches to the development of evolutionary theory, information on these birds, including that provided by Darwin, was based until recently on brief field studies or analyses of museum specimens. A long-term field study conducted by Grant (1986) rectified that situation and served to clarify some of Darwin's findings.

There are currently 14 recognized species of Darwin's finches. The morphological traits of these species vary widely. The greatest variation is in beak size. While beak size differences are apparent shortly after hatching, they become more evident as the animals mature. Grant demonstrated the ways in which beak size and shape influence the range of foods eaten by the finches. Intraspecific and interspecific differences in beak size and shape affect the efficiency with which these birds exploit foods in the environment.

Grant's study documented differential survival by various phenotypes. A phenotype is an individual's outward appearance, which is determined by the

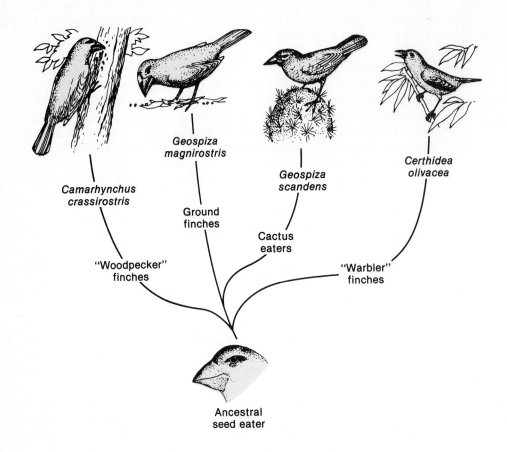

Figure 2-1 The adaptive radiation of the Galapagos finches.

interaction of the genotype (the genetic structure) with the environment. During stressful periods, such as times of drought, finches with larger body sizes and greater beak depths may have survived in greater numbers than did smaller finches, because larger birds were better able to manage larger and harder seeds. The differential survival of larger birds may have been further enhanced by a tendency among females to mate with larger males. Grant estimated that the combined effect of natural selection and preferential mate selection resulted in a 4 to 5 percent shift in the population toward the larger-bodied birds.

Darwin was unsure of the variability he observed in the animals and plants, and he noted that such variation would undermine the concept of the immutability of life. Upon his return from his voyage, one of his first projects was his *Journal of Researchers,* a descriptive narrative of his trip. This work contains only a slight hint of the intellectual turmoil he was beginning to experience. In 1857, Darwin wrote as follows:

> My theory would give zest to recent and fossil comparative anatomy; it would lead to closest examination of hybridity, to what circumstances favour crossing and what prevent it . . . this and direct examination of passages of structure in species might lead to laws of change, which would then be the main object of study, to guide our speculations with respect to the past and future. [quoted in de Beer, 1965:94]

Darwin wrote in his *Autobiography* that natural selection was the key to understanding the origin of new species. Arriving at this momentous conclusion, he refused to commit himself in print for some time. He wrote as follows in his *Autobiography:* "In June 1842, I first allowed myself the satisfaction of writing a very brief abstract of my theory in pencil in 35 pages; and this was enlarged during the summer of 1844 into 230 pages" (quoted in de Beer, 1965:119). This "abstract" was the first statement of Darwin's thoughts on evolution. In 1844, Darwin wrote as follows to his friend J. D. Hooker: "At last the gleams of light have come, and I am almost convinced (quite contrary to the opinion I started with) that species are not (it is like confessing a murder) immutable" (quoted in de Beer, 1963:135).

ALFRED R. WALLACE: A CODISCOVERER OF EVOLUTIONARY THEORY

Darwin eventually completed work on his momentous book *On the Origin of Species* partially as a result of having received a manuscript from one of his contemporaries, Alfred R. Wallace. Wallace's career paralleled Darwin's in many ways. The independent development of the theory of evolution by the means of natural selection by both men was more than mere coincidence. Both traveled widely and both observed in great detail the variety of plant and animal life. Both came to an understanding of the means by which selection works in nature from reading Malthus's work, and both were struck by the possibility that Malthus's ideas held the key to understanding the evolutionary

Figure 2-2 Variation in finch beaks as related to diet.

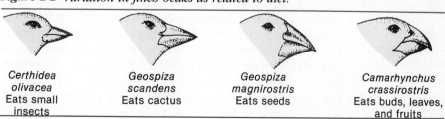

| Certhidea olivacea Eats small insects | Geospiza scandens Eats cactus | Geospiza magnirostris Eats seeds | Camarhynchus crassirostris Eats buds, leaves, and fruits |

process. Darwin and Wallace realized that those individuals who survive are somehow better adapted than those who do not. Both also realized that variations that increase an organism's ability to produce fertile offspring will be retained, while variations that decrease fertility will be selected against.

Both men provided a rational and convincing explanation for population diversity and change over time. Wallace provided his explanation in a paper entitled "On the Tendency of Varieties to Depart Indefinitely from the Original Type." This paper, also known as the Ternate paper, was mailed to Darwin in 1858 and seems to have forced Darwin to commit his own views to paper. Although both Darwin and Wallace drew similar and apparently independent conclusions about the process of change, it is Darwin who is usually credited with formulating the theory of evolution. This may not be entirely unfair because for 22 years, Darwin had meticulously recorded an overwhelming amount of evidence to support evolutionary change.

DEBUT OF THE THEORY OF EVOLUTION

After receiving Wallace's Ternate paper, Darwin fretted about a public unveiling of his views. Finally, his friends Hooker and Lyell prevailed upon him to submit a summary of his views, along with Wallace's Ternate paper, to the Linnaean Society. A joint paper was presented before the Linnean Society in London in 1858 and published in the society's *Journal of Proceedings* under the title "On the Tendency of Species to Form Varieties, and on the Perpetuation of Varieties and Species by Natural Means of Selection." What effect did that paper have on the world at that time? The idea of natural selection, which would later set the intellectual world ablaze and forever change our view of life, at first attracted little notice.

Darwin's ideas were developed and finally published in 1859 in his most famous book, *On the Origin of Species: The Preservation of Favoured Races in the Struggle for Life.* Darwin had spent more than 20 years writing this book. On the day the book appeared, the total edition of 1,250 copies was sold; a second edition was published in 1860. *On the Origin of Species* is a composite of two complementary theories, only one of which was original to Darwin (Kennedy, 1976). The idea that each species was not independently created and had descended from other forms was not original to Darwin. During his time, this idea was called the *transmutation doctrine.* Darwin built on this idea and insisted that the theory was incomplete until some mechanism was applied whereby this transmutation occurred. Others, such as Lamarck, had proposed mechanisms for change, but these explanations had little merit. For Darwin, the mechanism of change was natural selection, and his documentation of this process was Darwin's original contribution to evolutionary theory. Darwin's argument had a set of premises that subjected evolution to research. Previous arguments for organic change presented speculative systems but suggested little in the way of collecting evidence.

All life is related and has developed over time through the process of "descent with modification." That idea was fairly common among naturalists by the end of the eighteenth century. Darwin's grandfather, Erasmus, described it in great detail in an epic poem, *Zoomania,* in 1794. What Darwin added in *On the Origin of Species* was a theory of *how* such a thing could happen, *how* living things changed over time. His elegant *how*—natural selection—made the concept of evolution plausible for the first time.

In *On the Origin of Species,* Darwin characterized his theory as having the following features:

1. All species are capable of producing offspring more rapidly than can be compensated for by an increase in food supplies. (This idea was originated by Malthus.)
2. There is variation among all living things. Such variation is important in understanding why some individuals survive in their environment and others do not survive or do not survive as well.
3. In the struggle for existence, those individuals with the most favored variants—those that are best adapted—pass more of their traits to the next generation. This situation, whereby certain individuals have more offspring than others, is known as **differential reproduction.** (Keep in mind, however, that Darwin did not know how traits were inherited. That information was added by Gregor Mendel and is discussed in Chapter 5).
4. Over long time periods, successful variants may produce great differences that result in new species. This is the result of natural selection.

The two important aspects of Darwin's explanation of evolution by natural selection are (1) the struggle for existence and (2) descent with modification (that is, change over time). Darwin envisioned descent with modification as occurring slowly and over long time periods. In Chapter 6 we provide another possible alternative for the means of descent with modification.

A major tenet of Darwin's argument was his emphasis on the idea that the struggle for existence occurred among individuals, and that those individuals with favorable variations would survive and reproduce more readily than others. Darwin's emphasis on the individual and on the role of individual variability led him to natural selection as the evolutionary mechanism. Natural selection works on individuals, but the population is the unit of evolution.

Darwin's book is important not only for its account of how the evolutionary process works, but also for its vast compilation of data documenting the results of evolutionary change. In *On the Origin of Species,* Darwin described the living world as ever changing. He noted that species change gradually, and that new species emerge while others become **extinct** (die out). He postulated the idea of common descent.

Darwin made little mention of the possibilities of human evolution in *On the Origin of Species.* The possibility of human evolution did receive discreet recognition in the conclusion of the book, however. The implications of Darwin's 1859 work for understanding human evolution were largely unspoken until his 1871 book, *The Descent of Man,* wherein he offered some explicit arguments for the process of human evolution.

While Darwin's principal contribution to modern evolutionary theory was his insistence on the role of natural selection in evolutionary change, his principal failure was the fact that he could not explain how adaptive traits were transmitted from one generation to another. Darwin documented that populations exhibited variability and that this variability was the source of organic change, but he did not know how the variation was introduced into a population. It was Mendel who explained the mechanisms of genetic inheritance, and his contribution will be discussed in Chapter 5.

This chapter outlines some early ideas precedent to Charles Darwin's contribution to evolutionary theory. It was geologists such as Lyell who provided evidence for an expanded time period in which evolution could occur. Darwin's principal contribution to modern evolutionary theory was his insistence that natural selection played the key role in organic change.

Darwin's theory of evolution is based on the following facts: All species are capable of producing more offspring than survive; there is variation among all living things; and those individuals who are best adapted pass on more of their traits to subsequent generations. Darwin stressed that natural selection worked on individuals, but populations were the unit of evolution.

The missing element in Darwin's theory of evolution was his lack of an explanation about the means whereby variation is introduced into a population and how traits were transmitted across generations. Gregor Mendel provided that information; his contribution to modern evolutionary theory is discussed in Chapter 5.

BIBLIOGRAPHY

APPLEMAN, P. 1970. *Darwin.* New York: W. W. Norton & Co., Inc.
BRACKMAN, A. 1980. *A Delicate Arrangement: The Strange Case of Charles Darwin and Alfred Russel Wallace.* New York: Times Books.
DARWIN, C. 1958. *The Origin of Species.* New York: Mentor.
DARWIN, C. 1965. *The Expression of Emotions in Man and Animals.* Chicago: University of Chicago Press.
DEBEER, G. 1965. *Charles Darwin: A Scientific Biography.* New York: Natural History Library.
EISELEY, L. 1961. *Darwin's Century.* New York: Anchor.
EISELEY, L. 1972. The intellectual antecedents of *The Descent of Man.* In *Sexual Selection and the Descent of Man,* B. Campbell, ed., pp. 86–98. Chicago: Aldine.
GOULD, S. 1986. Evolution and the triumph of homology, or why history matters. *American Scientist* 74: 60–69.

GRANT, P. 1981. Speciation and adaptive radiation of Darwin's finches. *American Scientist* 69: 653–63.

GRANT, P. 1986. *Ecology and Evolution of Darwin's Finches.* Princeton, N.J.: Princeton University Press.

HIMMELFARB, G. 1959. *Darwin and the Darwinian Revolution.* New York: W. W. Norton & Co., Inc.

KENNEDY, K. 1976. *Human Variation in Space and Time.* Dubuque, Iowa: Brown.

LOVEJOY, A. 1936. *The Great Chain of Being: A Study of the Prehistory of an Idea.* New York: Harper & Row, Pub.

PETERSON, W. 1979. *Malthus.* Cambridge, Mass.: Harvard University Press.

WILSON, L. 1971. Sir Charles Lyell and the species question. *American Scientist* 59: 43–55.

Chapter
3
The Biological Basis
of Heredity

DNA DOUBLE HELIX

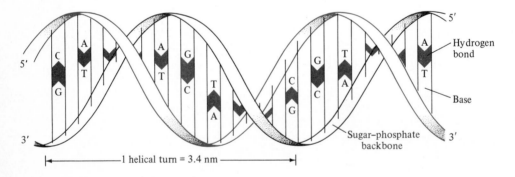

The human body is composed of cells. As the organism grows, cells proliferate through a cell-division process called mitosis. *In addition to carrying out essential metabolic processes, cells contain hereditary material which is passed from one generation to the next. A specialized form of cell division,* meiosis, *occurs in the testes and ovaries. Through meiosis, the genetic material of each parent is rearranged, providing eggs and sperm with a unique combination of traits. When the egg and sperm are fused, a new individual is created, with each parent contributing half of the genetic material. This chapter will discuss the process by which genetic variability is maintained and will describe the consequences of some of the errors that inevitably occur. The structure of the hereditary material will also be described, as will the mechanism by which inherited traits are expressed.*

THE CELL

Humans, like all living organisms, are constructed of cells. Cells are composed primarily of water, salt, proteins, lipids, and carbohydrates and contain numerous structures, all enclosed within a permeable membrane. Cells also contain nucleic acids, which play a crucial role in both the transmission and the expression of the hereditary material.

An animal cell is divided into two major parts—the **nucleus** and the **cytoplasm.** The nucleus serves as the control center of the cell, its contents separated from the rest of the cell by a thin membrane known as the **nuclear membrane.** The cytoplasm contains numerous structures, called **organelles,** that are involved in the activity of the cell (Figure 3-1). Two of these organelles

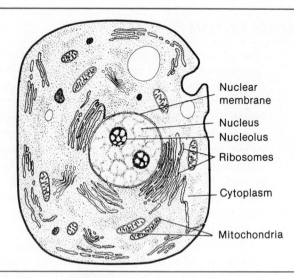

Nuclear membrane

Nucleus
Nucleolus

Ribosomes

Cytoplasm

Mitochondria

Figure 3-1 The structure of a human cell.

are the **mitochondria** and the **lysozymes.** The mitochondria are responsible for converting certain molecules found in the cell into the energy needed to perform other cellular activities. Lysosomes are sac-like structures that are attached to the cell membrane and are filled with digestive enzymes. When no longer needed by the cell, various types of large molecules are taken into the lysosomes and broken down into components which can be recycled by the cell.

The cytoplasm also contains particles called **ribosomes,** which are often attached to a complex structure known as the **endoplasmic reticulum.** The ribosomes are involved in the production of proteins, and the endoplasmic reticulum is involved in the transport of newly synthesized proteins out of the cell.

Located just outside of the cell nucleus are structures known as **centrioles,** which play an important role in cell division. Within the nucleus, separated from the cytoplasm by a thin membrane, are the **chromosomes,** complex structures which contain the instructions for the operation of the cell. In addition to directing the operation of an individual cell, the chromosomes also serve as the carriers of the hereditary material, a role which will be discussed in detail in Chapters 4 and 5.

While cells may differ substantially in structure and function, every cell in an organism contains an identical set of chromosomes. The chromosomes may instruct different types of cells to perform in different ways, yet each cell contains all of the instructions that are found in any other cell. The nuclei of all cells are identical because all of the cells in an organism are ultimately derived from a single cell.

CELL DIVISION: MITOSIS

Like all multicelled organisms, humans begin as a single cell, formed by the fusion of an egg and a sperm. This cell, called a **zygote,** undergoes a series of replications and divisions, resulting in geometric growth of the cell mass. A single cell divides into two cells, each of these divide into two more, and so on. Unless some kind of error occurs, each cell will be identical to every other cell. Eventually, the cells undergo the poorly understood process of differentiation, giving rise to the various types of tissues and organs found in a mature individual. The process by which **somatic** (body) **cell** growth occurs is called **mitosis.** Mitosis occurs in mature organisms as well; tissue growth (such as growth of hair and fingernails) occurs through mitosis. As somatic cells die, they are replaced through mitosis.

Although it is a continuous process, mitosis is usually described as occurring in several stages. The first stage, not actually considered part of mitosis, is called **interphase.** During interphase, the chromosomes are diffuse and threadlike, spread throughout the nucleus. Most of the metabolic activities associated with the cell occur during interphase, when the chromosomes are in this diffuse state. Also, during interphase, the chromosomes duplicate, so that upon entering mitosis, each cell has double the normal complement of genetic material.

During the first phase of mitosis, **prophase** (Figure 3-2), the chromosomes

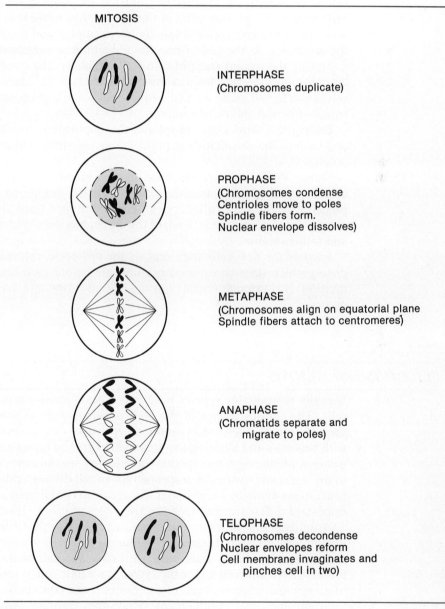

MITOSIS

INTERPHASE
(Chromosomes duplicate)

PROPHASE
(Chromosomes condense
Centrioles move to poles
Spindle fibers form.
Nuclear envelope dissolves)

METAPHASE
(Chromosomes align on equatorial plane
Spindle fibers attach to centromeres)

ANAPHASE
(Chromatids separate and
migrate to poles)

TELOPHASE
(Chromosomes decondense
Nuclear envelopes reform
Cell membrane invaginates and
pinches cell in two)

Figure 3-2 Cell division: mitosis.

begin to condense. Through repeated coiling and supercoiling, the dispersed chromosomes become tightly compacted into thick rodlike structures with each duplicate copy remaining attached to the original. The point on the chromosome where the two copies are attached is called the **centromere,** and each of the copies is referred to as a **chromatid.** Small structures called **centrioles,** which are located just outside the nuclear membrane, begin to migrate toward opposite sides of the cell. As they move into these positions, a series of elastic fibers, called **spindle fibers,** appear and form an arch between the centrioles. At the end of prophase, the nuclear membrane dissolves.

During the second stage of mitosis, **metaphase,** the condensed duplicated chromosomes migrate toward the center of the cell. They then align themselves end to end along the cell's equatorial plane and become attached to the spindle fibers at their centromeres.

During the third stage, **anaphase,** the duplicated chromosomes separate, and each of the chromatids is pulled along the spindle fiber toward opposite poles.

During the final stage, **telophase,** nuclear membranes re-form around each chromosomal cluster, and the cell membrane begins to invaginate. This pinching of the cell, called **cytokinesis,** continues until the single cell has divided into two new cells. Each of these daughter cells is identical to the other and to the original.

Each of the new cells then repeats the cell cycle, returning to interphase, during which their chromosomes duplicate before each undergoes a mitotic division. It is through repeated cycles of replication and division that growth occurs.

CELL DIVISION: MEIOSIS

Sexually reproducing species have two types of cells—**somatic cells** and **sex cells.** The various tissues of the body are composed of somatic cells which, through mitosis, increase in number, permitting damaged cells to be replaced with new ones and allowing the organism to grow. The sex cells, also known as **gametes,** are the eggs and sperm. Gametes are special types of cells, produced in the testes and ovaries by a special type of cell division called **meiosis.** While some stages of meiosis are similar to stages observed in mitosis, there are many important differences between the two types of cell division.

A fundamental difference between meiosis and mitosis is that meiosis is a "reduction" division. Instead of producing two cells identical to the original, meiosis produces four cells, each with only one-half of the genetic material found in a somatic cell. Since the zygote, a somatic cell, is formed by the fusion of an egg and a sperm, each of the gametes can contain only one-half of the total chromosomal complement. Since they contain only one-half of the genetic material, gametes are said to be **haploid.** Somatic cells are referred to as

diploid because they carry two copies of each chromosome, one inherited from each parent. Each of these copies is referred to as a **homolog,** and the pair of chromosomes (one from each parent) are said to be **homologous.** Humans have a total of 46 chromosomes, made up of 22 homologous pairs and one nonhomologous pair. The nonhomologous pair of chromosomes are the **sex chromosomes,** and they will be discussed in some detail in the next chapter.

Meiosis, which occurs only in the testes and ovaries, begins with a somatic cell. The chromosomes duplicate, and the cell enters the first stage of meiosis (Figure 3-3). In **prophase I,** the chromosomes condense and then pair with their homologs. The paired homologous chromosomes then become physically attached to one another. These attachments usually occur at several locations along the lengths of the chromosomes. This process of pairing and attachment, called **synapsis,** is unique to meiosis.

During synapsis, while the homologs are physically joined, genetic material may be exchanged between chromosomes. This exchange of genetic material, referred to as **crossing over,** is also unique to meiosis, and performs an important function. Prior to crossing over, each single pair of duplicated chromosomes consists of a total of four chromatids. Two are identical copies of the chromosome contributed by the individual's mother, and the other two are identical copies of the chromosome contributed by the father. Through crossing over, genetic material is exchanged between each of the parentally derived chromosomes, resulting in four chromatids, each bearing a unique combination of genetic material. An individual, then, has the potential to produce eggs or sperm carrying chromosomes that are different from either of those that were inherited. This capacity for generating variability is crucial to evolutionary change, as will be explained more fully in Chapters 5 and 7.

By the end of prophase I, the chromosomal pairs, still attached to one another, begin to migrate toward the center of the cell. In females, meiosis ceases at this point, and the sex cells are held in suspended animation for many years. Since meiosis begins in females before birth, all of the gametes that a female will ever possess are present at birth and remain "frozen" in prophase I until she begins ovulating. Since males begin to produce sperm at puberty and continue to do so throughout their lives, the meiotic cycle is unbroken and the sex cells move directly from prophase I to metaphase I.

During **metaphase I,** the spindles begin to form and the paired chromosomes line up at the equatorial plane. The orientation of the chromosomes in each pair is random with respect to parental origin. Thus the maternally derived chromosome 1 could appear either to the left or to the right of the paternally derived homolog. The position in which each homolog of chromosome 1 lies has no influence on the way in which the other chromosomal pairs arrange themselves. Thus it is possible that the maternally derived chromosomes 1, 4, and 7 could lie on the same side of the equatorial plane as the paternally derived chromosomes 2, 3, and 8. As will be discussed later, this **independent assortment** of chromosomes is an important source of variability in sexually reproducing species.

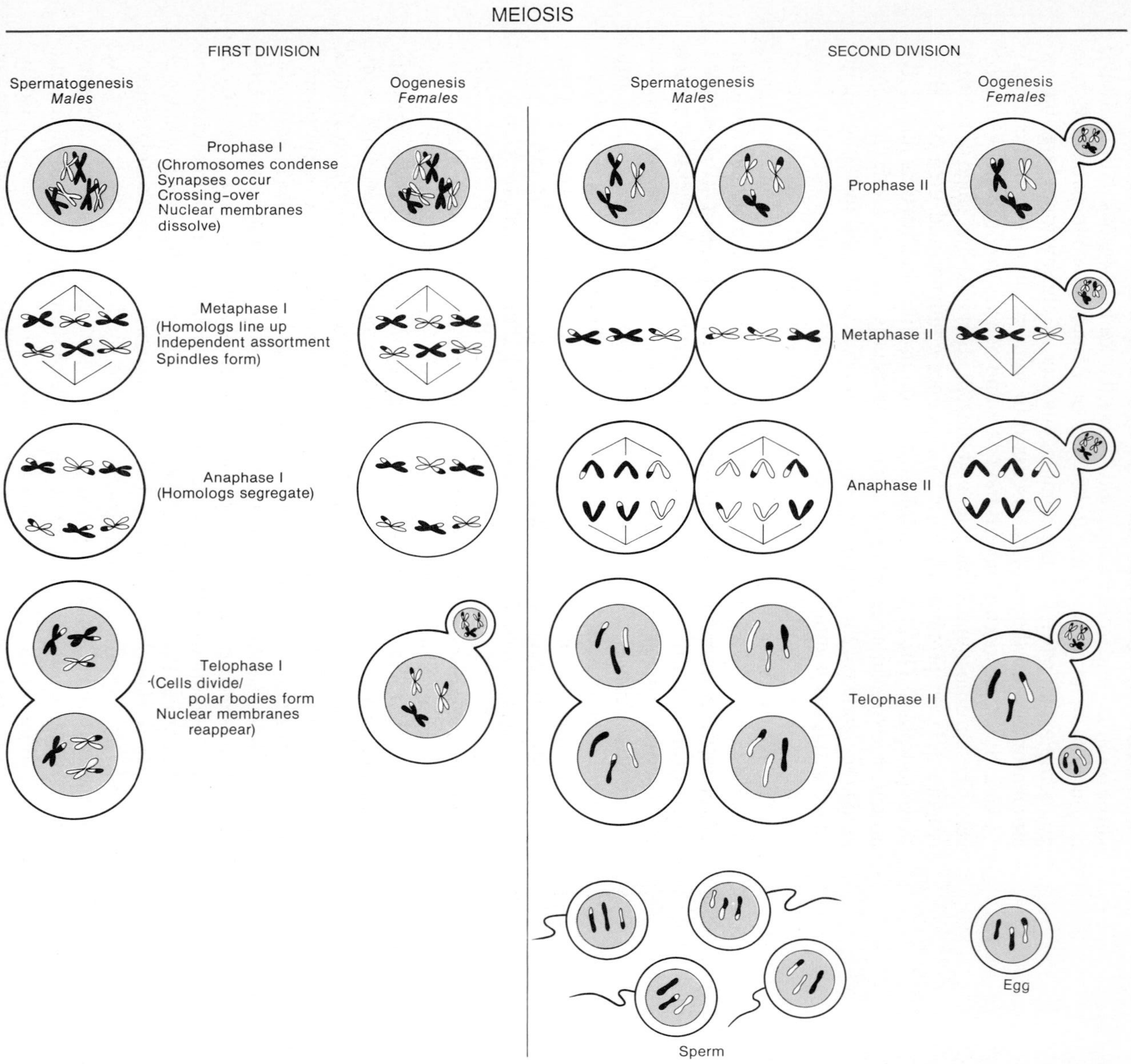

MEIOSIS

SECOND DIVISION

Oogenesis *Females*

Prophase II

Metaphase II

Anaphase II

Telophase II

Egg

Spermatogenesis *Males*

Sperm

FIRST DIVISION

Oogenesis *Females*

Spermatogenesis *Males*

Prophase I
(Chromosomes condense
Synapses occur
Crossing-over
Nuclear membranes
dissolve)

Metaphase I
(Homologs line up
Independent assortment
Spindles form)

Anaphase I
(Homologs segregate)

Telophase I
(Cells divide/
polar bodies form
Nuclear membranes
reappear)

Figure 3-3 Cell division: meiosis.

24

By the end of metaphase I, crossing over is completed and the synaptic points have moved to the tips of the chromatids. During **anaphase I,** the homologous members of each pair separate and are pulled along the spindles toward opposite poles. The sister chromatids do not separate. Thus one member of each (still doubled) chromosomal pair migrates to each side of the cell.

During **telophase I,** the cells divide, resulting in two haploid cells, each containing 23 duplicated chromosomes. In males, these two cells are approximately equal in size. In females, however, one of the cells keeps almost all of the cytoplasm, and the nucleus of the other is pinched off, forming a structure known as a **polar body.**

At this point, the dividing cells enter the second phase of meiosis, the stages of which are very similar to mitosis. In **prophase II,** the spindle begins to form in each haploid cell. Since the chromosomes are already duplicated, no additional duplication occurs.

During **metaphase II,** the chromosomes line up along the equatorial plane and attach to the spindle fibers. In females, approximately once a month, one or more eggs resume meiosis and progress to metaphase II. They remain at this stage until penetrated by a sperm. It is only after fertilization occurs that the egg proceeds to anaphase II. If fertilization does not occur, meiosis is not completed. In males, metaphase II is followed immediately by anaphase II.

During **anaphase II,** the duplicated chromosomes separate and the chromatids move along the spindle fibers to opposite poles.

In **telophase II,** the nuclear membranes re-form and the cells divide. In human females, if fertilization has occurred, the cell will divide. Once again, one of the new cells will gain most of the cytoplasm, and the second nucleus will be extruded as the second polar body. Thus, in human females, the process of meiosis results in the production of a single egg which contains one copy of each member of the chromosomal pair, a total of 23 chromosomes.

In males, each of the cells from the first meiotic division will have divided again. Thus, in males, the ultimate product of meiosis is four haploid cells, each containing a single copy of one member of each of the 23 original pairs. Because of independent assortment and crossing over, each of these cells is unique. After a few additional modifications, each of these haploid cells will become a sperm.

Meiosis is an extremely important process. By reducing the amount of genetic material by one-half, it produces a haploid cell, either an egg or a sperm, that contains exactly one-half of the genetic material necessary for an organism to function. Upon fertilization, the nuclei of the egg and sperm are fused. Since each gamete has contributed one copy of each chromosome, the full complement of 46 chromosomes is restored.

Even more important, however, meiosis ensures that each individual will be distinctly different from either parent. Through independent assortment and crossing over, it is virtually guaranteed that every egg and every sperm will be totally unique. As discussed in Chapters 5 and 7, this variability is an essential component of the evolutionary process. Without the variability produced through sexual reproduction, evolution could not occur.

AUTOSOMES AND SEX CHROMOSOMES

As noted earlier, the diploid human cell contains 46 chromosomes. These chromosomes occur in 23 pairs, with one member of each pair coming from each parent. In 22 of these pairs, the two chromosomes are homologous; that is, the chromosome inherited from the father contains instructions determining the expression of the same traits as found on the corresponding chromosome inherited from the mother. The 22 pairs of homologous chromosomes are called **autosomes** and are responsible for determining many different traits in humans.

The remaining pair of chromosomes are homologous in females but are not homologous in males. Because they differ from the autosomes in this respect, the members of the twenty-third pair of chromosomes are referred to as **sex chromosomes.** In normal humans, a female possesses two large X chromosomes and the male possesses one X and one smaller Y chromosome. Although the sex chromosomes are thought to play a crucial role in determining the sex of an individual, their role is not restricted to this function. The X chromosome (found in both males and females) is known to control the expression of a number of traits totally unrelated to sex determination.

Since only one member of each chromosomal pair is contributed to each gamete during meiosis, it is easy to see why it is always the father who determines the sex of the child. Since a female has two X chromosomes, all of her eggs will contain X chromosomes. Males, by contrast, would be expected to produce equal numbers of X-bearing and Y-bearing sperm. If a sperm carrying an X chromosome fertilizes an egg (which always contains an X chromosome), the resulting offspring will be female. Likewise, if an egg is fertilized by a Y-bearing sperm, the zygote will possess one X and one Y chromosome, resulting in a male offspring.

The fact that the autosomes are homologous and the sex chromosomes are not suggests that the sex chromosomes may function in a somewhat different manner. We know that both copies of each autosomal pair must be present in a normal individual. If, through an error in cell division, only one copy of a chromosome is present, the fetus rarely survives until birth. The possession of three or more copies of a chromosome is almost always lethal. Clearly, for proper growth and development, and for the proper expression of traits, two copies of each chromosome must be present. Yet the human male has only one copy of the X chromosome, which is known to contain the instructions for the expression of hundreds of important traits.

Since a male, possessing the X chromosome in a single copy only, expresses all of his traits as appropriately as the female, who possesses two copies, it seems apparent that only a single copy of a sex chromosome is necessary for proper expression. If this is the case, however, it would follow that the female, by carrying an extra X chromosome, would be expected to suffer the ill effects of possessing too many copies. However, females function quite well with two copies of the X chromosome. This apparent dilemma can be resolved by taking a closer look at the two X chromosomes in the female.

When stained chromosomes from a female are viewed under a microscope, one of the X chromosomes will appear to be more condensed and will stain darker. This darkly stained chromosome is inactive, and is referred to as a **Barr body.** The second X chromosome is apparently inactivated very early in the development of the embryo, with one X chromosome being randomly inactivated in each cell. While it is equally likely that either X chromosome will inactivate, it is clear that after inactivation occurs, all of the descendants of that cell will have the same active X chromosome (Lyon, 1962). Because the inactivation process is random, in approximately one-half of a female's cells, the active X chromosome will have been inherited from her mother; in the other half, the active X chromosome will have been inherited from her father. The role of X-chromosome inactivation in the expression of traits will be discussed in some detail in the next section.

THE DETERMINATION OF TRAITS: GENES AND ALLELES

As noted earlier, the chromosomes contain the instructions responsible for the expression of many of the traits present in an individual. The term **gene** is used to refer to that segment of a chromosome responsible for producing a single trait. In humans, the gene for the ABO blood type is found on chromosome 9; the genes responsible for producing hemoglobin are found on chromosomes 11 and 16.

In some cases the gene for a particular trait is the same in every individual. In many other cases, there are a number of alternate versions of a gene that an individual might possess. Each of these alternate versions of the gene is referred to as an **allele.** The ABO blood group gene, for example, has three possible alleles: A, B, and O. Only one version of a gene, one allele, is present on each chromosome. Since each of the autosomes are present in two copies, however, each individual will possess two copies of each gene and thus carry two alleles.

If an individual inherits a chromosome containing the A allele from his father and one carrying the B allele from his mother, then he is said to have the **genotype** AB. If he inherits an A from one parent and an O from the other parent, his genotype is AO. Within the human ABO system there are six possible genotypes: AA, BB, OO, AO, BO, and AB.

If the same allele is present on both chromosomes (for example, AA, BB, or

OO), the genotype is said to be **homozygous,** and the allele is expressed in the individual. If the two alleles in a genotype are different from each other, the genotype is said to be **heterozygous,** and whether one or both of the alleles are expressed depends on the dominance relationships among the alleles. If both alleles are expressed, the alleles are said to be **codominant.** In the ABO system, A and B are codominant; thus a person with the AB genotype will exhibit the blood type AB. If one allele is expressed and the other is not, the expressed allele is said to be **dominant** over the unexpressed one. The unexpressed allele is referred to as the **recessive** allele. In the ABO system, both A and B are dominant over O; thus the AO genotype produces blood type A, and the BO genotype produces blood type B.

The term **phenotype** is used to refer to the trait ultimately expressed in an individual. The phenotype is the product of the interaction of the two alleles present on the chromosomes (the genotype) together with the influence of the environment, if any, on the expression of that genotype. In the blood type example just described, the six genotypes, AA, AO, BB, BO, OO and AB, are responsible for producing four phenotypes; A, B, O, and AB.

As discussed earlier, since the sex chromosomes are nonhomologous, the genes found on those chromosomes are expressed somewhat differently from those found on autosomes. Since males possess only one Y chromosome and one X chromosome, and since the Y and X chromosomes do not appear to share any genes, a male will express whatever alleles are present on the single copies of each chromosome.

There are a number of interesting examples of genetic traits, found predominantly in males, whose frequency is the result of the fact that males possess only one X chromosome. Such traits are referred to as **X-linked** traits. One example of an X-linked trait is color-blindness. Color-blindness is caused by a recessive allele found on the X chromosome. Because color-blindness is recessive, it will be expressed in a female only if she is homozygous—that is, if she has the genotype aa. If she has the dominant normal allele (A) on either of her X chromosomes, she will exhibit normal vision. Since the recessive allele will usually be "hidden" in the heterozygous (Aa) genotype, few females will exhibit color-blindness. All heterozygous females will be **carriers** of the color-blindness allele, however, and one-half of their eggs will carry the recessive allele.

In order for a male to be color-blind, he need only possess one copy of the recessive allele, inherited from his carrier mother. Since there is not a second X chromosome, the single copy allele will always be expressed. By contrast, in order to be color-blind, a female would have to inherit a recessive allele from both parents, an unlikely occurrence if the allele is at all rare.

Since one of the X chromosomes is always inactivated in females, it is reasonable to ask how the female can be heterozygous for a particular trait when only one chromosome is supposedly active. As noted earlier, which of the two X chromosomes is inactivated in each cell line is entirely random. Although only one X chromosome is active in each cell, a female has approximately equal numbers of each and therefore has the opportunity to express the traits present on both chromosomes.

Usually, the inactivation of one X chromosome has no phenotypic effect in females. There is, however, an interesting example of how this phenomenon can sometimes affect the expression of certain traits. This example involves the genes for coat color in cats. Cats have a number of different genes which affect coat color. One of these genes is found on the X chromosome. If a male cat possesses a "black" allele, his coat color will be black; if he has an "orange" allele, he will be orange. If a female cat is heterozygous, that is, she carries both alleles, her coat color will contain a mixture of both colors, with the color of each patch determined by the allele on the X chromosome active in that cell line. This coloration, called calico, is thus found only in females.

NONDISJUNCTION AND CHROMOSOMAL ABNORMALITIES

Errors in cell division will occasionally occur, resulting in gametes with an abnormal number of chromosomes. If, for example, the sister chromatids of a given chromosome fail to separate during the second phase of meiosis, one of the resultant gametes will possess two copies of the chromosome, and one of the other gametes will not contain any copies of that chromosome. This type of error in cell division, characterized by the failure of the duplicated chromosomes to divide properly, is called **nondisjunction.**

When a gamete with an abnormal number of chromosomes is joined with a normal gamete, the newly formed zygote will possess either three copies of a particular chromosome or only one copy. Both are abnormal conditions, and the severity of the outcome depends on the chromosomes involved. The possession of a single copy of a chromosome is generally considered to be incompatible with survival. Fetuses having this chromosomal abnormality are usually spontaneously aborted at a very early stage. Those that survive longer are usually stillborn or die shortly after birth. It appears that normal differentiation and fetal development require the presence of two copies of each chromosome.

In those cases in which three copies of a chromosome are present, the severity of the condition may be related to the size of the chromosomes involved. It appears that the possession of three or more copies of any of the larger chromosomes is lethal. The possession of three copies of the smallest chromosome (chromosome 21) results in a condition known as **trisomy-21,** and affected individuals exhibit varying degrees of the traits associated with Down syndrome. Down syndrome is characterized by moderate to severe mental retardation and the presence of characteristic facial features, often accompanied by abnormalities of the heart and other organ systems. Unlike other individuals possessing an abnormal number of chromosomes, many individuals with trisomy-21 survive into adulthood. This is usually attributed to the small size of the chromosome and the assumption that the number of genes involved is also relatively small.

Nondisjunction is probably not a particularly rare occurrence. It has been suggested that at least one-half of all spontaneous abortions involve fetuses with an abnormal number of chromosomes. Trisomy-21 occurs in approximately 1 in every 500 to 600 births. Since the frequency of trisomy-21 increases with the age of the mother and seems to be independent of the age of the father, it is believed that most (but not all) of the cases are the result of nondisjunction during the formation of the egg. The fact that the egg may be suspended in the middle of the division process for 30 or more years lends support to the suggestion that the age of the egg may affect its ability to divide properly. It should be noted, however, that nondisjunction during the production of sperm cells has been documented and, while less common than nondisjunction in the egg, will result in an identical condition (Patterson, 1987).

Nondisjunction leading to an abnormal number of sex chromosomes has a much less deleterious effect than nondisjunction among the autosomes. The reasons for this may be twofold. First, when extra copies of the X chromosome are present, they are inactivated, apparently by the same process that produces the Barr body in normal females. In the case of the Y chromosome, its small size and the observation that it appears to possess very few genes suggest that multiple copies may not be particularly deleterious.

Females who possess three or more X chromosomes are generally considered to be normal, fertile females. The extra X chromosomes appear to inactivate without a noticeable effect on the phenotype. Likewise, males who possess an extra Y chromosome are generally indistinguishable from males with the normal XY combination. However, there have been a few studies which suggest that 47,XYY males are, on the average, slightly taller and may have slightly lower mental capacities than the average XY male.

An individual who possesses two X chromosomes and one Y chromosome (47,XXY) is phenotypically male. The presence of the Y chromosome seems to ensure that the individual develops secondary sex characteristics consistent with being male. The second X chromosome is inactivated and appears as a Barr body when the chromosomes are examined under a microscope. However, these 47,XXY males (a condition known as **Klinefelter syndrome**) are not phenotypically normal. These men usually have small, malformed testes and are infertile. They are often quite tall, with long arms and legs, and occasionally exhibit slight breast development. Some males with Klinefelter syndrome also exhibit decreased mental capacity. These traits suggest that the "inactive" X chromosome may have had some deleterious effect on the developing fetus before becoming inactivated.

In contrast, it appears that normal females must have at least two X chromosomes, both of which are active at some stage in fetal development. Although only one X chromosome is active in newborn females, with the other inactivated early in development, an individual who, through nondisjunction, possesses only one X chromosome will exhibit serious abnormalities. Individuals who exhibit the 45,XO condition, known as **Turner syndrome,** are phenotypically female, although they generally fail to develop secondary sex characteristics. Incomplete development of the ovaries leaves them infertile. Females with Turner syndrome are generally short in stature and exhibit a number of growth-related skeletal abnormalities. Defects of the heart and other organ systems often result in decreased life expectancy. Intelligence is usually normal, and many of the characteristic features of Turner syndrome may not appear until puberty. Most cases of Turner syndrome occur as the result of nondisjunction of the X chromosome in a parental gamete, although as many as 10 percent of the cases may result from the loss of an X chromosome due to a mitotic nondisjunction during fetal development. In the latter case, the individual will display a mosaic of normal (XX) and Turner (XO) cells, and will generally be less severely affected.

Males possessing only a Y chromosome and no X chromosome (45,YO) do not survive, suggesting once again that the presence of at least one X chromosome is essential to normal fetal development in both males and females.

THE STRUCTURE OF CHROMOSOMES

The chromosomes, as they appear during mitotic metaphase, are X-shaped. At this stage the chromosome is actually composed of two identical copies, called **chromatids.** The identical chromatids, often referred to as **sister chromatids,** are attached at the **centromere.** The centromere is a small, constricted region of the chromosome and as such is responsible for the X shape. While its position is constant for any particular chromosome, it varies among chromosomes. In fact, it is the position of the centromere which helps distinguish the various chromosomes from one another. The portions of the chromosomes on each side of the centromere are referred to as its arms. If the centromere is located near the center of the chromosome, the chromosome is classified as a **metacentric** chromosome. If the centromere is located near one end of the chromosome, the chromosome is said to be **acrocentric.** Smaller acrocentric chromosomes often appear to be V-shaped (Figure 3-4).

When stained with the appropriate dyes, the metaphase chromosomes are seen to possess distinctive banding patterns. The significance of these bands is not clearly understood, although they appear to be associated with areas of relative activity and inactivity in the chromosome. Genes that code for proteins tend to be associated with the more lightly stained bands. While the banding patterns are unique from chromosome to chromosome, homologous chromosomes will exhibit similar banding patterns. The position of the centromere and the banding patterns of each chromosome can be used to construct a **karyotype** for each individual. A karyotype is constructed from

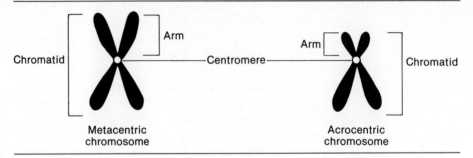

Figure 3-4 The structure of human chromosomes.

photographs of individual stained metaphase chromosomes. The individual chromosomes are matched with their homologs and then arranged in descending order by size (Figure 3-5). The human karyotype consists of 46 chromosomes, which occur in 23 homologous pairs. One member of each pair was contributed by the father, and the other was contributed by the mother. The first 22 pairs of chromosomes, the autosomes, are numbered 1 through 22, with pair 1 being the largest and pairs 21 and 22 being the smallest. The twenty-third pair, the sex chromosomes, are labelled X and Y. A human female has two X chromosomes; a male has one X and one Y.

When a metaphase chromosome is examined more closely, it is seen that each chromatid is composed of a highly condensed material known as **chromatin.** If all of the chromatin in a single somatic cell were to be unraveled and stretched end to end, it would be several feet long. The compaction of these long strands of chromatin into chromosomes involves several levels of coiling and supercoiling.

When examined closely, the long piece of chromatin is seen to be composed of approximately equal amounts of **deoxyribonucleic acid** (DNA) and a specific type of protein called **histone.** It is believed that there are five different types of histones in chromatin. Two copies each of four of these histones are grouped together in a rounded cluster. A strand of DNA, approximately 200 base pairs long, is wrapped around this histone cluster. This DNA-wrapped histone cluster is referred to as a **nucleosome.** The DNA makes approximately 1¾ to 2 full turns around the histone cluster. A strand of DNA approximately 140 base pairs in length is involved in this wrapping. The remaining length of DNA, approximately 60 base pairs, acts as a link between nucleosomes. The fifth histone, in a single copy, is attached to this piece of linker DNA (Figure 3-6).

The compaction of chromatin into nucleosomes results in approximately a seven-fold decrease in its overall length. The chromatin is further compacted through coiling and supercoiling (Figure 3-7). While the mechanism by which this occurs is not fully understood, the ultimate product is a chromo-

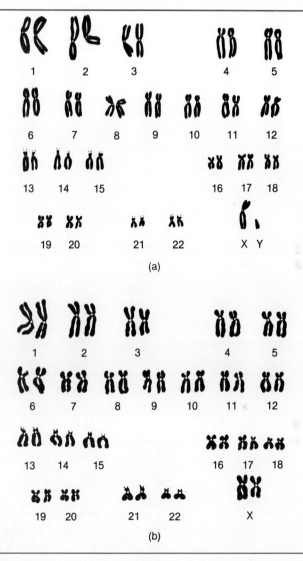

Figure 3-5 *The karyotypes of a normal human male (A) and female (B).*

some (or chromosomes) in which the genetic material has been compacted to less than 1/8,000 of its original length.

The highly compacted structures that are recognized as chromosomes appear in this form only during the active stages of cell division. Normally, the chromosomes are unwound and the chromatin is dispersed in thread-like form throughout the nucleus. There is strong evidence that DNA is relatively inactive in its compacted form. Most protein synthesis occurs when the chromatin is relatively loosely packed or in a dispersed state.

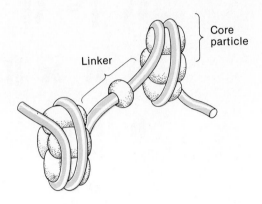

Figure 3-6 The structure of a nucleosome.

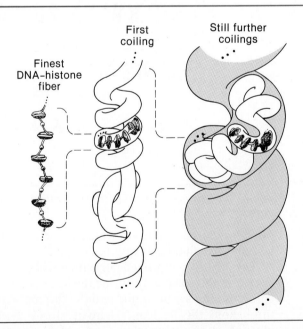

Figure 3-7 The compaction of chromatin into chromosomes through supercoiling.

THE STRUCTURE OF DNA

Chromatin, as just noted consists of approximately equal amounts of protein and DNA. The DNA, which is coiled around the histones, forming the nucleosomes, is itself helical in structure. A strand of DNA is composed of two vertical "backbones" formed by alternating molecules of **deoxyribose** (a sugar) and **phosphate groups.** These backbones are attached to each other by horizontal "rungs" formed by pairs of **bases.** This ladder-like molecule is then twisted into a helical structure, somewhat resembling a spiral staircase (Figure 3-8). This shape, described as a double helix, was initially recognized by James Watson and Francis Crick. Thus it is sometimes referred to as the Watson-Crick model. (For an interesting account of the discovery of DNA as hereditary material and the eventual "breaking" of the "genetic code", see Gribben, 1985.)

The bases are attached to the sugars on each backbone and project inward, toward the center of the helix. A single phosphate, sugar, and base complex is known as a **nucleotide.** The nucleotides forming each side of the DNA helix are joined by hydrogen bonds which form between the two bases (Figure 3-9). This **nucleotide pair** is the basic building block of DNA. A strand of DNA can be viewed as a series of stacked nucleotide pairs, connected to each other through the bonds which are formed between the alternating sugars and phosphates.

Four types of bases are found in DNA: adenine, guanine, cytosine, and thymine. Based on their size and structure, the bases are classified into two groups: the **purines** and the **pyrimidines.** The purines (adenine and guanine) have a double-ringed structure (Figure 3-10) and are larger than the pyrimidines (cytosine and thymine). Because of this difference in size and structure, a smooth, stable helix can occur only when a purine is bonded to a pyrimidine.

DNA DOUBLE HELIX

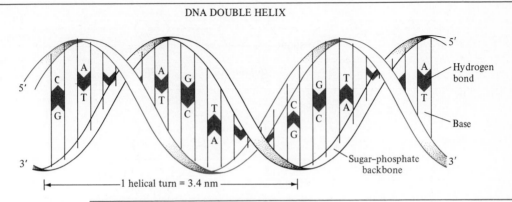

Figure 3-8 *The structure of DNA.*

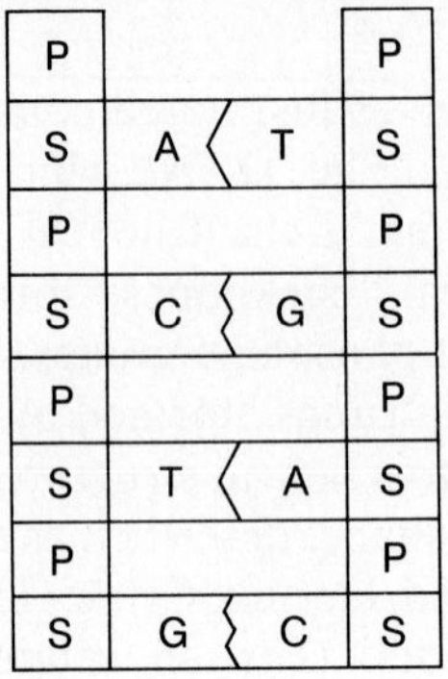

P			P
S	A	T	S
P			P
S	C	G	S
P			P
S	T	A	S
P			P
S	G	C	S

Figure 3-9 Base pairing in the DNA molecule.

If two bases from the same class were allowed to bond to each other, the helix would consist of a series of bulges and constrictions along its length, and its stability would be considerably reduced. Thus, one of the basic "rules" regarding DNA structure is that nucleotide pairs always consist of one purine bonded to one pyrimidine. Actually, the bonding is even more specific, with adenine always bonding to thymine, and guanine always bonding to cytosine. Bases that bond to one another are said to be complementary.

Since the base-pairing is very specific, it is often convenient to describe DNA in terms of the bases found along one side of the strand. At the level of the DNA molecule, a **gene** is defined as the specific sequence of bases responsible for producing a given trait. There are, in fact, two types of genes: structural and regulatory. **Structural genes** are those segments of DNA that are

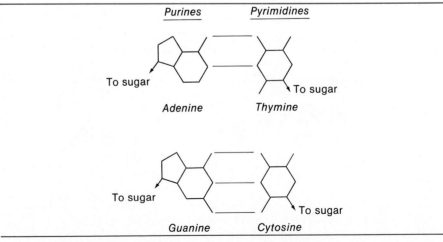

Figure 3-10 The structure of bases: purines and pyrimidines.

directly responsible for producing a specific trait. **Regulatory genes** consist of sequences of DNA that are responsible for controlling the activities of the structural genes. They are sometimes, but not necessarily, located near the structural genes which they control. A single regulatory gene may, in fact, control the expression of several different structural genes (Chambon, 1981).

Genes vary tremendously in length, from a few thousand to hundreds of thousands of base pairs. While it has been estimated that human chromosomes contain anywhere from 50,000 to 100,000 genes, the specific location of most genes is unknown. Despite the rapid, accurate sequencing techniques now available, the exact chromosomal location is known for less than 1 percent of all genes. Sequencing studies have confirmed, however, that the amount of DNA present in human chromosomes far exceeds that necessary to account for all of the genes. In fact, it has been suggested that structural and regulatory genes comprise less than 30 percent of all DNA. The remaining 70 percent seems to consist of nonfunctional "spacer" segments and numerous repetitive sequences of variable length. The function of these sequences is unknown, but the regularity of the pattern of bases in each sequence suggests that they are not merely "filler," but that they perform some kind of role either in the structure of the chromosome or in the expression of genes on it.

The locations of the nonfunctioning "spacer" segments are rather interesting. As might be expected, genes are separated from one another by such sequences. However, some of these spacer segments are also found within the genes themselves. When found within a structural gene, the nonfunctioning sequences are called **introns.** Whether or not these sequences originally served some function, they do not seem to interfere with the functioning of the gene. They are simply ignored or skipped over, as the gene's instructions are being "read." The possible evolutionary significance of these intervening sequences is discussed in the next chapter.

The hereditary material contained in cells is passed from one generation to the next through the process of sexual reproduction. By recombining the genetic material inherited from each parent and then reducing it by one-half, the process of meiosis ensures that variability will be maximized in each generation. Traits are inherited from each parent in the form of genes on chromosomes. Whether or not a particular version of a gene is expressed depends on the nature of the variants inherited from each parent. The function of the hereditary material, discussed in the next chapter, is in many ways a product of its structure, which is detailed in this section.

BIBLIOGRAPHY

*Carlson, E. A. 1984. *Human Genetics.* Lexington, Mass.: D. C. Heath.

Chambon, P. 1981. Split genes. *Scientific American* (May 1981).

*Cummings, M. R. 1988. *Human Heredity: Principles and Issues.* St. Paul, Minn.: West Publishing.

GRIBBEN, J. 1985. *In Search of the Double Helix: Quantum Physics and Life.* New York: McGraw-Hill.

LYON, M. F. 1962. Sex chromatin and gene action in the mammalian X chromosome. *American Journal of Human Genetics* 14: 135–48.

*MANGE, A. P., AND E. J. MANGE. 1980. *Genetics: Human Aspects.* Philadelphia: Saunders.

PATTERSON, D. 1987. The causes of Down syndrome. *Scientific American:* (August 1987), pp.52–61.

*SUTTON, H. E., AND R. P. WAGNER. 1985. *Genetics: A Human Concern.* New York: MacMillan.

*Recommended Reading (not cited)

The Function of

Hereditary Material

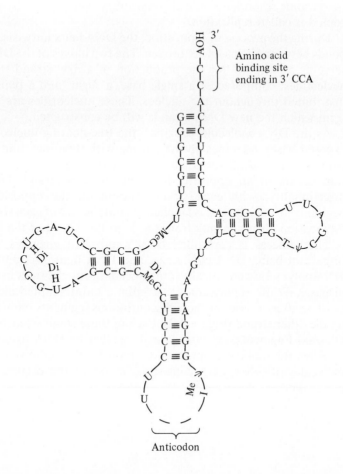

Anticodon

In the previous chapter, we described the structure of the genetic material, DNA. In this chapter, we will discuss the way in which this material functions as both the carrier of the hereditary material and the regulator of the expression of those traits. As with any organic system, errors occasionally occur. This chapter will also examine the evolutionary significance of the alterations and modifications that occur in the genetic material as a natural byproduct of its various functions.

DNA REPLICATION

In order to be transmitted across generations, a mechanism must exist by which the hereditary material can be duplicated. During both meiosis and mitosis, cell division begins only after the chromosomes are duplicated. The duplication process is really quite simple. The tightly packed chromosomes uncoil, exposing the strands of DNA. Each DNA strand is then copied, and the two strands recondense into chromosomes. The process by which the DNA is copied is called **replication.**

During the process of replication, the DNA helix untwists, and the chemical bonds between the bases are broken. The two halves of the DNA molecule each serve as a template for the production of a new strand (Figure 4-1). DNA **nucleotides,** composed of a single base, a sugar, and a phosphate group, are distributed throughout the nucleus. These nucleotides are the raw materials from which the new DNA strands will be constructed.

As the DNA molecule "unzips," the free-floating nucleotides bond to the exposed bases, adenines always pairing with thymines, and cytosines pairing with guanines. Both strands are replicated simultaneously, although replication occurs in an opposite direction on each strand. DNA strands have directionality, with each strand running in the opposite direction. The beginning of each strand is labelled 5′, and the end of each strand is labelled 3′. Replication always occurs from the 5′ to the 3′ end of the molecule.

This process is controlled by a number of enzymes, two of the most important being **DNA polymerase** and **DNA ligase.** As replication proceeds, DNA polymerase chemically joins each of the nucleotides in the growing chain of bases. While replication can continue uninterrupted along one strand, it must occur as a series of short discontinuous segments replicating "backward" up the other strand (Figure 4-2). Each of these small segments of DNA, called **Okazaki fragments,** are later joined together by DNA ligase.

When the replication process is complete, the end product is two identical molecules of DNA, each consisting of one of the original strands and one newly synthesized strand.

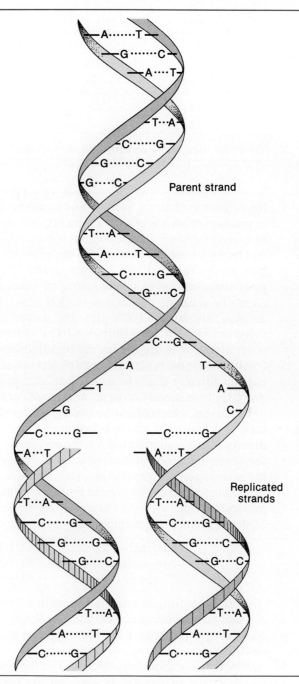

Figure 4-1 Replication of the DNA Molecule

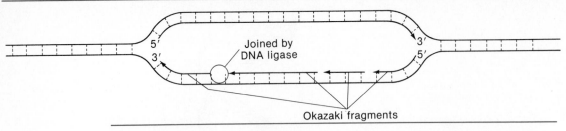

Figure 4-2 Okazaki fragments and the role of DNA ligase in replication of DNA.

MUTATION

Replication is characterized by an extremely precise pairing of bases. In order to produce an identical copy of the original molecule, the original strand must be copied faithfully. Occasionally, however, errors will occur. The wrong base will be substituted, a base on the template strand will be skipped, or an extra base will be inserted into the new strand. These errors in replication, called **point mutations,** alter the sequence of bases in a gene and may profoundly affect the ultimate expression of that gene. The genetic disorder sickle-cell anemia, discussed in Chapter 26, occurs in individuals who produce a defective form of hemoglobin A. The defective gene results from a single point mutation in a gene several hundred bases long.

Although most mutations are deleterious, some are not. Some mutations do not functionally alter the expression of a gene, and it should be noted that every allele originally arose as an altered form of an original gene.

Mutations are classified according to how they alter the gene. The simplest kind of mutation is a **base substitution.** This type of mutation occurs when a different base is substituted for the correct one. A base-substitution mutation can result in any one of three situations. In one instance, the mutation changes the meaning of the genetic message; this is a **missense mutation.** New alleles arise as the result of this type of mutation. **Nonsense mutations** occur when the mutation is such that the message becomes unreadable. These situations are analogous to altering a single letter in a simple sentence:

Original sentence: SUE SAW THE CAT
Nonsense mutation: SUE SRW THE CAT
Missense mutation: SUE SAW THE BAT

A base substitution can also result in a "neutral" mutation. In some cases, the sequence of bases can be altered slightly with no detectable effect on the trait being expressed. If the mutation has no apparent effect, it is said to be neutral.

When errors in replication result in the addition or deletion of a base, the effect on the expression of the gene is particularly great. These types of mutations are called **frameshift mutations** because they alter the reading frame, affecting all of the bases downstream from the insertion or deletion.

Original sentence:	SUE SAW THE CAT
After addition:	SRU ESA WTH ECA T
After deletion:	SES AWT HEC AT

Sometimes the term mutation is also applied to errors that occur at the chromosomal level. These "mutations" do not usually occur during replication, but are more frequently the result of errors that take place during the period of synapsis and crossing over that occurs during meiosis. During crossing over, entire segments of chromosomes are broken off and physically exchanged with the corresponding segments on the homologs. Occasionally, errors occur and pieces of chromosomes are lost **(deletions),** are attached to the wrong chromosome **(translocations),** or are rotated 180 degrees before being joined to the new chromosome **(inversions)** (Figure 4-3). The extent to which the individual is affected by mutations of this type depends on the size of the pieces and the particular genes involved. If a translocation or inversion brings a structural gene into contact with a different regulatory gene, the impact on the expression of the gene could be quite profound.

It has been suggested that chromosomal rearrangements of this sort may have played a significant role in the evolution of the higher primates (King and Wilson, 1975). Humans, chimpanzees, and gorillas have approximately 98 percent of their DNA in common. The two percent difference in DNA is responsible for a remarkable number of biological and phenotypic differences. It is suspected that differences in regulatory genes are largely responsible for these differences. A number of inversions and translocations distinguish ape chromosomes from those found in humans. It is possible that some of these chromosomal alterations reflect different relationships between the regulatory and structural genes present in each species.

It is important to recognize that mutations are of evolutionary significance only when they occur during meiosis. When a replication occurs during replication in a cell undergoing meiosis, the mutation will appear in the gamete and then ultimately in the offspring. Since additional variability is introduced into the system through gametic mutation, for a new allele to arise, or a new variant to appear, the mutation must occur during meiosis.

Mutations do occur during mitosis as well. Although this might cause some problem for the individual (for example, many cancers are characterized by uncontrolled mitosis, possibly due to a somatic cell mutation), a mutation of this type will not be passed on to the offspring and is thus of no evolutionary significance.

Mutations occur as a normal byproduct of a simple but necessarily precise replication process. Given the number of bases that must be found, matched to their counterparts on the original strand, and then attached to one another by enzymes, mistakes are not unexpected. Mutations occur regularly, with some genes apparently more prone to mutation than others. While some level of mutation is always expected, a number of environmental factors can markedly increase the rate at which mutations occur. Radiation, heat, and a variety of

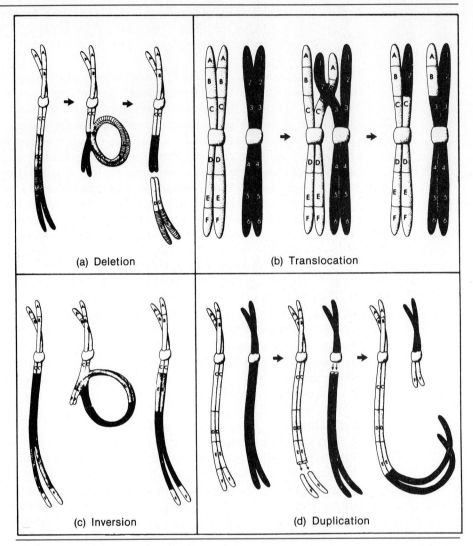

Figure 4-3 Types of chromosomal mutations.

both man-made and natural chemicals can all significantly increase the chance that replication will be disrupted.

DNA, TECHNOLOGY, AND EVOLUTION

Advances in DNA technology have given us the ability to sequence a given gene and compare it with others. New techniques that involve the isolation of particular genes, or portions of genes, have allowed scientists to develop new vaccines and medical treatments. Human insulin genes can be inserted into bacteria, which then incorporate the gene into their own DNA and produce human insulin. Other hormones and enzymes can be mass-produced in the same way, faster and at lower cost than synthetic versions can be produced. It may eventually be possible to directly alter defective genes in humans by introducing a copy of the normal gene into a developing fetus or an afflicted adult. While this kind of gene therapy is highly controversial, it is currently the focus of much of DNA research.

One of the results of this type of DNA research has been the development of techniques that allow the DNA of two different species to be compared. Fragments of DNA from two different species can be artificially combined into a hybrid segment. This technique, called **DNA hybridization,** involves the separation of each fragment of DNA into its two component strands. Each strand is then combined with the complementary strand from the other species, with bonds forming between the complementary bases. By analyzing the number of matches and mismatches between bases on the hybrid strands of each DNA fragment, it is possible to determine the degree of similarity between two species at the DNA level.

DNA hybridization studies have provided anthropologists with information regarding the genetic relationships among primates. The DNA of humans, chimpanzees, and gorillas differ from one another by approximately 2 percent; that is, when strands of DNA from any two of these species are combined, about 98 percent of the bases match exactly, with only 2 percent mispairing. By comparison, human DNA differs from that of orangutans by about 4 percent, and from baboons by about 8 percent. The exact degree of difference depends to some extent on the particular fragments of DNA being compared; thus different studies may give slightly different values.

Some studies have suggested that humans and chimpanzees are slightly more closely related than are humans and gorillas or gorillas and chimpanzees. Other studies have suggested that humans and gorillas may be slightly closer than either is to the chimpanzee. Still other studies indicate that the chimpanzee and gorilla are about equally distant from humans in terms of the sequence divergence of their DNA. Since these different interpretations are based on differences at the level of a fraction of a percent, and since the variation between samples in each study (using different fragments of DNA) often exceeds the variation between the species within each study, the relative relationship of the human, chimpanzee, and gorilla is currently unresolved (Cronin, 1983).

Although the degree of DNA difference among humans, chimpanzees, and gorillas is too small to clearly distinguish the order of their divergence, DNA hybridization studies have confirmed interpretations based on fossils regarding the order of divergence of the major primate groups. The differences between the DNA of two related species can be attributed to the cumulative effects of mutation in each lineage over time; thus the greater the difference in DNA, the more distant the relationship between the species. Based on the degree of similarity in their DNA, it appears that humans, gorillas, and chimpanzees are next most closely related to the orangutans, then to the gibbons, and much more distantly to the monkeys and prosimians (Figure 4-4).

While it is generally agreed that DNA hybridization allows anthropologists to determine the relative relationship among species, it is less clear whether this technique can be used to accurately assess the degree of that relationship. Some researchers have suggested not only that the degree of DNA similarity indicates a relative divergence time, but also that the degree of difference can be directly converted into a measure of the amount of time elapsed since the divergence occurred. The variability in DNA sequence between species then becomes the basis for a **molecular clock** (Wilson et al., 1974).

If the differences between two species are the result of accumulated mutations, and if these mutations have occurred at a constant, measurable rate, then it should be possible to determine the amount of time required for the mutations to have accumulated to the current level. Using this technique, researchers have suggested that the human, chimpanzee, and gorilla divergence occurred approximately 6 M.Y.A., that the orangutans diverged from the other great apes approximately 13 M.Y.A., and that the gibbons diverged from the other apes approximately 18 M.Y.A.

Critics of the molecular clock approach point out that it makes a number of assumptions which may not be entirely valid. For example, the calculations involved in converting percent difference in DNA to elapsed time are based on the assumption that the mutation rate has been constant throughout the

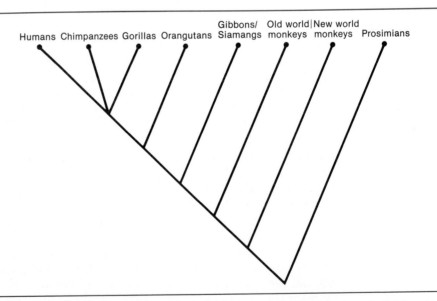

Figure 4-4 The relative divergence times of the primates based on hybridization data.

history of the lineage. If the average mutation rate has varied at different times, or if the rate was significantly higher or lower than presumed, then the molecular clock may be inaccurate.

It is likely, in fact, that the molecular clock underestimates the elapsed time in most lineages. This notion is supported by the fact that the fossil record suggests that while the relative divergence times are probably correct, the actual dates of divergence were probably somewhat earlier. Part of this apparent contradiction may stem from the fact that the calculations used in establishing the total number of mutations in each lineage assume that each mutation is unique, with only a single mutation occurring at each site. If the same base is subject to a series of mutations over time—for example, from an A to a T to a C and back to an A again—this series of three mutations is indistinguishable from a case in which no mutation occurred. Thus, measuring the amount of sequence difference does not necessarily reflect the number of mutations that actually occurred (Jukes, 1980). Likewise, there is no way of ever knowing whether the average mutation rate currently observed has been constant through time. It is simply not possible to determine what the average mutation rate of primate DNA was 30 million years ago.

Debate continues as to whether the molecular clock is a valid application of DNA hybridization techniques and data. Both proponents and critics agree that the similarity of DNA sequences between two species is indicative of the degree of evolutionary relationship between them. At issue is whether this technique can be used to establish an actual divergence date or whether it is capable only of establishing relative divergence times.

Interest in DNA sequencing and its ability to establish relative divergence times among species has naturally led investigators to question whether the techniques involved could be applied to the analysis of divergence patterns of populations within the human species. Since the differences in DNA sequence between various human groups is immeasurably small, standard DNA hybridization techniques do not provide useful divergence data.

Researchers interested in the patterns and times of divergence of various human populations have applied the techniques of DNA hybridization and the principles of the molecular clock to the analysis of human mitochondrial DNA (Brown, 1980). Mitochondria are involved in the energy metabolism of the cell. These organelles, found in the cytoplasm, are unusual in several respects. First, they have their own DNA, separate and distinct from that found in the cell's nucleus. When a cell undergoes mitosis, the mitochondria also replicate, with copies being allocated to the daughter cells. Second, mitochondria are maternally inherited; that is, all mitochondria are inherited from the mother. Since all mitochondria are maternally derived, there is no recombination during meiosis, and each egg theoretically receives identical copies of the mother's mitochondria. Thus every individual, male and female, carries copies of his or her mother's mitochondria.

Maternal inheritance, and the fact that they possess separate DNA, make mitochondria an ideal tool for tracing relationships among humans. Since there is no recombination, and since the mitochondria of only one parent are involved, any variation in the mitochondrial DNA across generations should be due to mutation. Another feature of mitochondrial DNA that makes it a particularly useful tool is the fact that it has a rather high mutation rate—much higher than that of nuclear DNA. Because it has a higher mutation rate, mutations should be expected to accumulate faster in mitochondrial DNA than in nuclear DNA. This higher rate of accumulated mutations should allow members of the same species to be compared with each other, something not possible with nuclear DNA.

The analysis of mitochondrial DNA has recently been applied to the problem of the origin and divergence of various populations of humans (Cann et al., 1987). Comparison of variability in sequences of mitochondrial DNA in various human groups may provide information that can be used to determine the relative divergence times, that is, the order of divergence of various human populations. Some researchers have taken this analysis one step further and, by applying the principles of the molecular clock, have tried to establish divergence dates for various human groups. While this approach suffers from many of the same problems as the nuclear DNA clock, it is a potentially useful tool for understanding some of the genetic relationships among humans.

GENES AND PROTEINS

Over 50,000 kinds of **proteins** are present in the human body. Proteins are involved in virtually every structural and metabolic process. Examples of functional proteins include **enzymes** and **hormones.** Proteins also serve structural roles as the major components of tissue. Proteins provide the structural framework of bones, muscles, ligaments, hair, skin, and other tissue. Proteins are also a crucial part of the cellular communication and transport network. **Hemoglobin,** a protein, is involved in the transport of oxygen by red blood cells. The **antibodies,** which play a major role in the effective function of the immune system, are also types of proteins.

Proteins are composed of strings of relatively simple molecules called **amino acids.** There are 20 different kinds of amino acids found in biological compounds. These, in various combinations, produce all of the different kinds of proteins. Some proteins are very simple, composed of a few hundred copies of only one or two amino acids. Others are quite complex, involving thousands of copies of many different amino acids. Amino acids are joined by chemical bonds, called **peptide bonds.** A chain of several amino acids is called a **polypeptide.** Some proteins are composed of a single polypeptide chain; others are composed of two or more polypeptides. Regardless of the complexity of the protein molecule, all proteins are composed of varying combinations of only 20 amino acids. Some of these amino acids are made by the organism, while others must be ingested in the form of animal or plant protein. The amino acids present in dietary protein are broken down by the cells, and the component amino acids are used to construct new proteins.

The construction of proteins from amino acids occurs in the cytoplasm of the cell, under the direction of genes present on chromosomes found in the nucleus. The relationship between the structure of the gene and the structure of a protein is now fairly well understood. As mentioned earlier, the term gene is used to describe that segment of DNA responsible for the expression of a single trait. More specifically, a gene is that segment of DNA responsible for producing a single protein. The information stored in the DNA determines the order in which specific amino acids are ultimately linked to produce a specific protein.

The order in which amino acids are linked to produce a particular protein is determined by the order in which the bases appear on a strand of DNA. Since there are 20 amino acids and only 4 bases, it is obvious that there cannot be a simple one-to-one relationship between base and amino acid. The **genetic code,** the specific way in which a sequence of bases represents a series of amino acids, must therefore involve some combination of the 4 bases, with groups of either 2 or 3 bases representing a single amino acid. If taken in pairs, there are still only 16 possible combinations, not enough to account for the 20 amino acids. If bases are taken 3 at a time, however, then 64 different combinations of bases are possible—enough to easily cover all 20 amino acids.

Each combination of 3 bases, called a **codon,** represents one amino acid. Since there are 64 possible codons, and only 20 amino acids, it is clear that the same amino acid is potentially represented by a number of different codons. Three of the codons serve as markers for the end of a coding sequence and are known as **stop codons.** The remaining 61 codons represent each of the 20 amino acids. The names of the amino acids, their abbreviations and corresponding codons are listed in Table 4-1.

The redundancy in the code means that it is possible for slightly different base sequences to "code" for the same protein. When a point mutation occurs in the DNA of a cell, the substitution of a new base will result in a different codon. If the new codon represents a different amino acid from that in the original, then a different protein will be produced. The hemoglobin variant found in sickle-cell anemia is due to the substitution of a single base, altering a single codon, changing the sixth amino acid in the 146 amino acid–long chain from a glutamic acid to a valine. This single change has major consequences for the structure and function of the hemoglobin molecule.

Not all mutations have a noticeable effect on the resultant protein, however. If a mutation results in a new codon that happens to code for the same amino acid, then the protein will not be altered. Mutations of this sort are referred to as **neutral mutations.**

The DNA, containing a sequence of codons specifying the order in which amino acids are to appear in the resultant protein, is found in the nucleus of the cell. The amino acids, which are ultimately assembled into the specified protein, are found in the cytoplasm. Since there is no direct contact between

Table 4-1 The Genetic Code.

Amino Acid Symbol	Amino Acid	DNA Codon	mRNA Codon
ALA	Alanine	CGA, CGG, CGT, CGC	GCU, GCC, GCA, GCG
ARG	Arginine	GCA, GCG, GCT, GCC, TCT, TCC	CGU, CGC, CGA, CGG AGA, AGG
ASN	Asparagine	TTA, TTG	AAU, AAC
ASP	Aspartic acid	CTA, CTG	GAU, GAC
CYS	Cysteine	ACA, ACG	UGU, UGC
GLN	Glutamine	GTT, GTC	CAA, CAG
GLU	Glutamic acid	CTT, CTC	GAA, GAG
GLY	Glycine	CCA, CCG, CCT, CCC	GGU, GGC, GGA, GGG
HIS	Histidine	GTA, GTG	CAU, CAC
ILE	Isoleucine	TAA, TAG, TAT	AUU, AUC, AUA
LEU	Leucine	AAT, AAC, GAA, GAG, GAT, GAC	UUA, UUG, CUU, CUC CUA, CUG
LYS	Lysine	TTT, TTC	AAA, AAG
MET	Methionine	TAC	AUG
PHE	Phenylalanine	AAA, AAG	UUU, UUC
PRO	Proline	GGA, GGG, GGT, GGC	CCU, CCC, CCA, CCG
SER	Serine	AGA, AGG, AGT, AGC, TCA, TCG	UCU, UCC, UCA, UCG AGU, AGC
THR	Threonine	TGA, TGG, TGT, TGC	ACU, ACC, ACA, ACG
TRP	Tryptophan	ACC	UGG
TYR	Tyrosine	ATA, ATG	UAU, UAC
VAL	Valine	CAA, CAG, CAT, CAC	GUU, GUC, GUA, GUG
Stop Codors		ATT, ATC, ACT	UAA, UAG, UGA

the DNA and the amino acids, assembly of a protein must be directed through intermediary substances that have the ability to carry the DNA message from the nucleus to the cytoplasm, and to then interpret the DNA message, directing the assembly of the protein. The substances involved in this process belong to a class of molecules called **ribonucleic acids** (RNAs).

RNA is similar to DNA in many respects, although it has a number of unique characteristics that allow it to function as both a carrier and interpreter of the DNA message. Like DNA, RNA is composed of sugar, a phosphate group, and bases. Three of the four RNA bases are identical to those found in DNA: adenine, guanine, and cytosine. The fourth RNA base, uracil, is similar to the thymine found in DNA and is complementary to adenine. As suggested by its name, RNA has a different type of sugar than is found in DNA. Unlike DNA, RNA is composed of only a single strand. A fragment of RNA looks very much like one-half of a segment of DNA, distinguishable by the different sugar and the presence of uracil instead of thymine.

There are three major types of RNA, all involved in the translation of the message contained within a DNA sequence into a protein. The three types of

RNA are **messenger RNA** (mRNA), **transfer RNA** (tRNA), and **ribosomal RNA** (rRNA). The mRNAs are involved in carrying the message from the DNA to the cytoplasm. The rRNAs are combined with proteins to form structures called **ribosomes,** which are involved in the assembly of the proteins. The amino acids themselves are attached to tRNAs, which play a crucial role in the ordering of the amino acids into proteins.

It has been stated that each DNA codon represents a single amino acid and that the order in which the codons appear on a strand of DNA determines the order in which amino acids will appear in the finished protein. The significance of this statement becomes clearer with an understanding of the relationship between tRNAs and DNA. As mentioned earlier, tRNAs are found in the cytoplasm of the cell. The single-stranded molecules are folded into a shape that in two-dimensional form resembles a clover leaf (Figure 4-5).

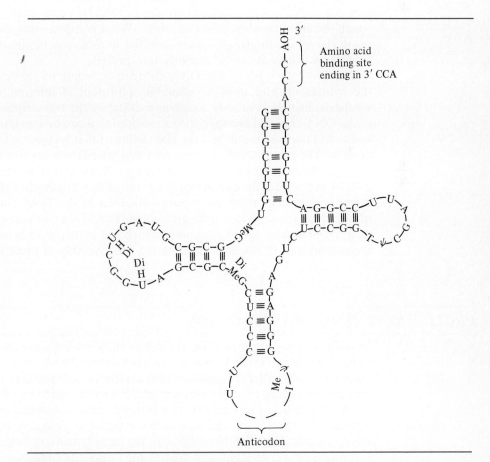

Figure 4-5 The structure of transfer RNA.

One end of the tRNA is attached to an amino acid. On one of the "arms" of the tRNA molecule is a sequence of three bases, called an **anticodon.** The anticodon on a particular tRNA is specific to the amino acid that it carries. For example, a tRNA with the anticodon CCG will attach itself only to a glycine, and a tRNA with an AAG will always carry a phenylalanine.

The anticodons on the tRNAs correspond directly to the codons found in the DNA, with the exception that RNA codons contain uracil, while DNA codons contain thymine. Thus the sequence AATCGTACC on a strand of DNA can be understood to specify that the amino acids carried by the tRNAs with the anticodons AAU, CGU, and ACC are to be assembled in precisely that order. Since the tRNA bearing the AAU anticodon carries a leucine, the tRNA with the CGU anticodon is attached to an alanine, and the ACC anticodon is found on the tRNA carrying a tryptophan, the DNA sequence AATCGTACC is essentially saying that the amino acids leucine, alanine, and tryptophan should be strung together to form a protein. Since each codon in a strand of DNA represents an anticodon on a particular tRNA, it is easy to see how the order in which codons appear in the DNA can specify the order in which the amino acids will be assembled. What is still missing, however, is the means by which the DNA sequence in the nucleus can be transmitted to the cytoplasm, where it can be properly interpreted.

The process by which the DNA-encoded instructions are read, carried to the cytoplasm, and used to assemble a protein is referred to as **protein synthesis.** Protein synthesis occurs in two stages: the **transcription** or copying, of the DNA-encoded message onto a medium that can be transported from the nucleus to the cytoplasm, and the **translation** of that message into a functional protein. The processes of transcription and translation involve the other two types of RNA described earlier, messenger RNA and ribosomal RNA. The mRNA molecule is unique in that it has the ability to pass through the nuclear membrane, transporting the message encoded in the DNA out to the cytoplasm where the protein is to be assembled. The rRNA combines with proteins to form structures called **ribosomes** which are involved in bringing together the mRNA and tRNA and coordinating the assembly of proteins.

PROTEIN SYNTHESIS: TRANSCRIPTION

In order to produce a protein, the DNA-encoded sequence must be copied onto a strand of mRNA, which can then leave the nucleus and enter the cytoplasm, where the message can be translated into a protein. The transcription process begins when the segment of DNA to be copied uncoils and the two DNA strands begin to separate. In a series of steps controlled by the enzyme **RNA polymerase,** RNA nucleotides are assembled along one of the exposed DNA strands. The RNA bases bond to the complementary bases on the DNA forming a strand of RNA that carries the "opposite" message from that on the DNA strand. Once the entire gene has been "copied" in this manner, the strand of RNA detaches from the DNA template and the DNA strands rejoin (Figure 4-6).

DNA double helix

Local unwinding

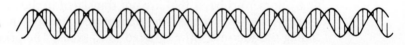

5′ RNA 3′

3′   5′

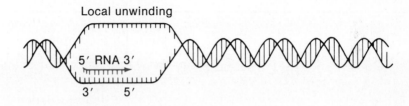

3′

5′

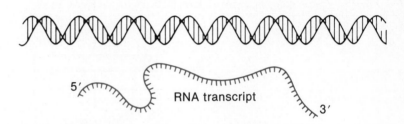

5′   RNA transcript   3′

Figure 4-6 Transcription of a messenger RNA on a DNA template.

This strand of RNA is referred to as a **primary transcript,** or sometimes as **premessenger RNA.** The base sequence of the primary RNA transcript is complementary to the sequence found in the DNA on which it was transcribed. Thus the DNA sequence ACGTACGGACCT would produce a primary RNA transcript with the sequence UGCAUGCCUGGA.

As discussed earlier, much of the DNA within a gene is noncoding. The series of codons that represent amino acids in the finished protein are broken up by numerous bases that are not translated in the final protein. Noncoding sequences, called **introns,** are interspersed throughout the gene, breaking the coding portion into units referred to as **exons.** The primary transcript copies the entire gene, including the introns. These noncoding regions are later spliced out so that only the coding portions, the exons, are translated (Figure 4-7).

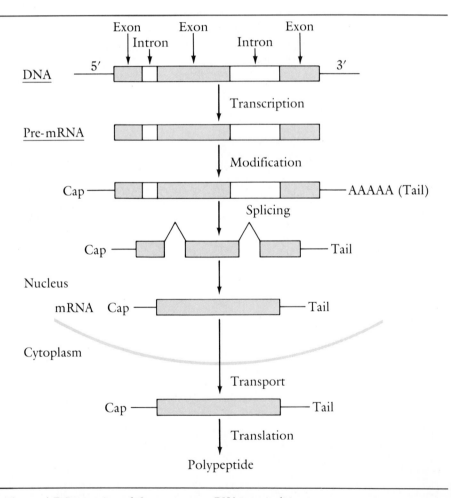

Figure 4-7 Processing of the messenger RNA transcript.

The primary transcript undergoes a series of modifications before it becomes a functional mRNA. First, a "cap" and a "tail" are added to the RNA transcript. The cap consists of a series of modified nucleotides, which are added to the 5′ end of the mRNA. The tail consists of a long series of adenines, which are added to the end of the mRNA strand. While the precise function of these added sequences is unknown, they appear to play an important role in the recognition and interaction of the mRNA with the ribosomes and tRNAs.

Once the cap and tail have been added to the mRNA primary transcript, the introns are spliced out, resulting in a segment of mRNA that contains only those codons that are to be translated into a protein. After undergoing these modifications, the mRNA leaves the nucleus and enters the cytoplasm, where the encoded message is translated into the appropriate protein.

This process, whereby a primary transcript is modified into a functional mRNA through the splicing out of noncoding segments, suggests a mechanism by which a single gene might actually be responsible for producing several different proteins. It is possible that a given sequence could act as an exon under some circumstances and as an intron under others (Borst and Grivell, 1981). Take, for example, a hypothetical gene composed of five exons and four introns. Let us assume that the normal gene product is specified by the codons contained in exons 1,2,3, and 4, and that exon 5 is normally spliced out along with the other introns. It is conceivable, however, that the primary transcript could be spliced differently, with exon 3 being spliced out and the mRNA consisting of exons 1,2,4, and 5. If the codon sequence in this secondary transcript produces a functional protein, then it is possible to have two different proteins, each deriving from the same primary transcript. The possibility that a single gene could code for more than one protein through the mechanism of differential processing of mRNA transcripts is of great interest to geneticists. It would mean that a relatively small amount of DNA could potentially code for an almost infinite number of different proteins. It is, in fact, believed that the extreme variability in proteins produced by the immune system is due to such a mechanism (Early et al., 1980). The way in which the immune system takes advantage of this phenomenon is discussed in Chapter 26.

PROTEIN SYNTHESIS: TRANSLATION

Once the primary mRNA transcript has been processed, the functional mRNA leaves the nucleus and enters the cytoplasm. There it attaches itself to a ribosome. Ribosomes are globular structures, composed of proteins and rRNA. Each ribosome consists of two subunits, with the smaller subunit "stacked" on top of the larger one. The mRNA attaches itself to a receptor in the smaller subunit. The mRNA attaches at the 5′ end such that the first codon fits into a groove in the surface of the ribosome (Figure 4-8).

On the other side of the ribosome there is a second receptor which is specific

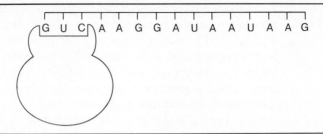

Figure 4-8 Protein synthesis: The first mRNA codon attaches to the ribosome.

to the anticodons of tRNAs. After the mRNA attaches its first codon to the ribosome, a tRNA with the complementary anticodon becomes attached to the other subunit of the ribosome, with a temporary bond forming between the mRNA codon and the tRNA anticodon. Once the appropriate tRNA has been brought to the ribosome, the next codon on the mRNA enters the ribosome's receptor. A second tRNA, with an anticodon complementary to the second mRNA codon, approaches the ribosome, and another temporary bond occurs. Each of the tRNAs at the ribosome are carrying amino acids. While the tRNAs are attached to the ribosome, peptide bonds form between the two amino acids.

After the first two tRNAs are attracted and the amino acids joined together, the ribosome continues to move down the length of the mRNA. The third codon enters the receptor, a third tRNA is attracted to the ribosome, and its amino acid is added to the growing chain (Figure 4-9). As the polypeptide chain grows, the bonds between the tRNAs and the amino acids are broken and the tRNAs are recycled, seeking out and binding to new amino acids.

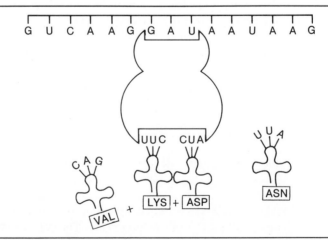

Figure 4-9 Protein synthesis: Amino acids are added to the polypeptide chain.

When the ribosome reaches the end of the mRNA and the last amino acid has been added to the polypeptide chain, the translation step of protein synthesis is complete. The mRNA may attach to another ribosome and synthesize another copy of the protein, or it may be broken down into nucleotides which can be recycled for use in another mRNA. The newly synthesized polypeptide chain may or may not undergo further modification before becoming a functional protein.

The process of protein synthesis is, then, a two-step process. The first step, transcription, involves the production of a mRNA, which carries a complementary copy of the DNA sequence. The mRNA sequence is complementary to both the DNA sequence and the tRNA's anticodon. Thus, through the intermediary role played by the mRNA, the sequence of DNA codons is able to specify the order in which the corresponding tRNAs are brought together and the protein is assembled. This process is presented schematically in Figure 4-10.

PSEUDOGENES AND EVOLUTION

Using enzymes that preferentially break bonds between particular pairs of bases, geneticists have been able to directly determine the base sequence of large segments of DNA. In addition to providing much information about the actual codons which comprise the functional portions of the gene, such studies have allowed geneticists to examine the introns and other noncoding sequences as well. Since such a large proportion of human DNA is composed of

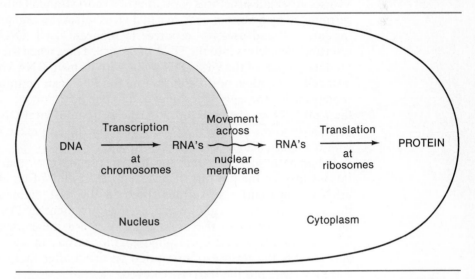

Figure 4-10 A schematic representation of the steps involved in protein synthesis.

noncoding sequences, its reason for existence is of great interest to geneticists. Studies of the sequences present in noncoding regions have in fact resulted in some very interesting insights into the evolution of certain genes (Blake, 1981; Hood et al., 1975).

In many instances, functional genes are separated by long stretches of DNA that do not code for proteins but which, when examined closely, show remarkable similarities to the adjacent functional genes. Some of the base sequences are virtually identical except for the presence of a few base substitutions that apparently prevent the sequence from being transcribed or translated. These noncoding regions which strongly resemble other, often adjacent, functional genes are called **pseudogenes.**

Pseudogenes exhibit too great a similarity to functional genes to exist by chance alone. Some pseudogenes include sequences that resemble both the introns and exons of the functional gene from which it apparently derived. It is thought that these pseudogenes may have originally arisen as the result of a process called **unequal crossing over.** This term refers to a situation that might result from an error occurring during meiosis, when the homologs trade genetic material. If an error occurs during crossing over in which the homologous chromosomes break at two different points and thus exchange unequal amounts of DNA, it is possible that one of the new chromosomes will possess two copies of some of the genes.

Some pseudogenes strongly resemble their functional counterparts, but curiously do *not* include the introns found in the functional gene. The presence of such sequences in the noncoding portion of the DNA may be explained as the result of the activity of an enzyme called **reverse transcriptase.** The activity of this enzyme is best understood from studies of how viruses infect cells. Viruses are small structures consisting of a short strand of either DNA or RNA surrounded by a protein coat. When a virus infects an organism, it takes over the host cell and uses its resources to replicate itself. DNA viruses act by inserting themselves into the DNA of the cell. Thus, when the cell replicates, it produces copies of the viral DNA along with its own. RNA viruses can use the host cell in a couple of different ways. The RNA can be translated into viral proteins using the cells' ribosomes and amino acids, or, as sometimes occurs, the viral RNA can be used to transcribe a strand of viral DNA, which can be inserted in to the host cell's DNA. Viruses are able to make DNA from RNA with the assistance of reverse transcriptase.

It has been suggested that the human pseudogenes that do not contain introns may be the product of reverse transcription of an already-processed mRNA. Apparently, at various times in the past, human mRNAs have, through reverse transcription, produced complementary DNA strands which have been inserted in the original DNA. Since these pseudogenes do not contain sequences that correspond to the introns in the original gene, it appears that the reverse transcription occurred after the primary transcript was processed and the introns removed.

Pseudogenes are of particular interest to those geneticists who study the evolution of genes. If pseudogenes originally formed by duplication or by reverse transcription, it is likely that the duplicated gene was functional, although unnecessary. A duplicate copy of a functional gene would be free to mutate randomly without conferring any disadvantage to the organism (Li, et al 1981). Over time, the duplicate gene would be expected to accumulate enough mutations to render it nonfunctional. Nevertheless, it would be expected to maintain a strong resemblance to the original. It is conceivable that on occasion, mutations occurring in duplicated genes could ultimately result in a functional, but different, gene.

There is strong evidence that a number of human genes are indeed derived from such duplicated genes. One of the best examples of such an occurrence involves the globin genes. Hemoglobin, a major component of red blood cells, is responsible for the binding and transport of oxygen through the bloodstream. In adult humans, each hemoglobin molecule is composed of four polypeptide chains. Two of these chains are identical copies of α **(alpha) chains** that are each 141 amino acids in length. The other two chains are identical copies of 146 amino acid–long β **(beta) chains.**

Three other types of hemoglobin are found in small amounts in the red blood cells of adults, but in greater quantities during embryonic and fetal development. In these variants, the hemoglobin molecule is still composed of four chains, with two copies of the alpha chain present in each. Instead of beta chains, however, these hemoglobin variants have two copies of either δ **(delta),** γ **(gamma),** or ϵ **(epsilon) chains.** These three variant chains are very similar to the beta chain and are believed to have derived from it by duplication. The genes coding for these chains appear to be adjacent to one another, forming what is referred to as a **gene cluster** or **gene family.** Pseudogenes found in this region suggest that there may have been several duplication events during the evolution of these genes, with some duplicates mutating into new genes and others becoming nonfunctional. The functional relationships among the members of a gene cluster is unclear. It is believed that in such cases, several structural genes may be under the control of a single regulatory gene. How genes are turned on and off and what determines the timing of their expression is still unknown, but is currently a major research focus.

Chromosomes, which carry the hereditary material, are composed largely of DNA. DNA is involved in two distinct but related processes: replication and protein synthesis. Both meiosis and mitosis require that the DNA in each cell be copied before it can be passed to the next generation of cells. While replication usually produces identical copies of the DNA molecule, errors occasionally occur. Such errors, called mutations, *can result in the altered expression of genes and can be of major evolutionary significance through the creation of new alleles.*

Protein synthesis, the process by which the instructions encoded in the DNA are translated into a functional protein, is of great interest to human biologists. The role of

DNA, enzymes, and the various types of RNA in protein synthesis have been discussed in some detail, as has the evolutionary significance of some of the observed changes in these genes.

BIBLIOGRAPHY

BLAKE, C. C. F. 1981. Exons and the structure, function and evolution of haemoglobin. *Nature* 291: 616.

BORST, P., AND L. A. GRIVELL. 1981. One gene's intron is another gene's exon. *Nature* 289: 439–40.

BROWN, W. M. 1980. Polymorphism in the mitochondrial DNA of humans as revealed by restriction endonuclease analysis. *Proceedings of the National Academy of Science, USA* 77: 3605–9.

CANN, REBECCA L., et al. 1987. Mitochondrial DNA and human evolution. *Nature* 325: 31–36.

*CRICK, F. H. C. 1962. The genetic code. *Scientific American,* Oct. 1962, pp. 66–77.

CRONIN, J. E. 1983. Apes, humans and molecular clocks: A reappraisal. In *New Interpretations of Ape and Human Ancestry,* R. L. Ciochon and R. S. Corruccini, eds, pp. 115–50. New York: Plenum.

*DARNELL, J. 1983. The Processing of RNA. *Scientific American,* Oct. 1983.

*DARNELL, J. 1985. RNA. *Scientific American,* Oct. 1985: pp. 68–87.

*DOOLITTLE, R. F. 1985. Proteins. *Scientific American,* Oct. 1985: pp. 88–99.

EARLY, P., et al. 1980. Two mRNAs can be produced from a single immunglobulin gene by alternate RNA processing pathways. *Cell* 20: 313–19.

*FELSENFELD, G. 1985. DNA. *Scientific American,* Oct. 1985: 58–67.

*GRIBBEN, J. 1985. *In Search of the Double Helix: Quantum Physics and Life.* New York: McGraw-Hill.

HOOD, L., et al. 1975. The organization, expression and evolution of antibody genes and other multigene families. *Annual Reviews of Genetics* 9: 305–53.

JUKES, T. H. 1980. Silent nucleotide substitutions and the molecular clock. *Science* 210: 973–78.

KING, M. C., AND A. L. WILSON. 1975. Evolution at two levels in humans and chimpanzees. *Science* 188: 107–16.

LI, W., et al. 1981. Pseudogenes as a paradigm of neutral evolution. *Nature* 292: 237–39.

*MILKMAN, R. (ed). 1982. *Perspectives on Evolution.* Sinaur.

*WATSON, J. 1976. *The Molecular Biology of the Gene,* 3d ed. Menlo Park, Calif.: W. A. Benjamin.

WILSON, A. C., et al. 1974. The importance of gene rearrangement in evolution: Evidence from studies on rates of chromosomal, protein and anatomical evolution. *Proceedings of the National Academy of Science, USA* 71: 3028–30.

*Recommended Reading (not cited)

Chapter

5

Principles of

Inheritance

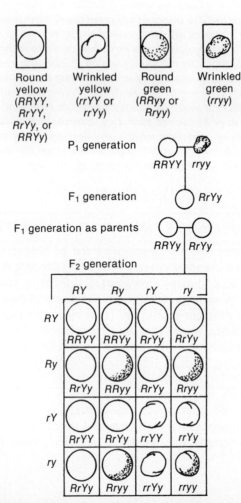

The transmission of inherited traits was a process that was recognized and manipulated long before it was even remotely understood. Artificial breeding of plants and animals had produced domesticated species that could be reliably maintained hundreds, perhaps thousands, of years before the demonstration of chromosomal inheritance. Throughout the nineteenth century, a number of misconceptions and myths persisted concerning the nature of inheritance, even though empirical efforts to breed domestic species had produced impressive results. Even Darwin was under the impression that determinants of physical characteristics were produced by the organs and tissues themselves rather than in the nuclei of the germ cells. The belief that a miniature version of an entire person could be found within each sperm was still widespread in the eighteenth and nineteenth centuries.

The elegant experiments of Mendel, using the domestic pea plant, demonstrated that inheritance involved the transmission of a determinant of each trait in some form of particle and that each individual received one determinant for each trait from each parent. By showing that an unexpressed trait could be transmitted intact to the next generation, Mendel was able to provide convincing evidence that some traits were dominant in the presence of others. Mendel's laws are still a fundamental part of the science of genetics even though the discovery of chromosomal inheritance did not occur until more than 40 years after he published the results of his experiments. Building on Mendel's work, geneticists have been able to unravel the mysteries of inheritance down to the molecular level. The occurrence of traits that are counted as well as those that are measured has led to the development of different approaches to the analysis of inherited traits. The distinction between discrete and continuous variables has been important in the development of biometric statistics, a branch of statistics that has been vital in the analysis of variation within and between populations. The mathematical elegance of Mendel's experiments set the stage for these applications of mathematical techniques to the study of biology.

THE TRANSMISSION OF TRAITS FROM ONE GENERATION TO THE NEXT

For evolution to occur, a species must be able to change in order to remain adapted to a changing environment. The concept of a changing earth is not an intuitive one, and many have found it difficult to accept. Before uniformitarian principles of geology were generally accepted (see Chapter 2), the idea of a drastically different earth populated by unfamiliar and sometimes grotesque creatures seemed more fanciful than scientific. Similarly, the notion of species evolving into other forms seemed absurd. In a world where species were fixed, or unchanging through time, the principle function of heredity would be to ensure that "like begot like." There would be no need for mechanisms to generate new variation in such a system, since deviations from the existing pattern would simply be "abnormal," and the future of the unfortunate possessor of abnormal traits was not promising.

If one accepts the "fixity of species," then the process of hereditary transmission of traits is primarily one of maintaining the continuity of the species. The major source of variation would be through hybridization, the mating of presumably unrelated individuals possessing different traits. Hybrids could be expected to be different from either parent but to bear some resemblance to each. The experience of animal breeders had long ago shown that intense inbreeding could be expected to enhance the expression of already-present characteristics. Breeds of dogs, domestic fowl, and horses had all been subjected to undeniably successful selective breeding programs long before the mechanisms of inheritance, as we now understand them, were comprehended. It should not be surprising that the idea that "all inheritance is blending" was widely accepted. It made sense, and it even agreed with much of the evidence derived from the empirical experiments that breeders were conducting as they "improved their breeds." In many instances, the mating of two individuals expressing extremes of a trait produces offspring who express intermediate values of it.

Contemporary biologists no longer believe in the fixity of species or in blending inheritance. As evidence for the occurrence of changes in the nature of the earth itself has accumulated, interest has shifted to mechanisms that permit species to change and thereby to survive. Thus the process of evolution demands that species be capable of "descent with modification." It is not sufficient, in a changing world, to merely perpetuate the characters already present. To avoid extinction, there must be a way for new and potentially useful traits to be produced, incorporated, and passed on to future generations. This crucial aspect of the biological makeup of species makes it possible for successful adaptations to spread through populations over time. It also provides species with some populations capable of surviving environmental shifts that might otherwise annihilate the entire species.

The science of genetics concerns itself with the processes by which inheritance and the production of new variations are achieved. Today, the science of genetics is subdivided into a number of subdisciplines, including molecular genetics and population genetics. A common thread runs through these subdivisions—namely, the basis for the transmission and expression of inherited traits. In recent years, major discoveries in physical chemistry and biochemistry have broadened our understanding of the molecular basis of inheritance. Earlier, developments in probability theory and statistics had opened the way to greater understanding of the distribution and spread of genes in populations. Developments in these areas of genetic research have been so impressive and striking that it is easy to forget that both are still concerned with a process that was elegantly described by an Austrian monk named Gregor Mendel (Figure 5-1) long before development of methods taken for granted by chemists and statisticians today. However, because Mendel's discovery of some of the "rules of the game" is so fundamental to an understanding of how inheritance works, the time taken to acquire some familiarity with the basic concepts of Mendelian genetics will be well rewarded when an understanding of molecular and population genetics is sought.

Figure 5-1 Gregor Mendel.

PRINCIPLES OF INHERITANCE

Lacking information about the molecular basis of inheritance and expression of traits, Mendel concentrated on the traits themselves. Mendel observed and recorded the transmission of well-defined characteristics from one generation to the next when individuals with distinct differences were bred with each other. Implicit in Mendel's strategy is a test of the hypothesis that "all inheritance is blending," since blending would eventually produce a sample population that was intermediate for each trait. For instance, a tall individual mating with a short individual would be expected to produce offspring of intermediate height. It would follow, of course, that if blending were the mechanism at work, medium-height individuals, when bred with other medium-height individuals, would necessarily produce only medium-height offspring. Also, a necessary result of blending would be permanent loss of a trait that disappears in any generation. It was known well before Mendel's time that traits could sometimes reappear after apparent disappearance. Blending did not explain such "throwbacks." The impressive thing about Mendel's experiments was that by a relatively simple series of breeding combinations, alternative explanations could be tested. The research design was straightforward enough that unambiguous outcomes could be analyzed by simple statistical procedures and interpreted with a high degree of confidence. Of course, these are all basic criteria for a well-designed scientific experiment, so it is worth taking a closer look at some of Mendel's experiments in order to gain an appreciation of how experimental science is conducted, as well as to see how some of the fundamental mechanisms of inheritance work.

PARTICULATE INHERITANCE

It had long been known that in sexually reproducing species, traits were inherited from both parents. It was by no means certain, however, that the contributions of the two parents to the hereditary makeup of the offspring were equal. Human families in which some children more closely resembled the father's or mother's side of the family were commonplace. Also, occurrence of a trait such as blue eyes in an offspring of two brown-eyed parents gave evidence that something other than blending of inherited characteristics existed. One explanation—the one that turned out to be correct—was that some sort of particle was transmitted to the offspring by each parent and that such particles could be present and transmitted by the offspring to their own offspring without necessarily being expressed in a given generation. When such unexpressed traits reappeared, they could be fully expressed, unchanged, despite a generation or more of nonexpression. Mendel chose a number of traits that could be followed through generations of experimental breeding and that expressed themselves in a clearcut way. The species of sexually reproducing organism that he selected was a garden pea *(Pisum sativum)* that he could grow in his monastery garden. It could also be protected from accidental pollination. Thus Mendel could cross-pollinate strains that possessed the traits he selected and be confident that the outcome of these hybridizations was not confused by uncontrolled fertilizations.

Mendel knew his garden peas well. On the basis of his experience in breeding them, he was able to identify seven traits, each possessing two well-defined alternatives, that could be followed through generations of cross-breeding. These traits are listed in Table 5-1. It was possible to follow the expression of each of these traits both individually and in the combinations that appeared in succeeding generations of breeding.

Table 5-1 Traits chosen by Mendel for breeding experiments with peas

Trait	Expression	
	Either	Or
1. Form of ripe seed	Round	Wrinkled
2. Color of pea	Yellow	Green
3. Color of seed coat	Gray	White
4. Form of ripe seed pod	Smooth	Constricted
5. Color of unripe seed pod	Green	Yellow
6. Position of flowers	Axial	Terminal
7. Stem length	Tall	Short (0.75 to 1.5 feet)

A strategy that made Mendel's experiments more successful than those of any of his predecessors was that he started with strains that were self-fertilized through enough generations that their offspring were uniform. Thus, for instance, he produced a strain that produced only long-stemmed plants when self-fertilized and another that produced only short-stemmed ones. From the perspective of a believer in blending inheritance, each of the strains might then be viewed as possessing maximum concentrations of tallness or shortness and would be expected to produce medium-height offspring.

What Mendel was able to show, however, was that when a parental strain producing only long-stemmed plants was cross-pollinated with a strain producing only short-stemmed ones, the offspring unfailingly produced long-stemmed plants. This was because tallness always expresses itself, whether inherited from one parent or from both. Thus it is a **dominant** trait, while shortness is a **recessive** trait.

Using another trait, round or wrinkled seeds, the experimental crosses can be traced through two generations, as shown in Figures 5-2 and 5-3. The first, or parental, generation is designated P_1. Their offspring are the first filial generation, designated F_1. The parental generation involved one parent that transmitted the round-seeds trait, while the other parent transmitted wrinkled seeds. All of the F_1 offspring of these matings produced round seeds. Thus round seeds is the dominant trait, and wrinkled seeds is the recessive trait. Although only round seeds are produced by the F_1 offspring, each of them remained capable of transmitting either round seeds or wrinkled seeds to their offspring. The offspring of the crossing of F_1 with other F_1 individuals produced an F_2 generation in which the wrinkled-seed trait reappeared in one-quarter of the individuals. These were the ones that inherited the wrinkled-seeds trait from both parents and were therefore **homozygous** for the recessive trait. Another one-quarter of the F_2 generation was homozygous for the round-seeds trait but were indistinguishable from the individuals in the F_2 generation who had received round seeds from only one parent. Thus, three-quarters of the F_2 generation was **phenotypically** of the round-seeds

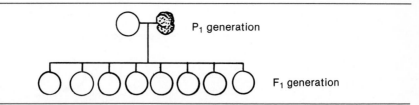

Figure 5-2 *Phenotypes of the F_1 generation when a round-seed producing plant was crossed with a wrinkled-seed producing plant.*

category and one-quarter of the phenotypically wrinkled-seeds category, the phenotype being the visible characteristics associated with the trait. However, the round-seed phenotypes were made up of two different **genotypes:** those receiving it from only one parent and those receiving it from both.

One of the features of Mendel's experiments was that the ratios of the phenotypes could be predicted (3 round seeds to 1 wrinkled seeds) and that these ratios permitted a reasonable explanation of how the trait was transmitted; that is, a particle possessed by a parent was transmitted intact to the next generation. These results also showed that each individual possessed two such particles, one inherited from each parent, and could transmit either one to a given offspring. We now call these particles **genes,** and when referring to the possible alternatives, the term **alleles** is now conventional. When the nature of the gene itself became known to be on a specific location on a chromosome, it became conventional to refer to it as a **locus.** Thus the locus for seed shape in Mendel's experiments exhibits two alleles: round and wrinkled. The genotypes produced by the mating of the F_1 heterozygotes are shown in Figure 5-4. Here *A* refers to the dominant allele (round), and *a* refers to the recessive allele (wrinkled).

Each of the traits Mendel selected behaved in a similar fashion when such breeding experiments were conducted. The 3-to-1 ratio seen when round and

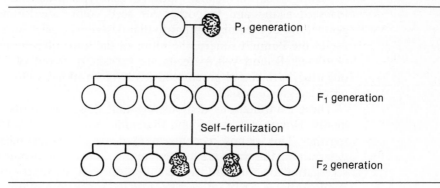

Figure 5-3 *The phenotypes produced in the F_2 generation when F_1 hybrids were allowed to self-fertilize.*

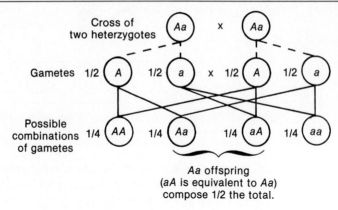

Genotypes of offspring are 1/4 *AA*, 1/2 *Aa*, and 1/4 *aa*,
a ratio of 1:2:1

Figure 5-4 The genotypes produced from a cross of two heterozygotes.

wrinkled seeds were inherited was also seen in the transmission of the traits for
seed color (3 yellow to 1 green), seed coat color (3 gray to 1 white), and so on.
Mendel had identified a general phenomenon.

When the behavior of two traits was observed at the same time, it became
evident that while both traits followed the same rules, each appeared to be
independent of the other. We know now that Mendel had been fortunate
enough to select loci that were located on different chromosomes. However,
Mendel did not know about chromosomes. The chromosomal basis for
inheritance would not be determined until 45 years after Mendel published his
results. Mendel arrived at his conclusions mathematically, without knowledge
of the structures located within the nucleus of the cell—a fact that makes his
research design especially impressive.

Figure 5-5 shows the distribution of genotypes produced when two loci, one
for seed shape and the other for seed color, are followed through two
generations of breeding similar to that described earlier for seed shape. By the
use of the Punnett square, the ratios of the four different phenotypes can be
predicted: Round yellow seeds are present in 9 out of 16 F_2 offspring; 3
offspring have round green seeds; 3 have wrinkled yellow seeds; and 1 has
wrinkled green seeds.

These combinations demonstrate that these two traits reassort independently. However, it was found that some other traits tended to be inherited
together. This we now recognize as evidence of **linkage,** meaning that the loci
determining the traits are located on the same chromosome and are therefore
segregating together and will remain together as chromosomes are reassorted.
While linkages are of interest because the separation of linked genes provides
evidence that chromosomes can on occasion exchange segments with their

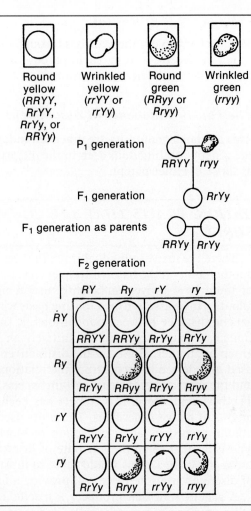

Figure 5-5 A Punnett Square showing how independent assortment was demonstrated.

partners, or homologues, the principles that Mendel discovered were best illustrated by the unlinked traits that were shown in Table 5-1.

MENDEL'S LAWS

From the elegant experiments he designed and conducted, Mendel derived certain general principles that are now known as Mendel's laws:

The Law of Segregation

The mechanism of inheritance is through the transmission of particles, one of which is received from each parent. One or the other can in turn be transmitted to the next generation without being changed.

The Law of Independent Assortment

This law holds that traits are inherited independently of one another and that the genetic combinations seen in the offspring need not therefore be the same as those in either parent.

DISCRETE VARIATION: TRAITS THAT ARE COUNTED AND NOT MEASURED

There are many individual traits that can differentiate one individual from another and, on the basis of frequencies, one population from another. A few of these have proven sufficiently useful in distinguishing probable genetic affinities to be assessed on a routine basis when attempts are made to assess the genetic distance between populations. It should be noted that none of these traits can be used to assign definitively an individual to one racial or ethnic group or another. However, the distinctiveness of their distributions has been used as a device to reconstruct the relationship of populations to each other and therefore to reconstruct certain aspects of human population movement. The best evidence in this respect has been that used to confirm the Asiatic origins of native Americans. The traits used in this area of reconstruction of human prehistory are a collection of biochemical and morphological characteristics that share the attribute of discrete inheritance. While many other traits and comparisons would serve to illustrate the potential uses of analysis of discrete variation, these will provide a useful example.

A genetic trait that produces a specific identifiable characteristic or some other specific alternative is called a **discrete** trait. Such traits are counted and their frequencies in the population are calculated in order to estimate the frequencies of the alleles that determine them. The traits that Mendel chose for his experiments were so informative because of their discrete character. The human blood groups have been valuable in comparing human populations because they also are discrete traits, and the frequencies of the alleles at a number of loci can be compared to assess the degree to which populations have become genetically different. Because such discrete traits are generally not susceptible to environmental modification in the way that continuous traits are, they provide a better opportunity to assess the genotypic characteristics of the individual or population directly from the phenotype. As shown by Mendel's experiments, discrete traits are frequently masked by the occurrence of dominance. This is the case when a person who has inherited both the allele for blood group O and that for blood group A is phenotypically type A.

Although the blood groups are the most frequently discussed of the discrete traits, there are many others that are of interest to human biologists. They are often used in combinations to assess **biological distance**—the degree of genetic divergence between two or more populations as determined by the application of the principles of Mendelian genetics in a population context. As the number of identifiable discrete traits has grown, they have become increasingly reliable indicators of individual genetic affinities as well, and with the most recently developed techniques, such problems as the establishment of true paternity are finding reliable answers.

Because no selective advantage has been demonstrated for many of the more well-known discrete traits, they are thought to be better indicators of genetic relationships between populations than are traits that can be modified by the environment. The production of **phenocopies,** or environmentally produced simulations of a genetic trait, is far less common in single-locus

Table 5-2 Summary of Principle Blood Group Distribution

System	Phenotypic Frequencies
ABO (including A_1 and A_2)	Type O most common, more than 50% of most individuals in a population. Type B nearly absent in American Indians and Australian aborigines. Type B present in up to 15% of Europe and 40% of Africa, Asia and India. A_2 limited primarily to Europe.
MNS-U	American Indians almost exclusively M; N most common in Australia and the Pacific. MS and NS absent in Australia. U-negative appears limited to Africa.
Rh (R_1, R_2, R_0, r, and others)	Rh negative (*rr*) rare or absent in most of the world, but found in 15% of Europeans. R_0, almost exclusively of African origin, found in 70% of Africans.
Duffy (*Fy^a^, Fy^b^, Fy*)	Most Australians and Polynesians and 90% of Asian populations. Duffy positive (*Fy^a^*) 90% in India, 85% to 90% in American Indians, 65% in England and America, 27% in American blacks. *Fy^a^* very low in Africa, but *Fy* gene is very common to about 80%.
Diego (*Di^a^, Di^b^*)	Diego-positive (*Di^a^*) limited to American Indians, 2%, to 20%, and Asians. Diego-positive is absent in Europe and Africa, and much of the Pacific and among Eskimos.
Kidd (*Jk^a^, Jk^b^*)	*Jk^a^*, Kidd-positive, is most common in West Africa and among American blacks, 90%. Also found in American Indians, 70% to 90%, Europeans, about 70%, and is least common among Chinese, 50% to 55%.

Source: Adapted from S. M. Garn, *Human Races,* 2d ed. (Springfield, Ill.: Chas. C Thomas, 1962), p.47.

discrete variation than in polygenic, continuous traits. Thus when the biological distance between populations is estimated, a constellation of discrete traits is usually preferred for comparison.

BLOOD GROUPS

Among the best-known traits of discrete variation in humans are the blood groups. More than 20 different blood groups are now known (see Tables 5-2 and 5-3). Some of these have clinical significance, but most are of interest mainly as genetic markers (traits that can be used to determine genetic affinities). The first blood group to be identified is that now known as the ABO system (see Table 5-3). It was discovered by a Viennese physician named Karl Landsteiner in 1900, but was referred to by an entirely different set of terms at the time. (Interestingly, Landsteiner was later awarded a Nobel prize for an entirely different area of research.) What Landsteiner identified was what he termed the "specificity of serological reactions" (Landsteiner, 1945). He had, as we now know, observed one form of an antigen–antibody reaction. The reaction could be identified by the occurrence of a clumping of red cells when a suspension of them was treated with the serum of an individual of a different blood type. This clumping is called an **agglutination reaction.** When the suspension is properly diluted, all of the red cells in it will agglutinate, leaving a clear fluid behind. It is now known that a successful agglutination reaction is the result of antibodies reacting with the antigenic sites on the surface of the red cells and attaching to them. Because each antibody has more than one antigen-binding site, some will simultaneously attach to two red cells linking them together tightly (cross-linkage) (Figures 5-6, 5-7, 5-8). When many cross linkages are formed, all of the cells in suspension can ultimately be drawn together.

Different blood-group antigens are recognized by different categories of antibodies. Not all of them will produce a straightforward agglutination reaction of the sort characteristic of the ABO test. For instance, testing for Rh blood types requires an additional step which produces agglutination by adding an additional antibody linking the Rh-specific antibodies attached to the red cells to each other. As the structure and function of antibodies has become better understood, the precision of blood typing has improved substantially, and it is likely that more blood groups will be discovered.

Table 5-4 shows frequencies of ABO blood groups in selected populations. Additional information about antibody structure can be found in Chapter 26.

HLA

The blood groups have proven to be useful markers for the identification of population affinities and of the biological distance of populations from each other. A more specific aspect of human variability at the level of the individual

Table 5-3 *History of Discovery of Red Blood Cell Antigens*

System	Year of Discovery	Number of Antigens Known
ABO	1900	6
MNS	1927	18
P	1927	3
Rhesus	1940	17
Lutheran	1945	2
Kell-Cellano	1946	5
Lewis	1946	2
Duffy	1950	2
Kidd	1951	2
Diego	1955	1
Xg	1962	1
Dombruck	1965	1

In addition to antigens of the major systems, there are also antigens found only in single families (private systems) or antigens which are common to most humans (public systems).

Private Systems		Public Systems
Levay	Romunde	1
Jobbins	Chr^a	Vel
Becker	Swann (Sw^a)	Yt
Ven	Good	Gerbich
Cavaliere	Bi (Biles)	Lan
Berrens	Tr^a	Sm
Wright (Wr^a)	Webb	
Batty		

SOURCE: Adapted from I. M. Lerner, *Heredity, Evolution, and Society, 2d ed.*, (San Francisco: W. H. Freeman & Company, Publishers, 1976), p. 354.

is seen in the HLA system. The antigenicity of human cells reflects the presence of specific **glycoproteins** (combinations of sugars and proteins) on their surfaces. Successful transplantation of tissues depends upon the degree to which the transplanted and host tissues differ with respect to these surface molecules. The properties of these glycoproteins are determined by four major genes, designated HLA-A, HLA-B, HLA-C, and HLA-D, all located on the short arm of chromosome 6. The glycoproteins coded by HLA-A, HLA-B, and HLA-C are found on the surface of all body cells that retain their nuclei. The HLA-D glycoproteins are found only on the surface of specialized cells, including macrophages, B lymphocytes, and activated T lymphocytes. The HLA-D site on the chromosome has three subregions: HLA-DR, HLA-DQ, and HLA-DP. A gene complex located on the same arm of chromosome 6 between the site occupied by HLA-D and those occupied by HLA-A, HLA-B,

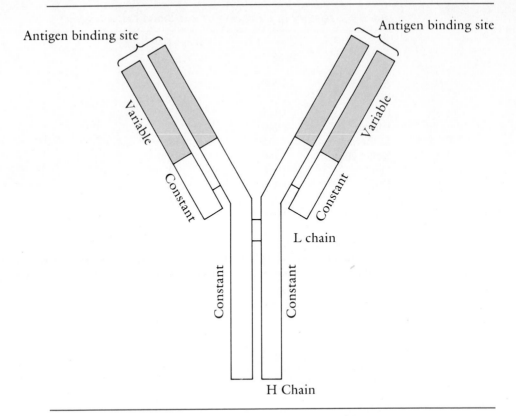

Figure 5-6 The structure of an antibody from the IgG fraction of human blood serum.

and HLA-C controls the production of **complement,** a substance necessary for the destruction of the target cell in a cell-mediated immune reaction.

When all of the complexes of genes controlling the entire range of HLA variability are taken into account, it can be seen to be the most polymorphic human genetic system. There are currently 23 known alleles of HLA-A, 47 alleles of HLA-B, 8 alleles of HLA-C, 14 alleles of HLA-DR, 3 alleles of HLA-DQ, and 6 alleles of HLA-DP. The nomenclature to designate the specific antigens present in this system uses the letter for the locus and a number for the allele at that locus. Thus there are alleles A1 through A23, B1 through B47, C1 through C8, DR1 through DR14, DQ1 through DQ3, and DP1 through DP6. Each of these alleles is codominant, and, since the genes for HLA are located so close together on the chromosome, they usually stay together without recombination during meiosis. With the chromosomes inherited from the two parents expressing all of the allelic variation the HLA system provides, millions of combinations are possible.

IgG

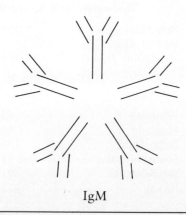

IgM

***Figure 5-7** Structure of an IgG antibody compared to that of an IgM antibody.*

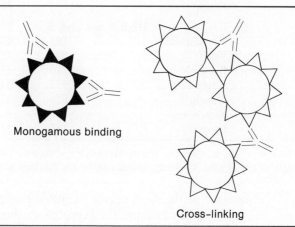

Monogamous binding

Cross-linking

***Figure 5-8** Comparison of a monogamous binding with a cross-linking reaction.*

Table 5-4 Frequencies of ABO Blood Groups

Population	Place	Number Tested	Blood-Group Frequency			
			O	A	B	AB
Low A, virtually no B						
American Indians:						
Toba	Argentina	194	98.5	1.5	0.0	0.0
Sioux	South Dakota	100	91.0	7.0	2.0	0.0
Moderately high A, virtually no B						
Navaho	New Mexico	359	77.7	22.5	0.0	.0
Pueblo	New Mexico (including Jemez)	310	78.4	20.0	1.6	.0
High A, little B						
American Indians:						
Shoshone	Wyoming	60	51.6	45.0	1.6	1.6
Bloods	Montana	69	17.4	81.2	0.0	1.4
Eskimo	Baffin Land	146	55.5	43.8	.0	0.7
Australian aborigines	South Australia	54	42.6	57.4	.0	.0
Basques	San Sebastian	91	57.2	41.7	1.1	.0
Polynesians	Hawaii	413	36.5	60.8	2.2	0.5
Fairly high A, some B						
English	London	422	47.9	42.4	8.3	1.4
French	Paris	1,265	39.8	42.3	11.8	6.1
Armenians	From Turkey	330	27.3	53.9	12.7	6.1
Lapps	Finland	94	33.0	52.1	12.8	2.1
Melanesians	New Guinea	500	37.6	44.4	13.2	4.8
Germans	Berlin	39,174	36.5	42.5	14.5	6.5
High A and high B						
Welsh	North Towns	192	47.9	32.8	16.2	3.1
Italians	Sicily	540	45.9	33.4	17.3	3.4
Siamese	Bangkok	213	37.1	17.8	35.2	9.9
Finns	Hame	972	34.0	42.4	17.1	6.5
Germans	Danzig	1,888	33.1	41.6	18.0	7.3
Ukrainians	Kharkov	310	36.4	38.4	21.6	3.6
Asiatic Indians	Bengal	160	32.5	20.0	39.4	8.1

SOURCE: Adapted from W. C. Boyd, "Genetics and the Human Race," *Science* 140: 1057–1064, 7 June 1963. Copyright © 1963 by the American Association for the Advancement of Science.

Because of the high degree of individuality inherent in the HLA system, HLA typing has become the accepted method of matching tissues for organ transplants. HLA antigenicity is the major element of the body's system of

Table 5-5 **Diseases Associated with HLA Alleles**

Disease	HLA Allele	Frequency in Affecteds (%)	Frequency in Nonaffecteds (%)
Ankylosing spondylitis	B27	90+	8
Rheumatoid arthritis	DR4	70	28
Psoriasis	B17	38	8
Reiter's syndrome	B27	75	8
Systemic lupus erythematosus	DR3	50	25

identifying self as opposed to nonself. And, for reasons that are still unknown, there is a high degree of association between certain HLA alleles and some diseases (see Table 5-5).

LACTOSE INTOLERANCE

Human milk is rich in lactose, which makes up 6.8 percent of its total volume. In a normal human infant, lactose is broken down to glucose and galactose by the enzyme lactase. In most humans, the production of lactase is highest in the perinatal period, declines in childhood, and is nearly absent in the adult (Kretchmer, 1981). Therefore, most adult humans cannot digest milk effectively and suffer bloating, flatulence, and diarrhea if milk is consumed in any significant quantity. In this respect humans are quite similar to most other mammals.

Lactose digestion occurs in the small intestine, at the brush border of the epithelium of the **villi,** or fingerlike projections that form the absorptive surface. It is thought that lactase is produced in the crypt cells of the small intestine (see Figure 5-9) and that these cells migrate outward on the villi with the enzyme attached to their membranes (Phillips, 1981). The enzyme is readily released from the membrane when protein digestion is taking place. The monosaccharides, galactose and glucose are readily absorbed when lactose is broken down and rapidly appear in the blood (Alpers, 1981). It is thought by some investigators (Flatz and Rotthauwe, 1977, Simoons, 1981) that the hydrolysis of lactose has an effect similar to that of vitamin D_3 on the enhancement of calcium absorption as well. This could have been a significant advantage in cloudy areas like northern Europe, where both vitamin D produced by the action of sunlight on the skin and that derived from food were in short supply during the winter months.

While most humans lose the ability to produce lactase in sufficient quantities to sustain lactose digestion, some populations retain the capacity

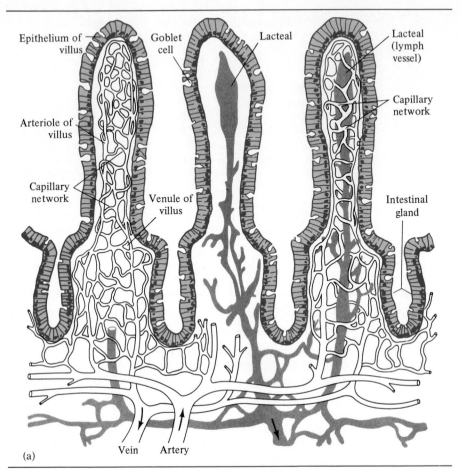

Epithelium of villus

Goblet cell

Lacteal

Lacteal (lymph vessel)

Arteriole of villus

Capillary network

Capillary network

Venule of villus

Intestinal gland

(a)

Vein   Artery

***Figure 5-9** The villi of the human small intestine.*

into adulthood. Human populations that exhibit continued lactase production have lived in areas where dairying and milk consumption have been important. Figure 5-10 compares the percentage of nondigestors of lactose in a number of populations. It can be seen that a European dairying population (the Danes) have only about 2 percent nondigestors while both African (Bantu) and Asian (Thai) nondairying populations have about 95 percent nondigestors.

An interesting exception to the low frequency of nondigestors seen in populations descended from peoples in traditional zones of milk consumption is the Arabs, 85 percent of whom are nondigestors. However, it seems likely that the practice in many parts of the Middle East of permitting milk to ferment, producing products such as yogurt, has eliminated the need for lactase, since fermentation breaks lactose down to simpler sugars before consumption through the action of bacterial enzymes.

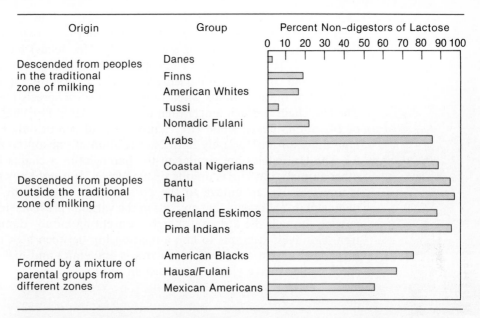

Figure 5-10 Percent non-digestor of lactose in dairying and non-dairying populations. (From D. Walcher and N. Kretchmer, Food Nutrition and Evolution *(New York: Masson Publishing, 1981), p. 5.*

The practice of dairying may have originated as many as 10,000 years ago (Simoons, 1981). The advantage of retention of lactase production into adulthood when a nutritious food resource such as mammalian milk became reliably available could have favored the mutant gene determining it. Its spread through the population could have been reinforced by improved calcium absorption associated with lactose hydrolysis. The gene for adult lactase production is a dominant one and is therefore expressed in every individual possessing it. There are a number of populations, particularly in modern-day India, in which the gene frequencies may still be in the process of change. As mentioned earlier, the Arabs may provide an example of cultural adaptation—fermentation of milk—making a genetic adaptation—retention of lactase production—unnecessary. This would be another example of a population's retaining the most flexible response of a series of graded responses to environmental conditions.

HAPTOGLOBIN

Haptoglobin is one of the proteins found in blood serum. Its function is to form complexes with hemoglobin that has been released from red cells, usually because of the destruction of the red cell. Haptoglobin, like hemoglobin, is a four-chain protein (tetramer) made up of two α and two β chains. The synthesis of the α and β chains is under the control of two separate loci. The locus controlling synthesis of α chains (the Hp_α locus) has three common alleles Hp_α^{1F}, Hp_α^{1S}, and Hp_α^2. The superscript *1F* designates a fast-migrating protein, and *1S,* a slow-migrating one. The migration speeds refer to the behavior of these proteins when tested by **electrophoresis** (see Figure 5-11). The Hp_α^2 chain is much longer than the Hp_α^{1F} or Hp_α^{1S}. Hp_α^2 chains are made up of 142 amino acids, while Hp_α^1 chains are made up of only 83 amino acids. Hp_α^{1F} differs from Hp_α^{1S} only in the substitution of one amino acid at position 54. The Hp_α^1 alleles are similar to the haptoglobin α chains in a number of other animals, but Hp_α^2 is unique to our species. It is not known whether there is any selective advantage to the possession of one or the other allele of haptoglobin. It appears that any one of the variants prevents hemoglobin from passing through the kidneys, thereby preventing kidney damage and loss of iron. However, attempts to find a relationship between high rates of red cell breakdown (as in areas where malaria is epidemic) and high frequencies of specific alleles have yielded inconsistent results.

TRANSFERRIN

Transferrin is a protein involved in the salvaging of iron freed by red cell destruction. Its normal function is to complex with and transport free iron in the blood to bone marrow, where new hemoglobin is synthesized.

There are twenty or more known variant forms of transferrin, but most are rare. The TfC form is the most common type. A variant that migrates slowly in a starch-gel electrophoresis is designated TfD, and a fast-migrating one, TfB. One slow variant, TfD_1, occurs with a frequency of 1 to 5 percent in populations in Africa, Australia, and New Guinea. It is thought that African and Australian TfD_1 possess the same amino acid substitution. Chinese, South East Asian, Sri Lankan, Indian, and some native American populations have a variant designated TfD_{chi}. Navajo Indians of the southwestern United States have been shown to possess a variant designated TfB_{0-1} at a frequency of about 8 percent.

It is not known whether any of the transferrin variants conveys a selective advantage through superior iron transport capacity. In this respect, transferrin and haptoglobin represent something of an enigma. Their functions are sufficiently important, and the environmental challenges of malaria and other red cell–destroying conditions sufficiently widespread, to create an apparent opportunity for natural selection to influence gene frequencies among the numerous variants exhibited by these proteins. It seems quite likely that more will be learned about these proteins.

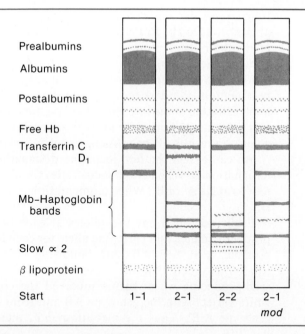

Prealbumins

Albumins

Postalbumins

Free Hb

Transferrin C
D_1

Mb–Haptoglobin
bands

Slow $\propto 2$

β lipoprotein

Start

1–1   2–1   2–2   2–1
mod

Figure 5-11 The pattern produced by serum proteins after starch-gel electrophoresis and staining.

QUANTITATIVE INHERITANCE OF CONTINUOUS TRAITS

The traits that Mendel used to demonstrate the laws of segregation and independent assortment were useful because they were characterized by the existence of two distinct alleles at each of the seven loci. However, many traits are determined by the simultaneous influence of more than one locus.

When the expression of a genetically determined trait is the result of the action of more than one locus, it is an example of **multiple-factor,** or **polygenic** inheritance. Such traits are called **continuous traits.** The term "continuous" in this context means that virtually any value within a certain range of values may occur. Continuous variables, such as height, are measured, as compared with **discrete traits,** such as blood group reactions, which are counted. The distinction between continuous and discrete traits is an important one because different statistical methods are needed to analyze data falling into one or the other category.

To see how multiple-factor inheritance produces continuous distributions of values, we can start with a simple example drawn from the plant genetics literature (Crow, 1976).

In one variety of wheat, seed colors range from white to very dark red. In crossing experiments using methods originally published by Mendel, a plant bearing very dark red seeds was fertilized by one bearing white seeds. All of the plants produced by this cross had seeds of medium-red color. We can call these plants the F_1 generation.

When the F_1 plants were used to fertilize each other, the next generation (F_2) produced five different phenotypes of seed color ranging from white to light red, medium red, dark red, and very dark red. If we use a notation that assigns a special value to the intensity of red pigmentation transmitted by each gamete and postulate the presence of two loci, each with two alleles determining seed color, the results of the crossing experiment are easily explained.

We can assign the first locus the designation A and the second locus the designation B. When either locus codes for intense pigmentation, we can refer to it as allele A^1 or B^1. When pigmentation is absent, the alleles are simply A or B.

Each individual has two alleles at each of the two loci, but it can only produce gametes that carry one allele for each locus. Four types of gametes are possible: A^1B^1, A^1B, AB^1, AB. Following Mendel's sweet-pea experiments, it can be assumed that the parental cross of the white and very dark red seed-producing wheat plants involved the combining of gametes from the white variety with the genotype AB and from the very dark red one with the genotype A^1B^1. Thus the medium-red F_1 plants all had the same genotype A^1A/B^1B.

When the F_1 plants are crossed with each other, all four kinds of gametes are possible, and, assuming that the recombination of alleles is random, the four kinds of gamete will be produced in approximately equal numbers. The use of a Punnett square will illustrate how the reassortments in the second, or F_2, generation occur (Table 5-6).

The presence of four primed alleles in only the first cell (upper left) means that individuals producing seeds of the very dark red color will occur in 1 out of 16 fertilizations. Similarly, the presence of no primed alleles in only the sixteenth cell (lower right) means that individuals producing white seeds will also occur in only 1 out of 16 fertilizations. Examination of the number of primes appearing in the remaining cells of the Punnett square reveals that three primes (dark red) occur in four cells; two primes (medium red) occur in six cells; and one prime (light red), in four cells.

Using this result, it is now possible to construct a histogram (Figure 5-12)

Table 5-6 Punnett Square for Cross of Medium-Red and Medium-Red Seed-Producing Wheat Plants

	A^1B^1	A^1B	AB^1	AB
A^1B^1	$A^1A^1B^1B^1$	$A^1A^1B^1B$	$A^1AB^1B^1$	A^1AB^1B
A^1B	$A^1A^1BB^1$	A^1A^1BB	A^1ABB^1	A^1ABB
AB^1	$AA^1B^1B^1$	AA^1B^1B	AAB^1B^1	AAB^1B
AB	AA^1BB^1	AA^1BB	$AABB^1$	$AABB$

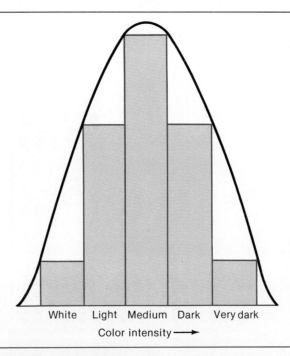

White   Light Medium Dark Very dark

Color intensity ⟶

Figure 5-12 Histogram of composition of F_2 progeny population of F_1 backcross of medium-red seed producing wheat plants.

that will allow us to illustrate how the range of color intensities in a hypothetical population of 16 individuals is distributed. It can be seen that the medium-red phenotype is the most common of the five possible phenotypes but that all five are represented.

Although with some imagination one can visualize something like a curve of frequencies around the seed-color histogram, it is a crude approximation and there are some large gaps under the curve.

However, if we extend the example to include one more locus, also with two alleles, we can see how polygenic traits can produce continuous distributions. For this example, again following Crow, we will use the pattern of the preceding example except that the three loci, A, B, and C, all transmit increased height when the primed alleles A^1, B^1, and C^1 are present. A Punnett square showing the outcome of the combinations of the eight possible gametes is shown in Table 5-7.

If, instead of color intensity, the primed alleles in this example transmit increased height, the range of values present begins at 60 inches (for individuals with 0 primes) and goes to 66 inches (for individuals with 6 primes). Reading from the Punnett square, it can be seen that only 1 of the 64 cells contains 6 primed alleles and would therefore produce a 66-inch individual. Similarly, only 1 cell contains 0 primed alleles and would produce a 60-inch

Table 5-7 Punnett Square for Cross of Medium-Height Plant 60 Inches, with Height Determined by Three Loci

	$A^1B^1C^1$	A^1B^1C	A^1BC^1	A^1BC	AB^1C^1	AB^1C	ABC^1	ABC
$A^1B^1C^1$	$A^1A^1B^1B^1C^1C^1$	$A^1A^1B^1B^1C^1C$	$A^1A^1B^1BC^1C^1$	$A^1A^1B^1BC^1C$	$A^1AB^1B^1C^1C^1$	$A^1AB^1B^1C^1C$	$A^1AB^1BC^1C^1$	$A^1AB^1BC^1C$
A^1B^1C	$A^1A^1B^1B^1C^1C$	$A^1A^1B^1B^1CC$	$A^1A^1B^1BC^1C$	$A^1A^1B^1BCC$	$A^1AB^1B^1C^1C$	$A^1AB^1B^1CC$	$A^1AB^1BC^1C$	A^1AB^1BCC
A^1BC^1	$A^1A^1B^1BC^1C^1$	$A^1A^1B^1BC^1C$	$A^1A^1BBC^1C^1$	$A^1A^1BBC^1C$	$A^1AB^1BC^1C^1$	$A^1AB^1BC^1C$	$A^1ABBC^1C^1$	A^1ABBC^1C
A^1BC	$A^1A^1B^1BCC^1$	$A^1A^1B^1BCC$	$A^1A^1BBCC^1$	A^1A^1BBCC	$A^1AB^1BCC^1$	A^1AB^1BCC	A^1ABBCC^1	A^1ABBCC
AB^1C^1	$AA^1B^1B^1C^1C^1$	$AA^1B^1B^1C^1C$	$AA^1B^1BC^1C^1$	$AA^1B^1BC^1C$	$AAB^1B^1C^1C^1$	$AAB^1B^1C^1C$	$AAB^1BC^1C^1$	AAB^1BC^1C
AB^1C	$AA^1B^1B^1C^1C$	$AA^1B^1B^1CC$	$AA^1B^1BC^1C$	AA^1B^1BCC	$AAB^1B^1C^1C$	AAB^1B^1CC	AAB^1BC^1C	AAB^1BCC
ABC^1	$AA^1B^1BC^1C^1$	$AA^1B^1BC^1C$	$AA^1BBC^1C^1$	AA^1BBC^1C	$AAB^1BC^1C^1$	AAB^1BC^1C	$AABBC^1C^1$	$AABBC^1C$
ABC	$AA^1B^1BCC^1$	AA^1B^1BCC	AA^1BBCC^1	AA^1BBCC	AAB^1BCC^1	AAB^1BCC	$AABBCC^1$	$AABBCC$

individual. Figure 5-13 shows a histogram with the distribution of height categories among the 64 progeny produced in this cross.

In this example, the intermediate category, individuals whose height is 63 inches, is most common: 20 individuals have that characteristic. There are 15 individuals that are 62 inches tall; 15 individuals that are 64 inches tall; 6 individuals that are 61 inches tall; 6 that are 65 inches tall; and only 1 that is 60 inches tall and 1 that is 66 inches tall.

Tracing a line around the histogram, as done in Figure 5-13, produces a closer approximation to a normal curve than the 2-locus, 2-allele model did. There are still large gaps under the curve. However, a 4-locus, 2-allele model would yield 16 kinds of gametes, and if a Punnett square were to be generated for this example, it would contain 256 cells that would yield 9 phenotypic categories and a histogram that would fit more closely under a curve. Adding more loci and more alleles at each locus would yield even closer fits of histograms and curves. If the influence of environmental factors on the growth process producing height is included in the estimate of possible phenotypic expressions, it soon becomes evident that polygenic traits expressed under varying environmental conditions can express a nearly infinite number of values between the minimum and maximum. We need not postulate excessive-

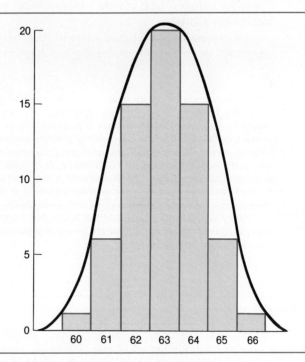

Figure 5-13 Histogram of height categories produced by the cross of medium height (63') individuals using a 3-locus, 2-allele model.

ly large numbers of loci or alleles to produce the normal curves that can generally be used to describe most continuous values.

HOW DO POLYGENIC DETERMINANTS OF CONTINUOUS TRAITS FUNCTION?

What do the multiple loci underlying a given continuous trait actually determine? This interesting question has led to much productive research. Since continuous traits are measurable traits and are often the product of the growth process as modified by environmental factors, questions concerning the determinants of size will raise ancillary questions about factors that modify growth. Thus, when discussing the possible number of loci involved in the determination of a trait like adult stature in humans, it is not possible to exclude such growth-limiting factors as intestinal absorption, disease susceptibility, kidney function, and endocrine balance (Sinclair, 1985). Each of these factors may have one or more genetic determinants and must therefore be taken into account when estimations of the proportion of the trait's expression that is inherited are attempted. Thus it would be misleading to talk about a "gene for tallness" as if it were simply a locus whose action translated directly into linear growth.

The process of growth and some of its genetic and environmental determinants will be discussed more fully in Chapters 22 and 23.

The inheritance of traits was shown by Mendel to involve the transmission of particles from both parents to offspring. The segregation of traits and their independent assortment makes it possible for a high degree of variation to be produced with a limited amount of genetic material. Some traits are determined by a single locus, and the frequencies of their alleles can be used to compare populations with each other. It is sometimes possible to identify a selective advantage for such discrete traits, but their chief interest usually lies in their existence as genetic markers by which the biological distance between populations can be estimated. Continuous traits, determined by the combined action of several loci, provide the basis for variables that are measured rather than counted. Continuous traits provide a measure of variation both within and between populations.

BIBLIOGRAPHY

ALPERS, D. H. 1981. Carbohydrate digestion: Effects of monosaccharide inhibition and enzyme degradation on lactose activity. In *Lactose Digestion: Clinical and Nutritional Implications,* D. M. Paige and T. M. Bayless, eds., pp. 58–68. Baltimore: Johns Hopkins University Press.

CROW, J. F. 1976. *Genetics Notes,* 7th ed. Minneapolis: Burgess.

CUMMINGS, M. R. 1988. *Human Heredity: Principles and Issues,* pp. 303–7. St. Paul: West Publishing.

FLATZ, G., and ROTTHAUWE, H. W. (1977). The human lactose polymorphism: physiology and genetics of lactose absorption and malabsorption. In A. G. Steinberg, A. G. Bearn, A. G. Motulsky, B. Childs, eds., *Progress in Medical Genetics,* NS, II. Philadelphia: Saunders, pp. 205–49.

KRETCHMER, N. 1981. The significance of lactose intolerance. In *Lactose Digestion: Clinical Nutritional Implications,* D. M. Paige and T. M. Bayless, eds., pp. 3–7. Baltimore: Johns Hopkins University Press.

PHILLIPS, S. F. 1981. Lactose malabsorption and gastrointestinal function: Effects on gastrointestinal transit and absorption of other nutrients. In *Lactose Digestion: Clinical and Nutritional Implications,* D. M. Paige and T. M. Bayless, eds., pp. 51–57. Baltimore: Johns Hopkins University Press.

RACE, R. R., and R. SANGER. 1975. *Blood Groups in Man,* 6th ed. Oxford: Blackwell Scientific.

SIMOONS, F. J. 1981. Geographic patterns of primary adult lactose malabsorption: A further interpretation of evidence for the Old World. In *Lactose Digestion: Clinical and Nutritional Implications,* D. M. Paige and T. M. Bayless, eds., pp. 23–48. Baltimore: Johns Hopkins University Press.

SINCLAIR, D. 1985. *Human Growth After Birth.* (4th ed.). Oxford: Oxford University Press.

Chapter
6
The Evolutionary
Process

Fish   Chicken   Human

The term evolution *generally refers to change in an organism over time. The evolutionary concept also refers to the fact that organisms are related by descent through a common ancestry. This latter notion presumes that life arose only once on Earth and that all life stems from preexisting forms. A key component of the evolutionary process is the appearance of new genes or gene combinations—called mutations. Early evolutionary concepts, such as the notion that ontogeny recapitulates phylogeny, were naive. The specific genetic mechanisms of evolution are discussed in Chapter 7.*

EVOLUTION

The word *evolution* refers to at least three concepts (Thompson, 1982).

1. Generally, the term *evolution* refers to change over time. There is a wealth of information about changes in the qualitative and quantitative diversity of organisms over time and space in the earth's history and a parallel set of data for changes in the earth's geology. These data verify a pattern of change, but make no statement or inference about the mechanism of change.
2. The term *evolution* also refers to the fact that organisms are related by descent through a common ancestry. Descent from a common ancestry is derived from the twin premises that life arose only once on Earth and that all life proceeds from preexisting forms.
3. The third meaning of the term *evolution* is currently confined to the particular explanatory mechanism provided by Darwin.

The essence of modern Darwinian evolutionary theory is this: Organisms vary through the process of the mixing of genes in sexual reproduction and through random mutation-copying errors in the genes. Some mutations are presumably beneficial to the organism in its environment, but most are not. In general, organisms that are better adapted will survive longer and leave more offspring. From one generation to the next, the gene frequencies of a population will change slightly for the better in a particular environment. As the environment changes, so will the proportions of various types of organisms inhabiting it because different qualities will prove advantageous. If this model is applied to the whole of life's history, most life forms can be explained as the result of gradual, adaptive change.

If evolution occurs, there should be evidence of the process. There should be similarities among species that have diverged from a common ancestor, for example. Nineteenth-century scientists sought evidence of evolution in comparative anatomy, comparative embryology, paleontology, and biogeography. Twentieth-century scientists add data from genetics, comparative biochemistry, ecology, and **ethology** (the study of behavior).

As currently used by geneticists, the term *evolution* refers to changes in gene frequency over time. When dealing with the fossil record, however, it is impossible to directly measure gene frequency changes between ancestral and descendant populations. Therefore, evolutionary interpretations based on the fossil record are primarily based on skeletal changes through time. Comparative anatomy—the study of the organs, tissues, and systems of related groups—has revealed many fundamental structural similarities and differences and has traditionally presented some of the strongest evidence in support of evolution. Because parts of the skeletal system, including the teeth, often fossilize, evolutionary relationships between living and extinct species are often based on comparative studies of the skeletal system and dentition.

Figure 6-1 shows the skeletal system of five vertebrates. Although their posture and general appearance differ, all the skeletons are constructed along the same plan: skull, spinal column, shoulder girdle, hip girdle, and limbs. The degree of similarity among the various forms is striking when we note that *Seymouria* has been extinct for more than 230 million years.

Equivalent structures derived from a common ancestor are called **homologous structures.** Each of the forelimbs in Figure 6-2 is adapted to a particular function, reflecting in its size and shape an adjustment to a particular life-style. Despite the wide range of functional adaptations, however, precisely the same bones occur in each forelimb.

All vertebrates begin life as a fertilized egg (or zygote). Comparisons of embryos at equivalent stages of development in different vertebrate groups reveal strong resemblances during their early stages of differentiation. For example, at 8 weeks gestation the human embryo has gill slits, a rudimentary tail, and a circulatory system more similar to that of a fish than to that of the human adult (Figure 6-3). Such traits are lost or greatly modified during later stages of development.

Early in the development of evolutionary theory, the presence of similar sequences in the embryonic development of diverse forms led to overgeneralizations, such as the statement that ontogeny (growth and development) recapitulates phylogeny (evolutionary history). The theory of recapitulation—the idea that the developmental stages of an organism repeat its evolutionary history—is a gross oversimplification. Although strict application of the theory of recapitulation to all events of embryonic development is impossible, similarities in vertebrate embryonic development may reflect the retention of genetic material from an ancestral evolutionary line.

THE ROLE OF POPULATION VARIABILITY IN THE EVOLUTIONARY PROCESS

Population variability, the large variety of possible genetic combinations, is essential to an evolutionarily successful population and is the basis of evolutionary change. New genetic material is introduced into a population by

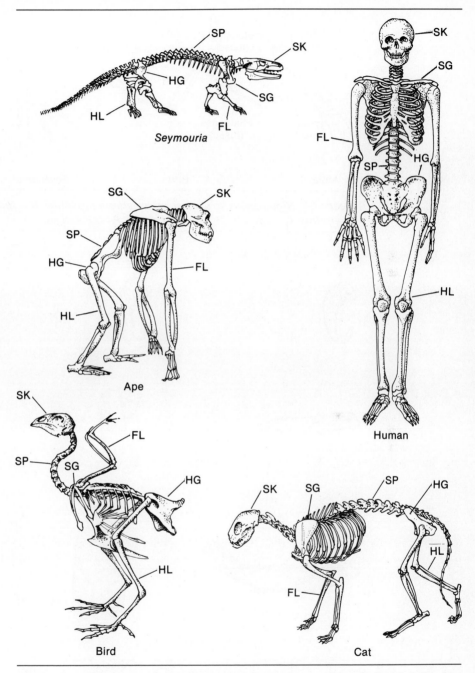

Figure 6-1 *Comparative skeletal anatomy of vertebrates. SK—skull; SG—shoulder girdle; SP—spine; HG—hip girdle; FL—forelimb; HL—hindlimb.*

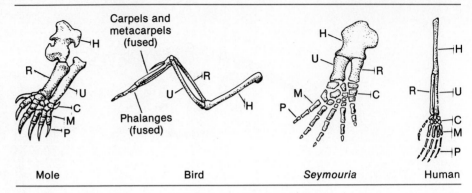

Figure 6-2 Homologous structures in vertebrate forelimbs. H—humerus; U—ulna; R—radius; C—carpals; MC—metacarpels; P—phalanges.

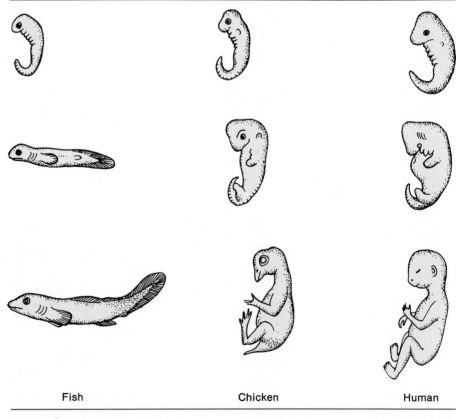

Figure 6-3 A comparison of fish, chicken, and human embryos during comparable stages of development.

mutation, a random change in the structure of a gene or chromosome. One long-term advantage of sexual reproduction is that it produces genetic variability by mixing the genes from both parents into new combinations. Recombination spreads new genes that have been provided by mutation throughout the population and develops new genetic combinations from existing genotypes. Recombination is the means by which a sexually reproducing population maintains genetic variability. Recombination enhances the effects of mutation by assembling a broad spectrum of genetic combinations that are affected by various forces, producing evolutionary change.

What is the significance of the variability produced by recombination? Most environments change over time. Therefore, in general, the more variable (that is, the more generalized) the population, the greater its long-term chances for survival. Variability enhances survivability in changing environments because of the possibility that some members of a variable population can meet the demands of a shifting environment. The more specialized an organism, the less its chances for survival in a changing environment. A good example of this tendency is the koala bear, whose major source of nourishment is eucalyptus leaves. Should something destroy this food source, the koala bears' survival would be threatened. If the environment does not change, the koala bear is well adapted, and no other animal is likely to out-compete it by making use of its specialized food niche. Compared to koala bears, humans are genetically variable. This genetic variability, along with our myriad of cultural adaptations, has enabled us to inhabit a great variety of climatic zones and to consume a great variety of foods. Humans are probably better able to face some catastrophic event than are koala bears.

NATURAL SELECTION

Darwin's primary contribution to evolutionary theory was the claim that natural selection was the mechanism of evolutionary change. Darwin's concept of natural selection stressed that individuals differ among themselves and that individual differences are influenced by hereditarily transmissible traits. Darwin was ignorant of the means by which such transmission occurred, however. Darwin noted that whenever individual differences impart greater or lesser fitness, those traits of the more fit individuals will be increasingly represented in succeeding generations. The fitness implied by Darwin's argument refers to an organism's success in leaving fertile and surviving offspring. Fitness is determined by the criterion of whether a trait that is expressed contributes to greater reproductive success.

Once change has occurred in the gene pool, those genes and gene combinations that aid an organism's adjustment to its environment are favored through reproductive advantage. Those individuals whose genotypes allow them to produce more viable offspring are said to enjoy the advantages of positive differential reproduction. Through natural selection, those genes or gene combinations that ensure the highest level of adaptive efficiency to environmental stress are the most numerous over time. The environment is the selective force in this process.

Natural selection is the principal force that operates over time to enable the development of new adaptations to the world's diverse environments. Natural selection is one of the factors responsible for the evolution of the present diversity of life. Natural selection is the impact of any element in the organism's environment that tends to produce genetic change over generations. Environments change, and thus the gene frequencies of organisms within the environment must also change in order to survive. A trait or behavior that may be adaptive at one point in time in one environment may be less adaptive or may even become maladaptive at another point in time in a different environment. Changing environments emphasize the importance of maintaining genetic variability to meet changing conditions.

Traits that are selected for or against are merely adaptive or nonadaptive; they aid or hinder, or may even be neutral, to an organism's survivability.

The mechanism of evolutionary change through natural selection can be summarized as follows:

1. Only inherited traits can be subject to natural selection. If a trait is not genetically linked, gene frequencies cannot change, and biological evolution does not occur.
2. Individual variation in traits is the key to understanding natural selection. Natural selection acts on individual variation by favoring the better-adapted traits. Such traits are passed to the next generation.
3. Traits that are considered favorable at one point in time may not be favored at another point in evolutionary time. The concept of favored traits is relative to the environmental context.

ADAPTATION

The term **adaptation** refers to an evolutionary change in a behavior or structure that produces an efficient interaction with the environment. Any trait that is advantageous to an organism's coping with its environment is said to be *adaptive.* An organism adapts to its total surroundings (the econiche), including all existing foods, competitors and enemies, and all other variables that affect it in any way. It must be noted that in terms of natural selection individual organisms cannot adapt. Biological adaptation occurs between generations as the result of differential reproductive success among all the reproducing individuals of the population. Biological adaptations are genetically based.

The order in which organisms move into a **habitat** (the area where a species lives) influences how they use the habitat. The first organisms moving into a new habitat theoretically have that whole habitat open to them because of a lack of competition from previous occupants. Subsequent inhabitants usually occupy successively narrower portions of a habitat, thereby reducing competition. Later occupants to a habitat tend to be more specialized than earlier inhabitants.

LEVELS OF EVOLUTIONARY CHANGE

Evolutionary rates are dependent on such factors as habitat type, generation time, and number of offspring. The rapidity and scope of change in the evolutionary history of an organism can vary (Simpson, 1953). **Microevolution** refers to the accumulation of small changes within a potentially continuous population which produce differences between related populations or in one population over time. An example of microevolutionary change is the array of human blood groups (see Chapter 24). Unlike microevolutionary change, which usually does not isolate breeding populations from one another, **macroevolutionary** change, or evolutionary change above the species level, usually results in the rise and divergence of discontinuous groups (Figure 6-4). The large-scale evolution studied by the paleontologist in the fossil record reflects macroevolutionary change. Quantum evolution refers to change that normally occurs in small, rapidly evolving populations moving into new habitats. Quantum evolution is characteristic of populations in temporary states of disequilibrium. Both macroevolution and quantum evolution result in genetic discontinuity.

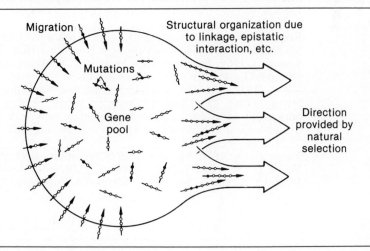

Figure 6-4 Illustration of the interaction of the basic features of evolution: (1) mutation; (2) recombination; (3) structural changes in the chromosomes and gene drift; and (4) natural selection.

Random mutations produce new genetic combinations, and those combinations that are adaptive increase an organism's survivability. Such adaptive genes or gene combinations are distributed through the process of recombination. Evolution working through the process of natural selection leads to an improvement in the adaptive relations between organisms and their environment. An adaptation is a behavior or structure that produces an efficient interaction with the environment. Any trait advantageous to an organism's coping with its environment is said to be adaptive.

Because environments change over time, populations that are successful over the long run are those that exhibit variability—that is, those that can adjust to shifting habitat conditions. Evolutionary rates are dependent upon many factors. Microevolutionary change refers to the accumulation of small changes within a potentially continuous population. Microevolutionary change does not isolate breeding populations from one another; however, both macroevolutionary and quantum evolutionary change do isolate populations.

BIBLIOGRAPHY

BODMER, W., and L. CAVALLI-SFORZA. 1976. *Genetics, Evolution, and Man.* San Francisco: Freeman & Company Publishers.

GRANT, V. 1963. *The Origin of Adaptations.* New York: Columbia University Press.

KING, J., and T. JUKES. 1969. Non-Darwinian evolution. *Science* 164: 788–97.

LERNER, I. 1968. *Heredity, Evolution, and Society.* San Francisco: W. H. Freeman & Company Publishers.

MAYR, E. 1974. Behavior programs and evolutionary strategies. *American Scientist* 62: 650–59.

RACLE, F. 1979. *Introduction to Evolution.* Englewood Cliffs, N.J.: Prentice-Hall.

RENSCH, B. 1959. *Evolution Above the Species Level.* New York: Columbia University Press.

ROSS, H. 1966. *Understanding Evolution.* Englewood Cliffs, N.J.: Prentice-Hall.

SALTHE, S. 1972. *Evolutionary Biology.* New York: Holt, Rinehart and Winston.

SAVAGE, J. 1969. *Evolution.* New York: Holt, Rinehart and Winston.

SIMPSON, G. 1951. *The Meaning of Evolution.* New York: Mentor Books.

———, 1953. *The Major Features of Evolution.* New York: Columbia University Press.

SMITH, J. 1966. *The Theory of Evolution.* Baltimore: Penguin.

SOLBRIG, O. 1966. *Evolution and Systematics.* New York: Macmillan.

STEBBINS, G., and F. AYALA. 1981. Is a new evolutionary synthesis necessary? *Science* 213: 967–71.

THOMPSON, K. 1982. The meanings of evolution. *American Scientist* 70: 529–31.

VOLPE, E. 1967. *Understanding Evolution.* Dubuque, Iowa: Wm. C. Brown.

WALLACE, B., and A. SRB. 1964. *Adaptation.* Englewood Cliffs, N.J.: Prentice-Hall.

Chapter

7

Population Biology in Evolutionary Perspective

The concept of genetic equilibrium is a direct outgrowth of the principles revealed by Mendel's experiments. Traits are inherited through the transmission of genes, which are reshuffled each time meiotic cell division occurs. Well-defined traits are segregated from one another and reassorted independently. Because the process is essentially one of chance events, prediction of the occurrence of genotypes on the basis of gene frequencies is possible through the application of probability theory. While the probability approach does not enable the prediction of the occurrence of a specific genotype, it works well for populations and best for large populations in which randomization of events is most nearly approached. When the probability approach is applied to the prediction of genotype frequencies, an underlying assumption is that the population is in equilibrium that is, that gene frequencies are stable from one generation to the next. When the prediction of genotype frequencies produces a different result than is actually observed, the assumption of equilibrium is not satisfied and the question of why there is a disequilibrium arises. The major forces of evolution are the usual suspects, although certain assumptions, such as large population size and random mating, may also be violated. The important evolutionary forces are selection, migration, mutation, and drift. Each of these forces can be responsible for a shift of gene frequencies, causing disequilibrium. Much can be learned of both theoretical and practical interest when the reasons for disequilibrium are sought. Methods of analysis are largely statistical, but the data to be analyzed can be obtained from many sources. Both field and laboratory research may be involved in pursuit of the answers to questions raised by the identification of a disagreement between predicted and observed genotype frequencies.

THE CONCEPTS OF MENDELIAN GENETICS APPLIED TO POPULATIONS

Population geneticists have historically thought of the effect of natural selection on living populations in terms of the elimination of less-fit alleles. The simplest feasible mathematical models have been required for testing hypotheses concerning gene frequency equilibrium. Substitutions of single alleles are, of course, the most easily manipulated models, even though they are less likely than more complex ones to reflect the realities of population biology. Population geneticists have used such simple models to test deviations from stable, or "equilibrium," gene frequencies. When deviations are identified, it is then sometimes possible to identify the factor or factors that cause them. Since changes in gene frequency associated with deviations from equilibrium values are the forces that drive the evolutionary process, the major causes of evolution have been specified as forces producing changes in gene frequency. These have conventionally been called the four forces of evolution. They are as follows:

Mutation
Selection
Migration
Drift

Before the effects of these forces can be considered, it will be necessary to examine the concept of equilibrium itself. It is this concept that allows the inference of changed gene frequencies over time to be made on the basis of a particular instant in time. Also, the concept of equilibrium in gene frequencies is one that spans the range of theoretical approaches in genetics, drawing from molecular as well as population biology to explain field observations.

The fundamental concept of the equilibrium approach to gene-frequency analysis is drawn directly from Mendel's work, which demonstrated that inheritance was by discrete entities that we now call **genes.** Because each individual in sexually reproducing organisms inherits the genetic determinants of all heritable traits from two parents, there is the chance that a different gene can be obtained from one parent than from the other. Many characteristics exhibit such differences, called **allelic variation.** Under certain environmental circumstances, one allele may be favored over others and therefore possess a selective advantage. This is referred to as superior **fitness.** Genes possessing even a modest advantage in fitness will, in time, replace their less-fit alleles. If such replacement is occurring, the frequencies of the two alleles will be in the process of change and will therefore not be in equilibrium.

Viewed from another perspective, if it is possible to determine that the frequencies of two alleles are not in equilibrium, it is possible that natural selection (see Chapter 6) is at work. This process will ultimately lead to the elimination of one and the **fixation** of the other. Is it possible to identify a disequilibrium without following the actual change of gene frequencies over a number of generations? The Hardy-Weinberg method is one way of approaching the problem. It is named for two researchers who applied the methods first developed by Mendel to the analysis of population data. Hardy was a mathematician, and Weinberg, a physician. In 1908, both independently arrived at the conclusion that a deviation from expected genotype frequencies indicates that the gene frequencies for that trait are not stable. William Ernest Castle, an American animal breeder, had already made that discovery in 1903, but he had not spelled out all of the criteria defining equilibrium. Although the Hardy-Weinberg method in and of itself cannot pinpoint whether selection, mutation, migration, or drift is predominant, it can reveal that one or more of these forces are at work. The method relies on certain basic assumptions and relatively simple calculations that allow the investigator to compare what is observed to what would be expected if equilibrium prevailed.

To describe and illustrate the concept of equilibrium and the Hardy-Weinberg method of analysis, we can use an example drawn from the study of human blood groups. One of the human blood group systems, called MN, has just two alleles, M and N. These alleles are **codominant;** individuals who have inherited different alleles from their parents will express both and are therefore readily identified as being of the genotype MN. This simple system yields just three phenotypes: M (individuals who have inherited the M allele from both parents), N (individuals who have inherited the N allele from both parents), and MN (individuals who have inherited M from one parent and N from the other).

Using this mode of inheritance in a population context, we can organize our data as follows:

Phenotype	Genotype
M	MM (homozygous)
MN	MN (heterozygous)
N	NN (homozygous)

In approaching the analysis of gene frequencies, it is conventional to assign the letters p and q to the frequencies of the alleles. In this example, we will assign the letter p to the frequency of the allele M and the letter q to the allele N. Since there are only two alleles at this locus, the frequencies p and q will account for 100 percent of the observations in the population. This then permits us to express our basic assumption of the frequencies of M and N in the population as $p + q = 1$. If there were more than two alleles, as is often the case for other traits, our calculations would be more complicated, but the principle at work would not change, as we will see later.

At this point we can see how Mendel's results can be put to work to generate descriptions of a population's genetic characteristics. If the population is in genetic equilibrium, the frequencies of the alleles will remain the same from one generation to the next. If mating in the population is random—that is, if mates are not chosen according to some bias such as a cultural preference for a particular skin pigmentation, for example, that is associated with the trait under investigation—genotypes will occur in similar frequencies from generation to generation as well. For a codominant trait like the MN blood group, frequencies of phenotypes will be as stable as the genotypes determining them.

If we put together the genes and the gene frequencies in a manner that allows them to be manipulated mathematically, they can be arranged like this:

Gene	Frequency
M	p
N	q

Genotype	Phenotype	Frequency
MM	M	$p \times p = p^2$
MN	MN	$(p \times q) + (q \times p) = 2pq$
NN	N	$q \times q = q^2$

When we view the genotype frequencies developed in this way, we are looking at the fundamental expression of the Hardy-Weinberg equilibrium. It can be arrived at through a somewhat different approach by thinking of the genotypes of all mating pairs in a population as being defined as the probability that each individual will possess each of the two alleles. Thus we can say that an individual's male parent had p probability of transmitting M, and q probability of transmitting N. The female parent also has p probability of transmitting M, and q probability of transmitting N. Their combined probabilities are therefore $(p + q) \times (p + q)$. If we multiply $(p + q) \times (p + q)$, we get $p^2 + 2pq + q^2$, and since these genotype frequencies will account for 100 percent of our observations in the population, we can say that $p^2 + 2pq + q^2 = 1$.

The probability that a specific individual drawn at random from the population will produce a gamete bearing the M allele is the same as the frequency of that allele in the population. The probability of producing a gamete bearing the N allele is, likewise, the frequency of the N allele in the population. If the frequencies of the two alleles in the population can be determined, it is then possible to forecast the frequency of the genotypes that will be found. The degree to which the prediction of genotype frequencies differs from those actually found will be a measure of disequilibrium, which, in turn, is an indication that one of the forces of evolution is at work. An example will show how this procedure of identifying the potential for evolutionary change works.

Since the MN blood group alleles are codominant, it is possible to use a technique called the *gene-count* method to estimate gene frequencies in a population. If we select a random sample of 100 individuals and draw blood samples from them, small samples of red blood cells can be prepared for testing with anti-M and anti-N antisera. Each blood sample is split, and half is tested with anti-M and the other with anti-N. Three results are possible when such tests are performed:

	Anti-M	Anti-N	Genotype
Reaction	+	−	MM
Reaction	+	+	MN
Reaction	−	+	NN

As a result of the tests of 100 randomly selected individuals, we identify the following genotype frequencies:

Genotype	Frequency	M Allele	N Allele
MM	27	54	0
MN	59	59	59
NN	14	0	28
	100	113	87

From this we can derive gene frequencies as follows:

$$M = p = \frac{113}{200} = 56.5$$

$$N = q = \frac{87}{200} = 43.5$$

If we estimate equilibrium frequencies for genotypes using the Hardy-Weinberg method, we predict the following:

$$MM = p^2 = (56.5 \times 56.5) = .32$$
$$MN = 2pq = 2(56.5 \times 43.5) = .49$$
$$NN = q^2 = (43.5 \times 43.5) = .19$$

However, the actual genotype frequencies were MM = .27, MN = .59 and NN = .14.

In order to assess the magnitude of the deviation from expected values, statistical tests of the result can be conducted. One such test, called the Chi-square test, is used to determine the significance of the difference between expected and observed values. This test shows that the genotype frequencies for MM, MN, and NN in the population under investigation do not deviate sufficiently from equilibrium values to permit the conclusion that a real change in gene frequencies is taking place. So the hypothesis of a change in gene frequencies due to natural selection, migration, mutation, or drift would be rejected on the basis of these data.

Since the turnover of generations in human populations requires about 25 years, the investigator does not have the option of merely waiting to see if gene frequencies have changed in the next generation. The appropriate use of the Hardy-Weinberg equilibrium method permits the identification of a transient state implying change. In a sense, the effect is comparable to examining a single frame from a motion-picture film and finding evidence of movement in the position of a person who cannot be at rest. It may not be possible to determine where the person is moving or why, but it makes it possible to predict that the image in subsequent frames will show additional changes.

Not all genetic loci behave in the clearcut way that the MN locus does. Some have more alleles, and some resemble the seed-color locus that Mendel studied in his sweet-pea experiments in that they possess the characteristics of dominance and recessivity. In Mendel's experiments, one of the most significant results was the disappearance of the recessive trait in the first filial (F_1) generation and its reemergence in the next generation when the heterozygotes were crossed with each other. This result demonstrated that inheritance is not a matter of blending, as many thought at that time, but is instead the product of the transmission of discrete particles that maintain their integrity even when the trait that they determine is not expressed. While the homozygous expression of recessive alleles made the nature of inheritance more understandable through Mendel's experiments, the determination of equilibrium gene frequencies is more complicated when one of the alleles at the locus in question is recessive. When there are more than two alleles and when one of them is also recessive, more sophisticated methods are needed. This is true of the well-known human ABO blood group system. In the ABO system, the A and B alleles are codominant, while O is recessive.

The usual way of determining an individual's ABO blood type is to divide a blood sample into two test tubes and, after diluting them with physiologic saline solution (0.9 percent sodium chloride), add a drop of anti-A serum to one tube and a drop of anti-B serum to the other. These antisera are produced by inoculating either rabbits or chickens with A or B substance. The antibodies that appear in the animal's blood will react with A or B substance either in the animal **(in vivo)** or in a test tube **(in vitro).** The antibodies are extracted from blood drawn from the animal, purified, and concentrated. Antisera are conventionally sold with a coloring agent added (blue for anti-A and yellow for anti-B) to prevent mistaken readings of positive reactions when simultaneous testing is done. The tubes are then spun on a centrifuge. If the red blood cells in the test tube carry the antigen of blood group A, they will clump together in an agglutination reaction that will result in all or most of the cells present in the tube forming a "button" on the bottom of the tube in the presence of antiserum A. Similarly, if the cells carry the antigen of blood group B, they will agglutinate in the presence of antiserum B.

	Anti A TUBE 1	Anti B TUBE 2	PHENOTYPE	GENOTYPE
Reaction	+	−	A	AA or AO
Reaction	−	+	B	BB or BO
Reaction	−	−	O	OO
Reaction	+	+	AB	AB

Using this type of test, it is possible to identify four different phenotypes: A, B, O, and AB. However, only two of these phenotypes permit the direct identification of the underlying genotype. The phenotype O is (with rare exceptions) expressed by individuals who have inherited the O allele from both parents and are therefore of genotype OO. Similarly, the phenotype AB occurs only when the individual has inherited the A allele from one parent and the B allele from the other. The problem in estimating gene frequencies arises because the O allele is recessive in the presence of A or B and is therefore undetectable in the heterozygote.

Despite the complications imposed by the presence of three alleles at the ABO locus and by the recessive nature of the O allele, it is possible to estimate gene frequencies in a population. The method used is somewhat more complicated and somewhat less precise than the gene-count method used for simple codominant traits like MN, but it does permit a reasonably close approximation of actual gene frequencies.

HARDY-WEINBERG EQUILIBRIUM AND THE FORCES OF EVOLUTION

In order for Hardy-Weinberg equilibrium values for genotype frequencies to occur, certain conditions must be met. These conditions are as follows:

1. The population must be large.
2. The choice of mates must be random, and the number of males and females in the population must be equal.
3. None of the four forces of evolution (selection, mutation, migration, and drift) is at work.

Such stringent conditions are seldom fully satisfied. For instance, no population is infinitely large. The question of the effect of small population size is an interesting one from an evolutionary standpoint since chance factors can exert a powerful influence on gene frequencies in very small populations. A simple example will illustrate why this is true.

If we were to forecast the outcome of flipping a coin 1,000 times, the percentage of error would be quite small, with heads and tails occurring in about equal frequencies. In the short run, however, as in the case of the five tosses of the coin, a run of five heads or five tails in a row would not be a very remarkable event. As a matter of fact, even after a run of four consecutive heads, the odds of heads coming up on the fifth toss are still 50:50. With a sufficiently large number of tosses, all of the short-term disturbances of the 50:50 ratio will balance each other and, if an infinite number of tosses were possible, the ratio of heads to tails would be precisely 1 to 1.

Similarly, chance factors can have important effects on gene frequencies when a population is small. The impact of small population size can be especially significant in the case of alleles that are present in low frequency. This is because the failure of the possessor of such an allele to reproduce can result in its disappearance from the next generation. Any chance event that prevents possessors of rare alleles in small populations from passing a rare allele on to the next generation can thus exert a strong influence on the genetic composition of succeeding generations. Recognition of the importance of chance events in the alteration of gene frequencies in small populations led to the incorporation of the concept of random genetic drift in modern evolutionary theory.

Sewell Wright developed mathematical methods to facilitate the theoretical treatment of random genetic drift, and James F. Crow, Motoo Kimura (1970), and Susumu Ohno (1970) have all developed applications that have permitted testing of hypotheses. As a result of the work of these geneticists and others, it has become widely recognized that many factors may modify the influence of natural selection on gene frequencies.

POPULATION BOTTLENECKS: A CAUSE OF GENETIC DRIFT

Small population size can occur as a result of a catastrophe that results in a sharp decrease in numbers, called a *population bottleneck*. Such a reduction can result in the disappearance of certain alleles in subsequent generations. The lost alleles cannot be replaced as long as the population remains isolated from other populations that do possess it. Even if population size increases, later frequencies for those alleles will differ from those in populations that have not passed through such a bottleneck.

FOUNDER EFFECT: ANOTHER CAUSE OF GENETIC DRIFT

The gene frequencies of a population can also reflect the occurrence of a nonrepresentative sample when a small population migrates. If, for example, the individuals that migrated to a new territory should by chance all lack the B blood group allele, future generations of the founding population would also lack the allele. This has been called the **founder effect.**

From these examples, it can be seen that population size can have an important effect on gene frequency changes. Such changes are most unpredictable when populations are very small, making random genetic drift possible. In small populations, it is not possible to assume that none of the forces of evolution is at work, since drift may well produce significant change.

RANDOM EVENTS: ANOTHER CAUSE OF GENETIC DRIFT

The carrier of a rare allele is almost always a heterozygote. Therefore, half of the carrier's gametes will possess the rare allele and half will carry the more common allele. The expectation would then be that half of the carrier's progeny would inherit the rare allele and half would inherit the more common one. However, each fertilization involving the carrier's gametes is a random event, much like the tossing of a coin. Therefore, it would not be especially remarkable if several consecutive offspring, or even all of them, were to receive the common allele. In a small population with only one carrier of the rare allele, the failure of that one carrier to transmit it would result in its loss to the population and in a fixation of its more common allele.

SAMPLING ERROR: YET ANOTHER CAUSE OF GENETIC DRIFT

Another interesting possibility is the fixation of a rare allele in a small population. This could happen through sampling error when a small group drawn from the population at large migrates to found a new population that is genetically isolated from other populations. It is possible for the migrant group to be composed of an unusually high proportion of carriers of a rare allele. If the carriers were exceptionally successful in leaving descendants (as was sometimes the case with a chief or tribal leader), chance factors leading to a high percentage of the carrier's offspring possessing the rare allele would yield a population in which the previously rare allele is more frequent than the previously common allele. If the disproportion in gene frequencies is great enough, and if the selective value of the two alleles in the new environment is relatively similar, the previously uncommon allele can drift to fixation. The result of this kind of drift would then be a population lacking an allele that was common in its parent population. Even if the migrant population dramatically increased in numbers in its new habitat, the lost allele would not be restored unless either an appropriate mutation occurred or a mating involving an individual from another population in which the lost allele was still predominant occurred.

Although these examples of loss or fixation of an allele are hypothetical, biologists have long suspected that certain of the more unusual gene frequencies seen in isolated human populations reflect just such chance events occurring in small populations. Since the vast majority of the history of our species was characterized by life in small, often isolated populations, opportunities did exist for the various forms of random genetic drift, population bottlenecks, founder effects, and chance loss and fixation of alleles to have a significant impact on human evolution. Due to the nature of human population structure, size, and tendencies to migrate, the genetic composition of our species was quite possibly highly influenced by such events.

An example of random genetic drift in a small population of human hunter-gatherers

Assume that the alleles of the human ABO blood group locus are of equal selective value. Further assume a population of 100 individuals in which the frequency of the B allele is 10 percent. During a period of poor hunting, the population disperses over a wide territory in order to improve the chance of taking enough game animals to survive. During the time of dispersal, groups of 10 to 12 individuals range widely, sometimes into new territory, and some become totally separated from the others. One or more groups may be totally lacking the B allele. If one such group became permanently isolated from the rest and became the founder of what ultimately was to become a large population, that population would lack the B allele. Many biologists believe that something like this happened early in the history of the American Indian. Human migrations out of Asia across the Bering Land Bridge during the late Pleistocene epoch are thought to have evolved small groups of hunter-gatherers from eastern Siberia (Laughlin, 1966). Some of these migrants moved north and east, ultimately to become the Eskimo of Alaska and Canada. Some migrated out along the Aleutian Islands and were the ancestors of the present-day Aleuts. Others moved south. Some of these migrants had reached what is now Arizona and New Mexico by 12,000 years B.P. They eventually populated all the rest of North and South America and made up the large group we call the American Indians. While Eskimo and Aleut populations still possess the blood group B allele, the American Indians populating the rest of North and South America lack it. For this reason, most biologists favor the hypothesis that a small group migrating out of Asia and lacking the B allele were the ancestors of all of the American Indians.

NON-RANDOM MATING

A second assumption underlying Hardy-Weinberg equilibrium genotype frequencies is that matings are random with respect to genetically determined traits. It is likely that this assumption is violated to some extent in most human populations. There is a tendency for mate selection to yield pairings in which some similarities exist. This is called positive **assortative mating.** Such mating does not by itself change gene frequencies in a population, but it can affect genotype frequencies by increasing the number of homozygotes for the traits being chosen. If reproductive success of the homozygotes differs from that of heterozygotes, selection will take place and gene frequencies will change. Although not itself one of the forces of evolution, assortative mating can create conditions conducive to evolutionary change and, if systematically practiced in a population, would prevent Hardy-Weinberg equilibrium genotype values from being attained.

The impact of assortative mating on gene frequencies is probably modest because the traits selected for are mostly of a polygenic nature. In addition to mate selection based on similarities (positive assortative mating), there is also the possibility of selection favoring dissimilarities (negative assortative mating) for certain characteristics. For instance, in the United States, marriages involving two red-haired individuals occur less frequently than would be predicted on the basis of the frequency of red-haired genotypes and random mate selection.

THE SEX RATIO

Another assumption upon which the occurrence of Hardy-Weinberg equilibrium genotype frequencies rests is that the sexes are present in equal numbers in the population. Although this assumption is generally valid in large populations of humans, disproportions can and do occur, and their occurrence is more likely in small populations. If one sex is represented by an unusually small number of individuals, representatives of the less common sex will experience a higher probability of transmitting their genes to the next generation than will those of the more common sex. Chance factors can affect the genotypes of individuals who for this reason disproportionately influence the gene frequencies of the next generation. Thus sex ratios can have an important effect on gene frequencies.

EFFECTIVE POPULATION SIZE

An important concept in estimating the likelihood of evolutionary change in small populations is that of **effective population size,** which is always less than the total size of the population, since not everyone in a population is equally likely to reproduce. Whereas a small number of females of reproductive age will limit the reproductive potential of the population, a severe disproportion in sex ratios favoring either males or females will have the effect of reducing the population's variability since the sex that is least represented will, if numbers are small enough, create a bottleneck. This will affect the range of variation in future generations in the same way that small overall population size does. In small populations in general, and in those in which a small number of individuals of either sex contribute a high proportion of the offspring in a given generation, it will be difficult for subsequent generations to avoid inbreeding. This is because a high proportion of prospective mates will share a common ancestor. Sustained inbreeding will further decrease variability as well as lead to the exposure of genetic defects that are expressed only by homozygotes for a recessive allele. Insofar as such traits are harmful or lethal, their exposure enhances the opportunity for selection to occur, eliminating the genetic contribution of their possessors and further reducing variability.

SELECTION

There is a tendency to think of evolution as being the result of natural selection. This is only partially true, however, since selection by itself is only the outcome of certain phenotypes being less fit than others. The term *fitness* can be thought of merely as the degree of success a given genotype has in passing its genetic traits on to the next generation. Since the fitness of a phenotype can differ under differing environmental circumstances, the environment can play an important role in reducing the amount of variability a population can retain. A severe environment will have a lower tolerance for phenotypic variation, and sustained exposure to strong environmental stress will narrow the range of a population's genetic heterogeneity.

DIRECTIONAL SELECTION

Selection can occur in several ways. One form has been designated **directional selection.** In directional selection, phenotypes on one or the other side of the mean value for a **continuous trait** have superior fitness to those at the mean or closer to the opposite extreme. A continuous trait is one that is determined by the combined effects of more than one locus and that can be measured over a continuous range of values. Height (stature) in humans is a continuous trait

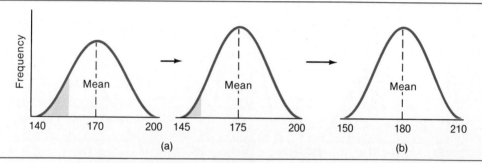

Figure 7-1a *"Directional selection for increased height. Shorter individuals suffer a selective disadvantage while taller ones enjoy greater reproductive success. The result is an increase of mean stature of the population."*

Figure 7-1b *"The mean stature of the population has increased by 10 centimeters but the range of values for stature is similar."*

under the influence of many loci. A sustained advantage in fitness for tall individuals would, in time, shift the population's mean value for stature upward. If no new variation was introduced into the population's gene pool, such as through new mutations or by mating with migrants drawing on a different gene pool, the range of variation for stature might be narrowed. The curve of distributions for stature would undergo the kind of alteration shown in Figure 7-1(a).

If new variation arising from recombination, mutations, or migration is incorporated into the gene pool, the advantage of being tall might lead to a further increase in mean statures by adding to the number of individuals at the extreme for tallness, as shown in Figure 7-1(b). Although the range of values is the same in Figure 7-1(b) as at the start, 60 centimeters (cm), the mean has shifted upward from 170 cm to 180 cm, and the tallest surviving individuals are now 210 cm tall instead of 200 cm tall. With continued superiority of fitness for tallness and with continued availability of new genetic variability that includes the potential for increased stature, the population could continue to increase its mean and maximum statures. This is a straightforward illustration of directional selection. Of course, at some point the fitness associated with tallness would begin to decline, and the limits of directional selection would be reached.

STABILIZING SELECTION

When the limits of directional selection are reached, directional selection would give way to a period of stabilizing (or normalizing) selection. In its definitive form, stabilizing selection is characterized by superior fitness being

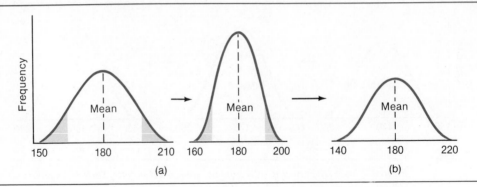

Figure 7-2a "Stabilizing selection wherein both very tall and very short individuals experience a selective disadvantage. The frequency of individuals expressing mean values for stature is increased while the range of values for stature is narrowed."

Figure 7-2b "Reduced selective pressure against both extremes of stature results in expansion of the range of values for stature with less clustering around the mean value."

associated with mean values for the trait. In Figure 7-1(b), individuals with statures of 180 cm would enjoy the greatest fitness. In the event of strong stabilizing selection, genotypes yielding either very tall or very short phenotypes would possess very low fitness values, and the range of values for stature would decrease as shown in Figure 7-2(a). Restriction of the range of values around the mean has changed the shape of the curve from a normal (normokurtic) one to one with a narrower base but similar height (leptokurtic). In the absence of stabilizing selection, there might be a reduction in the difference in fitness of the mean phenotype and restoration of the normokurtic distribution, or possibly even a tendency toward a flat (platykurtic) one with reduced central tendency, as shown in Figure 7-2(b).

SKEWED DISTRIBUTIONS

Even when a population maintains stable values for a continuous trait, the distribution may not be entirely symmetrical. This is because the fitness of one extreme of the distribution may be much lower than that at the opposite extreme. When such asymmetries occur, the curve of distribution exhibits what has been called **skewness.** A skewed curve of distribution is shown in Figure 7-3, which is drawn from the actual range of values for weight in the population of young males in the United States. It can be seen that while males weighing 25 kilograms (kg) less than the mean value of 62.5 kg are not represented, there are individuals weighing as much as 43 kg above the mean.

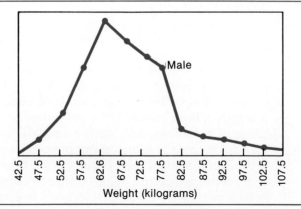

Figure 7-3 *"Skewed distribution of values for weight in 17-year olds in the USA, 1966-1970"*

MIGRATION

The maintenance of equilibrium genotype frequencies is not possible if there is migration from another population with different gene frequencies. Gene flow, or **introgression,** from another population can result in a shift in the gene frequencies of the host population that prevents equilibrium genotype frequencies from ever being attained. This is because one generation free of all factors that could alter gene frequencies is a prerequisite for Hardy-Weinberg equilibrium.

Movement of genes through a population need not always require movement of people. For instance, matings that take place across a boundary separating two populations can result in the acquisition of a new allele by one of the populations. Through matings involving individuals living farther from the boundary, the new allele can be gradually transported to the center of the population's distribution. The human tendency to avoid inbreeding through various cultural practices such as village exogamy (choice of mate restricted to individuals living outside one's own home village) facilitates the exchange of genetic material. The practice of choosing a wife from another village and requiring that she come to live with her husband's family is common in much of India. The interconnected network of small villages that is characteristic of the distribution of rural India's population ensures that there is exchange of genes even though groups are not migrating in the conventional sense.

MUTATION

Mutation is the source of all new variation. In its most elemental form, a mutation is an alteration in a single base pair. Sometimes, but not always, such alterations will lead to a significant change in the amino acid sequence of a protein. Many mutations do not yield changed proteins, however, and many remain undetected except when sophisticated techniques such as DNA sequencing are applied. The continual production of mutations is the inevitable result of copying errors that occur during DNA replication. The accumulation of these small and invisible errors over time is thought by many geneticists to provide a "molecular clock" that can be used to assess the degree of relatedness of two species that have undergone a period of evolutionary divergence. Both nuclear DNA and mitochondrial DNA undergo the accumulation of mutations, and much research is currently underway to apply the knowledge recently gained about these DNA sequences to the reconstruction of the evolutionary history of our species. Interesting as these mutations might be from the perspective of long-term evolutionary reconstruction, however, it is because they are rendered selectively neutral that they are able to accumulate. Therefore, from the perspective of ongoing evolutionary processes, this kind of mutation is irrelevant.

When a mutation produces a significant change in a protein, that change is usually harmful. Since surviving species are by definition adapted, they are usually endowed with traits that have been selected and have proven beneficial. Significant change in a beneficial trait, therefore, is usually detrimental and may be lethal. On the rare occasion where a mutation is beneficial, it could be expected to spread. Since the environment continually changes, a mutation that was undesirable in the past may prove beneficial against a new environmental background. Thus new variation in the form of mutations is essential for long-term survival. The price of maintaining a pool of new variation to ensure survival in a changing world is the decreased fitness of individuals carrying a deleterious mutation. This is a price that must be paid in order to permit the species to evolve and thereby survive. When a mutation produces a viable alternative to an existing allele, the first step in the alteration of gene frequencies at that locus has been taken. If a new and successful allele spreads through the population, gene frequencies will continue to change and Hardy-Weinberg genotype frequencies will not be observed.

Populations usually differ from the ideal in terms of size, mobility, mutations, and mating patterns. For most of the history of our species, populations have been small. Opportunities for random genetic drift, population bottlenecks, and disproportionate reproductive success by some member or members of the population have probably occurred frequently. Some differences between present-day human populations could have arisen through chance events that were followed by sufficient isolation to permit one population to become distinct in one or more genetically determined characteristics. The tendency for human populations to break down isolation barriers from time to time has generally resulted in a blurring of the boundaries, producing gradients of genetic differences rather than sharp disjunctures.

BIBLIOGRAPHY

BERNSTEIN, F. 1924. Ergebnisse einer biostatistischen zussammenfassenden Betrachtung über die erblicchen Blutskukturen des Menschen. *Klinische Wochenschrift.* 33: 1495–97.

BERNSTEIN, F. 1925. Zussammenfassende Betracktungen über die erblichen Blutstrukturen des Menschen. Zeitschrift *indukt. Abstamm u. Vererb Lehre Kererbgsl.* 37: 237–70.

*BODMER, W. F., and L. L. CAVALLI-SFORZA. 1976. *Genetics, Evolution, and Man.* San Francisco: W. H. Freeman & Company Publishers.

*BOYER, S. H. (ED.) 1963. *Papers on Human Genetics.* Englewood Cliffs, N.J.: Prentice-Hall. (Contains original 1908 Weinberg paper.)

CASTLE, W. E. 1903. The laws of heredity of Galton and Mendel and some laws governing race improvement by selection. *Proceedings of the American Academy of Arts and Sciences* 39: 223–42.

CROW, J. F., and M. KIMURA. 1970. *A Introduction to Population Genetic Theory.* New York: Harper and Row.

KIMURA, M., and T. OHTA. 1971. *Theoretical Aspects of Populations Genetics.* Princeton, N.J.: Princeton University Press.

LAUGHLIN, W. S. 1966. Genetical and anthropological characteristics of Arctic populations. In *The Biology of Human Adaptability,* P. T. Baker and J. S. Weiner, eds., pp. 469–95. Oxford: Clarendon Press.

LANDSTEINER, K. 1945. The Specificity of Serological Reactions. Cambridge: Harvard University Press.

OHNO, SUSUMU 1970. *Evolution by Gene Duplication.* Berlin: Springer-Verlag.

*PETERS, J. H. ED. 1959. *Classic Papers in Genetics.* Englewood Cliffs, N.J.: Prentice-Hall. (Contains original 1908 Hardy paper.)

*PIANKA, E. R. 1976. Competition and niche theory. In *Theoretical Ecology: Principles and Applications,* R. M. May, ed., pp. 114–41. Philadelphia: W. B. Saúnders.

*Recommended Readings (not cited)

Chapter
8
The Behavior
of Prosimians
and Monkeys

This chapter begins with a discussion of the types of primate groups and of sociobiology, a theoretical concept used to help explain social behavior. We will then discuss the behavior and social organizations of several species of prosimians and monkeys. Prosimians are the primates least closely related to humans. Although some prosimians are anatomically rather distinct, others exhibit monkeylike traits in their anatomy and behavior. Prosimians are restricted to Africa and Asia. Monkeys are found not only in Africa and Asia but also in Central and South America. Although they share many similarities in anatomy and behavior, some important anatomical traits distinguish New and Old World monkeys.

Because they have a closer phylogenetic relationship to humans, this chapter concentrates on the Old World monkeys. Beginning in the late 1950s a number of Old World monkeys were the subject of intensive study. The first monkey species to be studied with an intention of generating useful information for reconstructing early human social organization and behavior was the East African savanna-dwelling baboon. Other Old World monkeys that have been intensively studied include the Indian rhesus and the Japanese macaque, the Indian langur and the African green monkey. Some key features of the social organization and behavior of each species are presented. One shared trait of all these primates, and of primates generally, is that members reside in social groups. However, the size and the composition of the social groups of these species vary. In each of the species, male and female members have different roles within the social group.

OVERVIEW

As the creatures most closely related to humans, monkeys and apes have been studied intensely from various perspectives. Most early primate research was biomedical; only relatively recently has behavioral research become a focal point of nonhuman primate studies. Observers of behavior record what their subjects do—when, where, and for how long. Field researchers observe how animals react to changing social and environmental conditions, how they interact with one another, and how they obtain and process food, among other behaviors. If the animals are social—and almost all primates are—observers attempt to describe the social structure and function of the social group.

The scientific study of animal behavior is called **ethology.** The observer, the **ethologist,** searches for the functions of the observed behavior patterns, trying to understand what shaped their evolution. The ethological approach attempts to reconstruct the evolution of motor patterns and to explore processes underlying behavioral development. The ethological approach emphasizes the evolutionary significance of behavior.

Ethological studies begin with a description, an **ethogram,** of a species' behavioral repertoire. The ethogram should be a complete description of behavioral patterns, as well as a discussion of the form and function of the behavior. Ethologists seek to find recurring behavioral constellations. Behaviors within such constellations are considered to be closely related to one another. Ethologists are also concerned with comparing the behavior of different populations of the same species. Such intraspecific comparison indicates the range of the species' adaptations to different habitat conditions.

Naturalistic primate studies have collected data that advance our knowledge and understanding of the complex behavior of human and nonhuman primates. Field studies have provided a new appreciation of the variety and complexity of primate social behaviors and social organizations, and have demonstrated the remarkable variability and adaptability of social behavior.

TYPES OF PRIMATE SOCIETIES

Five types of nonhuman primate social organizations are generally recognized: (1) the noyau, (2) the territorial pair, (3) the one-male group, (4) the multimale group, and (5) one-male groups within a multimale group. The characteristics of these social groupings will be briefly discussed. (Table 8-1 lists another set of primate groupings).

In the noyau, males and females defend their **territory**—that is, the areas in which they reside. In the noyau, males are solitary, and females are often accompanied solely by their immature young. Each male has a territory overlapping those of several females with whom he mates. This organization typifies such nocturnal primates as pottos and bush babies.

The territorial pair, typical of most gibbons, which are the smallest and most arboreal of the apes, was viewed by some early investigators as the analogue of the human family. In most gibbon species, a male and female are paired in a territory that they defend against other pairs. The male and female of the territorial pair drive off their maturing offspring. This minimizes population concentrations in small areas and forces offspring to find unrelated animals with whom to mate. There is minimal sexual dimorphism in pair-organized species.

The one-male–multifemale group is found among some members of the Old World monkey genus *Cercopithecus,* some leaf-eating monkeys, and the savanna-dwelling patas monkey. All members of such social units forage and move together. Unattached males live either alone or in all-male groups (sometimes called bachelor groups). The entrance of such males into a bisexual group, a group containing members of both sexes, may precipitate considerable aggression and even infanticide in some species.

The multimale-multifemale group characterizes many nonhuman primates, and its appearance was once considered universal based on early studies of savanna-dwelling baboons. Multimale-multifemale groups, especially those living on the savanna, are large social organizations which may contain a few hundred animals. A dominance structure in which animals are ranked relative to others is typical of multimale groups.

Table 8-1 **Types of Nonhuman Primate Social Groups**

---

1. Solitary animals except for mother–infant pair and mating adults. Many primates in this category are arboreal and nocturnal.
   Examples: Bush babies, mouse lemur, loris, orangutan.

2. Monogamous pairs with their young. This type of social organization is most common among arboreal primates.
   Examples: Gibbon, marmoset, indri, titi monkey.

3. One-male–multifemale social group. One adult male in the group does all the breeding. In some species with this social organization, like langurs, all-male groups will invade and may kill all the resident infants.
   Examples: Some leaf-eating monkeys, patas monkey.

4. Single aggregate male groups with several single male units in a larger aggregation. Such groupings are most common in arid or semiarid country where food and sleeping sites are scarce.
   Examples: Hamadryas baboon, gelada.

5. Multimale-multifemale groups. Examples of this social organization are quite common and are found among both arboreal and terrestrial species. In such social groupings, the number of adult females is larger than the number of adult males. There is also usually considerable sexual dimorphism.
   Examples: Savanna baboons, macaques, vervets.

6. Diffuse groupings with considerable change in the social structure.
   Example: Chimpanzee.

In the one-male "harem," or polygynous group, one adult male lives with a number of females within a larger multimale structure. Residence within this larger social unit, which contains many polygynous groups, differentiates this social organization from the one-male–multifemale social units just discussed. In hamadryas baboons, for example, the leader male is the focus of the group, and he controls the behavior of his "harem." Mating with harem females is solely the prerogative of this male.

SOCIOBIOLOGY

Primatologists (researchers who study primates) try not only to provide a full description of the behaviors they witness, they also explain why certain behaviors occur. One of the theoretical perspectives used to explain behaviors is **sociobiology.** This term became widely known with the publication of E. O. Wilson's 1975 book entitled *Sociobiology: The New Synthesis.* Sociobiological theory provides a sweeping set of hypotheses about the evolution of social behavior. We will, for example, be referring to sociobiological explanations when we look at infanticide in langurs and the mating patterns of male chimpanzees (Chapter 9). Sociobiology has focused attention on the role of kinship in determining social relationships within primate social groups (see, for example, Richard and Schulman, 1982). Sociobiologists argue that the purpose of such behavior is the maximization of reproductive success. They assume that behavior has a genetic basis, and that its evolutionary impact can be measured by its influence on reproductive success.

Despite the fact that we accept the idea that some aspects of sociobiological theory can provide useful clues to understanding certain primate behaviors, we reject the notion that sociobiological theory can, or should, be used in a wider perspective to explain (or justify) social conditions in general. Theories that help to explain why insects or birds, for example, act in one way or another should not be called on to explain away human prejudices, class stratification, or other social injustices. Sociobiology has all too often been called on to justify intolerable human social, political, and economic conditions. We reject this misuse of sociobiology, as do anthropologists generally. As anthropologists, we also recognize the sweeping role that culture plays in the expression of human behavioral patterns.

Sociobiology is based on the concept of **inclusive fitness,** first discussed by the British zoologist William D. Hamilton in 1963. Hamilton demonstrated that genealogical relationships have important implications for social behavior. The concept of inclusive fitness implies that an individual's genetic **fitness** includes not only its own reproductive success, but also the reproductive successes of its relatives. The closer the kinship tie, the greater the number of genes shared. For example, because siblings have more genes in common than do cousins, it can be expected that siblings will aid, or at least not disrupt, one another's reproductive behavior more often than they will aid the reproductive behavior of less closely related animals or nonrelated animals. Gene-based behaviors that do this will be selected for.

Another important concept of sociobiological theory is that of **kin selection.** The concepts of kin selection and inclusive fitness are intertwined. For example, it can be argued that when an animal gives a warning call, it protects a number of individuals with whom it shares its genes. The gain in survival of its genes might be greater if relatives were saved than the loss that would be expected if the animal giving the warning call were itself killed. Such behavior has often been labelled altruism. The selective advantage of an individual's assisting a relative depends on three factors: (1) the risk to its own fitness— that is, how impaired its own mating performance will be, (2) the benefit of its behavior to its relative or relatives, and (3) the extent to which genes are shared by relatives. Theoretically, one should be more likely to assist parents and siblings than less closely related kin. Kin selection extends the concept of Darwinian fitness to include not only the reproductive success of an individual and its offspring, but also the reproductive success of all individuals in the social group with which the individual shares a genetic relationship.

Animals not related to one another, or only distantly related, occasionally help one another. Such aid cannot be attributed to kin selection. Trivers (1971) developed a model to help explain what appears to be altruistic behavior in nonrelatives. This model, called **reciprocal altruism,** refers to behaviors that are more beneficial to the recipient than costly to the provider, and assumes that a similar act in reverse or some kind of return could be expected in the future. Acts of reciprocal altruism are behaviors that occur between individuals independent of any genetic relationship. The idea of reciprocal altruism is based on the old adage "do unto others as you would have them do unto you." "Cheaters"—that is, those who do not act to help others—are supposedly removed because others remember their selfish behavior and do not mate with them or are less likely to aid them in the future. The major differences between the mechanisms of kin selection and reciprocal altruism are the mutual or reciprocal aspects of the latter, and the fact that the latter involves behavior without regard to genetic relatedness, as supposed by the former.

Robert Trivers (1972) has also attempted to use sociobiological explanations to explain parental behavior and male and female mating strategies. His model of parental investment has been incorporated into Hrdy's (1977) discussion of langur infanticide presented later.

PROSIMIANS

The Prosimii (Table 8-2) constitute a suborder of primates apart from the monkeys, apes, and humans. The study of the prosimians offers useful insights into the early stages of primate evolution because anatomically, some have changed little from the earliest primates. Most prosimians have smaller, flatter skulls than other primates. Their ears are pointed and mobile. A pointed muzzle is often tipped by a naked rhinarium, an area of moistened skin surrounding the tip of the nose. Naked rhinaria, not found in higher primates, who rely strongly on the visual sense, are usually found in animals who rely heavily on olfactory communication. Most prosimians are small. They live a great part of their lives in the trees. Some feed exclusively on insects, and some are nocturnal.

Although compared to other primates, their anatomy most resembles the nonprimate ancestral stock, prosimians clearly show their primate affinities with hands and feet adapted for climbing by grasping. The social structure of some of the lemurs that inhabit the island of Madagascar resembles that of monkeys. Like some monkeys, some lemur species have multiple adult male and adult female groups, and infants of both sexes remain lifelong members of a bisexual social group.

Living prosimians belong to one of three superfamilies: Tarsioidea, the tarsiers; Lorisoidea, the lorises; and Lemuroidea, the lemurs. Tarsiers are native to Southeast Asian tropical rainforests. They are small, nocturnal animals with long tails, greatly elongated hindlimbs adapted to leaping among the branches, and large, bulging eyes which assist in locating insect prey at

---

Table 8-2 **Prosimians: Distribution, Anatomy, and Social Organization**

Habitat

Asia and Africa. In Africa, many prosimians (the lemurs) are concentrated on the island of Madagascar.

Many are arboreal, nocturnal, and insectivorous.

Anatomy

Most have smaller, flatter skulls than other primates.

Many have pointed, mobile ears.

Nocturnal prosimians have large eyes and eye orbits.

Most are small-bodied.

Most have a pointed muzzle and a naked rhinarium.

Prosimians climb by grasping with the hands and feet.

Behavior/Social Organization

Many are solitary, but some lemurs live in bisexual social groups.

---

night. Tarsiers have a relatively large brain (compared with other prosimians) and an almost completely enclosed bony eye orbit. They are strictly arboreal, usually travel in small groups or pairs, and feed on fruits and small reptiles in addition to insects.

Lorises (Figure 8-1) are found in Africa and Asia. Like many of their prosimian relatives, lorises are mainly arboreal and nocturnal. They are largely insectivorous, which, in combination with their nocturnality, is perhaps one reason that they do not suffer from competition from monkeys even though

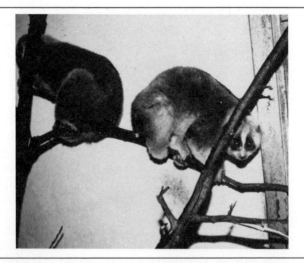

Figure 8-1 A pair of captive slow lorises (Nycticebus coucang) *from China. These are nocturnal primates.*

their range overlaps that of these larger and more intelligent primates. Some lorises, like the aptly named slow loris, are studies in slow motion. Some have enormous eyes (an adaptation to nocturnal life) and grooming claws on the second toe of each foot. The elongated heel and ankle bones of one of the lorises, the galago, is a specialization reflecting their pattern of locomotion, known as vertical clinging and leaping.

Lemurs, the most diverse prosimian group, are confined to the island of Madagascar, where their existence is threatened by human-induced habitat changes. They are the only primates inhabiting Madagascar, and they have evolved for millions of years in isolation from mainland African primates. Lemurs belong to one of three families: the Lemuridae, the Indriidae, and the Daubentoniidae. Although some members of the family Lemuridae are nocturnal and lead a solitary existence, the ring-tailed lemur is diurnal and lives in social groups. The Lemuridae combine primate anatomical features, such as fingernails on all the digits except the second toe of the foot, partly opposable big toe and thumb, and a heavy reliance on binocular vision, with traits rarely found in primates. For example, some lemur species estivate; that is, they sleep throughout the hot season, obtaining their nutrients from a large fat deposit at the base of the tail.

The family Indriidae, the most monkeylike of the prosimians, includes the indri, the avahi, and the sifaka. These species exhibit traits that are unusual in primates, such as webbed toes. Little is known about the indri's social behavior, but avahis are reputed to live in family units of two to four individuals.

The family Daubentoniidae contains only one species, the members of which are called aye-ayes. The aye-aye is distinctive in its possession of two large, chisel-like teeth in the front of the jaw and an elongated nail tipping a long, thin middle finger. The specialized teeth are used to tear open tree bark to find grubs, which are then "speared" with the elongated nail of the middle finger. Aye-ayes are nocturnal and often live in pairs.

NEW WORLD MONKEYS

New World monkeys (Table 8-3) are arboreal and inhabit a variety of rain forest niches in South and Central America. No New World monkey evolved a terrestrial adaptation. Although some New World monkeys closely resemble Old World monkeys, there are important facial and dental differences. New World monkeys have three premolars instead of the two present in Old World forms. The nostrils of New World monkeys are more widely spaced than in Old World forms, and are oriented toward the side rather than forward or down as in Old World forms. Some New World monkeys also have **prehensile** (grasping) tails, which can be used as a fifth hand for grasping. These monkeys will hang by their prehensile tails, leaving their hands and feet unencumbered for feeding or holding food. Some New World monkeys, such as the howler and spider monkeys, have long arms which they use to swing beneath branches, much like the brachiating Asian ape, the gibbon.

Despite behavioral and anatomical differences, New and Old World monkeys share an ancient evolutionary history because all primates had a common ancestry in North America about 60 M.Y.A. (Chapter 14). New World monkeys may trace their ancestry to an African primate stock dating to about 35 M.Y.A. Evidence for this ancestry lies in the sharing of an extra premolar by some Oligocene African primates and modern New World monkeys and the presence of a number of biochemical similarities. At about 35 to 40 M.Y.A., South America and Africa were much closer to each other than they are today, and it has been suggested that New World monkeys may have drifted from Africa to South America on some sort of natural raft. Many South American rodents and other fauna are also believed by some to be part of an African to South American migration.

New World monkeys belong to either one of two families: the Callithricidae or the Cebidae. Marmosets and tamarins (Figure 8-2, 8-3, and 8-4), primates small enough to be held in the palm of one hand, belong to the Callithricidae. Many of these monkeys have colored patches or hair tufts. Marmosets have a generalized primate diet which includes insects, small vertebrates, and fruits. They live in family groups of 3 to 8 members; however, larger groups have been observed. Marmosets usually give birth to twins, and paternal care is prevalent; both of these characteristics are quite rare among nonhuman primates.

Table 8-3 New World Monkeys: A General Summary of Distribution, Anatomy, and Social Organization

Habitat
Central and South America only.
All are arboreal forest-dwellers. There are no terrestrial forms.

Anatomy
Most have three premolar teeth in each quadrant of the jaw.
Nostrils face sideways.
Some forms have a prehensile tail.
Many have long arms associated with locomotor specializations.

Behavior/Social Organization
Titi monkeys: Strong, long-lasting monogamous pairs or small family groups averaging 3–5 animals. They may be territorial.

Marmosets: Family groups of 3–8 members. Larger groups are possible. They give birth to twins. Paternal care is the rule.

Howler monkeys: Groups average 18 members. Females outnumber males in the social group. Lone males are seen. They are territorial. Infanticide is reported among red howler monkeys.

Figure 8-2 A marmoset, Callithrix penicillata, *is shown clinging to the bark of a tree on which it has been feeding on sap. The holes which it has gouged in the bark with its teeth can be seen.*

Figure 8-3 A cotton-top marmoset adult male.

Figure 8-4 A male golden lion tamarin (Leontopithecus rosalia).

Marmosets and tamarins have two instead of three premolars, and claws instead of nails on most of their digits.

The Cebidae is a large and diverse group, one of whose members is the titi monkey (Figure 8-5 and 8-6). Titis are small, thickly haired monkeys. They live in strong, long-lasting monogamous pairs or small family groups averaging 3 to 5 animals. Each family inhabits a small forest patch that may be defended with vocalizations and threatening postures. Loud vocalizations emitted early in the morning signal a group's location and maintain group spacing.

Figure 8-5 A yellow-haired titi monkey, Callicebus torquatus, *in Amazonian Peru. Note the typically broad nose of a platyrrhine monkey.*

Figure 8-6 A South American night monkey, Aotus trivirgatus, *father carrying its month-old infant on its back. Among the night and the titi monkeys the father carries the infant except when the infant is nursing. Note the large eyes typical of nocturnal primates.*

Another member of the Cebidae is the howler monkey (Figure 8-7). This monkey is aptly named; it possesses a specialized larynx which permits a deep and booming vocalization. Most howlers are large animals with prehensile tails and long black, brown, or copper-red hair, depending on the species. Howlers live in groups averaging about 18 animals; however, groups may have as many as 45 animals. Females usually outnumber males, a common primate trait. (The number of adult females to adult males is expressed as the **socionomic sex ratio.** For example, 2:1 means two adult females for every adult male.) Although most howler groups are bisexual, males occasionally live alone. Each group moves within a fairly well-defined area defended against intrusion by other groups. **Territory**—that is, a geographical area that is defended against incursion by animals of another group—is maintained by howling and by shaking and breaking branches—acts that substitute for physical aggression. Howling also occurs early in the morning and is a means of locating and spacing adjacent groups. There is no clear pattern of male dominance, and both sexes care for the young.

The red howler monkey is one of six howler monkey species distributed from southern Mexico to northern Argentina. Although infrequently observed, violent fighting sometimes erupts among howler groups (Crockett, 1984). Red howler social groups average about nine animals, with one to two adult males, two to four adult females, and immature offspring. Unlike members of many primate species, red howler females emigrate from their natal group. About one in five females and very few males mature and

Figure 8-7 A brown howler monkey, Alouatta fusca, *in Brazil feeding on leaves, the most important part of its diet. Note how it uses its prehensile tail to stabilize itself while sitting on a branch. It may even hang by its tail while feeding.*

reproduce in the group in which they are born. Females emigrate only reluctantly. Among the many problems emigration poses for the female is the fact that emigrant females, while awaiting a chance to enter a new group, may delay their first pregnancies and thereby lower their genetic contribution to future generations.

Red howler group sizes appear to be limited by the restricted food supply in a given home range. The number of females per group is limited. If resources are scarce, females and their mothers may have more to gain if the daughter leaves to join another group in an area with more food. There may also be a conflict between a mother and daughter or between mothers, all of whom may favor keeping their own daughters rather than those of other females in the group. Conflicts between females occasionally escalate to physical fights. Females probably emigrate because the breeding opportunities within a group are limited, and breeding opportunities can be found elsewhere.

Typically larger than adult females, adult males compete with each other for entry into groups and access to females. They clash violently and occasionally kill each other. Assailants often invade a group in pairs, and these cooperating males have greater success in expelling resident males than does a single male invader. Invasion by males into an established bisexual group often leads to infanticide.

Infanticidal red howler males may have greater reproductive success than noninfanticidal males. Females conceive sooner after losing infants, and the average interbirth interval is reduced to 10.5 months as a result of infanticide. Killing an infant allows the male red howler to mate sooner. Since his tenure as a breeding male in a group is limited and unpredictable, the sooner the male produces his own offspring, the more likely the offspring are to survive. Female red howlers are not always willing accomplices to the male's infanticide. They can, and do, try to avoid new males if they already have young. This strategy is not usually effective, however. Of the infants Crockett studied, only 25 percent survived a change of male leadership. Since the odds are against the survival of her current infant, a female's best strategy after an infant dies would be to conceive as soon as possible after a new male takes over the group's leadership.

A third member of the Cebidae are the spider monkeys. Their long arms, hooklike hands, and prehensile tails allow them to be supreme arboreal acrobats. Spider monkey group sizes range from small family groups to large aggregations of 100 or more animals. Females outnumber males. Females with their offspring seem to form a cohesive subgroup within the larger social unit. Male dominance behavior is evident.

OLD WORLD MONKEYS

Major behavioral studies have been conducted on such Old World monkeys as the Asian macaques and langurs and the African baboons, green monkeys, and patas monkeys (Table 8-4). Old World monkeys are a diverse group belonging to the superfamily Cercopithecoidea. Old World monkeys share a number of distinguishing anatomical traits. Almost all have at least a short, nonprehensile tail. Their trunk is long and narrow from side to side and deep from front to back. This structure is related to their predominantly quadrupedal mode of locomotion, during which they rest on the palms of their hands and feet or on their finger pads, and not on their knuckles or fists, as apes do. Old World monkeys move through the trees quadrupedally and span distances by jumping. All Old World monkeys have three molar teeth in each quadrant of the jaw, with two pairs of cusps connected by crests, a configuration known as **bilophodont molars** (Figure 8-8). Like apes and humans, Old World monkeys have two premolars in each quadrant of the jaw, instead of the three premolars found in most New World monkeys. Old World monkeys have great efficiency of movement and strength in their opposable thumbs and big toes. Some Old World monkeys also have **ischial callosities,** calloused regions on the rump which appear to be an adaptation to sitting on hard surfaces for long periods of time.

There are two subfamilies of Old World monkeys: the Colobinae and the Cercopithecinae. The Colobinae contains mainly arboreal monkeys whose stomachs are specialized for ingesting leafy materials. Asian langurs (Figures 8-9, and 8-10) and African colobus monkeys belong to this group.

The Cercopithecinae is a diverse subfamily containing Asian and African

---

Table 8-4 Old World Monkeys: A General Summary of Distribution, Anatomy, and Social Organization

---

Geographical Location:

Africa and Asia

Wide range of adaptations, from arboreal to terrestrial forms and forest to savanna dwellers.

In Asia, Old World monkeys include the macaques and langurs.

In Africa, Old World monkeys include the baboons, cercopithecine, and colobus monkeys. There are also macaques in North Africa.

Anatomy:

Many have short tails, but some macaques, African cercopithecines, and the leaf-eating monkeys have long tails. None have prehensile tails.

Locomotion is quadrupedal. Most have long, narrow trunks.

Nostrils face downward.

Two premolars in each quadrant of the jaw. The molars are bilophodont.

Ischial callosities are adaptations to sitting.

Many macaques have cheek pouches as feeding adaptations.

Leaf-eaters have specialized stomachs as feeding adaptations.

All except leaf-eating monkeys have opposable thumbs in many forms.

Behavior/Social Organization:

Macaques: The size of the social group is species-specific and varies with the habitat and food supply. There are clearcut dominance hierarchies in most species. Social groups contain more females than males. Males can also be found living a solitary life or in all-male groups. Subgroups are evident. Social groups are matrifocal. Most macaque species have mating and birth seasons. Grooming and play are very important social behaviors.

Baboons: The size of the social group varies with the habitat. The hamadryas and geladas live in polygynous social groups. Mating and birth seasons are commonly found. Social groups contain more females than males. In many species the social groups are matrifocal. Dominance hierarchies and grooming and play behavior are usually quite evident.

Leaf-eating monkeys: There are different kinds of social groups, ranging from polygynous groups to multimale and multifemale groups. Solitary males and all-male groups are quite common. Territoriality is expressed in many species. Infanticide has been reported for many species. Infant-sharing among females is quite common.

---

species. Lacking the specialized stomach of the colobine monkeys, cercopithecine monkeys possess cheek pouches that serve a digestive function and can also be filled with food for leisurely eating in a different location. Cercopithecine monkeys usually spend more time on the ground than do colobine monkeys. Asian cercopithecines are commonly called macaques; African cercopithecines are a far more diverse group that includes baboons, green monkeys, patas monkeys, and others. Macaques and baboons have been among the most intensely studied of all primates.

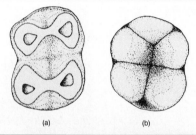

(a)   (b)

Figure 8-8 (A) Bilodophont molar typical of Old World monkeys showing the double ridge (loph) configuration. (B) The Y-5 pattern characteristic of hominoid lower molar teeth.

Figure 8-9 An endangered species, this leaf-eating langur (Presbytis johnii) *inhabits south India. An adult male is shown here.*

Macaques

Macaques are ubiquitous laboratory primates. They were used in biomedical research and psychological testing long before their natural behavior was studied. Macaques have a wide geographical and ecological distribution; they are remarkably adaptable animals. They inhabit various forest types, mangrove swamps, grasslands, and dry scrub areas. They range from being almost completely arboreal to almost completely terrestrial. Besides trees, they

Figure 8-10 Monkeys in India are often found living in the city alongside human inhabitants. These are hanuman langurs (Presbytis entellus) *from Jaipur, northern India.*

inhabit cliffs and rocky places, and in India they live in cities, villages, temples, and railroad stations.

Some of the longest-term information on macaques comes from **provisioned colonies,** social groups to whom humans provide food, in Japan and on the island of Cayo Santiago, Puerto Rico (Figure 8-11). The provisioning process ensures that the animals will return to a designated area to feed. By continually returning to a specified area, the animals eventually become readily identifiable. The provisioned colony on Cayo Santiago was established in 1938 when rhesus macaques were introduced from India. These animals have been studied for long periods of time since then. Provisioned colonies of Japanese macaques have been studied since the late 1940s. Data from these provisioned colonies have been especially revealing. Because of long and continuous observation, individual animals and their kin groups have become well known to researchers. This familiarity has allowed researchers to collect voluminous data. Provisioning can alter behavior and social organization. For example, because food is provided, social groups are often larger than those characteristic of nonprovisioned groups. Because the time spent locating food is reduced by provisioning, such behaviors as grooming can be more frequently expressed.

Most macaque species contain social animals residing in groups with rather clearcut **dominance hierarchies,** or rankings. Dominance ranking refers to the relative amount of power one animal has over another. Rank in the hierarchy is relative to rank over or beneath others. Despite earlier, rather naive concepts of dominance hierarchies, their establishment and function are quite complex, as will be discussed momentarily. As in most primate societies, adult male macaques appear to play the major role in keeping social order. On closer examination, however, among macaques and many other primates, social groups are actually female-focal. Females play a cohesive social role primarily because males emigrate from their natal group (the group in which they are born) while females remain. Females provide the social continuity accompanying long-term familiarity.

An understanding of macaque social order and behavior can be obtained only after the kinship network is understood. Many behaviors are strongly influenced by female kinship ties. Many monkey and ape societies are matrilineally structured (Figure 8-12).

Both the rhesus and Japanese macaque group structures contain a number of subgroupings. For example, the central part of the Japanese macaque group contains the highest-ranking males and females and their offspring. Lower-

Figure 8-11 Rhesus macaques (Macaca mulatta) *of various ages clustered around a feeding station on Cayo Santiago, Puerto Rico. The stuffed cheek pouches are visible on some animals.*

(a)

(b)

(c)

(d)

Figure 8-12 *Among macaques, there is a very strong tie between a mother and an infant and between related females. (A) and (B) show a mother and young infant rhesus macaque in northern India. (C) shows a female cluster among rhesus macaques in northern India. (D) shows a family grouping of female bonnet macaques* (Macaca radiata) *in southern India.*

ranking animals have limited access to the central part of the group; thus they have little to do with the highest-ranking males. Although macaques, usually the males, may try to rise in rank, a lower-ranking animal's attempts to gain status are often frustrated because of lack of support during altercations. Such frustration can lead to a male's emigration from the natal group; he may either move into another group or lead a solitary life. Subadult and young adult males often spend some part of their lives outside of a bisexual group, living alone or in all-male groups.

The rhesus dominance ranking is interesting. Animals acquire some of their ranking position from their mothers. Infants watch their mother's every move, including the tenor of her social interaction with others. Infants then interact with these same animals in the same manner as their mothers do. A dominant mother also supports her infant in social interactions; thus the infant of a dominant mother is less likely to be subordinate to others. Infants of dominant mothers have more opportunity to interact with animals of higher rank, and their very proximity to such animals affords them protection. Dominant mothers are less possessive of their infants, who have an opportunity for more social interaction with more animals at a younger age than do infants of subordinate, lower-ranking mothers. Infants born of dominant mothers in a kin group with many *female* relatives can expect support from female kin members, while infants of subordinate mothers are less likely to have a substantial number of kin in the social group and are essentially on their own.

Maturing females rank just below their mothers; the same is true for prepubertal males. At puberty, males either gain or lose rank or they leave their natal group. The dominance relationship between brothers and sisters is a function of age until the male is 3 or 4 years old; then he becomes dominant over his sister if he remains in the natal group. Females almost always rank beneath their mothers. If a female acts independently of her mother, she can sometimes achieve a higher rank than her mother has when the mother's rank declines, as it does with advancing age.

Rank can be expressed in unexpected ways. For example, evidence gathered over a 20-year period on a captive rhesus colony indicates that the newborn's sex may be tied to its mother's dominance rank (Simpson and Simpson, 1982). Mothers potentially able to devote substantially more time and energy to their offspring's development (those more able to protect them from others, for example) should bear offspring that most effectively repay high levels of maternal investment. A mother would leave more descendants through a daughter than a son if the former inherits her mother's high rank. Because rank is partially a reflection of the number of female relatives an individual has in a group, high-ranking females are those who have given birth to many daughters. A low-ranking mother, on the other hand, would leave more descendants through a son, who is likely to emigrate at puberty and not necessarily carry the liability of his low rank into a new group. Males born to low-ranking females are not likely to remain in their natal group because their low rank can negatively affect their breeding success.

Because rhesus females usually remain in their natal group and are closely allied with mothers and other female kin, a high-ranking daughter could contribute more to her mother's *fitness* by aiding in interfamily fights and by breeding more successfully. A son is unlikely to have the same positive effect because most males emigrate. Fitness is not only a measure of survival or longevity; it is also measured by the ability to successfully reproduce. The concept of fitness can be extended to include not only one's own reproductive success, but the reproductive success of one's relatives. This is called *inclusive fitness.* Under the broader definition of inclusive fitness, some of an individual's genes could be transmitted to the next generation through one's relatives even if the individual has no surviving offspring of its own. An individual can enhance its own fitness by behaving in ways that enhance the reproductive success of its relatives. The concept of inclusive fitness helps us understand, for example, why related rhesus macaque females will come to one another's aid and help care for and protect a relative's infants.

Daughters also bring costs to their mothers, by competing with each other within their own families, for example. A daughter of a low-ranking mother may share with her mother the disadvantages of low rank, including poorer breeding performance. An emigrating son, whose rank is not tied to his mother's rank, may gain sufficient status in his new social group to contribute to his mother's fitness. Being more involved in family strife and attracting more aggression to their mothers from other adults, daughters may be more costly to rear than sons. Because sons leave their mothers at an earlier age, mothers are slower to breed after having daughters than after bearing sons. Therefore, sons are more likely to be presented with a new sibling in their second year, and the presence or absence of a sibling can affect a youngster's development.

Primates generally spend a great deal of time in social interaction. Much of this social interaction occurs during **grooming** behavior (Figure 8-13), and many hours are spent in mutual grooming. Much mutual grooming occurs among related animals; thus grooming helps to reinforce kinship networks. Grooming also helps keep the hair and any wounds clean and free of debris. An animal will either groom itself (self-grooming) or present a part of its body to another animal for grooming. Grooming of one animal by another is called *social grooming,* or *allo-grooming.*

Play is one of the most important social behaviors for young primates (Poirier and Smith, 1974; Poirier, Bellisari, and Haines, 1978). Macaque youngsters spend a good part of each day in social play; most play groups consist of animals of the same age and sex. Young-infant play groups are sexually integrated; however, females leave the heterosexual play groups by 1.5 years of age. By 1.5 years of age, young males and females begin to undergo different socialization processes in preparation for adult social roles. Young females spend more time with their female relatives, with whom they are likely to have a life-long relationship. During this time they show an intense interest in newborn siblings, learning and practicing mothering behavior within the

Figure 8-13 *Two female rhesus macaques grooming.*

female subgroup. While female primates are biologically equipped for mothering (for example, they have breasts with which to nurse their young), they must learn mothering behaviors. Such behaviors are not innate; this is why, for example, many zoos experience problems when newborns are left with females who have neither experienced nor practiced and observed mothering behavior. Such females do not know how to respond to an infant's needs.

Rhesus mating behavior is neither random nor uncontrolled. As is the case among most nonhuman primates, mating rarely occurs between closely related animals. Mating between a mother and her adult son is quite rare, but there may be some sexual activity between them when the son is sexually immature. In the few cases in which the mother was the preferred partner, the male was in his first active mating season. The incidence of brother–sister mating is very low, and those instances that do occur usually involve young animals. Of 406 observed courtships among the rhesus monkeys on Cayo Santiago, only 11 percent involved genealogically related pairs (Missakian, 1972). There were only 9 cases of mother–son mating, 15 cases involving brother and sister, and 19 cases of other kin-related sexual encounters (Missakian, 1972). It is almost impossible to say anything authoritative about father–daughter matings because an ovulating rhesus female mates with many males, and it is often impossible for an observer to know which male fathered an offspring.

It has been noted that male macaques emigrate from their natal group. The emigrating males frequently transfer into the group to which their older, maternally related brothers or other male relatives belong. Brothers spend more time close to one another, form coalitions with one another more frequently than with nonrelated animals, and disrupt one another's interactions with sexually receptive females less frequently than would be expected by chance. Males with a brother in a group spend more time in that group than do males who have no brother in the group. When a male enters a group, he is more likely to breed with females who are already familiar to his brother. Brothers who behave nepotistically and noncompetitively (in this case by sharing breeding females) increase their inclusiveness fitness. Brothers also mate more often with females who are related to one another than randomly with any female (McMillan and Duggleby, 1981).

The pattern of nepotism is interesting and is not restricted to rhesus males. A similar pattern of group transfer is found among African vervet monkeys (Figure 8-14). When vervet males emigrate from their natal group, they are often accompanied by a brother. This raises an issue about the costs and benefits of transferring randomly as opposed to nonrandomly, and of transferring alone or accompanied by a brother or age mate. Male vervets are likely to repeatedly transfer among groups in which their male relatives reside.

Because social standing and reproductive success for male vervets, as for many primates, depends upon fighting skill and the ability to form alliances with other group members, there are obvious advantages to transferring to a new group accompanied by one's brother or moving into a group in which one's brother already resides. Brothers who transfer together can effectively avoid mating with close kin, especially if they retransfer when a brother's daughters reach sexual maturity. Brothers not only form alliances when entering their new group, but they also have a means by which they can keep track of close kin in order to avoid them as mating partners.

Mature male vervets who have resided in a group for five or more years tend to transfer again. Thus they avoid the danger of mating with their own or their

Figure 8-14 *A male vervet monkey* (Cercopithecus aethiops) *from Kenya.*

brother's offspring. In their second transfer, males may move farther afield and may move alone. As full-grown adults, they are less vulnerable to possible predation during the transfer; thus they are able to move to more distant groups. Fully mature adult males are also more likely able to defend themselves against any hostilities they may encounter when entering a new group, thereby lessening their need for an alliance with a brother or age mate. A male moving for the second time can adopt a more random mode of transfer than that in his first move and still have a low risk of mating with close kin. Older males provide a steady supply of migrants, and therefore new genes, across the clusters of neighboring groups. The more random transfer of single, older males means that "a population in which groups exchange males at high rates always received at least some migrants from different groups" (Cheney and Seyfarth, quoted in Lewin, 1983: 150).

Groups that frequently exchange males experience less intergroup aggression and more friendly encounters than groups that do not exchange males. The consequences of repeated, nonrandom male transfers between groups extend beyond the immediate social benefits enjoyed by the individual directly involved.

Baboons

Baboons (Figures 8-15 and 8-16), residents of Africa, have been the subject of numerous behavioral studies since Washburn and DeVore's (1961) pioneering study. Much has been written about baboon social life, and until relatively recently they were the model for our general knowledge about primate behavior.

Baboons are found from coast to coast throughout sub-Saharan Africa and in the Arabian peninsula. They occupy diverse vegetational zones including subdeserts, savannas, acacia thornveld, and rain forests. Other habitats include rocky cliffs, gorges, and seaside cliffs. Baboons inhabiting these diverse habitats exhibit different social organizations and behaviors that reflect adaptations to such environmental pressures as the type and dispersion of food resources, availability of sleeping sites, and the kind and amount of predation.

Five types of baboons are grouped in the genus *Papio:* the hamadryas, the Guinea, the yellow, the chacma, and the olive baboon. If given the opportunity—where their ranges overlap, for example, or in zoos—these types can interbreed and produce viable young. Three of these five types—the olive, yellow, and chacma, the so-called savanna baboons—have very similar social organizations. All live in large groups of between 20 and 200 animals that contain several adults of both sexes. Savanna baboons have a breeding system in which both females and males tend to mate with several different members of the opposite sex. Hamadryas baboons are polygynous, however; they live in one male–multiple female units in which the one male exclusively mates with several females.

(a)   (b)

Figure 8-15 (a) A male olive baboon (Papio anubis) *from Kenya. (b) A subadult olive baboon.*

Figure 8-16 A female olive baboon grooming another female with a month- or two-month-old nursing infant.

Baboons usually sleep in trees. However, the Ethiopian hamadryas baboons often converge a few hundred strong to sleep on isolated rock outcrops because of the dearth of trees in their habitat. Baboons are omnivorous; their diet includes fruits, grasses, seeds, roots, lizards, and occasionally other meat. There are troops in South Africa that kill domestic sheep, and some troops in East Africa occasionally prey on small ungulates and hares (Strum, 1975).

Savanna-dwelling baboons were among the first nonhuman primate models for reconstructing early human social organization and behavior. The assumed parallels suggested that early human ancestors moving out of heavily forested regions onto the savanna had to deal with problems similar to those of other terrestrial primates, such as the baboon. These problems included avoiding predators and coping with food resources that were more scattered than those in the tropical forests. However, while modern baboons can provide useful information for reconstructing human evolution (Chapter 10), neither they nor any primate can provide a clear picture of early human social organization and behavior.

Savanna baboon groups contain several adult males. Adult males are usually about twice the size of adult females. Adult females outnumber adult males by a ratio of from 4:1 to 14:1, depending on the species of baboon. Group sizes vary, but 40 to 80 animals is a common size range for savanna baboon groups.

As was true in almost all early primate studies, research on baboons emphasized the role of adult males in maintaining group cohesion. Only after many years of study was it realized that adult females formed the social core in savanna baboon groups. As in many primates, female baboons remain in their natal groups throughout their lives, whereas adolescent males generally move to another group. Females in a group are usually closely related to one another and tend to form kin-based subgroups. Members of the same matriline groom one another more frequently than they groom nonrelated animals; they spend more time in proximity to one another; and they support one another during aggressive encounters. Female kin and matriarchs are the core of the baboon's society.

Among baboons and other Old World monkeys with similar social organizations, female dominance rankings affect behavior (Smuts, 1985). Higher-ranking females have priority of access to resources that affect breeding success, such as food or water. In the short term, a female's rank affects a range of behaviors. For example, high-ranking females are groomed more frequently and are less vulnerable to harassment. While it has been suggested that higher rank increases a female's reproductive success (Cheney, Seyfarth, and Smuts, 1986), Strum (1987) found that among the females of the Pumphouse Gang baboon group, which she studied for 13 years, dominance rank did not influence reproductive success. Two factors were implicated in such success, however: age and food availability. Middle-aged females were the most fertile age group. Females of all ages produced fewer offspring when food was scarce. It can be argued that if dominance rank allowed access to food, then the more dominant females might have access to more or favored food, both during seasons of plenty and during those of scarcity, and might therefore have a slightly greater reproductive success.

Although rank and kinship are important factors in female–female relationships, female friendship bonds are also very significant. Unrelated females may form close bonds, and because baboon females are attracted to mothers with infants, all females go through periods of intense social interaction with other females. Adult males, on the other hand, rarely associate with other adult males except perhaps to threaten away a predator or to form a temporary alliance against another male (Strum, 1987). Male–male grooming is rare, and male dominance relationships are rarely as clearcut or stable as those of the females.

Smuts (1985, 1987) noted in her studies of East African olive baboons that particular females and particular males seemed to spend an inordinate amount of time together. To develop a formal definition of friendship, Smuts scored animals according to grooming behavior and by noting who was observed near whom. An animal who scored high on both grooming and proximity measures with another animal was considered to be a friend of that animal.

Several factors seemed to influence which animals befriended which. Most heterosexual friendships were between unrelated animals because males usually emigrate from their natal group. When heterosexual friendships did form between related animals, which was unusual, these related friends never mated. Age seemed to affect friendships. Animals usually befriended others of similar age. Regardless of either age or dominance rank, most females had just one or two male friends, but males had from zero to eight female friends. Dominant males did not have a greater number of female friends than their less dominant counterparts, however. Instead, it was the older males who had resided in a group longer who had the most female friends. When a male had several female friends, these females were often closely related to one another.

For a behavior to be evolutionarily significant, it should have benefits measurable in terms of differential survival and reproduction. What evolutionary benefits might friendship provide? From their male friends, females seem to gain protection from aggression by other males and from the less injurious but more frequent aggression of other females. Males are particularly protective of their friends' youngest infants when another male gets too close to the youngster or when a juvenile female plays too roughly with the infant.

A male–infant relationship develops out of the male's friendship with the infant's mother. As the infant matures, the male–infant relationship takes on a life of its own. Young infants seem to actively search out their male friends when the mother is a few yards away. A close bond with a male friend may improve an infant's nutrition. Adult males often monopolize the best feeding spots, but they will tolerate intrusion into their feeding areas by infants of their female friends. Males seem to become genuinely attached to their infant companions. If a male friend's infant is a female, the male will not mate with her when she matures. This avoidance of mating is similar to that which characterizes mothers and sons and maternal siblings.

In about half the friendships that Smuts observed, the male was likely to be the father of his friend's most recent infant. In the other half, however, the male was probably not the father; in fact, he was never seen to mate with the female. Smuts reports that males who were friends with the mother but not the likely father of her infant nearly always developed a relationship with the infant. On the other hand, males who mated with a female who was not a friend usually did not develop a relationship with her infant. Smuts (1987) concludes that friendship with the mother, and not paternity, seems to mediate the development of male–infant bonds.

Why would males protect an infant they may not have fathered? Smuts suspects that it has to do with female choice. She suggests that the female may prefer to mate with a male who has already demonstrated friendly behavior by, for example, protecting her infant even though it is not his own. For the male, such protective behavior toward an unrelated infant can result in his having access to a female willing to mate. By increasing both the male's future chance of mating and the likelihood that a female's infant will survive, friendship contributes to the reproductive success of both partners.

Friendships among baboons can help to explain certain aspects of human behavior. For example, long-term heterosexual bonds apparently can evolve in the absence of a sexual division of labor or food sharing. Contrary to the most commonly held theoretical position, heterosexual cooperation may rest not on an exchange of economic benefits, but rather on an exchange of social benefits.

Smuts's findings also suggest that intense heterosexual relationships can occur without sexual exclusivity. Human ancestors may have experienced intimate friendships long before they invented various forms of sexual exclusivity as exhibited, for example, in the nuclear family. Smuts's research also shows that male baboons provide mothers and infants with social benefits even when the males are unlikely to have fathered the infant. Females, in return for such benefits, provide friendly males with a variety of benefits, including increased acceptance into the social group and perhaps increased future mating opportunities.

Let us look more closely at the establishment and maintenance of female baboon dominance hierarchies. A female's rank at maturity is influenced by her mother's age, the interval between her birth and the births of her sisters, and other demographic factors (Hausfater, Altmann, and Altmann, 1982). Daughters usually begin to establish their adult rank when they are about 4 years old, approximately one year prior to menarche. Females are completely integrated into the adult dominance hierarchy by the time they are 5½ years old, nearly one year before the birth of their first infant. By 4 years of age, immature females begin to dominate one or more older females. Eventually they attain a rank among the adults that is nearly identical to the mother's rank.

As a result of the strong influence of maternal rank on the offspring's rank, female dominance relationships are highly consistent between successive years and generations. Rank relationships among females are consistent both within and between generations and may represent the single most important source of long-term stability and continuity in group organization.

A female's first ranking is also influenced by her mother's age. As females mature, they become increasingly less likely to constrain or limit the rise in rank of their maturing daughters. Advanced age seems to increase the probability that a female will decline in rank, but this is not always true.

Rank relationships within a family are interesting. The mother, or matri-arch, gives most of her time, attention, and protection to the youngest family member. Older offspring are shortchanged. A rank order develops within a family in which the mother is dominant, the youngest child is the next dominant, and so on, in reverse order of birth (Strum, 1987).

The rank position "targeted" by a maturing female may be the same as that of her mother in the year of the daughter's birth rather than the mother's rank at some later stage in the daughter's maturation. Young female baboons apparently attain their mother's rank, while young males must fight their way to whatever rank they can reach. As among rhesus monkeys, high-ranking mothers tend to bear more female infants, who are likely to be high-ranking themselves. Lower-ranking mothers tend to have more male infants, who have a chance to work themselves to a higher rank. Interestingly, male offspring of low-ranking mothers seem to have higher survival rates than female offspring do. The reason for this difference is unclear. The most protective mothers are the lower-ranking females. They are protective because their infant's safety is threatened more often than is the safety of offspring of higher-ranking infants.

A female's status comes from her mother and is not greatly affected by her relationships with males. A male's position within a group is affected by the tenor of his relationships with females, however. If a male fails to form friendships with females, he is unlikely to be integrated into a group even if he can dominate the group's activities. Once he becomes a resident in a group, a male's mating success depends in part on the number of female friends he has acquired. When a female establishes a relationship with a male, she and her immature infant acquire an ally in the troop who, because of larger size and superior fighting skills, may make a significant contribution to their survival. If females and infants benefit from a male's investment in them, and if a female tends to mate with males who have demonstrated their willingness and ability to protect her and her infants, then a male who forms special relationships with females may achieve increased reproductive success, even when a female's current infant is not his own (Smuts, 1983). Despite what was once thought, a male's mating success is a factor not so much of his aggressiveness in terms of competition for females, but of his responsiveness to the distress of a female and her offspring. Females may be more likely to mate with a nurturing male than with an aggressive one.

Strum (1987) demonstrated that male dominance ranking could be predict-ed from the length of time spent in a social group. Quite unexpectedly, newcomers, those who had recently emigrated into a group, were the most dominant males. Male short-term residents, those living in a group for about 1½ years, were next in dominance rank. The lowest-ranking males were the long-term residents, those who lived in the group for 3 years or more. It was once suggested that the highest-ranking, more aggressive males were those who had the highest reproductive rates. It was not the newcomers or the most aggressive and dominant males who had the greatest success in mating or in obtaining favored foods. Rather, it was the long-term residents, those males who had learned social strategies, who had more social ties and experience, and therefore less need for aggression to obtain their needs and desires, who were the most reproductively successful. "Short-term residents were on the way up; they had made friends and gathered social information, but it was the long-term residents who showed how much time and experience was needed in this male world . . . (Long-term male residents) . . . had wisdom, friendships, and an understanding of the subtle tactics necessary for success" (Strum, 1987:126).

Most males left a social group after a residence period of about five years. There were two peaks in male emigration from the Pumphouse Gang baboon group studied by Strum. The first peak was after about one year and included mainly those males who were unable to integrate into the group. This was followed by a lull in emigration, followed by another peak of exodus after about five years of residence. As Strum (1987) noted, if a male was reproductively successful during his first year or so after entry into a group, then after five years' residence, his eldest daughters would be approaching sexual maturity. Perhaps males were exiting the group to avoid inbreeding with their offspring. Similar observations of male exodus have been witnessed among macaques, and the same reasoning, inbreeding avoidance, has been applied.

One of the highest incidences of predatory behavior among nonhuman primates has been documented for the Pumphouse Gang baboon group (Strum, 1975, 1987). Predatory behavior was first noted in this group in 1970 and 1971, when 47 cases were witnessed during a period of 1,032 observation hours. During this time the animals preyed upon cape hares, birds, and young gazelles. All but three cases of predation involved adult males, and in all but one instance the adult male ate the meat.

From 1972 to 1974, Strum (1975) witnessed 100 cases of predation. During 1970 and 1971, males did 94 percent of the killing and 98 percent of the eating of the prey; adult females did only 6 percent of the killing and 2 percent of the eating. In contrast, two to three years later, males did 61 percent of the killing; females, 14 percent; juveniles, 16 percent; and 9 percent was done by an unidentified age and sex group. Over this short time period, a behavioral tradition had spread virtually throughout the age classes in the group.

The change in participation in predation also altered the profile of the prey. Individual idiosyncrasies affected participation in meat-eating and predation. Some animals were more interested in eating meat and hunting than were others. The interest of some females in the capture and consumption of meat equalled that of some males. Youngsters seemed to learn the pattern of meat-eating from watching adults. Kill sites soon became gathering places for youngsters. Once a youngster obtained a piece of meat, its interest in meat increased.

Hunting and meat-eating were important venues for understanding the flexibility of baboons' behavior and skills. For example, the animals learned from experience how to modify their hunting techniques for more success. Although it was once thought that humans were the only primates to hunt and share their prey, chimpanzees and baboons changed that notion (see Chapter 10). Baboon males in the Pumphouse Gang shared meat with others. "No one ever simply handed the meat over, but a male would scoot aside to allow a female friend a turn at the carcass, or a mother would let her infant join in the meal" (Strum, 1987:131). Although males hunted most often, they were never seen to share with one another, not even with another male who might have aided in the prey's capture. After reaching a peak, the incidence of hunting behavior declined in the Pumphouse Gang.

The social organization and behavior described is typical of the savanna baboon; however, both the gelada and hamadryas baboons have a different type of social organization. Both live in polygynous societies which are structured on three levels (Fedigan, 1982). The first level consists largely of small heterosexual reproductive units of one mature male, several adult females (an average of six) and their younger offspring, and perhaps several juvenile males. All mating occurs within these units and is restricted to the one leader male and the adult females. Also at this level are all-male groups (sometimes called bachelor groups), juvenile peer groups, and solitary males. Approximately 20 percent of the gelada reproductive units have a "follower," or semiattached male who may try to take females from the male leader of the reproductive unit. Such attempts are less likely to succeed if close bonds, as reflected in grooming behavior, exist between a resident male and the group's females. Among the hamadryas, a male is less likely to challenge another male if the latter is with a female that strongly prefers him.

This polygynous type of social unit is found among the savanna-dwelling African patas monkeys and the arboreal Indian leaf-eating Nilgiri langur. In contrast to these animals, however, there is another tier in the social organization of both the gelada and the hamadryas baboon. At night, smaller foraging units may join for sleeping purposes atop cliffs or large rock outcrops in groups as large as 600 animals. Although part of this larger unit, the smaller one-male units maintain their own integrity. Animals of different one-male units sleep near one another but have minimal social interaction with other one-male units in the large sleeping congregation. These large sleeping congregations are not social units per se, but rather are adaptations to the scarcity of available sleeping positions that offer protection against predation.

The gelada is a terrestrial vegetarian inhabiting the Ethiopian highlands, which are dominated by cliffs. As an adaptation to their cliff habitat, female geladas and their young move closest to the cliff edges, where the males protect them from predation. Whenever danger threatens, the group moves to the cliff edge. Females and their young descend the cliff face to a ledge, while the male remains behind as a shield above them.

The basic social group, the breeding and foraging unit among geladas, is the one-male unit. Such units are particularly evident during the dry season, when food is scattered. At this time, male-led units, containing from 4 to 12 animals, separate from one another and forage independently. In this way, they ensure that whatever food is available can be exploited with minimal competition.

Hamadryas baboon males vigorously preserve their one-male units. The male leader of the unit prevents mating between any younger males in the unit and the females. Young males delay breeding until the older, leader male either dies or allows them to breed. Young males may form their own group by "adopting" juvenile females. These females are a few years from sexual maturity, which suggests that these males delay reproductive activity in order to ensure that they will eventually have exclusive access to breeding females.

The male has a specialized behavior, the neck bite, which he uses to retrieve any female who strays from his group. The male approaches a female from his unit whom he wishes to have follow him, and he mouths or gums her neck without breaking the skin. The female immediately follows him back to her group. The male hamadryas's neck bite and the female's following response are communication mechanisms unique to the hamadryas that help maintain the one-male units. Savanna-dwelling baboon males do not exhibit the behavior, nor do the females exhibit the following response.

Leaf-Eating Monkeys (The Colobines)

The Colobinae, the other subfamily of Old World monkeys, inhabits Asia and Africa. Asian colobines, specialized leaf-eaters, are commonly referred to as *langurs,* while African forms are called *colobus monkeys.* Colobines usually inhabit thickly forested regions. In some areas, however, Asian species are secondarily adapted to forests that are rather extensively damaged by human activities, and even to semiarid and montane conditions, as well as urban settings. Like the macaques and baboons, colobines can adjust to some degree of human exploitation of the habitat by raiding garden plots and eating domestic crops (Poirier, 1969, 1970). This ability to adjust to new foods, one measure of behavioral plasticity, is a key primate trait. Colobines, like many forest-dwelling species, are under increasing pressure because of habitat destruction.

The members of the subfamily Colobinae share many morphological and behavioral traits, which stem from a shared folivorous (leaf-eating) diet and a largely arboreal habitat. The dietary preference for relatively unnutritious and hard-to-digest leaves is associated with a specialized stomach and large salivary glands adapted to breaking down cellulose found in leaves. Shared anatomical traits also reflect a common arboreal heritage. For example, the hands and feet of colobines are longer and narrower than those of the more terrestrial macaques and baboons. The colobine's thumb is usually reduced relative to that of most other primates. Leaf-eating monkeys generally show minimal sexual dimorphism, another manifestation of the arboreal habitat.

Colobine group sizes range from 2 to 3 animals in some species to over 100 animals in others, to possibly as many as 500 animals in one Chinese species, the snub-nosed golden monkey (Figure 8-17). Food availability, population density, the relative openness of the habitat, and the presence of predators are factors that influence group size (Poirier and Kanner, in press). Large groups are characteristic of species living in relatively open areas, and smaller group sizes are typical in forested areas.

Colobine groups are generally bisexual and contain one or several males (young adults or subadults) and several females, infants, and juveniles. In some species, however, one adult male–multiple adult female groups are common. In fact, multiple-male and one-male groups belonging to the same species may be found in proximity to one another. The mechanism that determines whether a group is one-male or multimale is not clearly under-stood. Males living a solitary existence are not uncommon. All-male ("bache-lor") groups are common and are the source of periodic intensive aggression with bisexual groups in some species. All-male groups are composed of recent male emigrants from a bisexual group or of males who may soon try to force their way into a bisexual group.

In many colobine species, social groups contain a number of rather independent subgroupings, such as those of adult females and infants,

Figure 8-17 The snub-nosed golden monkey (Rhinopithecus roxellanae) *inhabiting China is one of the world's most endangered primates. (Left) A young male about 5 or 6 years old. (Right) Three young females.*

juveniles and subadults, or juveniles. Social interactions generally occur within, rather than between, subgroups. This pattern of social interaction weakens overall group cohesion.

In addition to birth and death, male emigration and immigration account for changes in the composition of langur groups. In some species, aggression is common when either solitary males or all-male groups attempt to enter a bisexual group. This aggression is usually directed against the adult male or males of the bisexual group and the infants. If the take-over attempt succeeds, the resident male or males are often driven from the group, and all the infants are killed.

The pattern of infanticide among primates was first reported for langurs. Not all langur species practice infanticide, and the motives for such behavior are still not completely understood. Infanticide is not a common event in any langur species. When infanticide occurs, it is always practiced by a male or males shortly after entering a new social group. Infanticide has many effects, one of which is that a female who loses an infant (especially if it is nursing) to infanticide begins to ovulate soon after the infant's death.

Hrdy (see, for example, 1977) has been the leading proponent of the view that infanticide is a male reproductive strategy. She argues from the premise that the female and male's reproductive strategies are independent and often antagonistic. A male enhances his limited breeding span when he kills the offspring of rival males and hastens the female's ovulation. Thus the male quickly produces his own offspring before he also is subject to an all-male invasion and ejection from the group. The male is best served during his brief tenure as head of the group if the total reproductive period of females within his group is confined to his tenure. In the act of removing the offspring of his genetic competitor, the previous leader male, the new male increases his own chances of reproductive success.

Some have argued that infanticide is an inherited tendency. Therefore, any female who sexually boycotted infanticidal males would do so to the detriment of her own male progeny. Her sons would suffer in competition with the sons of less discriminating mothers whose sons were sired by an infanticidal male. Females benefit from letting their offspring die because they can then mate soon after with the new dominant male, who might then confer higher status and more protection to their infant.

If infanticidal males are to avoid killing their own young, they must have some means of recognizing their own paternity. Hrdy proposed that, by taking account of recent copulations with the mother, males show some capacity to avoid killing their own young. This allows females one possible infanticide counter-measure. They may copulate with several males at the time of conception and soon thereafter, especially during all-male invasions and before it is settled who the new leader male will be, and thus cloud the paternity of future infants. This is called *cuckoldry*.

There are alternatives to Hrdy's explanation of infanticide. For example, the sexual excitement and tension that accompanies the act of battling other males may be a stimulus behind infanticide. A male's postinfanticidal behavior is markedly relaxed, suggesting that infanticide reduces his tension.

Hrdy's position has other detractors. For example, it has been suggested that infanticide is a pathological result of extreme overcrowding, often associated with habitat destruction by humans. High population densities may lead to infanticide as a means for controlling population growth. Those arguing that infanticide is a pathological behavior note that during the violence that accompanies a male takeover, infants, the smallest and most vulnerable group members, are the most likely to be harmed.

The occurrence of infanticide raises such questions as whether it is an adaptive behavior, why it is manifested only in some species and not others, and how the possible evolution of such behavior would be explained. Despite the many unanswered questions, the occurrence of infanticide is being reported with greater frequency for many nonhuman primate species, as well as among humans (Burke, 1984). It deserves continued attention.

Two other behaviors, territoriality and infant sharing, are also common to colobines. Colobines often exhibit territorial behavior; that is, they defend a predefined location against incursion by other groups. In most species the male plays the major role in territorial displays. Seldom do territorial encounters lead to actual physical aggression. Most encounters consist of loud, booming vocalizations, wild jumps through trees, and running back and forth. Territorial behavior is not a means for extending a group's home range; rather, it is a means by which ranges are maintained. The major functions of territorial behavior appear to be the spacing of males and, indirectly, prevention of over exploration of resources and overcrowding.

Infant sharing (allomaternal care) is common. The mother subgroup, common to colobines as well as most primates, is usually composed of female relatives and is the primary social unit for the infant's protection and care. Infants are often passed from one female to another within this subgroup. In some species, mothers begin to pass their own infants to other females, or simply allow other females to take their infants, within a few hours after birth. Although allomaternal behavior is not restricted to langurs, it is an extremely common occurrence among them. Younger females, who have not yet borne their own infants, are often most active in these transfer sequences. It can be argued that allomothering among langur females is a form of kin selection when the allomothers are directly related to the infants for whom they care because allomothers may be promoting the survival of their kin. Allomothers, especially if they have not yet had their own infants, may gain practice in infant care as a result of such behavior. Mothers benefit from the transfer of their infants because such transfer temporarily relieves them of the almost continual burden of caring for an infant. Infants also benefit from such interactions by enlarging their social contacts and by having extra caretakers. This could be especially important if the infant's mother dies and the infant needs other adults for protection.

Some prosimians have monkeylike social organizations. Most prosimians have restricted habitats; the lemur, for example, lives solely on the island of Madagascar.

A number of anatomical traits separate Old and New World monkeys. Some anatomical differences are related to the fact New World monkeys never evolved a terrestrial adaptation. There are two families of New World monkeys. Marmosets, belonging to the family Callithricidae, are unique among primates because twinning is quite common and paternal care is the rule. The family Cebidae is a diverse group containing forms with prehensile tails.

Major behavioral studies of Old World monkeys have concentrated on Asian macaques and langurs and African baboons and vervets. The baboon's social organization and behavior was once considered an appropriate model of early human social organization and behavior. Early primate studies wrongly emphasized such behaviors as male dominance and aggression and downplayed the importance of female kinship networks. It is now recognized that female kin units are of key importance in troop cohesion. Infanticide, a rather common behavior among primates, was first reported for Asian langurs. There are a number of alternative explanations for the practice of infanticide.

BIBLIOGRAPHY

ALTMANN, J. 1980. *Baboon Mothers and Infants.* Cambridge: Harvard University Press.

ALTMANN, S., and J. ALTMANN. 1970. *Baboon Ecology.* Chicago: University of Chicago Press.

ANN ARBOR SCIENCES FOR THE PEOPLE EDITORIAL COLLECTIVE. 1977. *Biology as a Social Weapon.* Minneapolis: Burgess.

BERNSTEIN, I., and E. SMITH. 1979. In summary. In *Primate Ecology and Human Origins,* I. Bernstein and E. Smith, eds. New York: Garland.

BURKE, B. 1984. Infanticide: Why does it happen in monkeys, mice, and men? *Science* 84: 26–31.

CARPENTER, C. 1964. *Naturalistic Behavior of Nonhuman Primates.* University Park: Pennsylvania State University Press.

CHENEY, D., R. SEYFARTH, and B. SMUTS. 1986. Social relationships and social recognition in nonhuman primates. *Science* 234: 1361–66.

CROCKETT, C. 1984. Family feuds. *Natural History* 93: 54–63.

CROOK, J. 1966. Gelada baboon herd structure and movement. *Symposium Zoological Society of London* 18: 237–58.

DeVORE, I. (ED.) 1965. *Primate Behavior: Field Studies of Monkeys and Apes.* New York: Holt, Rinehart and Winston.

DOLHINOW, P. (ED.) 1972. *Primate Patterns.* New York: Holt, Rinehart and Winston.

FEDIGAN, L. 1982. *Primate Paradigms: Sex Roles and Social Bonds.* St. Albans, Vt.: Eden Press.

HAMILTON, W. 1963. The evolution of altruistic behavior. *American Naturalist.* 97: 354–56.

HAMILTON, W. 1964. The genetical theory of social behavior. *Journal of Theoretical Biology* 7: 1–52.

HAUSFATER, G., J. ALTMANN, and S. ALTMANN. 1982. Long-term consistency of dominance relations among female baboons *(Papio cynocephalus). Science* 217: 752–55.

HRDY, S. 1977. *The Langurs of Abu.* Cambridge: Harvard University Press.

JAY, P. (ED.) 1968. *Primates: Studies in Adaptation and Variability.* New York: Holt, Rinehart and Winston.

JOLLY, A. 1967. *Lemur Behavior: A Madagascan Field Study.* Chicago: University of Chicago Press.

JOLLY, C., and F. PLOG. 1979. *Physical Anthropology and Archaeology.* New York: Knopf.

KUMMER, H. 1968. *Social Organization of Hamadryas Baboons.* Chicago: University of Chicago Press.

LANCASTER, J. 1975. *Primate Behavior and the Emergence of Human Culture.* New York: Holt, Rinehart and Winston.

LEWIN, R. 1983. Brotherly alliances help avoid inbreeding. *Science* 222: 148–51.

LUFT, J., and J. ALTMANN. 1982. Mother baboon. *Natural History* 91: 30–39.

MAPLES, W. 1969. Adaptive behavior of baboons. *American Journal of Physical Anthropology* 31: 107–11.

MASON, W. 1971. Field and laboratory studies of social organization in *Saimiri* and *Callicebus.* In *Primate Behavior: Developments in Field and Laboratory Research,* vol. 2., L. Rosenblum, ed. New York: Academic Press.

MCMILLAN, C., and C. DUGGLEBY. 1981. Interlineage genetic differentiation among rhesus macaques on Cayo Santiago. *American Journal of Physical Anthropology* 56: 305–12.

MEIKLE, D., and S. VESSEY. 1981. Nepotism among rhesus monkey brothers. *Nature* 294: 160–61.

MISSAKIAN, E. 1972. Genealogical and cross-genealogical dominance relations in a group of free-ranging rhesus monkeys *(Macaca mulatta)* on Cayo Santiago. *Primates* 13: 169–80.

NAPIER, J., and A. WALKER. 1967. Vertical clinging and leaping, a newly recognized category of locomotor behaviour among primates. *Folia Primatologica* 6: 180–203.

POIRIER, F. 1968. The Nilgiri langur *(Presbytis johnii)* mother–infant dyad. *Primates* 9: 45–68.

POIRIER, F. 1969. Behavioral flexibility and intertroop variability among Nilgiri langurs of South India. *Folia Primatologica* 11: 119–33.

POIRIER, F. 1970. Nilgiri langur ecology and social behavior. In *Primate Behavior: Developments in Field and Laboratory Research,* vol. 1, L. Rosenblum, ed. New York: Academic Press.

POIRIER, F., A. BELLISARI, and L. HAINES. 1978. Functions of primate play. In *Social Play in Primates,* E. Smith, ed., pp. 143–69. New York: Academic Press.

POIRIER, F., and M. KANNER. 1989. A review of primate socialization. In *Perspectives on Primate Biology.* P. Seth and S. Seth, eds. New Delhi: Today and Tomorrow's Publishers.

POIRIER, F., and E. SMITH. 1974. Socializing functions of primate play behavior. *American Zoologist* 12: 275–87.

RICHARD, A., and R. SCHULMAN. 1982. Sociobiology: Primate field studies. *Annual Review of Anthropology* 11: 231–55.

ROWELL, T. 1972. *Social Behavior of Monkeys.* New York: Penguin.

SADE, D. 1965. Some aspects of parent–offspring and sibling relations in a group of rhesus monkeys, with a discussion of grooming. *American Journal of Physical Anthropology* 23: 1–8.

SADE, D. 1967. Determinants of dominance in a group of free-ranging rhesus monkeys. In *Social Communication Among Primates,* S. Altmann, ed. Chicago: University of Chicago Press.

SADE, D. 1968. Inhibition of son–mother mating among free-ranging rhesus monkeys. *Science and Psychoanalysis* 12: 18–38.

SIMPSON, M., and A. SIMPSON. 1982. Birth sex ratios and social rank in rhesus monkey mothers. *Nature* 300: 440–41.

SMUTS, B. 1982. Friendship: Long-term bonds between male and female baboons. *Anthroquest* 24: 10–13.

SMUTS, B. 1983. Special relationships between adult male and female olive baboons: Selective advantages. In *Primate Social Relationships,* R. Hinde, ed., pp. 262–66. Sunderland, Mass.: Sinauer.

SMUTS, B. 1985. *Sex and Friendship in Baboons.* New York: Aldine.

SMUTS, B. 1987. What are friends for? *Natural History.* February 36–44.

STRUM, S. 1975. Primate predation: Interim report on the development of a tradition in a troop of olive baboons. *Science* 187: 755–57.

STRUM, S. 1987. *Almost Human.* New York: Random House.

TRIVERS, R. 1971. The evolution of reciprocal altruism. *Quarterly Review of Biology* 46: 35–57.

TRIVERS, R. 1972. Parental investment and sexual selection. In Sexual Selection and the Descent of Man, B. Campbell, ed. Chicago: Aldine.

VOM SAAL, F., and L. HOWARD. 1982. The regulation of infanticide and parental behavior: Implications for reproductive success in male mice. *Science* 215: 1270–71.

WASHBURN, S., and I. DEVORE. 1961. The social life of baboons. *Scientific American* 204: 62–71.

WASHBURN, S. 1978. What we can't learn about people from apes. *Human Nature* 1: 70–75.

WILSON, E. 1975. *Sociobiology: The New Synthesis.* Cambridge, Mass.: Belknap.

Chapter

9

The Behavior of Apes

This chapter will discuss the behavior and social organization of the apes: the chimpanzee, gorilla, orangutan, and gibbon (Table 9-1). Studies of apes, especially the chimpanzee, have helped clarify our conception of early stages of human evolution and have helped redefine some of our ideas of what it means to be human.

Some apes, such as the gorilla, have been known to Europeans for only slightly more than 100 years. Early portrayals of the African apes, the gorilla and chimpanzee, as degenerate humans or ferocious killers have been proven wrong. Tales have also been woven about the Asian apes, the orangutan and the gibbon. In seventeenth-century Europe, tales were told of male orangutans abducting human females.

The continued survival of ape populations is uncertain. Some apes, such as the gorilla and orangutan, may not survive another 100 years. Habitat destruction is threatening all ape populations, whether they live in Africa or in Asia.

THE CHIMPANZEE

One of the first reports about chimpanzees comes from an anatomical description published in 1641. A report on one of the first live chimpanzees to be seen by Europeans was published in 1738 (quoted in Reynolds, 1967: 51). The name *chimpanzee* is about the only part of this highly fanciful description that modern studies have not dispelled.

> A most surprising Creature . . . taken at Guinea: It is a female about four foot high, shaped in every part like a Woman excepting its head. . . . She walks upright naturally, sits down to her food, . . . and feeds herself with her Hands as

Table 9-1. Classification and Distribution of the Apes

Family	Genus and Species	Common Name	Continent
Hylobatidae	*Hylobates lar**	Gibbon	Asia
	Hylobates syndactylus	Siamang	Asia
Pongidae	*Pongo pygmaeus*	Borneo orangutan	Asia
	Pongo abelii	Sumatra orangutan	Asia
	Pan troglodytes	Chimpanzee	Africa
	Pan t. verus		
	Pan t. schweinfurthii		
	Pan paniscus	Pygmy chimpanzee	
	Gorilla gorilla	Western lowland gorilla	Africa
	Gorilla g. beringei	Mountain gorilla	
	Gorilla g. graueri	Eastern lowland gorilla	

*This table does not include all the subspecies of *Hylobates*.

a human Creature. She is very fond of a Boy . . . and is observed always sorrowful at his Absence. She is clothed with a thin Silk Vestment, and shows great Discontent at the openings of her Gown to discover her Sex. She is called . . . Chimpanzee, or the Mockman.

Chimpanzees inhabit a wide range across equatorial Africa, from the west coast to within a few hundred miles of the east coast. The most adaptable of the apes, chimpanzees inhabit rain and mountain forests as well as dry woodlands, and sometimes even savannas with widely scattered trees. Because they inhabit such an ecological range, chimpanzee populations also experience a wide range of climatic conditions.

One of the best-known recent observers of chimpanzees is Jane Goodall, who began her studies in 1960 in the Gombe Stream Reserve, Tanzania. In the beginning, Goodall spent her days atop a rocky hill, where she could observe and be observed as a harmless, unassuming member of the forest community. Social acceptance by her fellow primates took a long time. On some days, Goodall spent 12 hours in the field, climbing up and down slopes and forcing her way through dense vegetation to view the chimpanzees. She often heard distant calls, but when she arrived the animals were gone. During the first few months of her study, chimpanzees ran from her as she approached to within 500 yards. Eventually she was accepted as an unobtrusive stranger, first merely avoided but later ignored by the chimpanzees.

Goodall's study is unique because of its long duration—more than two decades—and because of her familiarity with individual animals. She has documented changes within the chimpanzee's life cycle and has studied individual animals in their natural environment. Because of our close evolutionary relationship (reflected in anatomical, physiological, genetic, and behavioral traits), chimpanzees are particularly useful for understanding human evolution.

Prior to Goodall's work, the phrase "man the toolmaker" was a common anthropological definition of humans. Humans made tools, a trait that supposedly separated us from the rest of the primates. Goodall has documented a number of instances of chimpanzee tool use, however. Tool use has also been reported by Japanese researchers, who noted that chimpanzees use tools to probe for and "capture" ants and termites. Chimpanzees use objects in their environment as tools to a greater extent than any living primate except humans.

Goodall saw chimpanzees break off grass stems or thin branches, which they poked into termite holes to get at the termites (Figure 9-1). The chimpanzee then runs the probe across its front teeth and eats the termites that have become attached to it. If the probe does not fit the hole, the chimpanzee shapes it until it does fit. For example, leaves may be stripped from a stem to make a suitable tool. Chimpanzees not only use tools, but they also make them. Chimpanzees have used stout sticks as levers to enlarge the opening of an underground bee nest. Sticks were also used to pry open boxes stored at Goodall's camp, much to the chagrin of her staff.

A

B

C

D

Figure 9-1 *(A) Adult female chimpanzee at Gombe digs for safari ants. (B) Two adult males at Gombe fish for termites. (C) Adult male chimpanzee at Gombe fishes for termites. (D) Adolescent male chimpanzee at Gombe fishes for termites.*

Chimpanzees obtain termites almost exclusively through the use of tools. When chimpanzees spend long time periods fishing for and eating termites, as they do during certain months of the year, tool use is a normal part of the daily routine. Chimpanzees show individual variation in termiting ability, tool use and manufacture, and patience. Material chosen to make a tool is sometimes obtained from distances of 300 feet from the termite mound. The use of tools in termiting requires great skill, and dry-season termiting requires more skill and care than does wet-season termiting. Several tools are sometimes picked up at once. Those not put to immediate use are tucked into the groin or laid on the ground nearby for future use.

Chimpanzees have been observed chewing a wad of leaves to make it more absorbent and then using it as a sponge to sop up rainwater that cannot be reached with the lips. This modification of a handful of leaves is an example of tool use.

> Finding rainwater cupped in a fallen tree, but out of reach of his lips, Figan manufactures a "sponge." First he briefly chews a few leaves to increase their absorbency, then dips the crumpled greenery into the natural bowl and sucks out the liquid. By fashioning a simple tool he saves himself the bother of walking to a stream for a drink. [van Lawick-Goodall, 1967].

Chimpanzees have used leaves to wipe the remnants of a brain from the inside of a baboon skull or to dab at a bleeding rump wound. Leaves have been used as toilet paper when an animal has diarrhea, and some animals have used leaves to wipe themselves clean of mud and sticky foods.

Three traits differentiate chimpanzee and human tool use and manufacture: (1) Humans use tools to make other tools, while chimpanzees apparently do not; at least, they have not been seen doing so. (2) Humans use tools much more frequently, and in more circumstances, than do chimpanzees. (3) Humans depend on technology for survival; chimpanzees do not. Humans also make tools for later contingencies and save them for long periods. Chimpanzees do not, but they may not have to do so as long as natural materials are available. Perhaps when humans began to use scarcer materials, or materials that were more difficult to obtain, then we began to save them for future use.

Chimpanzee tool use is basically the provenience of females (McGrew, 1978). Males can make and use tools, but tool use and manufacture is a learned and practiced behavioral tradition usually passed from mother to daughter. Sons are less apt to learn these techniques because they spend less time with their mothers. Thus they have less time to observe how tools are made and used.

Female chimpanzees at Gombe spend much more time than do males searching for and feeding on termites. It follows, then, that they also use tools for feeding more frequently than do males. Although there is no evidence that females are more skillful in their tool use than are males, at one chimpanzee study site females showed more dexterity in their use of tools—rocks to break open nuts (Boesch and Boesch, 1981). Such a sex difference is significant with regard to the perpetuation of the tool-using culture. Females spend long periods using tools; thus their infants—future tool users—have ample time to learn the necessary skills. In chimpanzee society the female is the most likely to transfer from her natal community; in so doing, she not only widens the genetic pool, but she also takes with her behavioral traditions learned while a youngster. Female chimpanzees may take tool using traditions from one group to another.

Chimpanzee tool use and manufacture is also a function of their intelligence and manual dexterity. Although baboons relish the ants and termites eaten by the chimpanzees, and although they have ample opportunity to observe chimpanzees as they "termite fish" or "ant dip," as these activities are called, they seem unable to learn the techniques and apparently lack the necessary manual dexterity.

Chimpanzees have also been observed using tools as weapons. For example, one Gombe male, Mike, raised his social rank by intimidating other animals because he rolled empty kerosene cans during his charging display. The noise generated by the cans frightened the other animals. Although chimpanzees seldom used wood or rocks as weapons in serious fighting, there are undoubtedly occasions when the use of sticks or rocks cowed the victim.

Goodall (1970, 1973) has argued that differences in tool use patterns in various chimpanzee communities are culturally divergent traditions. Once a technique has become established in a community, it probably persists virtually unchanged for generations.

Until rather recently, it was assumed that humans were the only predatory, meat-eating, food-sharing primate. It is now known that chimpanzees hunt and eat meat, and they do so more frequently than originally assumed. "The Gombe Stream chimpanzees are efficient hunters; a group of about 40 individuals may catch over 20 different prey animals during one year" (van Lawick-Goodall, 1971: 281–282). Chimpanzee predatory behavior is of marked interest to anthropologists, who are accustomed to considering humans the sole predatory primate. (In fact, a number of nonhuman primates prey on birds, small reptiles, and small mammals.)

The hunting, killing, and eating of immature medium-sized mammals appears to characterize chimpanzees throughout their range—although the pattern is more common in some regions than others. In addition, cannibalism has been reported from two sites: Gombe and Mahale.

During a 12-month study of chimpanzee hunting at Gombe, Teleki (1973) witnessed 30 episodes of predation, 12 of which were successful. There is no evidence that chimpanzees take or even pursue animals weighing over 20 pounds. Japanese investigators (Toshiada, et al., 1979) witnessed 54 predation events by chimpanzees in the Mahale Mountains of Tanzania. Most prey were small animals, and there was a concentration on juvenile prey of solitary-living ungulates and small-sized group–living primates. The most likely prey at Gombe is the red colobus monkey; 20 to 30 such monkeys are taken annually (Figure 9-2). As many as 4 or 5 animals are captured during one

Figure 9-2 Adult male chimpanzee at Gombe feeding on a skull of a red colobus monkey.

hunting session. Not all chimpanzee hunts are successful; male colobus monkeys have ferociously attacked chimpanzees preying on juveniles. Adult bush pigs have repelled a number of chimpanzee predatory attacks on young bush pigs.

Chimpanzees usually prey on mammals; other than at Gombe, there are no more than a handful of reported cases of chimpanzees preying on birds (McGrew, 1983). The overall level of meat eating at Gombe was inflated by the high frequency of baboon kills during the period of heavy food provisioning in the early 1960s. When heavy provisioning of bananas for the chimpanzees ceased and baboons stopped frequenting the provisioning area, baboon kills dropped dramatically. Because baboons apparently were not preyed on by chimpanzees prior to provisioning in 1963, predation on baboons may have been a by-product of human intervention through banana provisioning. The decline in predation on baboons is due in part to the fact that the baboons themselves became vigilant to the possibility of chimpanzee hunting; that is, they learned how to protect their infants or to avoid potentially dangerous situations. There was an interesting increase in preying on baboons in 1979, which may be related to a fortuitous, opportunistic baboon kill when chimpanzees once again realized that baboons were a potential food source. All seven successful baboon kills between 1979 and 1981 involved chimpanzees preying on baboon troops that were unaccustomed to chimpanzee predation.

Chimpanzees prey heavily on social insects because insects constitute a sizable, concentrated, and often sedentary biomass. Exploiting insects as a food source is energetically efficient for the large-bodied chimpanzees. Many social insects have relatively impregnable homes, and among nonhuman primates, only the chimpanzee has solved the problem of getting into a bee's nest or termite's mound. There are population differences in the techniques used by chimpanzees to obtain termites and other insect prey. Although the same prey may be available to a number of chimpanzee populations, some populations do not exploit them. Social traditions apparently determine which insects are exploited.

Teleki isolated three major components of chimpanzee predatory behavior. The first event, the pursuit phase, takes various forms. Chimpanzees may take advantage of a fortuitous situation by lunging at and grabbing at nearby prey. Other forms of pursuit are chasing the prey, which may require a dash of 100 or more yards, and stalking, which can continue for more than an hour. Both chasing and stalking appear to be premeditated and occasionally involve the use of strategies and maneuvers that isolate or corner the prey.

The second event, the capture, is a brief period ending with the initial dismemberment of the prey. The third and longest event, consumption, involves sharing the prey with other hunters and with other group members who may beg for a piece of meat by staring at the animal that is holding the meat. Animals may also beg by extending an open hand and holding it beneath the mouth of an animal that is eating meat. Teleki once observed a consumption that involved 15 chimpanzees and lasted 9 hours. Meat is a highly desired food and is the only food shared among group members. There is often intense competition for a share of meat after a kill. Although Teleki documented the voluntary sharing of meat, other investigators have not observed this behavior. The sharing of meat seems to be a group-specific behavior. Based on his observations of meat sharing, Teleki suggested that chimpanzee hunting behavior is as much a social event as a food quest. Goodall disagrees and she believes that hunting is basically for food, an assessment bolstered by the observation of another chimpanzee population in which prey animals are only reluctantly shared with other group members.

Observers are unable to discern how chimpanzees coordinate their hunts. Although they are usually vocal, chimpanzees are quiet while hunting. "All remain silent until the prey is captured or the attempt is broken off. This means, of course, that the hunters do not coordinate their efforts by means of vocal signals" (Teleki, 1973:37). Hunting raises the excitement level of the chimpanzee. Chimpanzees kill their prey quickly. Prey that is captured by more than one animal may be literally torn apart as each captor tugs on a different limb.

A single chimpanzee may successfully hunt alone, but hunting is often a group activity. A lone chimpanzee who has made a kill usually remains silent so as not to draw attention to the kill, whereas loud calls typically mark the climax of a group hunt. The latter is far more likely to be detected by other animals who are not involved in the hunt.

Although some chimpanzees can and do hunt successfully on their own, the presence of other hunters is often beneficial and, particularly during hunts of baboons and large bushpig young, may even be essential to the hunt's success. The most sophisticated examples of group hunting involved predation on baboons. In some cases Goodall suggests that hunters sense that they will be unsuccessful on their own and elicit the help of other animals.

Although Teleki noted that the animal that made the kill was the one to get the brain, others have not observed such a preference and have witnessed the brain being shared. However, it is true that the brain was eaten first in almost all observed cases of a successful capture.

An intense debate revolves around the issue of what part of the early human diet was vegetable and what part consisted of meat protein. With regard to meat eating, the debate centers on whether humans hunted or scavenged their meat. Partially because humans seem to consider hunting a more noble pursuit and scavenging as demeaning, early humans were considered to have obtained a good portion of their meat through hunting (Chapter 10).

Chimpanzees can help put this debate in perspective. Some reported instances of chimpanzee hunting may in fact be scavenging behavior. In one chimpanzee population, animals ate meat that they were neither seen nor heard to kill. Chimpanzees may scavenge meat taken by carnivores. Evidence for scavenging among chimpanzees supports the contention that early humans also probably obtained some part of their meat through scavenging (see Chapters 12, 16, and 17).

Another common argument is that human males are the hunters and females are the gatherers. This argument ignores the fact that among modern hunter-gatherers, females often provide the bulk of the food—gathered vegetables. Chimpanzees again show that our conceptions of early human evolution need revision. Although adult males hunt far more often than females, female chimpanzees at Gombe hunt more often and eat much more meat than originally assumed. The first observed female kill at Gombe was in 1973. During the period from 1974 to 1981, females were seen to capture or steal, and then eat, at least part of 44 prey animals. They captured or seized additional 15 prey, but subsequently lost them (Goodall, 1986). A female travelling in a family unit with her dependent young or in a small male party is much more likely to be successful in obtaining meat than when she hunts in a party containing adult males, who are likely to appropriate any kill she makes or meat she obtains. On two occasions, however, adult females took prey from adult males. Adult males are likely to share meat with a begging female if she is in estrus. There may be some link between sharing meat and sexual access to the female.

Females do not hunt as vigorously when males are present, and this may account for the scant reports of hunting by female chimpanzees. When males are absent, females often hunt on their own. Female chimpanzees at Gombe have been observed scavenging meat killed by baboons. They are not deterred by the presence of a larger, male baboon.

Female chimpanzees from the Mahale mountains in western Tanzania are more predatory than female chimpanzees at Gombe. (Takahata, Hasegawa, and Nishida, 1984). They hunted alone and preyed primarily on bushpigs. Although a small group of male chimpanzees sometimes chases prey, definitive evidence of cooperative hunting at Mahale has not been obtained. This contrasts with Goodall's reports that male chimpanzees at Gombe hunt in small groups and that brothers cooperate in hunting.

McGrew (1978) notes sex differences in the chimpanzee's mode of food acquisition. Male chimpanzees at Gombe consume more meat from birds and mammals, while females consume more insects. This difference may be related to the female's more frequent ant dipping and termite fishing. McGrew categorizes the pattern of prey acquisition by male chimpanzees as hunting because it is a cooperative act and involves moving relatively great distances. He characterizes the female chimpanzee's behavior as gathering because it is an individual act of accumulating a food that consists of many small units and is concentrated at a few known permanent sources.

Instances of cannibalism have been reported. Between 1971 and 1984, six infant chimpanzees were killed and eaten by members of the group studied by Goodall. On three occasions the victims were young infants of females who did not belong to the community. In other cases, two females, Passion and her late adolescent daughter, Pom, killed and ate at least three babies born to females in their community. Although adult males were observed killing infants during an attack on the mothers, Passion and Pom's attack on a mother seemed to have been directed at seizing the infants. This behavior is unique to this mother and daughter, and although the reasons behind the behavior are not understood, one result was the removal of infants of potentially competitive reproductive females from the social unit.

The structure of chimpanzee social groups is of interest to anthropologists trying to reconstruct early human social groupings. The adaptability and flexibility of chimpanzee social groups may help to explain how early humans coped with environmental and predatory stress. Chimpanzees in the Budongo Forest of Uganda, for example, markedly change their behavior when approaching open terrain. In the forest they are relaxed and their social group is loose, but they become tense and vigilant in open spaces.

Chimpanzees may be found in any one of a number of different social groupings, or parties (Goodall, 1986):

1. *All-male party*—two or more adult and/or adolescent males.
2. *Family unit*—a mother and her dependents, with or without older offspring (Figure 9-3).
3. *Nursery unit*—two or more family units, sometimes these are accompanied by nonrelated childless females.
4. *Mixed party*—one or more adult or adolescent males with one or more adult or adolescent females, with or without dependents.
5. *Sexual party*—mixed party in which one or more of the females are sexually receptive; that is, they are in estrus.
6. *Consortship*—an exclusive relationship of one adult male with one adult female when they travel, with or without her offspring.
7. *Gathering party*—a group comprising at least half of the members of the community, including at least half of the adult males.
8. *Lone individual*—an animal completely alone.

The size of the party is determined by the number of estrous females. A sexually popular female, unless in a consortship with a male, will attract most or all of the community's males and many of the females. When several

Figure 9-3 *Among the closest and longest-lasting of all relationships among chimpanzees is the mother-infant bond.*

females are sexually receptive at the same time, party size is often even larger.

Ghiglieri (1985) provides an insightful look at the social ecology of chimpanzees. Chimpanzee communities may consist of 50 or more members who search for fruit-bearing trees and other foods. When fruit is scarce, community members may forage on their own. When fruit is abundant, however, chimpanzees tend to congregate in large parties to feed, mate, and socialize. This fusion-fission type of social organization, a relatively rare trait among nonhuman primates, may be an adaptation that maximizes the efficiency of the search for fruit, which accounts for approximately 78 percent of the diet. The size of the foraging group can increase with the number of fruit trees visited. The size of the foraging party is proportional to the crown volume of the tree. Large trees, which bear more fruit, are visited by more chimpanzees for a longer period of time.

Much of the chimpanzee's diet consists of rare species of fruit that tend to grow in clumps and are not uniformly distributed throughout the home range. Ghiglieri sees the chimpanzee's way of life as being based on finding a rare and quickly vanishing food supply before its competitors locate the same food source. The chimpanzee's acute memory and excellent sense of spatial relationships may be related to its feeding pattern.

Most nonhuman primate groups are composed of a number of relatively closed social groups, but in chimpanzee society both sexes have almost complete freedom to enter and leave groups as they please. The membership of temporary parties is constantly changing. Adults and adolescents may also choose to spend some time alone, but in general, chimpanzees are extremely social animals. This type of social organization means that the daily experiences of a chimpanzee are far more variable than those of almost any other primate.

A chimpanzee rarely sees all the members of its community on the same day and probably never sees all of them two days in succession. Some individuals may meet on a fairly regular basis, but others seldom meet. Each male is likely to encounter all other adult males of his community several times a week and may also encounter many females. Social relationships are characterized by unpredictability.

Although a female may be very social and may encounter many individuals during a week when she is sexually active, she becomes more solitary when she is no longer in estrus. More peripheral females encounter far fewer individuals in a week. Chimpanzee society is extraordinarily complex, with such factors as age, sex, and mother's personality influencing an individual's social relationships.

In most group-living primates, outbreeding is accomplished by the emigration of males from their natal group. In contrast, among chimpanzees (and among gorillas and some monkeys), young females may temporarily or permanently transfer to another group (Pusey, 1978). While both young females without infants and some older females may transfer temporarily, only the former, usually those in estrus, have been observed to permanently transfer to a new group. Females may range at the edges of two different groups and may associate with males and females of both groups.

There are permanent female transfers, and some females transfer to other than a natal group on a temporary basis. These females visit neighboring communities for relatively short periods, usually during consecutive periods of estrus, and then return to their original group. Certain peripheral females may continue to move back and forth between communities. It is not uncommon for females in late adolescence to transfer back and forth between neighboring communities, associating and mating with males of both. After giving birth, the female typically commits to one of the two groups. If her preferred area of movement is close to the boundary of both groups, however, she may continue to associate with both for a while. There is usually severe aggression if adult males encounter neighboring females and infants.

Unlike most nonhuman primate males, the chimpanzee male resides within his natal group for life. A male ultimately becomes part of the male community that patrols the group's borders and fathers the next generation. Whereas male chimpanzees in a community are closely related, females may not be closely related to other females in the group. This situation is rare among nonhuman primates.

Probably because of their close kinship ties, male chimpanzees in a group are generally noncompetitive with one another, even during mating. Male chimpanzees, unlike male orangutans and gorillas, spend little time vying with one another for mating opportunities. Female chimpanzees usually mate with several male group members during each estrous cycle. A female is normally sexually receptive for only a few weeks every five years. Thus, this pattern of male tolerance is striking given the fact that a male has only a limited opportunity to pass along his genes. Male tolerance toward reproductive competitors may be linked to the fact that the group's males are related to one another. All or most males are descended from the same small group of patriarchs. Any two males in a community are therefore likely to share the same father or grandfather. If one male successfully mates, some of his male relative's genes are also passed to the next generation.

When any male fathers an offspring, other males in the group share his success by way of increases in their inclusive fitness. Because males probably share a significant genetic ancestry, some of those shared genes are passed along whenever one of them successfully mates. Genetic relatedness and inclusive fitness may be key factors in the evolution of a chimpanzee community maintained by cooperating males. Cooperative defense of the range by genetically related males is one foundation of chimpanzee society. Community boundaries are determined by the activities of male bands who patrol the group's boundaries.

Female chimpanzees also have community interests. Within the community into which she has immigrated, a female tends to socialize only with a subset of other females. Some of these females may be relatives from the natal group. Female chimpanzees tend to travel together. Females may collectively repel strange females who try to enter their group. This implies the existence of a close female community; in fact, there may be a separate female community superimposed on the male chimpanzee community.

The pattern of chimpanzee social life obviously differs for each of the sexes. A male begins to leave his mother when he is about 8 years old, and he will spend many hours alone for the rest of his life. The amount of time that a male spends with individuals outside of his immediate family depends on his mother's personality and sociability. If a mother is friendly and contacts animals outside her family unit, it is likely that her son will also have contact with these animals. A female also spends time alone when she first begins to travel independently of her mother. After she gives birth, however, she is unlikely to spend any time completely alone for the rest of her life. At Gombe, the bond between mothers and daughters is extremely close. A female's close-knit family unit provides her with companionship, grooming, play, and support during aggressive interactions with other community members.

After giving birth to her first infant, a female typically becomes less sociable. She continues to associate with her mother but spends a good deal of time alone with her infant. When she once again commences breeding, she begins to associate with both males and females.

When compared to that of other nonhuman primates, chimpanzee society grants its members (those 9 years of age and older) relative autonomy. Once a male breaks his tie to his mother, he is free to associate with whomever he pleases. While a female also has some options in terms of association, her psychological dependence on her mother is stronger.

The freedom of association found among chimpanzees is important in reducing tension, especially among males. At the same time, the various social opportunities that are available impose unusual demands on the acquisition of social intelligence. Most primate youngsters are reared within a relatively stable social group, but a chimpanzee youngster may encounter new individuals every day. The chimpanzee youngster must learn to function in a highly complex social setting. Nevertheless, as is the case for most other primates, an animal's closest bonds are with family members—between a mother and her offspring, and between siblings.

One result of the fact that chimpanzees often roam far from their natal group is increased intercommunity aggression. At Gombe, for example, Goodall reports that on four occasions, attacks on females by males of another group led to the death of the female's infant. On three occasions these infants were eaten or partially eaten. A similar occurrence was documented at another chimpanzee research site. Unlike those langurs who practice infanticide, male chimpanzees do not seem to attack and kill infants in order to bring females into estrus.

Gombe has been roughly divided into two groups that were once part of the same group. There is a very fluid, overlapping area between the two new groups. During 1974 and 1975, four animals were attacked and killed for no apparent reason by a northern group that ventured deep into the southern area. Goodall speculated that the northern chimpanzees were on "patrol" at the time of the killing. A sense of territoriality and overcrowding produced by human destruction of the habitat may be linked to the killings. Goodall witnessed attacks by animals from one group on those from another. Such attacks lasted from 15 to 20 minutes. The violence attracts young males. When males returned to their own range, the members of the patrol seemed highly agitated and often began to hunt.

Goodall has documented the extension of the range of one of the larger groups at Gombe. At the same time, the range of another group shrunk from about 12 square kilometers in 1978 to about 8 square kilometers at the end of 1981. During that time three males from the smaller group disappeared, the most recent disappearance involving the leader (the alpha) male. All three males were healthy when last seen, and Goodall suspects that they were victims of an intercommunity clash with the larger adjacent group. During Goodall's study, one whole chimpanzee community was apparently decimated by its neighbors.

Goodall suggests that chimpanzees attack members of other communities because they have an aversion to strangers. The decimation of one community of chimpanzees by another at Gombe occurred through determined efforts to wound and batter in order to incapacitate animals of the other group. Among primates, only humans and chimpanzees seem to react so violently to strangers. Goodall suggests that the kind of aversion to strangers exhibited by chimpanzees may in fact be a precursor to armed conflict.

Chimpanzees differentiate between "us" and "them" and have a strong sense of group identity. Infants and females who are part of a group are protected even if the infants are sired by males of another community. Infants of females who do not belong to the community may be killed.

Sex plays an important role in chimpanzee society. A young female begins to travel away from her mother with adult males during her first estrous period. During adolescent sterility, which lasts 1 to 3 years, she mates (unsuccessfully, of course) not only with males of her own community, but also with at least some males from a neighboring social group. When she becomes pregnant, between the ages of 12 and 14, she typically makes a commitment to one community. At Gombe she often stays in her own natal group, with her mother, to give birth and raise her offspring, the first of whom may have been sired by a male from a neighboring community. A young male, in contrast, always remains in his natal group and competes with other resident males for mating rights. As a group, males protect their community females from neighboring males and try to recruit young females from adjacent communities to join them.

A male who maintains a consortship with a fertile female probably has a better chance to father her child than he would in a group situation, which would require him to compete with other males. During consortship, a male holds exclusive mating rights. A consort relationship may also be more conducive to fertilization, because the pair is away from the excitement and heightened aggression that typically characterize sexual behavior in a larger group. Consort couples that spend more time together seem more likely to have a successful mating.

One striking anatomical feature of mature female chimpanzees is the appearance of swelling around the anal-vaginal region, which indicates sexual receptivity. The swelling, which precedes ovulation by a few days, serves to alert neighboring males to a female's reproductive state and may elicit sexual rather than hostile behavior. At Gombe, no brutal attacks were ever pressed on females with sexual swellings. By facilitating a female's chances of mating with neighboring males, sexual swellings may be considered highly adaptive for female chimpanzees. (In fact, such swellings are also found among macaque and baboon females and seem to serve a similar function.) Females with a sexual swelling are accorded favors not given to other females. Females with sexual swellings are groomed more often by males and are more likely to gain meat by begging than are females without swellings.

Because of its fluid nature, a chimpanzee society is markedly affected by the presence or absence of receptive females. Party size, for example, tends to be larger when a sexually receptive female is present, and party size affects the frequency of aggression and other social interactions. The tendency of females to have their first postpartum sexual swellings at the end of the dry season results in huge gatherings of excited animals. These gatherings draw together animals who do not see one another for weeks on end for much of the year; it is a time for reacquaintance. Infants and juveniles, as a result of their mother's increased sociability, have rich opportunities for social interaction.

The chimpanzee mating pattern is flexible. Males have various options for maximizing their reproductive success, and some males can alter their mating strategies with respect to their position in the male dominance hierarchy. Some males will compete with others for access to a female within the community, while other males will lead females on a consortship and try to monopolize her mating. The calm and relaxed nature of the relationship of animals on a consortship, some of which last more than a month, suggests that chimpanzees have the potential for developing more permanent ties with nonrelated members of the opposite sex.

The availability of sexual partners also affects relationships between neighboring communities. Adult males, perhaps visiting peripheral areas in search of adolescent females for recruitment into their own communities, may come upon and brutally attack older females with young or may encounter neighboring males with resultant hostility. Consortship pairs, because they roam at the edges of the community's areas, risk being attacked by a patrol of males from a neighboring community.

Although parent–child or sibling–sibling mating was rarely observed, one male copulated with his mother. The mother at first resisted, but after being threatened she cooperated with her son.

The most salient features of chimpanzee social organization are as follows (Smuts, 1985):

1. Male chimpanzees born in the same community form a cooperative group whose goal seems to be to defend as large an area as possible against incursions by male groups from other communities. Intercommunity conflict can lead to severe aggression between male groups, which can result in the death of some animals.
2. Most adolescent females transfer from their natal group to a neighboring group. They usually remain in this new group for many years, perhaps forever, and they mate primarily with males whose range they share.
3. Mothers spend much of their time alone with their infants, but occasionally associate with males in large parties when they gather at a seasonally abundant food source. Male–female encounters in such situations are usually friendly and relaxed.
4. Aging females and infants are especially vulnerable to severe attacks by males from other communities. Females are especially vulnerable when near the boundary of another community's range and when the males of their own community are losing a prolonged struggle against males from another community. Females are generally safe within a community whose males can successfully defend the community's boundaries. Males also defend newly arrived females from female community residents. Because most females leave their natal group, they may join a group in

which they have no female relatives. Under such circumstances, females might be expected to compete with one another for reproductive opportunities. Because a female who bears an infant might not be a relative, females do not share in the inclusive fitness of having a related female give birth to an infant. Because a male's reproductive fitness is limited by the number of females in the community, they should be expected to try to keep as many females as possible in, and add females to, the community.

5. Females tend to choose male associates who effectively defend a large community range. If males are no longer able to defend community borders—for example, if there is a declining number of males—females may move en masse to an adjacent community containing males that are able to defend a boundary.

6. Female and male chimpanzees establish long-term, reciprocal relationships based on an association between individual females and an entire group of males (many of whom may be related to one another). In the context of such relationships, males make a substantial contribution to the welfare of females and infants by protecting them from males of other communities.

The foregoing description applies to the common chimpanzee (*Pan troglodytes;* see Table 9-2). The pygmy chimpanzee (*P. paniscus*) departs somewhat from this pattern. Both common and pygmy chimpanzees share elements of their social organization; for example, they live in large communities composed of smaller subunits. The smaller subunits differ between the two species, however. The pygmy chimpanzee's basic social unit contains roughly equal numbers of adult males and females together with immature animals (Kano, 1982). Pygmy chimpanzees live in larger social groups than do common chimpanzees. Among pygmy chimpanzees, the most common group size is 11 to 15 animals. Among common chimpanzees, group size is 2 to 4 animals at Gombe and 2 to 6 in the Budongo Forest (Reynolds, 1965).

Pygmy chimpanzees have higher male–female and female–female affinities than do common chimpanzees. Group cohesion is strong among pygmy chimpanzees and is maintained by such behaviors as genito-genital rubbing in females, a lengthened period of female sexual receptivity, high tolerance of group members by dominant males, and widespread food sharing (Susman, 1987).

Shea (1983) suggests that group cohesiveness among pygmy chimpanzees, coupled with reduced sexual dimorphism (Kinzey, 1984), may reflect a reduced level of intragroup aggression relative to that of the common chimpanzee. It may also reflect the more arboreal habitat of the pygmy chimpanzee and a more closed breeding system, wherein female pygmy chimpanzees migrate from their natal group but stay within their community.

Pygmy chimpanzees do not exhibit the common chimpanzee pattern of all-male parties patrolling large home ranges, nor are female pygmy chimpan-

Table 9-2. Highlights of the Social Organization and Behavior of the Common Chimpanzee

Distribution: Savannas and forests in eastern and western Africa.

Social Organization and Behaviors: Some tool use and manufacture, especially by females.
Predatory behavior in both sexes; some cooperative predation.
Various patterns of social groups and parties; some modification according to habitat type and food sources.
Party size determined by number of sexually active females in the group.
Killing of members of neighboring social groups in some regions.
Females emigrate from the natal group; males stay in the natal group.
Males cooperate to maintain social boundaries against males of other groups.

Status: Endangered in many locales because of human encroachment in the habitat.

zees frequently found alone with their offspring or with other females. The day ranges of chimpanzees at Gombe are larger than those of pygmy chimpanzees.

Pygmy chimpanzee society displays a number of traits common to forest rather than open-country forms. For example, compared to common chimpanzees, pygmy chimpanzees have a reduced day range, increased arboreal feeding, and spend less time feeding. Certain aspects of the pygmy chimpanzee's behavior, such as reduced levels of intraspecific aggression, increased sexual receptivity, and reduced sexual dimorphism, may be related to reduced stress on the pygmy chimpanzee's social organization when compared to that of the common chimpanzee. This, in turn, may be related to the pygmy chimpanzee's more stable forest habitat, with its reduced seasonality, relaxed feeding competition, and reduced predator pressure, compared with that of more open-country, terrestrial chimpanzees (Susman, 1987).

If *Australopithecus afarensis,* the earliest known human ancestor (Chapter 17), was more forest adapted and more arboreally adapted than its descendants, as some have suggested, then the pygmy chimpanzee may provide important clues to its anatomy and behavior. Pygmy chimpanzees provide one important source of data for models of early hominid behavior.

THE GORILLA

The first scientific description of the gorilla (Figure 9-4) appeared in 1847. Gorillas inhabiting east Africa were first discovered by Europeans as late as 1902. Three gorilla subspecies are usually recognized. Perhaps 35,000 lowland gorillas (*Gorilla gorilla gorilla*), the subspecies most often seen in zoos, inhabit Gabon, western Africa, alone. Some 1,000 miles to the east, in the Virunga Volcano region of Zaire, Uganda, and Rwanda, live the last surviving mountain gorillas (*G. g. beringei*). Only about 400 of these animals survive in

Figure 9-4 An adult male lowland gorilla. (A) Note the gray hair on the back and rump areas. This pattern is the reason for the name silver-backed male. (B) Note the large nuchal crest on the head and the large brow ridges of the adult male. Also note the hair on the powerful arms.

the wild. The third subspecies is the eastern lowland gorilla (*G. g. graueri*), of which there are about 4,000 surviving, mainly in eastern Zaire, and about 24 alive in captivity.

The first long-term scientific research on free-ranging gorillas was carried out by George Schaller (1963, 1964), who spent 10 months studying 10 gorilla groups containing a total of about 200 animals. At least partially because of their imposing body size, many had assumed that gorillas were ferocious animals. However, Schaller habituated gorillas to his presence by approaching them slowly, alone, and in full view. After repeated approaches he was accepted as an innocuous addition to the habitat. Once the gorillas realized that Schaller was not dangerous, curiosity replaced their fear; they observed Schaller observing them. His study demonstrated that gorillas could be observed. Schaller learned gorilla communicative gestures; if he frightened an animal, he merely shook his head, as subordinate gorillas do. He was then ignored. Schaller's study portrayed the gorilla as a lazy wanderer, one who likes to doze or sunbathe in midmorning. "Perhaps the worst that can be said about the temperament of the wild gorilla is that it is morose and sullen; at best it is amiable, lovable, shy, and gentle" (Reynolds, 1967:149). This view has been modified as data have accumulated. For example, gorilla males can be violent when protecting their group, as well as in other instances.

Gorilla social groups are relatively stable and cohesive. Group sizes vary from a low of 2 to about 20 animals (Table 9-3). An average group contains about 10 members according to Fossey (1985) and about 17 members according to Schaller (1963).

The composition of gorilla groups varies, but a representative group contains at least one silverback male (so-called because of graying of the hair about the rump and up the back). Some groups contain more than one silverback male. The second silverback is usually the son of an aging leader; some males may succeed their fathers as the group's leading silverback. The silverback is a sexually mature male, over 15 years old, who is the group's undisputed leader. He weighs about 375 pounds, twice the size of a female. The silverback male leads and controls the group; he determines when, where, and how fast it should travel. As the group's defender, a silverback male stays behind and intimidates intruders with a chest-beating display. The male will rise on his hind feet, soundly beat his resonating chest with his hands, and throw sticks and other nearby objects into the air. The act is meant to intimidate and seldom leads to direct attack. In multi–silverback male groups, the least dominant of the silverback males gives the display while the leader moves off with the rest of the group.

A typical group also contains at least one sexually immature blackback male between 8 and 13 years old and weighing about 250 pounds. Although blackback males are considered sexually immature in the natural state because they do not breed, they will breed in captivity if a silverback male is absent. The presence of the silverback male restricts the blackback male's mating. Young blackback males often leave their natal group to lead a wandering or

---

Table 9-3. Highlights of the Social Organization and Behavior of the Gorilla

---

Distribution: *Western Lowland Gorillas:* western Africa
Eastern Lowland Gorillas: eastern Zaire
Mountain Gorillas: Zaire, Uganda, Rwanda (Virunga Volcano Region)

Social Organization and Behavior: Relatively stable social groups.
Typical group has at least one silverback male, 1 sexually immature male. Females outnumber males; often 3–4 sexually mature females.
Mature females emigrate from natal group. Groups contain a number of unrelated females.
Males emigrate, but for different reasons than females.
Silverback males have exclusive mating access to females.
Males practice infanticide in formation of new groups.

Status: Highly endangered. Quite likely to become extinct before end of the twenty-first century.

---

solitary existence until they have succeeded in attracting females to form their own social group. If such males join an established group, they generally occupy a peripheral position.

Females outnumber males in gorilla groups, a typical primate pattern. An average gorilla group contains three or four sexually mature females over 8 years of age. Each mature female weighs about 200 pounds. If the females are not the daughters of the group's silverback male, each is ordinarily bonded to a silverback male for life. A typical group also contains between three and six immature animals, all of whom were probably fathered by the reigning silverback male.

A male–female pair does not constitute a gorilla group; a silverback male must attract more than one female to establish a stable breeding unit. Such females need not come from the same group, but the second female must join the silverback male shortly after the first or the first will leave to join another male. However, a single female will remain with a lower-ranking silverback in an established group in which she has the protection and help of other group members.

Each gorilla group moves over its own range, which is usually 10 to 12 square miles in size. The borders of these ranges can change as the silverback males explore and extend them. The vast wanderings about the range may be one way of ensuring an adequate food supply. The greater the range overlap with that of other groups, the more frequent the intergroup encounters. Because males try to add females from other groups to their own, intergroup encounters are frequent if there is a disproportionate ratio of males to females. These intergroup encounters can prove fatal, especially to youngsters, if a new male joins a group or succeeds in attracting a female to his group.

Mature females are likely to emigrate from their natal group, unlike most nonhuman primates, but like chimpanzees. Gorilla groups are composed largely of unrelated females that probably have not matured together. Adult female bonds are apparently quite weak; group cohesion is tied to the relationship between resident females and the silverback male rather than to female kinship ties, as is the case for many other primates.

Although established gorilla groups are cohesive over the long term, there are times in an animal's life when it may leave one group for another in order to maximize its reproductive potential. Females transfer from their natal group to groups that do not contain related males. Nulliparous females (those who have not yet given birth) often transfer to lone silverbacks or to small groups. Their rank order corresponds to the order in which they are acquired by dominant silverbacks. Females living in groups with a number of females may transfer to a group with fewer females, thereby raising their status.

Nearly all of the females in Fossey's study left their natal groups and almost immediately joined another group. Females may change their group affiliation more than once, but they initially transfer to a group with an overlapping range, thereby ensuring some familiarity with members of their new group. Resident males try to prevent female emigration by deterring the proximity of other males rather than by herding the females. Many female transfers were marked by aggressive displays or fights between the males of the competing groups.

All of the factors affecting a female's decision to emigrate are not clear. The quality of a male's range probably affects the female's decision to emigrate. Whether or not a female stays with a male is probably also influenced by their success in raising offspring. Because females produce only a limited number of offspring, it benefits them to be very selective about the conditions in which their infants are conceived and raised. (The average birth interval of 13 females in Fossey's study was 39.1 months. For viable births, the average interval was 46.8 months.)

Male gorillas also emigrate, but their reasons for doing so may be different from those influencing female emigration. Males first emigrate at about 11 years of age. Males remaining in their natal group are the leading males or perhaps the leading male's sons. Leader males inhibit the sexual behavior of young males, suggesting that competition for females encourages male emigration. There seems to be less conflict between a father and his son for access to breeding females or for dominance positions.

In order to understand gorilla social organization, one must understand their mating patterns. Silverback males retain exclusive sexual access to females; therefore, younger males may leave a group to form their own group rather than waste their reproductive years. Although a receptive female may have many potential mates, she has only one actual mate—the highest-ranking silverback in the group who is not closely related to her. Until conception, only he copulates with her. If other males attempt to compete for a receptive female, her partner stays close to her and keeps constant vigil. A male's reproductive success depends on maintaining exclusive mating rights to adult females, which he does by forming a permanent bond with each female in the group.

Possibly as a result of his proximity to his mate, other males have restricted access, and the pair mate repeatedly. The female will fight off another male's advance. If no other males are present, there is no close male–female contact and mating is much less frequent. Under these circumstances, the female often solicits mating.

After impregnation, the female's sexual life depends primarily on the presence of silverback males in her group that are lower ranking than her mate. If another male is present, the female often solicits copulation. Although another male may reply by mounting the female, he rarely achieves penile penetration. Such failure is not due to the female's efforts; in fact, after impregnation she often courts sexual behavior. The impregnating male often watches the female's activities, but he seldom intervenes.

Animals seldom mate with their close relatives. A daughter of a group's leader becomes the mate of the second-ranking silverback male in the group, provided he is not her full brother. If this is the case, she moves down the dominance hierarchy until she mates with a male that is not a full sibling. If no appropriate male is found, she emigrates. In a multi–silverback male group, female offspring of lower-ranking silverbacks may become mates of the group's leader. Mother–son matings probably do not occur, but matings between distant relatives are reported (Veit, 1982).

The exchange of daughters among males of the same group and between groups avoids inbreeding and reduces mate competition. No silverback competes with another for females that are his mother, full sister, or daughter. This system of mate exchange enables close kin to remain in a tightly organized group in which they can protect one another.

The female's proximity to a silverback male is most affected by the presence of an infant. Females with dependent young less than 5 years old spend more time with the silverback male than do females without dependent young. As infants mature, the mother's time near the silverback decreases, suggesting that proximity to the male offers some protection to a mother with dependent young.

The large silverback males are very gentle with infants and do not try to avoid them. One by-product of the male's tolerance of an infant's proximity is the protection of his genetic investment in the infant and an increased probability that females will remain in his group. If a female leaves the group, she may leave a weaned infant behind with the father.

Although the male is gentle with an infant born in his own group, this is not the case when a female attempts to join a new group with a dependent, or unweaned, infant. Infant loss is common in the process of the bonding of a new pair. If a silverback dies and the female and infant transfer to a new group, the infant is often killed by the resident male in the new group. Birth intervals are longer for primiparous females (first-time mothers) than for multiparous females (those who have had a number of infants) because younger females often transfer between silverbacks before settling down with one. Such transfers make young females more likely to lose an infant due to infanticide than would be the case for females who remain in one group during their childbearing years.

Infanticide among gorillas "seems necessary to maintain a healthy degree of exogamy, or outbreeding" (Fossey, 1981:512). Soon after infanticide, the now infantless mother copulates with the infanticidal male. Infanticide speeds a female's return to breeding, possibly because the cessation of nursing causes a resumption of ovulation. The infanticidal male ensures that all offspring born into a group are his, and the female ensures that a male will expend full effort to protect her infant, whom he has fathered.

A young gorilla male who is establishing his own group may kill infants of a low-status female living in a larger group led by an older male. The female may then abandon this group and join the young male to form a new group. By becoming one of the first to join the young male's group, the female gains high status if other females subsequently join. She receives more food and protection, and any young she has while in the group share the leader male's genes and are protected by him. In losing one infant, the female gorilla may gain a better chance of having more surviving offspring.

THE ORANGUTAN

Orangutans (Figure 9-5) live in Borneo and Sumatra; however, they are evolutionarily closer to the African gorilla and chimpanzee than they are to the other Asian ape, the gibbon. Unlike the gregarious chimpanzees, orangutans are shy. Older male orangutans look particularly striking because of their unique bulging, fleshy cheek pads. These cheek pads are a sexually dimorphic trait, and although their evolutionary significance is unclear, their presence may be reinforced by sexual selection. Some studies suggest that females seem more willing to mate with older males with cheek pads than with younger males without such pads.

There may once have been at least 500,000 orangutans inhabiting the forests from the Celebes to North China. About 2,000 years ago there were probably more orangutans than people in Borneo. Today the orangutan's numbers are dangerously depleted and its range severely restricted because of habitat destruction. The orangutan faces extinction.

Unlike most other anthropoids, the orangutan (Table 9-4) avoids long-term contact with others of its species and generally lacks the social group that is typical of the other apes. Horr (1977:293) notes:

> Young orangs do not mature in the context of a group or troop of several individuals of all ages and sexes in which long-term relationships are developed on the basis of daily, face-to-face contact. Not only is there no cohesive, geographically bounded "troop" . . . but there are apparently no instances in which a large number of orangutans come together for coordinated movement.

Galdikas (1979), on the other hand, has reported as many as nine orangutans in temporary company. She noted, however, that tension rises when more than five animals are together, and the group divides into smaller units. Orangutans do form social units, but units larger than a few animals are temporary.

The basic orangutan social unit is the mother–infant pair. Although a mother and her infant may meet another mother–infant pair and spend a day or two foraging near each other, there is minimal social interaction between the two units. A mother–offspring unit is usually composed of a female and one offspring, but two or three previous offspring may be in close association. The mother–offspring unit sleeps, moves, and feeds together.

The mother–offspring units move over small jungle areas, perhaps one-fourth of a square mile, that remain rather constant through time. Although the range is small, and a female could cross it within a day, movement is generally restricted to a limited area. The ranges of mother–offspring units may overlap. Even though such overlap must lead to some familiarity, it does not lead to larger social aggregations.

Maturing offspring leave the mother–offspring unit at age 4 or 5 to establish their own ranging patterns as adults. Juvenile females leave their mothers somewhat later than juvenile males, a rather typical primate pattern. Juvenile female orangutans may establish overlapping ranges with their mothers and may spend most of their lives in the same few square miles as their mothers.

Figure 9-5 The following photos of orangutans were taken at the Orangutan Research and Conservation Project at the Tanjung Puting National Park, Indonesia. (A), (B), (C) Adult female orangutan sharing food with her infant male. (D) Ex-captive female infant orangutan having a snack of rice. (E) Adult female (at least 22 years old).

Table 9-4. **Highlights of the Social Organization and Behavior of the Orang-utan**

Distribution: Restricted to certain forests in Borneo and Sumatra

Social Organization and Behavior: No large social groups. Major grouping is a mother and infant.
Mature males are usually solitary-living.
Adult males fight with one another over access to mature females.

Status: Highly endangered; extinction may be imminent.

Despite such proximity, they do not form the matriarchal groups that are typical of many monkeys. Juvenile males move farther from their mother (helping prevent inbreeding with their mothers and sisters) and are often alone in the forest. Young males may form brief "social" associations with other juvenile males, but there are no juvenile male peer groups. Juvenile females do not appear to travel independently, but temporary, nonbreeding young male–female pairs have been observed.

Adult male orangutans basically lead a solitary existence. Meetings between males often result from efforts to mate with a female and are usually accompanied by aggression. Males may be fatally wounded while competing for mating access to females. Unlike most primate males, the adult male orangutan is intolerant of infants, and mothers with youngsters avoid males until their offspring are large enough to survive independently.

Adult male orangutans range over larger areas than do adult females. Male ranges are 2 or more square miles in area and often overlap the ranges of several females. As males move over their range they emit loud, trumpeting vocalizations that carry for long distances. Such calls announce their presence and give females a chance to locate them and either join them or move away. Females can probably identify males according to their calls; thus females have some choice about with whom they mate. The calls also allow the other males in the vicinity to decide whether to avoid or challenge one another.

The orangutan social structure may be an adaptation to the fact that critical food items are thinly distributed throughout the forest (MacKinnon, 1979). Large concentrations of animals would rapidly exhaust the food supplies in any given region. Female–offspring ranges are the minimal area of support. Predation by animals other than humans is rare, and males do not defend the young. Permanent male–female bonds would further deplete food supplies and force females to move over larger ranges, where they may encounter risks to their own lives and to those of their young. Females are sexually receptive only about once each 2.5 to 3.5 years, and males further maximize their reproductive success by ranging over wide areas and contacting many females.

Although some amount of male–male competition over access to breeding females is not uncommon among nonhuman primates, rarely do such encounters produce the severe aggression common to orangutans. We have already noted that a male may be killed by a competing male. Competition among males for females is an important factor in orangutan adaptation. There is some disagreement among researchers as to whether younger or older males are the most sought-after mates. Galdikas (1979) reports that females may avoid subadult males because the fully mature and successful adult male may be the more fit partner. On the other hand, MacKinnon (1974) found that among Borneo orangutans, younger males sire more offspring.

Female orangutans show no external signs of ovulation such as the genital swelling found in female chimpanzees and many monkeys. A female orangutan reveals her hormonal state by certain "flirting behaviors." When a transient adult male finds a receptive female, he follows her for days. A male may stay within a range for several years and mate with a female with whom he spends several days each month. Some male consorts will even stay with females when they are pregnant. Certain males and females may spend much of their reproductive lives sharing a range.

MacKinnon (1979) defines two phases of the reproductive strategy employed by male orangutans. The first, the subadult sexuality stage, commences at about age 10 and continues to about age 15. During this stage, the young male's mating strategy is to maintain consortships with relatively willing females and to forcefully copulate with uncooperative females. The second phase, the full adult sexuality stage, begins when the orangutan is about 20 years old. In this phase the male can attract females, employ greater selectivity in mate choice, and consort with greater certainty of successful fertilization.

Rijsken (1978:266) identified two patterns in male orangutan sexual behavior: "rape" and cooperative mating. He notes:

> In its extreme form, the "rape" is a straightforward copulatory act, initiated by subadult males, in which females usually display distress and a lack of cooperation. . . . "Cooperative mating" is . . . usually initiated by the female . . . both partners show considerable coordination of movements before, during, and after copulation, while copulation itself is performed cooperatively.

Although it is not always easy to determine the level of cooperation, Rijsken argues that subadult males are especially prone to forceful copulation, and females generally avoid them. (MacKinnon disagrees, however.) Younger females are often the targets of subadult males. Some behaviors involved in the so-called rape, such as chasing, are tied to the length of the copulation (Maple, 1980). Copulations preceded by a chase were significantly longer than those not initiated by a chase. Males may be aroused by the chase, and the chase may be necessary for a successful copulation.

THE GIBBON

Gibbons, the smallest of the apes, live in southeast Asia in China, Burma, Thailand, Vietnam, and Kampuchea. In China, gibbons are very rare and may be nearing extinction (Ma, Wang, and Poirier, 1988). Early reports of gibbons concentrated on their loud and sonorous vocalizations and the fact that, unlike most primates, most gibbons live in monogamous family groups containing a male, a female, and their nonadult offspring.

Although the monogamous mating system found among some gibbons is less common than either polygamy or promiscuity, other primates (besides gibbons and some humans) are also monogamous (Table 9-5). Monogamy is widely distributed among primates, with at least 25 percent of all genera having at least one monogamous species. On the other hand, monogamy among the apes is limited to the gibbons (Table 9-6). Kinzey (1987) argued that monogamy among nonhuman primates is associated with relative behavioral and ecological inflexibility. Both Kinzey and Hrdy (1981) suggest that monogamous species are behaviorally more conservative than are polygamous and promiscuous species. This is at least partially due to the fact that in larger social groups there are many more potential social interactions and interactants. Monogamous primates are ecologically more restricted. Food resources that provide the bulk of their diet are limited and occur in dispersed small patches that can accommodate only a few feeding animals at any one time. Monogamous primates also tend to eat lower-quality foods (Fragaszy and Mason, 1983; Wright, 1985).

Kinzey suggests that among nonhuman primates, monogamy appears to have the least long-term adaptive value. The reasons for this are not altogether clear, but if it is true then it helps explain why monogamy is rarely encountered among primates. When monogamy occurs it is restricted to specific ecological situations.

Gibbons are supreme arboreal acrobats, brachiating through the trees propelled by their long arms. Unlike gorillas and orangutans, adult gibbons exhibit little physical sexual dimorphism. This reduced sexual dimorphism is a common feature of arboreal primates; both sexes are physically quite similar in size and often similar in behavior.

---

*Table 9-5. **Monogamy Among Primates***

New World Monkeys (Family Cebidae)		
Genus	Common Name	Occurrence
Aotus	Owl or Night Monkey	1 nocturnal species
Callicebus	Titi Monkey	3 species
Pithecia	Saki Monkey	2 to 4 species
Old World Monkeys (Family Cercopithecidae)		
Cercopithecus neglectus	De Brazza's Monkey	1 species
Presbytis potenziani	Mentawi Island Langur	1 species
Nasalis concolor	Simakobu Monkey	1 species
Gibbons (Family Hylobatidae)		
Hylobates	Gibbons	Most are monogamous
Humans (Family Hominidae)		
Homo	Humans	Culturally influenced

Table 9-6. Highlights of the Social Organization and Behavior of the Gibbon

---

Distribution: Forests of southeastern Asia.

Social Organization and Behavior: Most types of gibbons are monogamous.
Brachiation is the common mode of locomotion.
Highly territorial; both sexes participate.

Status: Endangered in some areas because of forest destruction.

One early gibbon study reported that males excluded their sons and females excluded their daughters from a family group when the youngsters reached sexual maturity. Sexually mature animals forced from the family group form their own mated pairs with others in a similar situation. More recent research suggests that subadult gibbons are forced out of the family unit by parental intolerance regardless of the sex of either the parent or the offspring. That is, mothers help force out sons as well as daughters, and fathers help force out daughters as well as sons. By forcing youngsters out of the family unit, inbreeding is avoided and overfeeding is prevented.

Gibbons are territorial; they defend the areas in which they live. Territorial defense usually involves an exchange of loud vocalizations and vigorous chasing. Each family knows its territorial boundaries; if this area seems in danger of encroachment by an adjacent group, the group rushes to the spot and calls and shakes branches until the trespassers retreat. Territorial encounters seldom lead to physical aggression.

Living apes are found in Asia and Africa. The Asian apes are the gibbon and the orangutan. The African apes are the gorilla and the chimpanzee. Although all ape species are under stress due primarily to habitat destruction, the orangutan and gorilla appear to be the most immediately threatened with extinction.

The group compositions of the apes vary. Unlike most nonhuman primates, most gibbons reside in monogamous family groups. At or somewhat prior to sexual maturity, youngsters of both sexes are forced from their family group. They must then form their own separate family groups with unrelated members of the opposite sex. The vast majority of nonhuman primates reside in bisexual social groups; however, the orangutan social organization is different. Orangutan males generally live solitary lives, while mothers and their infants live together for a few years. The range of a male orangutan overlaps that of several female and infant pairs. Orangutan males often fight viciously for access to a sexually receptive female.

One shared trait of gorilla and chimpanzee social organizations is the emigration of females from their natal group. This unusual pattern is found only in a few monkey species, for commonly it is the males who migrate. In most nonhuman primate societies, related females form the core of the social unit. Among chimpanzees, it is a group of related males that is the cohesive force of the social group. The fact that males in a social group are related may explain the lack of excessive overt male competition for mating access to females. While female chimpanzees move from group to group, males often attack males and infants, and sometimes females, of another group. These attacks can be so severe as to sometimes cause death or the decimation of a social group.

Gorilla females also leave their natal group. While some male gorillas may also migrate from their natal group, their migration may be due to different reasons than that of females. The most conspicuous member of the gorilla social unit is the silverback male. A stable social group must contain at least one silverback male. The silverback male fathers all the infants in the social group. He restricts the mating behavior of other males in his social group, unlike the chimpanzees, where many males mate with receptive females.

BIBLIOGRAPHY

BADRIAN, A., and N. BADRIAN. 1984. Social organization of *Pan paniscus* in the Lomako Forest, Zaire. In *The Pygmy Chimpanzee: Evolutionary Morphology and Behavior,* R. Sussman, ed., pp. 325–46. New York: Plenum.

BOESCH, C., and H. BOESCH. 1981. Sex differences in the use of natural hammers by wild chimpanzees: A preliminary report. *Journal of Human Evolution* 10: 585–93.

BUSSE, C. 1978. Do chimpanzees hunt cooperatively? *American Naturalist* 112: 767–70.

BYGOTT, J. 1972. Cannibalism among wild chimpanzees. *Nature* 238: 410–11.

BYGOTT, J. 1974. Agonistic behavior and dominance in wild chimpanzees. Ph.D. dissertation, Cambridge University.

CARPENTER, C. 1940. A field study in Siam of the behaviors and social relations of the gibbon (*Hylobates lar). Comparative Psychological Monographs* 16: 1–212.

CHIVERS, D. 1974. The siamang in Malaya. *Contributions to Primatology* vol. 4. New York: S. Karger.

ELLEFSON, J. 1968. Territorial behavior in the common white-handed gibbon, *Hylobates lar* Linn. In *Primates: Studies in Adaptation and Variability,* P. Jay, ed., pp. 180–200. New York: Holt, Rinehart and Winston.

FOSSEY, D. 1970. Making friends with mountain gorillas. *National Geographic* 137: 1, 46–68.

FOSSEY, D. 1978. Development of the mountain gorilla (*Gorilla gorilla beringei*): The first thirty-six months. In *The Great Apes,* D. Hamburg and E. McCown, eds., pp. 139–87. Menlo Park, Calif.: Benjamin/Cummings.

FOSSEY, D. 1981. The imperiled mountain gorilla. *National Geographic* 159: 501–23.

FOSSEY, D. 1985. *Gorillas in the Mist.* Boston: Houghton-Mifflin.

FRAGASZY, D., and W. MASON. 1983. Comparisons of feeding behavior in captive squirrel and titi monkeys *Saimiri sciureus* and *Callicebus moloch. Journal of Comparative Psychology* 97: 310–26.

GALDIKAS, B. 1979. Orangutan adaptation at Tanjung Puting Reserve: Mating and ecology. In *The Great Apes,* D. Hamburg and E. McCown, eds., pp. 195–233. Menlo Park, Calif.: Benjamin/Cummings.

GHIGLIERI, M. 1985. The social ecology of chimpanzees. *Scientific American,* June: 102–13.

GHIGLIERI, M. 1987. Sociobiology of the great apes and the hominid ancestor. *Journal of Human Evolution* 16: 319–358.

GHIGLIERI, M. 1988. *East of the Mountains of the Moon.* New York: The Free Press.

GOODALL, J. 1970. Tool-using in primates and other vertebrates. In *Advances in the Study of Behavior,* vol. 3, D. Lehrman, R. Hinde, and E. Shaws, eds., pp. 195–249. New York: Academic Press.

GOODALL, J. 1973. Cultural elements in a chimpanzee community. In *Precultural Primate Behavior,* vol. 1, E. Menzel, ed. New York: S. Karger.

GOODALL, J. 1979. Life and death at Gombe. *National Geographic,* 155: 592–620.

GOODALL, J. 1986. *The Chimpanzees of Gombe: Patterns of Behavior.* Cambridge, Mass.: Belknap.

GOODALL, A., and C. GROVES. 1977. The conservation of eastern gorillas. In *Primate Conservation,* Prince Rainier and G. Bourne, eds., pp. 599–637. New York: Academic Press.

HARCOURT, A. 1979. Contrasts between male relationships in wild gorilla groups. *Behavioral Ecology and Sociobiology* 5: 39–49.

HARCOURT, A. and K. STEWART. 1978. Sexual behavior of wild mountain gorillas. In *Recent Advances in Primatology,* vol. 6, D. Chivers and J. Herbert, eds., pp. 611–12. New York: Academic Press.

HARCOURT, A., K. STEWART, and D. FOSSEY. 1976. Male emigration and female transfer in wild mountain gorillas. *Nature* 263: 226–27.

HASEGAWA, T., M. HIRAIWA, T. NISHIDA, and H. TAKASAKI. 1983. New evidence on scavenging behavior in wild chimpanzees. *Current Anthropology* 24: 231–32.

HORR, D. 1975. The Borneo orang-utan: Population structure and dynamics in relationship to ecology and reproductive strategy. In *Primate Behavior: Developments in Field and Laboratory Research,* vol. 4, L. Rosenblum, ed., pp. 307–23. New York: Academic Press.

HORR, D. 1977. Orang-utan maturation: Growing up in a female world. In *Primate Bio-Social Development,* S. Cheavlier-Skolnikoff and F. Poirier, eds., pp. 289–321. New York: Garland.

HRDY, S. 1981. *The Woman That Never Evolved.* Cambridge, Mass.: Harvard University Press.

ITANI, J., and A. SUZUKI. 1967. The social unit of chimpanzees. *Primates* 8: 355–83.

KANO, T. 1982. The social group of pygmy chimpanzees (*Pan paniscus*) of Wamba. *Primates* 23: 171–88.

KANO, T. 1983. An ecological study of pygmy chimpanzees (*Pan paniscus*) of Yalosidi, Republic of Zaire. International *Journal of Primatology* 4: 1–31.

KAWANAKA, K. 1981. Infanticide and cannibalism in chimpanzees. *African Study Monographs* 1: 69–99.

KINZEY, W. 1984. The dentition of the pygmy chimpanzee, *Pan paniscus.* In *The Pgymy Chimpanzee: Evolutionary Morphology and Behavior,* R. Sussman, ed., pp. 65–88. New York: Plenum.

KINZEY, W. 1987. A primate model for human mating systems. In *The Evolution of Human Behavior: Primate Models,* W. Kinzey, ed., pp. 105–14. Albany: State University of New York Press.

MA, S., Y. WANG, and F. POIRIER. 1988. Taxonomy, distribution and status of gibbons (*Hylobates*) in southern China and adjacent areas. *Primates* 29: 277–286.

MACKINNON, J. 1974. *In Search of the Red Ape.* New York: Holt, Rinehart and Winston.

MACKINNON, J. 1979. Reproductive behavior in wild orangutan populations. In *The Great Apes,* D. Hamburg and E. McCown, eds., pp. 257–74. Menlo Park, Calif.: Benjamin/Cummings.

MAPLE, T., 1980. *Orang-utan Behavior.* New York: Van Nostrand Reinhold.

MAPLE, T., and M. HOFF. 1982. *Gorilla Behavior.* New York: Van Nostrand Reinhold.

McGREW, W. 1978. Evolutionary implications of sex differences in chimpanzee predation and tool use. In *The Great Apes,* D. Hamburg and E. McCown, eds., pp. 441–64. Menlo Park, Calif.: Benjamin/Cummings.

McGrew, W. 1983. Animal foods in the diets of wild chimpanzees (*Pan troglodytes*): Why cross-cultural variation? *Journal of Ethology* 1: 46–41.

McGrew, W., C. Tutin, and P. Baldwin. 1979. New data on meat-eating by wild chimpanzees. *Current Anthropology* 20: 238–40.

Nishida, T. 1968. The social group of wild chimpanzees in the Mahal Mountains. *Primates* 9: 167–224.

Nishida, T., and S. Uehara. 1980. Chimpanzees, tools, and termites: Another example from Tanzania. *Current Anthropology* 21: 671–72.

Pusey, A. 1978. Intercommunity transfer of chimpanzees in Gombe National Park. In *The Great Apes,* D. Hamburg and E. McCown, eds., pp. 465–80. Menlo Park, Calif.: Benjamin/Cummings.

Reynolds, V. 1965. *Budongo: A Forest and its Chimpanzees.* New York: Natural History Press.

Reynolds, V. 1967. *The Apes.* New York: Harper and Row.

Rijksen, H. 1978. *A Field Study on Sumatran Orangutans* (Pongo pygmaeus abelli *lesson 1827): Ecology, Behavior, and Conservation.* Wageningen, Netherlands: H. Veenman and B. V. Zonen.

Schaller, G. 1963. *The Mountain Gorillas.* Chicago: University of Chicago Press.

Schaller, G. 1964. *The Year of the Gorillas.* Chicago: University of Chicago Press.

Shea, B. 1983. Paedomorphism and neotony in the pygmy chimpanzee. *Science* 222: 521–22.

Smuts, B. 1985. *Sex and Friendship in Baboons.* Chicago: Aldine.

Sugiyama, Y. 1969. Social behavior of chimpanzees in the Budongo Forest, Uganda. *Primates* 10: 197.

Sugiyama, Y. 1972. Social characteristics and socialization of wild chimpanzees. In *Primate Socialization,* F. Poirier, ed., pp. 145–64. New York: Random House.

Susman, R. 1987. Chimpanzees: Pygmy chimpanzees and common chimpanzees: models for the behavioral ecology of the earliest hominids. In *The Evolution of Human Behavior: Primate Models.* W. Kinzey, ed., pp. 72–86. Albany: State University of New York Press.

Takahata, Y., T. Hasegawa, and T. Nishida. 1984. Chimpanzee predation in the Mahale Mountains from August 1979 to May 1982. *International Journal of Primatology* 5: 213–33.

Tanner, N. 1981. *On Becoming Human.* New York: Cambridge University Press.

Teleki, G. 1973. The omnivorous chimpanzee. *Scientific American* 228: 33.

Toshiada, N., S. Yehara, and N. Ramadhani. 1979. Predatory behavior among wild chimpanzees of the Mahale Mountains. *Primates* 20: 1–21.

van Lawick-Goodall, J. 1967. *My Friends the Wild Chimpanzees.* Washington: National Geographic Society.

van Lawick-Goodall, J. 1971. *In the Shadow of Man.* Boston: Houghton Mifflin.

Veit, P. 1982. Gorilla society. *Natural History* 91: 48–58.

Wrangham, R. 1974. Artificial feeding of chimpanzees and baboons in their natural habitat. *Animal Behaviour* 22: 83–93.

Wrangham, R. 1978. Sex differences in chimpanzee dispersion. In *The Great Apes,* D. Hamburg and E. McCown, eds., pp. 481–90. Menlo Park, Calif.: Benjamin/Cummings.

Wright, P. 1985. The costs and benefits of nocturnality for *Aotus trivirgatus* (the night monkey). Ph.D. dissertation, City University of New York.

Chapter

10

Analogues for Reconstructing Our Past

Because the fossil record limits the kinds of data that can be generated, scientists turn their attention to other sources of information to help reconstruct our past. Modern hunter-gatherers, for example, serve as analogues for reconstructing how our ancestors adapted to their environment and how they may have made and used tools. Nonhuman primates, our closest phylogenetic relatives, are studied to generate information about ecological and behavioral adaptations. Useful information can be had from watching social carnivores, for they live a mode of life—hunting—that characterizes part of our own past. Using nonhuman primate models stresses phylogenetic relationships while reliance on social carnivores stresses ecological relationships.

In the end, if any model proves useful in helping to reconstruct early human behavioral patterns and social organizations, it will have to be a unique model. We need, for example, not only to look for similarities between ourselves and nonhuman primates; we must also explore our differences. Models allow new inferences to be drawn and new insights to be reached. Models give new meaning to data. Without models little could be said about the behavior, diet, social organization, mating system, and so on, of long-extinct human ancestors.

OVERVIEW

This chapter will look at possible models for helping us understand and reconstruct early human behavior and social organizations. Models can be used in many ways, and various models have been proposed to enable us to understand human evolution. In this book, for example, various arguments (scenarios) have been proposed to try to help explain the appearance of a morphological or behavioral trait.

Many mistaken efforts have been made to rely on one model to explain unique traits in human evolution. Various definitions have been offered in an attempt to explain what it means to be called hominid, or human. One of the earliest explanations is the "man the hunter" hypothesis. In this scenario, first proposed by Darwin, hunting is promoted as the key behavioral feature redirecting human evolution. Among the many factors leading to the demise of this explanation was the realization that our earliest ancestors, the australopithecines, were more likely the hunted than the hunters (Chapter 17). Despite the many deficiences in the hunting scenario, it is clear that hunting and meat-eating played important roles at some point in human evolution and that hunting has affected our evolutionary history (Tooby and DeVore, 1987).

Another popular scenario has been Jolly's seed-eating hypothesis (the T-complex discussed in Chapter 10). According to this scenario, the basic early hominid dietary adaptation was feeding on seeds and other small objects. This diet purportedly led to a number of unique dental traits shared by both hominids and such monkeys as the gelada. A diet of seeds and small objects supposedly led to the initial divergence from a common ancestor of the human and ape lines. There is, however, evidence to refute this explanation.

A third scenario was proposed by Lovejoy, who argued that a key hominid innovation was monogamous pair bonding, leading to the early appearance of a nuclear family, and male provisioning, as enhanced by bipedal locomotion. Some problems with this scenario are discussed in Chapter 16. This scenario stressed the male's provisioning of a female and her youngster as an enhancement to their survival and the acquisition of bipedalism by males. Among other things, it failed to explain why females also became bipeds. An attempt to rectify this failure was provided by Tanner, in the "gathering by females" scenario. (This scenario is mentioned in several chapters in this book.) Tanner's gathering hypothesis has often been substituted for the hunting hypothesis. However, because both the gathering by females and hunting by males hypotheses stress the contributions of only one of the two sexes in our bisexual species, each fails as an explanation. An explanation cannot merely assert, as do both the gathering and hunting hypotheses, that one subsistence pattern is superior to or more reliable than another; it must show why such is the case.

Rather than propose here that one model or group of models is best for reconstructing human behavior and social organizations, we will present information from a number of models to show the kinds of information that can be gathered using a comparative approach. This approach is more eclectic. We look, for example, at the *possible* clues that can be provided from research on modern human hunter-gatherer populations, nonhuman primates, and social carnivores. Each of these sources presents certain kinds of information that can provide useful clues for reconstructing behavior and social organizations from bones and artifacts.

In using modern human populations and nonhuman primates as our models, we stress phylogeny (evolutionary relatedness) rather than ecology. When using social carnivores as models, we stress ecological relationships (hunting and meat eating) instead of phylogeny. When we stress analogies with nonhuman primates, we look at similar behaviors that have appeared in evolutionarily related species. When we stress analogies with social carnivores, we look at similar behaviors that have appeared in evolutionarily unrelated species. In the latter, any behavioral similarities are due to shared ecological pressures.

In the end, if any model proves useful in helping to reconstruct early human behavioral patterns and social organizations, it will have to be a unique model. Humans are unique animals, and we need to look at a number of models in order to reconstruct our past. (Both Kinzey, 1987, and Potts, 1987, make this point.) We must look not only for similarities between ourselves and nonhuman primates, but also for differences. Those differences, which make us unique, may be more important in helping to explain our evolutionary past than would long lists of similarities between humans and other phylogenetically or ecologically related species (Potts, 1987).

Despite the potential problems that accompany the use of models, the misuse of models, or the use of inappropriate models, models are necessary.

Models allow new inferences to be drawn and new insights to be reached. Models give new meaning to data. Without models, little could be said about the behavior, diet, social organization, mating systems, and so on of long-extinct human ancestors. According to Tooby and DeVore (1987:184), "models are essential for the reconstruction of hominid behavioral evolution." Models "offer the eventual prospect of alleviating the shortage of information about hominid evolution." The question is not whether we should use models; rather, the question is, what models are most useful and how can models best be used?

RATIONALE FOR USING A COMPARATIVE APPROACH

The fossil and archaeological record itself—that is, bones and traces of past behavior (artifacts) that have been preserved—is the major source of information about how human groups once looked and lived. This record is always incomplete, however (see Chapter 13), because it is based on relative degrees of preservation (Table 10-1). Furthermore, many aspects of behavior do not fossilize, and we are left to make inferences and educated guesses. Vital questions about the behavior and social organization of our ancestors can, at best, only partially be answered by the fossil and archaeological records. We seek more information and are not content simply to interpret preserved clues because behavioral and social changes are important in understanding our evolution.

The fossil record raises many questions, and the problem is to find the source or sources that are likely to yield the most appropriate answers. Studies of living species, including humans, have helped us to interpret archaeological findings and have supported arguments bearing on such major developments in human evolution as a bipedal gait, tool use and manufacture, scavenging and hunting, and social organization. The approach has been to rely on observable behavior as an aid for interpreting the behavior of extinct populations. Events in the prehistoric past cannot be observed directly; they can only be reconstructed from material evidence. Such reconstruction is based on analogy, whereby the identity of unknown forms or relationships are inferred from those already known.

Three main sources of information can help us to understand human evolution (see Table 10-2). For example, the few surviving groups of **hunter-gatherers,** people subsisting on wild plants and animals, have a way of life that is in some ways similar to the way all humans lived until about 15,000 years ago. No modern hunter-gatherer population provides a perfect model for reconstructing early human social organization or behavior. They can offer guidance in matters of interpretation, however. Contemporary hunting and gathering peoples are not living relics from the past. Like all other human cultural systems, they have been adapting to their environment for thousands

Table 10-1 Major Human Behavioral, Anatomical, and Physiological Changes Since the Human/Ape Divergence[*]

TRAIT	VISIBLE IN FOSSIL/ ARCHAEOLOGICAL RECORD	INFERRED
Anatomical/physiological traits		
Postcranial modification for bipedalism	X	
Modification of hands for effective tool use and manufacture	X	
Reorganization and enlargement of brain	X	
Reduction of face and jaws; remodeling of cranium, face, and jaws	X	
Reduction of body hair and changes in glands of the skin		X
Modified estrous (ovulation) cycle		X
Modification of vocal tract for speech	X	X
Changes relating to birth processes, i.e., lengthening of gestation, delayed maturation (seen in fossil record)	X	X
Behavioral social changes		
Development and consistent use of tools	X	
Inclusion of meat protein in diet; hunting behavior	X	
Temporarily defined home base	X	
Food-sharing and sexual division of labor	?	X
Controls on emotional displays		X
Larger social groups	X	
Permanent dwelling structures	X	
In much later periods we have evidence of art, symbolism, and spiritualism	X	
Extension of social bonding mechanisms	?	X

[*]These categories should not be considered absolute differentiators of human and nonhuman primates. For example, there are data on tool use and manufacture among some of the modern apes; consumption of animal protein, hunting, and scavenging among some monkeys and apes; and psychological attachment to a home area. It is more likely that the *combination* of these and other factors, rather than the presence of any one of them, is implicated in the differentiation of human and nonhuman primates. More items will be added as the volume of fossil and archaeological records increases.

of years. Nevertheless, of all existing societies, theirs is closest to the way of life that prevailed for most of human evolutionary history. Because humans lived as hunters and gatherers for most of our evolutionary history, it should be no surprise that some modern behavior has ancient roots.

Gifford (1980) discusses the contributions of **ethnoarchaeology**—that is, the use of living human populations as analogies for reconstructing the past. Although ethnoarchaeological research provides many clues for the study of extinct human populations, there is considerable debate concerning the nature and limits of ethnographic analogy for analyzing prehistoric behavior. For example, modern cultural systems probably do not reflect the full range of prehistoric cultural systems and behavior. Therefore, strict reliance upon analogy based on observations of modern hunter-gatherers severely limits the range of possible interpretations. Direct analogies between modern hunter-gatherers and earlier humans in terms of their cultural systems and organization may be misleading, because in some cases we may be studying the material effects of cultural behavior in adaptive systems vastly different from those of modern humans. The major problem with the comparative approach is an overreliance on the importance of material culture. Living societies whose technology is similar to that inferred from the archaeological record are sometimes incorrectly viewed as exact analogues for reconstructing the entire prehistoric culture.

Living nonhuman primates, especially the monkeys and apes, are an important source of information for reconstructing our past because of our shared evolutionary relationship and because some nonhuman primates, such as savanna baboons (Chapter 8), live in a habitat similar to that which was probably occupied by our early ancestors. The mode of adaptation of modern nonhuman primates to such habitat pressures as food getting and predator avoidance, and their social structures, are important clues for understanding human adaptations in similar environmental circumstances. Tool use and manufacture have been important features of human evolution for the past 2.5 million years, and until recently, most anthropologists believed that these behaviors were uniquely human. However, chimpanzees, our closest nonhuman primate relatives, make and use tools in a wide variety of circumstances (see Chapter 9). Our understanding of our evolutionary history is enhanced if we know how and in what situations the chimpanzee uses and makes tools. If we learn why chimpanzees make and use tools and many other nonhuman primates do not, we can begin to reconstruct the situation that led to our ancestors' commitment to tool use and manufacture.

Social carnivores, such as the hyena, hunting dog, and lion, are a third source of comparative data for reconstructing our evolutionary past. In contrast to nonhuman primates who are basically vegetarians with an occasional addition of meat to the diet, social carnivores provide clues for understanding the earliest hunting methods and the adaptiveness of food sharing. The archaeological record suggests that meat eating and tool using were important to human evolution. The social carnivores can provide useful insights when considering factors such as hunting techniques, the size of the home range, and the kinds and sizes of animals available to unsophisticated tool-using human hunters.

The point is not that we are, or ever were, nothing more than social carnivores, or that modern nonhuman primates are an adequate model for our evolutionary past. That would be nonsense, because modern social carnivores and nonhuman primates have evolved, as we have, and they can serve only as models. We have just as much to learn when such models clarify our uniquenesses as when they provide data highlighting our commonalities. The more we know about the evolutionary history and adaptations of our evolutionarily related primate relatives and the ecologically related social carnivores, the more we learn about processes that shaped our evolutionary past. Nonhuman primates, social carnivores, and extant hunter-gatherers provide an array of natural experiments with their various adaptations to multiple habitat demands.

The comparative method can help us to determine similarities and differences between certain phenomena in human and other animal species, and can enable us to begin to understand how we are similar to or different from other primates. It will not by itself establish the causes of such similarities and differences, however. Because the comparative method does not consider all possibilities, comparisons are open to a voluntarily or involuntarily biased selection of examples. Nonhuman primates, for instance, are so varied that it is not difficult to find one or several examples to bolster any view one espouses. Comparative discussions of social behavior are particularly prone to the introduction of culturally loaded generalizations, with the assumption that such generalizations are true of all people.

LESSONS LEARNED FROM MODERN HUNTER-GATHERERS

In 1966 it was estimated that there were 30,000 hunter-gatherers in a world population of about 4.5 billion. The number has since been reduced.

Australian Aborigines

One of the first to study hunter-gathering people with the idea of collecting data to help reconstruct the past was an archaeologist Richard Gould (1968a, b). Over a 15-month period, Gould studied a two-family group of 13 people. These groups were among the very few people in the world still regularly making and using stone tools. Gould noted how the group lived, collecting information on tool making, food sources, camping, and the like that might bear on the interpretation of prehistoric sites and the reconstruction of prehistoric social behavior.

During the height of the Australian summer (December and January), the day begins just before sunrise. Obtaining the daily food begins at around 6:00 or 7:00 A.M., before it becomes unbearably hot. The group divides into two parties in search of food; everyone leaves camp. The women gather plant foods and may walk 4 or 5 miles carrying nursing children on their hips or on their backs. While the women are out collecting, the men are hunting—generally a less dependable way of obtaining food in the desert. Hunting usually occurs by ambushing prey at or near a water hole used by such animals as the emu, kangaroo, or wallaby. On most occasions, all that the men have to show for their efforts is a lizard or other small game. Women are more apt than the men to provide the daily food requirements. Roughly 60 to 70 percent of the aborigine's diet is plant food.

Aborigines may use their teeth either as tools or for making tools. The

---

Table 10-2 Information that can be Gathered Using the Comparative Approach

---

Modern Hunting and Gathering Peoples

Site formation

Food sources

Methods of tool manufacture and tool use

Movement patterns; features (social or ecological) that influence movement

Use of the teeth as tools, and the resulting dental damage

Size of the social groups; social or natural mechanisms that affect group sizes

Sex roles; the part played by each sex in gathering foods, for example

Health, mortality and morbidity patterns

Nonhuman Primates

The range of social organizations and social behaviors

Ecological adaptations—helps to reconstruct behavior and social organizations

Food sources—helps to assess what part of the diet was plant protein and what part was animal protein

Sex roles

The importance of social life and learning of social behaviors

Social Carnivores

How to effectively hunt without tools and language

What the remnants of a social carnivore's meal looks like and what part of animals they eat—helps to interpret archaeological bone deposits

---

premolar teeth may be used to nibble flakes from stone; the teeth and the supporting jaw structure are quite strong. Aborigine tooth use is an example of how modern groups can help us understand some skeletal traits found in the fossil record. Because dental remains make up a large proportion of the fossil record and because a number of inferences are based on dental wear patterns, it is helpful to note how modern populations use their teeth. By observing the ways in which teeth are used as tools, we can see what types of wear patterns result. Records of various dietary patterns can help researchers understand what types of wear patterns result from different diets. A study of tooth use can also be helpful in explaining cranial morphology; for example, the researcher can observe the effect of the use of the teeth as tools on the chewing musculature and surface features of the skull or jaw.

Kalahari !Kung San

A long-term effort is being expended to gather information on the San people who lived in the Kalahari Desert of Botswana in southern Africa. Approximately one-third of all existing hunter-gatherers (some 9,000 people) once inhabited the Kalahari. One study concentrated on the inhabitants of one small area of this 350,000 square mile expanse. The study area had a radius of 20 miles, was surrounded by vast stretches of waterless expanse, and included 11 permanent water holes and wells, between 400 and 500 plant and animal species, and about 450 San people.

Researchers investigated the San's health and nutrition, family and group structure, personal relationships, tool technology, and general methods of coping with environmental pressures. Archaeologists excavated San living floors and asked questions about what they uncovered, hoping to generate alternative interpretations for prehistoric living sites. Garbage dumps were explored to analyze the kinds and amounts of accumulations left from meals and meal preparation. These data provide a clearer explanation of the many seemingly prehistoric "garbage dumps." They provide information on how many people and days it might take to accumulate debris and what items are most likely to be preserved.

Much time was spent recording what the !Kung San eat and how they obtain food. Prior to the study it was assumed that the hunter-gatherer's life bordered on starvation and that the task of finding food was all-consuming. For the San, the basic tools for food gathering include a pair of unworked hammerstones for cracking nuts and a digging stick. The most important item is the "kaross," a combination garment and receptacle made of antelope hide draped over a woman's shoulder. Into the pocket formed by the draping women put food, such as nuts, berries, and roots, and their children. (Because of its utilitarian value, some sort of carrying device may have been developed early in human evolution.)

A study was made of the factors affecting the choice of San living sites; and efforts were made to develop a clearer idea of the significance of living floor patterns found at long deserted sites. Researchers attempted to discern the factors that determine the choice of a living site and that force people to move from one camp to another. San camps are typically occupied for weeks or months before the San deplete the food supplies and are forced to move. Such very basic information may help to explain some of the migrations of prehistoric populations.

One result of studies of hunting and gathering societies has been the so-called magic numbers hypothesis (Birdsell, 1972). The "magic numbers" of 25 and 500 refer to hunter-gatherer band and tribe sizes, respectively. These numbers suggest the existence of social regularities that we do not yet fully understand. Birdsell, studying rates of population growth among Australian aborigines, noted that band sizes ranged from 20 to 50 people. He selected 25 as a representative number. Studies of the !Kung San and other hunter-gatherers support the finding that 25 is the average group size. Prehistoric populations also probably averaged close to 25 members per band. Although there is nothing absolute about the number 25, it may represent the most efficient size of working groups of adults, and it is generally consistent with the average size of many primate social groups.

The second "magic number," 500, is a purely human phenomenon and is an average for a dialect tribe of hunter-gatherers, all of whom speak the same dialect. The number 500 is not an absolute figure, and Birdsell has noted that the sizes of individual macrobands may range from as low as 200 to more than 800 persons. The number 500 becomes meaningful only after one considers the census figures for a large number of tribes.

The number 500 may reflect certain features of the human communication system. The unity of hunting and gathering societies depends on face-to-face contact, on close intimacy among members of its component bands. This unity creates the impression of belonging to an extended community, even though various bands may live miles apart and come together only at certain times of the year. The intimacy between the bands is based not only on sharing the same language, but also on a store of shared knowledge.

There seems to be a basic limit to the number of persons capable of knowing one another well enough to maintain a tribal identity at the hunter-gatherer level. Murdock (noted in Pfeiffer, 1969) has also demonstrated the relevance of the number 500 in many aspects of American society. For example, an architect's rule of thumb states that the enrollment of an elementary school should not exceed 500 pupils if the principal expects to know them all by name.

The underlying mechanisms accounting for the "magic numbers" is yet to be fully understood. The memory capacity of the human brain must be relevant, as must be the possibility that 500 people constitute the most effective breeding population.

Studies of modern gathering and hunting societies forced researchers to reassess a number of ideas about the social organizations and behaviors of our ancestors. For example, it was once argued that hunting was the pursuit that bonded males together and that it was the basis for an apparent male dominance in society. A strong male bias permeated theory building in human evolution. Hunting, primarily a male activity, was romanticized; hunting was supposedly an activity requiring considerable intelligence and a complex tool assemblage. Gathering, primarily a female activity, was supposedly a simple task requiring a simple tool assemblage and little specialized knowledge. Through a lack of information, and with apparent cultural biases, interpretations relegated females to a secondary role as food providers. Their role in human evolution was dismissed as peripheral largely through the error of omission or conscious disregard.

This unfortunate bias has begun to disappear. Plant gathering is not only a major economic strategy, with females often providing the majority of the food; it is also a complex activity requiring no less specialized knowledge than any other food-getting activity. Plant gathering requires a knowledge of where to find the plants, in what seasons they are edible, how to obtain hard-to-get plants, and how to prepare them. In a bisexual species, such as humans, both sexes are important for survival and evolutionary success. The sexual bias that characterized recent theories of human evolution reflected cultural biases and not biological realities. Studies of modern hunter-gatherers helped reveal this bias.

LESSONS LEARNED FROM THE NONHUMAN PRIMATES

As noted in previous chapters, monkeys and apes generally live in social groups that are organized on the basis of age, sex, relative dominance, and kinship. Life in a social group is a mammalian trait that predates the evolution of the primates. Primate groups are usually characterized by interanimal cooperation; status differentiation according to age, sex, and kinship ties; a rather complex communication system; and social traditions. Primate societies have certain unique traits that differentiate them from other animal societies. Primate groups are usually permanent, year-round, and bisexual, as opposed to the seasonal, sometime unisexual groupings of many other social animals. In many mammals it is exclusively the mother that rears the young; in contrast, the primate infant is raised and socialized in a stable social group (however, socialization is primarily left to the mothers and their female relatives [Poirier, 1972, 1973]). Social behavior is the key to understanding primate life, and life in a social group is the primate's key to evolutionary success.

Social living places a premium on learning. Many animals, such as birds and fish, have social behaviors that are largely dependent on fixed, genetically based cues. Primates, in contrast, respond not only to fixed cues but also to learned behaviors, which results in considerable behavioral flexibility. Because there is considerable individual and behavioral variability, a primate must be flexible and discriminating in its behavioral responses. One important adaptive trait common to primates is their high degree of behavioral flexibility and their ability to behaviorally adjust to rapidly changing social and habitat conditions (Poirier, 1969).

Because much of primate behavior results from learning, and because learned behavior may not be transferable to all segments of the population, primatologists have reported considerable intertroop behavioral variability within the same species. Intraspecific comparative studies are imperative before it can be stated with any degree of confidence that a behavior or social organization characteristic of one social group typifies the genus or even the species, or that it has significance for understanding human evolution. Behavioral variability was probably an essential trait that allowed early human ancestors to move from the forest to the savanna habitat.

The social group has long characterized primate evolution; indeed, the social group has long been a mammalian trait. Group characteristics, such as the degree of sociality, dominance expression, sexuality, and interanimal relationships, vary; however, most primates spend part of their life in close association with other members of their species. Within the social group an animal learns to adapt to its surroundings. Differences between primate societies depend not only on the species' biology but also to a great extent on the circumstances in which animals live and learn. Because most primates live a rather complex social life, they must learn to adjust to one another. Compared to most of the rest of the animal world, primate societies have the greatest differentiation of learned social roles.

Social living is requisite for the young primate to perform effectively as an adult of its species. Animals with restricted social experiences, such as those raised in isolation, exhibit some social maladjustment, especially in mothering, sexual, grooming, and aggressive behaviors. All of these are learned behaviors. The full development of a primate's biological potential requires the stimulus usually provided by other members of the social group.

Social life is important, but not all primates have the same degree of social life. Among arboreal primates, for example, protection may come not by cooperative group action, but instead by an individual's dashing through the nearest trees. If, as in some instances, a group existence does not result in reduction of predation or increased social behavior, why then do most primates still reside in social groups? A primary reason for group living may be an enhancement of learning; the group has a pool of knowledge and experience that far exceeds that of its individual constituents (Washburn and Hamburg, 1965). Group experience is transmitted across generations and becomes the basis of troop traditions. Troop traditions, the sum of individual learning experiences, are more advantageous for survival than individual learning in many situations, especially if a new behavior is difficult to acquire individually in direct interaction with the environment. Troop tradition assumes a long life expectancy, also a primate trait.

Within the social context, an animal learns about appropriate diet, existing predators, and the correct mode of behavioral interaction. Primates living in a social group benefit from the shared knowledge and experience of the species. The primary reinforcement for primate learning is the social context, the group in which the infant is born and nurtured. Even activities that indicate individual independence, such as observing, manipulating, and exploring, are facilitated or inhibited by the group setting. Individual behaviors are controlled by a continuous process of social learning arising from group interactional patterns. Animals whose behaviors do not conform sufficiently to group norms are less likely to reproduce.

LESSONS LEARNED FROM SOCIAL CARNIVORES

The search for clues about our past among nonhuman primates is reasonable on evolutionary grounds because we are genetically related; it is less reasonable on ecological grounds because social systems are strongly influenced by the habitat. Monkeys and apes are essentially vegetarians who live in groups confined to small home ranges. We assume, however, that our ancestors were widely roaming and were hunters and gatherers for a substantial part of our evolutionary history. This way of life is in strong contrast to that of modern nonhuman primates. Schaller and Lowther (1968) concluded that more could be learned about the genesis of our social system by studying phylogenetically unrelated but ecologically similar forms. Social carnivores were the obvious subjects. Some of the selective pressures influencing the existence of social carnivores also had an impact on human societies.

The analogy is imperfect, however. When we compare human hunting to carnivore hunting, we may miss the special nature of the human hunting adaptation. For example, human females do not hunt and then regurgitate the kill to their young upon their return to a den. Nor do human young stay in dens; they can be carried. Male wolves do not kill with tools, butcher, and share with others who have been gathering other food.

Some researchers are documenting what social carnivores, such as leopards, eat, and are especially interested in the remains of a meal. Which bones are eaten, which are left behind, and the state of the leftovers are all important clues in determining whether bone accumulations were left by an ancient hominid hunter or by an ancient carnivore. A study of the food remains of gnawing rodents can also help us understand old bone deposits. For example, porcupine burrows are being excavated to determine which bones porcupines store and how they eat these bones. The reason for such an approach is to determine which bone accumulations were left by humans and which by nonhuman predators and scavengers. The practical implications of such studies will be discussed later.

Few researchers would once have suspected that in order to learn about our past, anthropologists would be studying nonhuman primates, feeding leopards to study the composition of the leftovers, or crawling into hyena dens and excavating porcupine burrows to see what kinds of bones they collect.

Modern hunting-gathering populations have provided clues to the kinds of food resources exploited and the manner of food preparation. In their variety of social organizations, monkeys and apes provide clues to our ancestors' adaptations to differing habitat pressures. The remains of a social carnivore's meal may provide clues as to who accumulated bone assemblages in the fossil record. These are but a few of the lessons that can be learned through the judicious use of the comparative approach.

BIBLIOGRAPHY

BIRDSELL, J. 1972. *Human Evolution.* Chicago: Rand McNally.

CAMPBELL, B. 1976. *Humankind Emerging.* Boston: Little, Brown.

FREEMAN, L. 1968. A theoretical framework for interpreting archaeological materials. In *Man the Hunter,* R. Lee and I. DeVore, eds., pp. 262–67. Chicago: Aldine.

GHIGLIERI, M. 1987. Sociobiology of the great apes and the hominid ancestor. *Journal of Human Evolution* 16: 319–58.

GIFFORD, D. 1980. Ethnoarchaeological contributions to the taphonomy of human sites. In *Fossils in the Making: Vertebrate Taphonomy and Paleoecology,* A. Behrensmeyer and A. Hill, eds., pp. 94–107. Chicago: University of Chicago Press.

GOULD, R. 1968a. *Chipping Stone in the Outback.* Garden City, N.Y.: Natural History Press.

GOULD, R. 1968b. Living archaeology: The Ngatatjara of western Australia. *Southwestern Journal of Anthropology* 24: 101–22.

HARLOW, H. 1963. Basic social capacity of primates. In *Primate Social Behavior,* C. Southwick, ed., pp. 153–61. Princeton, N.J.: D. Van Nostrand.

HARLOW, H. 1966. The primate socialization motives. *Transactions and Studies of the College of Physicians of Philadelphia* 33: 224–37.

HOWELL, N. 1979. *Demography of the Dobe !Kung.* New York: Academic Press.

HRDY, S. 1981. *The Woman That Never Evolved.* Cambridge, Mass.: Harvard University Press.

JAY, P. (ed.) 1968. *Primates: Studies in Adaptation and Variability.* New York: Holt, Rinehart and Winston.

JOLLY, A. 1972. *The Evolution of Primate Behavior.* New York: Macmillan.

JOLLY, C., and F. PLOG 1976. *Physical Anthropology and Archaeology.* New York: Knopf.

KINZEY, W. 1987. Introduction. In *The Evolution of Human Behavior: Primate Models,* W. Kinzey, ed., pp. vii–xvi. Albany: State University of New York Press.

LANCASTER, J. 1975. *Primate Behavior and the Emergence of Human Culture.* New York: Holt, Rinehart and Winston.

LEE, R. 1978. *The !Kung San.* New York: Cambridge University Press.

LEWIN, R. 1988. New views emerge on hunters and gatherers. *Science* 240: 1146–48.

McGREW, W. 1972. *An Ethological Study of Children's Behavior.* New York: Academic Press.

MASON, W. 1965. The social development of monkeys and apes. In *Primate Behavior,* I. DeVore, ed., pp. 514–44. New York: Holt, Rinehart and Winston.

MORRIS, D. 1967. *The Naked Ape.* New York: McGraw-Hill.

PFEIFFER, J. 1969. *The Emergence of Man.* New York: Harper & Row, Pub.

PFEIFFER, J. 1972. *The Emergence of Man,* 2d ed. New York: Harper & Row, Pub.

POIRIER, F. 1969. Behavioral flexibility and intertroop variability among Nilgiri langurs of South India. *Folia Primatologica* 11: 119–33.

POIRIER, F. 1970. Nilgiri langur ecology and social behavior. In *Primate Behavior: Developments in Field and Laboratory Research,* vol. 1, L. Rosenblum, ed., pp. 251–383. New York: Academic Press.

POIRIER, F. 1972. Introduction. In *Primate Socialization,* F. Poirier, ed., pp. 3–29. New York: Random House.

POIRIER, F. 1973. Primate socialization and learning. In *Learning and Culture,* S. Kimball and J. Burnett, eds., pp. 3–41. Seattle: University of Washington Press.

POTTS, R. 1987. Reconstructions of early hominid socioecology: A critique of primate models. In *The Evolution of Human Behavior: Primate Models,* W. Kinzey, ed., pp. 28–47. Albany: State University of New York Press.

RADINSKY, L. 1975. Primate brain evolution. *American Scientist* 63: 656–63.

REYNOLDS, P. 1977. The emergence of early hominid social organization. I. The attachment system. *Yearbook of Physical Anthropology* 20: 73–95.

REYNOLDS, V. 1967. *The Apes.* New York: Dutton.

RICHARD, A., and S. SCHULMAN. 1982. Sociobiology: Primate field studies. *Annual Review of Anthropology* 11: 231–55.

SCHALLER, G. 1972. *The Serengeti Lion.* Chicago: University of Chicago Press.

SCHALLER, G., and G. LOWTHER. 1968. The relevance of carnivore behavior to the study of early hominids. *Southwestern Journal Anthropology* 25: 307.

SHARER, R., and W. ASHMORE. 1979. *Fundamentals of Archaeology.* Menlo Park, Calif.: Benjamin/Cummings.

THOMPSON, J. 1975. A cross-species analysis of carnivore, primate, and hominid behavior. *Journal of Human Evolution* 4: 113–24.

TIGER, L. 1969. *Men in Groups.* New York: Vintage.

TIGER, L., and R. FOX. 1971. *The Imperial Animal.* New York: Holt, Rinehart and Winston.

TOOBY, J., and I. DEVORE. 1987. The reconstruction of hominid behavioral evolution through strategic modelling. In *The Evolution of Human Behavior: Primate Models,* W. Kinzey, ed., pp. 183–237. Albany: State University of New York Press.

VAN LAWICK, H., and J. VAN LAWICK-GOODALL. 1970. *Innocent Killers.* New York: Ballantine.

WASHBURN, S. (ed.) 1961. *Social Life of Early Man.* Chicago: Aldine.

WASHBURN, S., and I. DEVORE. 1961. The social life of baboons. *Scientific American* 204: 62–71.

WASHBURN, S., and D. HAMBURG. 1965. Implications of primate research. In *Primate Behavior,* I. DeVore, ed., pp. 607–22. New York: Holt, Rinehart and Winston.

WASHBURN, S., and R. MOORE. 1974. *Ape Into Man: A Study of Human Evolution.* Boston: Little, Brown.

Chapter

11

Determining

Evolutionary

Relationships

MAMMALIA.

ORDER I. PRIMATES.

Fore-teeth cutting; upper 4, parallel; teats 2 pectoral.

1. HOMO.

Sapiens. Diurnal; varying by education and fituation.

    2. Four-footed, mute, hairy.   *Wild Man.*

    3. Copper-coloured, choleric, erect.   *American.*

        Hair black, ftraight, thick; *noftrils* wide, *face* harfh; *beard* fcanty; *obftinate*, content free. *Paints* himfelf with fine red lines. *Regulated* by cuftoms.

    4. Fair, fanguine, brawny.   *European.*

        Hair yellow, brown, flowing; *eyes* blue; *gentle*, acute, inventive. *Covered* with clofe veftments. *Governed* by laws.

    5. Sooty, melancholy, rigid.   *Afiatic.*

        Hair black; *eyes* dark; *fevere*, haughty, covetous. *Covered* with loofe garments. *Governed* by opinions.

    6. Black, phlegmatic, relaxed.   *African.*

        Hair black, frizzled; *fkin* filky; *nofe* flat; *lips* tumid; *crafty*, indolent, negligent. *Anoints* himfelf with greafe. *Governed* by caprice.

Monftrofus Varying by climate or art.

    1. Small, active, timid.   *Mountaineer.*

    2. Large, indolent.   *Patagonian.*

    3. Lefs fertile.   *Hottentot.*

    4. Beardlefs.   *American.*

    5. Head conic.   *Chinefe.*

    6. Head flattened.   *Canadian.*

The anatomical, phyfiological, natural, moral, civil and focial hiftories of man, are beft defcribed by their refpective writers.

Vol. I.—C   2. SIMIA.

An understanding of the world of living organisms requires the placement of the multiplicity of plants and animals into a rational and manageable system. Systematics *is the study of the types and diversity of living organisms and their interrelationships. The classification system that is used to place life forms into groups provides a simple means of reference.* Nomenclature *is the assignment of names to related groups of plants or animals. The two basic taxonomic units are the* species *and the* genus.

A species is a group whose members have the greatest genetic resemblance. A species is a group of individuals that can interbreed and produce fertile offspring. Under normal conditions, members of one species can not breed with members of another species. Groups of species sharing similar traits are placed into a single genus. The scientific name of an organism contains both a genus and a species referent. This is a called a binomial, which for modern humans is Homo sapiens.

LINNAEAN CLASSIFICATION SYSTEM

The eighteenth century was a time of considerable research in the fields of comparative anatomy and systematics. Eighteenth-century scientific inquiry was characterized by a concept known as **naturalism,** whereby humans were viewed as a natural phenomenon, as part of the universe and as governed by its laws. As early as 1732, Swedish botanist Carolus Linnaeus discussed the relationship between human and nonhuman primates. In the tenth edition of his book *Systema Naturae*, he placed humans within the Anthropomorpha, a group which included all other known primates. Although Linnaeus appreciated the morphological similarity between human and nonhuman primates, he did not understand the ultimate reason for this similarity; that is, he failed to realize their evolutionary relationship.

The presently used classification system is based on Linnaeus's work. The Linnaean classification system is hierarchical; that is, categories in the system are based on shared traits. Categories, such as kingdoms, containing the largest number of forms are the most inclusive, and categories such as species are the least inclusive. Organisms in the same kingdom, such as the Animal Kingdom, are less closely related than are organisms in the same species.

The process of classification is subject to many problems, not the least of which is the fact that the Linnaean system was not designed to convey evolutionary information. The Linnaean system was first seen to represent the "real world" as created by a Supreme Being. All species represented in the Linnaean system were thought to be permanent and immutable results of a special creation. The Linnaean system is so devised that **taxa** are unable to reflect the nature of evolutionary change. (A **taxon,** plural *taxa,* is any group of organisms within the classificatory system that is related to another group by descent from a common ancestor. This group is distinctive enough to be given a name to differentiate it from other groups.) Although evolution is a process of change linking one life form with another, the Linnaean system is able to

MAMMALIA.

ORDER I. PRIMATES.

Fore-teeth cutting; upper 4, parallel; teats 2 pectoral.

1. HOMO.

Sapiens. Diurnal; varying by education and fituation.
2. Four-footed, mute, hairy.   *Wild Man.*
3. Copper-coloured, choleric, erect.   *American.*
    Hair black, ftraight, thick; *noftrils* wide, *face* harfh; *beard* fcanty; *obftinate,* content free. *Paints* himfelf with fine red lines. *Regulated* by cuftoms.
4. Fair, fanguine, brawny.   *European.*
    Hair yellow, brown, flowing; *eyes* blue; *gentle,* acute, inventive. *Covered* with clofe veftments. *Governed* by laws.
5. Sooty, melancholy, rigid.   *Afiatic.*
    Hair black; *eyes* dark; *fevere,* haughty, covetous. *Covered* with loofe garments. *Governed* by opinions.
6. Black, phlegmatic, relaxed.   *African.*
    Hair black, frizzled; *fkin* filky; *nofe* flat; *lips* tumid; *crafty,* indolent, negligent. *Anoints* himfelf with greafe. *Governed* by caprice.

Monftrofus Varying by climate or art.
1. Small, active, timid.   *Mountaineer.*
2. Large, indolent.   *Patagonian.*
3. Lefs fertile.   *Hottentot.*
4. Beardlefs.   *American.*
5. Head conic.   *Chinefe.*
6. Head flattened.   *Canadian.*

The anatomical, phyfiological, natural, moral, civil and focial hiftories of man, are beft defcribed by their refpective writers.

Vol. I.—C   2. SIMIA.

Figure 11-1 Linnaeus' classification of the genus Homo.

represent only discontinuous relationships; it is a static, two-dimensional framework, whereas evolution is dynamic and multidimensional and results from change through time. Since Darwin's work, the zoological classificatory system has slowly been modified to incorporate the viewpoint that the living world is constantly changing, evolving new forms from old.

BASIC RULES OF NOMENCLATURE

Although various rules are used to establish categories within the classification system, it must be remembered that the system is arbitrary and that names are imposed on forms in nature for convenience. The procedures employed in determining the group, or taxon, to which an organism belongs usually include a subjective element, such as the determination of which traits are evolutionarily relevant. This subjective element produces many of the disagreements noted in the chapters on primate evolution, for example.

A set of rules embodied in what are called the "codes" of nomenclature must be followed when assigning a scientific name to an organism. These rules have been established over many years and function to ensure clarity and usefulness. The codes of nomenclature help eliminate or reduce confusion and ensure a common language in biological classification.

The smallest taxon regularly used in the classification scheme is the **species.** Species that are more similar to one another than to other species are grouped into a category called the **genus.** Likewise, many genera (the plural of *genus)* are grouped into families, families into orders, orders into classes, and classes into phyla. Most living organisms also belong to either the animal or the plant kingdom, the highest classificatory units. (See Table 12-1 for an example.)

All taxonomic groups of any one kind, like the family, are supposed to differ from related groups belonging to the same order by a roughly equal degree. The same degree of difference should be found in each order. In the modern taxonomic system, biological classification is usually intended to reflect degrees of evolutionary relationship. The system is not rigid; it is always subject to modification as more is learned about any organism within the system.

The two categories within the classification system to which we continually refer are the genus and the species. The species, which is also discussed in this chapter, is the group whose members have the greatest genetic resemblance. The term *species* usually refers to a group of individuals that can interbreed and produce fertile offspring but cannot breed with members of another species.

A **species** is a group of organisms whose ecologic and physiologic functions are the same and whose offspring are similar and capable of reproducing the same line. This definition of a species is imperfect. When the concepts of time and evolution are superimposed, we discover that in those cases in which complete lineages are known (ancestors and descendants through millions of years and many species), there is morphological and reproductive overlap through many populations.

The problem with the species concept is that the degree of reproductive isolation is sometimes unknown. It may not be possible to know, especially with fossil or paleospecies, whether two kinds of organisms were able to breed under natural conditions. Furthermore, organisms meeting the criteria for separate species under natural conditions may breed in artificial conditions such as zoos and laboratories. Taxonomists thus often recognize species on the basis of differences that are assumed to reflect the consequences of reproductive isolation.

Local differences can occur among members of the same species. These small differences, maintained by partial reproductive isolation, are recognized in classification as **subspecies.** Subspeciation can be the first step on the road to speciation.

Groups of species sharing similar traits are placed into a single genus. Species belonging to one genus usually share the same broad adaptive zone. This represents a general ecological life-style more basic than the more specialized niches characteristic of a species.

The ecological definition of a genus is very important to understanding the evolutionary relationships among fossil remains. For example, limb bones are often a good indication of the type of locomotion practiced, and locomotion is strongly tied to the habitat. If there are indications from the fossil record that a creature inhabited an ecological zone different from that of previously described creatures, then we are justified in supposing more than one genus.

The scientific name of an organism contains its genus and species designation. A subspecies might also be assigned. Assignment of generic and specific names follows the Linnaean system of establishing a binomial (that is, a two-term name) that must be applied to each newly described species. Taking as an example modern humans, the binomial reference is *Homo sapiens.* A third modifier, the subspecies designation, is used to distinguish modern humans from our ancestors. Thus, we establish the taxon of *Homo sapiens sapiens.* The genus designation always begins with a capital letter, the species and subspecies designations begin with a lowercase letter. The binomial always appears in italics or is underscored. Categories such as the family are not italicized or underscored, but they too begin with capital letters. Modern humans and their ancestors belong to the family Hominidae.

You might ask, why use the binomial? Why not refer to animals and plants by a common name, such as *horse* or *rose?* We cannot do this because there are many millions of different species of plants and animals alive today. In the past, there may have been many millions more. There are not enough common names to go around, and they differ in different languages. Scientific names are universally understood.

A **type specimen** must be designated whenever a new species is described. The type is a particular specimen—a single designated skull, for example—that establishes the criteria for a certain classification, and is the specimen to which all unidentified new finds are compared. Types are established at the species, genus, and family levels. The type of a species is an individual specimen; for a genus, the type is a species; and for a family, the type is established on a genus. The type specimen, being only one specimen, may not be typical of the group it is meant to represent because it is unlikely that one specimen can exhibit the range of physical variation characterizing a group. This poses a serious problem.

The concept of type grew out of the belief in the immutability of the species. An individual specimen was inappropriately idealized as a representative of all members of the species. The concept of type led to the false premise that a single specimen—the type—would be a sufficient sample for the species. With the development of population genetics, stressing that populations, and not individuals, are the evolutionary units, there was a shift from considering individual specimens to studying large samples. (Unfortunately, large samples are rarely found in the fossil record.)

Once a species becomes established, its status often becomes quite fixed in its classification. It must be borne in mind, however, that a biological entity, such as that represented by the Middle Pleistocene human group *Homo erectus,* is a dynamic, living creature and not a fixed type. *Homo erectus* eventually changed to the extent that scientists who discovered the remains of its descendants called them *Homo sapiens.* There was a biological continuum between *Homo erectus* and ourselves. Although scientific convention draws discrete boundaries between ourselves, *Homo sapiens,* and *Homo erectus,* these boundaries could not have existed in biological reality.

ESTABLISHING EVOLUTIONARY RELATIONSHIPS

The scientist follows a number of guidelines in evaluating evolutionary relationships among fossils. For example, there should always be an economy of hypotheses; all available, reliable material and their affinities should be embraced by a single scheme. If a new specimen is found, and if the evaluation of the form is inconsistent with present taxonomic schemes, it may be best to defer judgment until further material is uncovered.

Taxonomic assessments should be based on a well-authenticated, reliably dated, and fairly complete fossil sample. This criterion is often difficult to meet because we are extremely fortunate when we find a fairly complete sample that can be dated. (Dating methods are discussed in Chapter 13).

When evaluating evolutionary relationships among fossils, one must be aware of several potential problems. For example, the aging process can lead to considerable modification in the structure and proportions of the skeleton. Because age changes are so marked, it would be improper to compare, for example, a few measurements of the adult human skull to those of a juvenile ape and to infer from such a comparison that the former is not markedly different from the apes in general. Terrestrial primates generally exhibit considerable **sexual dimorphism**—that is, physical differences between males and females. (See Figure 11-2.) Because the degree of sexual dimorphism is an important consideration in evaluating fossil samples, male specimens must be compared with male specimens and female specimens with female specimens.

It is also important to keep in mind the possibility of **mosaic evolution,** a situation in which different morphological traits evolve at different rates. At different stages in the evolutionary history of the Hominidae, the human family, different morphological features were of different taxonomic relevance. For example, **bipedalism,** walking upright on two legs, is one of the taxonomically relevant features in distinguishing the earliest human ancestors from the apes. Although the earliest humans were bipedally erect, as are

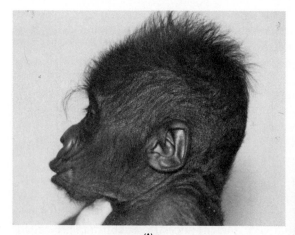

(A)

(B)

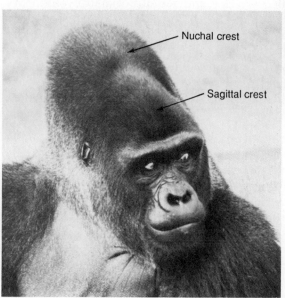

Nuchal crest

Sagittal crest

(C)

Figure 11-2 This series of three photographs shows the developmental and sexually dimorphic variability in the appearance of the sagittal crest in gorillas. (A) An infant male lowland gorilla (Gorilla gorilla gorilla) in whom the segittal crest has not yet developed. (B) A 28-year-old female lowland gorilla without a sagittal crest. The crest seldom appears in females because of lesser development of huge jaw muscles. (C) A 15-year-old male lowland gorilla with a large sagittal and nuchal crest.

modern humans, they differed significantly from modern humans in terms of the shape of their face and skull and in the size of their brain. Different parts of the human body evolved at differing rates.

Once all relevant features have been considered, organisms are fitted onto a **phylogenetic tree,** a branching diagram on which each species is represented as a separate branch. The branches on the tree are called **clades,** groups of species sharing a common ancestor. A number of assumptions are followed when determining where a form or species fits in terms of its evolutionary relationship to other known forms or species. These assumptions include the following:

1. Forms sharing detailed resemblances are usually closely related. In general, the more two forms resemble each other, the more recent their shared ancestry. Some resemblances are not due to a shared recent ancestry, however, but to a very ancient ancestry. Such traits are called *primitive traits.* For example, many animals share the human trait of five digits on the hands and feet. The fact that both turtles and humans have five digits does not reflect a close and recently shared evolutionary relationship. Such resemblances tell us about the function of turtle appendages and human appendages, rather than indicating a close evolutionary relationship.

2. Clades are recognized by the sharing of **derived traits,** which result from a recent adaptation. Shared derived characteristics not immediately related to function are more likely to reflect an evolutionary relationship than shared derived characteristics immediately related to function.

The researcher must take care to ensure that similar traits are not due to either **parallelism** or **convergence,** both of which may inappropriately imply close evolutionary relationships when none exists. Parallelisms, structural similarities within a related group, arise independently in more than one segment of a group. For instance, among primates, which are basically arboreal, long forearms have independently evolved a number of times in different lines as adaptations for hanging and feeding. Convergence occurs when remotely related forms come to resemble one another because of similar adaptations. When similarities in adaptive relationships or structures develop in species that are not closely related, they are said to have *converged.* Flippers in whales, seals, and sea cows exemplify convergent evolution.

SPECIATION

The species concept is the key concept in modern evolutionary biology. A *species* is a group of actually or potentially interbreeding organisms that are reproductively isolated from other such groups. Reproductive isolation, the principle criterion for defining a genetic species, is often correlated with geographical isolation. A population adapts to local environmental conditions. Such adaptations, molded by natural selection, may eventually result in genetic differences in local areas. Eventually, because of reproductive isolation, differences can accumulate and result in speciation.

The division of an evolutionary lineage into a temporal species is somewhat arbitrary, and is often a matter of definition and convenience. When enough change has occurred, it is convenient to divide the lineage into time segments and give them different species names. This division into segments and the assignment of names can lead to problems; some are discussed in the chapters on human evolution.

The transformation of one species from another of the same lineage is called **anagenesis,** or **phyletic evolution** (Figure 11-3). Anagenesis, the type of speciation envisioned by Darwin, results from the gradual accumulation of small changes caused by mutations over a long period of time. **Cladogenesis** (Figure 11-3), another form of speciation, involves the splitting of one lineage into two, such that one ancestral species gives rise to two or more descendant species. This splitting usually occurs when gene flow between populations is restricted.

Although the Darwinian concept of evolution holds that evolutionary change is slow and gradual, it can also occur rapidly. There sometimes appear to be rapid, short spurts of evolutionary change. This pattern of evolution, during which long periods of relative stability (stasis) are punctuated by short bursts of speciation, is referred to as **punctuated equilibrium.**

Although punctuated equilibrium allows for some transitional forms, unlike the Darwinian concept of evolution, punctuated equilibrium does not expect the existence of a long series of finely graded intermediates in the fossil record. In punctuated equilibrium, anatomical change occurs rapidly. A

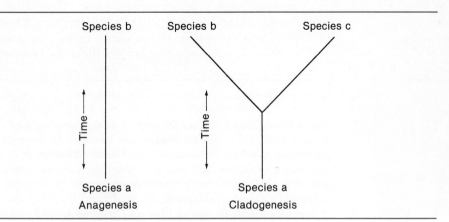

Figure 11-3 The comparison between anagenesis (phyletic evolution) and cladogenesis.

definition of rapid change is relative to a species' generation time. This transitional phase would be quite short compared with the species' total duration on earth. The rapidity of such change would explain the failure to find fossils of intermediate forms.

As envisioned by the punctuated equilibrium model, the origin of a new species is most likely to occur in a small group of organisms that is geographically isolated from the main population of the species. The new species may eventually dominate the territory occupied by the parent species. The punctuated equilibrium model recognizes the incomplete nature of the fossil record as reflecting a biological reality. Since fossilization is a rare event which never leaves a complete record of yearly changes, we would not expect to see a continuity of species in the fossil record.

EXTINCTION

A species can become extinct in a number of ways. For example, it can develop a way of life such that climatic change would prevent its continued existence. A species may also become extinct when it is out-competed for local resources by another species.

A number of factors influence extinction rates (Lewin, 1982). For example;

1. A species dependent on one food source is more vulnerable to extinction than a species with a more generalized diet.
2. Species with a very limited geographical range are more vulnerable to extinction through local catastrophes than are species with a wider distribution.
3. Species with short generation times are more plastic than those, such as humans, with long generation times. Generation time is sometimes linked to body size. Larger-bodied forms have statistically higher probabilities of extinction. For example, extinction rates of species of mammals are significantly higher than those for invertebrates.

Although taxonomy is a useful tool in understanding and cataloging plant and animal diversity, it has its limitations. The species concept, one of the most important concepts in modern evolutionary biology, is essential to any discussion of systematics and taxonomy. Speciation results from reproductive isolation, which primarily results from genetic incompatibility. There is currently a debate concerning the mode and tempo of speciation. The process of speciation may be one of slow and gradual transformation or the origin of new species may result from punctuated equilibrium, a pattern whereby long periods of little or no change are punctuated by short bursts of rapid speciation.

A type specimen must be designated whenever a new species is described. A number of the guidelines that must be followed when evaluating evolutionary relationships among fossils were discussed. Once all relevant features have been considered, organisms are fitted into a phylogenetic tree. The branches on the phylogenetic trees are called clades—that is, groups of species sharing a common ancestor.

BIBLIOGRAPHY

CRONIN, J., N. BOAZ, C. STRINGER, and Y. RAK. 1981. Tempo and mode in hominid evolution. *Nature* 292: 113–22.

EHRLICH, P., R. HOLM, and D. PARNELL. 1974. *The Process of Evolution.* New York: McGraw-Hill.

ELDREDGE, N., and I. TATTERSALL. 1982. *The Myths of Human Evolution.* New York: Columbia University Press.

ENDER, J. 1973. Gene flow and population differentiation. *Science* 179: 243–50.

HUXLEY, J., ed. 1940. *The New Systematics.* Oxford: Oxford University Press.

LEWIN, R. 1980. Evolutionary theory under fire. *Science* 210: 883–87.

LEWIN, R. 1982. Extinction leaves its mark on ecology. *Science* 218: 42–43.

LEWIN, R. 1986. Recognizing ancestors is a species problem. *Science* 234: 1500.

MAYR, E. 1969. *Principles of Systematic Zoology.* New York: McGraw-Hill.

SIMPSON, G. 1945. *The principles of classification and a classification of mammals. Bulletin of the American Museum of Natural History* 85: 1–350.

SIMPSON, G. 1951. *The Meaning of Evolution.* New York: New American Library.

SIMPSON, G. 1961. *Principles of Animal Taxonomy.* San Francisco: W. H. Freeman & Company Publishers.

SNEATH, P. and R. SOKAL. 1973. *Numerical Taxonomy.* San Francisco, W. H. Freeman & Company Publishers.

SOKAL, R. 1973. The species problem reconsidered. *Systematic Zoology* 22: 360–74.

SOKAL, R., and T. CROVELLA. 1970. The biological species concept: A critical evaluation. *American Naturalist* 104: 127–53.

SOKAL, R., and P. SNEATH. 1963. *Principles of Numerical Taxonomy.* San Francisco: W. H. Freeman & Company Publishers.

SOLBRIG, O. 1966. *Evolution and Systematics.* New York: Macmillan.

STANLEY, S. 1979. *Macroevolution: Patterns and Process.* San Francisco: W. H. Freeman & Company Publishers.

STANLEY, S. 1981. *Fossils, Genes, and the Origin of Species.* New York: Basic Books.

TATTERSALL, I. 1986. Species recognition in human paleontology. *Journal of Human Evolution* 15: 165–75.

VRBA, E. 1980. Evolution, species, and fossils: How does life evolve? *South African Journal of Science* 76: 61–84.

WILLIAMS, B. J. 1987. Rates of evolution: Is there a conflict between neo-Darwinian evolutionary theory and the fossil record? *American Journal of Physical Anthropology* 73: 99–110.

Chapter
12
Where Humans Fit in the Animal Kingdom

Modern humans, scientifically referred to as Homo sapiens sapiens, *belong to the kingdom Animalia, class Mammalia, order Primates, suborder Anthropoidea, family Hominidae, genus* Homo, *species* sapiens, *and subspecies* sapiens. *(See Table 12-1.) The reasoning behind some of these references is discussed in this chapter. Humans exhibit the following traits which are common to mammals: warm-bloodedness, the existence of four different kinds of teeth which are specialized for different functions, the expression of play behavior as an important means of environmental manipulation, a dependence on learned social behaviors, and a long period of infantile dependency. Humans share many anatomical and behavioral traits with the other members of the order Primates. Based on a number of shared anatomical, genetic, and behavioral traits, humans have an especially close evolutionary relationship with the modern African chimpanzee.*

Invertebrates, animals without backbones, were not abundant until approximately 600 million years ago (M.Y.A.). Since then, millions of invertebrates have lived and died. Approximately 80 percent of the 130,000 or so known species of fossil animals are invertebrates.

VERTEBRATE EVOLUTION

Humans are vertebrates; that is, we have a spinal column. The earliest vertebrates evolved hundreds of millions of years before humans first appeared. Vertebrates may have evolved 520 to 435 M.Y.A. The first vertebrates may have resembled the modern-day sea lancelet (*Amphioxus*), a small animal presently inhabiting coastal regions around the world. The sea lancelet has a **notochord** and a dorsal nerve cord. Vertebrates, such as the jawless fishes, the ostracoderms, dating to 435 M.Y.A., had a true spinal column enclosing the nerve cord and an internal skeleton composed of soft cartilage rather than bone.

There are five major categories of vertebrates: fishes, amphibians, reptiles, birds, and mammals. The fossil record is relatively complete for most of these groups, and the evolutionary relationships between major categories are apparent. The early and middle Paleozoic (beginning 520 M.Y.A.) can be regarded as the Age of Fishes; the upper Paleozoic-Mesozoic (280–145 M.Y.A.), the Age of Reptiles; and the Cenozoic (beginning 75 M.Y.A.), the Age of Mammals.

Many vertebrates are land-dwelling (terrestrial) creatures. All animals that successfully adjusted to terrestrial life had to first solve two problems: respiration and reproduction. Solutions to these problems varied as animal groups responded with different physiological and anatomical adaptations. The immediate problem to be solved if vertebrates were to survive on land was obtaining oxygen. Fish gills, for example, cannot function in air. Fish lack a protective covering to prevent water loss; they soon dehydrate when placed in the relative dryness of the atmosphere.

Among the many fish species populating the seas hundreds of millions of

Table 12-1. **Humans in the Animal Kingdom**

CATEGORY		TRAITS AND REPRESENTATIVES
Kingdom	Animalia	Multicelled animals; representatives that are mobile, ingesting, and have sense organs
Phylum	Chordata	Animals with notochords and gill slits
Subphylum	Vertebrata	Fish, amphibians, reptiles, birds, mammals
Class	Mammalia	Monotremes (egg-laying mammals), placental mammals (Eutheria), and others
Subclass	Eutheria	Rodents, carnivores, primates, and others
Order	Primates	All representatives of the order Primates
Suborder	Anthropoidea	Old and New World monkeys and the Hominoidea (apes and humans)
Superfamily	Hominoidea	Lesser apes (gibbons), great apes (orangutans, chimpanzees, gorillas), and the Hominidae (humans)
Family	Hominidae	Fossil and modern representatives of humans, i.e., *Australopithecus* and *Homo*
Genus	Homo	Fossil and modern representatives, i.e., *Homo habilis, H. erectus,* and *H. sapiens*
Species	sapiens	Fossil and modern representatives
Subspecies	sapiens	Modern representatives and their ancestors dating back to the late Pleistocene

years ago were the lobefins, or crossopterygians (Figure 12-1). Lobefins made a successful transition from an aquatic to a terrestrial habitat because of the unique structure of their fins and the presence of primitive lungs. The lobefin's fin structure permitted it to "walk" for short distances. This was important, for example, when it needed to move from a drying or stagnant pool to a more favorable location. The ability to move short distances on land meant the difference between survival and extinction.

While in the water, the lobefin obtained oxygen by breathing through its gills; while on land, it obtained oxygen by breathing with its primitive lungs. With gradual modification of the lungs into specialized organs capable of breathing air, lobefins extended the time they could spend on land.

Lobefins had other traits that aided their survival out of water. Their thick skin helped reduce water loss. Their spine, shoulder girdle, and limbs were strengthened and modified, which permitted them to move short distances over land. Changes in their skull and teeth allowed them to feed on land plants, and their senses of smell and hearing were improved. These changes accumulated and appeared in the first group of terrestrial vertebrates, the amphibians (Figure 12-2). Amphibians, a group including frogs, toads, and salamanders, are intermediate between fish and reptiles. Most amphibians pass through an aquatic stage early in their life cycle (tadpoles are an example).

Amphibians first appeared about 280 to 225 M.Y.A. Most amphibians are not

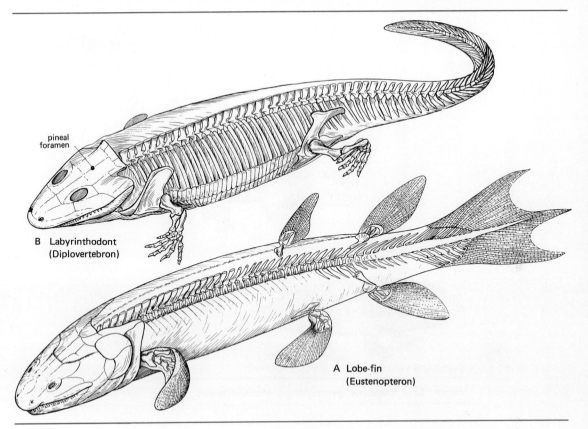

pineal
foramen

B Labyrinthodont
   (Diplovertebron)

A Lobe-fin
   (Eustenopteron)

Figure 12-1 A lobe-finned fish belonging to the genus Eusthenopteron.

completely terrestrial; they retain the external reproductive system of their ancestors and must return to water in order to reproduce. Female amphibians lay their eggs in or near water, and in most amphibian species the female's eggs are fertilized externally by the male. Water is essential to amphibian reproduction because their eggs lack a hard shell and they rapidly dry when exposed to air.

Between 225 to 200 M.Y.A., a new group of vertebrates, the reptiles, appeared. They were the first completely terrestrial vertebrates, evolving from an amphibian stock. The first reptiles were the primitive cotylosaurs, the stock from which all other reptilian forms are thought to have evolved. Reptiles showed several advances over the amphibian line; the most important was the development of the **amniotic egg** (Figure 12-3), an important adaptation to terrestrial living.

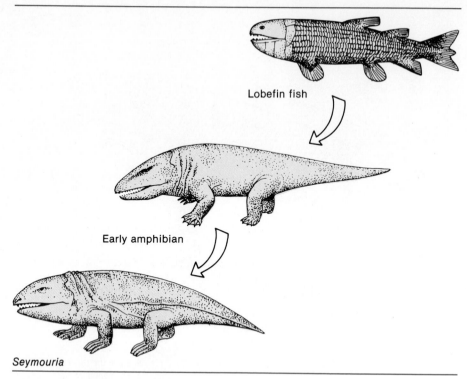

Lobefin fish

Early amphibian

Seymouria

Figure 12-2 *Stages in the evolution of amphibians.*

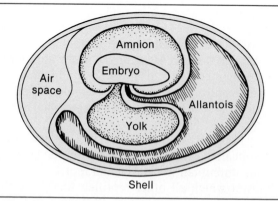

Figure 12-3 *Amniotic egg.*

With the evolution of an internal reproductive system, reptiles no longer needed to return to water to reproduce. Reptiles have an internal reproductive system in which the sperm is introduced into the female's body and fertilization occurs in the moist environment of the female's reproductive tract. After fertilization, the **embryo** (the early stage of development) is enveloped by a membranous sac, the amnion, which maintains a moist environment for the developing embryo. A second sac, the allantois, receives and stores the waste products of metabolism. In mammals, the allantois contributes to the formation of the placenta. The entire structure is surrounded by a shell of limelike material, which permits the exchange of oxygen and carbon dioxide while preventing water loss.

The amniotic egg permits the embryo to develop in its original environment by enclosing it in the liquid-filled sac, the amnion. The egg contains a food supply, the yolk, and membranous structures that allow the exchange of oxygen and carbon dioxide through the shell and the storage of waste materials from the embryo. These structures allow the reptile to develop into a nearly fully formed miniature adult by the time of hatching. This eliminates the larval stage of the amphibian life cycle and the necessity to return to a water environment. The amniotic egg is a major adaptation to a terrestrial life-style.

MAMMAL-LIKE REPTILES AND MAMMALIAN EVOLUTION

The earliest mammal-like reptiles belonged to a group called the Pelycosauria, animals distinguished by their large size and varied diet. According to tooth specializations, some were specialized carnivores (meat-eaters), and others were herbivores (plant-eaters). Some pelycosaurs had large dorsal sails—webs of membrane stretched across protruding spines on the body—which might have been a crude precursor of the internal temperature-control systems later found in mammals. Perhaps when the animal was cold, it turned its body to position the so-called sails to absorb more sunlight.

Pelycosaurs thrived for about 50 million years before becoming extinct. One pelycosaur suborder, the sphenacodonts, included the genus *Dimetrodon,* which may have given rise to the second subclass of mammal-like reptiles, the therapsids (Figure 12-4). Therapsids gave rise to more than 300 genera which contained species ranging from the size of a rat to the size of a rhinoceros. Some were carnivores, and others were herbivores.

An important mammalian feature is the ability to generate heat and maintain a constant body temperature. While some therapsids may have been warm-blooded, it is not known if they controlled their body temperature with any precision.

Therapsids may have reproduced like reptiles; that is, they may have laid eggs. Egg protection among mammal-like reptiles could have led to incubation

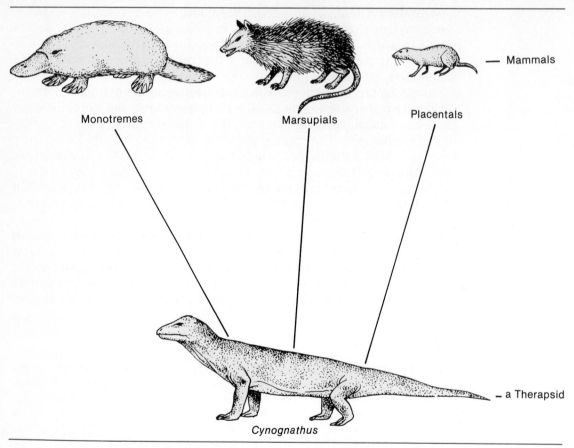

Figure 12-4 *Divergence of the mammals.* Cynognathus *is representative of therapsids from which the first mammals evolved.*

and parental feeding. This may have paved the way for longer egg retention within the mother and then, as in mammals, to live births.

The line with mammal-like features passed through the theriodonts, a diverse group of apparently efficient carnivores, to the cynodonts, from which the first true mammals evolved approximately 200 M.Y.A. Two major trends in cynodont evolution were an overall size reduction (they ranged in size from that of a rat to that of a wolf) and an increasing elaboration of mammalian features. The cynodonts were small and were apparently insect-eaters, like the mammals that are thought to have evolved from them.

Mammals exploited new evolutionary opportunities. They began to move into and exploit relatively unoccupied habitats, resulting in their rapid diversification, expansion, and proliferation. This process of rapid diversification and proliferation is known as **adaptive radiation,** and is one of the first stages in the evolution of new taxonomic groups.

Mammalian Traits

A number of characteristics of modern mammals were also typical of their earlier ancestors (Table 12-2). These common characteristics include the following:

1. Mammals are warm-blooded animals (a condition called **homeothermy**). Internal control of a constant body temperature allowed mammals to inhabit and exploit a range of environments wider than that available to reptiles.
2. Mammals have different kinds of teeth (Fig. 12-5) (a condition called **heterodontism**) specialized for different functions. Mammals generally have four types of teeth. The canines are for piercing or tearing; the incisors are for cutting and slicing; and the premolars and molars are for grinding.
3. Mammals express play behavior as an important means of environmental exploration and learning. As we will note later, play is an extremely important primate behavior through which youngsters practice survival skills, develop physical coordination, and learn social behaviors and communication skills.
4. Mammals are more dependent on learning than are their reptilian predecessors.
5. The mammalian mode of reproduction is also significant in understanding mammalian evolutionary success. The reproductive mode of one group, the placentals, allows an extensive period of prenatal development. Mammals also have fewer births per parturition, and those infants born are protected.
6. The developmental period among mammalian young is extended by nursing. Nursing young need not begin to feed themselves or defend themselves immediately after birth; therefore, they may be less prone to predation. The infant's longer period of attachment to its mother increases the opportunity for learning behaviors necessary for survival.

---

*Table 12-2. **Some Major Mammalian Evolutionary Traits***

---

1. Mothers nurse and protect their newborns.
2. Fewer young are born each birth period than is the case for amphibians and reptiles.
3. Most mammals give birth to live young; the monotremes are the exception.
4. There is a clear trend toward prolonged immaturity, which is correlated with the role of learning in behavioral development.
5. Mammals are homoiothermic, or warm-blooded; that is, they internally control their body temperature.
6. Many mammals lead social lives and are found in social groups.
7. Mammals are characterized by dietary differentiation and heterodontism.

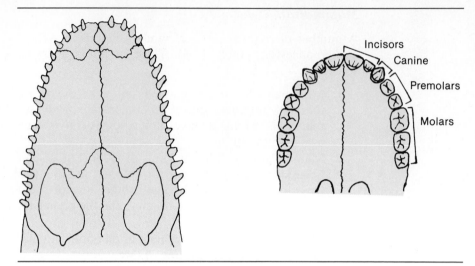

Figure 12-5 Dental differences between reptiles (left) and mammals (right).

These traits are not clear-cut indications of mammal status. For example, there is evidence to suggest that some dinosaurs were warm-blooded (de Ricqles, 1974; Desmond, 1975; Thomas and Olson, 1980). Of the mammalian traits just noted, fossil evidence is helpful primarily in regard to heterodontism.

Mammalian Types

Reproductive specialties differentiate the three mammalian groups (Table 12-3). One subclass, the Monotremata (monotremes), includes the duck-billed platypus and the spiny anteater. Like birds and reptiles, monotremes lay eggs.

A second subclass, the Marsupialia (marsupials), is more geographically widespread than the monotremes and includes the opossum, kangaroo, and koala bear. Marsupials are **viviparous;** they give birth to live young. Marsupial young are born at a very immature stage and migrate to the mother's pouch, where they attach themselves to her nipples. They remain within the pouch to develop further before they emerge.

The third subclass, the placental mammals (Eutheria), reproduce through a process whereby the egg is released from the mother's ovary, is fertilized by introduced sperm, and is then implanted on the walls of the mother's womb. In the early stage of the organism's development, a tissue is produced, the placenta (which is not present in monotremes and marsupials), which attaches to the wall of the womb. The placenta permits an interchange of fluids between the mother and the developing young. Whereas the bird's and reptile's egg must contain enough yolk to nourish the young until it has hatched, placental mammals use the mother's physiological mechanisms for these functions and for supplying oxygen to the tissues of the developing young.

Table 12-3. **Reproductive Specializations**

Amphibians	Reproduction is external, and water is an essential medium for reproduction. Many more young are born than survive. Parents do not care for young.
Reptiles	Amniotic egg obviates the need to return to water to reproduce. Fertilization is internal. Many more young are born than survive. Parental care is very unusual.

Mammals	Three different reproductive specializations are apparent:
	  Monotremes: Lay eggs, like birds and reptiles.
	  Marsupials: Are viviparous. Young are born very immature and mature in mother's pouch. Fertilization is internal.
	  Placentals: Females have specialized structure called *placenta.* Fertilization is internal. Development takes place in the mother's womb.
	
	Among mammals, fewer young are born at each birth period than is the case for amphibians and reptiles. Mammalian females nurse their young and protect them for various lengths of time.

INSECTIVORA

The insectivora (insect-eating forms) are the mammalian group most likely to have given rise to the order Primates about 60 or 65 M.Y.A. Living representatives of the insectivora, including moles, hedgehogs, and shrews, are found throughout tropical and temperate regions of both the Old and New Worlds. The evolutionary history of the insectivora goes back at least 130 M.Y.A. The earliest placental mammals were probably insectivores. The anatomical traits characteristic of insectivores make it likely that they were ancestral to several mammalian orders in addition to the order Primates. For example, insectivores may have been ancestral to rodents and bats.

Insectivores have a curious mix of anatomical traits. Like primates, they have five digits on their extremities. Unlike primates, however, the digits are tipped with claws, not nails. The southeast Asian tree shrew is one animal that has a combination of anatomical traits, some of which are like those of insectivores and some of which are like those of primates; thus it is difficult to classify tree shrews with either one or the other group. Unlike most insectivores, which live on the ground or burrow into the ground, tree shrews are **arboreal** (tree-living). Like primates, and unlike insectivores, tree shrews have large eyes and possess somewhat mobile hands and feet that can be used to grasp. They supplement their insectivorous diet with other foods. In common with insectivores, tree shrews have digits tipped with claws, no stereoscopic vision, multiple births, and a dental complement different from that of primates, among other traits. Most researchers are inclined to place tree shrews among the insectivores, but this was not always true. Because of the anatomical and behavioral traits that they share with primates, tree shrews are often the models to which researchers refer when trying to reconstruct the earliest stages of primate evolution.

Unfortunately, there is virtually no fossil record to document the evolutionary transition from insectivores to primates. We must rely on inferences from later fossils and living representatives of both insectivores and primates. If we rely on insectivores as a model for what early primates looked like and how they may have behaved, we can infer that the ancestors of the primates and the earliest primates themselves were small, were likely nocturnal, were insectivores, and depended more heavily upon the sense of smell than do modern primates. Primates diverged from the insectivores by becoming adapted to a mode of life that included an omnivorous diet and life in the trees. This new diet and habitat led to fundamental anatomical and behavioral changes, such as are noted in the following pages.

THE PRIMATES

A number of anatomical traits that characterize the order Primates (Table 12-4, Table 12-5) may be related to increased behavioral complexity. A shift from an olfactory (sense of smell) to a visual reliance led to a different perception of the world. The cerebral cortex of the brain increased in size and complexity. A lengthening of prenatal and postnatal life demands prolonged infant care and allows time for the offspring to learn how to exploit environmental resources.

Primates typically exhibit a combination of a number of the following traits.

Nails instead of claws on their digits.

Prehensile (grasping) hands and feet.

Pentadactyly—five fingers and toes.

Tendency toward complete bony enclosure of the eye orbits.

Forward placement of the eye orbits.

Opposability of toe and thumb to the remaining digits.

Enlarged cerebral hemispheres, which are related to the primate's sense organs.

One pair of thoracically placed mammary glands.

Well-developed **clavicles** (collar bones).

Reduced olfactory sense and enhanced visual sense.

A reproductive strategy that usually includes one infant each birth and extensive parental care.

Not all primates have all these traits, and other mammals have some of these traits. For example, some marsupials have nailed digits and prehensile hands and feet, and a number of mammalian orders have clavicles, partially

Table 12-4. **PRIMATE CLASSIFICATION***

	Some Living Examples
Order: Primates	
Suborder: Prosimii	
Superfamily: Lemuroidea	Lemurs, Indris, Sifakas (all found on island of Madagascar)
Lorisoidea	Loris, Bushbaby
Tarsiioidera	Tarsier (southeast Asia)
Suborder: Anthropoidea	
Superfamily: Ceboidea	New World monkeys: howler monkey, spider monkey, woolly monkey
Superfamily: Cercopithecoidea	Old World monkeys: macaques, baboons, langurs
Superfamily: Hominoidae	
Family: Hylobatidae	Gibbons, Siamangs (Asia only)
Family: Pongidae	
Genus: Pan	Chimpanzee (Africa only)
Genus: Gorilla	Gorilla (Africa only)
Genus: Pongo	Orangutan (Asia only)
Family: Hominidae	
Genus: Homo†	Humans

*Not all categories are listed in this table.
†The human genus *Homo* has existed for approximately 2.2 million years. It was preceded by the genus *Australopithecus* (see Chapter 17).

enclosed eye orbits, and thoracically placed mammary glands. In no other mammal, however, is there the concentration of these traits as there is in primates.

Primates are a good example of a diversified order. Most common primate traits stem from either (1) a retention of ancient or generalized vertebrate and mammalian traits or (2) the development of an arboreal adaptation. Primates are broadly distributed throughout the tropics of the Old and New Worlds. The order Primates can be subdivided into three groups: **prosimians** (the most primitive and earliest members), **platyrrhines** (New World monkeys), **catarrhines** (Old World monkeys, apes and humans). We also often refer to **hominoids**, a term embracing homids (humans), and **pongids,** a term referring to chimpanzees, gorillas, orangutans, and their ancestors.

THE HUMAN–APE RELATIONSHIP

The close relationship between humans and some apes was recognized as early as the middle 1800s. When we refer to a close human–ape relationship, we are especially referring to a relationship between humans and gorillas and

*Table 12-5. **Some Primate Characteristics***

1. **Locomotor Adaptations**
   a. Retention of ancestral mammalian limb structure; pentadactyly in hands and feet; separate ulna and radius; mobility of limbs.
   b. Mobile and grasping (prehensile) hands and feet; nails replacing claws in most forms.
   c. Retention of a tail in most monkeys. New World monkeys have a prehensile (grasping) tail which functions as an extra hand and is part of the feeding adaptation.
   d. Erect sitting posture, which was a precursor for structural uprighting; rotation of foramen magnum to a position beneath the skull.
2. **Sensory Adaptations**
   a. Enlargement of the eyes.
   b. Color vision and increased sensitivity to low light levels.
   c. Medial (forward) rotation of eye, which allows stereoscopic vision.
   d. Enclosure of eye in bone cup, which results in greater protection.
   e. Reduction of the snout and loss of the naked rhinarium, both of which indicate a decreasing reliance on olfactory senses.
   f. The increasing reliance on vision and decreasing reliance on olfaction are reflected by a reorganization of the brain's structure.
3. **Dental Traits**
   a. Simple cusp patterns on the molar teeth. Monkeys have bilophodont (four cusps in two parallel rows) lower molars. Apes and humans normally have a Y-5 lower molar cusp pattern, in which there are five instead of four cusps.
   b. All Old World monkeys, apes, and humans have 32 teeth: 2 incisors, 1 canine, 2 premolars, and 3 molars in each quadrant of the jaw. Most New World monkeys have 36 teeth because they have an extra premolar in each quadrant of the jaw.
4. **General Traits**
   a. Lengthened period of maturation, infant dependency, and gestation compared with most mammals; decreased number of young (usually one infant) per parturition; relatively long life span.
   b. Relatively large and complex brains, especially those regions controlling vision, manipulation of the hands and feet, muscle coordination and control, and memory and learning.
   c. Year-round, bisexual social groups organized on the basis of age, sex, and matrilineal kinship.

Source: Some data from B. Campbell, *Humankind Emerging.* (Boston: Little, Brown, 1982).

chimpanzees. In 1863, Thomas H. Huxley published a group of essays entitled *Evidence as to Man's Place in Nature,* in which he presented evidence for this relationship. Darwin supported Huxley's contention in his 1871 book, *The Descent of Man.*

The earliest evidence used to support the argument for a close human–ape relationship was a close skeletal and muscular similarity. Many of the shared features are **ancestral traits**—that is, traits inherited from their common ancestor. For example, the human trunk is similar to the chimpanzee's in arm length, trunk breadth, and shortness of the lumbar (lower back) region. There are a great many similarities in the upper bodies of humans and apes. We share with some apes major structural features of the trunk that enable such actions as stretching to the side and hanging comfortably by the arms. Humans and apes share a number of muscular similarities in the upper limbs, and these similarities are related to our ancestral locomotor pattern of **brachiation** (arm-swinging beneath branches) (Figure 12-6).

Besides comparing muscular and skeletal anatomy, there are other means of providing evidence for the close human–ape relationship. One is by analysis of deoxyribonucleic acid (DNA), the genetic basis of life (Chapter 3). DNA strands can be compared using the technique of **DNA hybridization,** in which the links between the double strands of the DNA helix are broken by heating.

Figure 12-6 A brachiating gibbon (Hylobates lar). *The long arms and hooked hands are adaptations to swinging beneath branches, which is a locomotor pattern known as brachiation. Note the longer arms and shorter legs.*

As DNA cools, the strands realign and pair again. The extent of relatedness of DNA strands is shown by the degree to which the strands of two different species hybridize. Single DNA strands from different species are placed together to determine to what degree they will bond. For example, the single DNA strands of humans and chimpanzees bond to each other; this is DNA hybridization. The next step compares human double-stranded DNA to the hybridized human–chimpanzee double-stranded DNA. Similarities and differences are measured in terms of thermal stability—that is, the difference between the temperature at which the hybridized chimpanzee–human DNA strands separate and the separation temperature of reannealed human DNA. DNA hybridization is useful for testing relationships of animals that are relatively closely related. Single DNA strands will not hybridize well if organisms are too distantly related. DNA hybridization research suggests that the chimpanzee is most closely related to the human, followed closely by the gorilla.

By most measures, humans and chimpanzees share the closest relationship among the living primates. As evidence of a close human–ape relationship accumulates, some revisions of their classification have been suggested. While most scientists still place apes and humans into two separate families—Hominidae for humans and Pongidae for apes (see Table 12-4)—some have suggested that humans, chimpanzees, and gorillas should be put into the same subfamily, the Homininae, and that these three should be separated from another great ape subfamily, the Ponginae, which would include only the orangutan. Placing humans, chimpanzees, and gorillas in the subfamily Homininae implies a closer evolutionary relationship than would be the case if humans were placed in one family (Hominidae) and the three great apes were placed in another family (Pongidae).

The most recent information from molecular genetics and DNA studies indicates that humans and chimpanzees are genetically closer to each other than either is to the gorilla. This view is supported by the divergence times of the different forms. Gorillas may have diverged from the common human–ape ancestor about 8 to 10 M.Y.A., while humans and chimpanzees may still have been united in the same evolutionary line until about 6.3 to 7.7 M.Y.A.

THE HUMAN PRIMATE

Evidence for inclusion of humans in the mammalian order Primates has been provided. What makes humans unique within the order Primates? Why are humans included in a different taxonomic family from other members of the superfamily Hominoidea? From an evolutionary perspective, the most significant modern human traits are (1) our completely erect posture and habitual bipedal gait, (2) our abstract and symbolic communication, known as language, (3) the presence of culture, providing as it does immense opportunities for enhancing learning, (4) our comparatively large brains, and (5) our consistent tool use and manufacture and our reliance on tools.

Other animals, especially nonhuman primates, learn by experience and observation. Some animals, including nonhuman primates, transmit learned behavior from one generation to another (Chapter 8); this transgenerational passing of learned behavior is the basis for culture. Furthermore, some animals, such as chimpanzees, make and use tools (Chapter 9)—an ability once thought to be limited to humans. Some animals also display behavioral patterns that humans readily understand. Yet there are dramatic differences between human and nonhuman primates. Humans can sit and speculate about these differences; this is one of our unique traits.

While curiosity is a major primate trait, humans are perhaps the nosiest of the nosy. Humans climb a hill simply to see what lies beyond. Dostoevski once wrote, "Man needs the unfathomable and the infinite just as much as he does the small planet which he inhabits." As far as we know, humans alone have the capacity for self-reflection. The British author G. W. Corner wrote, "After all, if he is an ape he is the only ape that is debating what kind of ape he is." Humans alone among the primates have the ability to communicate about the past and plan for the future; our language allows this unique trait. Probably humans alone have ethical and philosophical ideals. The British writer Hazlitt noted, "Man is the only animal that laughs and weeps, for he is the animal that is struck with the difference between what things are and what they ought to be."

In 1863, Thomas H. Huxley suggested that humans were closely related to the gorillas and the chimpanzees. The most sensitive measure of that close evolutionary relationship is through the means of DNA hybridization. This technique affirms that humans are most closely evolutionarily related to the African chimpanzee. Humans and chimpanzees may have diverged from a common ancestor as recently as 6 to 8 million years ago.

Despite the fact that humans are evolutionarily closely related to nonhuman primates, especially the chimpanzee, a number of features distinguish humans within the order Primates. For example, humans constantly locomote bipedally, have an abstract means of communication called language, and have a dependency on technology that is part of an elaborate survival mechanism called culture. Culture provides humans with an almost endless means of elaborating on our genetic capabilities. Humans are the contemplative primate, the philosophical primate that ponders life and death.

BIBLIOGRAPHY

BRUCE, E., and F. AYALA. 1978. Humans and apes are genetically very similar. *Nature* 276: 264–65.

CRAWSHAW, L., B. MOFFITT, D. LEMONS, and J. DOWNEY. 1981. The evolutionary development of vertebrate thermoregulation. *American Scientist* 69: 543–50.

DE RICQLES, A. 1974. Evolution of endothermy: Histological evidence. *Evolutionary Theory* 1: 51–58.

DESMOND, A. 1975. *Hot-blooded Dinosaurs: A Revolution in Paleontology.* New York: Dial Press.

FITCH, W. 1976. Molecular evolutionary clocks. In *Molecular Evolution,* F. Ayala, ed., pp. 160–78. Sunderlands, Mass.: Sinauer Associates.

GOODMAN, M. 1975. Protein sequences and immunological specificity. In *Phylogeny of Primates,* F. Luckett and F. Szalay, eds. New York: Plenum Press.

GOODMAN, M., R. TASHIAN, and J. TASHIAN, eds. 1976. *Molecular Anthropology: Genes and Proteins in the Evolutionary Ascent of the Primates.* New York: Plenum.

KEITH, A. 1925. *The Antiquity of Man* (2d ed.) London: Williams and Norgate.

KEMP, T. 1982. *Mammal-like Reptiles and the Origin of Mammals.* New York: Academic Press.

KLINGER, R., H. HAMMERTON, D. NUSTON, and E. LANGE. 1963. The chromosomes of the Hominoidea. In *Classification and Human Evolution,* S. Washburn, ed., pp. 235–42. New York: Viking Fund.

KOHNE, D. 1970. Evolution of higher organism DNA. *Quarterly Review of Biophysics* 3: 327.

LEWIN, R. 1987. My close cousin the chimpanzee. *Science* 238: 273–75.

MAHANEY, M., and P. SCIULLI. 1983. Hominid–pongid affinities: A multivariate analysis of hominoid odontometrics. *Current Anthropology* 23: 382–87.

MIYAMOTO, M., J. SLIGHTON, and M. GOODMAN. 1987. Phylogenetic relations of humans and African apes from DNA sequences in the $\psi\eta$-Globin region. *Science* 238: 369–73.

RACLE, F. 1979. *Introduction to Evolution.* Englewood Cliffs, N.J.: Prentice-Hall.

RESIZ, R., and M. HEATON. 1980. Origin of mammal-like reptiles. *Nature* 288: 193.

ROMER, A. 1950. *Vertebrate Paleontology.* Chicago: University of Chicago Press.

ROMER, A. 1970. *The Vertebrate Body.* Philadelphia: Saunders.

SARICH, V. 1971. A molecular approach to the question of human origins. In *Background for Man,* P. Dolhinow and V. Sarich, eds., Boston: Little, Brown, pp. 182-91.

SCHWARTZ, J. 1984. Hominoid evolution: A reassessment. *Current Anthropology* 25: 655–72.

SCHWARTZ, J. 1987. *The Red Ape: Orangutans and Human Evolution.* New York: Houghton-Mifflin.

SEUANEZ, H. 1979. *The Phylogeny of Human Chromosomes.* New York: Springer-Verlag.

SOCHA, W., and J. MOOR-JANKOWSKI. 1979. Blood groups of anthropoid apes and their relationship to human blood groups. *Journal of Human Evolution* 8: 453.

THOMAS, R., and E. OLSON (eds.). 1980. *A Cold Look at the Warm-Blooded Dinosaurs.* Boulder, Colo.: Westview Press.

WASHBURN, S., and R. MOORE. 1980. *Ape Into Human* (2d ed.). Boston: Little, Brown.

WILSON, M., and A. WILSON. 1975. Similar amino acid sequences in *Pan* and *Homo. Science* 188: 107.

YUNISH, J., and G. PRAKASH. 1982. The origin of man: A chromosomal pictorial legacy. *Science* 215: 1525–29.

Chapter

13

The Fossilization

Process and Dating

Methods

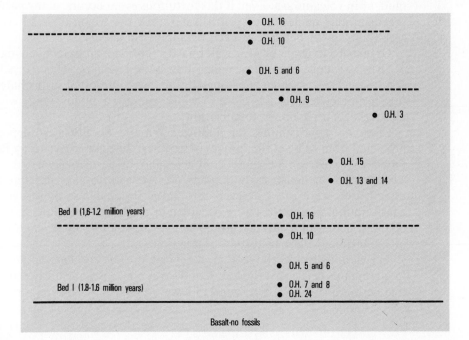

- O.H. 16
- O.H. 10

- O.H. 5 and 6

- O.H. 9
- O.H. 3

- O.H. 15
- O.H. 13 and 14

Bed II (1,6-1.2 million years)
- O.H. 16
- O.H. 10

- O.H. 5 and 6
Bed I (1.8-1.6 million years)
- O.H. 7 and 8
- O.H. 24

Basalt-no fossils

This chapter will discuss the fossilization process and dating techniques. The scientific value of an artifact or fossil depends on accurate dating. Various methods currently used to date fossil remains fall into two categories: relative dating and chronometric dating techniques. Chronometric dating techniques provide an actual numerical date for either the fossil itself or the deposit in which it is found. Relative dating establishes that one thing is older than another. Most evolutionary schemes have as their basis chronometric dates.

An exceedingly small number of all the plants and animals to have inhabited the earth have been fossilized. The fossilization process is a chance event requiring a specific set of environmental circumstances, such as deposition in mud or in a cave. Different parts of the body are more susceptible to fossilization—for example, the teeth.

FOSSILS AND FOSSILIZATION

Fossilization is rare, and fossil finds are an even rarer event. **Fossils** are either the remains or the imprints left in soil or rocks of plants or animals that once existed. The term *fossil* was once applied to rocks and minerals, as well as to organic materials. It eventually became apparent that rocks, minerals, and fossils had a different origin and nature.

The most common mode of fossilization involves the preservation of specific parts of an organism. At death a number of factors may quickly lead to an organism's destruction. Destruction can be prevented or minimized if the organism is protected, for example, by burial in a stream or lake, in a cave, in mud, or in volcanic ash. Even if this fortuitous event occurs, many parts of the organism may be destroyed prior to burial by the action of weather, by soil conditions, or by being scavenged by another organism.

Organisms living in or near water have a far better chance of leaving a trace of their existence than those inhabiting humid jungles, where fossilization conditions are very poor. Fortunately for those interested in primate evolution, primates tend to live close to water sources, a circumstance which has increased their chance of fossilization.

Caves are good sources for fossilized remains because cave deposits are protected from some of the ravages of weather, time, and scavengers. Remains found in caves can be quite complete and in a relatively good state of preservation. Although early humans do not seem to have inhabited caves, their bodies were often dragged into caves by predators or scavengers for consumption. Many caves were occupied or used over long time periods. The dirt and debris in a cave accumulates over time and may reveal a long and often startlingly clear history of occupation.

In general, the older the geological deposit, the less the chance of uncovering fossil remains because of the forces of destruction. This, in addition to the fact that earlier forms are often found in fewer numbers, are two reasons that the human fossil record of 2 to 4 million years ago is rather scanty when compared with the record of 50,000 years ago. Humans were more numerous 50,000 years ago, and they inhabited a wider geographical area; both factors increase their chance of recovery. Furthermore, in later stages of human evolution, the practice of deliberate burials contributed to fossilization.

Different body parts fossilize at different rates and incidences. The so-called hard tissues—the bones and teeth—are partially composed of inorganic materials, which makes them more likely to fossilize. Soft tissues, such as muscles, skin, and cartilage, are much less likely to fossilize. In general, the higher the bone's mineral content, the greater the chance of fossilization. Teeth, with over 90 percent mineral content, are the most commonly fossilized body parts. The harder and larger bones, such as the upper-leg bone (the femur) and the upper-arm bone (the humerus), are much more commonly fossilized than lighter and more fragile bones, such as the ribs. The fossilization process is also influenced by the type of soil in which the material comes to rest.

Taphonomy, the study of the fossilization process, has revealed a wealth of information that is very useful in helping to reconstruct the condition of a site. For example, taphonomic analysis can help determine whether a bone or any other kind of debris was disturbed pre- or postmortem by a predator or scavenger. By demonstrating how bones were deposited, taphonomic analysis can also reveal much about the environmental context of a site. Deposits disturbed by water contain a higher proportion of heavier than lighter bones, because the latter are more likely to have been washed away.

Taphonomic studies consider the geological and biological processes that help to accumulate, modify, and bury remains. Taphonomic analysis seeks to assess the contribution of geological events, human and nonhuman activity, and other factors to the formation of clusters of animal bones and artifacts. Taphonomic analysis helps to determine whether human activity is responsible for the pattern of deposition of the debris being excavated. If humans deposited at least some of the remains at the site, it is then necessary to assess the kind of activities that occurred at the site.

Bones can become distorted during fossilization. Many fossilized skulls, for example, have been distorted during the fossilization process by the weight of the earth pressing down on them. Soft tissue such as the brain, which is cradled by bone, may be destroyed, but the space left by the brain may be filled by mud or other material which then hardens and provides a mold or cast of the tissue. In the case of the brain, such a mold is called an **endocranial cast.**

Because the fossilization process is so dependent on local conditions, the process can occur with varying speed. Fossilization can occur quite rapidly in some areas and quite slowly in others. Despite the many variables affecting fossilization, and despite the rarity of fossils, fossil remains are the major evidence used to interpret evolutionary history.

DATING FOSSIL MATERIALS

When considering the age of a fossil specimen, researchers seek answers to two important questions: (1) What is the relationship of the fossil material to known geological, floral, faunal, and archaeological sequences? and (2) What is the chronological age of the specimen in years? The first query asks whether the remains are contemporaneous within their context, and therefore whether the site's faunal, climatic, and archaeological information can be properly associated with the find. The answer to the second query provides a figure—the chronometric age of the find.

Establishing a chronological sequence for fossil remains is fundamental to understanding their evolutionary relationship and significance. In order to establish the contemporaneity of fossil or archaeological material with the deposit in which it lies, it must be demonstrated that the deposit is undisturbed. It must be shown that there is no possibility of an intrusive burial or derivation from younger or older deposits. All dates must be viewed as suspect unless these conditions are met.

Two dating methods, **relative dating** and **chronometric dating** (see Table 13-1), are useful in different circumstances. Relative dating establishes that one object—a bone, a tool, or other remains—is older or younger than something else. Relative dating arranges objects in chronological order, although the total time span and interval between the objects is unknown. Relative dating establishes a chronological sequence of youngest to oldest; chronometric dating determines the age in terms of years. Chronometric dating determines the age of a specimen or source deposit and yields a numerical figure.

Cross-dating is an important element in any dating scheme. It establishes relationships between assemblages, or significant elements therein, from various geographic locales. Cross-dating ties sites into a preexisting scheme; sites must be cross-dated with other sites in order to establish temporal relationships.

RELATIVE DATING METHODS

Typological and Morphological Dating

It is important to determine whether archaeological or bone materials are contemporaneous with the deposit in which they lie. The site's stratigraphy, the relative vertical placement of objects in the soil, must be determined. Given an undisturbed site, materials at the lowest levels should be the oldest. In the absence of an undisturbed stratified site, less reliable means are available for determining a relative time sequence. For example, typological dating, based on the fact that manufactured objects undergo stylistic changes over time, can be used to arrange objects in a relative time sequence.

When an object is not associated with organic material useful in age determination, or when a fossil is found lying above ground out of context, it can sometimes be dated according to its form, or morphology. However, morphological dating should be attempted only when a large, well-known fossil series with a well-documented evolutionary history is available.

Fluorine, Nitrogen, and Uranium Dating

Buried bone undergoes changes in chemical composition that can be measured using fluorine, nitrogen, and uranium dating techniques. These dating methods are especially important in disturbed sites where it is necessary to establish contemporaneity of the buried remains. The relative age of bone can be determined by comparing its chemical composition with fossil bone of known ages either from the same site or of same age if they are preserved under comparable conditions. Bones buried at the same time and under comparable conditions should contain equal amounts of whichever of the three elements, fluorine, nitrogen or uranium, is being measured.

The primary value of fluorine, uranium, and nitrogen analysis lies in the fact that it enables us to determine the relative ages of bone or bone objects from the same deposit. It is usually impossible to use any of the three analyses as more than a rough guide to the geological age of an isolated specimen. Fluorine cross-dating is especially hampered by the fact that the amount of fluorine permeating bone depends on how much is present in the ground water, and this varies with the locale.

Paleomagnetism

Paleomagnetic dating is based on the fact that the earth's magnetic field periodically changes in direction and intensity. The magnetic pole is now oriented in a northerly direction, but this has not always been true. Paleomagnetic dating involves taking samples of sediments that contain magnetically charged particles. Such particles retain the magnetic orientation they had when becoming consolidated into rock.

The history of polarity changes over the past 4 million years or so has been determined with some precision. Such polarity changes, which can take as little as 5,000 years to occur, can leave natural records in rocks. Geomagnetic polarity epochs have been established that last between 0.5 million and 1.0 million years. Polarity was reversed between 0.5 and 2.5 M.Y.A. and before 3.4 M.Y.A. It is possible to determine the history of polarity changes over the past 4 million years or so with some precision and to construct what is called a "reversal chronology."

CHRONOMETRIC DATING METHODS

Radiocarbon Dating

The radiocarbon, or C^{14}, dating technique has been used since 1949. Although any organic material is theoretically subject to radiocarbon dating, the best substance is charcoal, which is common in more recent archaeological sites. Radiocarbon dating is fairly reliable, provided that proper precautions are taken in selecting samples and ensuring that they are not contaminated either in the laboratory or by additional radiocarbon from more recent material.

Wood charcoal is best for radiocarbon dating; 1 gram of charcoal is an adequate sample. Burned bone is often dated, but unburned bone is seldom submitted for dating. A fairly large sample of unburned bone is needed because it contains little carbon; however, unburned bone does contain a carbon-rich substance called *collagen* that can be extracted and dated. A few finds have been directly C^{14} dated but, because most skeletal assemblages are quite incomplete, researchers are hesitant to destroy the amount needed for the procedure. They rely instead on C^{14} dates of associated but more expendable materials.

Radiocarbon is present in the cellular structure of all plants and animals. Organisms lose C^{14} at a steady rate, but they also consume it. Plants maintain their C^{14} level during oxygen exchange with the atmosphere, while animals maintain their level by eating plants or other animals that have eaten plants. Radiocarbon intake is maintained as long as the organism lives; intake promptly ceases at death, and C^{14} levels begin to radioactively disintegrate.

In the disintegration process, C^{14} becomes nitrogen. Disintegration proceeds at a known rate, based on the C^{14} half life of 5,730 years. The length of time it takes for half of the original atoms to disintegrate (or, put another way, when half of the original atoms remain) is the *half-life.* After one half-life, the amount of radioactive isotope is halved. After the span of another half-life, half of the remaining atoms, or one-fourth of the original atoms, are present. This process of halving, the rate of radioactive decay, allows C^{14} to be used to date past events. By measuring the ratio of C^{14} atoms to nitrogen in dead organisms, it is possible to calculate the length of time in "radiocarbon years" that has elapsed since the organism died.

Table 13-1. *Some Major Chronometric Dating Techniques*

Time Period	Dating Method
Modern period to 2,500 B.C.	Historical documents, tree ring (dendrochronology)
Recent times to 50,000 years ago	Carbon^{14}
50,000 years ago to 500,000 years ago	No accurate chronometric dating techniques for this time period
500,000 years ago to age of Earth	Potassium-argon, fission track

Radiocarbon dates are expressed as a date midway between two points, which represents a margin of error of 1 standard deviation. The limits are indicated by a plus-or-minus sign. A typical date reads *40,000±1,000 years.* Radiocarbon dating is generally limited to an upper range of approximately 50,000 to 70,000 years.

There are three potential sources of C^{14} dating errors: (1) statistical errors, as are indicated by the plus-or-minus dates, (2) errors related to the C^{14} level of the sample itself, and (3) errors related to "contamination"—that is, laboratory storage, preparation, and management. It is important to have a series of dates to test for reliability.

Rather recently there has been some revision of the C^{14} chronology. For example, at times the rate of C^{14} production fluctuated so rapidly that samples of different ages showed an identical concentration of C^{14} decay even though the older sample would have been expected to have more radioactive decay. Fluctuations in C^{14} concentrations may be correlated with the level of solar activity. Climatic change may have influenced the concentration of C^{14} in the atmosphere. Volcanoes can add other forms of carbon to the atmosphere, temporarily lowering the proportion of C^{14}, which may result in a sample's being dated as older than it actually is.

Potassium-Argon Dating

Radiocarbon dating encompasses the most recent periods of human evolution, leaving a large percentage of our evolutionary history beyond its grasp. This period of time can be dated with other techniques, such as potassium-argon (K-Ar) dating. Potassium-argon dating ascertains the age of volcanic rocks and tektites (glasslike objects formed during the impact of large meteorites on the earth's surface). Potassium-argon dating dates the deposit, and not the fossil or cultural remains. Potassium-argon dates a time span from 500,000 years ago to 3 billion years ago.

Potassium contains a very small amount of the radioactive isotope potassium^{40} (K^{40}). Potassium^{40} decays slowly but with regularity to form the inert gas argon^{40} (Ar^{40}). Over time, a rock that contains potassium will steadily accumulate more argon^{40}, thereby providing a measure by which the rock can be dated. The greater the accumulation of argon^{40}, the older the rock. Volcanic deposits are particularly suited for K-Ar dating because during a volcanic eruption, all of the argon is expelled from the minerals, and the decay of potassium^{40} to argon^{40} begins anew. Measuring the amount of argon in a volcanic rock determines how long it has been since the volcano erupted.

Fission-Track Dating

Fission-track dating was originally devised to date manufactured glass, but it can also be applied to dating volcanically derived glasslike substances, such as obsidian. The procedure involves counting the number of tracks caused by the spontaneous fission of uranium[238] (U^{238}) during the lifetime of the sample. The date obtained depends on the density of such tracks and the number of uranium atoms, which is determined by the increase in track density produced by neutron irradiation and laboratory-induced fission of U^{235}. Fission-track dating can be used to verify K-Ar dates. If dates from the two methods agree, then a fairly accurate age determination is ensured. For example, material used to fission-track date Olduvai Gorge Bed I, an important early human site in Tanzania, consisted of specimens from the volcanic deposit used for the K-Ar date. Dates derived from the two methods are in close agreement.

DETERMINING PAST CLIMATIC CONDITIONS

Besides knowing the date of a fossil or archaeological assemblage, researchers also value information about climatic conditions at the time of fossilization or preservation. With this information scientists can reconstruct habitat conditions and can also feel more confident when assessing the functional significance of bone or artifact assemblages. Some means for assessing habitat conditions will be discussed next.

Glaciations

Climatic conditions associated with **glaciations** (periods of ice and cold) and **pluvials** (periods of heavy rainfall and higher lake levels) affected the evolution of many plants and animals, including humans. During the Pleistocene geological epoch, for instance, animal populations slowly migrated toward lower altitudes and warmer latitudes. The classic European glaciation scheme originally recognized four glacial periods, named after Alpine valleys: the Günz, Mindel, Riss, and Würm. These glacial periods were subdivided into cold phases, the stadials, and separated by warmer interstadials. Glaciations alternated with warmer periods, called interglacial periods. Glaciations were not periods of unrelenting cold, for temperatures fluctuated as the ice sheets advanced and retreated.

Pleistocene glaciations most drastically affected the higher latitudes in North America and Europe, while they had lesser effects in Asia and Africa. At their maximum, ice sheets covered up to three times as much land area as they do today. Less dramatic climatic shifts occurred in the more tropical latitudes of southern Asia and Africa. Climatic zones shifted depending on the extent of the Arctic zones. For example, during colder periods, the dry Sahara supported some grassland vegetation and the Mediterranean became a temperate sea. Snow lines were sometimes lowered on tropical mountain ranges, and rain forests expanded and contracted depending on the amount of rainfall. The vast ice sheets locked up enormous amounts of water, lowering sea levels to far below their present depths. Land bridges formed as the sea level dropped and exposed the continental shelf from the ocean now covering it. When the ice sheets melted, sea levels rose and flooded many regions.

The European glaciation scheme has been modified in recent years, and the names of the glacial periods have been changed. The three most recent northern European glaciations are now named after three German rivers: the Elster, the Saale, and the Weichsel. At the height of the Elster Glaciation, 32 percent of the world's land mass was covered with ice, and sea levels were lowered by as much as 650 feet below their present height. The Kansan Glaciation in North America is equivalent to the Elster in northern Europe.

The Holstein, or Great, Interglacial followed the Elster Glaciation. The climate was temperate and at times milder than that characterizing modern Europe. During the Great Interglacial, human settlement in temperate latitudes took hold as small bands exploited the rich game populations of European river valleys.

The Saale Glaciation coincided with the North American Illinoian Glaciation. The Saale Glaciation did not last as long as the Elster, and gave way to the last Interglacial, the Eem, about 125,000 years ago. The Eem Interglacial lasted about 50,000 years and was more temperate than the Holstein Interglacial. Temperatures at the height of the Eem may have been comparable to those of recent times.

The Weichsel Glaciation, the Wisconsin Glaciation in North America, formed the last great European Pleistocene ice sheet. About 70,000 years ago, the climate cooled rapidly and tundra replaced central European forests (Figure 13-1). By about 50,000 years ago the seas were about 350 feet lower than today.

Floral and Faunal Indicators of Pleistocene Climates

Palynology, the analysis of fossilized pollens, is one of the most valuable aids for determining past climatic conditions. When the nearly indestructible pollen granules settle to the ground, they become incorporated into the deposits and in the absence of lime are almost indefinitely preserved. Because pollens of various floral species are quite individualistic and can often be readily identified at the generic level, pollen analysis can be applied to solving problems relating to the paleoenvironment.

Because the composition of faunal assemblages often changes in response to climatic conditions, faunal remains can also be used to reconstruct paleoenvironments. The most useful mammalian groups for correlating Pleistocene deposits include the elephant, rhinoceros, bear, hyena, deer, and antelope. Elephants are important demarcators of Pleistocene subdivisions. The dating of virtually all European human fossil sites relies on associated fossilized elephant remains. Evolutionary changes in suids (pig-like forms) during the Pliocene and Early Pleistocene in Africa have been used to obtain relative dates for early human remains found in Africa.

Mammalian remains also aid the dating of deposits by indicating a climatic

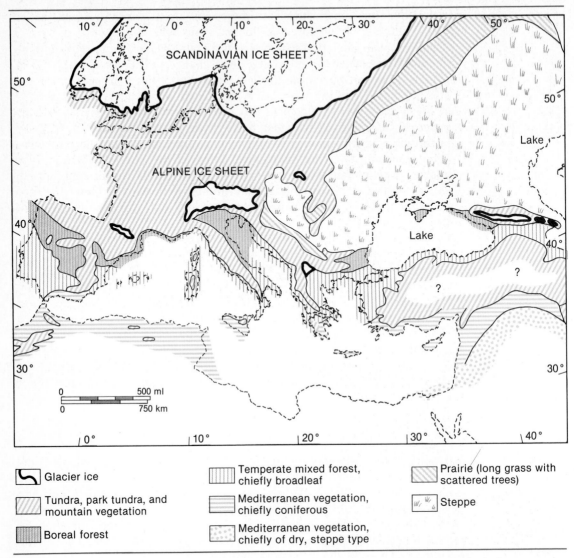

Figure 13-1 European vegetation at the height of the Weichsel Glaciation.

stage. For example, it can be inferred that a hippopotamus-bearing deposit is from a different time period than one containing a cold-climate form such as the musk ox. Fossil invertebrates, freshwater and land mollusks (such as snails), and insects are also valuable climatic indicators because they are highly sensitive to climatic changes.

Researchers seek not only to recover fossilized remains, they also seek to date these materials and to understand the preservation process. Without reference to a dated sequence, fossil and archaeological remains are of limited scientific value. The study of the fossilization process is called taphonomy. Taphonomic analysis seeks to assess the contribution of geological, human, and other agents to the formation of clusters of bones or artifacts.

When considering the age of a specimen, researchers seek to ascertain the relationship of the fossil material to known dated sequences and attempt to ascertain the chronological age of the specimen. Depending upon the geological context, specimens can be either relatively or chronometrically dated. Those specimens in radioactive geological contexts, such as volcanic deposits, are capable of being chronometrically dated. Such specimens are provided with a numerical date. The major chronometric dating techniques are C^{14} useful in dating organic materials to about 50,000 years ago, and potassium-argon, used to date radioactive geological strata from 500,000 years ago to 3 billion years ago. Fission track dating can be used to verify potassium-argon dates.

Researchers also need to understand the ecological context of their fossils or artifacts. The study of fossil pollens, palynology, is useful in this regard.

BIBLIOGRAPHY

BRILL, R., R. FLEISCHER, R. PRICE, and R. WALKER. 1964. The fission-track dating of man-made glasses. *Journal of Glass Studies* 6: 151.

BROCK, A., and G. ISAAC. 1974. Paleomagnetic stratigraphy and chronology of hominid-bearing sediments east of Lake Rudolf, Kenya. *Nature* 247: 344–48.

BUTZER, K. 1971. *Environment and Archaeology: An Introduction to Pleistocene Geography,* 2d ed. Chicago: Aldine-Atherton.

CORNWELL, I. 1970. *Ice Ages: Their Nature and Effect.* New York: Humanities Press.

COX, A., G. DALRYMPLE, and R. DOELL. 1967. Reversals of the earth's magnetic field. *Scientific American* 216: 44–54.

DAMON, P., C. FERGUSON, A. LONG, and E. WALLICK. 1974. Dendrochronologic calibration of the radiocarbon time scale. *American Antiquity* 39: 350–66.

DIMBLEBY, G. 1970. Pollen analysis. In *Science in Archaeology,* D. Brothwell and E. Higgs, eds. New York: Praeger.

FAGAN, B. 1977. *People of the Earth,* 2d ed. Boston: Little, Brown.

FLEISHER, R., L. LEAKEY, P. PRICE, and R. WALKER. 1965. Fission-track dating of Bed I, Olduvai Gorge. *Science* 148: 72–74.

FLINT, R. 1971. *Glacial and Quaternary Geology.* New York: John Wiley.

GROMME, C., and R. HAY. 1963. Magnetization of basalt, Bed I, Olduvai Gorge, Tanganyika. *Nature* 200: 560–61.

HIGGS, E. 1970. Fauna. In *Science and Archaeology,* D. Brothwell and E. Higgs, eds. New York: Praeger.

HOWELL, F. 1975. An overview of the Pliocene and earlier Pleistocene of the Lower Omo basin, southern Ethiopia. In *Human Origins,* G. Isaac and E. McCown, eds. Menlo Park, Calif.: W. A. Benjamin.

LIBBY, W. 1955. *Radiocarbon Dating.* Chicago: University of Chicago Press.

MUSSET, A., T. REILLY, and P. RAJA. 1965. Paleomagnetism in East Africa. In *East*

African Rift System: Report of the Upper Mantle Committee. UNESCO seminar, Nairobi, 1965. Part 2, pp. 83–94.

OAKLEY, K. 1953. Dating fossil human remains. In *Anthropology Today,* A. Kroeber, ed. Chicago: Aldine.

OAKLEY, K. 1966. *Frameworks for Dating Fossil Man.* Chicago: Aldine.

OAKLEY, K. 1970. Analytical methods of dating bones. In *Science in Archaeology,* D. Brothwell and E. Higgs, eds. New York: Praeger.

PRICE, P., and R. WALKER. 1963. A simple method of measuring low uranium concentrations in natural crystals. *Applied Physics Letters* 2: 32.

RENFREW, C. 1971. Carbon[14] and the prehistory of Europe. In *Avenues to Prehistory,* B. Fagan, ed. San Francisco: Freeman.

SHUEY, R., F. BROWN, and M. CROSS. 1974. Magneto-stratigraphy of the Shungura Formation, southwestern Ethiopia. Fine structure of the lower Matuyama polarity epoch. *Earth and Planetary Science Letters* 23: 249–60.

Chapter
14
Early Primate Evolution

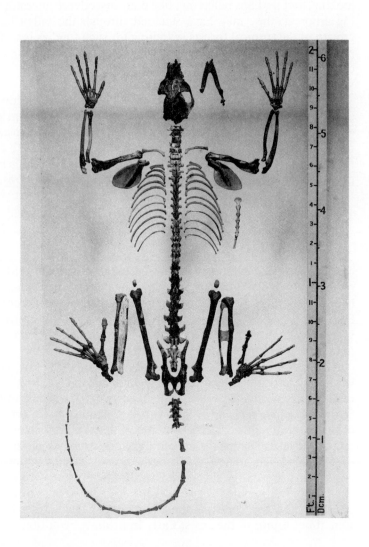

Primates probably first appeared in North America about 60 M.Y.A. In the initial stages of primate evolution, animals were forced from the ground into the trees because of competition for a terrestrial niche. Skeletal changes characterizing early primate evolution were primarily associated with diet; later skeletal modifications suggest locomotor changes that were probably associated with exploiting and exploring the arboreal habitat.

EARLY PRIMATES

Early primates were probably beady-eyed, whiskered, long-snouted animals looking, and perhaps behaving, like their insectivore ancestors. Before becoming arboreal, they may have scurried through the fallen leaves and undergrowth of the tropical forests searching for such food as insects. Early primate evolution coincided with a time when the Earth was undergoing extensive change. There seems to have been an enormous expansion in the number and variety of ivies, shrubs, and trees.

Early primates and insectivores probably intensively competed with one another for niches on the ground and in the trees. Early primates may have entered the trees as a refuge zone where competition from insectivores was less intense. In the trees, primates were forced to adapt to a life among the dense foliage, branches, and forest canopies. The adaptation to this new niche led the primates to develop a new set of environmental interactions.

PRIMATE DIET AND DENTITION

The majority of primate evolution occurred in the trees. Major adjustments required for tree living led to a shift in dietary preference and patterns of habitat exploration, including changes in the limb structure as noted in the Eocene (55–50 M.Y.A.) fossil record. Most foods within the arboreal habitat are vegetal, and most modern primates are essentially vegetarians who supplement their diets with insects and occasionally with meat.

The order Primates is first distinguished in the fossil record by a set of shared molar traits. Apart from these dental characteristics, ancestral primates retained primitive insectivore traits (Schwartz, Tattersall, and Eldridge, 1978; Szalay, Rosenberger, and Dagosto, 1987). Teeth, which form a major portion of the fossil remains of early primates, reflect an important dietary shift. The diet of the **insectivorous** (insect-eating) stock, from which the earliest primates probably evolved, included soft-bodied invertebrates (animals without backbones) that are easily sliced and swallowed. Insectivore teeth are long and sharp with well-defined **cusps** (elevations of the tooth crown surface) and are poorly suited for chewing the rough, tough-shelled seeds or fibrous fruit sometimes found in the trees. Early in primate evolution there was selection for teeth with shorter and more bulbous (rounded) cusps, which are better suited for grinding.

The dietary shift that characterized early primates was not an absolute shift away from an insectivorous diet; rather, it occurred through a relative increase in the importance of fruit, leaves, and other herbaceous materials, and a decrease in feeding on insects. Dietary changes characterizing the earliest stages of primate evolution may have occurred as a series of overlapping shifts. First, a large and sparsely inhabited frugivorous-herbivorous (fruit, bud, and leaf) niche must have been available. The changes necessary to adapt to these new foods were largely behavioral; for example, there was a slow shift in food preferences. Once a sustained interest in small fruits, berries, and leaves became established at the expense of a more insectivorous diet, selection favored populations that could most efficiently use these foods. Dependence on these new foods led to modification of the dentition and the digestive tract.

Modifications in the face and skull accompanied those of the chewing apparatus. One major change involved the reduction of the snout, which was probably related to a reduction in size and the crowding of the incisor, canine, and premolar teeth. There was probably an increasing reliance on the hands for picking up objects such as foods that were conveyed from hand to mouth. The cheekbones became broad and strong, probably because of an increasing bulk of the **masseter muscle** complex. The masseter muscles are chiefly concerned with the grinding mode of chewing. (If you touch your cheeks and grit your teeth, you can feel these muscles.) Major changes in the face and skull, such as the forward rotation of the orbits and a reduction of the snout, are associated with the development of **stereoscopic vision** (Figure 14-1) (the convergence of the two visual fields on one object) and an increasing reliance on vision and a reduction of the olfactory sense. Such changes are seen in Eocene primate fossils.

EVIDENCE OF PALEOCENE PRIMATES

The earliest fossil evidence of a possible primate stock comes from Paleocene deposits dating about 60 M.Y.A. from sites in Montana, Wyoming, Colorado, and New Mexico. These remains are assigned to the superfamily Plesiadapoidea (Table 14-1). An early genus of this group is *Purgatorius,* represented by a sample of 50 isolated teeth from a site in eastern Montana.

Dental patterns suggest that many Paleocene forms were adapting to a new diet, and further indicate entry into a new habitat. The variety of molar tooth patterns suggests that Paleocene primates were not specialized insectivores. Characteristics of the incisor and canine teeth suggest a specialized herbivorous or frugivorous diet. The emphasis on the development of the incisor teeth and a deemphasis on the canines indicates a general lack of predatory behavior.

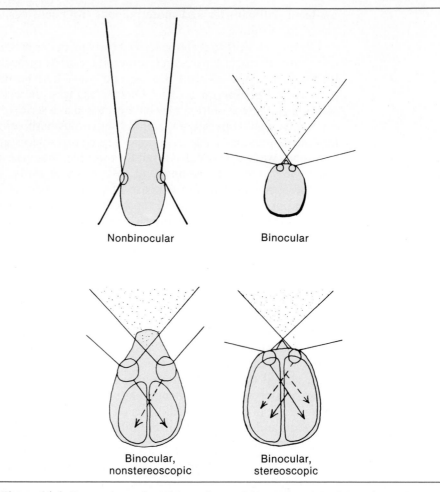

Nonbinocular

Binocular

Binocular,
nonstereoscopic

Binocular,
stereoscopic

Figure 14-1 Comparison of nonbinocular and binocular sight (above) and binocular, nonstereoscopic and binocular, stereoscopic vision (below). Primates possess binocular, stereoscopic vision.

PRIMATE EVOLUTION DURING THE EOCENE

A major adaptation to arboreal life was an adjustment to getting around in the trees, to exploiting this three-dimensional world. Major adjustments appear in the hands, feet, skull, and face of Eocene fossils dating from 50 to 36 M.Y.A. The Eocene epoch witnessed the maximal radiation (divergent development) of the early primates. As many as 43 genera and 3 families—the Adapidae (Figure 14-2), Tarsiidae, and Anaptomorphidae—have been recognized (Table 14-2).

Table 14-1. *Some Members of the First Possible Primate Superfamily, the Plesiadapoidea**

FAMILY	EPOCH	DISTRIBUTION	TRAITS
Plesiadapidae	Paleocene-Eocene	Europe, North America	Medium size, vegetarian, large chiseling incisors
Carpolestidae	Paleocene	North America	Rodent size, omnivorous, enlarged incisors and premolars
Paromomyidae	Late Cretaceous, Paleocene, Eocene	Europe, North America	Diverse group of rodent size, very long incisors
Picrodontidae	Paleocene	North America	Tiny mouselike animals, specialized teeth, nectar and insect feeders(?)

*Some reject this group as primates.
SOURCE: Adapted from C. Jolly and F. Plog, *Physical Anthropology and Archaeology* (New York: Knopf, 1976), p. 163.

Limb Structure

The general limb adaptations to arboreal life include grasping hands and feet equipped with nails instead of claws. The hands and feet of the early primates are characterized by pentadactyly (five digits) and by an opposable thumb and big toe. Grasping hands and feet are an adaptation to climbing by grasping, and they allow the young primate to cling to its mother, thereby reducing infant mortality in a species in which the mother is highly mobile. Foot bones belonging to a 52 million-year-old primate found in Wyoming and known as *Cantius trigonodus* are the oldest fossil evidence of a grasping big toe.

The primate forelimb is constructed from two separate bones—the ulna (on the outer side of the arm) and [the radius (on the thumb side)]. This allows forearm rotation and greater mobility, both of which are useful adaptations to the jumping and grasping necessitated by an arboreal life-style.

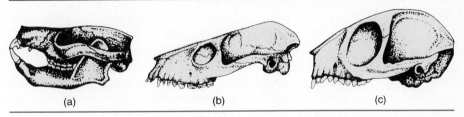

(a)   (b)   (c)

Figure 14-2 Comparison of the skull of the Paleocene form Plesiadapis *(A) with the Eocene forms* Adapis *(B) and* Necrolemur *(C) shows the reduction of the snout area.*

Table 14-2. **Some Members of the "Second Wave" of Primate Evolution**

TAXON	EPOCH	DISTRIBUTION	TRAITS
Family Adapidae	Eocene, Oligocene	Europe, North America, Asia, Africa	Diverse group of medium-size forms
Subfamily Adapinae	Eocene, Oligocene	Europe	Herbivores, some small, large-eyed forms
Subfamily Notharctinae	Eocene	North America, Asia, Africa	
Family Anaptomorphidae	Eocene, Miocene	Asia, Europe, North America	Small primates
Subfamily Anaptomorphinae	Eocene	North America	Small, large eyes, dentition suggests mixed diet
Subfamily Omomyinae	Eocene, Miocene	Asia, Europe, North America	Widespread group, generalized diet

SOURCE: Adapted from C. Jolly and F. Plog, *Physical Anthropology and Archaeology.* (New York: Knopf, 1976), p. 163.

Skull and Facial Structure

Major changes in the primate skull and face occurred in the Eocene. For example, both the reduction of the snout and the forward rotation of the eye orbits to a position in the front of the face suggest a reduction of reliance on the olfactory sense and increased reliance on vision. This shift in senses is emphasized by the lack of a naked rhinarium (the moistened, hairless, tactile-sensitive skin surrounding the nostrils in many mammals) in most modern primates. A shift from a reliance on olfaction to vision required a reorganization of the brain. There was a reduction of the olfactory brain center and an enlargement of the visual center.

Fossil evidence from Eocene primates, such as the shifting of the eye orbits from a lateral to a frontal position and the enclosure of the orbits by a protective bone casing, supports the argument for an increasing importance of the visual sense. Two Eocene primates, *Adapis* and *Notharctus* (Figure 14-3), show forward rotation of the orbits. Forward orbital rotation results in stereoscopic vision, which appears to be an adaptation to spatial orientation and may be associated with feeding and jumping from one tree limb to another. Leaping from branch to branch, for instance, requires that the tree-dweller continually make distance judgments. To the degree that visual fields overlap, image fusion and improvements of depth perception are necessary. Despite the advantages that accompany orbit rotation and stereoscopic vision, the Paleocene and Eocene primate record suggests that the order Primates began to diverge into perhaps a dozen or more forms before full forward orbital rotation was complete.

As a result of the shift in position of the orbits, the primate eye is

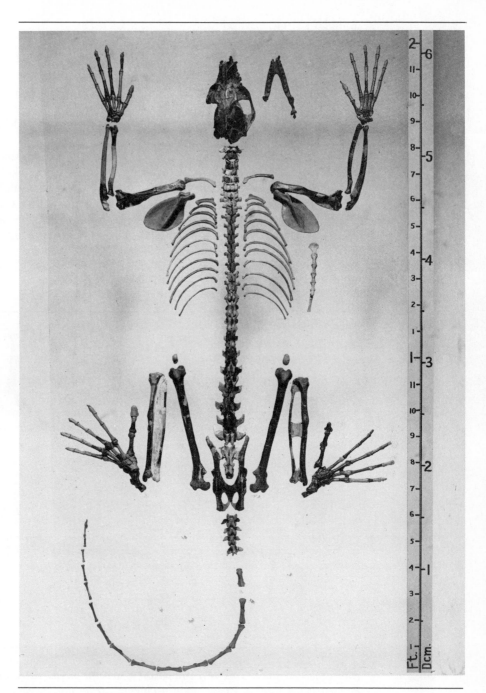

Figure 14-3 *Skeletal reconstruction of Middle Eocene primate* Notharctus osborni.

vulnerable. The eye of most prosimians (the first primates to evolve) is protected only by a slender bar of bone; but in monkeys, apes, and humans, the entire orbit is surrounded by a ring of bone, resulting in a distinct eye socket. One of the earliest possible primates, a form called *Plesiadapis* (Figure 14-4), lacks a complete bony orbit and still shows laterally diverged orbits. Some time during primate evolution, the structure of the eye itself was reorganized; most modern primates are **diurnal** creatures (active during the day) with some color vision.

Some Eocene primates show a shifting forward of the **foramen magnum** (the hole through which the spinal cord passes) to under the skull, which, when coupled with forelimb shortening, indicates that these animals kept an erect posture when sitting. Upright sitting, a major primate trait, is accommodated in some modern Old World primates by the presence of a specialized calloused skin on the rump called the ischial callosities. Ischial callosities are deadened areas of skin which allow those primates possessing them to sit comfortably on hard surfaces for endless periods of time. Upright sitting frees the hands for

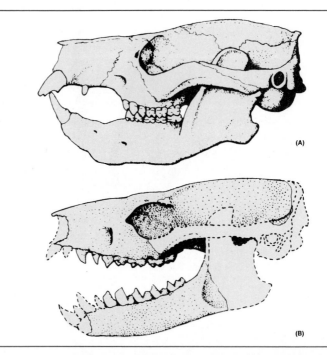

Figure 14-4 (A) Reconstructed skull of Plesiadapis tricuspidens *from the Late Paleocene of France. This is a composite of several published reconstructions. (B) Reconstructed skull of* Palaochthon nacimienti, *from mid-Paleocene of New Mexico (not to same scale). (B) modified from R. Kay and M. Cartmill,* Nature *(1984) 252:37-38.*

activities such as putting food to the mouth and exploring. These activities improve hand–eye coordination.

Changes in Ear Structure

It has been suggested that a major trend in early primate evolution was a reorganization of the structure and function of the middle ear that may have allowed better balance while leaping and may have enhanced the ability to make constant adjustments in body position. The ability to determine body position is important to an animal that habitually glides, leaps, or relies occasionally, but crucially, on exacting balance. The highly advanced middle-ear cavity of the Paleocene form *Plesiadapis,* especially in comparison with its relatively primitive postcranial (below the head) skeleton, suggests that its locomotion and feeding adaptations required a highly developed sense of balance and suggests an arboreal life-style. (Despite its advanced middle-ear structure, controversy exists as to whether *Plesiadapis* was arboreal.)

ALTERNATIVE HYPOTHESES

Arboreal Hypothesis

The arboreal hypothesis of primate origins links the major adaptations of early primates to the tree-dwelling habitat (Smith, 1912; Jones, 1916). According to the arboreal hypothesis, the primate's grasping hands and feet are related to grasping and hanging onto thin branches. The hands were the grasping and exploratory organs, and the hind limbs supported and propelled the body.

Jones argued that early in primate evolution the body's posture became upright, and grasping hands gradually replaced the jaws for obtaining food. The jaws and face became smaller, and the orbits shifted frontally. There were changes in the nervous system. The importance of the olfactory senses declined, and the visual senses became elaborated. This led to a restructuring of the brain and further anatomical changes in the face and jaw. Cartmill says of this view of primate origins, "The theory is persuasive, neat and fairly comprehensive. It does provide an explanation for most of the peculiarities of primates. I am going to argue, however, that it is not adequate" (1975b:15).

Visual Predation Hypothesis

Cartmill (1972, 1975b) offers the visual predation hypothesis as an elaboration of the arboreal hypothesis. Cartmill's theory concentrates on explaining the functions and evolution of the grasping hands and feet and the distinctive primate visual system. Grasping hands and feet are found only among arboreal mammals or their secondarily terrestrially adapted relatives. Most arboreal mammals have hands and feet more like those found among squirrels than among monkeys, however. Only some climbing mice, animals like the possum, and most nonhuman primates have a divergent and opposable big toe.

Cartmill argues that grasping feet help protect an animal against sudden falls and are well adapted for locomotion on slender branches. Grasping hands and feet might be adaptations to cautious movement among relatively slender branches on whose ends grow leaves, flowers, fruits, and nuts—growth that attracts insects and other invertebrates. If they could safely get out to the branch ends, primates would find a rich plant and insect food supply.

Feeding at the ends of branches does not itself require grasping hands and feet. But if an animal feeding there is a predator of invertebrates, it must be able to move quietly within striking distance of the prey and then either leap at or grab it with a swift movement of the hand and arm. Grasping feet allow an animal to move quietly and cautiously along relatively thin branches and, by anchoring the animal to a branch, allow it to lift both its hands to grab at the prey.

The primates' close-set eyes might also be an adaptation to predation. Among nonprimates, cats probably have the most primatelike visual system. In addition to their stereoscopic vision, cats resemble primates in other aspects of the visual system. Cats catch their prey by stalking and suddenly pouncing; they rely on visual cues, especially stereoscopic vision, to estimate the length of the pounce. Cartmill uses cat hunting behavior, with its anatomical modifications such as stereoscopic vision and close-set eyes, as a model for explaining primate predation and the evolution of their visual system. According to Cartmill (1975b:19), "the grasping hind feet and close-set eyes characteristic of primates originated as part of an adaptation to visually directed predation on insects among slender branches. . . ."

Visual predation can help explain the reduction of the primate olfactory sense. Reduction in olfaction may be a result of a convergence of the orbits. As the orbits move toward the middle of the face, they constrict nerves that pass between them from the brain to the nose. Olfaction appears to be most reduced in primates in which the eye sockets are closest together.

The replacement of claws by nails might also be an adaptation to moving on slender branches and feeding on fruits, seeds, nectar, and insects that are caught by hand. "Clawless digits, grasping feet and close-set eyes: These and other features common to most living primates all suggest that the last common ancestor of the living primates was a small visual predator. . . ." (Cartmill, 1975b:21).

Both the arboreal and the visual predation hypotheses agree that primates evolved in the trees. The hypotheses differ, however, in that Cartmill stresses what the primates did within the trees—that is, visually preyed on insects. Neither Jones nor Smith stressed feeding adaptations as crucial to explaining early primate evolution.

It is difficult to identify the earliest primate forms, which may have appeared during the late Paleocene. The earliest primates are identified by molar traits; later forms are recognized by changes in the limb, skull, and facial skeletons. Although primates evolved first in North America and spread from there to other regions of the world, by 40 M.Y.A. the center of primate evolution had shifted to Asia and Africa. During the latter time period, we witness the evolution of new primate forms, the monkeys and the apes. The evolution of the apes is discussed in Chapter 15.

Two different hypotheses have been offered to explain the appearance of major primate traits. The first hypothesis was offered in the early 1900s by G. Smith and F.W. Jones, who argued that the major primate anatomical traits were adaptations to life in the trees. Their suggestion is termed the arboreal hypothesis. M. Cartmill offered an elaboration of the arboreal hypothesis which is called the visual predation hypothesis. Cartmill's hypothesis concentrates on explaining the functions and evolution of the grasping hands and feet and the distinctive primate visual system.

BIBLIOGRAPHY

BARTH, F. 1950. On the relationships of early primates. *American Journal of Physical Anthropology* 8: 139–49.

BEECHER, W. 1969. Possible motion detection in the vertebrate middle ear. *Bulletin of the Chicago Academy of Science* 2: 155.

CARTMILL, M. 1972. Arboreal adaptations and the origin of the order Primates. In *The Functional and Evolutionary Biology of Primates,* R. Tuttle, ed. Chicago: Aldine-Atherton.

CARTMILL, M. 1975a. *Primate Origins.* Minneapolis: Burgess.

CARTMILL, M. 1975b. Primate evolution: Analyses of trends. *Science* 184: 436–443.

CLARK, W. E. 1969. *History of the Primates.* Chicago: Phoenix Books.

CLARK, W. E. 1971. *The Antecedents of Man.* Chicago: Quadrangle.

CONROY, G. 1980. Ontogeny, auditory structures, and primate evolution. *American Journal of Physical Anthropology* 52: 443–51.

HAINES, R. 1958. Arboreal or terrestrial ancestry of placental mammals? *Quarterly Review of Biology* 33: 1–23.

JOLLY, C., and F. PLOG. 1976. *Physical Anthropology and Archaeology.* New York: Knopf.

JONES, F. W. 1916. *Arboreal Man.* London: Arnold.

MACPHEE, R. 1982. *Auditory Regions of Primates and Eutherian Insectivores: Morphology, Ontogeny, and Character Analysis. Contributions to Primatology,* vol. 18. New York: S. Karger.

MARTIN, R. 1968. Towards a new definition of primates. *Man* 3: 377–401.

ROSE, M., and A. WALKER 1985. The skeleton of early Eocene *Cantius,* oldest lemuriform primate. *American Journal of Physical Anthropology* 66: 73–89.

SCHWARTZ, J., I. TATTERSALL, and N. ELDRIDGE. 1978. Phylogeny and classification of primates revisited. *Yearbook of Physical Anthropology* 21: 92–133.

SHAKLEE, A. 1975. Primate evolution: Analysis of trends. *Science* 189: 228.

SIMONS, E. 1972. *Primate Evolution: An Introduction to Man's Place in Nature.* New York: Macmillan.

SMITH, G. 1912. Presidential address to the anthropology section (H) of the Eighty-second Annual Meeting, British Association for the Advancement of Science, London.

SZALAY, F. 1968. The beginnings of primates. *Evolution* 22: 19–36.

SZALAY, F. 1972. Paleobiology of the earliest primates. In *The Functional and Evolutionary Biology of Primates,* R. Tuttle, ed. Chicago: Aldine-Atherton.

SZALAY, F. 1973. A review of some recent advances in paleoprimatology. *Yearbook of Physical Anthropology* 17: 39–64.

SZALAY, F., and E. DELSON. 1978. *Evolutionary History of Primates.* New York: Academic Press.

SZALAY, F., A. ROSENBERGER, and M. DAGOSTO. 1987. Diagnosis and differentiation of the order Primates. *Yearbook of Physical Anthropology* 30: 75–106.

VAN VALEN, L. 1965. Tree shrews, primates, and fossils. *Evolution* 19: 137–51.

VAN VALEN, L. 1969. A classification of the primates. *American Journal of Physical Anthropology* 30: 295–96.

VAN VALEN, L., and R. SLOAN. 1965. The earliest primates. *Science* 150: 743–45.

WILSON, J. (ed.) 1972. *Continents Adrift.* San Francisco: W. H. Freeman & Company Publishers.

Chapter

15

The Transition
to the Apes

The earliest ancestors of living apes seem to have appeared approximately 40 M.Y.A. in Eocene geological deposits in Burma. One Miocene ape group, the dryopithecines, was once considered to be the last common ancestor of humans and apes. Another Miocene fossil, once referred to as the genus Ramapithecus, *was considered to be the first ancestor on the hominid evolutionary line. The evolutionary roles of the dryopithecines and of* Ramapithecus *have been seriously undermined with the acceptance of a later divergence date—that is, 6 to 8 M.Y.A.—of humans and apes from a common ancestor.*

BURMESE FOSSILS

Southern Asia is a focal point for the earliest hominoid origins (Figure 15-1). This suggestion is based on finds dated to about 40 M.Y.A. and placed within the genera *Pondaungia* and *Amphipithecus,* both of which come from the Pondaung Hills, upper Burma. Since their original discovery in the mid-1930s, anthropologists have debated the evolutionary affinities of these fossils. Their discovery raised two questions: (1) Are they the earliest representatives of the ape evolutionary line? and (2) Was Asia the focal point of early ape evolution?

Supplemented with finds made in the 1970s, the fossil sample of *Amphipithecus* and *Pondaungia* consists of a few lower-jaw fragments and teeth. *Amphipithecus's* mandible is deep and heavy relative to its molars (Figure 15-2). Both halves of the lower jaw are fused, perhaps in response to heavy chewing stress. *Amphipithecus* has one extra premolar compared with modern apes, a trait found in modern New World primates. The chewing surfaces of the teeth suggest a diet including fruit (Ciochon, 1980). *Amphipithecus* was approximately the size of the smallest of the modern apes, the gibbon, and weighed 15 to 20 pounds (Figure 15-3).

OLIGOCENE HOMINOIDS

Oligocene deposits from the Fayum area south of Cairo, Egypt, yielded fossils of ancestors of living apes as well as fossils of monkeys. The Fayum habitat at 30 to 35 M.Y.A. was quite different from what it is today. The Fayum area is now desert, but studies of fossilized seed pods, pollens, and wood indicate that the Oligocene site was part of a tropical gallery forest. There were probably also areas of open savanna or coastal plains nearby. The Fayum faunal assemblage indicates a warm, well-watered lowland.

The Oligocene Fayum primates may have inhabited the forest canopy, as do most modern generalized primates. The suggestion that the environment consisted of tropical, lush, stream-watered growth is supported by the rarity of small mammalian fauna other than primates and rodents. Undergrowth near

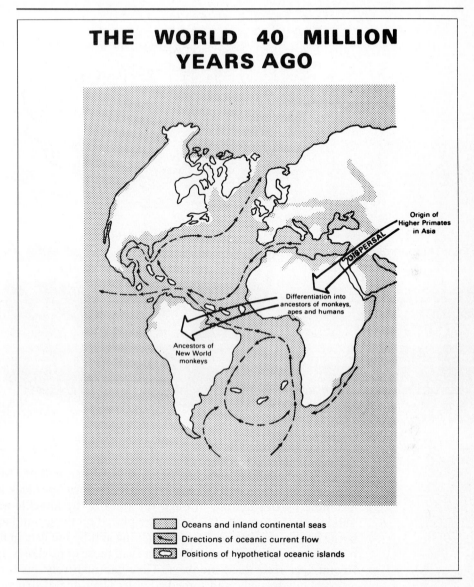

THE WORLD 40 MILLION YEARS AGO

Origin of
Higher Primates
in Asia

DISPERSAL

Differentiation into
ancestors of monkeys,
apes and humans

Ancestors of
New World
monkeys

Oceans and inland continental seas

Directions of oceanic current flow

Positions of hypothetical oceanic islands

Figure 15-1 The world as it looked about 40 million years ago. The arrows indicate the possible migration route of early primates out of Asia into Africa and then into South America.

the Oligocene streams was probably too dense or wet to maintain an abundance of small mammals. Primates and rodents, the most common fauna at the site, might have reached this relatively inaccessible riverbank area through the forest canopy.

Monkeys and apes are generally distinguished by anatomical traits related

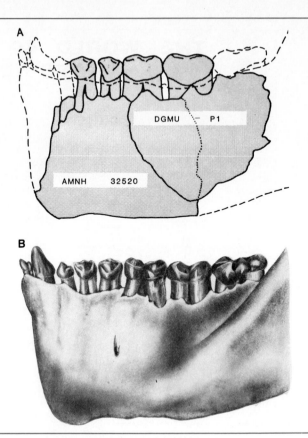

Figure 15-2 The reconstructed mandible of Amphipithecus.

to locomotor adaptations, dental characteristics, or both. Modern monkeys have tails and are generally quadrupedal; modern apes lack a tail, and some locomote by brachiating through the trees or by **knuckle-walking** and **fist-walking** on the ground. The hands are placed on the ground and the weight is borne by the knuckles in knuckle-walking and by the fists in fist-walking. The brain sizes of apes are generally larger than those of monkeys. In many respects Fayum apes resembled monkeys. They had relatively small brains and were arboreal quadrupeds, and some had tails. Their dental structure was uniquely apelike, however. These were monkeylike primates with apelike teeth.

A large portion of the Fayum primate assemblage consists of young animals. Their youth is indicated by the incomplete tooth eruption on many of the jaw fragments. Their skeletal remains allow us to make a number of morphological assumptions. For example, the frontal bones of the skull show that these primates had a comparatively narrow snout situated between relatively forward-positioned eyes, some forebrain expansion, and a relative reduction of the olfactory lobes. These primates relied on their visual sense.

Figure 15-3 Artist's reconstruction of Amphipithecus *based on actual fossil evidence and the order of development of anatomical features observed in primate evolution.*

Limb bones of the Fayum apes consist of toe and ankle bones, as well as a **humerus** and ulna (two forearm bones). These remains indicate that the Fayum primates were quadrupeds. Some Fayum apes had tails, unlike their modern descendants.

The oldest of the Fayum primates is *Oligopithecus savagei,* which has been dated to approximately 35 M.Y.A. The *Oligopithecus* fossil record consists of the left half of the mandible, from which both incisors and the last molars are missing. Simons (1962a or 1962b) reconstructs the **dental formula** as 2-1-2-3 (2 incisors, 1 canine, 2 premolars, and 3 molars in each quadrant of the jaw), like that of all modern Old World monkeys, apes, and humans.

Apidium, another Fayum genus, is represented by two species. The genera *Apidium* and *Parapithecus* form the family Parapithecidae. Simons (1960, 1972) suggests that they are ancestral to modern Old World monkeys. The genus *Apidium* forms the largest group of Fayum primate fossils. *Apidium* has an extra premolar when compared with modern Old World primates. Its dental formula, 2-1-3-3, a total of 36 teeth, is the same as that of most New World monkeys. Those holding to the possibility of continental drift as one explanation of the similarity between Old and New World monkeys point to the shared feature of 36 teeth characteristic of *Apidium* and New World monkeys as evidence of an African ancestry for New World primates.

The dental formula of *Propliopithecus,* which dates to 30 M.Y.A., is 2-1-2-3. Its canines are fairly short and small, and the premolars lack the sectorial (one-cusped) condition characteristic of modern apes. In primates with large upper canines, the canine overlaps the premolar in the lower jaw. The overlapping canines are accommodated by a gap, the **canine diastema** (Figure 15-4), between the premolar and canine and by the presence of one instead of two cusps, the **bicuspid** condition, on the premolar against which the overlapping canine rubs. The incisors of *Propliopithecus* appear to have been vertically implanted; they do not jut forward as is the case in most modern monkeys and apes. The face did not project far forward.

Propliopithecus was probably a small-faced arboreal ape. Most likely, this genus represented a large stock, some of whose members may have given rise to *Aegyptopithecus* and perhaps later to modern apes. Four species of *Propliopithecus* are now known from the Fayum. This indicates remarkable variability during the Oligocene period (Simons, Rasmussen, and Gebo, 1987).

Aegyptopithecus is dated to approximately 34 to 33 M.Y.A. More than 12 skull fragments, over 50 teeth, and several limb bones have been recovered. The cranial remains provide one of the best-preserved indications of early ape skulls. *Aegyptopithecus* males had large sagittal crests. The large sagittal crests, a bony crest along the top of the skull, to which chewing muscles attach,

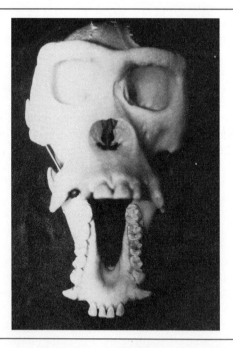

Figure 15-4 Skull, face, and lower jaw of an adult female gorilla. Note the large brow ridges and the lack of the large sagittal crest characteristic of male gorillas. On the lower jaw, the canine diastema is located between the premolar and the canine. You should also note that the incisor teeth are not vertically implanted as in humans, but jut forward.

develop in response to the heavy chewing musculature associated with large teeth. There are indications that *Aegyptopithecus* was increasing in size; the species *A. zeuxis* weighed 9 to 10 pounds. Numerous dental and facial similarities between *Aegyptopithecus* and the 20- to 16-million-year-old east African *Miocene* ape *Proconsul* suggest that *Aegyptopithecus* was in its ancestry (Simons, 1987).

An endocranial cast belonging to the genus *Aegyptopithecus* suggests that it possessed a rather small brain (Radinsky, 1973, 1977). The brain had a relatively large visual cortex, a relatively small olfactory region, and a smaller frontal lobe than that of modern apes. *Aegyptopithecus* had an increased emphasis on vision and a decreased reliance on smell, much like modern apes (Kay and Simons, 1980).

Besides the skull, *Aegyptopithecus* is known from four incomplete mandibles and about 50 teeth. Several dental traits suggest that it could have evolved from the earlier *Propliopithecus*. *Aegyptopithecus* shares a close morphological resemblance to the later dryopithecines. *Aegyptopithecus* has large canines for an animal its size, and the jaw is apelike.

In 1984, Simons announced newly discovered *Aegyptopithecus* remains which seem to contain members of both sexes. The jaws and canines assigned to males are larger than those assigned to females. In living primates in which such size differences exist, the animals live in bisexual social groups containing a number of adults. Like modern-day primates, *Aegyptopithecus* may have resided in relatively large social groups.

The limb skeleton of *Aegyptopithecus* is documented by more than a dozen arm bones and several leg and foot bones. There is a nearly complete right ulna which, in many ways, compares well with the ulnar length of the arboreal New World howler monkey or some of the Old World leaf-eating monkeys. *Aegyptopithecus* was well adapted to climbing and had some leaping ability. Two incomplete humeri also suggest that it was a robust, slowly moving arboreal quadruped (Fleagle and Simons, 1982).

Aegyptopithecus seems to be ancestral to the Miocene hominoids of the dryopithecine group. It seems to occupy an early position in the ape lineage. Although features of the skull and dentition suggest a relationship to later Old World primates, it must be emphasized that the postcranial skeleton differs.

Body weights of Fayum primates range from 1.3 pounds for *Apidium* to about 10 pounds for *Aegyptopithecus*. A similar range is found among modern New World monkeys. Body size is part of a species' adaptation to various food sources (Kay, 1973). The body sizes of Fayum primates tend to be larger than is common for modern arboreal insectivores, and this reduces the possibility of insect eating as a feeding strategy. The body size of *Aegyptopithecus* falls within the size range of such arboreal apes as the gibbon and very far below the range of terrestrial apes like chimpanzees and gorillas. This further indicates an arboreal habitat.

Although it has been argued that the Fayum forms precede the monkey–ape divergence (Fleagle et al., 1986), Simons (1987) argues that *Aegyptopithecus* is definitely an ancestral ape. The virtually simultaneous appearance of monkeys and ancestral apes in the Fayum deposits and the similarities of their small size, teeth designed for fruit eating, and quadrupedal posture indicate that they evolved either from a common ancestor or from a separate ancestor, but not one from the other (Whitten and Nickles, 1983).

MIOCENE HOMINOIDS

During the Miocene geological epoch of 25 to 6 M.Y.A., apes were represented by a number of genera which together are placed in a fossil group known as the dryopithecines. In Greek mythology, a *dryad* is a wood nymph, often said to have inhabited oak forests—a possible habitat for European dryopithecines. The most likely ancestor of the dryopithecines is *Aegyptopithecus.*

Dryopithecine is a generalized term for many Miocene apes. Although many different generic names have been applied, three separate dryopithecine genera or subgenera are generally recognized: the genus *Dryopithecus,* predominantly found in Europe; the genus *Sivapithecus,* found in Asia; and the genus *Proconsul,* found in Africa. There are also other forms which will be discussed.

Compared with the Oligocene primates, the Miocene apes show more similarities to modern apes. All of the Miocene apes have at least a few distinctly apelike traits. There is a considerable morphological gap between the early apes of the Fayum and the monkeys and apes of the early East African Miocene. The Miocene forms more clearly document the divergence of the monkeys and apes.

During the Miocene epoch, great mountain ranges arose and continents continued to drift apart. Africa and Eurasia were still one continent; however, volcanoes were actively changing the face of the African continent. A series of geological disturbances in Africa formed the Rift Valley. There seems to have been a mixture of wet and dry, warm and cool weather. The vegetation, which was a patchwork of forest and grassland not much different from modern African savannas, provided a rich environment of plant and animal foods.

Andrews (1981) suggested that the apes of the early Miocene, 20 to 18 M.Y.A., lived in quite different environments than did apes in the middle Miocene of 15 to 12 M.Y.A. The environment of early Miocene forms seems to have been more heavily forested, whereas that of the middle Miocene forms seems to have been dominated by temperate to tropical woodlands. This ecological shift is accompanied by skeletal changes in the primates, including the development of thickened tooth enamel, and skull and postcranial modifications. These changes probably reflected a changing dietary pattern and a new means of exploiting the environment. Although early Miocene apes retained many primitive traits, middle Miocene hominoids shared many traits with modern great apes and humans. They may have been able to exploit habitats beyond the range of modern apes.

The ancestors of modern great apes and humans passed through a very different adaptive phase that characterizes their present way of life. The members of one Miocene genus, *Sivapithecus,* were probably the size of modern orangutans. Animals of this size living in temperate or tropical woodlands must have been at least partially terrestrial because of discontinuities in the woodland canopy. Because woodland habitats have greater seasonal variation than do forests, fruits could be only a minor dietary item. The ecological evidence suggests that the middle Miocene apes were omnivorous and partially terrestrial (Andrews, 1981).

Fossils of Miocene apes are spread throughout the Old World: Africa, Asia, and Europe (Table 15-1). The first dryopithecine material, which was a lower jaw, was found in France in 1856. The first significant Asian ape fossil was a partial palate recovered and described in 1879.

As of 1979 (Pilbeam, 1979), the remains of about 300 individuals representing at least 7 ape species mostly belonging to the genus *Proconsul* had been recovered from 10 sites in Kenya and Uganda. Although some specimens may date to 20 M.Y.A., most probably date between 18.5 to 17.5 M.Y.A.

Table 15-1. **Distribution of Some Major Hominoid Sites**

Site	Genus	Age
Eurasia		
St. Gaudens, France	*Dryopithecus*	Mid-Miocene to Pliocene
Eppelsheim, Germany	"	
Vienna Basin, Austria	"	
Georgia, USSR	"	Early Miocene
Italy	*Oreopithecus*	Late Miocene
Siwalik Hills, India	*Sivapithecus*	Early Miocene
Lufeng, China	"	
Turkey	"	
Saudi Arabia	"	
Africa		
Maboko Island, Kenya	*Proconsul*	Early Miocene–Late Miocene
Rusinga Island, Kenya	"	
Songhor, Kenya	"	
Koru, Kenya	"	
Moroto, Uganda	"	
Napak, Kenya	*Micropithecus*	
Fort Ternan, Kenya	*Kenyapithecus*	
Kalodirr, Kenya	*Turkanapithecus*	Early Miocene
Kalodirr, Kenya	*Afropithecus*	Early Miocene
Maboko Island, Kenya	*Nyanzapithecus*	Early Miocene
Songhor, Kenya	*Rangwapithecus*	Early Miocene

Among the newest and most significant Miocene hominoid assemblages are the bones found at the Kaswanga Primate Site on Rusinga Island, Kenya. This site yielded 9 whole or partial *Proconsul* skeletons that were washed into a small gulley. The bones represent a sample of apes ranging in age from very small youngsters to adults of both sexes. Practically every part of the *Proconsul* skeleton is known from one or more of the individuals (Walker and Teaford, 1988). This assemblage has forced a rewriting of some earlier notions concerning the east African members of *Proconsul.*

The date of the large apes' appearance in Eurasia is still unclear; however, it seems to have occurred at less than 17 M.Y.A. Ape fossils from 300 localities in the Siwalik hills of Pakistan have been described (Pilbeam et al., 1977). The lower and middle Siwalik fauna can be separated into two groups: one dating around 12 M.Y.A. and another dating about 17 to 10 M.Y.A. The associated mammalian fossils suggest a woodland or bush habitat with open patches of grassland rather than extensive forests. In later times the habitat was open rather than extensively forested. The evidence suggests a shift from a mainly subtropical forest habitat to more open, less low-lying habitats and thus a nonevergreen forest context for at least some of the major primate localities.

At least two genera and four ape species have been identified at the Siwalik sites: *Sivapithecus punjabicus, S. sivalensis,* and *S. indicus,* and *Gigantopithecus bilaspurensis* (Pilbeam et al., 1977). *Sivapithecus* specimens range in age from 13 to 8 M.Y.A. and *Gigantopithecus* is dated to about 9 to 5 M.Y.A.

A lower jaw and four isolated teeth from Saudi Arabia date to 15 to 14 M.Y.A. (Andrews and Tobien, 1977). The faunal assemblage suggests a linkage with Africa. This is not surprising because migration occurred between Arabia and both North and East Africa at this time. These specimens have their closest morphological affinity to the Miocene apes of east Africa. Ape fossil material dating to 17 M.Y.A. has also been found in Saudi Arabia.

Because Saudi Arabia must have been close to migration routes between Africa and Eurasia, it is interesting that these specimens are not linked with contemporaneous species of *Sivapithecus* in Turkey. The Turkish deposits are similar in age to the Saudi deposit, but Turkish *Sivapithecus* species share traits with later Miocene *Sivapithecus* species from India and Pakistan. This indicates that the specimens from Saudi Arabia represent a primitive branch not directly related to later ape evolution.

Apes from the western part of Eurasia represent the genus *Dryopithecus* and date to about 13 to 9 M.Y.A. The material consists primarily of dental remains, although an ulna was found in France.

Western European apes were primitive forest or woodland forms and were probably quadrupedal arboreal dwellers. Larger species may have come to the ground to feed on relatively soft foods. Dryopithecine species disappeared from both Europe and East Africa about 9 M.Y.A., when climates cooled, foods became more seasonally abundant, and habitats provided less forest cover.

Although ape fossils are relatively rare, some major new fossils have been recovered in recent years, the evolutionary affinities of which were most unexpected. The Leakeys (1986a, 1986b) report the recovery of specimens from sediments along the western side of Lake Turkana, Kenya, at a small but rich early Miocene locality called Kalodirr. The estimated age of the deposits yielding the ape remains is 16 to 18 M.Y.A. The relatively complete material from Kalodirr is important in the new evidence it offers for morphological diversity in the Miocene Hominoidea.

The type specimen of one of the Kalodirr specimens, *Afropithecus turkanensis,* consists of the snout, facial skeleton, and some cranial fragments. The relatively large size of the canine teeth suggests that the specimen is a male. *Afropithecus* combines the traits typical of a variety of Miocene apes. This mosaic of traits suggests a greater complexity in the early Miocene ape fossil record than was previously apparent. *Afropithecus* shares some traits with the Oligocene form *Aegyptopithecus,* which may indicate a phylogenetic link (Leakey et al., 1988a).

The second new specimen from Kalodirr, *Turkanapithecus kalakolensis,* may be slightly smaller than a previously described female *Proconsul africanus* skull. It is reasonably complete and includes the facial skeleton, partial skullcap, and examples of all of the permanent maxillary teeth except the incisors. The associated lower jaw includes much of the left side and some teeth. A complete right femur and other bone fragments are probably associated with the skull and mandible. *Turkanapithecus's* relationship to other known fossil apes is not yet clear (Leakey et al., 1988b).

Other new material recovered in Kenya comes from Maboko Island (Harrison, 1986) and is assigned to a new genus, *Nyanzapithecus.* It dates to about 15 to 16 M.Y.A. *Nyanzapithecus* has a distinctive suite of traits, especially in the upper molars and premolars, which it shares with a late Miocene ape found in Italy called *Oreopithecus.* In both genera there is an increase in size from the first to the third molar. *Oreopithecus,* which dates from approximately 10 to 12 M.Y.A., has been called both a monkey and an ape. However, East African members of the genus seem to confirm its ape status.

Nyanzapithecus is a medium-sized primate with a highly distinctive dental morphology, a relatively short face with a low and broad nasal opening, and a relatively large jaw containing small and robust incisors. *Nyanzapithecus* and *Oreopithecus,* as well as a closely related form from Songhor, Kenya, called *Rangwapithecus,* which dates to about 17 M.Y.A., are placed in the family Oreopithecidae (Harrison, 1986), which seems to have diverged from the basal ape stock in Africa by at least the early Miocene.

Morphology

Much of the morphological reconstruction of Miocene apes is based on material gathered from around Lake Victoria in eastern Africa. This material probably represents bones washed into the deposits from which they were dug, perhaps after they were consumed by large carnivores and vultures. The primate population at this time was evidently large and diverse, and known specimens most likely represent only a minute portion of that population.

The presence of so many animal remains in shallow-water lake deposits raises the possibility that the animals were vulnerable when they came to the water to drink and that they were attacked there and killed. The relative absence of limb bones from the fossil assemblage may be because of their high marrow content. The majority of the limb bones were probably broken and eaten by carnivores. This would also account for the almost complete absence of skulls, which were liable to have been scavenged for their brain content.

The best-preserved Miocene East African ape skull belongs to *Proconsul africanus.* The skull is light in weight and rather small, suggesting a lightly built creature. Walker and Pickford (Walker, 1983) suggest a body weight close to 26 pounds, while others suggest a weight of 33 pounds. *Proconsul's* skull is different from that of modern apes. It lacks the heavy bony ridges characteristic of the **sagittal** (top of the skull) and **nuchal** (back of the skull) regions. When present, these crests are sites for the attachment of heavy chewing muscles and neck muscles, respectively. There is no heavy bone ridge *(supraorbital torus)* above the eye orbits, as is found in modern apes and large Old World monkeys.

Based on earlier, limited finds, it was suggested that the east African *Proconsul* had a limited degree of brain development. The general shape of the brain is similar to that of Old World monkeys. Walker and Teaford (1989) report a newer estimate of cranial capacity to be about 167 cc. They conclude that *P. africanus* was more encephalized than modern monkeys of comparable body size. The presence of a frontal air sinus or air space within the frontal bone of the skull is significant. Such air spaces are found in humans and African apes, but not in Asian apes or among the monkeys. The presence of a frontal air sinus in *Proconsul* suggests that these Miocene apes had at least some affinities with modern apes (Walker and Teaford, 1989).

A new sample of Miocene apes from Africa has dramatically increased the postcranial bone sample of these forms (Walker and Teaford, 1989). The new bones allow researchers to determine that the hands and feet exhibited both ape- and monkey-like features, and showed that *Proconsul* was a slow-moving quadruped. The limb proportions indicate both apelike and monkeylike features.

The unique combination of traits exhibited by *Proconsul* make functional interpretations a difficult task. There are no modern animal models of *Proconsul's* anatomy, and each of *Proconsul's* anatomical complexes are unique. For example, the ankle bones are slender and monkeylike while the big toe is robust and apelike. Similar unique combinations are found in the pelvis.

The original account of *Proconsul* concluded that it was an active, leaping quadruped which moved like today's Asian langurs and perhaps also had a limited ability to swing by the arms. The new fossils described by Walker and Teaford (1989) reveal a different story. *Proconsul* was a relatively slow-moving, arboreal species that had no obvious specializations for leaping, arm-swinging, or terrestrial living.

Much has been written about dryopithecine dentition, not only because teeth compose a large part of the fossil sample, but also because of the presence of the characteristic Y-5 mandibular molar crown pattern. The Y-5 pattern occurs, with variations, among modern and fossil apes and humans. This pattern has been persistent for at least 20 million years. Although some consider the Y-5 pattern to be an important diagnostic trait, others have raised doubts about its phylogenetic utility.

Evolutionary Relationships

The new East African finds associated with *Proconsul* show that this form was not a specialized ancestor of the modern chimpanzees or the gorillas. In fact, it has few special features linking it with these modern apes. *Proconsul* appears to have been a generalized ancestor of all the great apes and humans. For some time it was suggested that one member of the Miocene hominoid stock probably was ancestral to the first hominids. This view has been largely replaced based on the questioning of the hominid status of a form called *Ramapithecus* (discussed later) and on evidence suggesting a later human–ape divergence from a common ancestor than was originally thought.

The Miocene hominid called *Ramapithecus* was first found in 1934 by Lewis, who described fragmentary dental and jaw remains (Figure 15-5) and remarked on traits that appeared to be superficially associated with those of

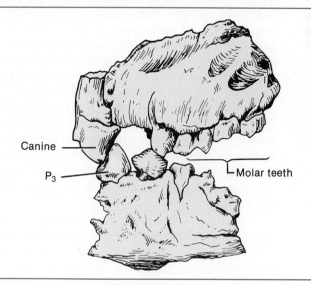

Canine

P₃

Molar teeth

Figure 15-5 Sivapithecus (= Ramapithecus) *mandible and maxilla articulated.*

early humans. That line of reasoning was later supported by L. Leakey (1968, 1969, 1970) on the basis of dental remains found in Kenya. Until rather recently, *Ramapithecus* was widely considered to be the first direct human ancestor, a form that diverged from the common ape–human line about 14 to 12 M.Y.A. *Ramapithecus* seemed to be in the right place—the Old World—and time—between the dryopithecines and *Australopithecus* (discussed in Chapter 17)—to be a human ancestor. Morphological traits that distinguish it from the earlier dryopithecines either parallel traits found in later human ancestors or foreshadow them.

The question of whether this fossil group belongs on the evolving human line depends in part on where one chooses to recognize the split of that line from the common human–ape stock. The boundary is likely to be somewhat arbitrary, and of the three sets of criteria used to differentiate humans from apes—postcranial features, dentition, and cranial and facial features—until recently only dental and jaw remains belonging to *Ramapithecus* were available.

In the last few years, researchers have stressed the nonhominid traits of *Ramapithecus* and have noted its close similarity to the orangutan ancestor, *Sivapithecus.* The demise of the *Ramapithecus*-as-hominid viewpoint began with the wide acceptance of the argument that the human–ape split occurred only about 8 to 6 M.Y.A., long after the first appearance of *Ramapithecus* at about 14 to 12 M.Y.A.

Most fossils originally placed in the genus *Ramapithecus* are now placed in the genus *Sivapithecus,* a fossil best known from deposits in Pakistan and China. *Sivapithecus* appeared during the middle Miocene, when some heavily forested areas gave way to mixed environments of dense forest, savanna, woodlands, and more open areas. Sivapithecids differed from the earlier dryopithecids, who lived in heavily forested regions of Africa and Europe. Dryopithecids may never have left these areas for more open habitats, whereas the sivapithecids may have lived on the boundary between the forest and open areas and may have exploited both for food.

In placing fossils first referred to as *Ramapithecus* in the human evolutionary line, too much emphasis seems to have been placed on a fragmentary fossil record. Until quite recently, all that remained of *Ramapithecus* were a few teeth and jaw fragments. A number of anatomical traits at first led to the conclusion that this form had a short, flat, deep face and a number of dental traits superficially resembling those of the first hominids, the australopithecines (Chapter 17).

More important in understanding the *Ramapithecus*-as-hominid viewpoint was the notion that the human and ape lines diverged from each other perhaps as early as 20 M.Y.A. The search ensued to find morphological traits to substantiate this argument. One trait used to distinguish ape and human ancestors was the thickness of the molar enamel. It turns out, however, that this trait is linked to diet and is of no importance for distinguishing between ape and human lineages (Martin, 1985).

Figure 15-6 The site of Lufeng, Yunnan Province, People's Republic of China. This site has yielded a vast amount of Sivapithecus *remains.*

Ramapithecus's inclusion within the genus *Sivapithecus* was supported by the recovery of a multitude of new fossils in Asia. Fossils from Shihuiba in the Lufeng Basin of Yunnan Province, China (Figure 15-6), constitute one of the most extensive ape fossil collections. There are nearly 1,000 specimens representing tens, if not hundreds, of individuals of both sexes dating to about 8 M.Y.A. There are 5 reasonably complete skulls, 6 fragmentary skulls, 9 mandibles (Figures 15-7, 15-8), a dozen or more upper-jaw fragments, many lower-jaw fragments, and isolated teeth.

Although there is some disagreement, many researchers place all the Lufeng hominoids into the taxon *Sivapithecus* and within the orangutan lineage (Pilbeam, 1986). The similarity to the orangutan is most evident in its facial features and anterior dentition (Figure 15-9).

A number of postcranial remains belonging to *Sivapithecus* come from the Siwaliks, including arm and leg bones and a few finger and foot bones (Pilbeam et al., 1980). Apparently the forearm and foot were very mobile. These forms could hang by their arms. The big toe was opposable and capable of powerful gripping, (Badgley, 1984). This limited evidence suggests that these forms were fully capable of moving through large and perhaps small branch zones of an arboreal habitat. The once-held view that they were evolving a bipedal gait is not based on any substantial evidence. This is most important because bipedalism is considered to be the human hallmark. Unless the fossil record unexpectedly forces us to reconsider the importance of

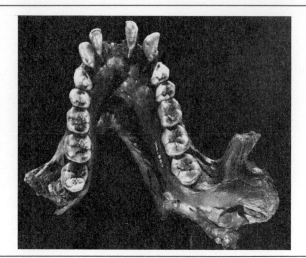

Figure 15-7 A Mandible of Sivapithecus *from Lufeng.*

bipedalism in human evolution, nonhominid forms such as *Sivapithecus* will probably not be considered to be within the Hominidae.

The view that some member of the sivapithecids might be ancestral to the Hominidae was further undermined when Pilbeam and his co-workers recovered an adult male *Sivapithecus* skull in Pakistan dating to about 8 M.Y.A. The skull, which includes about two-thirds of the facial bones, is distinctly

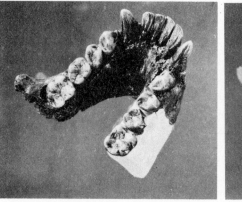

Figure 15-8 (left) Note the large canines and the canine diastema (situated between the canine and the first premolar) of this Sivapithecus *mandible. (right) A side view of the same mandible.*

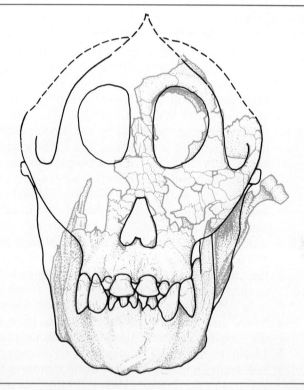

Figure 15-9 This partial face of Sivapithecus *was found in Pakistan and shows striking similarities to modern orangutans.*

nonhuman (see Figure 15-9) and looks very much like an orangutan's skull (Pilbeam, 1983; Preuss, 1982). Pilbeam also recovered a complete mandible with the entire dentition and most of the left side of the face intact. There were also a few unassociated postcranial remains.

The downfall of the argument that members of the Hominidae might be found among some middle Miocene apes began with the wide acceptance of a late divergence date of humans and apes and has been substantiated with fossil evidence found in China and Pakistan, and also recently in Africa. Not only was the form originally called *Ramapithecus* not an ancestral hominid, but it also was not distinct from *Sivapithecus,* into which genus it has now been placed. The sivapithecids may have already split from the common ape stock and may be ancestral to the orangutans rather than to the other great apes and humans. If dental similarities between the sivapithecids and the first humans, the australopithecines, are not indicative of an ancestral–descendant relationship, they are probably the result of parallelisms (Wolpoff, 1982).

GIGANTOPITHECUS

Of all primate fossils, the remains belonging to a form called *Gigantopithecus* have had perhaps one of the most colorful histories. *Gigantopithecus* has been called everything from an ape to a giant hominid. It has been suggested as a likely ancestor of the elusive Yeti, or Abominable Snowman, and linked to China's "Hairy Wildman" (Poirier, Hu, and Chen, 1983). Early mention of *Gigantopithecus* was made by von Koenigswald in 1935 on the basis of teeth found in a Chinese drugstore. The Chinese have collected fossilized teeth and bones, referred to as "dragon bones," for use in herbal medicines. Since the recovery of the original material, other *Gigantopithecus* remains were found in India as well as in China. *Gigantopithecus* is now known from a number of lower-jaw remains and well over 1,000 isolated teeth. *Gigantopithecus* may have weighed between 400 and 600 pounds and stood as much as 6 feet tall. It seems to have ranged in time from 9 to 5 M.Y.A. in India to as recently as 500,000 years ago in China. (In China, *Gigantopithecus* remains are found in the same deposits as those yielding bones belonging to the ancestors of the Giant Panda and the human fossils of *Homo erectus*).

In 1955, 47 *Gigantopithecus* teeth were found among a shipment of "dragon bones" in China. The process of tracing these teeth to their source resulted in the recovery of more teeth and a rather complete large mandible (Figure 15-10). Considerably more *Gigantopithecus* remains have come from central and southern China—both from warehouses for Chinese medicinal products and from cave deposits (Wang, 1980). Not all of the Chinese remains come from the same time period, and some species have larger teeth than others. The Chinese material is generally called *G. blacki.*

The Indian species of *Gigantopithecus* belongs to *G. bilaspurensis*—the species designation referring to a 1968 find in the village of Bilaspur. The Indian material dates to between 9 and 5 M.Y.A.

Ciochon (1984/1985) reports on new *Gigantopithecus* remains from northern Vietnam. This find represents the southernmost distribution of the genus and possibly its latest temporal occurrence. In China, *Gigantopithecus* is known to coexist with a very large fossil orangutan and occasionally with *Homo erectus.* Both genera also occur in Vietnam.

The *Gigantopithecus* teeth (Figure 15-11) are very large and have thick enamel. This is possibly an adaptation to heavy chewing of abrasive foods. The mandible of *G. blacki* is gracile compared with the size of its molars. Perhaps it was not as well adapted to chewing hard objects as is often suggested.

Jolly's (1970) seed-eating hypothesis, also known as the T-complex, has been called upon to explain *Gigantopithecus's* dental traits. The seed-eating hypothesis is based on the feeding behavior and dental adaptations of one type of African monkey, *Theropithecus gelada.* Jolly states that *Theropithecus's* dental traits are functionally related to and are a product of a diet involving the ingestion of large quantities of comparatively small, tough morsels like

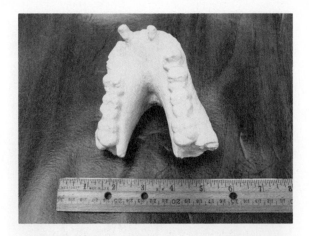

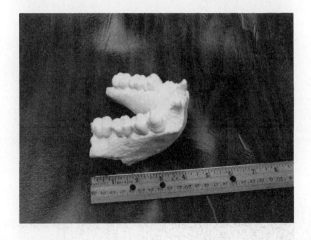

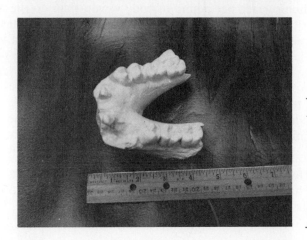

Figure 15-10 Photographs of a cast of a mandible of Giganto-pithecus blackii *from China. The missing teeth include the two medial incisors, the two canines, and the two third molars. The thickness of the jaw is clearly evident in these photos.*

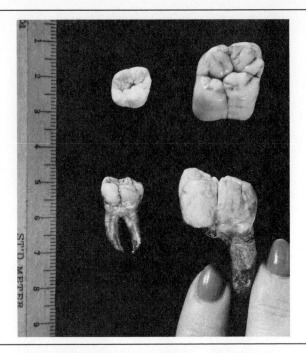

Figure 15-11 *Upper and lower molars of* Gigantopithecus *(right) compared with those of modern humans (left).*

grass seeds, stems, and rhizomes prepared by powerful and continuous chewing with the premolars and molars.

The gelada's dental traits include high-crowned molars, which are rapidly worn because of grit in the diet. The high-crowned molars supposedly provide more grinding surface per pound of body weight than do the molars of such primates as the common savanna-dwelling baboon. As geladas mature, their teeth become packed together in the jaws; this is associated with strenuous grinding. There is also vertical orientation of the incisors and some reduction in the size of the canines. The existence of similar dental traits in *Gigantopithecus* suggests that it may have fed on dietary items similar to those composing the gelada's diet.

In formulating the seed-eating hypothesis, Jolly notes the existence of a number of morphological and functional parallels between early humans and the gelada:

1. Both forms occupied a grassland–open country habitat.
2. Both have reduced incisors and canines relative to the premolars and molars.

3. Both show crowding of the molars and the presence of wear between the molar teeth.
4. Both have a robust, thick mandible beneath the molars.
5. In both forms there is a maximization of the chewing power and efficiency of muscles related to chewing.

Not all agree with Jolly's interpretations and the heuristic value of gelada dietary adaptations for understanding major components of human evolution. Wolpoff (1980) notes, for example, that powerful chewing is characteristic of mammals that are not seed eaters, and seeds are not the only food on the savanna that require powerful chewing. Wolpoff notes a number of difficulties involved in using the seed-eating hypothesis to help explain certain dietary adaptations of early humans. Although seed eating helps to explain some early human dental traits, it does not help us understand other human adaptations like tool use, bipedalism, canine reduction, and intelligence.

Gigantopithecus probably evolved first in India and spread north and east; the Indian species predates the Chinese species by millions of years. Although probably not ancestral to any modern apes, *Gigantopithecus* seems to be a relatively long-lived side branch of ape evolution. However, Eckhardt (1972, 1975), among a few others, suggested some close parallels between *Gigantopithecus* and early humans. If Jolly is correct, however, the similarities in jaws and teeth of *Gigantopithecus* and some early human ancestors are not indicative of a close evolutionary relationship, but are a reflection of independently acquired adaptations to a similar habitat and diet.

The interpretation of ape evolution is fraught with difficulties. The oldest possible ancestral apes come from Eocene deposits in Burma, but the most complete early evidence comes from Oligocene deposits in the Fayum region of Egypt. These forms had apelike teeth but were monkeylike in the rest of their morphology and locomotor behavior. They were small, quadrupedal, arboreal primates.

Aegyptopithecus was probably ancestral to the Miocene dryopithecines. Early and middle Miocene hominoids such as Proconsul *and* Dryopithecus *were in many respects quite different from later great apes. They were predominantly frugivorous or omnivorous, mainly arboreal, and lived mostly in forested habitats. Until quite recently, it was assumed that modern apes and humans diverged from the Miocene apes. Now, however, the ancestor–descendant relationship is considered to be more complex and is unclear.*

Gigantopithecus is an interesting form whose evolutionary position vis-à-vis other apes is unclear. Despite many attempts to connect Gigantopithecus *to the human lineage, the relationship has not been widely accepted.*

BIBLIOGRAPHY

ANDREWS, P. 1971. *Ramapithecus wickeri* mandible from Fort Ternan, Kenya. *Nature* 231: 192–94.

ANDREWS, P. 1981. Hominoid habitats of the Miocene. *Nature* 289: 749.

ANDREWS, P., and J. CRONIN. 1982. The relationship of *Sivapithecus* and *Ramapithecus* and the evolution of the orangutan. *Nature* 297: 541–46.

ANDREWS, P., W. HAMILTON, and P. WHYBROW. 1978. Dryopithecines from the Miocene of Saudi Arabia. *Nature* 274: 249–50.

ANDREWS, P., and H. TOBIEN. 1977. New Miocene locality in Turkey with evidence on the origin of *Ramapithecus* and *Sivapithecus*. *Nature* 268: 699–701.

BADGLEY, C. 1984. The paleoenvironment of South Asian Miocene hominoids. In *The Evolution of the East Asian Environment,* vol. 2, R. Whyte, ed. Hong Kong: University of Hong Kong.

BUTZER, K. 1977. Human evolution: Hominoids of the Miocene. *Science* 197: 224–46.

CIOCHON, R. 1980. *Amphipithecus* and *Pondaungia* as early anthropoids: The dental evidence. *American Journal of Physical Anthropology* 52: 24.

CIOCHON, R. 1984/1985. Paleoanthropological field research in Vietnam. *The Institute of Human Origins* 4: 6–7.

CONROY, G. 1972. Problems in the interpretation of *Ramapithecus:* With special reference to anterior tooth reduction. *American Journal Physical Anthropology* 37: 41–46.

CORRUCCINI, R., R. CIOCHON, and H. McHENRY. 1976. The post-cranium of Miocene hominoids: Were dryopithecines merely "dental apes?" *Primates* 17: 205–23.

ECKHARDT, R. 1972. Population genetics and human origins. *Scientific American* January: 94.

ECKHARDT, R. 1975. *Gigantopitheus* as a hominid. In *Paleoanthropology, Morphology, and Paleoecology,* R. Tuttle, ed. The Hague: Mouton.

ETLER, D. 1984. The fossil hominoids of Lufeng, Yunnan Province, The People's Republic of China: A series of translations. *Yearbook of Physical Anthropology* 27: 1–56.

EVERY, R. 1970. Sharpness of teeth in man and other primates. *Postilla* 143: 1–30.

FLEAGLE, J., and E. SIMONS. 1978. *Micropithecus clarki,* a small ape from the Miocene of Uganda. *American Journal of Physical Anthropology* 49: 427–40.

FLEAGLE, J. et al. 1986. Age of the earliest African anthropoids. *Science* 234: 1247–49.

FRAYER, D. 1974. A reappraisal of *Ramapithecus. Yearbook of Physical Anthropology* 188: 19–30.

GEBO, D., and E. SIMONS. 1987. Morphology and locomotor adaptations of the foot in early Oligocene anthropoids. *American Journal of Physical Anthropology* 74: 83–102.

GREENFIELD, L. 1979. On the adaptive pattern of *Ramapithecus. American Journal of Physical Anthropology* 50: 527–48.

GREENFIELD, L. 1980. A late divergence hypothesis. *American Journal of Physical Anthropology* 52: 351–66.

HARRISON, T. 1986. Fossil anthropoids from the middle Miocene of East Africa and their bearing on the origin of the Oreopithecidae. *American Journal of Physical Anthropology* 71: 265–84.

HURZELER, J. 1958. *Oreopithecus bambolii* Gervais: A preliminary report. *Verh. Naturf. Gesellschaft* 69: 1–438.

JOLLY, C. 1970. The seed-eaters: A new model of hominid differentiation based on a baboon analogy. *Man* 5: 5–26.

KAY, R. 1973. Mastication, molar tooth structure, and diet in primates. PhD dissertation. New Haven: Yale University.

KAY, R. 1983. *Ramapithecus* reclaimed. *The Sciences* January/February: 26–27.

KAY, R., J. FLEAGLE, and E. SIMONS. 1981. A revision of the Oligocene apes of the Fayum Province, Egypt. *American Journal of Physical Anthropology* 55: 293–322.

KAY, R., and E. SIMONS. 1980. The ecology of Oligocene African anthropoidea. *International Journal of Primatology* 1: 31–38.

LANGDON, J. 1987. *Functional Morphology of the Miocene Hominoid Foot.* New York: S. Karger.

LEAKEY, L. 1968. An early Miocene member of Hominidae. In *Perspectives on Human Evolution,* S. Washburn, P. Jay, ed. New York: Holt, Rinehart and Winston.

LEAKEY, L. 1969. Ecology of North Indian *Ramapithecus. Nature* 223: 1075.

LEAKEY, L. 1970. Newly recognized mandible of *Ramapithecus. Nature* 225: 199.

LEAKEY, R., and M. LEAKEY. 1986a. A new Miocene hominoid from Kenya. *Nature* 324: 143–46.

LEAKEY, R., and M. LEAKEY. 1986b. A second new Miocene hominoid from Kenya. *Nature* 324: 146–48.

LEAKEY, R., M. LEAKEY, and A. WALKER. 1988a. Morphology of *Afropithecus turkanensis* from Kenya. *American Journal of Physical Anthropology* 76: 289–300.

LEAKEY, R., M. LEAKEY, and A. WALKER, 1988b. Morphology of *Turkanopithecus kalokolensis* from Kenya. *American Journal of Physical Anthropology* 76: 277–88.

LEWIS, G. 1934. Preliminary notice of the new manlike apes from India. *American Journal of Science* 27: 161–81.

MARTIN, L. 1985. Significance of enamel thickness in hominoid evolution. *Nature* 314: 260–63.

MARTIN, L., and P. ANDREWS. 1982. New ideas on the relationships of the Miocene hominoids. *Primate Eye* 18: 4–7.

MAW, B., R. CIOCHON, and D. SAVAGE. 1979. Late Eocene of Burma yields earliest anthropoid primate, *Pondaungia cotteri. Nature* 282: 65–67.

OLSON, S., and D. RASMUSSEN. 1986. Paleoenvironment of the earliest hominoids: New evidence from the Oligocene avifauna of Egypt. *Science* 233: 1202–4.

PILBEAM, D. 1967. Man's earliest ancestors. *Scientific Journal* 3: 47–53.

PILBEAM, D. 1968. The earliest hominids. *Nature* 219: 1335–38.

PILBEAM, D. 1969. Tertiary Pongidae of East Africa: Evolutionary relationships and taxonomy. Bulletin 31, Peabody Museum of Natural History, Yale University, pp. 1–185.

PILBEAM, D. 1979. Recent finds and interpretations of Miocene hominoids. *Annual Review of Anthropology* 8: 333–52.

PILBEAM, D. 1983. *Ramapithecus* disowned. *The Sciences.* January/February: 24–25.

PILBEAM, D. 1984. Bone of contention. *Natural History.* June: 2–5.

PILBEAM, D. 1986. Hominoid evolution and hominoid origins. *American Anthropologist* 88: 295–312.

PILBEAM, D., et al. 1977. New hominoid primates from the Siwaliks of Pakistan and their bearing on hominoid evolution. *Nature* 27: 689–95.

PILBEAM, D., et al. 1980. Miocene hominoids from Pakistan. *Postilla* 181: 1–191.

POIRIER, F., H. HU, and C. CHEN. 1983. The evidence for wildman in Hubei Province, The People's Republic of China. *Cryptozoology* 2: 25–39.

PREUSS, T. 1982. The face of *Sivapithecus indicus:* Description of a new, relatively complete specimen from the Siwaliks of Pakistan. *Folia Primatologica* 20: 141–57.

RADINSKY, L. 1973. *Aegyptopithecus* endocasts: Oldest record of a pongid brain. *American Journal of Physical Anthropology* 39: 239–48.

RADINSKY, L. 1974. The fossil evidence of anthropoid brain evolution. *American Journal of Physical Anthropology* 41: 15–28.

RADINSKY, L. 1977. Early primate brains: Facts and fiction. *Journal of Human Evolution* 6: 79–86.

Robinson, J. 1972. *Early Hominid Posture and Locomotion.* Chicago: University of Chicago Press.

Schon Ybarra, M. 1984. Locomotion and postures of red howlers in a deciduous forest-savanna interface. *American Journal of Physical Anthropology* 63: 65–76.

Schwartz, J. 1984. Phylogeny of humans and orangutans. Paper given at 53d Annual Meetings of the American Association of Physical Anthropologists, Philadelphia, April 1984.

Simons, E. 1960. *Apidium* and *Oreopithecus. Nature* 186: 824–26.

Simons, E. 1961. The phyletic position of *Ramapithecus. Postilla* 57: 1–9.

Simons, E. 1962a. Fossil evidence relating to the early evolution of primate behavior. *New York Academy of Sciences* 102: 282.

Simons, E. 1962b. Two new primate species from the African Oligocene. *Postilla* 64: 1–12.

Simons, E. 1965a. The hunt for Darwin's third ape. *Medical Opinion and Review* November: 74–81.

Simons, E. 1965b. New fossil apes from Egypt and the initial differentiation of Hominoidea. *Nature* 205: 135–39.

Simons, E. 1967. The earliest apes. *Scientific American* 217: 28–35.

Simons, E. 1972. *Primate Evolution: An Introduction to Man's Place in Nature.* New York: Macmillan.

Simons, E. 1977. *Ramapithecus. Scientific American* 236: 28–35.

Simons, E. 1987. New faces of *Aegyptopithecus* from the Oligocene of *Egyptian Journal of Human Evolution* 16: 273–89.

Simons, E., and D. Pilbeam. 1965. Preliminary revision of the Dryopithecinae (Pongidae, Anthropoidea). *Folia Primatologica* 3: 81–152.

Simons, E., D. Rasmussen, and D. Gebo. 1987. A new species of *Propliopithecus* from the Fayum, Egypt. *American Journal of Physical Anthropology* 73: 138–47.

Straus, W. 1963. The classification of *Oreopithecus.* In *Classification and Human Evolution,* S. Washburn, ed., pp. 146–77. Chicago: Aldine.

Szalay, F. 1970. Late Eocene *Amphipithecus* and the origins of catarrhine primates. *Nature* 227: 355–57.

Szalay, F., and E. Delson. 1979. *Evolutionary History of the Primates.* New York: Academic Press.

von Koenigswald, G. 1969. Miocene Cercopithecoidea and Oreopithecoidea from the Miocene of East Africa. *Fossil Vertebrates of Africa* 1: 39–52.

Walker, A. 1983. The puzzle of *Proconsul. The Sciences* January/February: 22–23.

Walker, A., et al. 1983. The skull of *Proconsul africanus:* Reconstruction and cranial capacity. *Nature* 305: 525–27.

Walker, A. and M. Teaford. 1989. The hunt for *Proconsul. Scientific American* (January): 76–82.

Wang, S. 1980. Discoveries and expectations for the remains of anthropoid and human beings in Hubei Province. *Jiang-Han Archaeology* 2: 1–6 (in Mandarin).

Whitten, P., and M. Nickles. 1983. Our forebearer's forebearers. *The Sciences* January/February: 20–28.

Wolpoff, M. 1980. *Paleoanthropology.* New York: Knopf.

Wolpoff, M. 1982. *Ramapithecus* and hominid origins. *Current Anthropology* 23: 501–10.

Wu, R. 1984. The crania of *Ramapithecus* and *Sivapithecus* from Lufeng, China. In *Early Evolution of Man,* P. Andrews and J. Franzen, eds. Frankfurt: Senckenberg Museum.

Yinyan, Z. 1982. Variability and evolutionary trends in tooth size of *Gigantopithecus. American Journal of Physical Anthropology* 49: 21–32.

Zihlman, A., and J. Lowenstein. 1979. False start of the human parade. *Natural History* 88: 86–91.

Chapter
16
Trends in Human Evolution

The major trends in human evolution include an anatomical restructuring permitting upright bipedalism, exploitation of the terrestrial environment, increasing brain sizes, tool use and manufacture, and the addition of meat protein to the diet. Bipedal locomotion is the major trait differentiating early humans from the common ape–human ancestor. The first evidence of bipedality in the fossil record appears about 3.7 M.Y.A. The anatomical modifications allowing and accompanying bipedalism are discussed, as are some of the major hypotheses concerning the development and adaptive nature of bipedalism.

The effective exploitation of the terrestrial habitat by humans involved such behavioral adjustments as life in a social group, a sexual division of labor, and the development of a capacity for symbolic language. The increase in brain size in the human evolutionary lineage was neither rapid nor consistent. Increasing brain sizes are associated with increasingly complex social organizations and means of environmental exploitation. There is a feedback between these—for example, increasing cranial capacities probably allowed for more intense and diversified habitat exploitation, which, in turn, selected for increasing cranial capacities.

Stone tools first appear in the fossil record about 2 M.Y.A., approximately 2.5 million years after the first identified human fossil remains. Primate visual acuity and manual dexterity were preadaptations to human tool use and manufacture. Humans are the only primate to rely heavily on a tool technology for survival. While most primates are vegetarian, a substantial amount of the human diet includes meat protein. It is not entirely clear from the fossil record when meat began to play a large role in the human diet. At first, meat was probably obtained through scavenging. Consistent big-game hunting may not have developed prior to the appearance of H. erectus.

TREND 1: THE EVOLUTION OF BIPEDALISM

All major primate groups include species that sit or sleep in an upright position. Many primates also occasionally assume an upright walking posture. (So do birds and some lizards, and so did some dinosaurs.) Primate bipedalism usually is characterized by one of the following: 1) Consistent bipedalism characterized by standing erect with straightened knees is practiced only by humans. 2) Bipedal running occurs in many nonhuman primates. However, they use a bent-knee gait. Nonhuman primates cannot fully extend their legs at the knee. 3) Bipedal walking is less common among monkeys than among the great apes, whose bipedal gait is a bent-knee gait. Only humans can stand erect with their legs fully straightened for long periods of time. The distinguishing feature of human locomotion is that bipedalism is our normal mode of locomotion.

Because humans are the only primate to have intensively taken up bipedalism, we are interested in understanding how and why bipedalism evolved. Major changes in the lower limbs, feet, and pelvis accompanied the shift to habitual bipedalism in humans (Lovejoy, 1988). Structural changes in the lower limbs include an elongated femur (upper-leg bone) and changes in the foot. Among humans, the lower limbs are longer than the upper limbs, and the foot has shifted from the primate pattern of a grasping organ to a weight-bearing platform. Major anatomical changes in the foot region occurred early in human evolution. The structure of the human foot indicates that it evolved from the kind of foot typical of apes and atypical of a quadrupedal monkey (Figure 16-1).

A number of features distinguish the human from the ape pelvis. The pelvis actually comprises three distinct bones: the ilium, ischium, and pubis (Figure

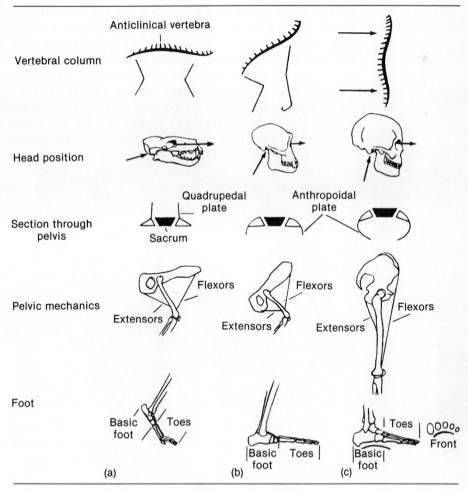

Figure 16-1 Structural changes resulting from bipedalism. (A) Quadrupedal animal; (B) Chimpanzee; (C) Modern human.

16-2). The structural basis of bipedal locomotion is anatomically complex, involving a reorganization of the pelvic region.

The major pelvic changes involved a shortening and broadening of the ilium; furthermore, the ilium tilted backward. The backward bending of the ilium allowed the trunk to be held vertically, followed by rotation of the sacral vertebrae (vertebrae at the end of the spinal column) and compensated for by a curving of the spine (referred to as a sigmoid or S-shaped curve). This change avoids obstruction of the birth canal while facilitating erect posture.

Muscular changes essential for the maintenance of balance and stabilization of the trunk accompanied skeletal reorganization. Although most human and ape thigh muscles do not differ with regard to the type of action produced, they do differ in the effect of the muscle's action. Of special importance are the gluteus maximus, the largest muscle in the human buttocks, and the hamstring muscles, which are important thigh extensors in humans and apes. Upon contraction, extensor muscles tend to straighten a bone around a joint. Extensor muscles are also powerful flexors of the leg at the knee joint (when they contract, they allow bending at the knee, decreasing the angle between the thigh and calf) and are important rotators of the thigh. The muscles that move the leg forward are the flexors, because they bend the leg at the hip; those that move the leg backward are the extensors, because they extend the leg at the hip joint. In humans, these muscles are developed to a relatively greater degree

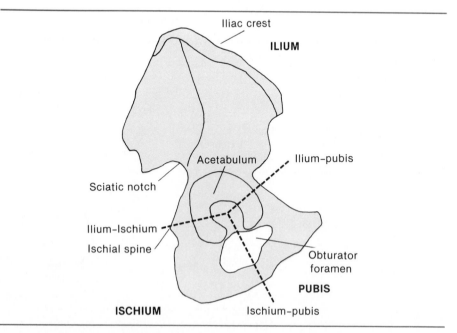

Figure 16-2 Anatomy of human pelvis.

than in other primates because humans alone depend on them for locomotion. The human leg is also proportionately heavier and larger.

The ape's ischium is relatively longer and the femur relatively shorter than in upright bipeds. This influences the functioning of the hamstrings and gluteus maximus. With a long moment arm (stable element)—the ischium—and a shorter lever arm (movable element)—the femur—the muscles produce a power action. In upright bipeds with the reverse proportions (short ischium and long femur), the hamstrings produce speed rather than power. The gluteus maximus is more a speed-of-action muscle in humans than it is among apes.

Power is apparently more valuable in animals that spend time climbing; speed and range of movement is of greater importance to a biped less dependent on tree life and more dependent on its ability to cover long distances in the shortest possible time. The upright biped sacrificed power of action for endurance.

Theories of the origin of human bipedalism require the reconstruction of many unknowns. Darwin (1871) argued that bipedalism arose when our ancestors "came to live somewhat less on trees and more on the ground," which was due "to a change in its manner of procuring subsistence, or to a change in the conditions of its native country." Many ideas have been proffered on the origin of bipedalism, but we will concentrate on the most recent.

Shipman (1984) suggests that bipedalism was an adaptation to the early human pattern of scavenging meat. Although bipedal running is neither fast nor efficient when compared with quadrupedal gaits, bipedal walking is more energetically efficient than quadrupedal walking. Bipedalism increased the energetic efficiency of human travel, and this increased efficiency was an important factor in the origin of bipedalism (Rodman and McHenry, 1980). Bipedalism is an efficient means of covering large areas slowly, and Shipman argues that it is an appropriate adaptation for a scavenger who must cover large areas. Bipedalism also elevates the head, thereby improving the ability to locate items at a distance. Combining bipedalism with agile climbing ability (of which there may be some evidence in such early human fossils as *Australopithecus afarensis*) further increases the opportunities to exploit the environment. Bipedalism frees the hands and makes them available for carrying. According to Shipman (pp. 26–27):

> Bipedalism is compatible with a scavenging strategy. I am tempted to argue that bipedalism evolved because it provided a substantial advantage to scavenging hominids. But I doubt hominids could scavenge effectively without tools and bipedalism predates the oldest known tools by more than a million years.

Lovejoy (1981, 1984) suggests that perhaps bipedalism was related to a new and effective reproductive strategy—pair bonding in a kind of rudimentary family unit. The potential link between reproductive strategy and bipedalism lies in primate sexual behavior. Some female monkeys and apes have a well-defined and rather short estrous period. Males attracted to estrous females seek the best chances of mating by competing (not necessarily through physical altercation) for them. The degree and form of such competition varies among species. Except among human males and the New World monkey, the marmoset, if primate males provide infant care they usually do so with minimal skill and interest. The offspring's care is almost exclusively left to the mother, who usually cannot care for more than one infant at a time and who normally does not become sexually receptive again until the infant can forage on its own.

Birth rates of monkeys, whose offspring mature rapidly, are not much reduced by a mother's preoccupation with her infant. For apes and early humans, however, the problem is and was more critical. An ape mother may spend five years raising one infant; this lowers the birth rate because primate mothers rarely give birth to another infant while still nursing previous offspring. Because of long birth intervals among apes, when compared with monkeys, Lovejoy argues that apes would be at an evolutionary disadvantage if they were in direct competition with monkeys.

According to Lovejoy, the solution to this dilemma is to space infants more closely, as monkeys do, while still providing each infant with quality care. That necessitates adopting a better strategy offspring care—for example, providing the mother with a food supply so that she does not have to forage for her own and her infant's needs. The mother would then be able to care for two or more infants simultaneously. Because she moves less, her offspring may have a greater chance of survival.

One possible auxiliary food source is the male. If an adult male is to be incorporated into a food-sharing role, his attention must turn to the female and infants—or to one female and one infant. If he became monogamous, he could indirectly help his infant survive by bringing food to its mother, thus giving her more time to be a protecting parent. To provide greater quantities of food, the male must be able to carry it; thus he would find bipedalism to be adaptive.

According to Lovejoy's scenario, a female benefited from male provisioning in a number of ways. For example, her ability to care for her offspring was increased. She could spend less time searching for food and more time directly caring for and protecting her young. The provisioning bipedal male could obtain food farther away from the area occupied by the female and infant; thus he increased their food supply without depleting local food resources. The female was thereby able to collect more foods locally, reducing dangers that both she and her young might encounter by roaming over a larger area.

Because the bipedal male increased the female's food supply through his provisioning behavior, she had more energy available for parenting. According to Lovejoy (1984:26), "Therein lies the ultimate advantage of provisioning." Females who benefited from provisioning were better able to manage overlapping offspring. Selection would rapidly have favored females that chose mates whose interest in them continued after fertilization. Any behavior of a potential mate that improved a female's reproductive rate would be favored.

Lovejoy's hypothesis concentrates on the acquisition of bipedalism by males as a means of supplying food for a female who is encumbered by a slowly maturing infant. Tanner (1981) suggests a hypothesis that centers on the acquisition of bipedalism by females. Tanner notes that bipedalism accommodated the increased infant dependency on its mother (pp. 157–58):

> With effective baby and child care, the young can be born more physically immature—which was certainly fortunate, for this was becoming necessary due to changes in the pelvis for bipedalism. Because infants and young must in any case be cared for already, increasing immaturity at birth would not be selected against.

The ability to walk great distances while carrying items was essential to early humans. Mobility over long distances for both females and males and effective carrying were made feasible by the development of bipedalism. There was much to be carried by the gathering females—their infants, digging implements, and the gathered foods. Because of these demands on the female, some sort of carrying device was a likely first tool.

Tanner argues that with the development of bipedalism, learning to walk required more time to develop motor coordination prior to independence (pp. 156–57). Prolonged infant dependency on the mother became necessary.

> This meant that the mother—or older sibling, mother's sibling, or mother's friend—had to carry a child that could no longer cling as effectively because the changed anatomy of bipedalism required loss of the foot's ability to grasp the mother. Even young who were already able to walk would have to be carried frequently and often, because they would tire.

Tanner's hypothesis suggests a restructuring of social life in response to the rigors imposed by bipedalism.

Sinclair and co-workers (1986) suggest that bipedalism developed along with long-distance migration, and they agree with Shipman that scavenging was important to the evolution of bipedalism. Sinclair and colleagues argue that early hominids scavenged migrating ungulate (hooved mammals) populations—the only animals that existed in large enough numbers to provide sufficient food for scavengers. Because many migratory animals die from starvation, their carcasses would be available to scavengers, who would not necessarily have to contend with predators for a kill. A migratory scavenger has access to an abundant and constant food supply.

There was an unfilled niche in Africa for a mammalian scavenger that could follow migratory ungulates. If the scavenger was a bipedal human, however, it had to carry its young. Access to a rich and constant food supply encouraged bipedalism among early hominids. Those who developed the ability to walk long distances rapidly increased their numbers and displaced the less numerous sedentary quadrupeds that were dependent on plant gathering.

Sinclair and colleagues' (1986) protohominid was a quadrupedal plant gatherer and occasional scavenger, much like the baboon. Two adaptations are needed for such a form to follow migrating ungulates. First, the young had to be carried. Among humans, this carrying was accomplished by using the arms, which had been freed from locomotion by assuming upright posture. A prolonged upright stance for efficient carrying required adaptations of the pelvis, such as those in the first member of the human family, *A. afarensis,* and subsequent forms. Second, they must be able to travel long distances efficiently. The primate foot, with its opposable big toe, changed to the modern human foot as a propulsive lever. This change must occur coincident with the hip changes.

The migration hypothesis suggests that habitual tool use developed from a need to speed up the butchering of carcasses in order to avoid competition with stronger mammal predators. The opportunity for hominid migration was enormous because savanna Africa was dominated by migration ecosystems.

TREND 2: EFFECTIVE EXPLOITATION OF THE TERRESTRIAL HABITAT

Behavioral adjustments were necessary to cope with the terrestrial habitat. One means of coping was to reside in social groups, a typical pattern of primate residence in both arboreal and terrestrial niches. Based on comparative data, early humans may have lived in social groups averaging 25 members per group. There was probably a sexual division of labor.

Tanner's (1981) picture of early human communities assumes that early humans had a basic plant-gathering economy and that mothers were the most regular gatherers. Tanner suggests that the early human social group probably contained a mother and one or several offspring. This genealogical unit could have held three generations: an old mother, adult daughter(s), and her infant or juvenile offspring. Because generations were short and these creatures were relatively short-lived, units of more than three generations would be rare. This mother-centered (matrifocal) genealogical unit would probably travel and gather together. Several units, especially those composed of sisters, may have met frequently and camped together with some regularity around well-known water sources.

Among most nonhuman primates, each animal is a separate subsistence unit. Once infants are weaned, they normally depend on their own skills in food acquisition for survival. Among humans, however, the weaned young still depend on adults for food. Because of this long-term dependence, much of the time during the day for both male and female humans is spent in activities that provide food for the young. "Because of the long-term dependence of children, a division of labor evolved in which the adventurous, wandering male became the hunter and the female developed the less mobile role of gatherer and mother" (Lancaster, 1975:78–79).

Females have the major responsibility for the early care, feeding, and rearing of the young. Therefore, any sexual division of labor that increases reproductive fitness (that is, the infant's survival) is beneficial. The human infant is born at a relatively immature stage and is unable to fend for itself. The human mother also lacks body hair (common to nonhuman primates) that the infant can grasp, allowing the mother the usual range of movement. The human mother must carry the infant. Given the long period of immaturity among human infants, once hunting and gathering developed as a way of life, a division of labor may have occurred between the sexes.

The division of labor provided a flexible system of joint dependence on plant and animal foods, which were provided by both sexes. The division of labor among humans was an efficient coping strategy quite different from that characterizing nonhuman primates. Although there is skeletal evidence of sexual dimorphism, there is no archaeological evidence supporting the contention that early humans exhibited a sexual division of labor. The adaptive advantages provided by this system suggest that such a division existed, however. A sexual division of labor may help explain why early humans could successfully compete and establish themselves in their new habitat.

The concept of the home base, an area to which group members return, may have developed in human evolution as an important aid to survival. (Until quite recently, there appeared to be early evidence for a home base at Olduvai Gorge, Tanzania, at a site dated to about 1.7 M.Y.A. This interpretation of the remains is now questioned: Home bases may not have appeared as early as once suggested.) A home base provides a location at which injured or sick individuals could remain and to which other group members could return at night. Among savanna-living baboons, with no home base, sick or injured animals must move with the troop or be left behind to die or be killed by a predator. A home base also becomes important because of the human infant's slower maturation rate; extended maternal care is needed to ensure survival. A home base can provide a relatively safe area where a female and her infant could remain for a few days, thus enhancing the survivability of both the mother and the infant.

The acquisition of tool use among humans, with its concomitant muscular and neurological requirements, helped initiate other adaptations for effective environmental manipulation and exploration. Tool use and terrestriality probably placed a premium on the development of an effective signaling system. Language acquisition may have been a partial response to continuing pressures to communicate effectively about increasing complexities of life—for example, making tools, finding food, and passing social traditions from a mother to her infant.

Although much has been written about the evolution of language, we do not know when language first evolved. Furthermore, few of the anatomical modifications necessary for human speech have fossilized because many of the speech structures are either muscle or cartilage.

Many have tried to link an increasing brain size with the onset of language, which was in turn supposedly tied to coordinating hunting behavior. Calvin (1983) has a unique perspective. He argues that it was the sequential skills and coordination developed in throwing that subsequently made language possible. Calvin suggests that learning to throw with one hand produced the very first lateralization of the brain, the first concentration of a brain function in one hemisphere. Language skills eventually became lateralized, and both throwing and language are most commonly concentrated in the brain's left hemisphere. Many people who have a language impairment suffer from damage to the left hemisphere of the brain. Calvin further suggests that the lateralization of throwing behavior spurred rapid brain enlargement. He sees a link between the muscle sequencing and visual perception that allowed one to hit a rapidly moving distant target by throwing a rock with one hand and an increasingly sophisticated tool complex.

Laitman (1984) attempts to explain the anatomical modifications involved in the evolution of human language by noting the shift in the position of the larynx (voice box) in the neck. The larynx determines how an animal breathes, swallows, and vocalizes. In almost all mammals, at all stages of development, the larynx is situated high in the neck, lying roughly opposite the first to third cervical vertebra. In this position, the larynx allows the direct passage of air between the nose and lungs. While an animal is breathing, liquids can still be swallowed. A nonhuman primate, for example, can simultaneously breathe and swallow liquids. However, the position of the larynx severely limits the range of sound production.

In modern human infants, the position of the larynx shifts downward around the second year of life. From birth to approximately age 2, the human larynx is high in the neck, much like that of any other mammal. The human newborn can breathe, swallow, and make sounds, much like monkeys and apes. At around age 2, however, the larynx begins to descend, altering forever the way in which the child breathes, swallows, and vocalizes. Once descent occurs, the larynx is in a position unlike that of any other mammal. In human adults, the larynx can be positioned anywhere between the fourth to almost the seventh cervical vertebra.

Although human adults cannot breathe and drink simultaneously, the descent of the larynx has produced a greatly enlarged pharyngeal chamber (the pharynx is the internal passage from the nose to the throat) above the vocal folds. Sounds produced in the larynx of human adults can be modified to a greater degree than is possible for newborns and any nonhuman mammal. The expanded pharynx seems to be the key to our articulate speech.

Laitman suggests that the first members of the human family, the australopithecines, (Chapter 17) had a laryngeal position approaching that of monkeys or apes. Consequently, they probably had a very restricted vocal repertoire compared with modern humans. The high position of their larynges would have made it impossible for them to produce some of the universal vowel sounds found in human speech, and it is unlikely that they could speak the way we do today.

Laitman suggests that the modern laryngeal condition allowing articulate speech appeared first among archaic *H. sapiens.* Until very recently there was no solid fossil evidence that could be used to help solve the dilemma of which early humans had speech. However, the discovery of a well-preserved human hyoid bone from Kebara cave, Israel, dating to about 62,000 years ago suggests that the Neanderthals had the capacity for human speech (See Chapter 20). The hyoid is a small bone to which the tongue is anchored at its base. The fossilized hyoid is almost identical to the modern human hyoid bone in its size and shape. The discovery of this fossil bone negates any arguments against the Neanderthals having speech (Arensburg, et al. 1989).

TREND 3: INCREASING BRAIN SIZE AND COMPLEXITY

There has been a trend toward increased brain size and complexity during human evolution; however, the trend was neither consistent nor steady. The size increase was slight during the approximately 3 million years of the evolutionary history of the *Australopithecus* and early *Homo* lineages but rather rapid during the middle Pleistocene in *H. erectus* and later *H. sapiens.* Increased brain size and complexity were probably related to such factors as tool use and manufacture, increasing environmental challenges, and more complex social groups.

Increased brain size and complexity may also be related to the infant's slower maturation rate, which required extended parental investment. Extending the period of maternal care allowed more time for infant socialization and placed a premium on learning abilities (Poirier and Hussey, 1982). Learning may have been enhanced by increasing brain sizes and complexity. It is also possible that increases in brain size led to earlier births and thus required longer learning times.

Culture has as a major component learned behavior that is transmitted across generations. One prerequisite for culture is adequate memory storage to facilitate relatively complex learning. A threefold increase in brain size occurred from early human forms to modern humans (Table 16-1), which is likely to have enhanced the capacity for information storage and the ability to learn. Although our early human ancestors had relatively small brains, even the smaller-brained forms had relatively larger cranial capacities than modern apes. The functional significance of the large cranial capacities of later humans is that they probably reflect increased technological abilities and long-term memory.

For a long time, anthropologists have speculated on the degree of feedback between increased brain size and complexity and tool use and manufacture. Although some aspects of this interaction have been questioned (see, for example, Holloway, 1967), there is little doubt as to its importance. Figure 16-3 shows how the feedback may have occurred. Tool use and manufacture are best understood as related to cerebral specialization, especially brain lateralization (the specialization of the right and left hemispheres for different functions). We cannot say which appeared first, hemispheric specialization or

Table 16-1. Increasing Brain Sizes

Taxa	Average Cranial Capacities (cc)	Estimated Weight (kg)
P. troglodytes		
(chimpanzee)	395	45
Humans		
A. afarensis	400	30
A. africanus	442	30
A. robustus	520	60
H. habilis	640	30
H. erectus	1,000	55
H. sapiens	1,400	57

manual dexterity. However, the whole complex of increasing verbal skills, skilled tool use and fabrication, and later cerebral specialization probably evolved together (Tunnell, 1973).

Martin (in Lewin, 1982) suggests that the upper limit of brain development is determined when the infant is still in the womb. After birth the brain follows a set growth trajectory, which in nonhuman primates typically involves doubling of the brain's weight; in humans the brain weight quadruples. Differences in gestation times apparently have consequences for or are the consequence of potential brain growth.

Milton (1981) hypothesizes that the element of predictability associated

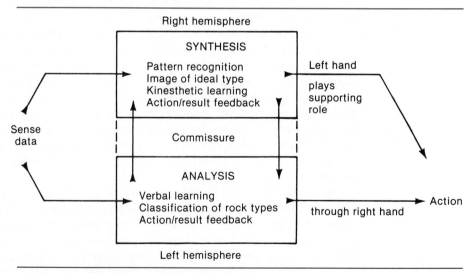

Figure 16-3 Tool use flow chart showing interaction of cerebral hemispheres in normal functioning.

with the spatial and temporal distribution patterns of plant foods in tropical forests stimulated primate intelligence. What appears to set primates apart from most other relatively long-lived and large-brained animals is their ability to store and retrieve a great amount of independently acquired information about their environment (Eisenberg, 1973). Milton (1981, p. 535) notes, "The extreme diversity of plant foods in tropical forests and the manner in which they are distributed in space and time have been a major selective force in the development of advanced cerebral complexity in certain higher primates."

Given the dynamic nature of tropical forests, it seems maladaptive for a tropical-forest dweller to genetically code a large variety of dietary information. What appears to be required is a great deal of behavioral flexibility, allowing a response to continually changing forest conditions. Increasing mental complexity, which places a strong emphasis on learning and retention, might have been selected for.

Milton notes that among later members of the human line—the genus *Homo,* for example—a behavioral shift favoring an increased ability to exploit mobile big game so that it could become a dependable addition to the diet may have required some major changes in certain areas of the brain. In addition, mobile prey typically evolve at the same rate or at a faster rate than their predators. "Lacking powerful jaws and claws characteristic of hunting carnivores and already predisposed to solve their dietary problems primarily through behavioral rather than morphological or physiological adaptations, these hunting hominids may have depended heavily on mental acuity to outwit and capture prey" (p. 544).

Holloway (1982, 1983) questions the commonly held assumption that the brain was one of the last structures to change in human evolution. He suggests that the brain was reorganized early in human evolution and that only the enlargement of the brain occurred late. The development of bipedalism was probably integrated with neuropsychological restructuring. Tobias (1982) notes that brain enlargement was not striking for the first 100,000 generations of human existence, but cerebral changes other than enlargement occurred.

Given Holloway's position, analyses examining brain size alone are likely to provide misleading and possibly erroneous conclusions regarding the dynamics of human evolution. Natural selection has operated on the evolution of the human brain, and the selection pressure has been in the realm of social behavior. Holloway suggests that selection pressure on brain organization and size continued throughout most of human evolution, or at least until the Neanderthals appeared about 125,000 years ago. The brain was not the terminal organ to evolve in the overall mosaic of human evolution, according to Holloway, unless one talks only about absolute size and ignores relative brain size, cerebocortical organization, and cerebral asymmetry. Absolute and relative increases in brain size were probably interspersed with evolutionary episodes of brain reorganization and other changes.

Falk, like Holloway, has spent years studying primate endocranial casts (or endocasts); however, her views differ from those of Holloway. She (1984) notes that endocasts belonging to members of an early hominid lineage, the South African australopithecines, resemble ape brains in both size and external form. This does not mean, however, that the australopithecine and the ape had the same thought patterns or mental capacities. Because of the scanty nature of australopithecine endocasts, it is not possible to reconcile the opposing views of Falk and Holloway.

Australopithecine brains retained a number of apelike traits. The earliest example of a humanlike endocast dates to about 2 M.Y.A. and belongs to a more advanced species, *Homo habilis,* from northern Kenya. This endocast exhibits a humanlike frontal lobe, including what appears to be Broca's area. Broca's area is crucial for human language, and its apparent presence in *H. habilis* suggests the possibility that this species had language. This is contrary to Laitman's argument, presented earlier. Falk (p. 39) suggests that until early humans acquired language, they "may not have been very human."

TREND 4: EXTENSIVE MANIPULATION OF NATURAL OBJECTS AND THE DEVELOPMENT OF MOTOR SKILLS TO FACILITATE TOOL MAKING

Extensive manipulatory behavior was facilitated by hands freed of locomotor functions, stereoscopic vision, increasing brain size, and more effective hand-eye coordination. The selective pressures for extensive environmental manipulation probably grew out of increasing tool use, which was, in turn, related to increasing problems of survival. A major advantage of the primate hand is that it permits detachment of objects from the environment. Among other things, knowledge about our environment stemmed from just naturally picking up objects and examining them. Manipulation of the environment was an outgrowth of primate inquisitiveness.

Grooming, another primate behavioral pattern, (Figure 16-4) involves the use of the hands to pick through another primate's hair and requires sophisticated hand–eye coordination. Most nonhuman primates who engage in grooming can oppose the thumb to the forefinger. Such opposability is required in holding and handling objects. These seemingly inauspicious beginnings involving grooming behavior were a **preadaptation** to picking up and examining objects. In time, this may have led to tool use and manufacture. Although other arboreal animals have some of the same adaptations to the arboreal niche as nonhuman primates, rarely do any approach the fine manipulative abilities and hand–eye coordination of primates.

Let us return to the proposition that the ability to detach objects from the environment using the hands is a major advance that was most important for the development of primate perceptual skills. We owe recognition of different kinds of objects to our visual acuity and tactile ability. Given the upright sitting position of nonhuman primates, vision became "a supervision, a guide and control of fine manipulations" (Spuhler, 1957:41). The relationship

A

B

C

Figure 16-4 (A) Closeup of one adult male chimpanzee grooming another. Note the close work of the thumb and first finger. Grooming was a preadaptation for tool use and manufacture. (B) Adolescent male at Gombe grooms sexual swelling of adult female. (C) Adult male grooms adult male who grooms adult female (left to right) at Gombe. Grooming cements social ties among nonhuman primates.

between the evolution of keen vision—which was possibly an adaptation to locomoting through the trees and grasping at swift insects (Cartmill, 1975)—and fine manipulation is two-dimensional. Vision itself became more refined, and intellectual absorption and mental utilization was more complete and lasting as the skilled movements became more complex and efficient (Polyak, 1957).

Primates extract objects from the environment with their hands; they smell and taste them, visually and tactically examine them, and then perhaps replace them. Primates "have come to see the environment not as a continuum of events in a world of pattern but as an encounter with objects that proved to make up these events and this pattern" (Campbell, 1966:129).

TREND 5: THE ACQUISITION OF MEAT PROTEIN

Although most nonhuman primates are noncarnivorous vegetarians, some kill and eat other vertebrates. The time when meat first assumed importance in the human diet is not known. Consistent meat eating required behavioral adjustments and changes in dentition and jaw musculature. Once meat became basic to the diet, means would have developed whereby it could be most efficiently obtained and butchered. Methods for carrying meat, rules for sharing (perhaps one of the first sets of societal rules), and maybe a linguistic system naming those who were to receive shares would have appeared.

Analyses of tooth surfaces sometimes indicate the role of certain foods in an animal's diet. Using an electron microscope, one can examine the minute scratches left on tooth enamel and dentine as the animal chews and crushes food. Tooth surfaces of an early human ancestor, *Australopithecus robustus* (Chapter 17), for example, suggest that it was basically vegetarian in its diet. More precisely, the tooth wear patterns resemble those of chimpanzees. Because the chimpanzee ingests a wide variety of dietary items, the statement that the teeth of *A. robustus* resemble those of a chimpanzee under an electron microscope does not conclusively define their diet. It does, however, exclude grass eating, bone crushing, and root eating, all of which would have left distinctive scratches and pits on the tooth's enamel.

A shift in enamel wear patterns on the teeth of a later human form, *Homo erectus,* suggests that a large amount of grit was incorporated into its diet. Perhaps this grit came from the discovery that roots and tubers were good food sources. The grit may also have been adhering to meat that was lying on the ground.

Increased meat consumption seems to have had some of its own hazards, as seen in *H. erectus* material (from Kenya) dated over 1 M.Y.A. One of the leg bones of this specimen is malformed, and the bone shafts are patchily encrusted with new bone. This bone may reflect the presence of a condition due to hypervitaminosis A, a toxic overdose of vitamin A. The condition is rare and is most commonly contracted by eating large quantities of raw liver, which is rich in vitamin A.

Too much emphasis seems to have been placed on the importance of hunting as a factor in human evolution. With most interest focused on the hunting half of the hunter-gatherer food-getting complex, gathering has been underemphasized. Many researchers have ignored the importance of gathering vegetable foods or have dismissed its results as "casually collected foods." Coon (1971) referred to the primacy of hunting and contended that it had more impact on social structure than did gathering. However, Lee (1968), among others, criticized this view. Food sources other than those offered by meat were important, and it is very unlikely that any human group ever relied primarily on a diet of meat.

The composition of the human salivary proteins supports the contention of an overreliance on meat eating and hunting in our theory building. Apes and humans have similar salivary proteins—the Pb proteins and related PPb (or post-Pb) proteins (Azen, Leutenegger, and Peters, 1978). Apes are primarily fruit and leaf eaters, whereas humans have an **omnivorous** diet. The diet probably did not change enough during human evolution for there to be strong selection for a change in salivary proteins from that of the apelike ancestors. Early humans probably shared with early apes the type of salivary proteins useful in processing a diet high in plant carbohydrates. Because human salivary proteins still resemble those of apes, there is a strong probability that gathered plant food remained important during human evolution.

When scenarios of human evolution refer to ingestion of meat protein, they usually refer to meat that has been hunted. The idea that scavenging might have represented a complete ecological adaptation has only recently come to the forefront. Several researchers, such as Richard Potts (1984), who worked with animal bones found at the 1.8 million-year-old Bed I site at Olduvai Gorge, Tanzania, have indicated that scavenging was probably quite an important component of early human life.

Based on an analysis of more than 2,500 antelope bones from Bed I, Olduvai Gorge, Shipman (1984) suggests that "instead of hunting for prey and leaving the remains behind for carnivores to scavenge, perhaps hominids were scavenging from carnivores" (p. 24). Scavenging has different costs and benefits than does hunting. For example, the scavenger can be relatively certain that the prey is dead, for predators have already performed the task of chasing and killing the prey. However, "while scavenging may be cheap, it's risky" (p. 24). Both predators and scavengers face the danger of possibly fighting over a carcass. The major energetic costs to scavengers come from the fact that they must survey much larger areas than predators to find food. Predators tend to be specialized for speed; scavengers, for endurance. Scavengers also need an efficient means of locating carcasses. Shipman suggests that bipedalism was an adaptation to this need for endurance and for locating carcasses.

There are few full-time mammalian scavengers. The bulk of the scavenger's diet comes either from other food sources or from hunting small game. Such game as rats or hares are consumed on the spot, eliminating the problem of having to defend a carcass against larger carnivores. Because small carnivores, such as jackals and striped hyenas, often cannot defend a carcass, much of their diet consists of fruit and insects. (As previously noted, there is dental evidence that part of the early human diet included fruits.) Shipman notes (p. 27), "The evidence of cut marks, tooth wear, and bipedalism, together with our knowledge of scavenger adaptations . . . is consistent with the hypothesis that two million years ago hominids were scavengers rather than accomplished hunters." Hunting as a major way of life may not have appeared until 1.5 M.Y.A. with *H. erectus.* There is evidence of hunting among *H. erectus* populations.

Blumenschine (1987) has provided an interesting discussion of the potential niche of an early hominid scavenging strategy, although he, like others, is not convinced that early hominids actually did scavenge. Hominid scavenging success would have been influenced by the size of the carcass scavenged in relation to the animals scavenging from the carcass and the degree of competition for the carcass.

If early hominids did scavenge meat, they would have secured most carcasses during the dry season from within or on the margins of riparian woodlands (that is, woodlands on the banks of rivers or streams). Most carcasses that would have been encountered there would be from medium-sized adults that were killed, partially eaten, and abandoned by felids during the dry season.

Major hypotheses dealing with human evolution tend to fall into two distinct categories (Cheney, 1982). One emphasizes "man the hunter," arguing that the development of hunting had a profound affect on human evolution. This hypothesis suggests that males are both the cooperative and competitive sex, cooperating with one another in pursuit of big game and competing (this competition is often mistakenly viewed as aggressive physical confrontation) for access to female mates. Male bonding (Tiger and Fox, 1971) is viewed as having an old evolutionary history, and females are portrayed as infant-producers, whose reproductive functions demand neither cooperation nor competition with members of their sex.

This long-standing interpretation of human evolution has been vigorously challenged by those arguing that food gathering, traditionally viewed as a female task, was easily as important as hunting in the evolution of human behavior. Food gathering exerted strong selective pressure on intelligence and technological skills, but proponents of this view are divided about the importance of competition and cooperation in the evolution of human behavior. Female reproductive success is assumed to be less dependent than that of males on competition for mates, and it is often argued that there has been little selection for competition or aggression in females. This stress on noncompetitive females ignores the important element of competition among females for access to the "most desirable" male mates.

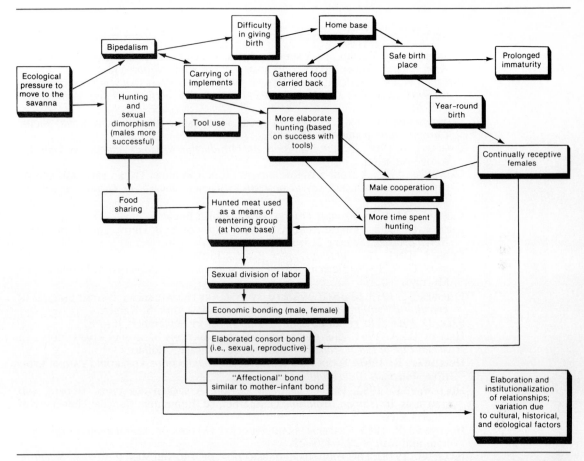

Figure 16-5 Interaction of physical, behavioral, and cultural pressures in primate evolution.

There are five major trends in human evolution. Skeletal and muscular modification are associated with the acquisition of bipedalism. While the earliest humans were bipeds—the first evidence of bipedalism being footprints dated to about 3.7 M.Y.A. and bones dated to about 3.2 M.Y.A.—there are differing opinions on why bipedalism developed. A sexual division of labor wherein both sexes contributed to the daily larder enhanced the exploitation of the terrestrial niche. Although meat protein became increasingly important in the human diet, the role of gathered plants cannot be overlooked, nor can the role that females played in gathering such foods. The male's role and the concept of "man the hunter" have been greatly overemphasized in past theoretical constructs of human evolution. Another feature characterizing human evolution was an increase in brain size and complexity. In neither case was the trend consistent or rapid. Brain lateralization and increasing complexity seem to have preceded a dramatic enlargement of the brain, which occurred only during later stages of human evolution.

BIBLIOGRAPHY

ARENSBURG, B.; TILLIAN, A.; VANDERMEERSCH, B.; DUDAY, H.; SCHEPARTZ, R. AND Y. RAK, 1989. A MIDDLE PALEOLITHIC HUMAN HYOID BONE. *Nature* 338: 758-60.

AZEN, E., W. LEUTENEGGER, and E. PETERS. 1978. EVOLUTIONARY AND DIETARY ASPECTS OF SALIVARY BASIC (PB) and POST PB (PPB) PROTEINS IN ANTHROPOID APES. *Nature* 273: 775–78.

BLUMENSCHINE, R. 1987. CHARACTERISTICS OF AN EARLY HOMINID SCAVENGING NICHE. *Current Anthropology* 28: 383–408.

CAMPBELL, B. 1966. *Human Evolution: An Introduction to Man's Adaptation.* Chicago: Aldine-Atherton.

CALVIN, W. 1983. A STONE'S THROW AND ITS LAUNCH WINDOW: TIMING PRECISION AND ITS IMPLICATIONS FOR LANGUAGE IN HOMINID EVOLUTION. *Journal of Theoretical Biology* 104: 121–35.

CARTMILL, M. 1975. *Primate Origins.* Minneapolis: Burgess.

CHENEY, D. 1982. FEMALES AS STRATEGISTS (REVIEW OF S. B. HRDY, *The Woman That Never Evolved). Science* 215: 1090–91.

COON, C. 1971. *The Hunting Peoples.* Boston: Little, Brown.

DARWIN, C. 1871. *The Descent of Man, and Selection in Relation to Sex.* London: John Murray.

EISENBERG, J. 1973. MAMMALAIN SOCIAL SYSTEM: ARE PRIMATE SOCIAL SYSTEMS UNIQUE? In *Precultural Primate Behavior,* E. Menzel, ed. New York: S. Karger.

FALK, D. 1984. THE PETRIFIED BRAIN. *Natural History* September: 36–39.

HALLOWELL, A. 1961. THE PROTOCULTURAL FOUNDATIONS OF HUMAN ADAPTATIONS. In *Social Life of Early Man,* S. Washburn, ed. Chicago: Aldine.

HOLLOWAY, R. 1967. TOOLS AND TEETH: SOME SPECULATIONS REGARDING CANINE REDUCTION. *American Anthropologist* 93: 63–67.

HOLLOWAY, R. 1982. HUMAN BRAIN EVOLUTION: A SEARCH FOR UNITS, MODELS, AND SYNTHESIS. IN *Human Evolution,* G. Sperber, ed. Edmonton, Canada: University of Alberta Press.

HOLLOWAY, R. 1983. CEREBRAL BRAIN ENDOCAST PATTERN OF *Australopithecus afarensis* hominid. *Nature* 303: 420–22.

ISAAC, G. 1978. THE FOOD-SHARING BEHAVIOR OF PROTOHUMAN HOMINIDS. *Scientific American* 238: 90–109.

LAITMAN, J. 1984. THE ANATOMY OF HUMAN SPEECH. *Natural History* 93: 21–27.

LANCASTER, J. 1975. *Primate Behavior and the Emergence of Human Culture.* New York: Holt, Rinehart and Winston.

LEE, R. 1968. WHAT HUNTERS DO FOR A LIVING, OR HOW TO MAKE OUT ON SCARCE RESOURCES. IN *Man the Hunter,* R. Lee and I. DeVore, editors, Chicago: Aldine-Atherton.

LEWIN, R. 1982. HOW DID HUMANS EVOLVE BIG BRAINS? *Science* 216: 840–41.

LOVEJOY, O. 1981. THE ORIGIN OF MAN. *Science* 211: 341–50.

LOVEJOY, O. 1984. THE NATURAL DETECTIVE. *Natural History* October: 24–27.

LOVEJOY, C.O. 1988. EVOLUTION OF HUMAN WALKING. *Scientific American.* November: 118–25.

McHENRY, H. 1982. THE PATTERN OF HUMAN EVOLUTION: STUDIES ON BIPEDALISM, MASTICATION, AND ENCEPHALIZATION. *Annual Review of Anthropology* 11: 151–73.

McHENRY, H., and L. TEMERIN. 1979. THE EVOLUTION OF HOMINID BIPEDALISM: EVIDENCE FROM THE FOSSIL RECORD. *Yearbook of Physical Anthropology* 22: 105–31.

MILTON, K. 1981. DISTRIBUTION PATTERNS OF TROPICAL PLANT FOODS AS AN EVOLUTIONARY STIMULUS TO PRIMATE MENTAL DEVELOPMENT. *American Anthropologist* 83: 534–48.

NAPIER, J. 1967. THE ANTIQUITY OF HUMAN WALKING. *Scientific American* 216: 56–66.

POIRIER, F., and L. HUSSEY. 1982. NONHUMAN PRIMATE LEARNING: THE IMPORTANCE OF LEARNING IN AN EVOLUTIONARY PERSPECTIVE. *Anthropology and Education Quarterly* 12: 133–48.

POLYAK, S. 1957. *The Vertebrate Visual System: Its Origin, Structure and Function.* Chicago: University of Chicago Press.

POTTS, R. 1984. HOME BASES AND EARLY HOMINIDS. *Scientific American* 72: 338–47.

RODMAN, P., and H. McHENRY. 1980. BIOENERGETICS AND THE ORIGIN OF HOMINID BIPEDALISM. *American Journal of Physical Anthropology* 52: 103–6.

SHIPMAN, P. 1984. SCAVENGER HUNT. *Natural History* 93: 20–27.

SINCLAIR, A., M. LEAKEY, and M. NORTON-GRIFFITHS. 1986. MIGRATION AND BIPEDALISM. *Nature* 324: 307–8.

SPHULER, J. 1957. SOMATIC PATHS TO CULTURE. *Human Biology* 31: 1–13.

TANNER, N. 1981. *On Becoming Human.* New York: Cambridge University Press.

TIGER, L., and R. FOX. 1971. *The Imperial Animal.* New York: Holt, Rinehart and Winston.

TOBIAS, P. 1971. *The Brain in Hominid Evolution.* New York: Columbia University Press.

TOBIAS, P. 1982. HOMINID EVOLUTION IN AFRICA. IN *Human Evolution,* G. Sperber, ed. Edmonton, Canada: University of Alberta Press.

TUNNELL, G. 1973. *Culture and Biology: Becoming Human.* Minneapolis: Burgess.

VON BONIN, G. 1963. *The Evolution of the Human Brain.* Chicago: University of Chicago Press.

WASHBURN, S., 1960. TOOLS AND HUMAN EVOLUTION. *Scientific American* 203: 62–75.

WASHBURN, S., and C. LANCASTER. 1968. THE EVOLUTION OF HUNTING. IN *Man the Hunter,* R. Lee and I. DeVore, eds. Chicago: Aldine-Atherton.

WILEY, J. 1984. PHENOMENA, COMMENT AND NOTES. *Smithsonian* 15: 38, 40, 42, 44.

WUNDRAM, I. 1986. CORTICAL MOTOR ASYMMETRY AND HOMINID FEEDING STRATEGIES. *Journal of Human Evolution* 1: 183–88.

ZIHLMAN, A. 1967. HUMAN LOCOMOTION: A REAPPRAISAL OF THE FUNCTIONAL AND ANATOMICAL EVIDENCE. PhD DISSERTATION. BERKELEY: UNIVERSITY OF CALIFORNIA PRESS.

ZIHLMAN, A., and L. BRUNKER. 1978. HOMINID BIPEDALISM: THEN AND NOW. *Yearbook of Physical Anthropology* 22: 132–62.

Chapter

17

The Earliest Human

Ancestors

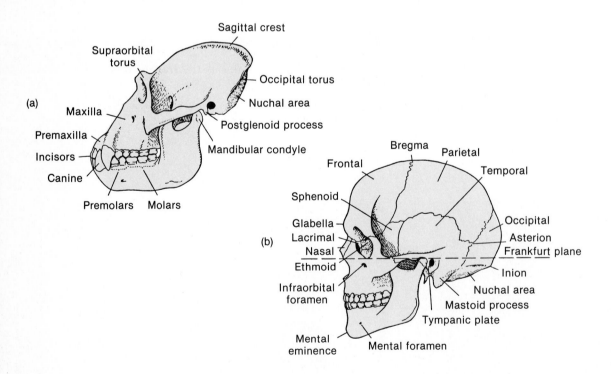

(a)

Sagittal crest

Supraorbital torus

Occipital torus

Nuchal area

Maxilla

Postglenoid process

Premaxilla

Incisors

Mandibular condyle

Canine

Premolars   Molars

(b)

Bregma   Parietal

Frontal   Temporal

Sphenoid

Glabella

Lacrimal   Occipital

Nasal   Asterion

Ethmoid   Frankfurt plane

Infraorbital foramen   Inion

Nuchal area

Mastoid process

Tympanic plate

Mental eminence   Mental foramen

In 1925, Dart first announced the recovery of early human remains from South Africa. Until the 1950s, few accepted his contention that there was an early African ancestor in human evolution. After many years and many discoveries in eastern and South Africa, the fossil group, most of whom are collectively known as the australopithecines, has been accepted into human ancestry.

Africa has yielded an array of pivotal early human fossils dating between 5.5 and 1 M.Y.A. Their skeletal variability has stimulated many evolutionary scenarios. The currently accepted position is that the earlier members of the group belong to the genus Australopithecus, *which has a number of species. The first forms belonged to A. afarensis. The anatomically more modern and later members belong to the genus and species of* Homo habilis.

These early hominids share the same bipedal locomotion as their descendants. The major differentiating traits of the two genera— Australopithecus *and* Homo *—and the various species are found in the skull, face, teeth, and cranial capacity. Some members of the early hominid group made and used stone tools belonging to the Oldowan tool tradition. All early hominids were restricted to Africa, the vast majority of the remains coming from east and southern Africa. The anatomies, life-ways and evolutionary relationships of the various forms are discussed.*

A BRIEF HISTORY

Dart first announced the discovery of early human remains from the country of South Africa in 1925. His description was based on a skull with a face and an associated endocranial cast of a juvenile of about 5 years of age, which were found in 1924 at a site called Taung, or Taungs. Dart was convinced that this skull belonged to some "manlike ape," as he called the find. He named the fossil *Australopithecus africanus* and stated, "The specimen is important because it exhibits an extinct race of apes intermediate between living anthropoids and man" (Dart, 1925a).

Few scientists accepted Dart's claims. At that time there were many competing theories of human evolution, all based on fragmentary remains. The Taung fossil was rejected because it did not fit into the theories then being championed by recognized scholars (Lewin, 1985). Besides belonging to a juvenile—and it is improper to propose a new taxon based on immature specimens—the fossil was, in light of then-championed theories, found in the wrong place, dated too late in time, and had the wrong morphology. In 1925, Asia, and not Africa, was considered the site of human origins—despite Darwin's earlier emphasis on Africa as the cradle of human evolution.

At the time of the Taung specimen's discovery, most scientists assumed that humans had appeared early in primate evolution. Because of incorrect ideas as to the dating of Taung and the overall time span of mammalian evolution, many argued that Taung had appeared too late in the evolutionary sequence to be of much consequence in terms of defining an early human ancestor.

Another preconceived notion that led to Taung's rejection was the long-held belief that the brain preceded the rest of the body in evolving toward a human form. Taung's small brain did not fit this notion. Furthermore, Taung had a more human face and teeth than were expected.

The recovery of the South African remains from Taung and other sites initially raised a number of disturbing questions. Were they apes, as most contended, or were they humans, as Dart argued? What was their mode of locomotion? Were they bipedal or quadrupedal? What was their evolutionary history? With continued recovery of more fossils, answers were provided to these and other questions, as we will discuss later in this chapter.

Not all of Dart's contemporaries sided against him. While Dart's interpretations concerning the nature of early human evolution in Africa were being rejected, Broom soon became convinced that Dart was correct. From other deposits in South Africa, Broom uncovered a remarkable series of human fossils to support Dart's contentions. Despite Broom's additional evidence, other scientists were still unconvinced that Africa was the human homeland. This situation lasted until the late 1950s, at which time the Leakeys began to uncover human remains dating to 1.8 M.Y.A. at a place called Olduvai Gorge in Tanzania.

GEOGRAPHICAL DISTRIBUTION

The earliest members of the human family, the australopithecines, first appeared about 5.5 M.Y.A., during which time the earth was a geologically restless planet. About 3 to 2 M.Y.A., there were violent geological changes and a general cooling of the climate. Africa was marked by continued shrinking of the forests and an expansion of savanna grasslands. In some areas, wet periods alternated with drier times. Major earthquakes opened the Rift Valley in East Africa and lowered or emptied many lake beds. Although the southernmost part of Africa remained relatively stable, northern areas experienced convulsive changes.

Australopithecine remains are found throughout East and South Africa (Table 17-1, Figure 17-1). As previously noted, the first remains to come to light were from South Africa, where five major sites are located in three widely separated regions. All five sites were uncovered by quarrying operations, and because the remains were not found in context, dating is problematic. Attempts to date the remains have yielded various figures.

Taung, the site of the first recovered australopithecine materials, is a limestone area into which animal bones and sand have fallen. Sterkfontein is a South African cave site that had a hole in the roof during australopithecine times. The three other South African sites are caves.

A number of important and spectacular finds of early human remains come from the extensive East African Rift Valley system (Table 17-2). Some of the

Table 17-1 **Plio-Pleistocene Sites Discussed in Text**

GEOGRAPHICAL REGION	GENERA, SPECIES	DATE OF FIRST APPEARANCE (MILLION YEARS AGO)
East Africa		
Ethiopia		
Omo	*A. africanus*	3.0–2.5
	A. boisei	2.1
	H. habilis	1.85
Hadar	*A. afarensis*	3.3
Tanzania		
Laetoli	*A. afarensis*	3.7–3.5
Olduvai Gorge, Bed 1	*A. boisei* and *H. habilis*	1.8
Kenya		
Tabarin	*Australopitheus sp?*	4.0–5.0
Lake Baringo	*Australopithecus sp?*	3.5–2.8
Kanapoi	*Australopithecus sp?*	4.0–3.0
Lake Turkana	*A. africanus*	?
	A. boisei	2.5
	H. habilis	1.9–1.8
South Africa		
Sterkfontein, MB 4	*A. africanus, A. robustus*	2.8–2.4(?)
Makapansgat	*A. africanus, A. robustus*	3.3–2.5(?)
Taung	*A. africanus* or *A. robustus*	perhaps 1.0
Swartkrans	*H. habilis* or *H. erectus*	2.0–1.5(?)
Kromdraai	*A. robustus* and/or *Australopithecus sp.*	2.0–1.0

most important of the Rift Valley sites are found at Olduvai Gorge (Figure 17-2). Olduvai Gorge is a steep-sided gorge stretching for about 25 miles across the Serengeti Plain in northern Tanzania. Olduvai Gorge is about 300 feet deep and geologically stratified into five beds (Figure 17-3). Bed I, the oldest and lowest bed, dates to the early Pleistocene of about 1.8 M.Y.A. The first important australopithecine discovery at Olduvai was made in July 1959, when Mary Leakey found a piece of a skull and two very large premolar teeth. This discovery helped to change forever our interpretations of human evolution and firmly established Africa as the center for human evolution.

Laetoli, Tanzania, located about 30 miles south of Olduvai Gorge, has yielded important human remains dated to about 3.77 to 3.5 M.Y.A. (M. Leakey et al., 1976). These remains were first recovered in 1975. Animal fossils at Laetoli are similar to those found today. Animal footprints of 17 taxonomic groups have been recognized.

Laetoli provided a rich collection of human teeth and jaw fragments representing at least 26 individuals. The two most complete remains are a child's mandible and the mandible of an individual about 15 years old. In

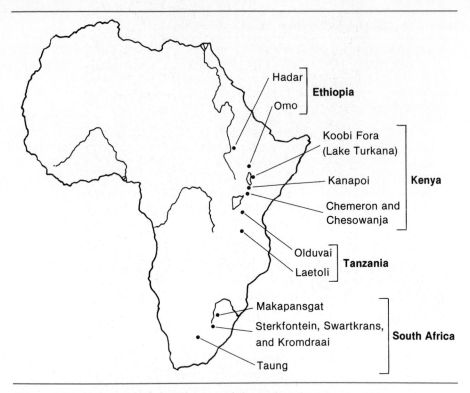

Figure 17-1 Geographical distribution of the earliest human ancestors.

1979, human fossil footprints belonging to at least 3 individuals—2 adults and a child—that dated to 3.5 M.Y.A. were discovered (M. Leakey, 1979). The best-preserved footprint trail contains 34 prints covering a distance of 7.6 feet. These footprints were apparently made by an anatomically modern foot and

Table 17-2 **Dates of Early East African Hominid Sites**

Date of First Appearance (Million Years Ago)	Olduvai	Omo Tuffs	Turkana Tuffs	Others
1.0–0.5	Bed IV			
1.5–1.0	Bed III	L	Chari	
2.0–1.5	Beds I, II	I_2, G, F	Okote, KBS (12) KBS (130/131)	Cheswonja, Natron, Kenya
2.5–2.0		E, D		
3.0–2.5		A. B. sands		Chemeron, Kanam, Kenya
3.5–3.0			Tulu Bor	Hadar, Ethiopia
4.0–3.5				Laetoli, Tanzania
5.5–5.0				Tabarin, Kenya

Figure 17-2 Looking into Olduvai Gorge.

suggest that when the individuals walked, they transmitted their body weight and propulsive forces in a manner similar to modern humans. The footprints are the oldest evidence of human bipedalism (Day and Wickens, 1980).

Laetoli is in a wooded area located near a volcanic mountain. When ash from the volcano mixed with rain and then dried in the sun, it set like cement. Following the rain, various animals left their prints in the deep volcanic ash. If a light rain had not fallen, the ash probably would have blown away. If there had been more rain, the impressions would have been washed away. The fossilization of the footprints was a fortuitous and rare event.

North of Tanzania is Kenya, a major source of early hominid fossils. One of the most important sites is in northern Kenya at Lake Turkana. As a result of the research of Richard Leakey and Kamoya Kimeu, human fossil remains from Lake Turkana have been known since 1968. Lake Turkana is the largest known source of late Pliocene and early Pleistocene human fossil sites (Figure 17-4). Fossil beds have yielded a series of comparatively well-preserved human skull and postcranial bones which show remarkable variability in size and morphology. The oldest human remains at Lake Turkana date to about 2 M.Y.A., and stone tools dating to the same time (Figure 17-5) were found in association with some cranial remains. Several locations at Lake Turkana appear to be occupation sites—that is, areas where humans made tools and engaged in other activities.

The Lake Baringo region of northern Kenya has yielded some of the oldest human remains. A 2-inch-long lower jaw fragment containing two molars was

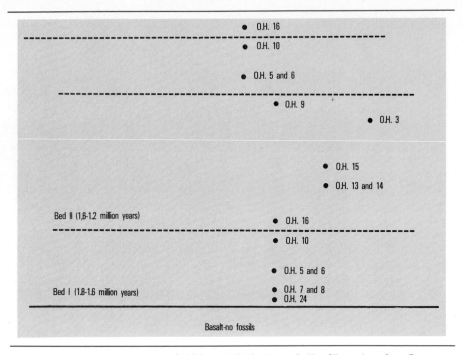

Figure 17-3 Representation of Olduvai Beds I and II. (Drawing by Georgette Goldberg Haydu. Data from M.D. Leakey, "Preliminary survey of the cultural material from Beds I and II, Olduvai Gorge, Tanzania," 1967. In W. Bishop and J.D. Clark, eds., Background to Evolution in Africa.

Figure 17-4 A view of the Koobi Fora region, Lake Turkana.

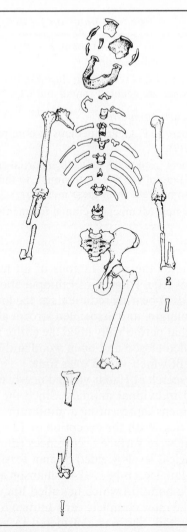

Figure 17-5 Skeletal remains of one of the most complete early human remains, "Lucy," from Hadar, Ethiopia. "Lucy" was small-brained and short in stature, and she walked bipedally.

recovered there. This material, from a site called Tabarin, places hominids in Africa by at least 5 M.Y.A. (Hill, 1985). Other fossil beds in the Lake Baringo Basin have yielded human remains dating between 3.5 and 2.8 M.Y.A.

Just north of this region is Ethiopia. The Omo Valley in Ethiopia is a significant hominid fossil locale. As of 1976, 17 locales yielding human remains of different types dating between 3.1 and 1 M.Y.A. have been recognized (Table 17-3). Mammalian faunal assemblages from Omo indicate that the past climate was quite different from today's parched conditions.

Table 17-3 **Hominid Materials from the Omo Valley**

Usno Formation and Members B through F and Lower Units of G from the Shungura Formation

This material is referred to *Australopithecus* with affinities to *A. africanus.* The oldest specimens are generally small and have a simple dental morphology.

Shungura Formation

Members E, F, G, and perhaps L: hominids attributed to robust australopithecine, *A. boisei* (?).

Members from G, H, and Mb: a partial cranium with maxillary dentition comes from Mb. Material G-28 is quite similar to that of *Homo habilis* (OH 7, 13) from Olduvai. Also some teeth from these members.

Uppermost Member K; cranial fragments with features diagnostic of *H. erectus.*

One of the most famous of all human fossil sites is located in the west central Afar Triangle of Ethiopia about 188 miles northeast of Addis Ababa. The fossil-bearing sediments at the location of Hadar generally represent lake, lake margin, and associated stream and river deposits related to an extensive lake that periodically filled the entire area. There was a mosaic of habitats that included closed and open woodland bush and grassland, the relative proportions of which varied over time.

Research at Hadar yielded nearly 6,000 specimens representing as many as 4,000 individual animals. Since the first field season in 1973, 240 human specimens representing a minimum of 35 individuals were collected from 26 localities. With the exception of 13 excavated fossils, human specimens from Hadar were surface occurrences (they lay exposed on the ground). Fourteen geological levels yielded human fossils dated about 3.3 M.Y.A.

In late December 1974, Johanson announced the discovery from Hadar of a female hominid which he called Lucy (Figure 17-5). Lucy is one of the oldest and the most complete early human fossil discoveries. She was about 3 feet, 10 inches tall. She was considered to be an adult, although by modern growth standards she would have been only a young teenager. Approximately 40 percent of her skeleton was recovered, but because humans (like all mammals) are bilaterally symmetrical, 80 percent of her skeleton was easily reconstructed.

Faunal remains indicate that Lucy lived in a lush grassland environment that was perhaps associated with open savanna woodlands. Fossilized turtle and crocodile eggs were found, along with fossilized crab claws. Such remains are consistent with a lakeshore environment.

The success at Hadar continued in 1975 with the recovery of the remains of 13 individuals, dubbed the "first family," from the same area. This cluster of remains raised a number of questions. For example, were the 13 individuals members of one family? Did they all die at the same time, and how did they die? The lakeshore and riverine deposits at the site suggested to some researchers that perhaps the group died in a flash flood. Other researchers suggested that they may have succumbed to a virulent disease. It was also proposed that the bones are the remnants of a leopard's meal, perhaps dropped from a tree into a waterhole below, where they were subsequently fossilized in the mud. However, because the bones apparently were deposited over a period of time, not fossilized contemporaneously with one another, they are obviously not a family and no particular explanation is needed for their deposition.

The "first family" assemblage consists of jaws, teeth, leg bones, hand and foot bones, a fossilized footprint, ribs, a partial adult skull, and the nearly complete lower jaw of an infant. There is evidence of old and young adults and children.

In 1981, 5 skull fragments and the upper part of a femur dated to 4 M.Y.A. were found in the Middle Awash Valley about 45 miles south of Hadar. The femur suggests bipedalism, and the skull fragments indicate a cranial capacity of about 400 cubic centimeters.

SITE LOCATION

Most early human sites are located near fresh water. Our early ancestors apparently chose to live alongside or near water sources until they had some means of carrying water. Sites located near water offered the best area for collecting certain food plants, for seizing some unsuspecting prey when it came to drink, and for obtaining the round stones favored for making tools.

Occupation sites at Olduvai Gorge show little evidence of human occupation on the savanna and barren floodplains. Human occupation occurs principally with evidence of perennial fresh water and relatively abundant game and vegetation. All 20 sites from Bed I, dating to about 1.8 M.Y.A., are situated along the lake margin. When much of the lake was no longer existent (during the deposition of Bed II), human activity was more widespread.

In contrast with those of East Africa, South African remains come largely from ancient caves and fissures. Sediments washed into these caves indicate ongoing environmental change, but it is likely that open grasslands were prevalent. Early human sites in South Africa were apparently located in open, grassy environments with local or scattered tree growth and uniform precipitation in the range of 600 to 800 millimeters per year.

Despite differences between East and South African sites, all are found in a semiarid or subhumid climate and are characterized by alternating wet and dry seasons and savanna vegetation. If further finds occur in Zaire, where early stone tools were found in a forest context, then it can be suggested that early humans also occupied forested environments. The environments occupied by early humans provided plentiful food and new evolutionary opportunities.

LIFEWAYS

Tool Use and Manufacture

Stone implements were found associated with human remains at the South African sites of Swartkrans and Sterkfontein and in East Africa at Olduvai Gorge, Omo, Lake Turkana, and Hadar. Where identification of the fossil remains is possible, almost all the tools appear to be associated with fossils classified as *Homo habilis* (pp. 327-34). Stone tools are not usually directly associated with the genus *Australopithecus.* Stone tools continued to appear in the archaeological record long after *Australopithecus* became extinct. When hominid fossils and stone artifacts are present at the same level, at least some fossils belong to the genus *Homo.* This circumstantial evidence, plus the larger cranial capacities of *Homo* compared with *Australopithecus,* are used to argue for *Homo* as the earliest tool makers.

Despite the fact that most have argued that the only early human tool user was the form called *H. habilis,* there is the possibility that at least one member of the genus *Australopithecus* also could have made stone tools (Lewin, 1988; Susman, 1988). The argument that *H. habilis* is the first stone tool maker is based primarily on the fact that the earliest occurrence of stone tools in the archaeological record is close in time to the earliest appearance of the genus *Homo.* This is circumstantial evidence of a causal relationship. The earliest hominids, *Australopithecus afarensis,* which first appear about 3.75 M.Y.A., are not found with stone tools. Stone tools may first appear about 2.5 M.Y.A., about .5 million years prior to the earliest fossil evidence of the genus *Homo.*

Susman (1988) argues that at least some members of the robust australopithecine lineage had the ability to make stone tools. He argues that recently discovered finger bones attributed to *A. robustus* (which he calls *Paranthropus robustus)* from the site of Swartkrans in South Africa indicate the ability to make stone tools. The new fossil evidence consists of 22 hand bones dating to about 1.8 M.Y.A. Although both the genera *Australopithecus* and *Homo* are found at the Swartkrans site, the context yielding the hand bones has mostly yielded *Australopithecus* remains. Susman's argument for tool manufacture by *A. robustus* is based on the width of its fingertips. Human fingertips are quite broad, in contrast to the narrow pattern found among apes and the earliest human species, *Australopithecus afarensis.* The broad human fingertip has a large pad of tissue which is richly supplied with blood vessels and sensory nerve endings, which allow fine control in object manipulation. Susman argues that *A. robustus* had the broad fingertips characteristic of modern humans.

It may be impossible to prove Susman's claim that *A. robustus* had broad fingertips. If, however, it is finally shown that more than one early human form made and used stone tools, then the manufacture of stone tools cannot be held responsible for the survival of one lineage and the demise of another. Until Susman's suggestion of possible stone tool manufacture, it was assumed that the robust australopithecine line lacked the intellect and the impetus to manufacture stone tools. It was this failing that supposedly led to its extinction. (This contention for an inability to manufacture stone tools was not based on anatomical evidence—previously there were no hand bones—but mainly on assumptions about the relationship between brain volume and intelligence and the relationship of these to culture.) However, if Susman is correct, then we must look for other reasons for its extinction. We may be forced eventually to reassess the long-held notion that the advent of stone tool manufacture and culture separated the early members of the genus *Homo* from its contemporaries in the genus *Australopithecus.* If the robust australopithecine lineage was making stone tools, perhaps such tools were being used for plant procurement and plant processing. The large molar teeth of the robust forms suggest that they were specialized for eating vegetable materials. There are bone artifacts from the Swartkrans site that show signs of having been used for digging.

Anatomical traits in the hand bones support the claim for tool use and manufacture by early hominids. Napier (1962a, 1962b) concluded from his study of *H. habilis* hand bones from Bed I Olduvai Gorge that these bones allowed a **power grip**—that is, the sort of grip used when wielding a hammer. They may also have allowed a **precision grip**—that is, the grip used in holding small objects such as a pen by opposing the thumb and fingers to one another. Napier demonstrated that the power grip was sufficient not only for making tools called **pebble tools,** but even for making the more advanced tools called **hand axes.** Only the precision grip could have been used on the small flakes found at Olduvai, however.

Once it was realized that early humans made and used tools, artifacts were assigned names based on their probable functions. The first such tool accordingly named was the hand axe. Other names, such as *blade, point,* and *scraper* have been applied to tools because such names reflect the tool's supposed use. Although such names have wide usage, until recently there was little experimental verification.

Microwear analysis, based on studies of microscopic traces of wear on a tool's working edge, reveals the functions of early stone tools. Keeley (1979), who designed a set of experiments to analyze the functions of a series of tools, found that different activities produced a characteristic kind of work polish on the tool being used. Keeley established six broad categories of polishes—wood polish, bone polish, hide polish, meat polish, antler polish, and non-woody plant polish—whose presence on a tool edge helps identify the tool's use.

Early tools are difficult to recognize, probably because the earliest tool use consisted of taking a stone, bone, or stick from the environment, using it once or a few times, and discarding it. Many of the earliest examples of tools are lost because such materials as wood or bone have decayed. It should be mentioned that a few suspected wood-working tools have been recovered that date to 1.5 M.Y.A. (Keeley and Toth, 1981).

The earliest stone tools are referred to the **Oldowan tradition.** The **chopper**

(Figure 17-6), a tool typically found in Lower Pleistocene sites, is often a smooth, rounded cobblestone or oblong block given a rough cutting edge by knocking flakes from both sides. This manufacturing technique is called **bifacial flaking.** Most of the earliest choppers found at Olduvai (where their earliest date is approximately 1.75 M.Y.A.) are about the size of a tennis ball or slightly smaller. Some tools must have been held between the thumb, middle, and index fingers and were probably used to prepare small pieces of plant or animal food. The Olduvai sites also contain possible early examples of bone tools.

Most researchers have argued that, for early tool makers, the core was the primary tool and that the associated flakes and fragments are largely waste material. Toth (1987) has suggested, however, that too much emphasis has been put on cores at the expense of flakes. He suggests that the traditional relationship might be reversed: Flakes may have been the primary tools, and the cores were the by-product of flake manufacture.

Toth also suggests that cores were probably transported from place to place and worked on a bit at a time. Early hominids may have carried partially flaked cores with them, perhaps in simple containers. At resting places the cores may have been chipped. Places of prolonged and frequent occupation would contain heavier concentrations of flaked material. Toth believes that this is the pattern that appears at Koobi Fora, Kenya. The fact that early hominids seem to have transported tools or potential tools over long distances differentiates human and chimpanzee tool use. The latter rarely transport objects farther than 100 meters.

Jones (1979) provided experimental data concerning the manufacture and use of the bifacially flaked tools at Olduvai. Obsidian or chert bifaces are efficient tools because their edges remain sharp during use and can easily be resharpened by secondary flaking. Such bifaces are highly efficient for cutting

Figure 17-6 Stone tools from Lake Turkana.

and skinning. Although the primary flake edges of basalt bifaces are easy to produce, they cannot be effectively resharpened. This limits the usefulness and life span of tools made from basalt.

The mechanical properties—that is, the propensity for fracture, sharpening, and so on—of the materials used to make the Oldowan tools at Olduvai vary. This has led to differences in work capabilities and, as previously noted, the apparent effectiveness of some rocks from which tools were made. The size, shape, and flaking properties of the raw materials used in tool manufacture must be considered when assessing the tool manufacturer's technological sophistication. Some tools considered to be crude or primitive are, according to Jones's data, the products of sophisticated and efficient techniques of stone tool manufacture.

Dart, who analyzed several thousand South African bone fragments, suggested that the earliest humans possessed what he called an osteodontokeratic tool assemblage. That is, they made tools not only from stone but also from bone, teeth, and antlers. Dart suggested that the **osteodontokeratic culture** was a pre-stone-making stage of intensive *tool use,* which was transitional to *tool making.* According to Dart, many of the bone fragments served as weapons: The long bones of the arms and legs of large ungulates were used as clubs; splintered and sharply pointed bones, antelope horns, and canines were used as daggers; and shoulder bones and jaws of larger animals became scrapers and sawlike blades. He argued that some long bones showed definite evidence of having been used to scrape and rub animal hides.

Dart has demonstrated that early humans could have used bones as tools. However, not everyone agrees that they did so or that the osteodontokeratic culture is evidence of the use of bones as tools. Brain (1967, 1968) offered an alternative explanation to Dart's osteodontokeratic culture. He concluded that one of the South African bone assemblages suggested by Dart to reflect usage of bones as tools may instead represent human and carnivore hunting activity associated with hyena scavenging behavior. Brain raises serious questions about Dart's osteodontokeratic culture because Dart maintained that early humans selectively collected particular skeletal parts for tools. Brain, on the other hand, argues that the South African sites were not actual human occupations but that the bone accumulations were the result of feeding by hyenas and porcupines.

Leopards also seem to have played some role in the South African bone accumulations. Brain (1981) concludes that the South African cave deposits contain mostly the remnants of carnivore meals. Modern leopards carry their prey into trees to avoid scavengers and to consume the food leisurely. Trees in the high veldt of South Africa today are frequently situated near cave openings. If this was true in the past, some leopard prey remains may have fallen into these caves. In fact, Brain (1970) has shown that the two puncture marks on a partial skull of an early human from Swartkrans, South Africa, match nicely with the mandibular canines of a fossil leopard.

This interpretation that the South African cave remains are the result of predation by carnivores and not purposeful bone accumulation by humans has received clarification. An analysis of bone fragments from Swartkrans revealed that the proportion of primates such as baboons, other monkeys, and a robust form of early human were unusually high. Based on the behavior of modern baboons, it has been suggested that primates at Swartkrans stayed in the caves during the cold spring and autumn nights. They must have been relatively easy prey for an agile carnivore, such as a leopard or sabre-toothed cat.

Other Possible Cultural Remains

Other evidence of possible cultural remains has been recovered. Volcanic ash, an excellent preservative, covers most of the **living floors** (places where objects remain in their original context) at Olduvai. Mary Leakey analyzed a 2,400-square-foot living floor at the Olduvai site of FLK which is dated to 1.8 M.Y.A. Her mapping of the area shows that an oblong central area of densely concentrated and very fragmentary remains is surrounded by a relatively barren area, beyond which debris again becomes more plentiful and more complete than remains in the central area. The central area may have been enclosed by a thorn fence or a windbreak. This would account for the barren zone, while objects found outside the area might have been thrown over the "fence" by the site's occupants. Two adjacent circular areas containing concentrated areas of artifacts and faunal remains were uncovered in the uppermost occupation level at site FLK North. At Olduvai site FC West in Middle Bed II, a living floor occurred on soils similar to those in Bed I. Artifacts and faunal remains were concentrated within two roughly circular areas, lying close together and reminiscent of the pattern seen at FLK North.

A stone circle found at Olduvai site DK and dated to about 1.8 M.Y.A. may have formed the base of a rough windbreak or simple shelter (Figure 17-7).

Figure 17-7 View of so-called stone circle living site (DK) in Olduvai Bed II. Rock pile at rear contains stones originally taken from the supposed circle wall.

The evidence suggesting an artificial structure are small heaps of stones that might have formed part of the circle and the fact that occupation debris did not appear in comparable density within the circle and surrounding areas.

According to Mary Leakey's (1971, 1976) interpretations, the sites in Beds I and II at Olduvai may represent seasonally occupied home bases. The accumulated remains may suggest that the inhabitants achieved a new type of social stability and possessed a sense of belonging to a particular group. This interpretation makes the social organization of the early inhabitants at Olduvai Gorge similar to modern hunter-gatherer populations. The home-base interpretation implies long-term behavioral continuity between early and modern humans. The early existence of supposed campsites apparently inhabited for an extended period of time implies that a hunter-gatherer subsistence pattern existed. If the early campsites were home bases, the modern hunter-gatherer adaptation would seem to represent an ancient way of life.

The home-base interpretation accords well with prominent ideas about human evolution. For example, increased meat consumption is often seen as a significant dietary change in human evolution. According to Leakey's home-base interpretation of the Olduvai sites, early hominids were obtaining meat and returning with the food to a home base for butchering and sharing.

After reviewing the same data, Potts (1984) offered a far different interpretation of the evidence found in Beds I and II. He questions whether food sharing, meat consumption, and tool use—behaviors which are associated with home bases—existed as early as 2 M.Y.A. The composition of the animal remains, the preponderance of limb bones, and the lack of evidence to suggest that whole or nearly whole carcasses were transported to the sites implies a pattern of opportunistic foraging by scavenging and hunting, without food sharing at a home base. "The available evidence suggests that hominids would have minimized the time spent at these sites, rather than have used them as the primary focus of social activity" (Potts, 1984:344–45).

Potts suggests that the so-called stone circle at site DK, the assumed earliest possible representation of a shelter and the basis for the home-base interpretation, may in fact have been produced by rocks ensnared in a radial distribution of tree roots. The rocks were caught in the roots of a tree that, when it decayed, left the rocks in a circular pattern. Potts also suggests that the appearance of stone flakes and bone fragments found within the circle could have been caused by water flow through the site.

Potts also suggests the possibility that the accumulations of stone and bone at the so-called home bases could have resulted from the simultaneous use of multiple caches of stone tools. He argues that stone caches were an energetically efficient way to use both stone and food sources at the same time. "Thus, the accumulation of stone artifacts and animal bones at the same locations does not necessarily mean that hominids used these sites as home bases" (Potts, 1984:345). According to this viewpoint, stone raw materials and manufactured tools were carried and left at various places in the foraging area. As a result, multiple stone caches were created, useful for processing carcasses and other foods. The time spent at the stone caches was minimized to prevent interaction with scavengers drawn to the meat. In contrast to modern hunter-gatherers, who occupy their campsites for up to several months, hominids hastily abandoned their stone cache areas. The use of the stone caches as processing areas implies that social activity was not focused there, as is true in modern hunter-gatherer campsites. As areas to which resources were carried, however, these caches were the precursors of home bases.

Potts argues that the bones found at several Olduvai sites dated between 1.85 and 1.7 M.Y.A. accumulated over a period of at least 5 to 10 years. Although early human inhabitants returned to these sites over a number of years, there is no clear indication of how often meat was eaten at these places, whether food sharing or other social activities occurred, or what proportion of the bones were the result of hunting as opposed to scavenging.

Potts also notes that the bones at the Olduvai sites contain both tooth marks of carnivores and cut marks made by tools. He feels that both humans and social carnivores modified the same bones over about the same time period through a succession of occupations or visits to each site.

Potts's interpretation contrasts with the suggestions of Binford, who argues that the Olduvai remains largely represent animal death sites rather than bone collections transported by humans. Binford holds that humans scavenged from carcasses abandoned by carnivores and consumed more bone marrow than meat.

DIETARY PATTERNS

Although it is difficult to assess the exact nature of the food sources, early humans were probably foragers, scavengers, and small game hunters, in that order of importance. Although most researchers suggest that early humans were to some degree carnivorous, vegetable foods were probably the dietary staples. Some 60 to 80 percent of the food of most modern hunters and gatherers consists of vegetable matter, and the early human diet probably consisted primarily of vegetable materials.

Certain segments of the woodland-bushland habitat probably played a role in early dietary adaptations. In the dry season, plant harvesting from various woodland-bushland tree legumes and from a variety of bush tree and liana species in thickets and groves could have supported relatively large numbers of humans. During the dry season, human scavenging and hunting may have occurred where game was concentrated near water holes in rivers and at springs.

While plant foods were probably the dietary staples, a number of studies have described evidence for meat eating early in human evolution at such sites as Koobi Fora at Lake Turkana, and Olduvai Gorge (Bunn, 1981; Keeley and

Toth, 1981; Potts and Shipman, 1981). These sites date to about 1.8 M.Y.A. The evidence consists of scattered stone tools and fragmentary animal remains. Analysis of bone assemblages from these sites seems to reveal direct evidence of butchering and marrow-processing activities.

Microscopic examination of bone assemblages from Olduvai and Koobi Fora showed three major categories of modification: (1) human-induced damage, including butchery (cut) marks and fracture patterns; (2) carnivore- and rodent-induced damage, including gnaw marks and tooth-derived fracture patterns; and (3) weathering and post-depositional alterations. A series of very fine linear grooves on the bone surfaces supposedly resulting from scraping by stone tools provide the clearest evidence to argue for human involvement with the bones (Bunn, 1981).

The presence of what may be cut marks and percussion marks on significant numbers of bone at Olduvai and Koobi Fora seem to document the involvement of early humans in cutting animal carcasses and breaking open bones, presumably to obtain meat and marrow, at about 2 M.Y.A. This evidence of early butchering allows us to dismiss models of human evolution that do not incorporate meat as some part of the diet. The mode of acquisition of this meat, whether it was hunted or scavenged, or both, remains uncertain. Such evidence also does not indicate the frequency of meat eating and hunting.

In a sample of 75 bones with 85 surface markings from 12 excavated levels in Beds I and II at Olduvai Gorge, 24 percent had what have been called cut marks (Potts and Shipman, 1981). Several bones in the assemblage had what appear to be both slicing marks and tooth scratches, suggesting that in some cases humans and carnivores used the same parts of the carcass.

Bunn and Kroll (1986) argue that butchering activities by the Olduvai hominids were common and that they had access to carcasses of many animals prior to any substantial meat or marrow loss through feeding by predators and scavengers. They believe that the Olduvai hominids were butchering carcasses by an efficient and systematic technique that involved skinning, dismemberment, and defleshing. Bunn and Kroll suggest that active confrontational scavenging at large predator kill sites might have enabled ancient hominids to achieve at least temporary control of carcasses during the time when high-yield meaty limbs were available. They contend that the data support a subsistence strategy combining the hunting of at least small animals, and the transporting of portions of carcasses to favored locales for later consumption.

Although scenarios of human evolution frequently refer to probable occasional scavenging, only recently has it been suggested that scavenging represented a complete ecological adaptation (Shipman, 1986b). The scavenging hypothesis argues that the early inhabitants at Olduvai were poor hunters, infrequently capable of killing and defending their prey. They relied instead on scavenging to obtain meat, skin, and other products of the carcass. Scavenging supplemented plant food foraging and was not a major source of food. Shipman estimates that about 33 percent of the diet was provided by scavenging.

One major problem in trying to interpret the incidence of meat eating in early human diets by relying on evidence of cut marks on bone is the fact that natural forces can produce marks on bone that are remarkably similar to those produced by human activity (Behrensmeyer, Gordon, and Yanagi, 1986; Hill, 1986; Morell, 1986). The type of soil in which bone lies is important because trampling by hooved animals of bone lying on sandy ground can produce marks quite indistinguishable from those produced by a stone tool cutting meat and tendon from bone. Sand lodged in an animal's hoof cuts across bone, leaving deeply grooved scratch marks. Trampling alone will not produce these scratches, "but a hoof with sand on it leaves a mark that . . . is indistinguishable from those made with a stone tool" (Behrensmeyer, quoted in Morell, 1986, p. 71). Although it is unlikely that multiple trample scratches could be mistaken for slicing or scraping marks, isolated trample marks might easily be misidentified as cut marks. Because of the low incidence of identified cut marks in bone assemblages attributed to human action, the misidentification of even a few trample marks could seriously affect interpretations of early human behavior by overestimating the amount of meat either eaten or butchered.

THE SKELETAL EVIDENCE

The early stages of human evolution are represented by a fossil assemblage manifesting considerable skeletal variability. In terms of overall body weight, the smaller members of the sample weighed 66 to 70 pounds, and the larger members may have weighed 160 pounds. The weight of the most complete individual, Lucy, is estimated at 60 pounds. Lucy was about 3 feet, 10 inches tall. There are height estimates for other hominids as well. A female australopithecine from South Africa is estimated to be 4 feet tall, and an early member of *Homo* from Lake Turkana is estimated to be 4 feet, 11 inches tall.

The Pliocene–early Pleistocene hominid fossil sample contains an estimated 405 to 617 individuals. One fact, often overlooked when discussing the early hominid skeletal evidence, is that interpretations are often skewed by the nature of the remains. Some sites yield a disproportionate amount of remains. One well-preserved specimen, like Lucy, makes a major difference to the sample's composition. Although skeletal remains of early hominids are numerous, some parts are poorly represented. The remains of a small number of well-preserved specimens often predominate.

Dental Remains

Because teeth preserve particularly well, dental traits of the earliest hominids have received more attention than any other skeletal features. The total dental pattern of all the early hominids conforms with that of the family Hominidae (Figure 17-20 on p. 329). Although essentially human, the teeth do differ from the teeth of modern *H. sapiens*. For example, the premolar and molar teeth are large; the third lower molar commonly exceeds the length of the second. The canine teeth in the Hadar and Laetoli samples are particularly noteworthy because of their large size.

The teeth of early humans are characterized by relatively vertically implanted incisors, relatively large premolars, and large molars with thick enamel. Members of the earliest human lineage, *Australopithecus,* have molar and premolar teeth that are 1.7 to 2.3 times larger than those of modern humans of similar body size (McHenry, 1984). Dental variability increased over time, and forms such as the large *A. robustus* (Figure 17-8) from South Africa and its large contemporary in East Africa, *A. boisei,* developed hyperrobust cheek teeth and large chewing muscles. These large muscles were supported by prominent crests of bone, the sagittal crests, along the top of the skull. Such crests made the skulls of the largest members of the early human line very distinctive. The teeth of later and anatomically more modern forms, such as *H. habilis,* were more similar to those of later humans.

Bromage and Dean (1986; Bromage, 1987) and Smith (1986) argue that the teeth of early hominids were apelike in their overall growth pattern. Others vigorously disagree with this interpretation (Grine, 1987). This disagreement over tooth growth patterns is dependent upon one's interpretation of the growth patterns of early hominids. By comparison with modern apes, modern humans have an extended period of infancy, which is important for greater intellectual and social nurturing. If our earliest ancestors also had prolonged

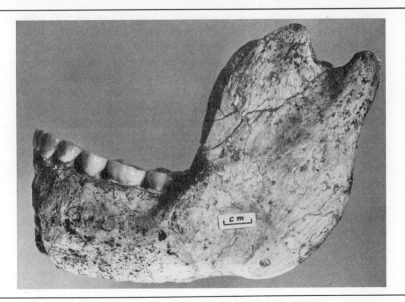

Figure 17-8 Lateral view of the mandible of A. robustus *(a robust australopithecine) from South Africa.*

infancies, then they were experiencing a different social life than that of modern apes. Signs of prolonged immaturity should appear in tooth eruption patterns.

If the suggestion by Bromage and Dean and by Smith that the teeth of hominids living 2 M.Y.A. were more apelike than humanlike in their matura-tion patterns is correct (and this is not certain), it has implications for our reconstruction of early hominid behavior patterns and society. If the eruption sequence was more like that of apes than of humans, it reduces the social gap between apes and early human ancestors. The implication is that the period of infancy in early hominids is not much prolonged, if at all, over that of apes. In fact, Bromage and Dean and Smith hold that there is no evidence for prolonged immaturity even among the earliest members of the genus *Homo* (that is, *H. habilis* and perhaps even *H. erectus)*. In both, however, increases in absolute brain size are documented.

Skull and Face

The morphology and dimensions of its skull first invited the suggestion that *Australopithecus* was an ape allied with the gorilla or chimpanzee rather than an early member of the human family. The small brain case and massive, projecting jaws produce a resemblance to apes (Figures 17-9, 17-10, 17-11, 17-18 and 17-19). As more skulls were recovered and critically examined, however, this resemblance was found to be superficial and functionally related to surface changes associated with the stresses imposed by the large muscles associated with heavy grinding of food.

The head and the face are highly integrated structures, and changes in one area result in changes in the other. Development of any of the muscles, especially the chewing muscles, attached to the skull or the face produces tensions in the bony architecture that affect its form. Bone is quite plastic; it changes in size and shape in response to stresses imposed on it by the muscles attached to its surface.

The australopithecine face can easily be distinguished from the faces of modern humans. The most prominent traits of the australopithecine's face are the large ridges of bone above the orbits, the brow ridges or supraorbital tori. These large brow ridges may have provided some protection against the stresses imposed on the face by the heavy chewing muscles. The other distinguishing feature is the extreme prognathism, the jutting forward of the face and lower jaw. Much of this prognathism was the consequence of the presence of large teeth. As our teeth reduced in size, so did the amount of prognathism. Neither the earlier australopithecines nor the later *Homo habilis* has a chin or a projecting nose. These traits did not appear until recently.

The most distinctive skulls and faces belong to the robust australopithe-cines. These forms are characterized by massive sagittal and nuchal crests and brow ridges (Figure 17-12). One of the surprises of the skull of the most

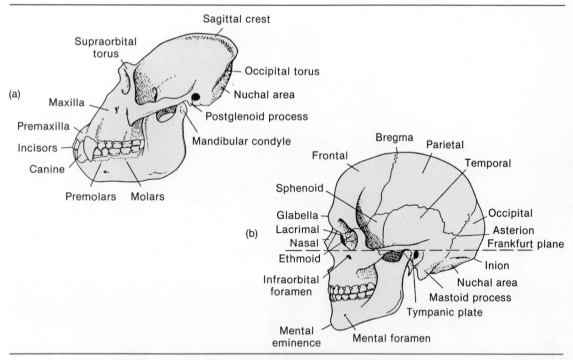

Figure 17-9 Skull of a male gorilla (A) and modern Homo sapiens *(B), seen from the side, illustrating some anatomical landmarks.*

massive of these robust forms, the specimen WT 17000, is that the skull walls were uniquely thin. Coupled with a massive jaw, this unique combination is not found elsewhere in the hominid fossil record.

Brain

At first, many scientists argued that the brain size of the australopithecines was too small to justify including them within the family Hominidae. The range of variation in cranial capacities (an approximation of the actual brain size) is from approximately 375 to less than 600 cubic centimeters in the earliest and morphologically least advanced forms belonging to the genus *Australopithecus* to over 700 cubic centimeters for some members of the species *Homo habilis*. This compares with a range of 1,000 to 2,000 cubic centimeters for modern humans. The hominids belonging to the genera of *Australopithecus* and *Homo* had relatively small cranial capacities when compared with those of modern humans. However, even the earliest hominids had relatively larger cranial capacities than their ape contemporaries. Modern chimpanzees, who are

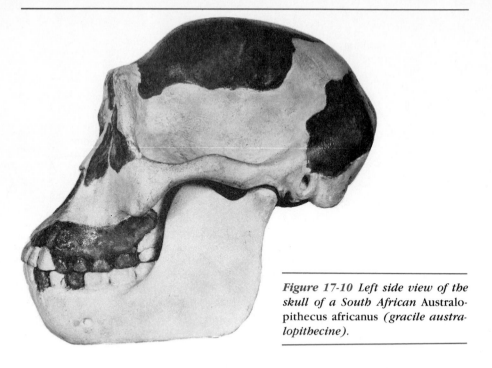

Figure 17-10 Left side view of the skull of a South African Australopithecus africanus *(gracile australopithecine).*

approximately the same size as the larger early hominids, have cranial capacities ranging from 320 to 484 cubic centimeters, with a mean of 394 cubic centimeters for a sample of 144 individuals.

Holloway (1974, 1975) has indicated a number of important ways in which the australopithecine brain differed from that of an ape. For example, there

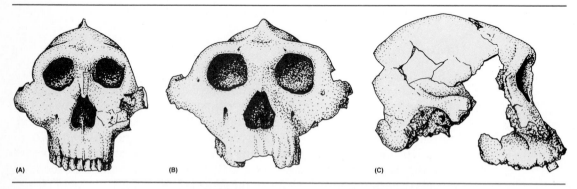

Figure 17-11 Skulls of three large australopithecines from east Africa: (A) A. boisei *from Olduvai Gorge—a robust australopithecine; (B) Similar skull from Koobi Fora, Kenya; (C) Half-skull from Koobi Fora that may have belonged to a female of the robust australopithecine lineage.*

Figure 17-12 A robust australopithecine skull (A. boisei) *from Lake Turkana, Kenya.*

was an expansion of the posterior **parietal** association areas, which receive connections from the three sensory areas: the auditory, somatic, and visual, concerned respectively with hearing, touch, and vision. There is a greater complexity of the frontal lobes, especially in some of the speech areas. There is also an expansion of the **temporal lobes,** which appear to be concerned with visual analysis and auditory memory. In modern humans, the temporal lobes are involved with recording and recalling experiences—that is, memory.

Holloway argues that the australopithecine brain differed from ours more in size than in organization. (This is discussed in more detail in Chapter 16.) He also states that although the brain was humanlike, this does not mean that it was a modern human brain. There is no indication from any of the endocasts that the earliest human brains had the areas necessary for speech.

The Locomotor Skeleton

No part of the postcranial anatomy shows more contrasts between modern apes and humans than the pelvis (Figure 17-13). A primary feature reflecting the evolutionary separation of the human and ape lineages was the modification of their locomotor skeletons for different life-styles. The human pelvis was modified to accommodate an upright bipedal posture. The limb and pelvic structure of early hominids is relevant to the determination of their taxonomic status. Australopithecine pelvic remains from South Africa exhibit hominid traits, although they differ from modern human pelves (Figure 17-14). The same is true for the Lucy pelvic material.

Lovejoy (1973, 1975) argued that the early hominid female pelvis was

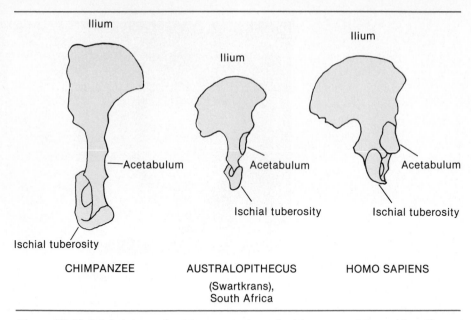

Figure 17-13 Pelvic bones of a chimpanzee, Australopithecus, *and the modern* Homo. *Note the differences in the ilium and ischium.*

better adapted to bipedalism than that of modern *H. sapiens* females. Given the small cranial capacities of early hominids, there was less conflicting pressure on the female birth canal selecting for effective bipedalism on the one hand and a large birth canal on the other. In modern human females, pelvic shape is the result of adaptive pressures both for effective bipedalism and for a birth canal that can accommodate the birth of a large-headed infant. Lovejoy argues that in modern humans the selective pressures from giving birth to large-brain infants is stronger, and therefore pelvic adaptations for bipedalism are compromised. Lucy's pelvis, for example, allowed bipedalism but would not permit the birth of a large-headed infant. The modern human male pelvis, adapted only to bipedalism and not to the birth process, more accurately reflects the ancestral pelvic shape than does the modern female pelvis.

One of the major differences between human and ape **pelves** is in the shape of the **ilium,** the large, flat bone that forms the upper part of the pelvis. The ilium is one of three bones composing the pelvis; the others are the **ischium** and the **pubis.** The human ilium is broadened compared to the elongated and narrow ape ilium. The broadened ilium extends the area for the attachment of the gluteal (buttocks) muscles. A change in the configuration of the crest of the ilium brings the largest of the human gluteal muscles, the gluteus maximus, into a position that allows it to function as an extensor of the thigh. This extension of the thigh is essential to walking erect.

Other postcranial remains support the interpretation that early humans were capable of bipedalism. An almost complete foot skeleton of the species *H.*

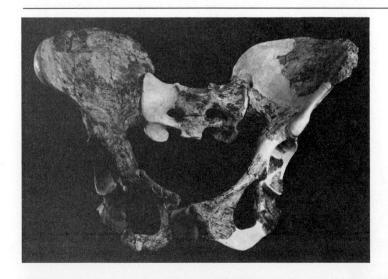

Figure 17-14 (left) Pelvis of Australopithecus *from Sterkfontein, South Africa. (below) Pelves of* Homo sapiens *(left) and* Australopithecus *(right) from Sterkfontein, South Africa.*

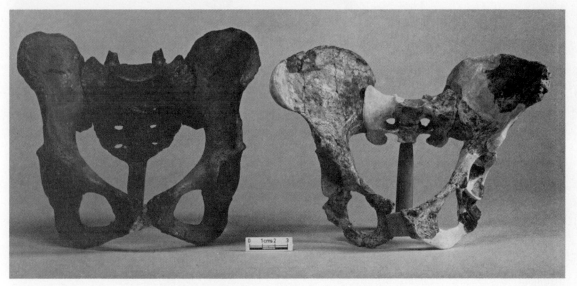

habilis (Figure 17-15) was found in Bed I of Olduvai Gorge. The foot is small but shows an anatomical resemblance to the modern human foot. The divergence of the first and second toes that is typical of the ape's grasping foot is not present in this specimen. The foot differs from that of modern humans because the transmission of weight and propulsive effort through the forepart of the foot was not identical to that in modern humans. In fact, some researchers (Oxnard and Lisowki, 1980) argue that the anatomy of the foot indicates that these creatures spent some time in the trees. They suggest that

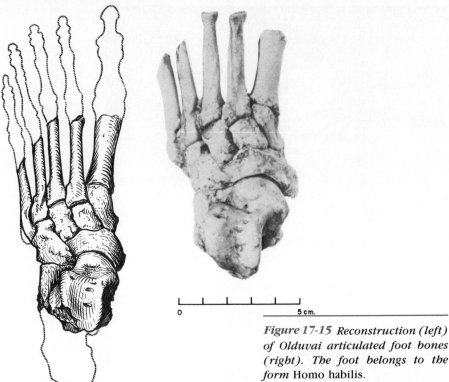

Figure 17-15 Reconstruction (left) of Olduvai articulated foot bones (right). The foot belongs to the form Homo habilis.

the foot belongs to an animal that was capable of climbing and other arboreal activities. They visualize a creature capable of both arboreal and terrestrial activities, but they reject the notion that the foot is from a strictly terrestrial creature. Prost (1980) suggests that early humans were adapted to life in the trees by climbing, but they moved on the ground as we do.

The 37 foot bones and fragments from Hadar make up the largest and most complete collection of early foot bones. They present a distinctly human pattern. This, along with the Laetoli footprints, contradicts the stand of Oxnard and Lisowki (1980) and Prost (1980). A study of the heel bone (calcaneus) of *A. afarensis* failed to support the argument for a degree of arboreality for this species. The Hadar foot displays traits that can only be accounted for by habitual bipedality.

Evidence from the upper limbs and the hand is somewhat contradictory, but there is no indication of a specialization for a strictly arboreal life-style. The thumb of *A. afarensis* is relatively short compared to that of modern humans but relatively long compared to that of modern apes (Bush, 1980). Susman and Stern (1979) argue that the hand had the functional capacity to allow suspensory locomotor behaviors. They suggest that "early hominids may have retained a capacity for climbing even past the point at which the foot became adapted for bipedalism" (p. 572). Lovejoy (1988) strongly disagrees. They also suggest that there was sexual dimorphism in locomotor patterns and that the smaller females were more arboreal than the larger males. While there is an example of such a dichotomy among the living orangutans, its existence among the early australopithecines awaits proof.

There is little evidence of the upper limbs, but some forelimb remains from Olduvai Gorge and Hadar retain primitive traits. The structure of the forelimbs indicates the possibility that early humans spent more time in the trees (perhaps for sleeping and food gathering) than is probably true in later stages of human evolution. The adoption of bipedalism may have led to a relatively rapid reorganization of the hindlimbs but to slower changes in the forelimb, an example of mosaic evolution.

The forelimb proportions of Lucy are similar to those of modern humans, but her hindlimbs are relatively much shorter. The elongation of the hindlimbs represents a major evolutionary change in later human evolution. Lucy's bodily proportions are compatible with bipedalism, but some argue that functional equivalence with the bipedalism of modern humans seems improbable (Jungers, 1982). Lucy's relatively short hindlimbs may imply differences in the bipedal gait when compared with modern humans. The relative elongation of the hindlimbs in later humans permitted an increase in the velocity of the gait at only a slight increase in energy cost because increased speed can be achieved by increased stride length rather than by increased step frequency. Selection to reduce the energy costs of bipedalism would have favored hindlimb elongation.

Early humans were bipedal; this characteristic distinguished them from the apes. Whether they were indistinguishable from modern humans in this regard is still open to debate (Abitbol, 1987). The major changes that occurred in early human postcranial anatomy were in the lower limbs. Some traits of the upper limbs, the thumb, and the shoulder girdle, along with the length of the forelimbs, may indicate a more arboreal mode of life than that of modern humans. It must be remembered, however, that even the most committed bipeds, modern humans, can and do spend time in the trees.

EVOLUTIONARY RELATIONSHIPS

The early hominid fossil record reveals considerable morphological diversity, as indicated by the various taxonomic schemes devised to accommodate the material. Some researchers recognize one long-lived evolutionary line of *Australopithecus* containing various species. Others recognize two genera: the earlier and skeletally more primitive *Australopithecus,* and a later, more modern-looking group called *Homo,* which is directly ancestral to later hominids. For some, the skeletal differences are due to the fact that some early hominids were exceptionally robust. They are called the robust australopithecines, or *A. robustus,* in South Africa and *A. boisei* in East Africa. The smaller and less robust group are the gracile australopithecines, *A. africanus.* Some researchers argue that size differences within the sample do not deserve recognition at the species levels but are instead merely a reflection of the extremes of sexual dimorphism.

One Genus

Some researchers argue that all early hominids can be placed in the genus *Australopithecus,* with a number of species distinctions. A minority of this group of researchers suggests that all early hominids belong in the genus *Homo.* Those adhering to the one-genus interpretation believe that anatomical differences within the sample are not of the same degree as those usually regarded as adequate for generic distinctions. They recognize anatomical distinctions within the sample, but they argue that such differences are to be expected given their long evolutionary history and the extent of their geographical range. The differences that exist may permit only a broad subdivision within the two main groups (Table 17-4). The human sample from Kromdraai and Swartkrans in South Africa and some material from Olduvai Gorge, Omo, and Lake Turkana appear to be larger, with more massive skulls, faces, jaws, and teeth. A second, anatomically more gracile group is found at the South African sites of Taung, Sterkfontein, and Makapansgat and the East African sites of Olduvai Gorge, Omo, and Lake Turkana.

Adherents to the single genus hypothesis recognize three species. One species, *A. africanus* (Figure 17-16),the gracile australopithecine, is smaller, lighter, and more gracile in skeletal anatomy. It is also argued that it has smaller molars and premolars, and has a smaller cranial capacity associated with its smaller body size. The other species, *A. robustus* and *A. boisei* (Figure 17-17),the robust australopithecines, are larger and have pronounced bony ridges and crests on the skull associated with larger molars and chewing

Table 17-4 **Some Traits Characteristic of Gracile and Robust Australopithecines**

Gracile	Robust
Smaller and less robustly built	Larger, more heavily built
More rounded and vertical skull	Flatter and tear-drop shaped
Little evidence of crests on skull	Clear sagittal and nuchal crests
Large front teeth	Smaller front teeth
Large rear teeth	Large rear teeth
4.0 to 4.6 feet tall	4.6 to 5.0 feet tall
Body weight approximately 60 pounds	Body weight approximately 100 pounds
Bipedal	Bipedal
No evidence of tool use	Minimal evidence of tool use
Cranial capacity of 450 cubic centimeters for a sample of 7	Cranial capacity of 504 cubic centimeters for a sample of 5

muscles. *A. africanus* may have appeared earlier; *A. robustus* and *A. boisei* are considered to be more specialized and somewhat divergent from the main line of human evolution.

The issue over relative body sizes of the robust and gracile australopithecines has recently been reopened. There are suggestions that the robust forms were no larger in body size than the gracile forms. Perhaps the so-called robust forms were robust only in reference to the size of their molars and premolars. If this is verified, then it will necessitate a reanalysis of dietary patterns and other assumptions about both forms, as such assumptions rest on supposed body size differences.

Dietary Hypothesis

The dietary hypothesis was first expounded by Robinson (1954, 1963), who originally maintained that differences among the australopithecines warrant recognition of two genera, *Australopithecus* and *Paranthropus*. He later (1972) suggested that *Australopithecus* be included in the genus *Homo* and that *Paranthropus* be recognized as a genus distinct from fully bipedal, erect, culture-bearing animals. Robinson suggests that the robust variety of australopithecines were vegetarians and that the gracile form, *Homo*, was omnivorous, with meat forming a substantial part of the diet.

The dietary habits of the two forms are based on habitat differences, which are supposedly reflected in dental and skull traits. Robinson argues that the large crests on the top and back of the skull of the robust form are associated with heavy muscles and large molars that were specialized for chewing vegetable materials. He argues that the size disparity between the anterior and posterior teeth in the robust form reflects this dietary specialization. The relatively larger canines and incisors in the gracile form supposedly reflect its omnivorous diet, and the larger molars and reduced canines and incisors in the robust form indicate its vegetarian diet. Robinson argues that the molars of the robust form are specialized for crushing and grinding food; he supports this contention by pointing out areas where enamel flakes were detached from their grinding surfaces. He argues that the enamel was chipped by grit adhering to roots and tubers that supposedly formed a large part of the diet. A more recent analysis of the molars of the gracile and robust forms tends to support Robinson (Grine and Kay, 1988). The wear on the molars of the robust forms suggests a diet of hard items like seeds. The molar wear of the gracile forms suggests a diet more of leaves and fleshy fruits.

Robinson has argued that something similar to the gracile form was ancestral to later hominids and that the robust form is a specialized offshoot that changed relatively little during its evolutionary history. It eventually became extinct. The lack of change witnessed in the robust form may be related to its not being a tool maker and possibly only a nominal tool user. It had less need for tools because it apparently exploited a richer environment than the gracile form. The gracile form, by contrast, lived in poorer environ-

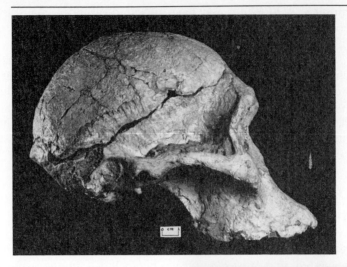

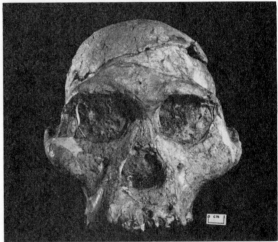

Figure 17-16 Side view (above) and frontal view (right) of the skull of A. *africanus (a gracile australopithecine) from South Africa.*

ments and faced more obstacles to survival. It made and used tools and possibly hunted.

Central to Robinson's argument is a postulated habitat difference between the two forms. Other researchers find little evidence to support this contention, however. Others reject Robinson's position that the robust and gracile forms were specialized for different dietary regimens. They argue that all skeletal and dental differences between the two forms can be attributed to overall size differences. The robust australopithecines are estimated to be 10 to 25 percent larger than the gracile forms. Perhaps **allometry** (differential growth of body parts in relation to the growth of the total organism) explains the differences in the face, skull, and teeth. If allometry occurred among the australopithecines, then the large molars of the robust form only represent the

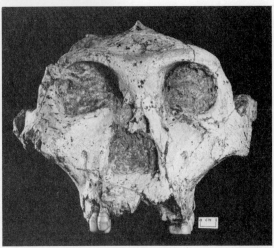

Figure 17-17 Side view (above) and frontal view (right) of the skull of A. robustus *(a robust australopithecine) from South Africa.*

needed tooth area to provide for a larger animal, and do not represent evidence for dietary differences.

Homo habilis

The proposal that a more advanced type of early human, called *Homo habilis* (Figure 17-21), coexisted with the genus *Australopithecus* is most closely associated with its originator, Louis Leakey. In 1961 he announced the recovery of material dated about 1.8 M.Y.A. from Bed I, Olduvai Gorge. He named this material *Homo habilis*. Assignment of this fossil to the genus *Homo* (Table 17-5), to which we belong, reflected Leakey's belief that it was a precursor of modern humans. A number of specimens from Olduvai, Lake

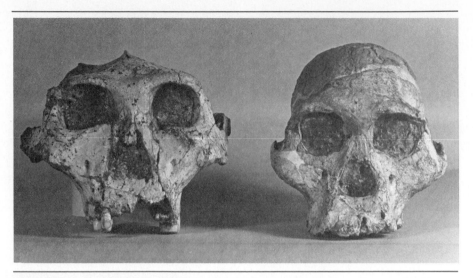

Figure 17-18 Frontal view of the skulls of Australopithecus robustus *(left) and* Australopithecus africanus *(right) from South Africa.*

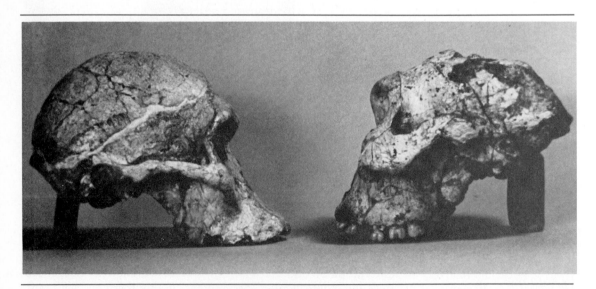

Figure 17-19 Side view of the skulls of Australopithecus africanus *(left) and* Australopithecus robustus *(right) from South Africa.*

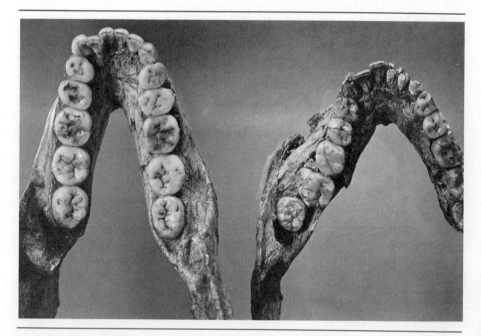

Figure 17-20 Occlusal view of the mandibles of A. robustus *and* A. africanus *from South Africa.*

Turkana, Omo, and South Africa have now been assigned to this taxon. See Table 17-6 for *H. habilis* sites.

The skeleton of *H. habilis* is a mosaic of primitive and more advanced traits, indicating that it walked bipedally erect. Its hand bones are consistent with tool-making abilities. In fact, all the tools now found in East Africa are attributed to *H. habilis. Homo habilis* had a larger brain (estimated to be at least 600 cubic centimeters) than did *Australopithecus* and a less robust skull compared with the robust australopithecines. *H. habilis's* teeth are also considered to be more modern than those of contemporaneous hominids.

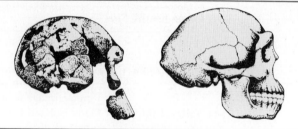

Figure 17-21 Homo habilis *(left) and* Homo erectus *(right).*

Table 17-5 *Major Anatomical Traits Differentiating Early* Homo *from* **Australo-pithecus**

Early *Homo*	*Australopithecus*
Small face relative to size of skull vault.	Large, heavy face.
Average cranial capacity for 6 specimens was 646 cubic centimeters.	Average cranial capacity for 7 gracile australopithecines was 450 cc; for a sample of 5 robust forms it was 504 cc.
Less postorbital constriction than among *Australopithecus* forms. Smaller brow ridges.	More postorbital constriction than seen in *Homo.* Larger brow ridges.
Smaller and less massive mandible than seen among *Australopithecus.*	Larger and more massive mandible than seen among *Homo.*
Front teeth generally larger relative to the size of the rear teeth, which are still large in *some* Homo specimens.	Generally larger posterior teeth, especially among robust species.
Bipedal.	Bipedal.

Opinions on the taxonomic ascription of fossils that Louis Leakey called *H. habilis* differ. Some researchers see *H. habilis* as a variable but well-defined taxon. Other researchers contend that *H. habilis* refers to such a heterogeneous collection of material that the taxon has little real meaning. Since 1964 at least a dozen specimens from Olduvai have been attributed to *H. habilis.* Other African sites, like Swartkrans and Sterkfontein in South Africa and Omo and Koobi Fora in East Africa, have also contributed material.

The most recent material added to the *H. habilis* taxon was recovered in 1986 at Olduvai Gorge not far from the site (FLK NN) of the Leakeys' original *H. habilis* find (Johanson et al., 1987). The newest materials, referred to as OH 62, consist of teeth and bone fragments from the right arm, skull, and both legs, and date to 1.8 M.Y.A. (Johanson et al., 1987; Wood, 1987). This is the first time that skull and limb bones attributed to *H. habilis* were recovered from the same site. The bones belong to an adult female.

Table 17-6 **Homo habilis** *Sites*

SITE	REMAINS
Olduvai Gorge, Tanzania	Eight specimens comprising several teeth, jaws, and skull fragments as well as hand bones and a foot; range in age from 1.8 to 1.5 M.Y.A.
Omo River Valley, Ethiopia	Many isolated teeth, five jaws, two skulls, femur, and part of ulna.
Lake Turkana, Kenya	Skull and postcranial bones; dated to 1.9 to 1.8 M.Y.A.

OH 62 provides a new and unexpected view of materials called *H. habilis.* Until the OH 62 find, *H. habilis* was considered to be taller and to have had a more modern-looking postcranial skeleton; that is, it looked more like its possible successor *H. erectus* than the O.H. 62 find suggests. OH 62 is only 3.6 feet tall, approximately the same height estimated for Lucy (*A. afarensis*). The long arms of OH 62 were especially unexpected. The upper arms are 95 percent as long as the legs; they probably reached almost to the knees. By comparison, the ratio in the much older Lucy material, who also had long arms compared to her legs, is 85 percent. The arm length is 70 to 75 percent of the leg length in modern humans.

The similarities in body size and arm length between OH 62 and *A. afarensis,* which predated OH 62 by more than 1 million years, suggests that little change occurred in the postcranial bones over a long period of time. The long arms of OH 62 also suggest that it spent time in the trees, despite its basically bipedal pattern.

OH 62's teeth offer evidence regarding the relative size of the posterior teeth. It has been suggested that there was a size reduction in the molars of *H. habilis* when compared with those of *Australopithecus.* If OH 62 is *H. habilis,* then initial measurements of her teeth suggest that this is not the case.

While Johanson and his colleagues (1987) suggest that OH 62 is *H. habilis,* the new material also shares important traits with *Australopithecus.* Including OH 62 in the taxon *H. habilis* further confuses the status of *H. habilis* and may make the range of variation of material included within early *Homo* from East Africa too great to be encompassed within one taxon (Wood, 1987). The case for including OH 62 with *H. habilis* rests on the affinities of the OH 62 face and skull with suggested *H. habilis* material from Sterkfontein, South Africa. However, the South African material has merely been likened to *H. habilis* and not formally attributed to the taxon (Wood, 1987).

Some materials included within the *H. habilis* taxon have large brains, relatively large dentition, and less prognathic faces than others in the species. Other materials belong to small-brained creatures with more lightly built faces. OH 62 belongs with the latter and not only fails to narrow the differences between the two groups, but confuses the taxonomic issue still further.

If OH 62 belongs in *H. habilis,* as Johanson and his colleagues suggest, then its shared traits with *Australopithecus* present some interesting problems. The time span of the East African *Homo habilis* fossils is approximately 2 to 1.5 M.Y.A. Some of the earliest *Homo erectus* fossils in East Africa date to 1.6 M.Y.A. (This material is discussed in Chapter 18.) If OH 62 is *H. habilis,* and if *H. habilis* is ancestral to *H. erectus,* as many accept to be the case, then the morphological change from *H. habilis* to *H. erectus* was completed in the relatively short period of about 200,000 years. This change, especially involving some significant changes in the limbs, is more rapid than researchers had previously believed.

H. habilis apparently lived alongside the robust australopithecines in East Africa about 2 to 1 M.Y.A. Louis Leakey argued that *H. habilis* represented a very old human evolutionary lineage. He was convinced that *H. habilis* was on the direct line to modern *Homo* and that other early hominids (including *Australopithecus)* were not. The contemporaneous australopithecines would represent an evolutionary dead end. A minority view maintains that *H. habilis* is just a gracile australopithecine. They view *H. habilis* as an advanced member of the gracile line.

Although the genus *Homo* may have descended from one of the *Australopithecus* species, it is not clear what led to the evolution of the genus *Homo.* Perhaps environmental changes precipitated the evolutionary change. There appears to have been a rather marked climatic change in Africa about 6 to 5 M.Y.A. and again about 2.5 M.Y.A. The former climatic change may be implicated in the first appearance of the hominids.

Approximately 6 to 5 M.Y.A., vast regions of Africa turned cooler, and heavily wooded areas gave way to advancing grasslands and scattered clumps of low trees producing a vegetational situation similar to that of modern-day East African savannas. These vegetational changes obviously affected the fauna, which are dependent on the vegetation for food and shelter. Forest and bush-dwelling antelope species disappeared and were replaced by open-country, grazing antelopes. The new climate and vegetation led to the extinction of many groups and the emergence of others, among whom may have been the australopithecines.

Following this change, the climate again warmed, to be followed about 2.5 M.Y.A. by a sharp temperature plunge reflected in the re-expansion of the Antarctic ice sheets. In Africa this cooling resulted in increased aridity, a reduction in the extent of wooded areas, and the appearance of more open and widespread grasslands.

As with previous climatic shifts, significant faunal changes occurred. In South Africa, at least, there was apparently a peak in the number of extinctions and the appearance of new species at about 2.5 M.Y.A. Closely following these events, the genus *Homo* first appeared. It seems reasonable to associate these climatic changes with the appearance of *Homo* and the eventual extinction of the genus *Australopithecus.*

Lake Turkana Sample

One of the most complicated pictures of early human evolution comes from Lake Turkana, where, in 11 years of searching, workers have found more than 5,000 fossils. Of the human remains fewer than 20 are whole bones, 9 are reasonably complete skulls, 30 or so are mandibles in varying states of preservation, and the rest are isolated teeth and other skeletal fragments.

Most Lake Turkana fossils were surface collected. By the end of 1973, at least three human groups appeared to be contemporaneous at Lake Turkana. The early *Homo* materials date to about 1.8 M.Y.A. and are referred to the taxon *H. habilis.* Robust australopithecine specimens are assigned to the taxon *A. boisei.* There is a fossil sample that shares many similarities with the South

African *A. africanus* and a *H. erectus* sample that is discussed in the next chapter. There is some evidence for ecological differences in the deposition of the human remains. For example, specimens assigned to the genus *Homo* appear to be significantly more common in lake margins than in riverine deposits. Material attributed to the robust australopithecines, *A. boisei,* is equally common in river and lake margin deposits.

Richard Leakey and colleagues (1978) describe the Lake Turkana sample as follows: The robust form, *A. boisei,* is distinct from the South African robust form *A. robustus. A. boisei* became extinct about 1.22 M.Y.A. It is a very distinctive form, with hyperrobust molars and premolars compared to its anterior teeth, a hyperrobust mandible, a cranial capacity of less than 550 cubic centimeters, and sexual dimorphism suggested by the presence of sagittal and nuchal crests.

One of the most recently discovered australopithecine skulls, labelled WT 17000, comes from the west side of Lake Turkana, Kenya, and dates to 2.5 M.Y.A. The skull closely resembles that of the East African robust australopithecine, *A. boisei.* WT 17000 is the oldest firmly dated robust australopithecine skull yet recovered (Walker et al., 1986). This skull and face have a wide palate, huge molars, enormous cheek bones, and a very pronounced sagittal crest. WT 17000 has the largest cranial crests of any early hominid yet recovered. The crests are a direct result of combining powerful jaw muscles and large teeth in a long, protruding face. The large size of the crests is partly due to the small cranial capacity of 410 cubic centimeters. The suite of facial traits associated with WT 17000 was previously thought to have evolved at a later date.

This find has generated considerable debate (Eckhardt, 1986; Falk, 1986; Lewin, 1986; Shipman, 1986a). WT 17000 certainly shows that the hyperrobust australopithecine lineage extended further back in time than was previously imagined. This discovery suggests that the *A. boisei* line is a separate lineage evolving in parallel with *A. africanus* (the gracile australopithecines) and *A. robustus* (the South African robust australopithecines), and not the end product of an *A. africanus–A. robustus* evolutionary lineage, as many suggest.

The general resemblance between *A. robustus* and *A. boisei,* the incredibly massive craniofacial and dental complex, may be due to parallelism. This raises some serious questions, including the issue of what happened to make this unlikely set of adaptations arise twice, independently. Two separate lines of australopithecine evolution demand a great deal of parallel evolution, and more evidence will be necessary to indicate that this occurred.

In a number of traits, WT 17000 resembles *A. afarensis,* from which it may have evolved. The WT 17000 skull suggests the presence of four distinct early hominid lines: *H. habilis, A. africanus, A. boisei,* and *A. robustus.* The presence of four lines of early hominids would indicate rapid diversification by other primate evolutionary standards. This raises the question of what happened about 3 M.Y.A. to account for this rapid diversification? Perhaps the climate changed and created new niches—a suggestion supported by evidence in South Africa. Because WT 17000 is apparently a separate evolutionary line evolving in parallel with *A. africanus, A. robustus,* and *H. habilis,* and not its final product, as was once assumed, a three-pronged fork formed early in human evolution. *A. africanus* and *A. robustus* appear to be going in one direction, *A. boisei* in a second direction, and *H. habilis* in a third direction. Although there are differences in the three evolutionary lines, each is undergoing dramatic facial shortening, so that instead of protruding like an ape's, the face becomes more vertical, like that of modern humans. In addition, the cranial base in each line is becoming more flexed, which is probably related to tucking under of the face. Facial shortening in the *A. robustus* and *A. boisei* lines is accompanied by an expansion of the size of the cheek teeth and a diminution of the front teeth (Lewin, 1986).

The small-brained gracile australopithecines at Lake Turkana had a close morphological affinity to the South African *A. africanus.* The traits of this group at Lake Turkana need further definition. This sample had a cranial capacity of 600 cubic centimeters or less, rarely showed a sagittal crest, and had smallish molars, premolars, and mandible.

The early *Homo* sample dates to 1.8 M.Y.A. It exhibits relatively large anterior teeth, a moderately robust mandible, and a cranial capacity sometimes exceeding 750 cubic centimeters. The skull has slight postorbital constriction and no sagittal crest. Postcranially, it is similar to modern *Homo.*

There are also materials that have not yet been classified and fall into what has been called an indeterminate category. Several of these specimens do not show traits entirely consistent with either *Australopithecus* or *Homo.* There is also a form that Leakey argues is distinct from both *Australopithecus* and *Homo.*

The human fossil sample from Lake Turkana is complex and perplexing. Many issues involving classification and dating remain to be resolved. Confusion exists not only on these grounds, but also concerning the ranges of individual and population variation and sexual dimorphism.

Australopithecus afarensis

The first human species to be named in many years is *A. afarensis,* a species based on specimens from Hadar, Ethiopia, and Laetoli, Tanzania (Johanson and White, 1979, 1980; Johanson, White, and Coppens, 1978). Johanson and White (1979, p. 325) argue that *A. afarensis* constitutes the oldest indisputable evidence of hominids and represents

> . . . the most primitive group of demonstrable hominids. . . . Although clearly hominid in their dentition, mandible, cranium, and postcranium, these forms retain hints of a still poorly known Miocene ancestry. Bipedalism appears to have been the dominant form of terrestrial locomotion employed by the Hadar and Laetoli hominids.

The erection of the taxon *Australopithecus afarensis* generated, and continues to generate, controversy (Lewin, 1987c). For example, Mary Leakey and some others are disturbed that the type specimen for *A. afarensis* is a jaw from Mary Leakey's site at Laetoli. Mary Leakey, because she does not accept that the Laetoli material belongs with *A. afarensis,* was quite disturbed that Johanson chose one of her fossils as the type specimen. Leakey and others who support her stand question the wisdom of joining two sets of fossils that are separated by over 1,000 miles and more than one-half million years. Johanson and White, his collaborator, countered that the Laetoli material is diagnostic of *A. afarensis.*

Many questioned the motives of considering the Laetoli material the type specimen and instead suggested that the more complete Lucy material is a more appropriate type specimen. Johanson has replied that while there may be more bone remains belonging to Lucy, the basic distinction between *A. afarensis* and the other australopithecines lies in the teeth and cranial anatomy, and not with such bones as the ribs, vertebrae, and so on which are found with Lucy but are not diagnostic. Because Lucy's dental and cranial remains are scarce, she does not make a good type specimen.

Others have questioned the choice of the species name *afarensis,* selected to honor the Ethiopian region where Lucy and the first family were found. Given the geographical and time separation between the Ethiopian and the Laetoli remains, the joining of these two samples might mask some important differences. It has been argued that it is inappropriate to join samples from totally different localities and time periods and give them the same name; rather, one should choose the type specimen from the geographical locality from whence the name is derived. A rebuttal to this argument would be that paleoanthropologists have long considered geography and time of secondary importance to anatomy in identifying relatedness. For example, while some criticize the taxonomy, fossils dating 1.8 M.Y.A. in East Africa and 0.5 M.Y.A. in China are both referred to as *Homo erectus* because they share a suite of anatomical traits and not because of contemporaneity or geographical proximity.

On the central issue of the fossils themselves, researchers remain divided and continue to raise questions such as the following. Do the fossils represent only one species? Is this species ancestral to *all* later hominids? Or does this fossil sample represent two or more species? While questions continue, and disagreements must be noted, the argument made by Johanson and his colleagues is followed here. The fossils are referred to as *A. afarensis* and are considered the ancestral species to all later hominids.

Johanson and White suggest that *A. afarensis* is the basal hominid stock from which *A. africanus* and *A. robustus* diverged in one direction, eventually becoming extinct, and *H. habilis* diverged in another direction, giving rise to subsequent hominids (Figure 17-22). *A. afarensis* is touted as the basal hominid because it shares a suite of dental, mandibular, and cranial traits with Miocene hominoids such as *Sivapithecus* that make it a good intermediate form between Miocene hominoids and subsequent hominids.

Johanson and White indicated that *A. afarensis* exhibited a good deal of

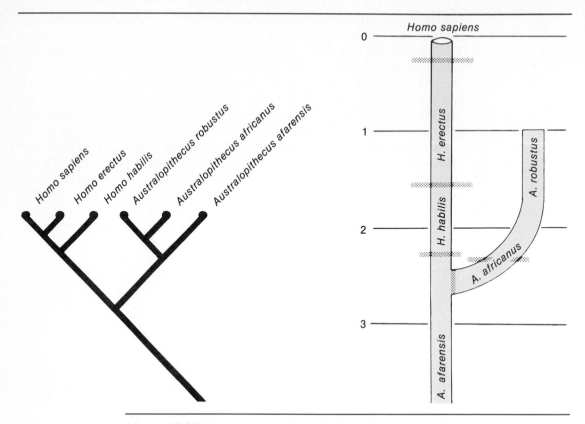

Figure 17-22 Two representations of the evolutionary placement of A. afarensis *proposed by D. Johanson and T. White to accommodate the Pliocene fossil hominids from Hadar and Laetoli.*

sexual dimorphism. Stern and Susman (1983) noted sexual dimorphism in the postcranial bones of *A. afarensis,* especially differences in the lower limbs and pelvis. Leonard and Hegmon (1987) noted sexual dimorphism in the lower first premolar of *A. afarensis.* Such sexual dimorphism might signal sexual differences in habitat exploitation. For example, Leonard and Hegmon and Stern and Susman suggest the possibility that female members of *A. afarensis* may have been more arboreal than were male members of the species.

If females were more arboreal, there would have been selection for smaller body sizes and limb proportions suited to a partially arboreal existence. Such differences have been noted in the *A. afarensis* fossil sample. One of the supposed advantages accruing to the arboreal females would be access to a higher quality of food and greater protection of their dependent young against predators. (Poirier noted in his study of southern Indian Nilgiri langurs that mothers with young infants usually left the youngsters in the trees when they went to the ground to eat.) Selective pressures on the more terrestrial males would favor larger body sizes and increased molarization of the teeth as an adaptation to a terrestrial habitat with a high proportion of low-quality foods (Leonard and Hegmon, 1987).

A model of sexual differentiation in habitat exploitation does not negate the argument for bipedalism among female *A. afarensis.* Rather, it suggests that there was not a complete overlap in habitat use by both sexes. It has been suggested that the orangutan on Borneo is a good example of sexual differentiation of habitat use. Male orangutans tend to exploit the ground and lower levels of the canopy more fully than do the females. Males consume a larger amount of low-quality foods than do females. While the orangutan may be a useful example, the degree of sexual dimorphism in body size among orangutans is not seen in *A. afarensis.*

The major traits of *A. afarensis* include the following:

1. There is considerable morphological variation in the *A. afarensis* sample —enough so that Mary Leakey declines to place the Laetoli materials within *A. afarensis.* Size variation is greater among the fossil assemblage from Hadar than from Laetoli. The smallest adult specimen, Lucy, stood about 3 feet 10 inches tall and weighed about 60 pounds. The largest adults stood about 5 feet tall and weighed up to 150 pounds. In addition to overall size variation, sexual dimorphism is exhibited.
2. The bones were thick for the overall body size, and they have markings that indicate that the individuals were heavily muscled.
3. *A. afarensis* was fully bipedal.
4. In proportion to their bodies, the arms of *A. afarensis* were slightly longer than the arms of modern humans.
5. Their hands were like those of modern humans, except for the tendency of the fingers to curl slightly. Certain aspects of the wrist bones were extremely apelike.
6. Their brains ranged in size from 380 to 500 cubic centimeters.
7. They had large, prognathic faces.
8. *A. afarensis* has the most primitive dentition of all hominids. The molars and premolars are large. The canines are somewhat pointed and have large roots. There is a small diastema in the upper jaw, and the first lower premolar is not bicuspid in the modern sense.
9. There is no evidence that *A. afarensis* made or used stone tools.

Overall, *A. afarensis* had "smallish, essentially human bodies with heads that were more ape-shaped than human-shaped. Their jaws were large and forward-thrusting. They had no chins. The upper parts of their faces were small and chimplike. The crowns of their skulls were very low" (Johanson and Edey, 1981: 275).

As noted earlier, questions have been raised about the evolutionary scheme presented by Johanson and White. Some question the validity of grouping the Hadar and Laetoli materials into one species. Richard Leakey sees two species at Hadar: a larger species which was a primitive form of *Homo,* and a group of

Table 17-7 Some Traits of Early Members of the Hominidae

AUSTRALOPITHECUS

Australopithecus afarensis. This is probably the earliest australopithecine species and appears over 3.5 M.Y.A. Johanson and White consider this form to be ancestral to later species of *Australopithecus* and *Homo habilis.* The species is found at both Hadar, Ethiopia, and Laetoli, Tanzania.

1. The form has a small skull and brain size of 380 to 500 cubic centimeters and a large prognathic face.
2. The teeth are quite large. The canine is somewhat pointed and has large roots. There is a small diastema in the upper jaw, and the first premolar has only a small lingual secondary cusp.
3. There is considerable sexual dimorphism in the dentition.
4. The arms are relatively long compared to the legs. The fingers are slightly curved.
5. They are powerfully built creatures with thick bones and robust muscle markings.
6. They are bipedal.

Australopithecus africanus. The first *Australopithecus* form to be named, it is known primarily from South Africa but may also appear at Lake Turkana, Kenya, and Omo, Ethiopia.

1. The molars and premolars are smaller and the canines larger than its contemporary, *A. robustus.*
2. They had a less robust face and skull than the robust forms and do not have a sagittal crest. The face and skull show a number of primitive traits.
3. Their cranial capacity is less than 600 cubic centimeters.
4. These are bipedal.

Australopithecus robustus and Australopithecus boisei. *A. robustus* is a South African form and *A. boisei* is an East African form. These species are larger (they may have weighed up to 150 pounds) and appear later than *A. africanus.* These forms are also bipedal.

A. robustus has heavy jaws. It exhibits small canines and incisors and larger molars compared with *A. africanus.* There is a very evident sagittal crest that functions to anchor the large chewing muscles.

A. boisei is a superrobust form. The sagittal crest is more pronounced than in the South African. *A. robustus;* this probably reflects larger chewing muscles. The mandible is hyperrobust. The molars and premolars are large relative to the anterior teeth. The cranial capacity is less than 500 cubic centimeters. Sexual dimorphism is exhibited in such structures as the sagittal and nuchal crests.

HOMO

Homo habilis. This is the first species of the genus *Homo* and first appears in East Africa about 1.80 M.Y.A. at Olduvai Gorge and Lake Turkana. This is perhaps the form that made the earliest stone tools found in East Africa. *H. habilis* is apparently the direct ancestor of *H. erectus.*

1. Compared with the genus *Australopithecus, H. habilis* has smaller posterior dentition, although the facial and mandibular bones still show adaptations to powerful chewing.
2. There is an increased cranial capacity. Males had cranial capacities of over 700 cubic centimeters and females had cranial capacities of 500 to 600 cubic centimeters. This is an expansion of about 15 percent over the genus *Australopithecus.*

smaller forms belonging to some previously unknown *Australopithecus.* Others question whether the material is distinctive enough to justify a new species, saying that it could have been just as adequately assigned to an existing species of *Australopithecus.*

Mary Leakey insists that the Laetoli material belongs in the genus *Homo.* Both she and Richard Leakey reject the notion that differences within the *A. afarensis* sample can be explained by sexual dimorphism. They believe that the differences warrant separation into the genera of *Australopithecus* and *Homo* which, they argue, coexisted over 3 M.Y.A. (Table 17-7).

Sexual Dimorphism

It has already been noted that there was significant sexual dimorphism in the early hominid sample. At issue is whether the dimorphism is so great that it can explain all the morphological variability. In other words, instead of the variation representing different genera (as argued by the Leakeys and Johanson and White) or dietary differences (as argued by Robinson), might it instead reflect the ranges of male and female phenotypes? This position has been taken by some researchers. The proposition that the extremes of morphological variation in early hominid populations can be accounted for by sexual dimorphism has not yet been put to a systematic test.

There is a long sequence of dated sites in East Africa. Hominid remains from about 5.5 to 4 M.Y.A. are relatively scarce, although they appear at Tabarin from about 5 M.Y.A. and in Ethiopia and Tanzania from about 4 M.Y.A. Human remains of bipedal creatures from 3.77 to 3.59 M.Y.A. appear at Laetoli, and remains from about 3.2 M.Y.A. appear at Hadar. Human remains from 3 M.Y.A. appear in South Africa.

The pattern of early human evolution in Africa appears to have taken the following course. A. afarensis is apparently the ancestral stock. Later came the gracile australopithecines, A. africanus, and the more advanced gracile form H. habilis, on the one hand, and the superrobust forms, A. robustus and A. boisei, on the other. H. habilis apparently evolved into H. erectus by at least 1.9 or 1.8 M.Y.A., and the robust australopithecines became extinct about 1 M.Y.A.

Some early forms, most likely H. habilis, made and used the stone tools found in Africa by at least 2 M.Y.A. As primitive as their skulls and faces were, and as small as their brains were, the postcranial anatomies of both H. habilis and Australopithecus were similar to those of modern humans. They were bipedal, although they may have spent more time in the trees than do modern humans.

BIBLIOGRAPHY

ABITBOL, M. 1987. Evolution of the lumbosacral angle. *American Journal of Physical Anthropology* 72: 361–72.

BEHRENSMEYER, A. 1975. Taphonomy and paleoecology in the hominid fossil record. *Yearbook of Physical Anthropology* 19: 36–50.

BEHRENSMEYER, A., K. GORDON, and G. YANAGI. 1986. Trampling as a cause of bone surface damage and pseudo-cutmarks. *Nature* 319: 768–71.

BOAZ, N. 1979. Early hominid population densities: New estimates. *Science* 206: 592–95.

BRAIN, C. 1967. Bone weathering and the problem of bone pseudo-tools. *South African Journal Science* 63: 97.

BRAIN, C. 1968. Who killed the Swartkrans ape-man? *South African Museums Association Bulletin* 9: 127–39.

BRAIN, C. 1970. The South African australopithecine bone accumulation. *Transvaal Museum Memoir* 18.

BRAIN, C. 1981. *The Hunters or Hunted? An Introduction to African Cave Taphonomy.* Chicago: University of Chicago Press.

BROMAGE, T. 1987. The biological and chronological maturation of early hominids. *Journal of Human Evolution* 16: 257–72.

BROMAGE, T., and M. DEAN. 1986. Re-evaluation of the age at death of hominids at Olduvai Gorge, Tanzania. *Current Anthropology* 27: 431–52.

BROOM, R. 1925a. Some notes on the Taungs skull. *Nature* 115: 569.

BROOM, R. 1925b. On the newly discovered South African man-ape. *Natural History* 25: 409–18.

BROWN, F. 1983. Tulu Bor Tuff at Koobi Fora correlated with the Sidi Hakoma Tuff at Hadar. *Nature* 300: 631–33.

BUNN, H. 1981. Archaeological evidence for meat-eating by Plio-Pleistocene hominids from Koobi Fora and Olduvai Gorge. *Nature* 291: 574–77.

BUNN, H. and E. KROLL. 1986. Systematic butchery by Pleistocene hominids at Olduvai Gorge, Tanzania. *Current Anthropology* 27: 431–52.

BUSH, M. 1980. The thumb of *Australopithecus afarensis. American Journal of Physical Anthropology* 52: 210.

BUTZER, K. 1974. Paleoecology of South African australopithecines: Taungs revisited. *Current Anthropology* 15: 367–82.

BUTZER, K. 1977. Environment, culture, and human evolution. *American Scientist* 65: 572–84.

CAMPBELL, B. 1967. *Human Evolution.* Chicago: Aldine.

CAMPBELL, B. 1968. The evolution of the human hand. In *Man in Adaptation: The Biosocial Background,* Y. Cohen, ed. Chicago: Aldine.

CAMPBELL, B. 1979. *Humankind Emerging.* Boston: Little, Brown.

CLARK, J. 1976. African origins of man the toolmaker. In *Human Origins,* G. Isaac and E. McCown, eds. Menlo Park, Calif.: W. A. Benjamin.

CLARK, W. L. G. 1964. *The Fossil Evidence for Human Evolution.* Chicago: University of Chicago Press.

CLARK, W. L. G. 1967. *Man-apes or Ape-men?* New York: Holt, Rinehart and Winston.

CURTIS, G., R. DRAKE, T. CERLING, and A. HAMPEL. 1975. Age of KBS tuff in Koobi Fora Formation, East Rudolf, Kenya. *Nature* 258: 395–98.

DART, R. 1925a. *Australopithecus africanus:* The man-ape of South Africa. *Nature* 115: 1195–99.

DART, R. 1925b. The Taungs skull. *Nature* 116: 462.

DART, R. 1926. Taungs and its significance. *Natural History* 26: 315–27.

DART, R. 1957. The osteodontokeratic culture of "Australopithecus prometheus." *Transvaal Museum Memoir* 10.

DART, R. 1960. The bone tool manufacturing ability of "Australopithecus prometheus." *American Anthropologist* 62: 134–43.

DART, R. 1971. On the osteodontokeratic culture of the Australopithecinae. *Current Anthropology* 12: 233.

DAY, M. 1976. Hominid postcranial remains from the East Rudolf succession: A review. In *Earliest Man and Environments in the Lake Rudolf Basin,* Y. Coppens, F. Howell, G. Isaac, and R. Leakey, eds. Chicago: University of Chicago Press.

DAY, M., M. LEAKEY, and T. OLSON. 1980. On the status of *Australopithecus afarensis. Science* 207: 1102–3.

DAY, M., and J. NAPIER. 1964. Hominid fossils from Bed I, Olduvai Gorge, Tanganyika: Fossil foot bones. *Nature* 201: 967.

DAY, M., and E. WICKENS. 1980. Laetoli Pliocene hominid footprints and bipedalism. *Nature* 286: 385–87.

DAY, M., and B. WOOD. 1968. Functional affinities of the Olduvai hominid 8 talus. *Man* 3: 440.

DELSON, E. 1987. Evolution and palaeobiology of robust *Australopithecus. Nature* 327: 454–55.

ECKHARDT, R. 1986. Hominid evolution. *Science* 233: 11.

FALK, D. 1979. On a new australopithecine partial endocast. *American Journal of Physical Anthropology* 50: 611–14.

FALK, D. 1986. Hominid evolution. *Science* 233: 11.

GRAY, T. 1979. Environmental and chronological implications from the Hadar formation fauna. *American Journal of Physical Anthropology* 50: 444–45.

GRINE, F. 1987. On the eruption pattern of the permanent incisors and first permanent teeth in *Paranthropus. American Journal of Physical Anthropology* 72: 352–60.

GRINE, F., and R. KAY. 1988. Early hominid diets from quantitative image analysis of dental wear. *Nature* 765–68.

HARRIS, J., and F. BROWN. 1985. New hominid locality west of Lake Turkana, Kenya. *National Geographic Research* 1: 289–97.

HARRIS, J., and G. ISAAC. 1976. The Karari industry: Early Pleistocene archaeological evidence from the terrain east of Lake Turkana. *Nature* 262: 102–7.

HAY, R. 1976. *Geology of Olduvai Gorge.* Los Angeles: University of California Press.

HAY, R. 1980. The KBS controversy may be ended. *Nature* 284: 401.

HAY, R., and M. LEAKEY. 1982. The fossil footprints of Laetoli. *Scientific American* 246: 50–57.

HEIPLE, K., and C. LOVEJOY. 1971. The distal femoral anatomy of *Australopithecus. American Journal of Physical Anthropology* 35: 75.

HILL, A. 1985. Early hominid from Baringo, Kenya. *Nature* 315: 222–24.

HILL, A. 1986. Tools, teeth and trampling. *Nature* 319: 719–20.

HOLLOWAY, R. 1974. The casts of fossil hominid brains. *Scientific American* 231: 106–15.

HOLLOWAY, R. 1975. The role of human social behavior in the evolution of the brain. Forty-third James Arthur lecture on the evolution of the human brain. New York: American Museum of Natural History.

HOLLOWAY, R. 1980. The OH 7 (Olduvai Gorge, Tanzania) hominid partial brain endocast revisited. *American Journal of Physical Anthropology* 53:267–74.

HOWELL, F. 1968. Omo research expedition. *Nature* 219: 567–72.

HOWELL, F. 1969. Remains of Hominidae from Pliocene Pleistocene formations in the lower Omo Basin, Ethiopia. *Nature* 223: 1234–39.

ISAAC, G. 1978. Food sharing and human evolution: Archaeological evidence from the Plio-Pleistocene of East Africa. *Journal of Anthropological Research* 34: 311–25.

ISAAC, G., R. LEAKEY, and A. BEHRENSMEYER. 1971. Archaeological traces of early hominid activities east of Lake Rudolf, Kenya. *Science* 173: 1129–34.

JOHANSON, D., and M. EDEY. 1981. *Lucy: The Beginnings of Humankind.* New York: Simon & Schuster.

JOHANSON, D., and M. TAIEB. 1976. Plio-Pleistocene hominid discoveries in Hadar, Ethiopia. *Nature* 260: 293–97.

JOHANSON, D., M. TAIEB, and Y. COPPENS. 1982. Pliocene hominids from the Hadar formation, Ethiopia (1973–1977): Stratigraphic, chronologic and paleoenvironmental contexts, with notes on hominid morphology and systematics. *American Journal of Physical Anthropology* 57: 373–402.

JOHANSON, D., and T. WHITE. 1979. A systematic assessment of early African hominids. *Science* 203: 321–30.

JOHANSON, D., and T. WHITE. 1980. On the status of *Australopithecus afarensis. Science* 207: 1104–5.

JOHANSON, D., T. WHITE, and Y. COPPENS. 1978. A new species of the genus *Australopithecus* (Primates: Hominidae) from the Pliocene of eastern Africa. *Kirtlandia* 28: 1–14.

JOHANSON, D., et al. 1987. New partial skeleton of *Homo habilis* from Olduvai Gorge, Tanzania. *Nature* 327:205–9.

JONES, P. 1979. Effects of raw materials on biface manufacture. *Science* 204: 835–36.

JUNGERS, W. 1982. Lucy's limbs: Skeletal allometry and locomotion in *Australopithecus afarensis. Nature* 297: 676–78.

KEELEY, L. 1979. The functions of Paleolithic flint tools. Reprinted in *Human Ancestors,* G. Isaac and R. Leakey, eds. San Francisco: W. H. Freeman & Company Publishers.

KEELEY, L., and N. TOTH. 1981. Microwear polishes on early stone tools from Koobi Fora, Kenya. *Nature* 293: 464–65.

LATIMER, B., J. OHMAN, and C. LOVEJOY. 1987. Talocrural joint in African hominoids: Implications for *Australopithecus afarensis. American Journal of Physical Anthropology* 74: 155–76.

LEAKEY, L. 1958. Recent discoveries at Olduvai Gorge, Tanganyika. *Nature* 181: 1099–1103.

LEAKEY, L. 1959. A new fossil skull from Olduvai. *Nature* 184: 491–93.

LEAKEY, L. 1960. The affinities of the new Olduvai australopithecine. *Nature* 186: 456–58.

LEAKEY, L. 1963. Very early East African Hominidae and their ecological setting. In *African Ecology and Human Evolution,* F. Howell and F. Bourliere, eds. Chicago: Aldine.

LEAKEY, L. 1966. *Homo habilis, Homo erectus,* and the australopithecines. *Nature* 209: 1279–81.

LEAKEY, L. 1967. *Olduvai Gorge,* vol 1. Cambridge: Cambridge University Press.

LEAKEY, L., P. TOBIAS, and J. NAPIER. 1964. A new species of the genus *Homo* from Olduvai Gorge. *Nature* 202: 5–7.

LEAKEY, M. 1971. *Olduvai Gorge,* vol. 3. Cambridge: Cambridge University Press.

LEAKEY, M. 1976. A summary and discussion of the archaeological evidence from Bed I and Bed II, Olduvai Gorge, Tanzania. In *Human Origins: Louis Leakey and the East African Evidence,* G. Isaac and E. McCown, eds. Menlo Park, Calif.: W. A. Benjamin.

LEAKEY, M. 1979. Footprints frozen in time. *National Geographic* 155: 446–57.

LEAKEY, M., R. HAY, G. CURTIS, R. DRAKE, M. JACKES, and T. WHITE. 1976. Fossil hominids from the Laetoli beds. *Nature* 262: 460–66.

LEAKEY, R. 1970. In search of man's past at Lake Rudolf in Kenya. *National Geographic* 137: 712–32.

LEAKEY, R. 1976. East Rudolf: An introduction to the abundance of new evidence. In *Human Origins,* G. Isaac and E. McCown, eds. Menlo Park, Calif.: W. A. Benjamin.

LEAKEY, R., M. LEAKEY, and A. BEHRENSMEYER. 1978. The hominid catalogue. In *Koobi*

Fora Research Project, vol. 1, M. Leakey and R. Leakey, eds. Oxford: Clarendon Press.

LEAKEY, R., and A. WALKER. 1980. On the status of *Australopithecus afarensis. Science* 207: 1103.

LEONARD, W., and M. HEGMON. 1987. Evolution of P_3 morphology in *Australopithecus afarensis. American Journal of Physical Anthropology* 73: 41–63.

LEWIN, R. 1983. Ethiopian stone tools are world's oldest. *Science* 211: 806–7.

LEWIN, R. 1984. Man the scavenger. *Science* 224: 861–62.

LEWIN, R. 1985. The Taung baby reaches sixty. *Science* 227: 1188–90.

LEWIN, R. 1986. New fossil upsets human family. *Science* 233: 720–21.

LEWIN, R. 1987a. Debate over emergence of human tooth pattern. *Science* 235: 748–50.

LEWIN, R. 1987b. The earliest "humans" were not like apes. *Science* 236: 1061–63.

LEWIN, 1987c. *Bones of Contention.* New York: Simon and Schuster.

LEWIN, R. 1988. A new tool maker in the hominid record? *Science* 24: 724–25.

LOVEJOY, C. 1973. The gait of australopithecines. *Yearbook of Physical Anthropology* 17: 147–61.

LOVEJOY, C. 1975. Biomechanical perspectives on the lower limb of early hominids. In *Primate Functional Morphology and Evolution,* R. Tuttle, ed. The Hague: Mouton.

LOVEJOY, C. 1988. Evolution of human walking. *Scientific American.* November: 118–25.

LOVEJOY, C., K. HEIPLE, and A. BURSTEIN. 1973. The gait of *Australopithecus. American Journal of Physical Anthropology* 38: 757–80.

McHENRY, H. 1982. The pattern of human evolution: Studies on bipedalism, mastication and encephalization. *Annual Review of Anthropology* 11: 151–73.

McHENRY, H. 1984. Relative cheek–tooth size in *Australopithecus. American Journal of Physical Anthropology* 64: 297–306.

McHENRY, H. 1986. The first bipeds: a comparison of the *A. afarensis* and *A. africanus* postcranium and implications for the evolution of bipedalism. *Journal of Human Evolution* 15: 177–91.

McHENRY, H., and R. CORRUCCINI. 1980. On the status of *Australopithecus afarensis. Science* 207: 1103–4.

MORELL, V. 1986. The unkindest cut. *Science* 86: 771–72.

NAPIER, J. 1962a. Fossil hand bones from Olduvai Gorge. *Nature* 196: 409–11.

NAPIER, J. 1962b. The evolution of the human hand. *Scientific American* 207: 56–62.

OXNARD, C., and P. LISOWSKI. 1980. Functional articulation of some hominoid foot bones: Implications for the Olduvai (hominid 8) foot. *American Journal of Physical Anthropology* 52: 107–17.

PILBEAM, D., and S. GOULD. 1974. Size and scaling in human evolution. *Science* 186: 892–901.

POIRIER, F. 1987. *Understanding Human Evolution.* Englewood Cliffs, N.J.: Prentice Hall.

POTTS, R. 1984. Home bases and early hominids. *American Scientist* 72: 338–47.

POTTS, R., and P. SHIPMAN. 1981. Cutmarks made by stone tools on bones from Olduvai Gorge, Tanzania. *Nature* 291: 577–80.

PROST, J. 1980. Origin of bipedalism. *American Journal of Physical Anthropology* 52: 175–89.

RAK, Y. 1985. Australopithecine taxonomy and phylogeny in light of facial morphology. *American Journal of Physical Anthropology* 66: 281–88.

ROBINSON, J. 1954. The genera and species of the Australopithecinae. *American Journal of Physical Anthropology* 12: 181–200.

ROBINSON, J. 1963. Adaptive radiation in the australopithecines and the origin of man. In *African Ecology and Human Evolution,* F. Howell and F. Bourliere, eds. Chicago: Aldine.

ROBINSON, J. 1966. The distinctiveness of *Homo habilis. Nature* 209: 953–60.

ROBINSON, J. 1972. *Early Hominid Posture and Locomotion.* Chicago: University of Chicago Press.

SHIPMAN, P. 1986a. A baffling limb on the family tree. *Discover* September: 87–93.

SHIPMAN, P. 1986b. Scavenging or hunting in early hominids: Theoretical frameworks and tests. *American Anthropologist* 88: 27–43.

SHIPMAN, P. 1989. The gripping story of *Paranthropus. Discover* 10:66-71.

SMITH, H. 1986. Dental development in *Australopithecus* and early *Homo. Nature* 317: 525.

STERN, J., and R. SUSMAN. 1983. The locomotor skeleton of *Australopithecus afarensis. American Journal of Physical Anthropology* 60: 279–318.

SUSMAN, R. 1988. Hand of *Paranthropus robustus* from Member 1, Swartkrans: Fossil evidence for tool behavior. *Science* 24: 781–83.

SUSMAN, R., and T. BRAIN. 1988. New first metatarsal (SKX 5017) from Swartkrans and the gait of *Paranthropus robustus. American Journal of Physical Anthropology* 77: 7–16.

SUSMAN, R., and J. STERN. 1979. Telemetered electromyography of flexor digitorum profundus and implications for interpretation of the OH 7 hand. *American Journal of Physical Anthropology* 50: 565–74.

TANNER, N. 1981. *On Becoming Human.* New York: Cambridge University Press.

TOBIAS, P. 1967. *Olduvai Gorge,* vol. 2. Cambridge: Cambridge University Press.

TOBIAS, P. 1971. *The Brain in Hominid Evolution.* New York: Columbia University Press.

TOBIAS, P. 1972. Progress and problems in the study of early man in sub-Saharan Africa. In *The Functional and Evolutionary Biology of Primates,* R. Tuttle, ed. Chicago: Aldine-Atherton.

TOBIAS, P. 1974. The Taung skull revisited. *Natural History* Dec: 38.

TOTH, N. 1987. The first technology. *Scientific American* 256: 112–21.

WALKER, A., and R. LEAKEY. The hominids of East Turkana. *Scientific American* 239: 54–66.

WALKER, A., et al. 1986. 2.5 Myr *Australopithecus boisei* from west of Lake Turkana, Kenya. *Nature* 322: 517–22.

WHITE, T. 1980. Evolutionary implications of Pliocene hominid footprints. *Science* 208: 175–76.

WHITE, T., and G. SUWA. 1987. Hominid footprints at Laetoli: Facts and interpretations. *American Journal of Physical Anthropology* 72: 485–514.

WOLPOFF, M. 1970. The evidence for multiple hominid taxa at Swartkrans. *American Anthropologist* 72: 576–607.

WOLPOFF, M. 1976a. Primate models for australopithecine sexual dimorphism. *American Journal of Physical Anthropology* 45: 497–510.

WOLPOFF, M. 1976b. Some aspects of the evolution of early hominid sexual dimorphism. *Current Anthropology* 17: 579–606.

WOLPOFF, M. 1980. *Paleoanthropology.* New York: Knopf.

WOOD, B. 1987. Who is the "real" *Homo habilis? Nature* 327: 187–88.

WOOD, B., and C. STACK. 1980. Does allometry explain the differences between "gracile" and "robust" australopithecines? *American Journal of Physical Anthropology* 52: 55–62.

Chapter

18

Homo Erectus

Fossil remains of Homo erectus *were first recovered by E. Dubois in Indonesia in 1891.* Homo erectus *skeletal and cultural remains have since been found in Africa, Asia, and Europe.* H. erectus *lived from approximately 1.8* M.Y.A., *when it first appeared in East Africa, to about 150,000 years ago in North Africa and perhaps India.* H. erectus *is the fossil group widely accepted as intermediate between* H. habilis *and* H. sapiens. *By the time of* H. erectus, *human evolution appears to have been increasingly influenced by culture.* H. erectus *may have been big-game hunters; in addition, they were users of fire, makers of dwelling structures, and inhabitants of previously unoccupied areas such as Asia and perhaps Europe.*

FIRST DISCOVERY

Prior to the discovery of *Australopithecus,* most scientists accepting the possibility of human evolution turned to Asia to find evidence, despite Darwin's suggestion that the earliest human ancestors would be found in Africa, because this is where our closest nonhuman primate relatives, the chimpanzees and gorillas, live. In 1891, Dubois, a Dutch physician, traveled to Indonesia, then under Dutch colonial rule. Soon after his arrival in Indonesia, Dubois reported the discovery of a skullcap, femur, and several other bone fragments at Trinil, a site on the Solo river in Java.

Dubois's contention that he had recovered remains of an ancestral human was poorly received at first because scientists were hesitant to accept the association of an archaic skullcap with a relatively modern-looking femur. Nevertheless, based on the anatomy of the femur, Dubois concluded that his "ape-man," as he referred to the find, walked bipedally erect like modern humans. He called his new discovery "Pithecanthropus erectus," the species name indicating its upright posture. This material, along with subsequent finds in Asia, Africa, and Europe, is now called *Homo erectus,* a taxon considered to be morphologically and geneologically intermediate between the African *Homo habilis* and *Homo sapiens.*

SKELETAL EVIDENCE

The cranial capacity of *H. erectus* varies from 750 cubic centimeters to 1,250 cubic centimeters. The lower end of the range characterizes earlier forms, and the higher end of the range characterizes later forms. Some part of the increase in cranial capacity over time can probably be related to increased body size over the time span of *H. erectus* evolutionary history (Wolpoff, 1980).

The *H. erectus* skull vault is flattened. The face is characterized by large brow ridges behind which there is marked **postorbital constriction;** that is, there is an indentation of the skull behind the large brow ridges. This area is elevated in modern populations because of an increased brain size and reconstructed face and skull. The *H. erectus* skull is widest at its base, whereas it is widest higher on the skull vault in modern humans; this may be due to the thinner bone, reduced mass of the chewing muscles, and increased cranial capacities found in modern humans. A sagittal ridge highlights the midline of the *H. erectus* skull. The *H. erectus* skull bones are thick relative to those of *H. sapiens;* the nasal bones are flat and the face protrudes more than in modern populations (Figure 18-1, 18-2).

The heavily built *H. erectus* mandible lacks a chin. The mandible reduced in size during the long history of *H. erectus.* The teeth are larger than those of modern populations. Premolar and molar size reduction also occurred over the time span of *H. erectus.* The canines are sometimes slightly overlapping.

The limb bones are essentially modern. However, based on early *H. erectus* remains from Africa, there are some differences between the postcranial anatomy of *H. erectus* and that of modern humans. Nevertheless, there is no doubt that *H. erectus* was bipedal.

The assumption that *H. erectus* is ancestral to *H. sapiens* is based on the following observations: (1) Morphologically, *H. erectus* conforms well with what would be expected as an intermediate stage between *H. habilis* and *H. sapiens.* (2) The existence of *H. erectus* in the early part of the Pleistocene, antedating any well-authenticated *H. sapiens,* provides an antiquity that conforms well with its supposed evolutionary relationship. (3) Some *H. erectus*

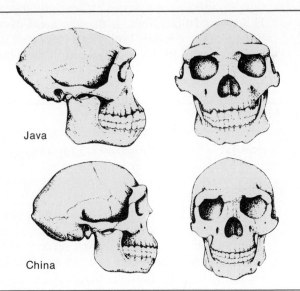

Java

China

Figure 18-1 *Comparison of* Homo erectus *skulls from Java and China. Note the large brow ridges, the sagittal ridge, and the cranial flattening on the side of the ridge (known as platycephaly), the constriction of the skull behind the brow ridges, and the amount of prognathism.*

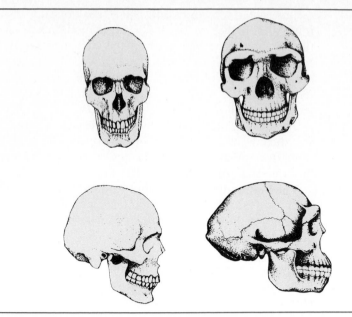

Figure 18-2 Comparison of modern skull (left) with that of Homo erectus *(right).*

samples illustrate a series of morphological changes from *H. erectus* to *H. sapiens*. In fact, there is disagreement over the assignment of some fossils because they contain both *H. erectus* and *H. sapiens* traits. (This will be discussed later in this chapter and in the next chapter.)

REVIEW OF SITES

(See Table 18-1 and Figure 18-3 for a review of sites.)

Africa

The oldest *H. erectus* remains come from Lake Turkana, Kenya. These remains include a pelvic fragment and two incomplete upper leg bones (femora) that date to about 1.8 M.Y.A. The most recently recovered *H. erectus* remains from Lake Turkana were found in 1984 at a site known as Nariokotome III. (See Figure 18-4.) The remains belong to a 12-year-old male and are dated to approximately 1.6 M.Y.A. (Brown and Fiebel, 1985; McDougall et al., 1985). The boy's chronological age estimate is based on tooth wear and tooth eruption patterns which are equivalent to those of a modern 12-year-old. The skeletal remains, given the catalog number WT 15000, are the most complete

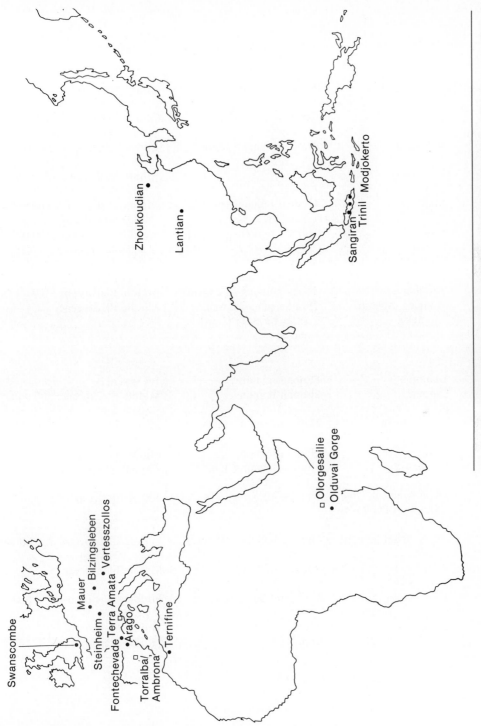

Figure 18-3 Some sites of Homo erectus and early Homo sapiens. The latter are found at Swanscombe, Steinheim, Bilzingsleben, Arago, and Terra Amata. These are discussed in Chapter 19. The dot indicates that human fossils are found at the site, and the box indicates that tools are found.

Swanscombe
Mauer
Steinheim
Bilzingsleben
Vertesszollos
Fontechevade Terra Amata
Torralba Arago
Ambrona
Ternifine
Olorgesailie
Olduvai Gorge
Zhoukoudian
Lantian
Sangiran
Trinil Modjokerto

Table 18-1

	SITE	EVIDENCE	DATE
Africa			
Kenya	Lake Turkana	Human remains, footprints	Lower Pleistocene, 1.8–1.5 M.Y.A.
	Olorgesailie	Tools, living site (possibly *H. erectus)*	Middle Pleistocene, 480,000–425,000 years ago
Tanzania	Olduvai Gorge	Human remains, tools	Lower Pleistocene, Bed II, 1.2 M.Y.A.
			Middle Pleistocene, Bed IV, 700,000–400,000 years ago
	Ndutu	Human remains (may be early *H. sapiens*)	Middle Pleistocene, 600,000–400,000 years ago
Ethiopia	Bodo	Human remains	Middle Pleistocene, 500,000–200,000 years ago
	Plain of Gadeb	Tools	Lower Pleistocene, 1 M.Y.A.?
South Africa	Swartkrans	Human remains	Middle Pleistocene
	Namibia	Tools (perhaps *H. erectus*)	Middle Pleistocene
North Africa	Morocco, Algeria, Tunisia	Human remains, tools (may be early *H. sapiens*)	Middle Pleistocene
Asia			
China	Yuanmou	Human remains	1.7 M.Y.A.(?)
	Lantian	Human remains	Middle Pleistocene, 500,000 years ago(?)
	Zhoukoudian	Human remains, tools, fire	Middle Pleistocene, 360,000 years ago
	Hexian	Human remains	Middle Pleistocene
	Jinniushan	Human remains, tools (*H. sapiens?*)	200,000 years ago (?)
Vietnam	Tham Khuyan, Tham Hai, Nui Do, Quan Yen	Human remains, tools	400,000 years ago (?)
Java	Djetis, Trinil faunal beds	Human remains, tools (?)	Middle Pleistocene, 700,000–600,000 years ago
Soviet Central Asia		Tools	Middle Pleistocene
India (?)		Tools and bones (?)	Middle Pleistocene (150,000 years ago)
Malaysia (?)		Tools (?)	Middle Pleistocene
Burma		Tools	Middle Pleistocene

Table 18-1 (Continued)

Europe (Some researchers reject the existence of *H. erectus* in Europe)

Germany	Mauer	Human remains, tools (?)	Middle Pleistocene, 300,000–250,000 years ago
Hungary	Vértesszöllös	Human remains	Middle Pleistocene, 400,000 years ago (?) perhaps as recent as 185,000 years
Italy	Fontana Ranuccio	Human remains, tools	Middle Pleistocene, 700,000 and 450,000 years ago
France	Montmaurin	Human remains	Middle Pleistocene, 300,000 years ago (?)
Spain	Torralba, Ambrona	Tools, butchered faunal remains	Middle Pleistocene, 500,000 years ago

*Not all the remains I am referring to the taxon *Homo erectus* are universally regarded as such. Some forms, most especially those in North Africa and Europe, are often referred to the taxon *Homo sapiens.* Such disagreement stems from the fact that some forms show traits of both taxa.

known for *H. erectus.* The missing parts are the left arm and hand, the right arm from below the elbow, and most of both feet.

One of the most interesting features of WT 15000 is his estimated adult height. At age 12, he was 5 feet, 4 inches tall. This is the body size previously postulated for adult *H. erectus.* If the growth rate is similar to that of modern humans, WT 15000 might have reached a height approaching 6 feet. WT 15000 would thus be much taller than previously predicted for any of our early

Figure 18-4 A reconstruction of WT 15000 (Homo erectus) from Lake Turkana.

ancestors. In fact, WT 15000 was taller than many modern humans. It will be interesting to see whether any future *H. erectus* finds confirm this body size or indicate that WT 15000 is an unusual specimen.

WT 15000's skull was assembled from about 70 pieces. The youngster's skull is small, and his cranial capacity may be 900 cubic centimeters. There are some interesting anatomical details associated with WT 15000. For example, the overall shape of the upper region of the thigh is different from that of modern or extinct humans. The vertebrae show some interesting differences from those of modern humans. The Turkana youngster has a narrow, flared pelvis and a combination of a large head and neck on the femur. These features of the upper leg are not found in other human femora, and the functional significance in terms of locomotion is unknown.

Richard Leakey (1970a, 1970b) announced the recovery of *H. erectus* remains from Lake Turkana in the form of an almost complete skull, KNM-ER 3733 (Figure 18-5) that is dated to 1.5 M.Y.A. Slightly older than KNM-ER 3733 is a very similar skull assigned the catalog designation of KNM-ER 3833. Its brow ridges, nuchal region, mastoids, and cranial base are somewhat thicker than similar areas in KNM-ER 3733. (The mastoids are bony protuberances found on each side of the skull behind the ear, to which the sternomastoid muscles attach. These muscles allow humans to rotate the head sideways.) KNM-ER 3733 may be a female and KNM-ER 3833 may be a male specimen (Wolpoff, 1980).

Another skull from Lake Turkana dates to approximately 1.5 M.Y.A. The face is broken away, the brow ridge is missing, and there is an associated

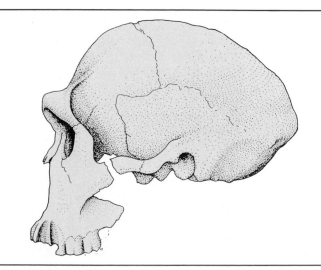

Figure 18-5 KNM-ER 3733, a Homo erectus *skull from Koobi Fora.*

mandible. This skull is morphologically closer to preceding australopithecine remains than other *H. erectus* remains at Lake Turkana.

In addition to the skeletal remains, there are also 7 human footprints from Lake Turkana attributed to *H. erectus* and dating to 1.5 M.Y.A. The prints were made by an individual about 5 feet to 5 feet, 6 inches tall and weighing about 120 pounds. Stone tools were also recovered from the same site.

H. erectus remains also come from Olduvai Gorge, Tanzania, the site of robust australopithecine and *H. habilis* remains. In Bed II at Olduvai, near the margin of an ancient lake, Louis Leakey recovered a *H. erectus* skullcap dated to approximately 1.2 M.Y.A. This skullcap shows many similarities to the KNM-ER 3733 material from Lake Turkana. The Lake Turkana remains may come from a population ancestral to the *H. erectus* remains from Olduvai.

Artifactual and skeletal remains have also been recovered from Bed IV, Olduvai. A left femoral shaft and hip bone of *H. erectus* were found associated with the *H. erectus* Acheulian tool industry. This is the first direct association at Olduvai of a well-defined tool assemblage with *H. erectus* skeletal remains. The leg and pelvic bones confirm that *H. erectus* was an erect and habitual biped.

A fairly well-preserved *H. erectus* skull was also found at the site of Ndutu, Tanzania, and dated to about 600,000 to 400,000 years ago. The skull vault is thick, with prominent brow ridges and a rather vertical forehead. The back of the skull (the occipital region) is thick. There is no sagittal ridge across the midline. The skull resembles material from Olduvai Gorge and later material from Zhoukoudian, China. The skull is morphologically intermediate between *H. erectus* and later *H. sapiens.* Some researchers place the skull with the latter species.

There are also *H. erectus* skeletal remains from South Africa (Figure 18-6). *H. erectus* materials were recovered in North Africa from Morocco, Algeria, and Tunisia from late Middle Pleistocene geological strata. These materials are apparently the last members of the *H. erectus* lineage in Africa.

One of the more interesting of the *H. erectus* skeletal samples comes from the Bodo region of Ethiopia. Human remains, including approximately 53 percent of a skull and face, were found associated with stone tools. Recent estimates place Bodo at a time between 500,000 and 200,000 years ago. There are indications that the Bodo individual camped near the edge of an ancient lake.

The Bodo material is morphologically intermediate between *H. erectus* and some early *H. sapiens* samples in such traits as the thickness and total breadth of the brow ridges and face. Electron microscopic studies of the Bodo skull have revealed a series of cut marks on the forehead and cheek bones. Bodo appears to have been intentionally defleshed after its death. The marks on the bone were left by the cutting edge of a stone tool (White, 1986).

The **Acheulian** tool tradition that is associated with *H. erectus* is found at sites in Ethiopia. Acheulian tools recovered from the southeast plateau of Ethiopia suggest that humans appeared on the Ethiopian high plateau about

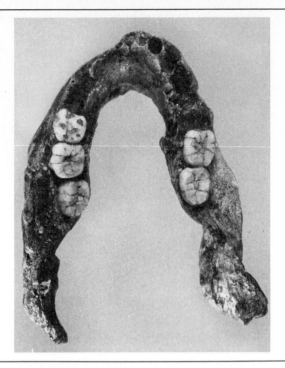

Figure 18-6 Mandibular specimen of Homo erectus *(SK 15) from Swartkrans, South Africa.*

1 M.Y.A. (Clark and Kurashina, 1979). This is the earliest date for human habitation in such environmental conditions.

A rich archaeological site is located at Olorgesailie (Figure 18-7), a site in the Rift Valley about an hour's drive from Nairobi, Kenya. Because of the lack of human skeletal remains, it is not clear that this is a *H. erectus* site. A date of between 700,000 and 900,000 years ago and the presence of tools of the Acheulian tradition suggest occupation by *H. erectus*. (See Figure 18-8).

Certain areas at Olorgesailie contain stone and bone accumulations that may have coincided with natural boundaries such as the bank of a sandy runnel or the limit of shade provided by larger trees. Smaller areas may have been occupied by four or five adults in a group; larger areas may have accommodated more than 20 adults. Based on the accumulation of a ton or more of stone artifacts and manuports (material that has been carried into a site, but that does not necessarily show use), it is estimated that the sites were continuously occupied for two or three months.

Olorgesailie contains such an abundance of baboon bones that it was initially suggested that the site represented continued, extremely successful hunting of a single baboon troop. The composition of the bone remains allows for differing interpretations, however. One analysis dismisses the contention that the animals were somehow killed as a troop by humans, but stresses that butchering did occur (Shipman, Bosler, and Davis, 1981). Another analysis (Binford and Todd, 1982) suggests that the primates were initially preyed on or at least scavenged by a relatively small predator-scavenger. The bones were later subjected to considerable attritional breakage by nonbiological agents or by trampling. In other words, humans may have had little to do with the bone accumulations.

Asia

Asian *Homo erectus* sites are found primarily in China and Java. The oldest Asian remains are found in Java. The oldest human fossiliferous beds in Java are the Djetis faunal beds, which date over 900,000 years ago and which have yielded a number of remains, all of which are probably *H. erectus.* The Trinil faunal beds (the source of Dubois's finds) overlay the Djetis beds. There are morphological differences between *H. erectus* fossils from the two strata.

The Trinil beds contain fossils of widely varying ages, and this raises doubts about the relationship between the skullcap and femur that Dubois found and assigned to the same individual. The exact geological derivation of the Trinil femur is uncertain, and its antiquity was inferred from its supposed associa-

Figure 18-7 The catwalk around part of the Homo erectus *site at Olorgesailie, Kenya.*

Figure 18-8 These photos are of stone tools of the Acheulian tradition from the site of Olorgesailie, Kenya.

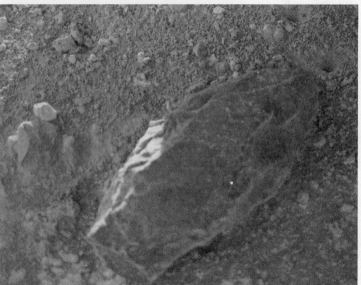

Figure 18-8 (Continued)

tion with the skullcap and the femur's supposedly archaic features. Many of Dubois's critics originally suggested that the femur was too modern-looking to belong with the skullcap, as Dubois had suggested. Relatively recent studies indicate that Dubois had, unfortunately, mixed materials from two different geological levels; the skullcap and femur from Trinil were not from contemporaneous creatures. It is ironic that the femur used to support *H. erectus's* bipedality probably derives from *H. sapiens*. Later *H. erectus* finds do, however, support claims for bipedalism in *H. erectus*.

The earliest human remains in China belong to *H. erectus* and possibly date to 1.7 M.Y.A. However, there is another date from the site that is only 500,000.

The material comes from the Yuanmou Basin, Yunnan Province, in southwestern China. The fossils consist of teeth and some limb fragments. The incisors (Figure 18-9) are large and may belong to a young male. The material has been referred to the subspecies of *H. erectus yuanmouensis* (Zhou, 1987).

In the 1920s and 1930s, an international team excavating at the cave site of Zhoukoudian (originally spelled *Choukoutien*), which is located about 25 miles from Beijing (Peking), uncovered the remains of approximately 40 individuals associated with tools, evidence of fire, thousands of animal bones, and fossilized pollen. The human remains, first called "Peking Man," are now considered to be a subspecies of *H. erectus* and are classified as *H. erectus pekinensis.* The Zhoukoudian remains consist of skullcaps, teeth, jaws, and postcranial remains. Unfortunately, no facial bones were preserved at the site. Consistent with their date of at least 400,000 to 350,000 years ago, the human remains from Zhoukoudian are more modern-looking than the oldest Javan *H. erectus.* The Javanese fossils are placed in the subspecies *H. erectus erectus.*

The earliest *H. erectus* deposits at Zhoukoudian include 14 skullcaps, 12 mandibles, 147 teeth, and some fragmentary skull remains. Although the material was broken, there were enough large pieces to allow for a rather complete reconstruction. All of the original materials were lost in the late 1930s during the confusion resulting from the Japanese invasion of China. Work resumed at Zhoukoudian in the 1950s, and additional material was recovered.

Animal remains, especially deer bones, were abundant. Bison, saber-toothed tigers, tigers, leopards, cheetahs, horses, wooly rhinoceroses, striped

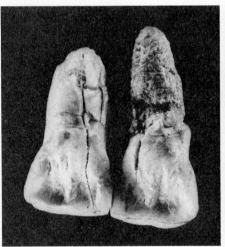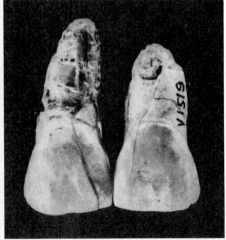

Figure 18-9 Two views of the incisors from Homo erectus *from Yuanmou, Yunnan Province, People's Republic of China.*

hyena, sika deer, giant beaver, and elephants inhabited the area. There was a big river and possibly a lake to the east which contained various water species; reeds and plants grew along the shorelines. Buffalo, deer, otter, and beaver inhabited the area. Some of these species may have contributed to the diet of *H. erectus,* for many of the associated animal bones are broken and splintered. In addition to bones from large species there are numerous bones from small animals such as hedgehogs, frogs, and hare. Ash layers in the cave abounded with the bones of these and other animals, including hamsters, mice, black rats, and harvest mice. There are also fragments of ostrich eggs. These remains have traditionally been interpreted as the residue of cooked meals by *H. erectus.* As will be noted in a moment, there are questions about this interpretation.

Both the floral and faunal evidence suggest a temperate environment. On the mountainous areas to the north and west grew mixed forests of pine, cedar, elm, hackberries, and Chinese rosebud. Evidence from different cave layers suggests climatic shifts during the long history of occupation at Zhoukoudian, first by *H. erectus* and much later by *H. sapiens.* There is disagreement, however, among Chinese researchers concerning the climate during *H. erectus* occupation at Zhoukoudian.

Numerous small quartz stone tools were recovered from the lower layers of Zhoukoudian. There are also large and crudely worked stone tools, a few of which display an even, uniform cutting edge. The artifacts' manufacturers often selected oval-shaped pebbles to make single- or double-edged axes called *chopping tools.* Such tools are found in most layers in the cave deposit.

Based on a reanalysis of the preserved remains, Binford and Ho (1985) and Binford and Stone (1986) question many of the notions once associated with the *H. erectus* finds at Zhoukoudian. They doubt that the lack of faces and enlarged foramen magnum, both supposedly due to efforts to extract the brain, were actually evidence that cannibalism occurred at Zhoukoudian as has been suggested. They also doubt that *H. erectus* at Zhoukoudian cooked their food, and that they used an array of plant and animal foods. Binford and Ho doubt that *H. erectus* had much to do with accumulating the bone materials at Zhoukoudian. They suggest that such materials were instead accumulated by other predators, especially the hyena.

Although many have stated that *H. erectus* used fire and perhaps cooked their food, an argument based on the accumulated ash remains associated with animal bones, Binford, Ho, and Stone suggest that the traces of fire at Zhoukoudian do not reflect purposeful burning and do not indicate the use of hearths. According to them, the ash found throughout the cave is the result of natural fires, perhaps caused by spontaneous ignition of vast amounts of organic materials (such as bird droppings) that are found in the cave.

Binford and Ho question whether humans deposited many of the animal bones at the site and whether such bone depositions indicate that *H. erectus* at Zhoukoudian was a big-game hunter. They argue that the deposits, including the human bones, were the remains of carnivore activity.

If Binford and Ho are correct, then the notion that *H. erectus* at Zhoukoudian used fire to cook its food, cannibalized the brains of its peers, and hunted big game must be altered. Instead, *H. erectus* at Zhoukoudian was perhaps simply another member of a faunal assemblage collected by a nonhuman predator. The view suggested by Binford and his colleagues awaits further testing. The major problem in settling the disagreements is that much of the original materials are lost. Newer excavations at Zhoukoudian might be helpful in reconciling the differing opinions.

A *H. erectus* mandible dated at 900,000 to 700,000 years ago was recovered in 1963 from the site of Chenjiawo (Ch'en-chia-wo) in Lantian District, Shaanxi Province, China. In 1964 at Gongwangling, 12.5 miles away, facial fragments, a tooth, and a skullcap were recovered; the material apparently belonged to a single individual (Figure 18-10). Gongwangling may predate both Lantian and Zhoukoudian and may be contemporaneous with the Javan Djetis faunal beds. The older date of the Lantian and Gongwanling materials is consistent with their more robust appearance when compared with the Zhoukoudian sample. Some scientists refer this material to the subspecies of *H. erectus lantianensis.*

The first *H. erectus* fossils found in southern China were unearthed in 1980 at Hexian, Anhui Province (Wanpo, Dushe, and Yongziang, 1981). The remains consist of 9 human teeth, the left part of a lower jaw with 2 intact molars, a heavily fossilized skull, and other fragmentary remains. As many as

Figure 18-10 The skullcap and mandible of Homo erectus *from Lantian, People's Republic of China. Photographed at the Institute of Vertebrate Paleontology and Paleoanthropology Beijing.*

4 individuals may be represented by the fossilized remains. The skull is similar to *H. erectus* from Java, suggesting that Hexian is older. Chinese paleontologists refer the material to the subspecies of *H. erectus hexianensis.* The associated fauna consist largely of animals that inhabited forest and woodland zones. There are indications that the climate at this time in the middle late portion of the middle Pleistocene, perhaps 200,000 years ago, was cool.

Some possible Chinese *H. erectus* materials were discovered in 1984 at Jinniushan (Gold Ox Hill) in Liaoning Province in northeast China. The remains are that of an almost complete 25- to 30-year-old male skeleton and are particularly important because the bones of the hands, feet, spine, ribs, and ulna are all unique specimens. The estimated date is 200,000 years ago. A few stone tools, burned animal remains, and burned clay and carbon were also recovered, which suggests the use of fire by *H. erectus.*

The recovery of the postcranial remains and the rather complete skull is very important because these *H. erectus* remains are in short supply, especially from Chinese sites. The postcranial remains should further confirm the presence of bipedalism, and the completeness of the skull will provide more reliable data for the reconstruction of cranial and facial features. Some Chinese researchers have cautioned that the remains may belong to an early *H. sapiens* and not to *H. erectus.*

Fossil evidence of the presence of middle Pleistocene humans has recently been reported from Vietnam. The preliminary date for the human remains is about 400,000 years ago (Ciochon, 1984/1985).

Putting the Javan and Chinese *H. erectus* remains in the same species affirms their close evolutionary relationship. The major features that differentiate the Zhoukoudian and Javan specimens are in the skull and teeth; the cranial capacity of the Zhoukoudian fossils is larger, and the teeth are significantly reduced in size compared with the earlier material. Asian *H. erectus* samples are quite similar in their postcranial anatomies.

All Asian *H. erectus* skulls are characterized by thick skull bones and projecting faces with large brow ridges and zygomatic arches. All had teeth larger than commonly found in modern populations. Cranial capacities vary; the earlier forms in Java generally have smaller cranial capacities than the later Chinese forms. Postcranially the *H. erectus* material approaches that of modern humans, except that the *H. erectus* material is more robust.

Sites in the Soviet central Asian region of Tadzhikstan dating to perhaps 250,000 years ago show that early humans, perhaps *H. erectus,* inhabited arid and climatically harsh regions in Asia. The inhabitants adapted to harsh semiarid uplands, and nowhere else in the Old World is a similar cultural adaptation known at this time. There are indications that humans inhabited this region during optimum climatic conditions. The inhabitants were probably wide-ranging bands of foraging hunter-gatherers who may have occupied small, temporary camps.

Europe

The task of defining a *H. erectus* sample in Europe is frustrated by the fragmentary nature of the human remains. Inclusion of European specimens within the *H. erectus* taxon is more a matter of tradition than the result of any distinctive morphological complex (Wolpoff, 1980). Some paleontologists suggest that all European fossil humans belong to *H. sapiens;* however, some fossils show a number of *H. erectus* features, and a good case can be made for including them within this taxon.

The first human fossil material recovered from Middle Pleistocene Europe is the Heidelberg or Mauer mandible, found in Germany. This lower jaw was recovered in 1907 from a sandpit in the village of Mauer, 6 miles from Heidelberg. It lay 78 feet below the surface in deposits dated to about 360,000 years ago. The Mauer mandible is approximately the same geological age as *H. erectus* from Locality 1, Zhoukoudian.

The chinless mandible is well preserved; most of the teeth are moderately worn. The mandible is one of the largest and most massive yet found. Its most striking trait is the great width of the ascending ramus (the bone which underlies the back of the cheek). The breadth of the ramus suggests powerful jaw muscles and wide, strong cheek bones. The size of the teeth is proportionately small compared to the robust mandible. This material is often assigned to the taxon *H. erectus heidelbergensis,* or to early *H. sapiens* by some researchers.

Sixty years after the Mauer find, an occipital bone and deciduous teeth were recovered from Vértesszöllös, a site dating to about 350,000 years ago or as recently as 185,000 years ago and located west of Budapest, Hungary. Vértesszöllös appears to have been a campsite. Perhaps because of its proximity to a hot spring, it seems to have been inhabited during the cool seasons of the year. Pebble tools were collected in and around the site, as was charred bone, indicating the presence of fire. This is the oldest cranial evidence from Europe. The bone is rather thick and possesses a well-marked nuchal ridge at the rear of the skull for neck muscle insertion. Nevertheless, some researchers believe that the bone belongs to a member of the *H. sapiens* population, rather than to *H. erectus.* One cranial capacity estimate of 1,400 cubic centimeters is above the maximum *H. erectus* cranial capacity and within the range of modern *H. sapiens.* The potential importance of the Vértesszöllös specimen lies in the information it provides concerning evolutionary changes at the end of the *H. erectus* lineage or the very beginning of the *H. sapiens* lineage.

A Middle Pleistocene site at Fontana Ranuccio in Italy has yielded Acheulian stone tools dating to 700,000 years ago and a bone tool industry dating to 450,000 years ago. The human remains, two teeth, date to the latter level. This is the earliest well-dated association of Acheulian stone tools with human remains to be found in Italy (Serge and Ascenzi, 1984). It is not clear whether the material comes from a member of the *H. erectus* population, although the 700,000-year-old date for the stone tools is in the *H. erectus* time span.

The Montmaurin mandible from France may date to about 300,000 years ago. It resembles the Mauer mandible in its robustness but is about the same size as the early *H. sapiens* mandible from Steinheim, Germany (Chapter 19). The mandible has no chin, and in other features closely resembles *H. erectus.*

That European Middle Pleistocene humans may have been hunting big game as early as 500,000 years ago is suggested by remains at the Spanish sites of Torralba and Ambrona. The Ambrona valley was part of a major migration route for large herds of deer, horses, and elephants. Torralba and Ambrona are located out in the open. The archaeological and fossil record indicates that humans may have visited this area seasonally to hunt and gather plant foods.

There are a considerable number of elephant bones at the site. It is widely held that many of the elephant bones exhibit marks caused by cutting, hacking, scraping, and other forms of human alteration. More than one researcher has stated, however, that few of the bones at Torralba and Ambrona show cut marks made by humans.

Binford (1981, 1985, 1987) argues, for example, that since it is not known how long a time is represented at Torralba, the animal remains could have been accumulated through a natural process of attrition in the population and not through hunting. Binford suggests that the animal assemblage at Torralba indicates a pattern of scavenging and not hunting, with the occasional exploitation of naturally occurring carcasses of elephants and horses for small amounts of meat.

One 270-square-foot area contained the left side of a large adult elephant with tusks and most bones in place; the head and pelvis were missing. Four flake tools found at the site indicate that the elephant was butchered there. The intriguing question involves why half the elephant's body was missing. Perhaps the elephant was caught in a muddy swamp and struggled to get free, and when it finally fell exhausted on its side, it was killed and butchered. It is not clear whether the elephant wandered into or was herded into the swamp. Torralba lies in a steep-sided valley where the water table rises to within a few inches from the ground's surface and where animals could become mired in the mud. The terrain 500,000 years ago was even wetter than it is today. Perhaps human hunters stood on the high ledges overlooking the valley, following the herd movements. Perhaps an unwary animal wandered from the herd and found itself caught in mud; it would be relatively easy to run down the hill and make the kill.

Perhaps humans played an active role by driving the animals into the swamp. There is evidence of burned grass and brush over an extensive area. Perhaps fires were deliberately set to drive the animals into the mud. Once mired in mud, they would have been relatively defenseless.

ACHEULIAN TOOL TRADITION

The Acheulian tool tradition associated with *H. erectus* first appeared about 1.5 M.Y.A. in Africa. Aside from the preceding Oldowan tool tradition, which first appeared in Africa about 2 M.Y.A. and is usually associated with *H. habilis,* the Acheulian is the most widespread and long-lasting stone-tool cultural tradition. Acheulian tools were made from a wider range of raw materials than were Oldowan tools. This may indicate a greater awareness on the part of the tool makers of their environment, as well as greater technological skills. In contrast to what appear to be all-purpose Oldowan tools, Acheulian tools were apparently tailored for different purposes. The basic Acheulian tool kit includes a versatile range of cutting, scraping, piercing, chopping, and pounding tools used to prepare plant and animal materials. Bones and ivory also seem to have been used as tools, as perhaps was wood.

The precision in manufacture of the Acheulian tools apparently resulted from a new flaking technique, the **soft-hammer technique,** whereby a stone flake is detached from the core with a wood, bone, or antler hammer (Figure 18-11). The use of these softer materials as a hammer allowed more control of the final product in terms of flake length, width, and thickness. The core surface was flaked all over, resulting in a bifacial flat and pear-shaped tool with longer, thinner, and more regular edges. With this development in manufacture, a new type of core tool—the cleaver, a U-shaped tool with a straight transverse cutting edge—was developed.

USE OF FIRE

The control of fire is probably one of the most momentous and far-reaching of human discoveries. The controlled and purposeful use of fire required conquering the fear of fire that is common to all mammals. With the purposeful use of fire, humans began to shape the world according to their design. For example, by bringing fire into its living space, *H. erectus* carved zones of light and warmth out of darkness, and thus provided relative protection from predators.

It is not clear when humans first began to use fire. The earliest evidence of fire with possible human connections comes from sites at Lakes Baringo and Turkana in Kenya. Burnt clay from these sites dates between 1.5 and 1.4 M.Y.A. Although some researchers (for example, Gowlett et al., 1981) suggest an association between this evidence and human occupation, most researchers are unconvinced of such a purposeful association. It is not difficult to find traces of fire early in Africa, but the problem is in distinguishing between controlled fire used by humans and naturally occurring fire.

If the evidence of fire at Lakes Baringo and Turkana is not associated with humans, then the earliest possible evidence of the use of fire associated with

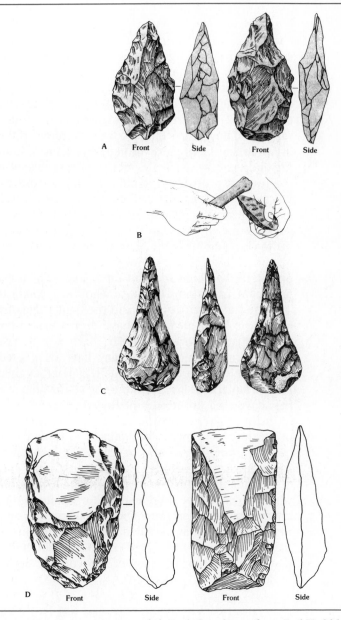

Figure 18-11 Hand ax production. (A) Early hand axes from Bed II, Olduvai Gorge. (B) Use of an animal bone to make a hand ax. (C) Acheulian hand ax from Swanscombe, England, one-third actual size. (D) Acheulian cleavers, one-half actual size.

humans may be recent discoveries from the South African cave site of Swartkrans, dated to about 1 M.Y.A. (Brain and Sillen, 1988). The Swartkrans site contains skeletal remains of both *A. robustus* and *H. erectus,* and it is not certain which group was using the fire. Evidence of fire use from other parts of the world is only found associated with *H. erectus,* however.

The evidence for controlled use of fire at Swartkrans is in the form of burned bone which is found in several distinct layers of limestone within the cave. The 270 charred bone fragments were found to have been heated to a range of temperatures that occur in campfires. If the evidence of controlled use of fire in South Africa is verified, this is the oldest incidence of humans using fire and the first verified evidence of early use of fire in Africa.

Fire was probably originally obtained from such ready-made sources as volcanic eruptions, brush fires, or gas and oil seepages. Humans may have camped near fire and learned to use it. When they moved, they may have taken smouldering embers with them; perhaps each band had a fire-bearer responsible for keeping the flame. Control of this potent material may have conferred an aura of respect and invincibility on its keeper. Such an individual had the potential to become an important leader. The use and control of fire may also have conferred status on those who knew where to find and how to use fire. The use and control of fire, and the knowledge of where to find it and how to keep the embers alive, may have been a prized possession, guardedly passed from generation to generation.

From the beginning, fire may have been used to keep away predators. Humans also seem to have used fire when they themselves were the predators. For example, evidence from the site at Torralba in Spain suggests that humans may have used fire to stampede their prey.

Introducing fire into the living spaces created an artificial day independent of the sun's movements for light and warmth. Our fascination with fire may be of ancient origin. Fire may have been a potent stimulant, and as such it would have served to enhance ceremonial occasions.

We can raise a number of unanswerable questions at this time. For example, what did early cave dwellers think of shadows dancing on dark cave walls as they sat around their fires? Did willowy shapes on the walls lead cave dwellers to thoughts that may have had magical or ritualistic overtones? Were any of the shadows construed as friends or foes, as animals of the hunt? Did the place that fire now holds in many of the world's religions have such beginnings as these? We can only speculate.

Homo erectus *remains from Africa and Asia exhibit a common morphological characteristic that can be used to designate the species. The oldest* H. erectus *samples appear in East Africa, where they date to about 1.8* M.Y.A. *Most of the Asian sample dates to about 400,000 years ago. (See Table 18-2.)*

Table 18-2. **Some Features Associated with Homo erectus**

Time Span 1.8 M.Y.A. to perhaps 150,000 years ago in North Africa. The earliest forms date to East Africa.

Distribution Africa, Asia, and perhaps Europe.

Associated Tool Culture Acheulian tool industry. Soft-hammer technique used for first time.

Life-ways Use of fire. Inhabited caves and built shelters. Evidence of big-game hunting. Entered new habitats such as plateau and semiarid regions.

Anatomy

Cranial capacity: 750 cubic centimeters in the earlier and perhaps smaller-bodied forms to 1,250 cubic centimeters in the latest and perhaps larger-bodied forms.

Face and skull: Flattened skull vault.
  Greatest width of skull low on the skull.
  Thick skull bones.
  Sagittal ridge is common.
  Large brow ridges and marked postorbital constriction.
  Flat nasal bones.
  Prognathism, heavy mandible lacking a chin, large teeth.

Limbs: Essentially modern limb structure and pelvis. There are some differences, but the functional significance of these is unknown. Bipedal.

---

*Homo erectus **is chronologically and morphologically intermediate between the lower Pleistocene African** H. habilis **materials and the later** H. sapiens **fossils. Some specimens, such as those in Europe, indicate a** H. erectus **to** H. sapiens **transition. For this reason, there is considerable disagreement over how to classify the European fossils.***

*Homo erectus **cultural associations such as the Acheulian tool tradition are elaborations of earlier cultural associations. Some morphological features distinguishing** H. erectus **from earlier forms, such as increases in brain size, facial morphology, and perhaps dental structure, may be related to changes in culture and tool manufacture. Cultural elaboration and the physical evolution of** H. erectus **are probably interrelated, although we are still unsure of exactly how the interrelationship functioned.***

BIBLIOGRAPHY

ANDREWS, P. 1984. An alternative interpretation of the characters used to define *Homo erectus*. In *The Early Evolution of Man,* P. Andrews and J. Frazen, eds. Frankfurt: Senckenberg Museum.

BARTSTRA, G. 1982. *Homo erectus erectus:* The search for his artifacts. *Current Anthropology* 23: 318–20.

BEHRENSMEYER, A., and L. LAPORTE. 1981. Footprints of a Pleistocene hominid in northern Kenya. *Nature* 289: 167–69.

BINFORD, L. 1981. *Bones.* New York: Academic Press.

BINFORD, L. 1985. Human ancestors: Changing views of their behavior. *Journal of Anthropological Archaeology* 4: 292–327.

BINFORD, L. 1987. The hunting hypothesis, archaeological methods, and the past. *Yearbook of Physical Anthropology* 30: 1–9.

BINFORD, L., and C. HO. 1985. Taphonomy at a distance: Zhoukoudian, The cave home of Beijing Man? *Current Anthropology* 26: 413–42.

BINFORD, L., and N. STONE. 1986. Zhoukoudian: A closer look. *Current Anthropology* 27: 453–75.

BINFORD, L., and L. TODD. 1982. On arguments for the "butchering" of giant geladas. *Current Anthropology* 23: 108–10.

BROWN, F., and C. FIEBEL. 1985. Stratigraphic notes on the Okote Tuff complex at Koobi Fora, Kenya. *Nature* 316: 788–92.

BRAIN, C.K., and A. SILLEN. 1988. Evidence from the Swartkrans cave for the earliest use of fire. *Nature* 336: 464–66.

BYE, B., et al. 1987. Increased age estimate for the Lower Paleolithic hominid site at Olorgeisailie, Kenya. *Nature* 329: 231–33.

CHANG, K. 1979. Chinese paleoanthropology. *Annual Review of Anthropology* 6: 137–59.

CIOCHON, R. 1984/1985. Paleontological field research in Vietnam. *Newsletter, The Institute of Human Origins* 4: 7–8.

CLARK, J. 1982. Our roots in time: Significant new hominid discoveries. *The L. S. B. Leakey Foundation Newsletter* 23: 17–19.

CLARK, J., and H. KURASHINA. 1979. Hominid occupation of the East-Central highlands of Ethiopia in the Plio-Pleistocene. *Nature* 282: 33–39.

DAVIS, R., V. RANOV, and D. DODONOV. 1980. Early man in Soviet Central Asia. *Scientific American* 243: 130–38.

DAY, M. 1971. Postcranial remains of *Homo erectus* from Bed IV, Olduvai Gorge, Tanzania. *Nature* 232: 383–87.

DELSON, E. 1985. Paleobiology and age of African *Homo erectus. Nature* 316: 762–63.

DUBOIS, E. 1896. *Pithecanthropus erectus:* A form from the ancestral stock of mankind. In The Annual Report for the Smithsonian Institute for the Year Ending June 30, 1898. Washington, D.C.: U.S. Government Printing Office.

EISLEY, L. 1954. Man the fire-maker. *Scientific American* 191: 52–57.

GOWLETT, J. 1987. New dates for the Acheulean age. *Nature* 329: 200.

GOWLETT, J., et al. 1981. Early archaeological site, hominid remains and traces of fire from Cheswonja, Kenya. *Nature* 294: 125–29.

HOLLOWAY, R. 1981. The Indonesian *H. erectus* brain endocasts revisited. *American Journal of Physical Anthropology* 55: 503–21.

HOWELL, F. 1960a. European and northwest African middle Pleistocene hominids. *Current Anthropology* 1: 175–232.

HOWELL, F. 1960b. *Early Man.* New York: Time-Life Books.

HOWELL, F. 1976. Some views on *Homo erectus,* with special reference to its occurrence in Europe. Paper presented at Davidson Black Symposium, Canadian Association of Physical Anthropologists, Toronto.

HOWELLS, W. 1966. *Homo erectus. Scientific American* 215: 46–53.

HOWELLS, W. 1980. *Homo erectus*—who, when and where: A survey. *Yearbook of Physical Anthropology* 23: 1–24.

HUANG, W D. FANG, and Y. YE. 1981. Preliminary observation on a fossil hominid skull found in Longtan cave in Hexian County, Anhui Province. *Kexue Tongbao* 26: 1116–20 (in Chinese).

ISAAC, G. 1968. Traces of Pleistocene hunters: An East African example. In *Man the Hunter,* R. Lee and I. DeVore, eds. Chicago: Aldine.

ISAAC, G. 1969. Studies of early cultures in East Africa. *World Archaeology* 1: 1–28.

ISAAC, G. 1975. Stratigraphy and cultural patterns in East Africa during the middle ranges of Pleistocene time. In *After the Australopithecines,* K. Butzer and G. Isaac, eds. The Hague: Mouton.

ISAAC, G. 1977. *Olorgesailie: Archaeological Studies of a Middle Pleistocene Lake Basin in Kenya.* Chicago: University of Chicago Press.

JACOB, T. 1967. Recent "Pithecanthropus" finds in Indonesia. *Current Anthropology* 8: 501.

JACOB, T., R. SOEJONO, L. FREEMAN, and F. BROWN. 1978. Stone tools from mid-Pleistocene sediments in Java. *Science* 202: 885–87.

JIA, L. P. 1975. *The Cave Home of Peking Man.* Peking: Foreign Languages Press.

JING, J. 1984. "Apeman" clue to evolution. *China Daily,* November 30, p. 1.

KRETZOI, M., and L. VERTÉS. 1965. Upper Biharian (Intermindel) pebble-industry occupation in western Hungary. *Current Anthropology* 6: 74–87.

LEAKEY, L. 1966. *Homo habilis, Homo erectus,* and the australopithecines. *Nature* 209: 1279–81.

LEAKEY, M. 1971. Discovery of postcranial remains of *Homo erectus* and associated artifacts in Bed IV at Olduvai Gorge, Tanzania. *Nature* 232: 380–83.

LEAKEY, R. 1970a. New hominid remains and early artifacts from northern Kenya: Fauna and artifacts from a new Plio-Pleistocene locality near Lake Rudolf in Kenya. *Nature* 226: 223.

LEAKEY, R. 1970b. In search of man's past at Lake Rudolf. *National Geographic* 137: 712.

LEWIN, R. 1984. Unexpected anatomy in *Homo erectus. Science* 226: 529.

LI, Y., and H. JIP. 1981. Environmental change in Peking Man's time. *Vertebrata Palasiatica* 19: 347 (in Mandarin with English summary).

LU, Z. 1984. How *Homo erectus* was found. *China Daily,* November 30, p. 5.

MANN, A. 1971. *Homo erectus.* In *Background for Man,* P. Dolhinow and V. Sarich, eds. Boston: Little, Brown.

MCDOUGALL, I., et al. 1985. Age of the Okote Tuff Complex at Koobi Fora, Kenya. *Nature* 316: 792–94.

OAKLEY, K. 1955. Fire as a Paleolithic tool and weapon. *Proceedings of the Prehistoric Society* 21: 36.

OAKLEY, K. 1961. On man's use of fire, with comments on tool making and hunting. In *Social Life of Early Man,* S. Washburn, ed. Chicago: Aldine.

PFEIFFER, J. 1971. When *Homo erectus* tamed fire, he tamed himself. In *Human Variation,* H. Bleibtreu and J. Downs, eds. Beverly Hills, Calif.: Glencoe Press.

PILBEAM, D. 1975. Middle Pleistocene hominids. In *After the Australopithecines,* K. Butzer and G. Isaac, eds. The Hague: Mouton.

POIRIER, F. 1987. *Understanding Human Evolution.* Englewood Cliffs, N.J.: Prentice Hall.

RIGHTMIRE, G. 1979. Cranial remains of *Homo erectus* from Beds II and IV, Olduvai Gorge, Tanzania. *American Journal of Physical Anthropology* 51: 99–116.

RIGHTMIRE, G. 1983. The Lake Ndutu cranium. *American Journal of Physical Anthropology* 61: 245–54.

SERGE, A., and A. ASCENZI. 1984. Fontana Ranuccio: Italy's earliest middle Pleistocene hominid site. *Current Anthropology* 25: 230–33.

SHAPIRO, H. 1971. The strange, unfinished saga of Peking man. *Natural History* 80: 8, 74.

SHAPIRO, H. 1974. *Peking Man.* New York: Simon & Schuster.

SHIPMAN, P., W. BOSLER, and K. DAVIS. 1981. Butchering of giant geladas at an Acheulian site. *Current Anthropology* 22: 257–68.

STRINGER, C. 1984. The definition of *Homo erectus* and the existence of the species in Africa and Europe. In *The Early Evolution of Man,* P. Andrews and J. Franzen, eds. Frankfurt: Senckenberg Museum.

TOBIAS, P. 1971. *The Brain in Hominid Evolution.* New York: Columbia University Press.

WALKER, A., and R. LEAKEY. 1978. The hominids of East Turkana. *Scientific American* 239: 54–66.

WEIDENREICH, F. 1943. The skull of "Sinanthropus pekinensis." *Paleontolgia Sinica.* 10: 1–229.

WHITE, T. 1986. Cutmarks on the Bodo cranium: A case of prehistoric defleshing. *American Journal of Physical Anthropology* 69: 503–9.

WHITEHEAD, P. 1982. Hominid discovery in the Awash Valley. *Explorers Journal* 60: 123–25.

WOLPOFF, M. 1977. Some notes on the Vérteszöllös occipital. *American Journal of Physical Anthropology* 47: 357–64.

WOLPOFF, M. 1980. *Paleoanthropology.* New York: Knopf.

WOO, R., and WU, X. 1982. Human fossil teeth from Xichuan, Henan. *Vertebrata Palasiatica* 20: 8–16 (in Chinese with English summary).

WU, M. 1983. *Homo erectus* from Hexian, Anhui found in 1981. *Acta Anthropologica Sinica* 2: 110–16 (in Chinese with English summary).

WU, R., and X. DONG. 1980. The fossil human teeth from Yunxian, Hubei. *Vertebrata Palasiatica* 17: 149 (in Chinese with English summary).

WU, R., and X. DONG. 1982. Preliminary study of *Homo erectus* remains from Hexian, Anhui. *Acta Anthropologica Sinica* 1: 2–13 (in Chinese with English summary).

WU, X., and L. WANG. 1985. Chronology in Chinese Paleoanthropology. In *Paleoanthropology and Paleolithic Archaeology in the People's Republic of China.* New York: Alan R. Liss.

ZHEN, S. 1983. Micromammals from the Hexian Man locality. *Vertebrata Palasiatica* 20: 239–40 (in Chinese with English summary).

ZHOU, G. 1987. The first man in China: Yuanmou Man, his date and living environment. Unpublished manuscript.

Chapter
19
Early Homo sapiens

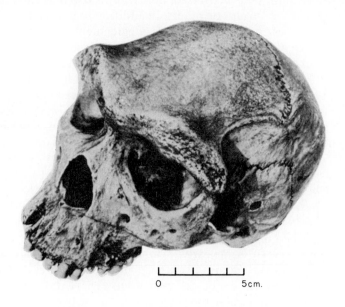

0   5cm.

The evolutionary relationships of many of the forms discussed in this chapter are unclear because they show intermediate anatomical traits. Some anatomical traits are characteristic of H. erectus *and some are typical of* H. sapiens. *The dating of many of these specimens is unclear, and this complicates the interpretation of their evolutionary relationships. These specimens are referred to as early* Homo sapiens *rather than late* Homo erectus *because of changes in skull size and shape and, to a lesser degree, changes in facial skeleton. The faces and skulls of a number of early* H. sapiens *specimens are less robust than those of the preceding* H. erectus *sample. The general time span is perhaps 250,000 or 300,000 years ago to 100,000 years ago.*

OVERVIEW

There is a lack of agreement as to which anatomical traits define early *Homo sapiens.* There are a series of African and Eurasian fossils that are different from *H. erectus* and yet are not clearly modern *H. sapiens* (Table 19-1). Some of these remains have large cranial capacities, approaching and even exceeding the size of those of modern *H. sapiens.* Nevertheless, some are robustly built and have large faces, jaws, and teeth (Table 19-2 on page 383). Following Wolpoff's (1980) lead, these materials are referred to here as early *H. sapiens.*

The dating and classification problems associated with a number of these fossils cannot be overstressed. Some forms listed as early *H. sapiens* here are listed with *H. erectus* by others. In addition to uncertainty about the dating of some of these materials, this lack of agreement is attributable to the fragmentary state of the materials and the equivocal nature of some of the anatomical traits exhibited. Although a number of these specimens have been attributed to early *H. sapiens* on scanty evidence and debatable grounds, there are important differences between these fossils and *H. erectus.* The major problem in trying to decide on either the *H. sapiens* or the *H. erectus* designation is related to the fact that we are arbitrarily subdividing an evolutionary continuum. There is a continuity between the earliest members of *H. sapiens* and the latest *H. erectus* fossils in areas with large samples. There will probably always be specimens that cannot be satisfactorily placed within any one group.

The main anatomical differences between the early *H. sapiens* and late *H. erectus* fossil assemblages are found in skull size and shape and, to a lesser extent, in the face. Dental changes from *H. erectus* include a reduction in the size of the posterior teeth and an expansion in the size of the anterior teeth (Wolpoff, 1980). Some early *H. sapiens* specimens do have immense posterior teeth, however, some surpassing the average size among *H. erectus.* Postcranially the major difference between *H. erectus* and *H. sapiens* is a reduction in muscular robusticity.

The cranial capacity of early *H. sapiens* averages 1,166 cubic centimeters, representing an 11 percent increase over that of *H. erectus.* Some early

Table 19-1. **Early** Homo sapiens *Sites Discussed in Text*

COUNTRY	SITE	REMAINS	DATE
Africa			
South Africa	Saldanha	Human remains, tools	100,000 years(?)
Zambia	Kabwe (Broken Hill)	Human remains, tools	130,000(?), 800,000–600,000(?)
Asia			
Indonesia	Solo	Human remains, tools	250,000(?) or much later into Upper Pleistocene
Europe			
England	Swanscombe	Human remains, tools	225,000–200,000
German Democratic Republic	Bilzingsleben	Human remains, tools, dwellings(?)	225,000
	Steinheim	Human remains	250,000(?)
Greece	Petralona	Human remains	debated
France	Terra Amata	Tools, dwellings	less than 300,000
	Arago (Tautavel)	Human remains, tools	200,000 + (?)
	Biache	Human remains	200,000 + (?)

H. sapiens cranial capacities fall below those of some later *H. erectus* specimens, however. Most changes in the skull from *H. erectus* to *H. sapiens* appear to result from increasing cranial capacities and the reduction of areas of muscle attachment. Brain size increases appear to reflect actual evolutionary changes in the brain; they are not just a reflection of body-size increases.

REVIEW OF SITES

Sub-Saharan Africa

The mixture of anatomical traits, some belonging with *H. erectus* and others with *H. sapiens,* and the uncertain dating of sub-Saharan remains confuses their evolutionary placement. The forms discussed here, Kabwe (or Broken Hill) from Zambia and Saldanha from South Africa, are referred to either a late *H. erectus* or an early *H. sapiens* evolutionary lineage. The latter designation is used here. The Kabwe specimen was found in 1921. While some date the fossil to 130,000 years ago, Murrill (1983) suggests a date of 800,000 to 600,000 years ago. If he is correct, then this material most likely belongs with *H. erectus.* Given our current fossil evidence, it is unlikely that *H. sapiens* appeared at such an early date.

The Kabwe skull (Figure 19-1) has a complete face which shows a combination of robust (archaic) and gracile features. The skull has a very large brow ridge, a low forehead, and a well-developed occipital region—all traits of

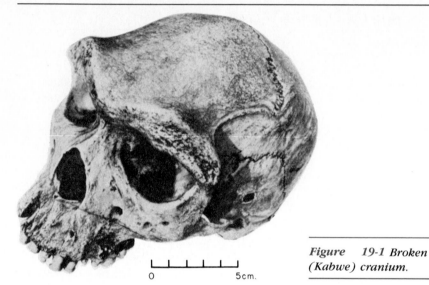

0   5cm.

Figure   19-1 Broken   Hill (Kabwe) cranium.

H. erectus. On the other hand, the skull exhibits several traits seen in early *H. sapiens,* including a cranial capacity of about 1,300 cubic centimeters, thinner skull bones, and a gracility of the structures supporting the facial musculature (Wolpoff, 1980).

The Saldanha skull is quite similar to that of Kabwe, although its face and base are not preserved. Although the date is not firmly established, it may date to about 100,000 years ago.

Asia

Possible early *H. sapiens* remains have been found in Indonesia. Referred to as the Solo fossils because they come from the banks of the Solo river, 13 skulls and skull fragments, lacking faces, were found between 1931 and 1941. There are also two incomplete lower leg bones (tibias). The skulls are similar to the Kabwe specimen and have marked cranial flattening, like *H. erectus,* and marked brow ridge development. Unlike Kabwe, the Solo skulls have thick cranial walls. Cranial capacities range between 1,150 and 1,300 cubic centimeters. The Solo skulls are generally larger than those often found among *H. erectus.* Wolpoff (1980) suggests an average 10 percent increase in cranial capacity over *H. erectus.*

Dating the Solo specimens has been a problem, but some estimates suggest an age of 250,000 years ago. Although there are broad similarities between the Solo remains and Chinese *H. erectus* material from Zhoukoudian, the Solo sample exhibits the gracility of skull features that characterized *H. sapiens* samples. The material may be transitional between *H. erectus* and *H. sapiens.*

Europe

European remains of possible early *H. sapiens* are the most numerous of this otherwise scanty set of fossils. They come from a time span roughly delineated by the Second or Hoxnian Interglacial and the Riss Glaciation, from 300,000 to 250,000 years ago to less than about 100,000 years ago. Although there are numerous European sites, the number of fossils is limited and there continues to be a question about their dating. Some remains like those from Petralona in Greece and Bilzingsleben in the German Democratic Republic, for example, have been referred to as *H. erectus* by some researchers.

The Swanscombe site is a gravel pit located near London along the Thames river. The area appears to have been a favorite hunting site for prehistoric populations, as several hundred thousand stone tools have been recovered there. The first human material came to light in 1935, when stone quarriers discovered an occipital bone protruding from a gravel bank.

A second fossil was discovered the following March near the site of the original find. This time a left parietal (the parietals are the two bones on the top of the skull) was uncovered, and it belonged with the 1935 occipital. The third skull fragment, the right parietal, was recovered in 1955, 75 feet from the original 1935 find. It also belonged to the same individual (Figure 19-2).

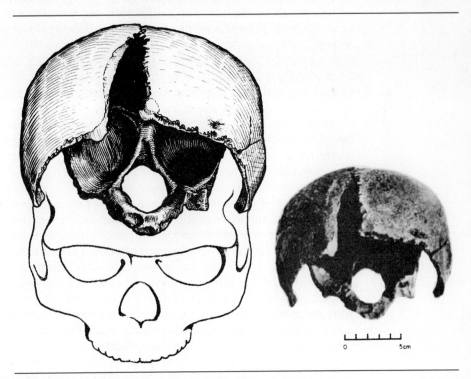

Figure 19-2 Swanscombe partial cranium.

Deposits yielding the Swanscombe remains appear to be of interglacial age and thus date to about 225,000 years ago. The associated fauna includes elephants and rhinoceroses. Fluorine analysis of the faunal remains indicated a middle Pleistocene date (Oakley, 1952). Stone implements associated with the skeletal remains have been assigned to the early middle Acheulian industry, usually associated with *H. erectus* fossils.

Swanscombe was inhabited during a temperate climatic period. The presence of elephants and rhinoceroses indicates that the English climate was warmer than it is today. African fauna migrated across the Dardanelles land bridge and browsed in the warm Thames valley along with wild boar, deer, and other woodland types. The approach of colder times is indicated by a decrease in the tropical African fauna assemblage and an increase in open-grassland species, the latter of which indicate a forest recession. This preceded the Riss Glaciation.

The three Swanscombe skull bones (an occipital and two partietals) were well preserved. The skull's sutures were still open. Based on the age of suture closure in modern populations, the individual is estimated to be 20 to 25 years old. The cranial capacity was probably between 1,275 and 1,325 cubic centimeters according to Coon (1962) or closer to 1,250 cubic centimeters by other estimates. This is within the range of cranial capacities of modern populations. Two major features differentiating Swanscombe from modern *H. sapiens* are the thickness of the skull bones and the heavy brow ridges found in Swanscombe.

Swanscombe's advanced traits, particularly the rather large cranial capacity, have led to some confusion regarding its classification. The larger brain and general suggestion of rounded and expanded skull contours typical of the Swanscombe skull approach modern conditions. On the other hand, the relatively low brain case height and certain other traits suggest a form morphologically intermediate between *H. erectus* and *H. sapiens.* Swanscombe is referred to as an archaic member of *H. sapiens.* Some paleontologists refer these specimens to the subspecies of *H. s. swanscombensis.*

Four skull fragments and a single molar were recovered from the site of Bilzingsleben in the German Democratic Republic (Vlček, 1978). The skull morphology approaches that of the African *H. erectus* from Olduvai Gorge. The brow ridges are well developed, the skull bones are thick, and the occipital is marked by a strong horizontal strut of bone. The bones were associated with a flake stone industry and numerous butchered animal bones. The approximate age is 228,000 years (Harmon, Glazek, and Nowack, 1980).

The interglacial character of the Bilzingsleben deposit is well established from the abundant floral and faunal remains; 10 plant species, 15 snail species, and 12 vertebrate species have been recovered. The fossil specimens indicate a forest environment with a climate slightly warmer than the present and without winter frost (Harmon, Glazek, and Nowack, 1980).

Some researchers suggest that the Bilzingsleben remains belong to an archaic middle Pleistocene *H. sapiens;* others classify the material as *H.*

erectus. The Bilzingsleben material is similar to that of Vértesszöllös, which is probably *H. erectus* but also bears some resemblance to *H. sapiens* material from Petralona, Steinheim, and Swanscombe.

Over 60,000 stone implements, as well as bone and antler tools were found. Evidence of two possible dwelling structures have been recognized. The presence of fish bones suggests possible freshwater fishing that was previously unknown at this early date.

The Petralona skull was recovered from a Greek cave in 1959. The skull is encrusted with limestone and, although fragmented, it is well preserved. The dating of the Petralona cave material is disputed. Based on paleomagnetic determination, however, Kurtén (1983) suggests a date of about 800,000 years old. Based on studies of associated faunal remains and skull morphology, Murrill (1983) suggests that the site dates from 800,000 to 600,000 years ago. Dating problems primarily stem from the fact that the fauna have been variously attributed to different time periods. Henning and colleagues (1981) question whether the faunal remains are associated with the human skull. They suggest that the human fossils actually date to less than 200,000 years ago.

The Petralona skull is large; however, cranial capacity estimates are disputed. Although estimates of 1,440 cubic centimeters and 1,383 cubic centimeters have been proposed, Howells (1973) believes an estimate of 1,220 cubic centimeters is more accurate. Murrill (1981), who spent a number of years working on the Petralona skull, estimates a cranial capacity of 1,155 cubic centimeters. Howells (1973) suggests that the skull is a specimen in the *H. erectus* lineage that differs from the Olduvai and Far Eastern *H. erectus* samples. The Petralona skull exhibits many features found on the Hungarian Vértesszöllös and Zambian Kabwe specimens.

Arago cave in France has yielded cultural and bone material and is dated to about 200,000 years ago. It may be somewhat older, however. The presence of a large archaic horse, a small wolf, a large panther, and fragments of extinct rodents date the site to the very beginning of the Riss Glaciation, about 200,000 years ago (de Lumley and de Lumley, 1973). The Arago human remains consist of many isolated teeth, phalanges, skull fragments, a mandible with 6 teeth (Arago 2), a half mandible with 5 teeth (Arago 13), the anterior portion of an adult skull, and some fragmentary postcranial remains. At least 23 individuals, including at least 8 youngsters, may be represented.

The most complete specimen (Arago 21) consists of the front portion of a skull with a complete face and a crushed frontal bone. Arago 21 has massive brow ridges, a flat forehead, and a narrow, elongated brain case (Figure 19-3). The skull has traits reminiscent of Far East *H. erectus* specimens. Because of the absence of maxillary tooth wear, the skull is thought to belong to a young adult approximately 20 years old.

Two mandibles, probably belonging to a male and a female, were found in 1969 and 1970 at approximately the same level. Neither of them appears to be associated with the Arago 21 skull. The mandibles seem to have been prognathic, and there are indications of considerable chewing stress. The

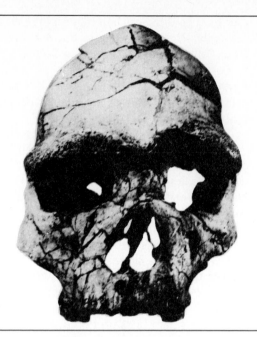

Figure 19-3 A skull from Arago cave, France. It shows a mixture of H. erectus *and* H. sapiens *traits.*

Arago 2 mandible may belong to a female, and it shows one of the earliest traces of a possible chin. The mandibles are considerably thicker than the older Mauer mandible.

The teeth of Arago 13 are among the largest found in the human fossil record, and the posterior dentition surpassed the size for *H. erectus.* The teeth of Arago 1 and 13 are large (Wolpoff, 1980). Arago's posterior dentition is reduced in size compared to that of *H. erectus.*

Among the most complete of the skulls dated to the Riss Glaciation, the Biache skull from France shows many similarities to the Swanscombe material. In addition to the parietal and occipital bones, the Biache fossils also include the back of the temporals (the bone found on the side of the skull), a palate and posterior teeth. Unlike Swanscombe, the Biache skull is flattened in the area where the occipital meets the parietals. The skull vault is small and fairly low, the area for nuchal (neck) muscle attachment is weakly developed, the occiput is rounded, and the mastoids are small. The Biache specimen may belong to a female.

The Steinheim skull and face (Figure 19-4) were found in 1935 from approximately 25 feet deep in a gravel pit located north of Stuttgart in West Germany. The material has been dated to roughly 250,000 years ago; however, the material may not be that old. There is considerable resemblance between the Steinheim and Swanscombe remains. The Steinheim skull was badly damaged behind the left eye; it also has a sizable hole in the base of the skull which suggests the possibility of cannibalism. The skull materials were associated with many nonhuman bones, but no tools were found.

As a result of being covered by wet earth before fossilization, the skull was warped and crushed. The left side, forward of the ear opening, had caved in, and much of the left side of the face was detached. The shape of the occipital bone is similar to that of Swanscombe, but the cranial capacity appears to be smaller. It is estimated at between 1,150 cubic centimeters and 1,175 cubic centimeters, similar to preceding *H. erectus* materials. The skull differs from *H. erectus* in several respects. The occipital bone is smoothly rounded, and the markings of the neck muscle attachments are slight and set low, like those of modern skulls. This indicates more gracile neck muscles.

Steinheim has heavy brow ridges and a low forehead, but the condition is not quite as archaic as that found among *H. erectus.* Although low, the forehead is fairly steep. Although large and heavy, the brow ridges are slightly separated over the nose. Steinheim's face is less prognathic than that of the Chinese *H. erectus* but more prognathic than that of modern populations. The nose also seems to have been rather broad.

The front teeth are missing, but the posterior teeth appear to be modern in size. The teeth are moderately taurodont; that is, there is a tendency toward an enlarged pulp cavity and perhaps fusion of the molar roots. Except for taurodontism, nothing notable distinguishes these teeth from those of modern Europeans.

Steinheim exhibits a combination of advanced and archaic traits. The skull is small and low, the cranial capacity is low, and the brow ridges are large. Along with these features typical of *H. erectus* are features of a more modern

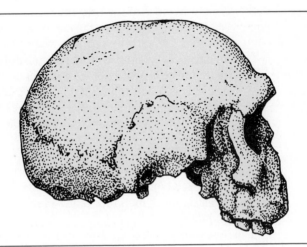

Figure 19-4 Early Homo sapiens *skull from Steinheim, West Germany. It is badly crushed, but it has modestly developed brow ridges and the teeth are small.*

aspect. The face is relatively small and has minimal prognathism. The skull also appears to be tucked under at the brow ridges. Maximal skull breadth is higher on the occiput than in earlier *H. erectus* specimens, indicating that although the skull is small, it morphologically approaches *H. sapiens.* The teeth are small, the third molar is reduced, and the occipital bone is rounded. All of these are modern features.

LIFE-WAYS

Two French sites provide the best data concerning the life-ways of early *Homo sapiens* populations. Arago Cave is located at the southern tip of the Corbieres Mountains, near the village of Tautavel in the Pyrenees. The fossil material from Arago dates to about 200,000 years ago. Arago is a large cave: It is 15 feet deep and 33 feet wide at its maximum. Nonhuman bones were recovered there as early as 1838. One cave level was formed during a dry, cold period when the cave was intermittently occupied. When it was abandoned, sand blew in, covering the human relics and providing a clean floor for subsequent inhabitants.

The de Lumleys (1973) hypothesize that the cave was inhabited by groups of prehistoric hunters who returned regularly to an established camp. The inhabitants lived in a dimly lit area, some distance from the cave's entrance, in a sandpit between a dune accumulating in the entry and another dune being formed at the cave's rear. The habitation areas are littered with bone fragments and flint or quartz tools; in some areas the abundance and disposition of the remains suggest a tool-making work area. In other areas are piles of bone debris more than 50 centimeters deep. There are stone slabs that the de Lumleys state were brought into the cave and may have been used by the inhabitants to avoid sinking into the sand. More than 100,000 artifacts were uncovered. Arago yielded many stone tools. Handaxes, an important component of *H. erectus* living sites, were rare.

One of the best examples of a later middle Pleistocene site is located at Terra Amata in the city of Nice on the French Riviera (de Lumley, 1969). The site, which dates to less than 300,000 years ago, was first uncovered in 1959 during construction of a shipyard. A few years later, during the building of apartments, bulldozers uncovered an extensive sandy deposit containing many tools.

Little is known about the physical appearance of the inhabitants of Terra Amata. The only clue is provided by an imprint of a right foot, 9.5 inches long, which is preserved in the sand. The individual who made the print is estimated to have been 5 feet, 1 inch tall. Some place the site with *H. erectus* and others with *H. sapiens.*

The landscape during the time of occupation was quite different than it is today. The backdrop of the Alps was much the same, but the seas reached further inland. Although temperate, the climate was brisker and more humid than it is today.

Superimposed living floors were uncovered in 3 separate locales: 4 on a beach section that formed a sandbar, 6 on the beach, and 11 on a dune island. On the slopes of an ancient sand dune, de Lumley uncovered the remains of a number of oval huts that ranged from 26 to 49 feet long and from 13 to 20 feet wide and may have housed 10 to 20 people. The huts may have been constructed of sturdy branches, bent to interlock at the top, with an entrance at one end and a hole in the top to allow smoke to escape. Presumably the branches were supported by posts, with rocks of varying sizes placed against the posts.

A basic feature of each hut was a hearth at its center. The hearths were usually shallow pits scooped from the sand, a foot or two in diameter. A low wall, made of piled pebbles, stood alongside the northwest quadrant of each hearth and may have served as a windscreen. Areas closest to the hearths were cleared of debris, indicating that people may have slept there. The hearths were apparently designed for rather small fires; however, judging from the larger accumulations of charcoal and ash, those located in the huts closest to the seas may have accommodated larger fires. Perhaps more people gathered in these huts, or perhaps it was just colder there because of the wind off the ocean.

Faunal remains include birds, turtles, and eight mammalian species. There is abundant evidence that the inhabitants were big-game hunters. Based on the relative abundance of the faunal remains, they preferentially hunted stag, elephant, wild boar, ibex, and Merck's rhinoceros. Most faunal remains were those of younger animals. There are also indications that the inhabitants ate oysters, mussels, and limpets, the shells of which are present. The presence of fish bones suggests that the Terra Amata inhabitants also fished.

The types of pollen present suggest that the inhabitants were seasonal migrants who arrived in late spring and early summer. Perhaps they chose the sheltered cove as a campsite because of the presence of nearby fresh water. On their arrival they erected huts and built hearths and windscreens. They probably hunted for a day or two, gathered seafood, and left. A short stay is indicated by the fact that the living floors do not show the signs of compaction characteristic of longer occupation, and by the fact that the huts probably collapsed soon after they were erected.

When either the previous year's inhabitants or new inhabitants visited the site the following year, little of the previous year's occupation floors remained. However, evidence suggests that the visitors erected their new huts on or near the old locations. Perhaps they found the old locations by using the previous year's hearth windscreens, which protruded above the sand, as landmarks. Eleven of the living floors are so precisely superimposed that they seem to represent 11 consecutive years of occupation. All this suggests that the inhabitants had a stable and fairly complex social organization.

Stone tools are abundant at the site. Some tools were probably locally made; the hut floors show evidence of tool-making activity. The tool maker's place in the hut is indicated by a patch of living floor surrounded by a litter of tool-manufacturing debris. There are also some bone implements.

Some domestic furnishings were also uncovered. Flattened limestone blocks may have provided convenient surfaces for sitting or for breaking animal bone. A semispherical imprint left on the sand dune is filled with a whitish substance, which may have been an impression left by a wooden bowl. If so, it would be the earliest trace of a container. Near the imprint, excavators found lumps of the natural pigment red ocher. The ends of several of these lumps were pointed and worn smooth, like a pencil. The "pencils" may have been used to color the body. Velo (1984) suggests that ocher could also have been used to treat wounds and to stem bleeding and to tan hides.

The red ocher found at Terra Amata is not the only evidence from this time period indicating possible artistic decoration. The earliest direct evidence of such decoration, perhaps art, is found in Riss-dated layers at Pech de l'Aze, France, along with an Acheulian tool complex. An engraving from Pech de l'Aze consists of a series of connected double arcs running from left to right. The marks were made by different tools, and perhaps at different times. Other simple marks were added, including a series of angles and double marks that resulted in a complex set of engravings. Although the marks are not completely understood, they may signify a complex cultural context (Marschak, 1972).

---

*Table 19-2. **Some Features Associated With Early** Homo sapiens*

Time Span The dating of many of these fossils is disputed. The time span usually given is from 300,000 to 100,000 years ago; however, at least one researcher suggests that Petralona may date to 800,000 years ago.

Distribution Africa, Asia, and Europe

Life-Ways They lived in caves and dwellings. They may have used aquatic foods and hunted big game. They may have decorated their bodies.

Anatomy These fossils are morphologically intermediate between the earlier *H. erectus* and the subsequent *H. sapiens* fossils. For this reason there is dispute over their taxonomic status.

      Cranial capacity: The largest is about 1,325 cubic centimeters. Average cranial capacity is 1,166 cubic centimeters—an 11 percent increase over that of *H. erectus*. Some early *H. sapiens'* cranial capacities are smaller than those of *H. erectus,* however.

      Face/skull: Some show reduced brow ridges; others show large brow ridges. Some show thinning of the skull bones; others show skull bones as thick as those of *H. erectus.*

Some forms have a low forehead and a flat skull vault like those of *H. erectus.* There is a marked decrease of robust musculature on the back of the skull of many of these forms. There is prognathism and a lack of a chin in all except possibly Arago 2. There is evidence of decreasing bulk of the chewing muscles. Many forms have immense molar and premolar teeth, while others show a reduction in molar and premolar tooth size.

      Postcranial: They were bipedal and had less robusticity in the lower limbs.

Different taxonomic assignments have been suggested to accommodate the fossil specimens discussed in this chapter. This lack of agreement is due to the facts that these specimens combine traits typical of both Homo erectus *and early* Homo sapiens, *and that the dating and context of many of these specimens is debated. Until we better understand the selective factors working on various anatomical complexes, we will be unable to positively attribute these specimens to one or the other species.*

Evidence of the life-ways of some of these fossils has been recorded in France. The site of Arago cave reveals artifacts. The site of Terra Amata has yielded information on dietary patterns, dwelling structures, and domestic furnishings. The evidence of the possible use of red ochre at Terra Amata is intriguing because of red ochre's potential role in artistic decoration.

BIBLIOGRAPHY

COON, C. 1962. *The Origin of Races.* New York: Knopf.

DE LUMLEY, H. 1969. A Paleolithic camp at Nice. *Scientific American* 220: 42–50.

DE LUMELY, H., and M. DE LUMLEY. 1973. Pre-Neanderthal human remains from Arago Cave in southeastern France. *Yearbook of Physical Anthropology* 17: 162–68.

HARMON, R., J. GLAZEK, and K. NOWACK. 1980. ^{230}Th/ ^{234}U dating of travertine from the Bilzingsleben archaeological site. *Nature* 284: 132–35.

HEMMER, H. 1972. Notes sur la position phylétique de l'homme de Petralona. *L'Anthropologie* 76: 155.

HENNING, G., W. HERR, E. WEBER, and N. XIROTIRIS. 1981. ESR-dating of the fossil hominid cranium from Petralona Cave, Greece. *Nature* 292: 533–36.

HOWELLS, W. 1973. *Evolution of the Genus Homo.* Reading, Mass.: Addison-Wesley.

KURTÉN, B. 1983. The age of Petralona Man. *Anthropos* 10: 16–17.

LEWIN, R. 1986. Recognizing ancestors is a species problem. *Science* 234: 1500.

MARSCHAK, A. 1972. *The Roots of Civilization.* New York: McGraw-Hill.

MURRILL, R. 1981. *Petralona Man: A Descriptive and Comparative Study, With New Information on Rhodesian Man.* Springfield, Ill.: Chas. C. Thomas.

MURRILL, R. 1983. On the dating of the fossil hominid Petralona skull. *Anthropos* 10: 12–15.

OAKLEY, K. 1952. Swanscombe man. *Proceedings of the Geological Association of London* 63: 271.

OVEY, C. (ed.). 1964. *The Swanscombe Skull: A Survey of Research on a Pleistocene Site.* London: Royal Anthropological Institute.

TATTERSALL, I. 1986. Species recognition in human paleontology. *Journal of Human Evolution* 15: 165–80.

VELO, J. 1984. Ochre as medicine: A suggestion for the interpretation of the archaeological record. *Current Anthropology* 25: 674.

VLČEK, E. 1978. A new discovery of *Homo erectus* in Central Europe. *Journal of Human Evolution* 7: 239–52.

WOLPOFF, M. 1980. *Paleoanthropology.* New York: Knopf.

Chapter

20

The Neanderthals

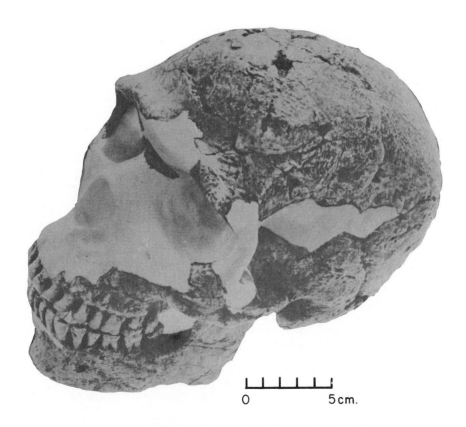

0   5 cm.

The remains of European Neanderthals were first recovered in the 1800s. Neanderthal remains have been and continue to be the source of considerable taxonomic debate. The Neanderthals are currently referred to either as **Homo sapiens neanderthalensis,** *making them direct ancestors to ourselves, or as* **Homo neanderthalensis,** *which would make them a side branch on the evolutionary line to modern* **Homo sapiens.** *The taxonomic argument has swung back and forth, but recent finds in the Middle East provide some of the strongest evidence for not including the Neanderthals in our own species. As noted in Chapter 21, there is evidence in Africa and the Middle East to suggest that modern* **Homo sapiens** *are not derived from a Neanderthal population.*

The Neanderthals are fairly well-known to researchers because of the array of the cultural remains they left behind. The tool assemblage commonly associated with European Neanderthals is called the Mousterian. For the first time in human history, there is evidence of extensive burials accompanied by rituals. This evidence is particularly intriguing at certain Middle Eastern sites.

Neanderthals are anatomically distinctive from modern humans because Neanderthals have larger cranial capacities, exhibit features of the facial skeleton suggesting strong chewing muscles, and some have a distinctive cranial morphology. These and other anatomical traits are most markedly shown in the colder regions of western Europe. Neanderthals in eastern Europe and the Middle East, those outside the influence of the western European glaciation, exhibit less robusticity in facial and skull traits.

THIRD INTERGLACIAL FOSSILS

A number of mostly fragmentary European fossil remains immediately precede the appearance of the Neanderthals. (See Table 20-1.) These remains date to the Third Interglacial period, about 150,000 years ago, and are found in France, Germany, and Italy. These hominids were once considered to be morphologically more modern than the succeeding western European Neanderthals and were used to support a separate and rather long-lived evolutionary line of modern *H. sapiens* in Europe. This position has been refuted, one reason being that anatomically modern humans seem to have evolved first in Africa and then perhaps migrated to Europe.

Third Interglacial remains from France come from the site of Fontéchevade, which yielded fragmentary remains of the skulls of two individuals. The Fontéchevade fragments most resemble the Swanscombe material in skull thickness.

The Ehringsdorf skull was found in Germany in 1925. The major remains consist of a parietal bone and a broken, faceless braincase. The cranial capacity is estimated at 1,450 cubic centimeters. The brow ridges are heavily built, as in Steinheim, but somewhat thicker and approach the size and shape found in later Neanderthals. The braincase is low and has a well-developed **occipital bun** (a bony protruberance at the rear of the skull), a characteristic that appears with regularity among later Neanderthals from western Europe. Ehringsdorf most closely resembles Steinheim and Swanscombe.

Table 20-1. **Fossils Belonging to the Neanderthals and Their Immediate Predecessors**

GEOGRAPHICAL AREA	SITE
Eemian (Riss-Würm) Interglacial Sample	
France	Fontéchevade
Germany	Ehringsdorf
Yugoslavia	Krapina
Würm Glacial Sample	
Central and Eastern Europe	
Yugoslavia	Vindija
Czechoslovakia	Ochoz, Sipka, Gánovce, Kůlna, Šala
Hungary	Subalyuk
Western Europe	
France	Hortus, La Ferrassie, Le Moustier, La Chapelle-aux-Saints, St. Césaire
Italy	Monte Circeo
Middle East	
Israel	Tabün, Skhül, Kebara, Pafzeh
Iraq	Shanidar
Asia	
China	Possibly Ma-pa (Ma-ba), Da-li (Ta-li), Changyang

The Yugoslavian site of Krapina yielded 800 shattered skull fragments, postcranial skeletal remains from practically every part of the body, 200 teeth, and more than 1,000 stone tools. (Figure 20-1). The dental and skeletal remains represent about 80 individuals. Krapina is the largest human fossil sample ever recovered from a single site. All adult skulls have a strong brow ridge development. (Figure 20-2). In some skull and jaw features the Krapina remains resemble those of the Neanderthals. The Krapina skulls exhibit

Figure 20-1 Stone tools from the Krapina site.

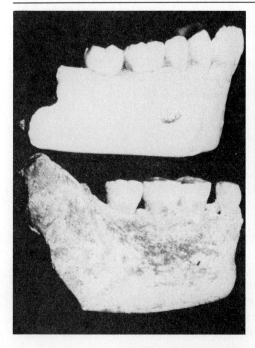

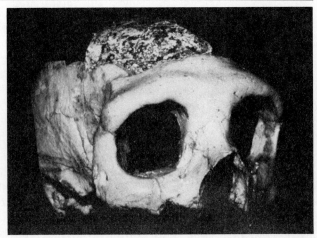

Figure 20-2 (Left) Two mandibles from Krapina, Yugoslavia. (Right) Partial skull and face from Krapina.

variation in some traits. In postcranial traits, the Krapina sample resembles the Neanderthals.

The bone breakage on the Krapina specimens was thought to indicate cannibalism, but Russell (1987a) refutes this contention. The breakage is more likely due to postdepositional events such as sedimentary pressure or roof falls. Russell (1987b) also presents evidence that the Krapina hominids were burying their dead with ceremony. The cut marks on the bones are consistent with a pattern of defleshing in preparation for secondary burial. Trinkaus (1985) also believes that the Krapina remains were buried. The Krapina remains "represent one of the oldest, as well as the largest samples of human burials yet known" (Trinkaus, 1985:213).

OVERVIEW: THE NEANDERTHALS

The Neanderthal fossil sample long confused anthropologists until the temporal, geographical, and cultural boundaries were delineated and the physical variability in the sample was analyzed and understood. The image maintained by many researchers in the early twentieth century of an overnight disappearance of the western European Neanderthals and their replacement by what seemed to be anatomically modern populations from outside Europe smacked of catastrophism.

By the 1950s, the image of the Neanderthals as savage or brutish was replaced with a newer characterization, typified by the following description (Howell, 1965:123):

> Of all the different kinds of prehistoric peoples, certainly the one who projects the clearest image is Neanderthal man. For most of us he is Stone Age man, the squat, shaggy, beetle-browed fellow that inevitably comes to mind when we think of our ancient relatives. We see him standing in the mouth of a cave—stone axe in hand, a few rough furs over his shoulder, some mammoth bones piled in the background—staring out over a snow-choked landscape as he ponders the ever-present problems of the ice age.

This image of the Neanderthal has persisted. The Neanderthals exhibited morphological differences from modern humans. Some of them lived in caves and wore skins; some inhabited cold, harsh climates. The first fossil skull positively identified as belonging to an ancient human was that of a Neanderthal. With nothing to compare it to but the skulls of modern humans, scientists were struck by the differences between them.

The discovery of the first Neanderthal remains occurred around the time of the publication of Darwin's evolutionary theory. Because of the timing of their discovery, Neanderthal remains drew more attention than they might otherwise have. Researchers began to search for the so-called missing link; the Neanderthals filled that vacuum. They were characterized as big, burly, and hairy, with sloping heads and backs—club-wielding creatures dragging their mates to caves.

The term *Neanderthal* refers to a quiet valley in western Germany. This was a favorite spot of Dusseldorf composer Joachim Newmann, who signed some of his works *Neander,* the Greek translation of his name. After his death, local inhabitants began to call the valley, spelled *thal* in German, Neanderthal—Neander's valley. The valley has since lent its name to a major group of human fossils.

A few Neanderthal finds came to light in the late 1800s. In 1866 a jaw in association with a **Mousterian** cultural assemblage was recovered from a Belgian cave. Darwin described this find in *The Descent of Man.* Skulls were later recovered (Figure 20-4). Most early finds were considered to be the remains of individuals who suffered from some kind of physical deformity which gave them their distinctive appearance.

The years prior to World War I witnessed the recovery of much European Neanderthal material, most coming from southwestern France. Other finds came from Spain, Italy, southeastern Europe, Russia, and the Middle East (Figure 20-3). French paleontologist M. Boule described the material in detail, but erroneously noted what he considered to be its highly uniform, specialized nature. Until the 1930s it was assumed that the European Neanderthals were slowly driven to extinction by subsequent populations, specifically the modern-looking populations in the Middle East.

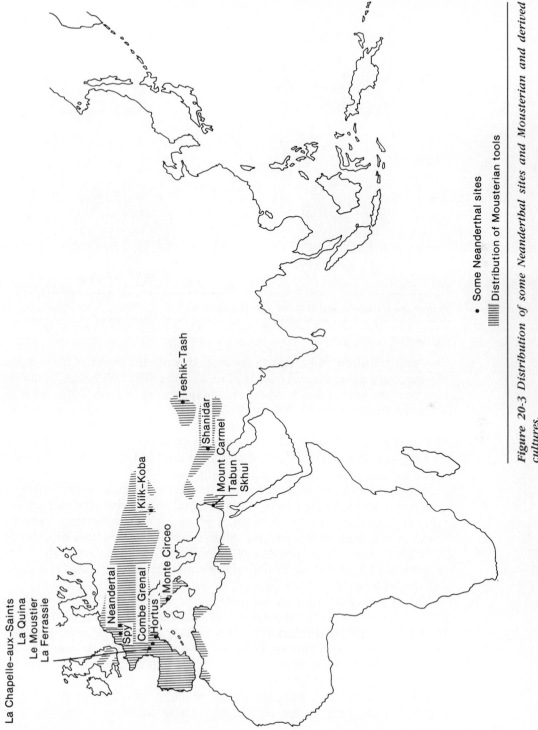

La Chapelle-aux-Saints
La Quina
Le Moustier
La Ferrassie

Neandertal
Spy
Combe Grenal
Hortus
Monte Circeo

Kiik–Koba

Teshik-Tash

Shanidar

Mount Carmel
Tabun
Skhul

• Some Neanderthal sites
▥ Distribution of Mousterian tools

Figure 20-3 Distribution of some Neanderthal sites and Mousterian and derived cultures.

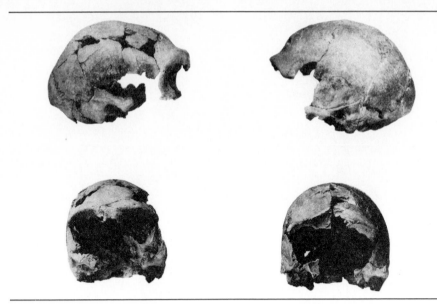

Figure 20-4 Human skulls from Spy, Belgium.

Lifeways

The tool tradition most closely associated with the Neanderthals is the Mousterian, a name derived from the French village of Le Moustier, where the type site (the site to which others are compared) is located. Dates from Le Moustier range from 58,000 to 42,000 years ago. The Mousterian tool tradition is characterized by the development of prepared core techniques for tool production. Stone tools were made from flakes produced by precisely striking thin, fine flakes of a predetermined size and shape. The core from which the flake was removed was not the primary tool.

Mousterian tools are characterized by careful manufacture, which may have been due to an increased number of skilled craftsmen producing new artifact types to accommodate a wider range of activities. Although similar tools are found in northern Africa and the Middle East, the European Mousterian includes a greater proportion and diversity of highly refined tools. The geographical range of Mousterian implements is primarily limited to Europe and the Middle East.

Not all European Neanderthal remains are associated with a Mousterian cultural assemblage. The latest-appearing Neanderthal is the skeleton excavated at St. Césaire, in southwestern France, dating to only 32,000 years ago. Tools associated with this anatomically Neanderthal type belonged to the Upper Paleolithic assemblage usually found with the *H. s. sapiens* populations that followed the Neanderthals.

Certain Neanderthal implements were probably used for hide preparation and butchering. Points—broad, triangular, retouched flakes—may have been tied to wooden spears to improve their penetrating power. Stone balls may have been used as bolas. Skins could have been used as rawhide lashings and thongs. Neanderthals may have trapped their prey; evidence from the Neanderthal site at Shanidar Cave, Iraq, suggests that animals were slaughtered by running grazing herds either over cliffs or into blind canyons.

Neanderthals were big-game hunters, and animal meat may have provided a large portion of their dietary intake. Evidence from such open-air sites as Lebenstedt, Germany, supports the assumption that during the summer some Neanderthal groups followed herds of grazing animals northward onto the open tundras. There is some evidence to suggest that Neanderthals were also scavengers, raiding the kills of other predators. Some Neanderthal groups may have adapted to a life-style involving seasonal movement, following herds into the forest in winter and returning with them onto the broad tundra expanse in summer. Other Neanderthal groups appeared to be sedentary; some sites in southwestern France were probably occupied year-round. Perhaps migration was confined to marginal populations inhabiting tundra fringes, whereas groups in less severe climates and where good shelter was available were basically sedentary. Seasonal movement seems to be a localized adaptation to certain environmental stresses.

Faunal remains associated with Neanderthal assemblages indicate the success of the Neanderthal hunters. The wooly mammoth and rhinoceros were successfully hunted; the presence of fish and bird remains at the Lebenstedt site underscores the Neanderthals' hunting success. At the Drachenhöhle site (Dragon's Cave) at Mixnitz, Austria, it appears that hibernating bears, including females with young, were attacked and killed on numerous occasions.

For the first time in the fossil record, the Neanderthals present an extensive record of deliberate burial accompanied by ritualistic behavior. Burials have been found in western and eastern Europe, Iraq, and central Asia. The French sites of Le Moustier (dating 56,000 to 40,000 years ago), La Ferrassie, and La Chapelle-aux-Saints (dating 75,000 to 60,000 years ago) yield Neanderthal burials. A male of between 15 and 20 years of age was buried in a cave at Le Moustier. He was lowered into a trench on his right side, his knees slightly drawn and his head resting on his forearm. Several stone implements and charred animal bones were buried with him.

One of the most interesting of the many Neanderthal burials is at Shanidar Cave, Iraq (Solecki, 1971). It has been argued that one Shanidar skeleton may have been buried with flowers. Pollen analysis suggests that the floral remains were small, brightly colored wild flowers. The flower burial was an unexpected find. "With the finding of flowers in association with Neanderthals, we are brought suddenly to the realization that the universality of mankind and the love of beauty go beyond the boundary of our species. No longer can we deny the early men the full range of human feelings and experience" (Solecki, 1971:250). However, others argue that the bones and flowers are not contemporaneous (Gargett, 1989).

Burials mark a new stage in human evolution; life and death seemingly held new value. Burial implies a concern for the deceased. Such concern is further suggested by the recovery of individuals who survived serious injuries and who must have been cared for by their contemporaries. Perhaps the individuals who received this care had special knowledge of magic, rituals, or hunting techniques, which indicates a complex and extensive social organization.

THE NEANDERTHAL FOSSIL SAMPLE

Western European Neanderthals

Western European Neanderthals were a heterogeneous group (See Table 20-2 on p. 402). Wolpoff (1980) attributes much of the skeletal variation to sexual dimorphism. Cranial capacities were large, ranging from 1,525 cubic centimeters to 1,640 cubic centimeters in 6 male skulls and 1,300 to 1,425 cubic centimeters in the smaller female skulls. The skulls were larger than those in modern populations and may have accommodated a larger brain than is common among modern *Homo sapiens.* The larger Neanderthal brains, compared with those of modern populations, may be related to the Neanderthal's heavier body and to the fact that cranial capacity averages for modern populations include a much more heterogeneous and larger sample than that which characterizes the western European Neanderthals. The Neanderthal skull was shaped differently; it had a low crown and achieved its interior shape by bulging on the side and back. A fairly characteristic trait is the presence of an occipital bun at the rear of the skull.

Four features distinguish the European Neanderthal's face: a receding chin, or no chin; large cheek bones; prominent brow ridges connected across the nasal bridge; and a rather large nasal cavity. The jaws are large and suggest strong muscle attachments. Certain dental traits suggest that the Neanderthals might have used their teeth as tools. Neanderthal incisors, which are broader than those in modern populations, may have been important tools in environmental manipulation. As such, they required robust roots and supporting structures, features seen in the Neanderthal fossils.

The Neanderthal face is extraordinarily robust. Rak (1986) suggests that the reason for this robustness is mechanical; the face is constructed to counteract the considerable forces that Neanderthals developed between their upper and lower teeth. Prior to Rak's suggestion, two other reasons were offered for the robustness of the Neanderthal face. The first explanation, developed in the 1950s, argued that the enlarged nasal chamber was a response to cold stress. The second proposal appeared in the 1960s and invoked dental biomechanics as the selective agent for the protruding face. Rak's model is an extension of this proposal. Neanderthals have very large canines and incisors relative to their molars and premolars. Individuals exhibit very heavy wear on the front teeth, indicating that heavy chewing stresses (perhaps because of chewing hides or other materials) were at work. Rak feels that the Neanderthal's face is morphologically more similar to preceding humans than to the subsequent *H. s. sapiens.*

The presence of an occipital bun, or chignon at the back of the skull, has long been considered a diagnostic Neanderthal trait. Occipital bunning appears to have attained its highest incidence among western European Neanderthals. There is variation even among these forms, however, with some forms having large, projecting buns and others having relatively small buns.

The presence of an occipital bun does not automatically indicate inclusion in the western European Neanderthal sample. An occipital bun also appears among earlier European, African, and European Upper Paleolithic samples. Some Middle Eastern Neanderthals exhibited buns, and some evidence of a bun also appears in recent humans.

Various interpretations have been forthcoming concerning the origin or function of the occipital bun. Trinkaus and Le May (1982) suggest that the occipital bun is dependent on the timing of brain growth relative to the sequence of the development of the bones of the skull vault. An occipital bun may result from a significant increase in brain size relatively late in the normal development of the childhood brain, especially in relation to the growth patterns of the skull bones. The occipital bun is a product of normal human neurocranial development, and only the high incidence and large size of the occipital bun among some Neanderthals is unique to Neanderthals. Trinkaus and LeMay suggest that the occipital bun is related to a slightly delayed pattern of brain growth relative to the timetable of modern humans. An additional contributory factor in the incidence of the occipital bun may be the relatively large brain size of many of the individuals exhibiting a bun.

Postcranial skeletons of European Neanderthals suggest that they were powerfully built, stood over 5 feet tall, and weighed up to 160 pounds. Their extremities were short compared with those of modern populations. A preserved Neanderthal footprint in the wet clay of an Italian cave shows that their feet were structurally similar to ours.

Some western European Neanderthal traits might be adaptations to cold weather. Nasal prognathism, for example, is seen as an adaptation to the cold conditions found throughout southwestern Europe at the time of Neanderthal habitation. The size and shape of the nose are related to the function of warming and moistening inspired air (Steegman, 1972). Nasal breadth is also affected by the breadth between the canines, because the roots of these teeth run along the sides of the nose. Among Neanderthals, the breadth between the canines is large because of the large incisors. This feature may also account for the large nasal breadths in early *H. sapiens* samples. Thus, there was a background of broad nasal openings in *H. sapiens* even before the emergence of cold-adapted Neanderthals, (Wolpoff, 1980).

There is a rough gradient of what are considered Neanderthal traits; the most extreme expressions are prevalent in the cold regions of Europe and diminish to the south and east into the Middle East. Western European Neanderthal populations are most readily identified because western Europe is where climatic selection was maximized.

Central and Eastern European Neanderthals

Neanderthal finds from eastern and central Europe are extremely important. Neanderthal remains from this area of Europe have blurred the boundary between western European Neanderthals and fully modern *H. sapiens* populations. Major eastern and central European Neanderthal fossils come from Czechoslovakia, Yugoslavia, and Hungary. Some refer to these fossils specimens as transitional specimens between modern and Neanderthal populations.

Vindija Cave, Yugoslavia (Figure 20-5), yielded 88 human specimens which are, unfortunately, in a fragmentary state. The earliest stratigraphic layer at Vindija dates from 40,000 to 32,000 years ago. The Vindija human remains can be divided into three groups. The first group of 34 specimens belongs to the modern subspecies of *H. s. sapiens*. The only remarkable feature of this group is the somewhat unusually thick cranial vault. The second group contains 4 specimens which are morphologically close to the Neanderthals, but they could also be accommodated within an early *H. s. sapiens* sample. The third group of 40 specimens is placed within the Neanderthals. In some

Figure 20-5 The Vindija cave site, Yugoslavia.

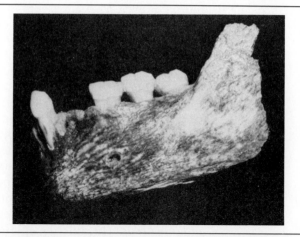

Figure 20-6 A mandible from the Vindija cave site. (Courtesy The Yugoslavian Academy of Sciences and the Arts; photo by Dr. F.H. Smith.)

respects, however, they are intermediate between the central European early *H. s. sapiens* condition and older central European Neanderthals. Those specimens preserving the brow region exhibit a characteristic Neanderthal ridge in all adults.

The Vindija Neanderthals represent an intermediate condition between most central European Neanderthals and early *H. s. sapiens.*

> [The] existence of such a group of comparatively late-dated Neanderthals, along with the Neanderthal-reminiscent morphology exhibited by certain early Upper Paleolithic specimens, . . . strengthens the hypothesis of a direct ancestral position for at least central European *H. sapiens neanderthalensis* in the lineage of *H. sapiens sapiens* in Europe. [Malez et al., 1980:367]

Not all researchers agree.

To varying degrees, central and eastern European Neanderthals display many traits found in anatomically modern populations. Chronologically, this fossil sample extends to the time period in which some of the oldest finds of fully modern *H. sapiens* appear. Furthermore, even those forms in this sample that are designated fully modern *H. sapiens* exhibit cultural and morphological links to the past.

The central European sample shows typical Neanderthal traits (Smith, 1982). The only systematic difference that appears to exist between western European and early central European Neanderthals is in average body size. Postcranial remains from central Europe are smaller, but this may be due to an overabundance of subadult material from one site.

Late Neanderthal material from central Europe has basically the same morphological pattern as the early sample. The late sample approaches the early *H. s. sapiens* anatomical condition to a consistently greater degree than the early group, however. The late group, for example, shows a reduction in certain facial features. The early modern *H. sapiens* sample from central Europe exhibits several traits that indicate a close connection with central European Neanderthals. There is considerable morphological similarity between early *H. s. sapiens* and late Neanderthal specimens from central Europe.

This later transition to *H. s. sapiens* in Western Europe leaves open the possibility that gene flow from outside western Europe was responsible for the anatomical change to *H. s. sapiens* in western Europe. This is an old puzzle that has not been resolved. Rak (1986) contends that the anatomy of the western European Neanderthal face precludes their being our direct ancestor. A case has been made that the change through time in the Neanderthal tool assemblage indicates such a basic difference between their intellect and that of modern *H. sapiens* that the former should not be considered a member of our species. That is, they should be classified *Homo neanderthalensis* and not *H. sapiens neanderthalensis.* The differing opinions about classification have not yet been resolved.

Middle Eastern Neanderthals

Many factors contributed to making the Middle East an evolutionary focal point. Game has always been abundant, and its concentration in the Middle East seems to have allowed rather heavy local human population centers to develop. A climatic shift to somewhat drier conditions at approximately 45,000 to 40,000 years ago led to local concentrations of grazing animals and their hunters. The richest human fossil sites are in areas where vegetation and game were most abundant—in the valleys along the western slopes of the coastal ranges, for example.

Middle Eastern specimens such as the es-Skhūl 5 skull (Figure 20-7) from Israel closely approach anatomically modern *H. sapiens;* other specimens, such as et-Tabūn from Israel and Shanidar I from Iraq, which date to an earlier time, anatomically approach western European Neanderthals. Some researchers consider Middle Eastern forms to be examples of a Neanderthal group transitional to *H. s. sapiens.*

The human fossil site at Mount Carmel, Israel, is located 12 miles from Haifa. The two major sites at Mount Carmel are the cave of et-Tabūn and the cave of es-Skhūl. Skulls found in both caves show pronounced brow ridges; however, they display remarkable variability in the degree of development of other features typically associated with Neanderthals. In some anatomical respects they rather closely resemble *H. s. sapiens.*

Tabūn cave yielded a male mandible and a female skeleton dated to between 50,000 and 60,000 years ago, although there is a suggestion that some et-Tabūn specimens may date to 70,000 to 80,000 years ago. The et-Tabūn woman had a low skull, arched brows, and a heavy, continuous brow ridge like her western European contemporaries. She lacked an occipital bun; her cranial capacity is estimated at 1,270 cubic centimeters, and her mandible lacks a chin. The male

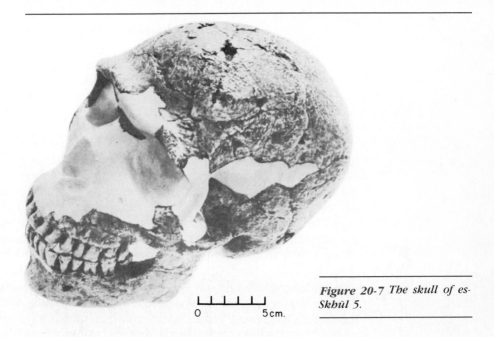

L_____L_____L_____L_____L
0   5 cm.

Figure 20-7 The skull of es-Skhūl 5.

mandible is large, deep, and rather square in front. Morphologically, the et-Tabūn material falls between the central and western European Neanderthals and possesses some traits seen at et-Skhūl.

The es-Skhūl cave site contained 10 skeletons in various states of preservation. Originally thought to be contemporaneous with et-Tabūn, the es-Skhūl remains seem to have been deposited about 10,000 years later, following a climatic interval that included the local disappearance of hippopotamuses and rhinoceroses. The et-Tabūn group manifests some classic Neanderthal traits, but remains from es-Skhūl show a general similarity to *H. s. sapiens.* The es-Skhūl brain cases are similar to those of modern humans in size and shape. They are high, round, and lack an occipital bun. The frontal bone is reminiscent of earlier Neanderthals; the brows are large, but they are not heavy or bulbous like those of earlier Neanderthals. The mandible has a chin, and the incisor teeth are large.

We have, fairly late in time, a Neanderthal population (et-Tabūn) giving way to a more modern form as typified by es-Skhūl skull number 5. The es-Skhūl remains are morphologically and temporally closer to modern *H. sapiens* than are the et-Tabūn remains. It has been suggested that such a population as et-Tabūn was replaced by a more modern population like that at es-Skhūl.

Although there are suggestions based on the archaeological and human remains found in the Mount Carmel caves that *H. s. neanderthalensis* evolved into *H. s. sapiens,* the more recently excavated Kebara cave in the same region casts doubt on this possibility (Valladas et al., 1987 a & b). Kebara cave is located about 15 kilometers south of et-Tabun Cave and contains a well-dated archaeological and human burial assemblage. The archaeological material is dated to about 62,000 to 52,000 years ago, older than previously thought for this part of the world. If the Neanderthals arrived late to this part of the world, then an evolutionary line from the Neanderthals to the earliest *H. s. sapiens* here would be a less likely possibility because the Neanderthals would have arrived after *H. s. sapiens* was already becoming established. (see pages 400-401).

Shanidar is a huge cave in the western Zagros Mountains of northern Iraq that has been occupied for about 60,000 years. Due to local earthquakes or the formation of ice on the ceiling, limestone slabs have periodically plummeted from the cave roof, killing many of the cave's inhabitants. The remains of a number of inhabitants who occupied the cave from 60,000 to 46,000 years ago are available for study. An infant's skeleton was found in 1953; in 1957 three adult skeletons were recovered; and in 1960 three more skeletons were found.

Four adults from Shanidar, numbers 1, 3, 4, and 5, exhibit evidence of predeath traumas. Shanidar number 3 seems to have been killed by a projectile point embedded in his ribs. He was subsequently buried against the cave wall. Shanidar number 1, a partial skeleton, is one of the most severely traumatized human fossils known. He suffered multiple fractures of the skull, right humerus, toes, right knee, and ankle, and also suffered from degenerative joint disease which might have been trauma related. Shanidar 1 shows signs of having had his right arm amputated. He was severely wounded by blows from some sharp instrument around and above the right eye. Despite these infirmities, which probably affected his ability to contribute to the social group, he survived and apparently died after being crushed by a slab of falling limestone.

A critical factor in understanding these traumas is the age of demise of these individuals. All four died at what at that time was a relatively advanced age. The average age of the four Shanidar adults was about 40 years old. The high prevalence of traumas may be largely a reflection of the number of elderly individuals in the sample.

The risk of injury seems to have been high among this population. Every currently available Neanderthal skeleton of advanced age shows bone trauma. The fact that individuals suffered such traumas suggests that Neanderthal life was harsh. On the other hand, the fact that they survived despite these injuries suggests that the disabled individuals were cared for by other members of the group. Shanidar 1 and 3, for instance, lived many years with severely debilitating injuries which would have prevented their normal participation in contributing to the group's survival. Perhaps they contributed in an indirect way to the group's well-being.

Based on their burial practices and on the fact that the Neanderthal sample at Shanidar cave and La-Chapelle-aux-Saints in France, which dates between 75,000 to 60,000 years ago, shows physical incapacitation, much has been made of what appears to be altruistic behavior among the Neanderthals.

Tappen (1985), however, chides those who overemphasize this apparent altruism. His close examination of the dentition of the Neanderthal skeleton belonging to the so-called old man (aged 40 to 45 years) from La Chapelle casts doubt upon overly ambitious attempts to document altruism. It had been argued that the "old man" had lost many of his teeth before death, and that someone prepared his food before giving it to him. Tappen argues, however, that the tooth loss suffered by La Chapelle-aux-Saints occurred after death and could not, therefore, have been a factor affecting his survival. La Chapelle may have been able to chew with moderate effectiveness up to the time of his death. Tappen argues that since the case for altruism is weak with regard to La Chapelle-aux-Saints, it may also be weak in other instances. For example, Tappen (1985:50) notes that "evidence of advanced social organization and cultural capacities is strikingly tenuous."

The skull contours of Shanidar 1 and 5 suggest deliberate cranial deformation (Trinkaus, 1982b). The most noticeable features of their cranial vaults are the flattened frontal region and parietal curvature, features commonly associated with cranial deformation among recent humans. The inferred presence of artificial cranial deformation among the Shanidar Neanderthals suggests the possibility of a heretofore poorly documented personal esthetic sense. The appearance of cranial deformation at the same time in human evolution as the first evidence of intentional burial of the dead and prolonged survival of the infirmed suggests a behavioral pattern allied with that of early anatomically modern humans.

Possible Chinese Neanderthals

The Ma-pa (or Ma-ba) skullcap was recovered from a cave in southern China in 1958. It may be contemporaneous with the European Neanderthals, with whom it shares some traits. The skullcap consists of the frontal, parietal, and nasal bones, and the lower border of the right eye socket. A number of Chinese paleontologists doubt that Ma-pa is a Neanderthal.

The Da-li (or Ta-li) cranium (Figure 20-8) appears to be a more complete version of the Ma-pa skullcap. The Da-li cranium may date between 71,000 to 41,000 years ago. However, an age estimate of 250,000 to 128,000 years ago has also been suggested. The skull presents a mosaic of archaic and more advanced traits.

EVOLUTIONARY RELATIONSHIPS

There is considerable disagreement about the meaning of the skeletal variation between the western and eastern European Neanderthal samples and between the former and some Near Eastern fossil assemblages. Morphologically, some of the Neanderthal specimens from eastern and central Europe and the Middle East are intermediate between the earliest *H. sapiens* and the earliest *H. s. sapiens* populations.

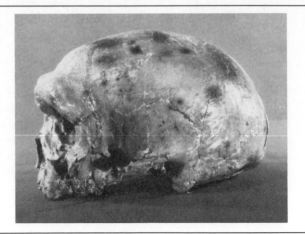

Figure 20-8 Side view of the Da-li cranium and face.

The European Neanderthals were replaced by modern *H. sapiens* populations about 35,000 years ago. Some European remains postdating the Neanderthals continue to show such Neanderthal traits as large brow ridges and large teeth. The continuance of such traits may be due to genetic admixture with the Neanderthals, or they may be retentions from more primitive ancestors elsewhere. Similarly, the more advanced traits found in some Neanderthal populations in eastern Europe and Asia may be the result of evolution or genetic infiltration from a more modern contemporaneous population. A skull fragment from Hanofersand, West Germany, dated to 36,000 years ago, has been interpreted as a Neanderthal–modern *H. sapiens* hybrid.

While the European Neanderthals retained a number of archaic traits, there are specimens in Africa and the Middle East that are clearly members of our subspecies, *H. s. sapiens*. Based on new evidence from the Middle East, for example, it is quite possible that *H. s. sapiens* populations moved out of Africa and into the Middle East and then entered Europe. The earliest *H. s. sapiens* samples date between 120,000 to 90,000 years ago and come from eastern and southern Africa (Stringer and Andrews, 1988). (They are discussed in the next chapter.)

Europe may have been a backwater in terms of human evolution. Stringer and Andrews (1988) contend that the Neanderthals genetically contributed little or nothing to modern populations. Because modern *H. sapiens* in Africa predates the Neanderthals, the notion that the Neanderthals evolved into modern humans is thrown into question. Stringer and Andrews argue that there is no evidence in any part of the world for a morphological transition from the Neanderthals to modern *H. sapiens*.

There is evidence of stone tools and human remains from Qafzeh Cave in Israel that also suggests that *H. s. sapiens* evolved outside of Europe (Stringer,

1987; Valladas et al., 1987a,b). This evidence dates to about 92,000 years ago and suggests that *H. s. sapiens* lived in the Middle Eastern region for at least twice as long as was generally accepted. This evidence conflicts with the suggestion that a Neanderthal population, such as that found at et-Tabūn, dated to perhaps 55,000 years ago, evolved into a modern population, such as that found at es-Skhūl and dated about 10,000 years later than et-Tabūn. The Qafzeh Cave evidence appears to establish that some *H. s. sapiens* preceded the Neanderthals in the Middle East. Therefore, the evolutionary model of Neanderthals evolving into *H. s. sapiens* lacks credence.

Prior to the discoveries at Qafzeh cave, Neanderthals were most commonly viewed as members of our own species. They are distinguished from modern humans by a subspecies designation—that is, they are called *Homo sapiens neanderthalensis.* However, if the dating at Qafzeh holds, and if the view that all modern humans can be traced to a rather recent African ancestry (on the order of 200,000 years ago) holds, these facts have implications for the classification of the Neanderthals. If Neanderthals and members of the modern species of *Homo sapiens* lived in the Levant and maintained their separate gene pools for at least 60,000 years before the Neanderthals were replaced by modern *Homo sapiens* in Europe, then the Neanderthals and modern *Homo sapiens* are members of separate species and not separate subspecies. If there was genetic separation for a long period of time, as is suggested at Qafzeh, then the Neanderthals should be classified as *Homo neanderthalensis* rather than *Homo sapiens neanderthalensis.*

It is still quite unclear why, if *H. s. sapiens* evolved in Africa by at least 100,000 years ago, they took so long to reach Europe and replace the European Neanderthals. Perhaps there was a climatic impediment to movement into Europe. Perhaps early *H. s. sapiens* populations entered Europe and we have yet to find their remains. There is also evidence to suggest that the Neanderthal tool tradition, the Mousterian, remained virtually unchanged over a long time period, in marked contrast to the speed with which the *H. s. sapiens* tool industries changed. This may suggest a fundamental difference in Neanderthal and *H. s. sapiens* societies, making it difficult for some investigators to accept that the Neanderthals evolved into modern humans.

When they were first recovered, the significance of the European Neanderthals and their role in the evolution of H. s. sapiens *was uncertain and subject to much debate. That condition still obtains. Some researchers categorize the Neanderthals within the subspecies* H. s. neanderthalensis, *which would place them within our evolutionary lineage. Others argue that the Neanderthals are a separate species,* H. neanderthalensis, *outside of our immediate evolutionary lineage. There is fossil and genetic evidence to suggest that* H. s. sapiens *arose outside of Europe, in Africa, and that the Neanderthals should be excluded from the* H. s. sapiens *evolutionary lineage.*

Table 20-2 Some Features Associated with Neanderthals

Time Span	Approximately 75,000 to 35,000 years ago.
Distribution	Primarily in Europe and the Middle East, possibly in Asia and Africa.
Life-Ways	They used the Mousterian tool tradition, which is characterized by the development of the prepared core technique. They were big-game hunters. They buried their dead and may have used personal ornamentation.
Anatomy	Varies somewhat depending upon location. Western European Neanderthals are the most robust members of the sample.
Cranial Capacity:	1,525–1,640 cubic centimeters for males; 1,270–1,425 cubic centimeters for females.
Face/skull:	In many European forms the skull is low and has a flat crown. In some Middle Eastern forms the skull has a high crown. An occipital bun is quite common, especially in European fossils. Large brow ridges are common in many fossils. Nasal prognathism is common to Western European forms. Chin is receding or absent. Jaws are large and robust. Anterior teeth are broader than those found in modern populations.
Postcranial:	Short and powerfully built.

BIBLIOGRAPHY

BINFORD, S. 1968. Early Upper Pleistocene adaptations in the Levant. *American Anthropologist* 70: 707.

BORDAZ, J. 1968. *The Old Stone Age.* New York: McGraw-Hill.

BRACE, C. 1962. Refocusing on the Neanderthal problem. *American Anthropologist* 64: 729–41.

BRACE, C. 1964. The fate of the "classic" Neanderthals: A consideration of hominid catastrophism. *Current Anthropology* 65: 3–43.

BRACE, C. 1968. Ridiculed, rejected, but still our ancestor, Neanderthal. *Natural History* 77: 38–42.

BRACE, C. 1971. Digging Shanidar. *Natural History* 80: 82.

BRAUER, H. 1984. The "Afro-European *sapiens* hypothesis," and hominid evolution in East Asia during the late middle and upper Pleistocene. In *The Early Evolution of Man,* P. Andrews and J. Franzen, eds. Frankfurt: Senckenberg Museum.

BROSE, D., and M. WOLPOFF. 1971. Early upper Paleolithic man and late Paleolithic tools. *American Anthropologist* 73: 1156–94.

CAMPBELL, B. 1976. *Humankind Emerging.* Boston: Little, Brown.

DEMES, B. 1987. Another look at an old face: Biomechanics of the Neanderthal facial skeleton reconsidered. *Journal of Human Evolution* 16: 297–303.

DENNELL, R. 1983. A new chronology for the Mousterian. *Nature* 301: 199–200.

GARGETT, R. 1989. Grave shortcomings: The evidence for Neanderthal burials. *Current Anthropology* 30: 157-90.

GREENE, D., and L. SIBLEY. 1986. Neanderthal pubic morphology and gestation length revisited. *Current Anthropology* 27: 517–18.

HOWELL, F. 1951. The place of Neanderthal man in human evolution. *American Journal of Physical Anthropology* 9: 379–416.

Howell, F. 1957. Pleistocene glacial ecology and the evolution of "classical Neanderthal" man. *Quarterly Review of Biology* 32: 330–47.

Howell, F. 1960. European and Northwest African middle Pleistocene hominids. *Current Anthropology* 1: 195–232.

Howell, F. 1965. *Early Man.* New York: Time-Life Books.

Howells, W. 1974. Neanderthals: Names, hypotheses, and scientific method. *American Anthropologist* 76: 24–38.

Howells, W. 1976. Explaining modern man: Evolutionist versus migrationist. *Journal of Human Evolution* 5: 477–95.

Jelinek, J. 1969. Neanderthal man and *Homo sapiens* in central and eastern Europe. *Current Anthropology* 10: 475–503.

Jelinek, J. 1976. A contribution to the origin of *Homo sapiens sapiens. Journal of Human Evolution* 5: 497–500.

Jelinek, J. 1982. The Tabūn cave and Paleolithic man in the Levant. *Science* 216: 1369–75.

Jolly, C., and F. Plog. 1976. *Physical Anthropology and Archaeology.* New York: Knopf.

Keith, A., and T. McCown. 1939. *The Stone Age of Mount Carmel,* vol. 2. Oxford: Clarendon Press.

Kennedy, K. 1975. *Neanderthal Man.* Minneapolis: Burgess.

Leroi-Gourhan, A. 1975. The flowers found with Shanidar IV, a Neanderthal burial in Iraq. *Science* 190: 562.

Lewin, R. 1986. A new look at an old fossil face. *Science* 234: 1326.

Lewin, R. 1988. Modern human origins under close scrutiny. *Science* 239: 1240–41.

Malez, M., et al. 1980. Upper Pleistocene hominids from Vindija, Croatia, Yugoslavia. *Current Anthropology* 21: 365–67.

McCown, T., and A. Keith. 1939. *The Stone Age of Mount Carmel,* vol. 1. Oxford: Clarendon Press.

Mellars, P. 1973. The character of the middle-upper Paleolithic transition in southwest France. In *The Explanation of Culture Change,* C. Renfrew, ed. London: Duckworth.

Mellars, P. 1986. A new chronology for the French Mousterian period. *Nature* 322: 410–11.

Poirier, F. 1987. *Understanding Human Evolution.* Englewood Cliffs, N.J.: Prentice Hall.

Rak, Y. 1986. The Neanderthals: A new look at an old face. *Journal of Human Evolution.* 15: 151–64.

Rak, Y., and B. Arensburg. 1987. Kebara 2 Neanderthal pelvis: First look at a complete inlet. *American Journal of Physical Anthropology* 70: 227–31.

Russell, M. 1987a. Bone breakage in the Krapina hominid collection. *American Journal of Physical Anthropology* 72: 373–79.

Russell, M. 1987b. Mortuary practices at the Krapina Neanderthal site. *American Journal of Physical Anthropology* 72: 381–97.

Schoeninger, M. 1982. Diet and evolution of modern human form in the Middle East. *American Journal of Physical Anthropology* 58: 37–53.

Sergi, S. 1967. The Neanderthal palaeanthropi in Italy. In *Selected Essays 1949–61,* W. Howells, ed. New York: Atheneum.

Smith, F. 1982. Upper Pleistocene hominid evolution in south-central Europe: A review of the evidence and analysis of trends. *Current Anthropology* 23: 667–86.

Solecki, R. 1971. *Shanidar: The First Flower People.* New York: Knopf.

Steegman, A. 1972. Cold response, body form, and craniofacial shape in two racial groups of Hawaiians. *American Journal of Physical Anthropology* 37: 193–221.

Stringer, C. 1984. Fate of the Neanderthal. *Natural History* December: 6–12.

Stringer, C. 1987. The dates of Eden. *Nature* 331: 565–66.

STRINGER, C., and P. ANDREWS. 1988. Genetics and fossil evidence for the origin of modern humans. *Science* 239: 1263–68.

TAPPEN, N. 1985. The dentition of the "old man" of La Chapelle-aux-Saints and inferences concerning Neanderthal behavior. *American Journal of Physical Anthropology* 67: 43–50.

TRINKAUS, E. 1973. A reconsideration of the Fontéchevade fossils. *American Journal of Physical Anthropology* 39: 25–35.

TRINKAUS, E. 1978. Hard times among the Neanderthals. *Natural History* 87: 58–63.

TRINKAUS, E. 1982a. The Shanidar 3 Neanderthal. *American Journal of Physical Anthropology* 57: 37–60.

TRINKAUS, E. 1982b. Artificial cranial deformation in the Shanidar 1 and 5 Neanderthals. *Current Anthropology* 23: 198–99.

TRINKAUS, E. 1983. *The Shanidar Neanderthals.* New York: Academic Press.

TRINKAUS, E. 1985a. Neanderthal public morphology and gestation length. *Current Anthropology* 25: 509–14.

TRINKAUS, 1985b. Cannibalism and burial at Krapina. *Journal of Human Evolution* 14: 203–16.

TRINKAUS, E. 1985c. Pathology and the posture of the La Chapelle-aux-Saints Neanderthal. *American Journal of Physical Anthropology* 67: 19–42.

TRINKAUS, E. 1986. The Neanderthals and modern human origins. *Annual Review of Anthropology* 15: 193–218.

TRINKAUS, E., and M. LE MAY. 1982. Occipital bunning among later Pleistocene hominids. *American Journal of Physical Anthropology* 57: 27–35.

TRINKAUS, E., and M. ZIMMERMAN. 1982. Trauma among the Shanidar Neanderthals. *American Journal of Physical Anthropology* 57: 61–76.

VALLADAS, H., et al. 1986. Thermoluminescence dating of Le Moustier (Dordogne, France). *Nature* 322: 452–54.

VALLADAS, H., et al. 1987a. Thermoluminescence dates for the Neanderthal burial site at Kebara in Israel. *Nature* 330: 359–60.

VALLADAS, H. et al. 1987b. Thermoluminescence dating of Mousterian Proto-Cro-Magnon remains from Israel and the origin of modern man. *Nature* 331: 644–46.

VALLOIS, H. 1952. Monophyletism and polyphyletism in man. *South African Journal of Science* 49: 69–79.

VALLOIS, H. 1954. Neanderthals and presapiens. *Journal of the Royal Anthropological Institute* 84: 111–30.

WOLPOFF, M. 1968. Climatic influence on the skeletal nasal aperature. *American Journal of Physical Anthropology* 29: 405–23.

WOLPOFF, M. 1980. *Paleoanthropology.* New York: Knopf.

This chapter deals with the appearance of H. s. sapiens, the subspecies to which we belong. H. s. sapiens colonized the Americas and some of the Pacific Islands, as well as Africa, Asia, and Europe. The cultural tradition of the early H. s. sapiens is the Upper Paleolithic. No single cultural tradition emerges as clearly as the Upper Paleolithic, during which there is a noticeable acceleration of cultural and technological innovation and a flowering of artistic expression.

The earliest possible evidence of H. s. sapiens comes from Africa about 120,000 to 100,000 years ago. H. s. sapiens populations moved into the Americas and Australia considerably later in time.

UPPER PALEOLITHIC LIFE-WAYS

Dietary Patterns

Upper Paleolithic people were primarily big-game hunters. Their weapons included spears, javelins, harpoons, clubs, stone missiles, and boomerangs or throwing sticks. Bolas were probably slung at the legs of animals; snares and pitfalls almost certainly trapped big game; and herds of gregarious animals were chased off cliffs.

Although fishing long preceded the Upper Paleolithic, the technique was refined during that time with the introduction of harpoons. Aquatic foods may have formed a sizable part of some local diets.

Reindeer played a large role in the hunting economies of some later Upper Paleolithic populations; in fact, some sites contain evidence indicating that their human inhabitants strongly relied on reindeer for food. Reindeer supplied the hides for clothing and tents, sinew for thread, bones and antlers for tools and weapons, and teeth for ornaments. There is evidence of reindeer antlers being fashioned into harpoons. The frequency of bone sewing needles, bodkins (large-eyed blunt needles), and belt fasteners suggests that wearing apparel, presumably of tanned hides and furs, was common.

Group hunting economies may have been specialized for locally abundant animals. While the reindeer was certainly the most important food item in France and Germany, the wooly mammoth was important to populations farther east. Horses were important locally as a dietary item. If the game were seasonal migrants, their predatory hunters presumably followed the same pattern. If the herds of gregarious animals were sedentary, semipermanent dwellings were possible.

Dwellings

Upper Paleolithic populations inhabited a variety of dwellings; rock shelters (that is, rock overhangs, as distinguished from deep caves) were widely used. Trees were felled and propped against the rock face, perhaps trellised by branches and skins. Large caves were inhabited, and huts or tents built inside caves were heated with wood or bone fires. Where rock shelters are rare, as in central and eastern Europe, there are remains of permanent dwellings. At Pushkari, in the Soviet Union, there are long huts, some of which were sunk into the ground. One hut measures 39 feet by 13 feet. At another site there are traces of two dwellings, each 120 feet by 49 feet. There are also nine hearths situated on the long axis, and numerous silos of varying shapes and heights. It is unlikely that this complex was accommodated under one roof.

Artistic Expression

One reason we know so much about the culture of European Upper Paleolithic populations is that their art, of which they left numerous traces, tells us much about their daily life, ritual practices, and concerns. As Pfeiffer (1983:37) notes:

> It came with a bang, apparently out of nowhere and with almost no foreshadowing in the archaeological record: the world's first and longest-lived art movement.
> . . . Art appeared all of a sudden, culminating in the magnificent cave paintings and engravings of Western Europe.

About 200 sites containing art have been discovered in Western Europe; 90 percent of these are located in France and Spain. Upper Paleolithic art can be divided into two categories: mobile art applied to small objects normally found in archaeological deposits (Figure 21-1), and cave art restricted to the walls, roof, and occasionally floors of caves and rock shelters. France alone has more than 70 cave art sites dating from 28,000 to 10,000 years ago. Cave art took the form of both engraving and painting. Reliefs were made by cutting away the rock to varying depths. There are examples of drawings on clay films on cave walls, ceilings, and floors, and the modeling of clay figurines. Coloring consisted of various kinds of ocher, manganese, and charcoal.

Much Upper Paleolithic art is placed on walls located deep in relatively inaccessible caves and is quite difficult to see (Figure 21-2). Caves were probably entered by people using artificial light from torches or fat-burning lamps to illuminate their way. Much of the art is in areas badly situated for viewing—in narrow niches, behind rock bumps, and sometimes in areas that must have been dangerous for both the artist and the viewer to enter. This suggests that the art may have served some ritualistic purpose.

Some researchers view Upper Paleolithic art as related to the food quest, as examples of magical rituals associated with the hunt. Much of the art is zoomorphic; it is concerned with animal representations. Some art seems to depict masked figures, with animal heads, antlers, and skins strapped over a human form (Figure 21-3).

Although naturalistic animal forms have always generated interest, there is much more to Paleolithic art than carved or painted animals. Among 1,200 engraved bones and antlers that came from 26 sites, including Altamira in

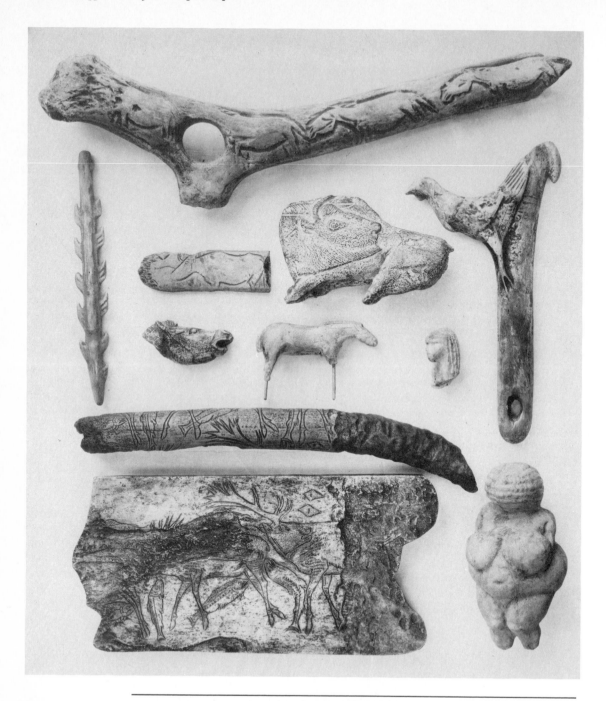

Figure 21-1 Examples of Upper Paleolithic mobile art.

Figure 21-2 Artists in the cave of Font-de-Gaume, France.

Spain, only 70 animal depictions were identifiable. Upper Paleolithic art may not be an attempt at self-amusement or self-expression. Much of the artistic expression reflects concerns with food procurement (Figure 21-4). Many animal figures are painted with spears in them or marked with blows from clubs. The French cave of Font-de-Gaume has several drawings of traps or enclosures with animals caught in them. One depicts a mammoth in a pitlike trap. Furthermore, Delporte suggests, (Lewin, 1986) as a result of an examination of more recent representations of animals in pottery and sculpture, and quite to the contrary of what is often assumed, that artists tend to paint or carve images of animals they do not eat. If this was always true, then it contradicts the possibility that the art was a magical ritual to ensure the success of the hunt.

If these paintings are actually attempts at sympathetic magic—that is, a way of ensuring a good hunt—then were there also Upper Paleolithic magicians? There are some 50 paintings of human figures clad in animal skins, some wearing animal heads or horns. Many of these are depicted in the midst of a dance.

Although most attention concerning cave art focuses on Europe, there are also cave paintings in North Africa and south of the Sahara in Tanzania and South Africa. Unlike European art, however, African paintings are often disregarded and are studied less often. The longest artistic tradition seems to have occurred in neither Europe nor Africa, but in Australia. Some present-

Figure 21-3 A human draped with animal skin and headdress.

day Australian aborigines still paint symbols that first appeared in Australia as early as 30,000 to 40,000 years ago.

Upper Paleolithic artists also engaged in sculpture and engraving; there are incised animal outlines on cave walls, some produced in bas relief. At Cap Blanc, France, there is a set of horses carved in bas relief; the natural rock curves accentuate the sides of the horses' bodies.

Female statuettes of bone, stone, and ivory and of varying design and merit are found in Europe. Their most obvious trait is an exaggeration of the torso, focusing on the stomach, breasts, and buttocks. The head and limbs are disproportionately small. These statuettes have been interpreted as tiny fertility figurines by some researchers. A major example is the so-called Venus of Willendorf, a 4-inch-high statuette, with a wavy hairdo and accentuated breasts, stomach, and thighs (Figure 21-5).

Of the hundreds of carved figures, not all are females with exaggerated proportions like the so-called Venus figurines. Some figures are of males, but

Figure 21-4 Archers painted in the Paleolithic rock shelters of Saltadora and Alpera, eastern Spain.

most are sexless. The idea of a continent-wide fertility cult has probably been greatly overstated.

Some of the most astonishing examples of sculpture date to at least 15,000 years ago and were found quite by accident in the French cave of Le Tuc d'Audoubert. Access to this cave is by way of an underground river. Two molded clay bison, each about a meter long, were found propped up in the middle of a low, round chamber within a larger chamber filled with stalactites. A third, smaller bison lay on the floor close to the main figures. The clay from which the figurines were made came from a pit in the cave floor. Human footprints were preserved in the wet clay of a side chamber.

Another cave in the Pyrenees, the Grotte de Montespan, also contains clay figures. Although these figures have deteriorated with age, one can still recognize a clay lion and clay bears which lie against the walls of a cavern some 1.2 miles from the cave's entrance. Once again there is a scattering of footprints, some belonging to children.

An exciting site, El Juyo, dating to about 14,000 years ago, was located in Spain (Freeman, et al, 1983). The site includes about 1,100 square feet of undisturbed strata. Faunal remains show that shellfish were gathered in large numbers. The hunting of such animals as red and roe deer, bison, horses, and ibex seems to have been very important. The most important animal in the diet seems to have been the red deer, probably because of its local abundance.

Level 4 at El Juyo reveals structures that might have been used for ceremonial purposes. The most remarkable feature was a free-standing stone sculpture crudely made from a stone block. The right half of the sculpture reveals the visage of a benign, smiling human male, with a simple curved nose, a moustache, and a beard. However, the left side reveals features of a large member of the cat family, perhaps a lion or leopard. The cat's features are seen in a deeply chiseled tear duct, a long and deliberately polished muzzle, a single projecting fang, and lines of black dots, which hint at the roots of whiskers.

The dualism expressed by the El Juyo sculpture and the depiction of opposed natures by using a left–right polarity are commonly found among living peoples but are rarely discernible in prehistoric artifacts. Level 4 has been viewed as a "space that has been symbolically structured and set aside for

Figure 21-5 *Willendorf Venus. Cast.*

the performance of patterned religious rituals dedicated to one or more culturally postulated supernatural beings. These rituals were not everyday activities essential to the economic survival of the group" (Freeman, Klein, and Echegaray, 1983:52).

While Neanderthal burials and some Upper Paleolithic cave paintings have also been viewed as possibly religious in nature, the El Juyo sanctuary provides stronger evidence for religious practices. The stone face may be the most convincing depiction of a supernatural being yet discovered in Paleolithic art.

There has been much discussion about the functions of Upper Paleolithic art. Although some of the cave art depicted animals of the hunt, it is unlikely that all the meanings and all the activities represented by Paleolithic art can be attributed to control over the hunted resources. There is some connection between the art and the subsistence pattern, but the latter activities apparently do not alone cause or create art.

Pfeiffer (1983) notes that it is necessary that we remember that Upper Paleolithic human populations were illiterate; thus they could store knowledge only by memorizing it. He argues that without writing, everything had to be dramatized. Our ancestors organized ways to attach emotion to information for memory's sake. Pfeiffer argues that cave art helped to achieve this end.

Pfeiffer suggests that cave art may have involved elaborate and systematic planning. Three stages may have been followed: (1) leading the uninitiated through an eerie and difficult route, "a kind of obstacle course to soften them up for indoctrination" (Pfeiffer, 1983:39); (2) catching and holding the viewer's attention with shocking and frightening displays; and (3) using every technique to imprint information indelibly in the memory system.

To prepare people for indoctrination, it helps to place them in a strange environment, a place without familiar landmarks and which produces a sense of loss. Caves meet these requirements. To further increase the sense of awe inspired by a cave and its paintings, early populations may have provided further assaults to the senses. Soviet archaeologists recovered a set of red-painted mammoth bones which may have been used as drums and other percussion instruments. Bone and ivory instruments resembling bull-roarers were found in some caves. Bull-roarers produce an eerie sound that may have further stimulated the senses and increased the sense of awe.

Circumstantial evidence that cave art may have served as an educational tool comes from children's footprints found in some caves. Children may have been undergoing training in some of the caves that are adorned with artistic works.

Prehistoric art may be a reflection of increased social complexity. It appeared at a time when there was a range of change in the economy, in tool-making traditions, and in social behavior. Paleolithic art may be an expression of an entire organizational, perceptual world view, a cosmology, a system of thought (Leroi-Gourhan, 1967). This system may be based in part on the division of the natural world into female and male components. Certain parts of caves, as well as certain groups of animals and signs, may have had a masculine or feminine association.

Paleolithic artists were selective in their choice and placement of subject matter. A closer look at the placement of such art challenges long-held beliefs that most cave art is to be found in the deep, dark, inaccessible regions of presumably sacred caves. Some specific forms or themes, such as depictions of females, tended to have been placed in rock-sheltered or daylit locales. Among the mobile art, some themes or depictions were significantly correlated with certain artifact types or forms. Horses, for example, are found on most kinds of artifacts except harpoons, whereas bison do not appear on spears.

Tool Inventory

Upper Paleolithic populations produced a culture that far exceeded in variety and style anything of its predecessors. Upper Paleolithic tool makers produced fine stone tools and delicately worked bone. The European Upper Paleolithic was essentially a blade-tool assemblage characterized by an abundance and variety of long, parallel-sided implements called "blades" (Figure 21-6). Specific tools of the blade-tool industry were devised for working bone and wood. **Burins** (chisel-shaped blades) were probably used for engraving and working wood, bone, or antlers that may have been employed as handles or shafts. Various types of scrapers may have been used to scrape wood or hollow out wood or bone.

European Upper Paleolithic industries are characterized by a shift in manufacturing technique and an emphasis on bone and wood-working tools. Stone tools reflect only a small portion of the cultural changes that occurred during this period, although differing styles and the appearance and frequency of different tool types is used to define Upper Paleolithic cultural traditions. What was once considered to be a progressive series of industries, each changing into or being replaced by another, may be a single industrial stage representing basic adaptive strategies.

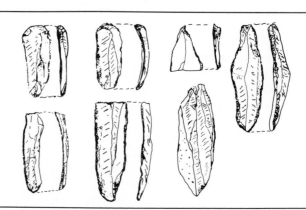

Figure 21-6 *Upper Paleolithic blade tools.*

New items, such as polished pins or antler awls, are found in Upper Paleolithic tool kits. Points were probably hafted to sticks. The later tool tradition, the *Magdalenian* (a cultural complex from Western Europe dating from 17,000 to 12,000 years ago), included hooked rods employed as spear throwers, barbed points and harpoons, fish hooks, needles, bone and ivory bodkins, belt fasteners, and tools of undetermined use. Many tools were highly decorated with animal forms, and may have served as ceremonial items.

The major cultural features of the Upper Paleolithic are as follows:

1. The population density exceeds that of previous times.
2. Stone artifacts are more stylized. Stylistic differences in tools may have played a role in information exchange (for example, in noting territorial or social boundaries), in the context of ritual, in support of ethnicity, or in maintaining and strengthening mating networks, exchange relationships, and structural processes (Wobst, 1977).
3. There is a far greater emphasis on the use of bone and antler, and there is a proliferation of bone tools. The use of bone may reflect a shift toward the hunting of large numbers of herd animals, like deer, in which both sexes have antlers for most of the year.
4. There is a broadening of the subsistence base to include more fish and birds.
5. There are indications of the use of personal ornaments. In addition to bones and antlers, shells and stones were used for ornamental purposes.
6. At the beginning of the Upper Paleolithic, humans began to obtain materials from distant sources, presumably through structured exchange networks.
7. Art appears rather suddenly in some parts of the world.

There seemed to be a restructuring of social relationships across the Middle/Upper Paleolithic boundary, in the course of which group affiliation and individual identity became important and are noted by regional differences in worked stone, antler, and bone, in the fabrication and wearing of ornaments, and in the regular aggregation of a set of otherwise dispersed local groups (White, 1982). The desirability of antlers as a communicative and technological medium is reflected in a shift to the hunting of large numbers of reindeer. Structured relationships between inhabitants of different geographical areas are evident in the presence of materials from distant sources. There may have been an increase in population density.

THE HUMAN FOSSIL SAMPLE

Every anatomical feature characteristic of early *H. s. sapiens* populations appears in lower frequency in preceding populations. *H. s. sapiens* fossils are distinguished from previous fossils such as the Neanderthals by reduction in the size of the anterior teeth, facial and brow ridge reduction, and increased cranial height. In all early *H. s. sapiens* samples, these attributes are less marked than in today's populations. The morphological changes that characterize *H. s. sapiens* occurred at different times in various parts of the world (See Table 21-1). For example, the brow ridge in the East African sample was already much reduced, while in their European contemporaries, especially among males, the brow ridge region was large and well developed (Wolpoff, 1980) (Table 21-2 and Figure 21-7).

The Upper Paleolithic human fossils had gracile faces, broad, high foreheads, protruding chins, and a mean cranial capacity estimated at 1,590 cubic centimeters. Their height has been variously estimated as between 5 feet, 4 inches and 6 feet tall.

Africa

Most African *H. s. sapiens* remains come from East and South Africa. There are problems with interpreting early African *H. s. sapiens* populations. Although the dating of the sites seems sound, the context of the remains from such sites as Border Cave, South Africa, and the Omo Kibbish Formation in

Table 21-1 **Some** Homo sapiens sapiens *Fossil Sites*

Geographic Region	Site	Date
Africa	Eyasi, Tanzania	130,000
	Omo, Ethiopia	130,000
	Laetoli, Tanzania	120,000 +/− 30,000
	Border Cave, South Africa	115,000–90,000
Asia	China, Java	20,000–10,000
Europe	France, Italy	ca. 30,000
	Czechoslovakia	30,000
	Yugoslavia	33,000
Australian region	Huron Peninsula, New Guinea	40,000
	Lake Mungo, Australia	32,000 (?), 28,000 (?)
	Devil's Lake, Australia	35,000
	Bluff Cave and ORS 7, Tasmania	32,000
	Fraser Cave, Tasmania	20,000–15,000
North and South America	Boqueiro do Sitio da Pedra Furada, Brazil Most Early PaleoIndian sites are disputed because of dating and context problems. The same can be said for Middle PaleoIndian sites dating between 28,000 and 11,500 years ago. Late PaleoIndian sites dating from less than 11,500 years ago are quite common in North and South America.	32,000

Table 21-2 *Features Distinguishing* **Homo sapiens sapiens** *from the Neanderthals*

---

1. In *H. s. sapiens* the forehead is more vertical, and the brow ridges are absent or reduced and never continuous.

2. *H. s. sapiens* has a higher skull vault, shows little or no evidence of an occipital bun, and has thinner skull bones.

3. *H. s. sapiens* shows relatively little prognathism. A distinct chin is present.

4. *H. s. sapiens* exhibits reduced bone thickness throughout the body, which is probably related to reduced muscle mass.

5. *H. s. sapiens* shows size reduction in the incisors.

Ethiopia are questionable. Even if the ages of the specimens are correct, there is considerable morphological difference from later-occurring European *H. s. sapiens* samples.

Perhaps the best evidence for the early appearance of *H. s. sapiens* in sub-Saharan Africa comes from the valley of the Omo River in Ethiopia. In 1976 Richard Leakey recovered parts of three skeletons, including two broken skulls and some postcranial bones, plus skull fragments of a third individual. Although Omo 1 and 2 show some variation in skull morphology, they should probably be classified together (Rightmire, 1975). Omo 1, which, unfortunate-

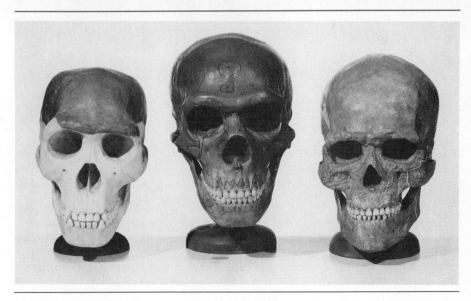

Figure 21-7 Skulls of human fossils. Left to right: Homo erectus, Neanderthal, H.s. sapiens.

ly, lacks a face, is quite heavily built and has a long, low cranial vault (Figure 21-8). There is a well-developed ridge of bone across the back of the occipital region of the skull. Omo 2 is more modern in appearance.

Associated faunal remains may be of Middle Pleistocene derivation. Although an age of 130,000 years ago has been obtained for the geological formation containing the skulls, the dating method used is not considered to be especially reliable.

An almost complete skull (called L.H. 18), including bones of the skull vault, much of the skull base, both temporals, parts of the face, and the upper dentition comes from Laetoli, Tanzania. The material is estimated to be approximately 120,000 years old. The age at death is estimated to be 20 to 30 years old. The skull shows a mix of modern and archaic traits. The good state of preservation of the face and its dating add considerably to its importance as a fossil near the root of the evolution of *H. s. sapiens* in East Africa.

The Border Cave remains suggest the possibility of *H. s. sapiens* in southern Africa about 115,000 years ago. The most important of the skulls did not come from a controlled excavation, however. Although it was found in a dump outside the cave, sediment wedged into cracks in the skull bones matches most closely sediment that yielded the 115,000 year date. In 1974 a fully modern adult jaw was excavated from a layer dated to about 92,000 years ago.

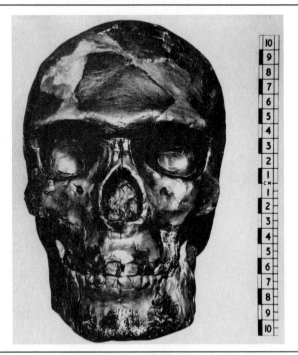

Figure 21-8 A recent reconstruction of the Omo 1 skull from southern Ethiopia. Possibly one of the earliest H.s. sapiens *skulls known.*

One of the newest attempts to unravel the origins of *H. s. sapiens* comes not from the study of fossils, but from the study of mitochondrial DNA (mtDNA). Unlike nuclear DNA, which one inherits from both parents, mtDNA is inherited from ones mother. Mitochondrial DNA is found outside the cell nucleus, in ones mitochondria, which produce most of the energy needed to maintain the cell's life. Because mtDNA is inherited only from the mother, it is useful for tracing genealogy. Mitochondrial DNA is not a mixture of both parents' genes, like nuclear DNA. MtDNA can be altered only by mutation.

Three biochemists, Cann, Stoneking, and Wilson, analyzed the mtDNA of 147 women from five world geographic regions—Africa, Asia, Europe, Australia, and New Guinea—and they discovered that the differences among the whole set were very small (Cann, Stoneking, and Wilson, 1987; Lewin, 1987a; Wainscoat, 1987). This finding indicated that all the women, despite the diversity of their geographical origins, shared a relatively recently inherited complement of mtDNA. The different populations separated out, one set was formed by women of African origin only and another set by individuals of all the other groups. It appears that in terms of mtDNA, all humans are more closely related than almost any other mammalian species.

More diversity in the mtDNA was found in the women with an African ancestry, suggesting that their mtDNA had accumulated more mutations because it was the oldest form. In other words, this was the longest branch of the human family. Apparently, the mtDNA tree began in Africa and then spread to the rest of the world. An African origin of all modern mtDNA agrees with the fossil record, which strongly suggests that all modern human populations can ultimately trace their roots to Africa, perhaps to such fossil representatives as are found in Tanzania, Ethiopia, and South Africa and dating between 120,000 and 90,000 years ago.

According to the proposal by Cann and colleagues all human females can trace their ancestry (at least their mtDNA ancestry) back to a woman who resided in Africa approximately 200,000 (the range is actually 290,000 to 140,000) years ago. This mtDNA "Eve," as she has unfortunately been dubbed, has "mothered" the entire population of modern women. Her genetic structure, through the reproductive success of her female line, overrode the genetic structure of all females in all other populations. As her female relatives fanned out from Africa some time about 100,000 years ago, they replaced local populations. There are many ramifications of this proposal; one of the most important is the fact that all of the world's populations are closely related to one another—no matter the phenotypic (outward) appearance. We all truly belong to one big family.

Not everyone accepts all of the conclusions of Cann and colleagues. For example, some paleoanthropologists question the time scale for the origin of modern *H. s. sapiens* as postulated by the mtDNA data. Fossil evidence suggests a more recent origin of 120,000 or 130,000 to 90,000 years ago rather than the 200,000-year-ago figure of the mtDNA data. Others question the possibility that one female and her female relatives could genetically swamp the genotypes of the world's females. (Mathematically, it is possible.) Still others question the rapidity of the genetic swamping that the Cann group's data suggest. And others contend that the similarity in mtDNA might be due not to a common ancestor, but to the effects of random genetic drift. There are few, however, who question that Africa is the site of the appearance of every new stage in human evolution. Both the fossil and the genetic evidence point in that direction.

The biochemical data generated by Cann and her colleagues have provided a fascinating new insight into human origins. (Not for the first time, however, if you recall how the biochemical data led the way in the eventual rejection of *Ramapithecus* as the earliest possible human ancestor.) Some researchers are now looking at the male Y chromosome in the hope of finding something comparable to the mtDNA inherited from ones mother. This should prove to be a more difficult challenge because the Y chromosome is found within the cell's nucleus, where there are many more genes than are found in the mitochondria.

Asia

Asian Upper Paleolithic human remains are not abundant. Materials do come from Zhoukoudian, China and Wadjak, Java. Both areas have also yielded *H. erectus* materials. There are also fossils from Taiwan and Japan, both of which were connected to the Asian mainland for much of the Pleistocene. The Upper Cave of Zhoukoudian yielded a number of human fossils dated to about 10,000 years ago.

Southern China from 100,000 to 70,000 years ago was probably the area for the dispersal of the earliest generalized type of *H. s. sapiens* in Asia. This population already had some recognizable Asian dental traits. Beginning perhaps about 70,000 years ago, populations from southern China radiated south, moving throughout insular southeast Asia and reaching Australia by as early as 50,000 or 40,000 years ago.

Europe

European Upper Paleolithic human remains were first found in the nineteenth century, but were thought to be modern burials. In 1868 the Cro-Magnon rock shelter, located in France, yielded some of the first finds: 6 skeletons—3 males (Figure 21-9), 2 females, and 1 youngster. Other remains of the Upper Paleolithic population from France come from the sites of Combe Capelle and Chancelade. The Combe Capelle fossils had long faces and long, high, narrow foreheads. They seem to have been of medium to small body size. The Chancelade specimen was short (about 4 feet, 11 inches tall) and had wide cheek bones and a heavy jaw, possibly indicating heavy chewing stress. The skull was long and narrow, and the nose was narrow.

There are many remains from central and eastern Europe. Three major finds come from the Czechoslovakian sites of Prědmosti, Brno, and Lautsch. The Prědmosti site is a common grave containing 18 or 20 individuals and may date to more than 30,000 years ago. Some skulls show primitive traits such as large brow ridges. The material was associated with more than 1,000 mammoth bones. The Brno skull, an adult male, exhibits some archaic traits when compared with the French remains. It had more accentuated brow ridges and other skull features resembling the preceding Neanderthals.

The right half of a frontal bone comes from the cave site of Velika Pecina, northwestern Croatia. The human specimen dates to about 33,000 years ago. The site also contained an enormous collection of fauna—138 different species and subspecies.

Australian Region

The colonization of Australia raises a number of questions: When did humans first enter Australia? To what Asian forms are they related? What are the relationships between Australia, Tasmania, and New Guinea on the one hand, and Indonesia on the other? Australia's original colonizers may have arrived by boat and foot via two major island routes: (1) Java via Timor or (2) Borneo via the Celebes, and the Moluccas. The widest distance to be crossed over water, about 50 miles, was probably navigated in small rafts or boats. There are broad anatomical relationships between modern Australian aborigines and fossil materials from Java, New Guinea, and Borneo.

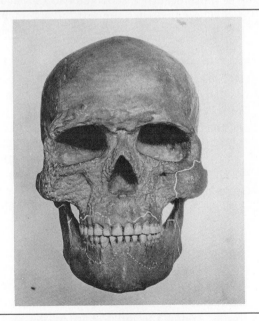

Figure 21-9 "Old Man" skull from Cro-Magnon shelter, France.

The geographical location of New Guinea suggests that it may have been an early point of origin for the Pleistocene settlement of Australia from the Indonesian-Indochina region. New Guinea's position as a point of origin for the colonization of Australia is strengthened with the discovery of artifacts on the island dating to about 40,000 years ago.

The oldest likely dates for human occupation of Australia range from 35,750 years ago to perhaps 28,000 years ago from the site at Lake Mungo. The remains include human cremations and hearths containing burnt animal bone and stone artifacts. If the old date at Lake Mungo proves unacceptable, a date of 35,000 years ago for the Devil's Lair site in southwestern Australia would be the oldest date for human occupation in Australia.

To understand why the colonization of Australia did not occur prior to 40,000 years ago, it must be remembered that the Sahul landmass, consisting of Australia, Tasmania, and New Guinea, has been separated from Sunda Land, the combined landmass of southeast Asia and much of Indonesia, by an island zone of Wallacea for about 50 million years. This water barrier prevented movement of people into Greater Australia. Even during the maximal low sea levels at 55,000 and 22,000 years ago, the shortest route across Wallacea, via Timor and onto the northwest Australian coast, would have involved at least eight boat voyages, the last being about 50 miles long. By this time, however, humans were intelligent enough and had the technology to make the crossing.

Once in Australia, humans crossed the Bass Strait and colonized Tasmania. The most recently discovered two sites in Tasmania date to about 32,000 years ago. These two sites support the argument that Tasmania and Australia may have been intermittently connected during the past 50,000 years. Human migrants may have reached Tasmania about 36,000 years ago when a drop in sea level of 55 meters exposed a land bridge from Australia to Tasmania (Cosgrove, 1989).

The Fraser Cave site in southwestern Tasmania, dating about 20,000 to 15,000 years ago, provided evidence of a specialized hunting economy focused on the large wallaby. Tool types are similar to those found in Australia.

Fraser Cave's inhabitants were the most southerly dwelling humans in the world. About 20,000 years ago they were as close to the great Antarctic ice sheet, then 1,000 kilometers south, as some European Upper Paleolithic populations were to the northern ice sheets. The early Tasmanians probably lived in tundralike conditions similar to those that existed in parts of northern Europe.

The Americas

The date of entry of human populations into the New World is hotly disputed. Populations probably entered the Americas by way of an emergent Bering land bridge connecting Siberia to Alaska and then moved south through Canada. Because continental glaciers grow at the expense of sea waters, sea levels are lowest when glaciations are at their maximum. During glaciation the

Bering land bridge (also called Beringia) created a Siberia-to-Alaska migration route.

Some argue that a smooth and unbroken land bridge wider than present-day Alaska joined the Old and New Worlds during much of the Pleistocene. Large animals may have crossed the land bridge during the 80,000 years of the Wisconsin Glaciation. The first humans probably crossed the bridge before the end of the Wisconsin Glaciation in pursuit of game slowly spreading out of Asia into Alaska.

Some suggest that the bridge first appeared only 28,000 to 25,000 years ago. After a period it closed and reopened again at between 14,000 and 8,500 years ago. The bridge may have opened and closed several times in conjunction with the retreats and advances of ice during deglaciation. Resolution of the dating of the opening and closing of the Bering land bridge is of major importance to settling the story of New World occupation.

Whatever the true nature of the migration, it probably occurred as two or three major waves. Besides glacial ice, there seems to have been no impediment to movement in the New World. The abundance of game speeded the human dispersal by providing food. Anywhere from 8,000 to 2,000 years has been estimated as the time for the journey from Alaska south to the tip of South America.

According to Aigner (1984), Beringia from 30,000 to 14,000 years ago was low-lying, with a mosaic of vegetational communities. A steppe-tundra environment of about 40,000 years ago was productive for supporting animals. By 30,000 years ago Beringia was treeless. At 10,000 years ago the habitat was even more impoverished. The best time for human movement across Beringia was the earlier period during the mid-Wisconsin Glaciation, which lasted from 60,000 to 25,000 years ago.

Evidence that humans may have entered the New World by about 40,000 years ago comes from a site in Brazil dating to perhaps 32,000 years ago. Researchers face difficulties in obtaining dates for the oldest inhabitants of North America because of the destructive nature of the glaciations and because the permanently frozen ground in the far north makes excavation all but impossible. However, glaciers never reached South America. Furthermore, in such areas as Brazil, earth tremors or volcanic activity is quite rare, and many areas are relatively undisturbed. There is also the Monte Verde site in Chile, which may date to 33,000 years ago.

The New World human fossil record is often divided into three periods: the Early, Middle, and Late Paleo-Indian periods. Many possible Early and Middle Paleo-Indian sites are disputed, and some researchers will not accept any evidence of New World habitation prior to about 13,000 years ago. Most Early and Middle Paleo-Indian sites are plagued by context problems (including poorly excavated samples and controversial dating techniques) and by a lack of agreement about what constitutes reasonable evidence for an ancient New World presence. Until these matters are settled, evidence for early New World sites will not gain wide acceptance.

One of the most recent attempts at redating early Paleo-Indian sites was made by Taylor and colleagues (1985). Over the last decade, human remains from at least 13 localities in the New World—most in southern California—have been assigned dates exceeding 11,000 years ago. The number of such sites has been drastically reduced with Taylor and colleagues' new dating.

If it is proven to exist, the Early Paleo-Indian period began prior to 30,000 years ago. There are scant remains from this time. Although the geological age of possible Early Paleo-Indian sites is reasonably well understood, either the association or the nature of possible artifacts and skeletal remains is questionable (Diamond, 1987).

Given the amount of disagreement among researchers, what will it take to prove that a site is an old site? The following criteria are often accepted (Grayson, in Lewin, 1987b): (1) The site must have undoubted artifacts or human skeletal remains; (2) such human relics must be in undisturbed deposits; (3) the associated dates must be secure; and (4) the site must have been excavated and published in such a way that other scholars can determine whether the preceding criteria were properly met.

The Middle Paleo-Indian period dates from 28,000 to 13,500 years ago. Human bones are generally lacking from this time period. No site has yet produced any quantity of cultural material, and there is scant evidence of a cultural sequence. Possible Middle Paleo-Indian sites come from California, Idaho, Oregon, and Texas. A number of Middle Paleo-Indian sites have also been reported in Mexico and South America.

The earliest site for human occupation in the eastern United States is the Meadowcroft Rock Shelter, located 47 miles west of Pittsburgh (Figure 21-10). The dates from the earliest habitation layers strongly support arrival of inhabitants in the New World over 20,000 years ago because some of the immigrants reached the upper Ohio River at Meadowcroft by at least 19,000 years ago.

The most complete evidence of New World occupation comes from numerous sites belonging to the Late Paleo-Indian period dating from about 13,000 years ago. By the Late Paleo-Indian period, humans were well established in the New World, with hunting sites and camps appearing from Tierra del Fuego in South America to Nova Scotia in Canada. The earliest part of this period is characterized by the remains of technologically advanced and highly skilled hunters who used a distinctive projectile point known as the *Clovis* point for killing mammoth and other big game.

Usually located near bogs or marshes, sites of Clovis-tradition hunters contain implements manufactured from materials whose source was sometimes as far as 200 miles away from the site. This indicates either a large nomadic range or trade. The Clovis tradition is closely related to kill sites. Because of their location and size, these sites appear to be associated with mammoth hunting. The strategy of the Clovis mammoth hunters seems to have been to ambush their prey along the route to one of its feeding or watering areas. Once wounded, the animal would probably head for the nearest water source, where the hunters could complete the kill.

The transition from the Clovis to the **Folsom** point about 11,000 years ago coincides with the extinction of much of the New World megafauna, such as mammoths, horses, and camels. There is a great deal of controversy concerning the role that Folsom-tradition hunters may have played in this extinction, however. The first Folsom point, which was found in 1926, comes from the Folsom site located in New Mexico.

Folsom points are distinctive; they are pressure flaked, about 2 inches long, thin, more or less leaf-shaped, and have a concave base. A long flake was apparently removed from each side, giving them a fluted shape. Grooves or channels extend from one-third to almost the whole length of the flake. Why these points were fluted is a matter of debate.

Folsom hunters took advantage of a distinct behavioral trait of their most frequent prey, the bison. The extinct bison is thought to have behaved in much the same way as its modern descendant did. When frightened, these animals

Figure 21-10 (Top) The view across Meadowcroft Rockshelter, looking west, in 1973 before excavations began. Piles of stones in the center of the photo mark the location of a recent hearth used by campers and hikers. The presence of these features testifies to the continuing importance of the site as a shelter for humans. (Bottom) The east face of Meadowcroft. Each small white tag marks the location of an archaeological feature or stratum, or the locus of one or more soil, pollen, or geological samples.

stampede. Adapting to this behavior, Folsom hunters used the jump and the surround-kill hunting techniques. In the jump technique, hunters stationed themselves downwind from the animals and stampeded them toward a high cliff, from which the bison would fall to their death. Many kill sites associated with the Folsom tradition are located at the bases of such cliffs. In the surround-kill technique, animals were herded into a canyon or other enclosed area, where they were killed and butchered.

Folsom settlement patterns were geared toward bison hunting. Camps were located on ridges overlooking bison grazing areas. Camps were also located near canyons. Folsom-tradition sites are most densely spaced just east of the Rockies, in areas where the bison may have wintered (DeGarmo, 1970).

The **Plano** tradition dates between 10,000 and 6,000 years ago and occurs from the Rockies to the Atlantic and from Mexico to Canada. Plano points are not fluted; instead they bear parallel pressure-flaked scars. Some of the oldest Paleo-Indian housing remains date to Plano occupations in Wyoming. The houses seem to have been circular and from 6 to 8 feet in diameter. The most recent structure is dated between 8,400 and 8,000 years ago. (The oldest evidence of dwelling structures in the New World dates to about 10,000 years old and are found in California.) Manufacturers of the Plano points were big-game hunters. They used the jump and the surround-kill techniques. Most big game hunted by Plano-tradition people belonged to modern species.

Not all Paleo-Indian groups were primarily hunters. More perishable foods, like flora and small animal remains, may have either decayed or been destroyed. There is archaeological evidence from southern Arizona suggesting that Paleo-Indians were both gatherers and hunters.

---

*Table 21-3 **Some Features Associated with** Homo sapiens sapiens*

Time Span Perhaps as early as 125,000 years ago in Africa and 92,000 years ago in the Levant; 40,000 to 35,000 years ago elsewhere.

Distribution Worldwide. Populations enter Australian region about 35,000 to 40,000 years ago and enter the New World perhaps as early.

Life-Ways Upper Paleolithic tool assemblage. New tools include materials made from bone, antler, and wood. Fishing appears. Art and sculpture are found. They inhabited a variety of dwellings and may have engaged in trade and magic or religious practices.

Anatomy Included in the same subspecies as modern humans but show anatomical differences from modern populations. There is a reduction in facial robusticity and in the brow ridges, especially in the East African sample. There is reduction in tooth size, increase in brain size, and the apparance of a chin.

Postcranial: Body build is less robust than that of the Neanderthals.

The earliest evidence of H. s. sapiens *remains comes from East and South Africa and dates between 120,000 and 90,000 years ago. It is thought that all modern populations can be traced back to these earlier African ancestors.*

During the time period of the Upper Paleolithic, perhaps about 35,000 years ago, populations moved into Australia. Ancestral American Indian populations moved out of Asia and entered North America across the Bering land bridge perhaps as early as 40,000 years ago. However, this date for a New World occupation is hotly contested by some researchers, who favor a date no earlier than about 20,000 to 13,000 years ago.

Major cultural changes are associated with H. s. sapiens *populations. New tool categories and new forms of expression—painting, engraving, and sculpting—appear.*

BIBLIOGRAPHY

ADOVASIO, J., and R. CARLISLE. 1984. An Indian hunter's camp for 20,000 years. *Scientific American* May: 130–36.

ADOVASIO, J., and R. CARLISLE. 1988. The Meadowcroft Rock Shelter. *Science* 239: 713–174.

AIGNER, J. 1984. The Asiatic–New World continuum in late Pleistocene time. In *The Evolution of the East Asian Environment,* vol. 2, R. O. Whyte, ed. Hong Kong: University of Hong Kong.

BADA, J., and H. HELFMAN. 1975. Amino acid racemization dating of fossil bone. *World Archaeology* 7: 160–73.

BADA, J., R. SCHROEDER, and G. CARTER. 1974. New evidence for the antiquity of man in North America deduced from aspartic acid racemization. *Science* 184: 791–93.

BAHN, P. 1985. Ice age drawings on open rock faces in the Pyrenees. *Nature* 313: 530–31.

BAILEY, G. 1982. Late Pleistocene life in Tasmania. *Nature* 301: 30.

BARBETTI, N., and H. ALLEN. 1972. Prehistoric man at Lake Mungo, Australia, by 32,000 years B.P. *Nature* 240: 346–48.

BORDEN, C. 1979. Peopling and early cultures of the Pacific Northeast. *Science* 203: 963–71.

BOWLER, J., A. THORNE, and H. POLACK. 1972. Pleistocene man in Australia: Age and significance of Mungo skeleton. *Nature* 240: 348–50.

BRAY, W. 1986. Finding the earliest Americans. *Nature* 321: 726.

BRYAN, A. 1969. Early man in America and the late Pleistocene chronology of western Canada and Alaska. *Current Anthropology* 10: 339–65.

CANN, R., M. STONEKING, and A. WILSON. 1987. Mitochondrial DNA and human evolution. *Nature* 325: 31–37.

CLARK, C. 1967. *The Stone Age Hunters.* New York: McGraw-Hill.

CONKEY, M. 1981. Altamira: The study of Paleolithic art. *L. S. B. Leakey Foundation News* 21: 16–18.

COSGROVE, R. 1989. Thirty thousand years of human colonization in Tasmania: New Pleistocene dates. *Science* 243: 1706-1708.

DAY, M. 1969. Omo human skeletal remains. *Nature* 22: 1135–38.

——— 1971. The Omo skeletal remains. In *The Origin of* Homo sapiens, F. Bordes, ed. Paris: UNESCO.

DAY, M., M. LEAKEY, and C. MAGORI. 1980. A new hominid skull (L. H. 18) from Ngaloba Beds, northern Tanzania. *Nature* 284: 55–56.

DeGarmo, G. 1970. Big-game hunters: An alternative and a hypothesis. Paper presented to 35th Annual Meeting of Society for American Archaeology, Mexico City, May 1970.

Dennell, R. 1986. Needles and spear-throwers. *Natural History* October: 70–78.

Diamond, J. 1987. Who were the first Americans? *Nature* 329: 580–81.

Dumond, D. 1980. The archaeology of Alaska and the peopling of America. *Science* 209: 984–91.

Duncan, R. 1972. The Cochise culture. MA thesis. Davis: University of California Press.

Fladmark, K. 1979. Routes: Alternative migration corridors for early man in North America. *American Antiquity* 44: 55–69.

Fladmark, K. 1986. Getting one's bearings. *Natural History* 95: 8–19.

Freeman, L., R. Klein, and J. Echegaray. 1983. A Stone Age sanctuary. *Natural History* 92: 47–52.

Groube, L., et al. 1986. A 40,000-year-old human occupation site at Huon Peninsula, Papua New Guinea. *Nature* 324: 453–55.

Griffin, J. 1960. Some prehistoric connections between Siberia and America. *Science* 131: 801.

Gurdon, N., and G. Delivrias. 1986. Carbon14 dates point to man in the Americas 32,000 years ago. *Nature* 231: 769–71.

Haag, W. 1962. The Bering Strait land bridge. *Scientific American* 206: 112–23.

Habgood, P. 1986. A late Pleistocene prehistory of Australia: The skeletal material. *Physical Anthropology Newsletter* 5: 1–5.

Haynes, C. 1969. The earliest Americans. *Science* 166: 709.

Heizer, R., and S. Cook. 1953. Fluorine and other chemical tests of some North American human and animal bones. *American Journal of Physical Anthropology* 10: 289–304.

Irving, W., and C. Harington. 1973. Upper Pleistocene radio-carbon dated artifacts from the northern Yukon. *Science* 179: 335–40.

Jelinek, J. 1969. Neanderthal man and *Homo sapiens* in central and eastern Europe. *Current Anthropology* 10: 475–504.

Jennings, J. 1978. Origins. In *Ancient Native Americans,* J. Jennings, ed. San Francisco: W. H. Freeman & Company Publishers.

Kiernan, K., R. Jones, and D. Ranson. 1982. New evidence from Fraser Cave for glacial age of man in southwest Tasmania. *Nature* 301: 28–32.

Kirk, R., and A. Thorne (eds.). 1976. *The Origin of the Australians.* Canberra: Australian Institute of Aboriginal Studies.

Leroi-Gourhan, A. 1967. *Treasures of Prehistoric Art.* New York: Abrams.

Lewin, R. 1986. Myths and methods in Ice Age art. *Science* 234: 936–38.

——— 1987a. Africa: Cradle of modern humans. *Science* 237: 1292–93.

——— 1987b. The first Americans are getting younger. *Science* 238: 1230–32.

Lynch, T., et al. 1986. Chronology of Guitarrero cave, Peru. *Science* 229: 864–67.

MacNeish, R. 1976. Early man in the New World. *American Scientist* 64: 316–27.

Martin, P. 1987. Clovisia the beautiful! *Natural History* October: 10–13.

Pfeiffer, J. 1982. *The Creative Explosion: An Inquiry into the Origins of Art and Religion.* New York: Harper & Row, Pub.

Pfeiffer, J. 1983. Was Europe's fabulous cave art the start of the Information Age? *Smithsonian* April: 36–45.

——— 1986. Cro-magnon hunters were really us, working out strategies for survival. *Smithsonian* October: 75–85.

Poirier, F. 1987. *Understanding Human Evolution.* Englewood Cliffs, N.J.: Prentice Hall.

Protsch, R. 1978. *Catalog of Fossil Hominids of North America.* New York: Fischer.

RIGHTMIRE, G. 1975. New studies of post-Pleistocene human skeletal remains from the Rift Valley, Kenya. *American Journal of Physical Anthropology* 42: 351–70.

———— 1979. Implications of Border Cave skeletal remains for later Pleistocene human evolution. *Current Anthropology* 20: 23–35.

SMITH, F. 1976. A fossil hominid frontal from Velika Pecina (Croatia) and a consideration of Upper Pleistocene hominids from Yugoslavia. *American Journal of Physical Anthropology* 44: 127–34.

———— 1982. Upper Pleistocene hominid evolution in south-central Europe: A review of the evidence and analysis of trends. *Current Anthropology* 23: 667–86.

SMITH, M. 1987. Pleistocene occupation in arid central Australia. *Nature* 238: 710–11.

STEWART, T. 1973. *The People of America.* New York: Scribner's.

TAYLOR, A., et al. 1985. Major revisions in the Pleistocene age assignments for North American human skeleton by C[14] accelerator mass spectometry: None older than 11,000 C[14] years B.P. *American Antiquity* 50: 136–40.

THORNE, A., and P. MACUMBER. 1972. Discoveries of Late Pleistocene man at Kow Swamp, Australia. *Nature* 238:316–19.

WAINSCOAT, J. 1987. Out of the garden of Eden. *Nature* 325: 13.

WHITE, P., and J. ALLEN. 1980. Melanesian prehistory: Some recent advances. *Science* 207: 728–33.

WHITE, P., and J. O'CONNELL. 1979. Australian prehistory: New aspects of antiquity. *Science* 203: 21–28.

WHITE, R. 1982. Rethinking the Middle/Upper Paleolithic transition. *Current Anthropology* 23: 169–92.

WOBST, H. 1977. Stylistic behavior and information exchange. University of Michigan Museum of Anthropology Papers 61.

WOLPOFF, M. 1980. *Paleoanthropology.* New York: Knopf.

Chapter

22

Human Growth and Development

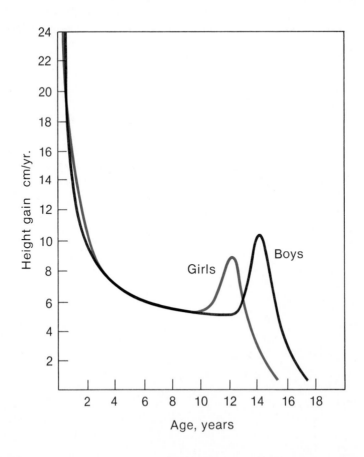

In a sexually reproducing species, the formation of a new organism requires the contributions of both parents to produce a fertilized egg. Early growth in large animals, including humans, involves many cell divisions. By the time a human infant is born, the fertilized egg has divided often enough to yield a total of 2.5 trillion cells. However, as the term "growth and development" implies, there is much more to the process than cell division or increase in size. Much specialization is necessary to produce the interdependent system of tissues and organs that constitute an organism. The phases of growth that yield an embryo, a fetus, and a newborn infant include a number of threshold events that determine the degree of its vulnerability to environmental influence. Many fertilized eggs are lost. It is believed that many of those lost would have been defective if they had developed into full-term infants. An environmental factor that damages the fetus will have the most profound impact early in the pregnancy. Later damage will have more localized effects. The human growth process is different from that of other mammals, even those of nonhuman primates, in the long period of dependency experienced by the human infant. This period of helplessness, with the extraordinary demands it makes on the infant's parents, has the compensating advantage of permitting the infant to spend much time learning. The complex process of learning language and culture is made possible by the lengthy and intensive care devoted to children by their human parents.

FERTILIZATION: THE BEGINNING OF LIFE

Nowhere are the competing forces of evolution—production and maintenance of variation versus selection—more clearly illustrated than in the production and fusion of the gametes that will become a **zygote,** an **embryo,** a **fetus,** a **neonate,** an infant, and ultimately an adult. The male **gamete,** or spermatogonium, after undergoing maturation to become a primary spermatocyte, divides to produce two secondary spermatocytes, which divide again, forming two **spermatids,** which then mature. After maturing, the single-celled, tadpole-shaped **spermatozoon** is really little more than a haploid set of chromosomes enclosed in a membranous capsule and propelled by a long **flagellum,** or whip-like tail. It is a model of economy with little excess baggage accompanying the essential cargo, the genetic material, on its journey to the fallopian tubes, where fertilization, the encounter with the **ovum,** or mature egg, usually occurs. The formation and development of each spermatozoon permits the reassortment of chromosomes during meiosis (see Chapter 6). The **haploid** sets of chromosomes carried by the millions of sperm in competition to fertilize each egg therefore represent enormous variation in terms of permutations and combinations of the original parental chromosomal complement as well as the occasional crossover during meiosis. The process is one that maximizes variation at the gamete level while wasting very little substance in an individual spermatozoon, millions of which are, after all, simply superfluous.

The process by which the maternal gamete, the ovum, is produced is quite different. The difference between the processes by which male and female gametes are produced is significant in terms of the maintenance of variability. The primary oocyte divides asymmetrically, with the two products of the division being of very different size(Figure 22-1). The larger one will go on to mature into the ovum. The smaller one, called a **polar body,** contains a haploid set of chromosomes and a small amount of cytoplasm. Polar bodies are seldom fertilized and, because of the small complement of cytoplasm they contain, would be unlikely to be able to support the many cell divisions that must take place after fertilization in the early stages of **embryogenesis.** If fertilized, the mature ovum will divide asymmetrically one more time, producing a second polar body, which again will contain a haploid set of chromosomes and a small amount of cytoplasm.

The asymmetry of the two cell divisions that the ovum undergoes acts to preserve the advantage of chromosome reassortment, which is essential to maximizing variation in the maternal genetic complement. At the same time, little of its important cytoplasmic content is wasted on the much smaller polar bodies, which will not develop into embryos. The contrast between this process, which yields a large ovum (about 100 micrometers in diameter) and substantial cytoplasmic mass, and the process by which the tiny spermatozoon is produced is clear evidence of the biological importance of producing with maintaining variation in the genetic complement contributed by each individual. However, there are constraints on the degree to which the production of variation can be favored over the survival of the individual gamete. These constraints are minimal in the production of spermatozoa, which can perform their function of seeking and fertilizing the ovum while containing very little cytoplasm. The constraints on miniaturization are much greater in the case of the ovum. The device of producing nonviable polar bodies has evolved to circumvent the constraints imposed by the need of the fertilized egg, or **zygote,** to divide many times and to distribute the original cytoplasmic mass over many cells in early embryo formation. This device maximizes the zygote's chances of successfully yielding a viable new individual and minimizes the cost of maintaining variation. The great difference between the gametes produced by males and females can then be understood in evolutionary terms.

FETAL LIFE

Growth during the embryonic period is characterized by a rapid increase in cell number (called **hyperplasia**). During subsequent stages of intrauterine growth, called the *fetal period,* cell *number* increase will gradually give way to a predominance of cell *size* increase (**hypertrophy**). By the second month of gestation, all of the tissues and organs that will be present in the adult are already in place, even though they will undergo much change in size and shape. The cells that make up the specialized tissues of the various organs of the body

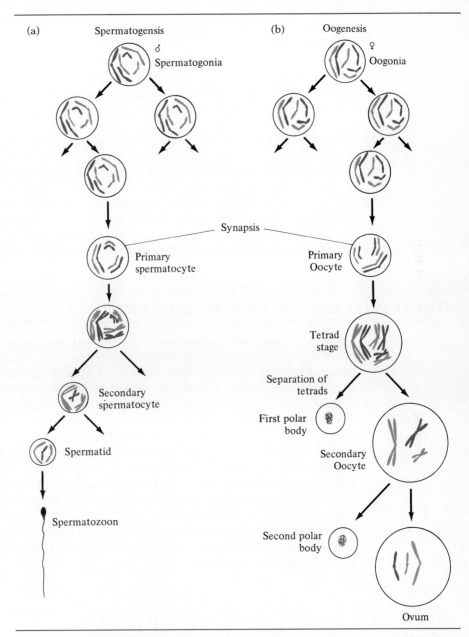

Figure 22-1 Gamete formation producing a spermatozoon (left) and an ovum and two polar bodies (right)

can now grow and begin their specialized functions. This, again, is the outcome of a complex variety of intercellular interactions that at first direct the formation, and later the function, of organs.

VULNERABILITY AND EARLY GROWTH

The fundamental nature of the growth and development that occurs during the embryonic stage of life makes it a time of considerable vulnerability. Trauma experienced in these formative stages often results in early spontaneous abortions. Inherited defects may also lead to early loss. Many early embryos are lost, and at least half of them have inherited some sort of genetic defect. Thus, selection against defective genotypes is an intrinsic characteristic of the human reproductive system. Although certain hereditary defects do result in stillbirths and neonatal mortality, the great majority of losses occur early in gestation, sometimes so early that the mother is unaware or uncertain that a pregnancy has occurred. From the perspective of biological costs, early death of a defective embryo is far less costly than stillbirth of a full-term infant or, worse yet, neonatal or infant mortality. It is also true that the emotional costs of loss increase with the length of time that growth and development continue.

EVOLUTIONARY SIGNIFICANCE OF ABORTIONS

From an evolutionary perspective, the continuation of an unsuccessful pregnancy has the undesirable consequences of preventing a fertile woman from becoming the mother of a healthy child for a longer time than would an early spontaneous abortion. At this time, when a major concern is limiting the size of the world's population, reducing the total number of children a woman may have hardly seems a major consideration. During most of the evolutionary history of our species, however, when infant and child mortality was high and women seldom lived long enough to complete reproductive life, factors that prevented reproductive-age women from having children would have threatened survival of the population and consequently would have been the focus of natural selection. There is no reason to believe that humans are different from other species in this respect. The current concerns for overpopulation and fertility control are quite recent and have not had sufficient time to be reflected in biological changes in processes of such fundamental importance as those by which the species perpetuates itself.

DIFFERENTIAL GROWTH OF ORGANS AND SYSTEMS

As the organs and organ systems that have been formed during embryogenesis grow and mature, the cells that perform specialized functions begin their work. Some systems are much more advanced than others, and some organs—the lungs, for instance—do not actually function until after birth. The fetus receives its nutrients directly into the circulatory system. Therefore, the digestive system is not functional until food is ingested by mouth, although some small amounts of amniotic fluid find their way into the stomach and intestines before birth. Almost all of the waste products produced by the developing fetus' metabolic activities are removed via the maternal blood after they cross the placental membrane. The filtration activity of the fetal kidney, although established, does not result in the production of any significant amount of urine. The fecal content of the fetal intestine is limited to a small amount of a sterile accumulation of the solid components of intestinal secretions and amniotic fluid.

THE FETAL SUPPORT SYSTEM

Although many of the organ systems function at a very low level throughout fetal life, the continuing increase in cell number and cell size is reflected in a steady increase in energy and protein requirements and a concomitant increase in the waste products of **metabolism.** Fetal growth must therefore be accompanied by placental growth, and one of the important determinants of the end of gestation is the limited ability of the placenta to diffuse the gases, nutrients, and waste products that must be exchanged to support the metabolic demands of the fetus. The work done by the placenta in supplying these demands is truly remarkable, since the rate of growth taking place around the time of midgestation, about 4½ months after fertilization, is the most rapid a human will ever experience—on the order of 11 centimeters per month (Sinclair, 1985). This rate does not persist, however, and the length of the fetus increases at the rate of only 2 centimeters a month after the eighth month. Table 22-1 on p. 438 shows the growth in length of the embryo and fetus.

The gestation period is generally divided into trimesters; the second and third trimesters constitute the fetal period. The second trimester is the time of maximal increase in the length of the fetus, while the third trimester is a time when the fetus gains weight, acquires body fat, and elaborates certain features such as hair, eyebrows, and the velvety surface of the tongue. During the second trimester, the musculoskeletal system undergoes a great deal of growth and change as the **cartilage models** of bones give rise to primary **ossification** centers, where the formation of true bone that will replace the cartilage begins. The heart and other muscular organs also grow rapidly at this time, adding many new contractile elements that permit the fetus to move more and more vigorously. As these movements increase within the amniotic sac, they ultimately become perceptible to the mother, confirming the presence of life.(Figure 22-2)

From the beginning of embryonic life, growth takes place along a gradient that favors the head over the lower portions of the body.(Figure 22-3) This gradient persists throughout gestation and remains evident at birth, when the head of the human newborn is disproportionately large and the limbs,

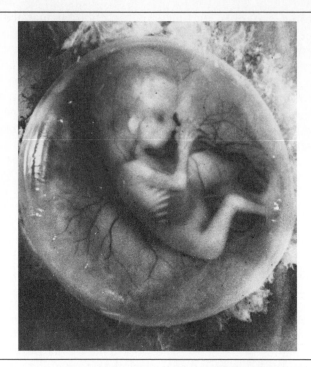

Figure 22-2 The in utero *appearance of a 36mm human embryo*

particularly the lower limbs, are very small and poorly developed. The spinal column ossifies and differentiates the vertebrae from intervertebral disks in early fetal life, but only two spinal curvatures—the thoracic and sacral curvatures—are present at birth. Two more curvatures, the **cervical** and the **lumbar,** will appear after birth. The cervical curvature appears when the baby starts to raise its head when lying in a prone position. The second, the lumbar curvature, develops when the baby starts to walk. Its function is to place the mass of the viscera over the pelvis and permit balance in the upright position. The tissues of the immune system are elaborated and have the potential for rapid growth during the second trimester but will not achieve maximum growth until early childhood.

BIRTH

At the end of the gestation period, approximately 280 days after the egg and sperm have united, birth (parturition) occurs. The factors that lead up to the initiation of labor are not fully understood, but it is generally believed that both the mother and the infant participate in the process through the production of chemical messengers that signal the end of the fetal period of

Series of Human Embryos and Fetuses
Drawn to Proportionate Size

A. Nine embryos arranged
   in series. (Estimated age:
   ca. three weeks to ca.
   two lunar months.)

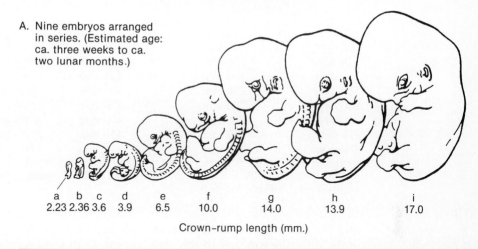

```
  a    b    c    d     e      f          g          h          i
2.23 2.36 3.6  3.9    6.5    10.0       14.0       13.9       17.0
```

Crown–rump length (mm.)

B. Seven fetuses arranged
   in series. (Estimated age:
   ca. early third lunar month
   to five months.)

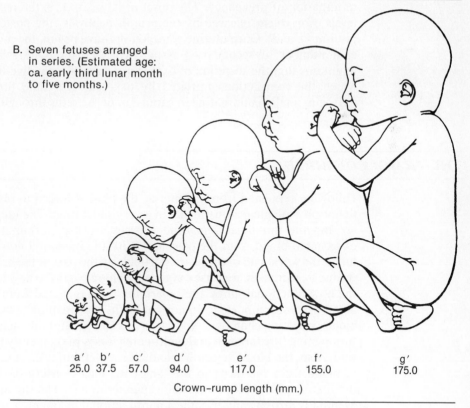

```
  a′   b′    c′    d′     e′         f′          g′
25.0  37.5  57.0  94.0   117.0      155.0       175.0
```

Crown–rump length (mm.)

Figure 22-3 Development of the human embryo (A) and fetus (B)

Table 22-1 *Growth of the Human Embryo and Fetus*

Age	Length (Crown to Rump)	Total Length	Weight
60 days	30 mm	40 mm	5 gm
90 days	55 mm	70 mm	20 gm
120 days	100 mm	150 mm	120 gm
150 days	150 mm	228 mm	300 gm
180 days	200 mm	300 mm	635 gm
210 days	230 mm	350 mm	1,220 gm
240 days	265 mm	400 mm	1,700 gm
270 days	300 mm	450 mm	2,240 gm
280 days	310 mm	470 mm	3,000 gm

Source: Adapted from W. J. Hamilton, J. D. Boyd, and H. W. Mossman, *Human Embryology,* 3d ed. (Baltimore: Williams and Wilkins, 1962), p. 120.

life. The size of the fetus, the increase in intrauterine pressure, and limitations in the diffusing capacity of the placenta are all thought to play a part in the termination of pregnancy. The onset of labor itself is the result of increased levels of **oxytocin** released by the **neurohypophysis** (the posterior part of the pituitary gland). Once uterine contractions have begun, the mother experiences a number of secondary physiological changes. One school of thought maintains that the secretion of oxytocin is part of a positive-feedback loop in which the contractions initiated by oxytocin stimulate further release of oxytocin, finally culminating in expulsion of the fetus through the birth canal.

THE TRAUMA OF BIRTH

Following expulsion from the uterus, the fetus is forced to make a number of major physiological adjustments in a very short time. The lungs must fill with air and the umbilical veins and arteries are lost, terminating the flow of oxygenated blood from the placenta. With the increased flow of blood to the lungs, the work load of the heart, particularly the part of the heart that supplies the lungs, increases. Because oxygenated blood begins to flow to the heart from the now-functional lungs, the separation of oxygenated from nonoxygenated blood becomes important. In normal births, the opening between the **atria,** or blood-collecting chambers of the heart, is closed, and the membrane covering the opening (the **foramen ovale**) ultimately fuses permanently to the interatrial wall. Also, the blood vessel that had, during fetal life, short-circuited the flow of blood from the heart to the lungs, the **ductus arteriosis,** is closed off by the first surges of blood into the expanded lungs. The ductus arteriosis will eventually atrophy and become a nonfunctional ligament. These fundamental physiological changes are, not surprisingly, accompanied, and in part facilitated, by the baby's first cry.

NEONATAL LIFE: THE FIRST 4 WEEKS

Reflexes

The newborn human is helpless in many respects, but it enters the world equipped with a set of reflexes that help it to survive. These reflexes are conventionally checked by the attending physician to assess the infant's neurological development (Lowrey, 1978). One of the earliest reflexes to appear is the sucking reflex, which is present in full-term infants and in all but the smallest premature infants. Newborns will not only suck vigorously on a fingertip placed in their mouths, but they will also turn their heads in the direction of a light touch on the cheek. This is called the "**rooting reflex,**" which, combined with the **sucking reflex**, allows the newborn to find and feed from the mother's breast. Another reflex present by the end of a normal gestation is the **Moro reflex,** which is an embracing motion of the arms in response to removal of support for the head when the baby is lying on its back. Newborns also reflexively "walk" when supported vertically with the soles of the feet on a flat surface and moved slowly forward. If the outside of the sole of a full-term infant's foot is stroked from heel to toe while the baby is lying on its back, the big toe will curl downward. This is called the **Babinski reflex.** An object placed in the hand of a full-term newborn will stimulate a grasp sometimes so strong that the baby can be lifted into the air while holding on to an adult's thumbs. Normal newborns can also blink, sneeze, cough, and gag, all reflexive responses that can protect them from eye damage, choking, and asphyxiation.

HUMAN HELPLESSNESS

When compared to other newborn mammals, humans come into the world with a very small behavioral repertoire. The responses that do occur all serve to permit the infant to maintain contact with its mother, to feed, and to avoid accidental injury. The newborn's most frequent and most effective behavior is its cry, which is well tuned to its mother's hearing and generally elicits a prompt response from any adult within earshot.

The aspect of human helplessness that most differs from that of other mammals is the length of its persistence. Humans are by far the slowest-maturing primate. The burden that such helpless and slow-maturing infants create for their parents must always have been a demanding one, especially during the thousands of generations that preceded the advent of agriculture. Indeed, the burden of transporting the helpless infant may have been implicated in the onset of bipedalism. Considering the magnitude of this burden and its potential for threatening the survival of both parents and infants, the offsetting advantages associated with it would have to be significant. As mentioned earlier, one such advantage is a prolonged learning period. As the subsequent discussion of human growth and development will reveal, the human newborn, helpless as it is, is superbly equipped for learning. Its long period of dependency and its highly evolved central nervous system provide it with the capacity for the complex behavioral patterns that make language and culture possible. It takes a great deal of time to acquire the tools needed to function as an effective member of any human culture, and the slow maturation rate that characterizes our species makes that time available.

THE PHASES OF POSTNATAL GROWTH

1. Infancy

At birth, the average human infant weighs about 3.4 kilograms (7.5 pounds) and is about 51 centimeters (20 inches) long. Full-term females are about 140 grams lighter and 4 millimeters shorter than full-term males. Its proportions differ from those of any later time in life. Its head and neck make up 25 percent of its total length, compared to the 10 percent normally seen in the adult. The newborn's arms are weak and poorly developed, and its legs are even more poorly developed. Whereas the lower limbs represent about half of the total length of the adult, they are only about a third of the newborn's length, and their tendency to be drawn up against the body makes them appear even shorter. Approximately 72 percent of the newborn's weight is water, as compared to about 60 percent in the adult. Of the total body water, the newborn has 37 percent inside its cells, compared to 58 percent in the adult. Extracellular fluid decreases continuously throughout the growth process. Table 22-2 shows the relative sizes of body parts at several ages up to adulthood.

The human newborn's disproportionately large head reflects the greater maturity of the head, or **cephalic** end, of the embryo and fetus compared to the tail, or **caudal** end. This difference in maturity, called the **cranial-caudal gradient,** is an important aspect of prenatal human growth since it results in the presence of a large and relatively well-developed brain early in life. At

Table 22-2 **Percent of Total Body Length of Major Sectors at Various Ages**

Age	Head and Neck	Trunk	Upper Limbs	Lower Limbs
Birth	30	45	10	15
2 years	20	50	10	20
6 years	15	50	10	25
Adult	10	50	10	30

birth, the brain represents from 10 to 12 percent of the total body mass compared to 2 percent of the total body mass at adulthood. The newborn's brain is a rapidly growing organ that will double its weight during the first year of life and will approximate adult size (about triple its weight at birth) by around age 10. Under normal circumstances, the infant's total body weight will double in the first 5 months, will have tripled by the end of the first year, and will be about ten times birth weight by around age 10.

Postnatal growth of the brain takes place through the increase of cell size with virtually no increase in cell number. Important changes in brain function arise from the lengthening of cell processes of the nerve cells (**neurons**) and the establishment of connections (**synapses**) between neurons. One of the features that distinguishes the human brain from that of other mammals is the large number of synaptic connections present and the development of major associative areas where information derived from several sensory channels and from memory is integrated and processed through numerous synapses. In addition to the increase in the length of neurons and the establishment of complex areas of association, the brain also grows by the addition of insulating sheaths of **myelin,** a fatty substance produced by specialized cells. The myelin sheath surrounding major **tracts,** or bundles, of neurons greatly accelerates the transmission of electrical impulses from one area to another. The myelin-ization process therefore enables the increasingly sophisticated areas of association in the maturing brain to receive more information faster than would be possible if neurons were unsheathed.

Other organs besides the brain grow rapidly during the first year of life. Most impressive is the growth of the thymus, a gland located in the chest behind the sternum, or breast bone. The thymus achieves about 40 percent of its adult weight in the first year of life. It will continue to grow rapidly until about the age of 12 years, when it is usually about double the size it will be at age 20. The thymus gland is a very important component of the developing immune system, playing a major role in the "education" of T-cells, which are crucial to the defense against many infections as well as cancers.

During the first year of life, both head circumference and chest circumference will increase by about one third. In a normal, well-fed baby, chest circumference will exceed head circumference for the first time at around the sixth month. In poorly fed or sickly babies, this may not happen until much later, a fact that is often used to assess the nutritional status of infants.

Height, or length, increases by about 50 percent during the first year of life, although the rate of height increase (growth velocity) actually declines from shortly after birth until the onset of the adolescent growth spurt. The most rapid increase in length had occurred in mid-gestation, when for a short time the fetus was growing at a rate of 11 centimeters a month. Figure 22-4 shows the rate of increase in length during gestation. Figure 22-5 shows the increments in height recorded for British girls and boys from birth until adulthood. It can be seen from these curves that postnatal growth is really a gradual process, with the exception of the period preceding puberty, when a

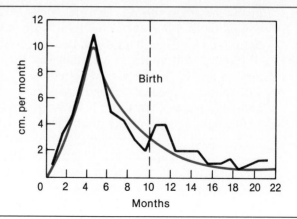

Figure 22-4 The rate of growth in length of the human embryo, fetus and infant

brief acceleration occurs and finally gives way to the total cessation of growth marking the attainment of adulthood. Seasonal variation in the rate of height increase has been reported, with faster growth occurring during the spring and summer months (Tanner and Whitehouse, 1982).

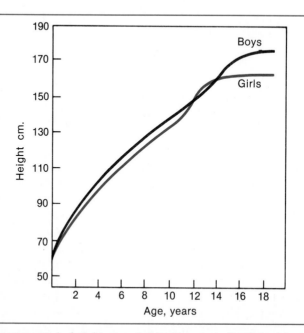

Figure 22-5 Increments in height recorded by Tanner in English girls and boys from birth to adulthood

2. Childhood

Childhood, for the most part, is characterized by rapid neurological development and gradual increases in organ sizes, height, and weight. Following the attainment of upright posture at around 1 year of age, the infant progresses to the toddler stage, during which neuromuscular control improves steadily. Learning to speak is also a major milestone for the toddler. Some students of human growth and development believe that the reflexes present at birth form the foundations for both neuromuscular and intellectual development, with the increasing recruitment of neurons and the addition of synapses underlying both processes. There is little doubt that the human child processes, stores, and analyzes a remarkable amount of information each day. One aspect of that processing, the acquisition and use of language, is an impressive accomplishment that is still not fully understood. Tables 22-3 and 22-4 show some of the critical phases in human language attainment.

The rate at which neurological development takes place varies considerably from one individual to another, just as physical growth does. It also appears that the process can be retarded, perhaps with long-term consequences, when serious deprivation, trauma, or disease intrudes. As mentioned previously, the human brain attains adult size by about 10 years of age. In this area of growth, as in all others, the average female is closer to the completion of growth than the average male of the same age. This sex difference in maturity is already present at birth and remains about 10 percent up to and including the occurrence of sexual maturation and the final cessation of growth. Thus, the part of the life cycle that we have designated "childhood" is of greater duration in boys than in girls. Differences in size and proportion that characterize male and female adults are largely the result of the longer period of childhood growth that boys experience.

Table 22-3 **Vocabulary Development of Children up to 6 Years of Age**

	AGE	
Year	Month	Number of Words
1	0	3
1	3	19
1	6	22
2	0	272
2	6	446
3	0	896
3	6	1222
4	0	1540
5	0	2072
6	0	2562

SOURCE: G. H. Lowrey, *Growth and Development of Children* (Chicago: Year Book Medical Publishers, 1978), p. 184.

Table 22-4 *Pattern of Normal Language Development*

Age	Vocalization and Speech	Response and Comprehension
1 month	Much crying and whimpering; produces some vowel and few consonant sounds.	Smiles; decreases activity; startles at loud sounds.
3 months	Different cries for pain, hunger, and discomfort; decreased crying time; some repetitive sounds ("ga, ga, ga"); coos and sighs.	Vocal gurgle in response to soothing voice; some imitative response to speech.
5 months	Babbles; vocal play; many repetitive sounds; all vowels, *m, k, g, b,* and *p;* laughs out loud.	Imitative response to speech decreased; turns and looks to sound; recognizes familiar voice; vocalizes displeasure.
7 months	Considerable variety in babbling, loudness and rhythm of all vocalizations; adds *d, t, n,* and *w* to repertory of sounds; talks to toys.	Gestures increase as part of vocal responses to stimuli; response to sound is increasingly influenced by visual factors.
9 months	Cries to get attention; increasing variations in pitch; "mama," "dada" and "baba" part of vocal play but not associated with a person or object.	Retreats from strangers, often accompanied by crying; may imitate hand clapping.
11 months	May use one word correctly; imitates sounds and correct number of syllables; little crying.	Comprehends "no no"; responds to "bye-bye" or "patty-cake" with appropriate gestures.

The most noticeable changes that childhood growth produces are those of increased height and increased length of the legs. Children grow by increasing the length of the long bones of the legs and arms and by increasing the height of individual vertebrae of the spinal column. This form of growth is called **epiphyseal growth** because it involves the presence of epiphyses, the growing ends of long bones separated from the shaft by a cartilaginous plate.

When growth occurs at an epiphysis, length increases even though the bone serves as a weight-bearing structure and may be subject to shocks and trauma from activity. Figure 22-6 shows a radiograph of the knee of a 10-year-old boy. The two epiphyses in this radiograph are located at the distal (lower) end of the femur (thigh bone) and at the proximal (upper) end of the tibia (shin bone). Both epiphyses appear to be open spaces because cartilage is not mineralized to the extent that bone is and is therefore not opaque in a radiograph. The growth that occurs on the end of the long bones is an extension of the end of the shaft through the formation of first a collagen framework and then the

Table 22-4 ***Pattern of Normal Language Development (continued)***

Age	Vocalization and Speech	Response and Comprehension
1–2 years	Much unintelligible jargon; all vowels present; improves articulation so that 25% of words intelligible; names many objects by 24 mo; much echolalia.	Recognizes 150–300 words by 24 months, responds correctly to several commands, ("sit down," "give me that," "stand up," "come here," and so on).
2–3 years	Tries new sounds but articulation lags behind vocabulary; 50–75% of words intelligible; often omits final consonants; jargon nearly absent.	Comprehends 800–1,000 words by 3 years, responds to many commands using "on," "under," "up," and so on.
3–4 years	Speech nears 100% intelligibility; faulty articulations of *l* and *r* frequent; uses 3–4 words in sentences; uses a few plurals by 4 years.	Recognizes plurals, sex differences, adjectives, and adverbs; comprehends complex sentences.
4–6 years	Syntax correct by 6 years forms 5- or 6-word sentences that are compound or complex (with some dependent clauses); fluent; articulation good except for *sh, z, ch,* and *j;* can express temporal relations; voice well modulated in conversation.	Understands 2,500–3,000 words; carries out commands involving 3–4 actions; comprehends "if," "because," and "why."

SOURCE: From G. H. Lowrey, *Growth and Development of Children* (Chicago: Year Book Medical Publishers, 1978), p. 185.

deposition of bone mineral on the framework. The epiphysis and the cartilage plate move farther from the mid-point of the shaft as the end of the shaft grows.

As the long bones are increasing in length, they are also increasing in diameter. To increase the diameter of the long bones, bone-forming cells (osteoblasts), similar to those that form the collagen matrix at the epiphyses, lay down and mineralize layers (lamellae) of bone on the outer surface of the shaft. A fibrous membrane called the **periosteum** surrounds the bone, adhering tightly to it. The inner layer of the periosteum (the **osteogenic layer**), is made up of cells, including the osteoblasts that lay down new bone.

Although the predominant factor in the increase in height during childhood is the growth of the long bones of the lower limbs, the spine increases in length as well. Each vertebrae increases in height through growth occurring at the **annular epiphyses.** This aspect of growth is slow and persistent, and the last epiphyses to close are generally those of the thoracic vertebrae. As a conse-

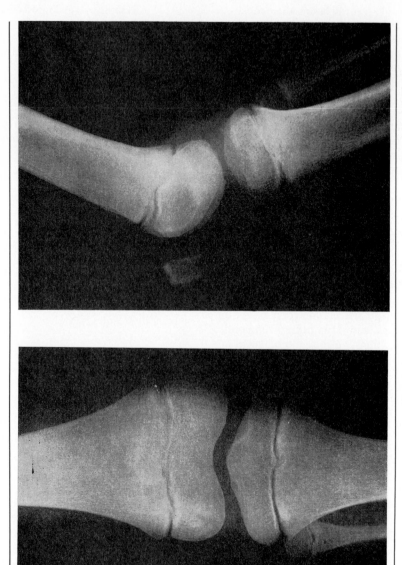

Figure 22-6 Radiography of the knee of a ten year old boy showing the cartilaginous plates of epiphyses which appear as dark lines

quence of the sequencing of epiphyseal closures, growth of the spine persists after growth of the legs has stopped, and the sitting height will make up a larger proportion of total height in the adult than was the case in late childhood.

The skull, mandible, and dentition also undergo major changes during childhood growth. By age 10, the size of the skull is nearly that of an adult, but much change will take place in the face and jaws later. The eruption of the deciduous (or milk) teeth begins during the first year of life, and some of the permanent teeth (the 6-year molars) appear in midchildhood. Figure 22-7 shows the eruption times of the permanent dentitions of boys and girls.

Because girls begin adolescence earlier than boys by an average of two years, boys have more time to increase the length of the legs. As a result, men are usually not only taller than women but also have proportionately longer legs.

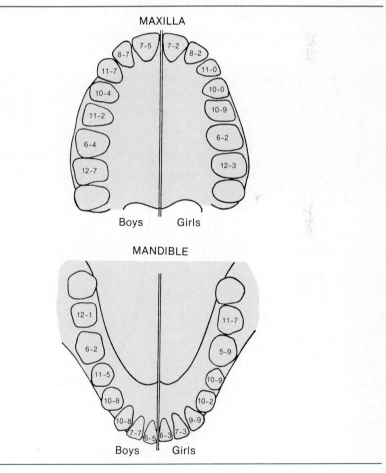

Figure 22-7 Eruption times (in years and months) of the permanent dentition of girls and boys

3. Adolescence and Puberty

The slow, steady growth of childhood eventually gives way to an accelerated phase of growth called the **adolescent growth spurt.** This growth spurt is the result of changes in endocrine function and hormone secretion that will lead to sexual maturation. In both sexes the adrenal cortex begins to secrete androgenic hormones at this time. In girls, higher concentrations of the hormone estrogen lead not only to more rapid growth but also to a major change in body composition, as well as to the development of secondary sexual characteristics. The first indications of puberty are usually an increase in weight followed by an acceleration of growth in height. In girls, this acceleration can usually be detected at around age 11, while in boys it happens at around age 13. It is in this age group that girls are frequently taller than many of their male classmates. In boys, the growth spurt is a response to increased secretion of testosterone by the Leydig cells of the testes.

The adolescent growth spurt in both sexes is usually completed within a 2-year period. At its onset, the rate of growth in height is the lowest since the first trimester of intrauterine life, on the order of 6 centimeters a year. At the peak of the growth spurt, about a year after its onset, **peak height velocity,** the most rapid period of postnatal growth, occurs and for a brief period may approximate 10 centimeters a year. Peak height velocity occurs, on the average, at age 12 in girls and at age 14 in boys (see Figure 22-8). It is followed

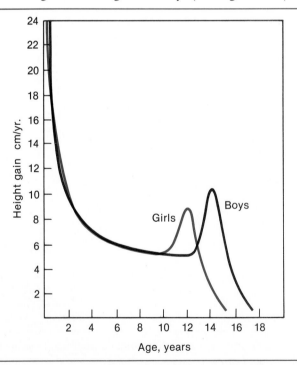

Figure 22-8 Velocity curves for growth in height in girls and boys

by a year of declining growth and finally by cessation of growth in height in both sexes (Figure 22-9). After growth in height has ceased, there is still a period of changing body composition as adult values are gradually attained. It is significant that the occurrence of a lengthy quiescent period followed by an adolescent growth spurt is a pattern unique to humans. Tables 22-5 and 22-6 show the weight and height percentiles for girls and boys in the United States from birth to age 18.

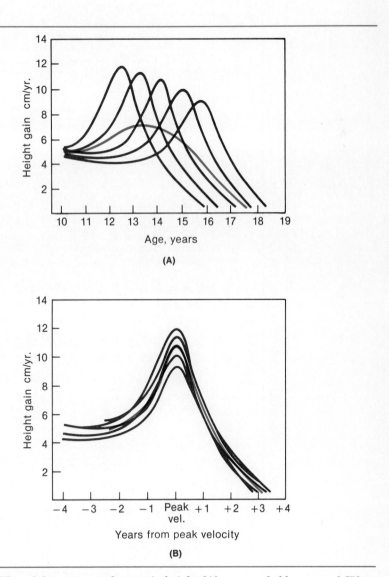

Figure 22-9 The adolescent growth spurt in height (A) as recorded by age and (B) as measured from peak height velocity

Table 22-5 Weight and Height Percentile Table for Girls up to Age 18

Weight in pounds			Weight in kilograms			Age	Height in inches			Height in centimeters		
10%	50%	90%	10%	50%	90%		10%	50%	90%	10%	50%	90%
6.2	7.4	8.6	2.81	3.36	3.90	Birth	18.8	19.8	20.4	47.8	50.2	51.0
8.0	9.7	11.0	3.30	4.20	5.00	1 months	20.2	21.0	22.0	50.4	52.8	55.0
9.5	11.0	12.5	4.10	5.00	5.80	2 months	21.5	22.2	23.2	53.7	55.5	59.6
10.7	12.4	14.0	4.85	5.62	6.35	3 months	22.4	23.4	24.3	56.9	59.5	61.7
12.0	13.7	15.5	5.30	6.20	7.20	4 months	23.2	24.2	25.2	59.6	61.0	64.8
13.0	14.7	17.0	5.90	6.80	7.70	5 months	24.0	25.0	26.0	60.7	64.2	67.0
14.1	16.0	18.6	6.40	7.26	8.44	6 months	24.6	25.7	26.7	62.5	65.2	67.8
16.6	19.2	22.4	7.53	8.71	10.16	9 months	26.4	27.6	28.7	67.0	70.1	72.9
18.4	21.5	24.8	8.35	9.75	11.25	12 months	27.8	29.2	30.3	70.6	74.2	77.1
21.2	24.5	28.3	9.62	11.11	12.84	18 months	30.2	31.8	33.3	76.8	80.9	84.5
23.5	27.1	31.7	10.66	12.29	14.38	2 years	32.3	34.1	35.8	82.0	86.6	91.0
25.5	29.6	34.6	11.57	13.43	15.69	2½ years	34.0	36.0	37.9	86.3	91.4	96.4
27.6	31.8	37.4	12.52	14.42	16.96	3 years	35.6	37.7	39.8	90.5	95.7	101.1
29.5	33.9	40.4	13.38	15.38	18.33	3½ years	37.1	39.2	41.5	94.2	99.5	105.4
31.2	36.2	43.5	14.15	16.42	19.73	4 years	38.4	40.6	43.1	97.6	103.2	109.6
32.9	38.5	46.7	14.92	17.46	21.18	4½ years	39.7	42.0	44.7	100.9	106.8	113.5
34.8	40.5	49.2	15.79	18.37	22.32	5 years	40.5	42.9	45.4	103.0	109.1	115.4
38.0	44.0	51.2	17.24	19.96	23.22	5½ years	42.4	44.4	46.8	107.8	112.8	118.9
39.6	46.5	54.2	17.96	21.09	24.58	6 years	43.5	45.6	48.1	110.6	115.9	122.3
42.2	49.4	57.7	19.14	22.41	26.17	6½ years	44.8	46.9	49.4	113.7	119.1	125.6

Table 22-5 Weight and Height Percentile Table for Girls up to Age 18 (continued)

Weight in pounds			Weight in kilograms			Age	Height in inches			Height in centimeters		
10%	50%	90%	10%	50%	90%		10%	50%	90%	10%	50%	90%
44.5	52.2	61.2	20.19	23.68	27.76	7 years	46.0	48.1	50.7	116.8	122.3	128.9
46.6	55.2	65.6	21.14	25.04	29.76	7½ years	47.0	49.3	51.9	119.5	125.2	131.8
48.6	58.1	69.9	22.04	26.35	31.71	8 years	48.1	50.4	53.0	122.1	128.0	134.6
50.6	61.0	74.5	22.95	27.67	33.79	8½ years	49.0	51.4	54.1	124.6	130.5	137.5
52.6	63.8	79.1	23.86	28.94	35.88	9 years	50.0	52.3	55.3	127.0	132.9	140.4
54.9	67.1	84.4	24.90	30.44	38.28	9½ years	50.9	53.5	56.4	129.4	135.8	143.2
57.1	70.3	89.7	25.90	31.89	40.69	10 years	51.8	54.6	57.5	131.7	138.6	146.0
59.9	74.6	95.1	27.17	33.79	43.14	10½ years	52.9	55.8	58.9	134.4	141.7	149.7
62.6	78.8	100.4	28.40	35.74	45.54	11 years	53.9	57.0	60.4	137.0	144.7	153.4
66.1	83.2	106.0	29.98	37.74	48.08	11½ years	55.0	58.3	61.8	139.8	148.1	157.0
69.5	87.6	111.5	31.52	39.74	50.58	12 years	56.1	59.8	63.2	142.6	151.9	160.6
74.7	93.4	118.0	33.88	42.37	53.52	12½ years	57.4	60.7	64.0	145.9	154.3	162.7
79.9	99.1	124.5	36.24	44.95	56.47	13 years	58.7	61.8	64.9	149.1	157.1	164.8
85.5	103.7	128.9	38.78	47.04	58.47	13½ years	59.5	62.4	65.3	151.1	158.4	165.9
91.0	108.4	133.3	41.28	49.17	60.46	14 years	60.2	62.8	65.7	153.0	159.6	167.0
94.2	111.0	135.7	42.73	50.35	61.55	14½ years	60.7	63.1	66.0	154.1	160.4	167.6
97.4	113.5	138.1	44.18	51.48	62.64	15 years	61.1	63.4	66.2	155.2	161.1	168.1
99.2	115.3	139.6	45.00	52.30	63.32	15½ years	61.3	63.7	66.4	155.7	161.7	168.6
100.9	117.0	141.1	45.77	53.07	64.00	16 years	61.5	63.9	66.5	156.1	162.2	169.0
101.9	118.1	142.2	46.22	53.57	64.50	16½ years	61.5	63.9	66.6	156.2	162.4	169.2
102.8	119.1	143.3	46.63	54.02	65.00	17 years	61.5	64.0	66.7	156.3	162.5	169.4
103.2	119.5	143.9	46.81	54.20	65.27	17½ years	61.5	64.0	66.7	156.3	162.5	169.4
103.5	119.9	144.5	46.95	54.39	65.54	18 years	61.5	64.0	66.7	156.3	162.5	169.4

SOURCE: From G. H. Lowrey, *Growth and Development of Children* (Chicago: Year Book Medical Publishers, 1978), p. 448.

Table 22-6 Weight and Height Percentile Table for Boys up to Age 18

Weight in pounds			Weight in kilograms			Age	Height in inches			Height in centimeters		
10%	50%	90%	10%	50%	90%		10%	50%	90%	10%	50%	90%
6.3	7.5	9.1	2.86	3.40	4.13	Birth	18.9	19.9	21.0	48.1	50.6	53.3
8.5	10.0	11.5	3.80	4.60	5.20	1 months	20.2	21.2	22.2	50.4	53.0	55.5
10.0	11.5	13.2	4.60	5.20	6.00	2 months	21.5	22.5	23.5	53.7	56.0	60.0
11.1	12.6	14.5	5.03	5.72	6.58	3 months	22.8	23.8	24.7	57.8	60.4	62.8
12.5	14.0	16.2	5.60	6.30	7.30	4 months	23.7	24.7	25.7	60.5	62.0	65.2
13.7	15.0	17.7	6.20	7.00	8.00	5 months	24.5	25.5	26.5	61.8	65.0	67.3
14.8	16.7	19.2	6.71	7.58	8.71	6 months	25.2	26.1	27.3	63.9	66.4	69.3
17.8	20.0	22.9	8.07	9.07	10.39	9 months	27.0	28.0	29.2	68.6	71.2	74.2
19.6	22.2	25.4	8.89	10.70	11.52	12 months	28.5	29.6	30.7	72.4	75.2	78.1
22.3	25.2	29.0	10.12	11.43	13.15	18 months	31.0	32.2	33.5	78.8	81.8	85.0
24.7	27.7	31.9	11.20	12.56	14.47	2 years	33.1	34.4	35.9	84.2	87.5	91.1
26.6	30.0	34.5	12.07	13.61	15.65	2½ years	34.8	36.3	37.9	88.5	92.1	96.2
28.7	32.2	36.8	13.02	14.61	16.69	3 years	36.3	37.9	39.6	92.3	96.2	100.5
30.4	34.3	39.1	13.79	15.56	17.74	3½ years	37.8	39.3	41.1	96.0	99.8	104.5
32.1	36.4	41.4	14.56	16.51	18.78	4 years	39.1	40.7	42.7	99.3	103.4	108.5
33.8	38.4	43.9	15.33	17.42	19.91	4½ years	40.3	42.0	44.2	102.4	106.7	112.3
35.5	40.5	46.7	16.10	18.37	21.18	5 years	40.8	42.8	45.2	103.7	108.7	114.7
38.8	45.6	53.1	17.60	20.68	24.09	5½ years	42.6	45.0	47.3	108.3	114.4	120.1
40.9	48.3	56.4	18.55	21.91	25.58	6 years	43.8	46.3	48.6	111.2	117.5	123.5
43.4	51.2	60.4	19.69	23.22	27.40	6½ years	44.9	47.6	50.0	114.1	120.8	127.0
45.8	54.1	64.4	20.77	24.54	29.21	7 years	46.0	48.9	51.4	116.9	124.1	130.5
48.5	57.1	68.7	22.00	25.90	31.16	7½ years	47.2	50.0	52.7	120.0	127.1	133.9
51.2	60.1	73.0	23.22	27.26	33.11	8 years	48.5	51.2	54.0	123.1	130.0	137.3

Table 22-6 Weight and Height Percentile Table for Boys up to Age 18 (continued)

Weight in pounds			Weight in kilograms			Age	Height in inches			Height in centimeters		
10%	50%	90%	10%	50%	90%		10%	50%	90%	10%	50%	90%
53.8	63.1	77.0	24.40	28.62	34.93	8½ years	49.5	52.3	55.1	125.7	132.8	140.0
56.3	66.0	81.0	25.54	29.94	36.74	9 years	50.5	53.3	56.1	128.3	135.5	142.6
58.7	69.0	85.5	26.63	31.30	38.78	9½ years	51.4	54.3	57.1	130.6	137.9	145.1
61.1	71.9	89.9	27.71	32.61	40.78	10 years	52.3	55.2	58.1	132.8	140.3	147.5
63.7	74.8	94.6	28.89	33.93	42.91	10½ years	53.2	56.0	58.9	135.1	142.3	149.7
66.3	77.6	99.3	30.07	35.20	45.04	11 years	54.0	56.8	59.8	137.3	144.2	151.8
69.2	81.0	104.5	31.39	36.74	47.40	11½ years	55.0	57.8	60.9	139.8	146.9	154.8
72.0	84.4	109.6	32.66	38.28	49.71	12 years	56.1	58.9	62.2	142.4	149.6	157.9
74.6	88.7	116.4	33.84	40.23	52.80	12½ years	56.9	60.0	63.6	144.5	152.3	161.6
77.1	93.0	123.2	34.97	42.18	55.88	13 years	57.7	61.0	65.1	146.6	155.0	165.3
82.2	100.3	130.1	37.29	45.50	59.01	13½ years	58.8	62.6	66.5	149.4	158.9	168.9
87.2	107.6	136.9	39.55	48.81	62.10	14 years	59.9	64.0	67.9	152.1	162.7	172.4
93.3	113.9	142.4	42.32	51.66	64.59	14½ years	61.0	65.1	68.7	155.0	165.3	174.6
99.4	120.1	147.8	45.09	54.48	67.04	15 years	62.1	66.1	69.6	157.8	167.8	176.7
105.2	124.9	152.6	47.72	56.65	69.22	15½ years	63.1	66.8	70.2	160.3	169.7	178.2
111.0	129.7	157.3	50.35	58.83	71.35	16 years	64.1	67.8	70.7	162.8	171.6	179.7
114.3	133.0	161.0	51.85	60.33	73.03	16½ years	64.6	68.0	71.1	164.2	172.7	180.7
117.5	136.2	164.6	53.30	61.78	74.66	17 years	65.2	68.4	71.5	165.5	173.7	181.6
118.8	137.6	166.8	53.89	62.41	75.66	17½ years	65.3	68.5	71.6	165.9	174.1	182.0
120.0	139.0	169.0	54.43	63.05	76.66	18 years	65.5	68.7	71.8	166.3	174.5	182.4

SOURCE: From G. H. Lowrey, *Growth and Development of Children* (Chicago: Year Book Medical Publishers, 1978). p. 447.

4. Menarche

In girls, the adolescent growth spurt is part of the process of sexual maturation that also includes the occurrence of **menarche,** the first menstrual period. Menarche occurs after growth in height has started to decline. There is some evidence that menarche cannot occur until there is a sufficient level of body fat. It is known that girls who have proportionally more body fat experience menarche earlier and that girls whose body composition is especially lean, as is the case with some female athletes, may experience menarche much later than the average. Even in adulthood, women who exercise heavily and maintain very low body fat levels experience irregular menstrual periods and, on occasion, amenorrhea, or the absence of menstrual periods. It is thought that body composition and menstrual periods are related through the differences in metabolic rate that characterize fat versus lean tissue as well as through the tendency for fatty tissues to store and synthesize certain estrogenic hormones. Since the carrying of a fetus to term and successful lactation thereafter make severe demands on the mother's energy reserves, it might be anticipated that mechanisms would exist to delay reproduction until some chance of success existed. The steady decline in the age of menarche that was recorded in Europe and the United States from the mid-nineteenth to the mid-twentieth centuries was associated with a substantial improvement in nutritional status of those populations and with the opportunity to accumulate energy reserves earlier in life. Similar trends toward earlier menarche have been seen in a number of other populations in recent times as nutritional status has improved.

GROWTH AND DEVELOPMENT AS MECHANISMS FOR MAINTAINING PHENOTYPIC PLASTICITY

The preceding discussion of growth and development provides the background for consideration of the manner by which environmental factors can play a part in shaping the adult organism. The growth process has been described as a target-seeking one. For instance, the genotype may have the potential to produce a phenotype whose stature is 180 centimeters (70 inches). If the environment is ideal, growth will take place in an orderly sequence that will end when the stature of 180 centimeters has been attained. However, factors that prevent the normal rate of growth from occurring may require that accelerated growth occur to compensate for a preceding delay. Such periods of "catch-up growth" have often been observed in human children, and it is thought that in cases of short delays followed by provision of adequate resources to sustain catch-up growth, there is a good chance that the process will be back on target and that subsequent stages of growth and development will be unaffected. When this happens, the genetically programmed stature of 180 centimeters may still be attained. However, catch-up growth does not always occur. When there is failure to restore the trajectory of the growth process to normal, one of two possible causes can be inferred.

First, the delay may have been the result of a factor or factors that intruded on a critical, sensitive aspect of the growth process and therefore produced an irreversible change in its outcome. The impact of iodine deficiency on the development of the fetal brain resulting in cretinism is one such factor. In such cases, a stature of under 150 centimeters (58 inches) may be all that can be attained before growth stops permanently.

A second possibility is that the length of time that the growth process was delayed was long enough to allow other aspects of the process to cross critical thresholds, so that the opportunity to catch up is foreclosed. An example of the second category would be the reductions in stature that are seen in communities where malnutrition is a chronic condition. In such circumstances, childhood growth slows and even stops for a considerable length of time. Epiphyseal growth may lag behind normal by months or even years, and epiphyses may close, ending long bone growth permanently before the genetically programmed height has been attained. In such cases, symmetrical reductions in body size pervade all tissues and organs to some extent, but the most pronounced effects can be seen in the overall reductions in skeletal muscle development.

In the extreme, long-term undernutrition can produce "nutritional dwarfism," a condition in which the arrest of growth is severe and prolonged enough to result in a greatly miniaturized but nonetheless symmetrical adult. In such cases, there is little or no evidence of an adolescent growth spurt, and sexual maturation may be delayed until the late teens or early twenties.

CHRONIC MILD UNDERNUTRITION

In less extreme cases of chronic but mild undernutrition, body size may be reduced, the adolescent growth spurt delayed and attenuated, and sexual maturation delayed in both sexes. Chronic mild undernutrition, although less dramatic in its impact on human health and survival than severe undernutrition, is nonetheless a major worldwide concern since so many children are affected by it. There is no question that much of the world's population has experienced some degree of growth retardation over much of recent human history. The dramatic increases in body size and acceleration of sexual maturity that have been occurring over the past 100 years give evidence that environmental constraints had been preventing human growth from attaining its genetically determined potential before improvements in food production and distribution and public health care became widespread. The range of values for average stature that have been recorded in human populations over time is strong evidence of human "phenotypic plasticity," the shaping of the phenotype by environmental modification of the genetically-transmitted program of growth and development. As will be discussed later, the phenomenon of phenotypic plasticity may, under certain circumstances, have considerable adaptive significance.

ENDROCRINE FACTORS CONTROLLING GROWTH

Childhood growth is regulated by the secretion of growth hormone by the pituitary gland. Human growth hormone is species-specific. Therefore, until recently, the only sources of growth hormone to treat children with a growth hormone deficiency were human cadavers. Developments in biotechnology have now made it possible to synthesize the hormone artificially. Human growth hormone stimulates bone growth and, in the presence of sufficient insulin, stimulates the uptake of amino acids by growing cells. These amino acids are used by cells to synthesize proteins in a process called **anabolism,** which is essential to growth. Growth hormone is in many cases associated with increased cell division, resulting in increased cell number (hyperplasia).

In order for normal growth to occur, it is also essential that the thyroid gland, located in the neck, produce sufficient thyroid hormones. Thyroid hormones are produced in response to the release of thyroid-stimulating hormone from the pituitary gland and can only be produced in the necessary quantities when sufficient iodine is present. When there is an insufficiency of iodine in the diet, the thyroid gland will increase in size in an attempt to compensate. The thyroid can become extremely enlarged, a condition called *goiter.* When chronic iodine deficiency is experienced prenatally, the newborn may exhibit the symptoms of **cretinism.** This condition is characterized by very small body size and severe and irreversible mental retardation, since brain growth is most affected by the inability of neurons to absorb nutrients in the absence of sufficient thyroid hormone. Metabolic rate, the rate at which cells release and use energy and synthesize proteins, is strongly influenced by thyroid hormone, and such important functions as adjusting to cold temperatures by raising the metabolic rate depend upon the proper function of the thyroid gland.

The **androgenic hormones,** produced by the adrenal cortex in both sexes and in the Leydig cells of the testes, stimulate the growth of muscle cells. This growth is *hypertrophic,* meaning that growth occurs through the uptake of amino acids by existing muscle cells rather than by the division of cells to increase cell number, as is the case in the response to growth hormone. Muscle-cell size increase serves to increase the diameter of muscle fibers. Since the contractile force generated by a muscle is proportional to its diameter, the hypertrophic growth of muscle under the influence of androgens translates directly into increased strength. The dramatic increase in strength that occurs in males after puberty is in large part explained by the fact that at the onset of puberty, males begin to secrete increased amounts of androgenic steroids in the adrenal cortex at the same time that the Leydig cells of the testes secrete large amounts of testosterone. Male pubertal growth therefore differs from female pubertal growth in that males are, in effect, subjected to a "double dose" of androgenic steroids and therefore experience greater hypertrophic growth of skeletal muscle and other connective tissue. Females, on the other hand, produce androgenic hormones only in the adrenal cortex and therefore experience a more modest spurt of hypertrophic muscle growth.

Estrogenic hormones produced in the ovaries of the female exert their effects on a number of target organs where growth is stimulated during puberty. Specific target organs include the uterus and the breasts, both of which experience substantial increases in size preceding the occurrence of menarche. With respect to skeletal growth, the major effect of estrogens is on closure of the epiphyses in females, the timing of which is determined by estrogen levels. While the gonads of both sexes produce estrogens throughout life, the amount produced in the testes after puberty is relatively small, and the effect of estrogens on male epiphyseal closure appears to be minor. In fact, the determinants of epiphyseal closure in males are still poorly understood.

The advantages that slow growth and late maturation confer on the human child center on the ability to learn and become enculturated. Because growth is so prolonged, there are mechanisms to protect the growing organism from environmental damage even though the growth process itself must be delayed. When growth is delayed for a short time, a period of catch-up growth will often occur. When conditions are severe enough to delay growth for a lengthy period, a permanent reduction in size may occur. The alteration of body size seen when environmental conditions severely retard growth is one example of human phenotypic plasticity. It may be expressed in delay of maturation as well as in reduction in size. The ability to alter the phenotype in this way may have important evolutionary consequences.

BIBLIOGRAPHY

EDELMAN, G. M. 1984. Cell adhesion molecules: A molecular basis for animal form. *Scientific American* 250: 118–29.

HAMILTON, W. J., J. D. BOYD, and H. W. MOSSMAN. 1962. *Human Embryology,* 3d ed. Baltimore: Williams & Wilkins.

GORDON, R., and A. G. JACOBSON. 1978. The shaping of tissues in embryos. *Scientific American* 6: 106–13.

GROBSTEEN, C. 1979. External human fertilization. *Scientific American* 6: 57–67.

LOWREY, G. H. 1978. *Growth and Development of Children.* Chicago: Year Book Medical Publishers.

PIAGET, J. 1969. *The Psychology of the Child.* New York: Basic Books.

SCAMMON, R. E. 1953. Developmental anatomy. In *Morris' Human Anatomy,* 11th ed. J. P. Schaeffer, ed., (New York: McGraw-Hill), pp. 11–62.

SINCLAIR, D. 1985. *Human Growth after Birth,* 4th ed. Oxford: Oxford University Press.

TANNER, J. M., and R. M. WHITEHOUSE. 1982. *Atlas of Children's Growth.* London: Academic Press.

Chapter

23

The Biology of Human Diversity

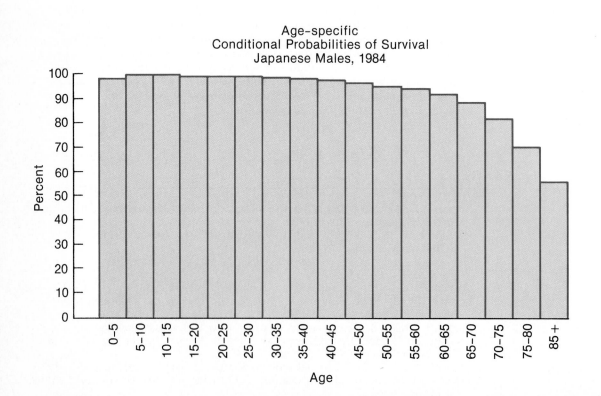

Age-specific
Conditional Probabilities of Survival
Japanese Males, 1984

Human populations were small through most of species history. The current trend of rapidly increasing population size is recent and unprecedented. The effect that large populations of humans is having and will have on human evolution and on the future of life on this planet is a matter of increasing concern as the limitations of the earth's resources and the tolerance of the environment are tested. The expansion of the human population is the result of the success humans have achieved in buffering themselves from the stresses of the environment. Contemporary human demography must be viewed as representing a transient phase differing vastly from that of earlier periods. The demographic profiles of developed and less-developed countries are still different, but there appears to be a trend toward increased life expectancy everywhere. As reductions in birthrates and infant mortalities occur in less-developed countries, their demographic profiles are becoming more similar to those of the developed countries. The impact of infectious disease on human mortality is changing. The causes of death in populations that have more old people differ from those that have more young people. The potential evolutionary significance of the changing demographic characteristics of the world's population is a matter of both practical and theoretical interest. As the population of the world grows larger and more interconnected, the factors that produced biological diversity among human populations are becoming less important. An unprecedented opportunity to accumulate new genetic variability is one of the consequences of the current phase of human population biology. What this may mean for the future of human diversity is one of the most engaging questions in modern biology.

DEMOGRAPHY: THE STUDY OF LIVING POPULATIONS

One of the major features of twentieth-century biology has been its emphasis on populations as opposed to individuals. While many biological phenomena must be examined in individuals or in small samples at best, it is always recognized that the results of such studies must be interpreted cautiously since the samples chosen may not be representative of the overall population from which they were drawn. The same issue was raised when discussing taxonomic placement of fossil populations (Chapter 7). In the development of the physical sciences, events involving millions of molecules were studied to develop a theoretical basis on which to predict the outcome of an experimental procedure. Through successful application of the experimental method, it was shown that many events, such as the diffusion of gases from one chamber to another, could be predicted with a high degree of precision even though the behavior of a single molecule would remain unknown. Realization that the **probabilistic** approach, so successful in the physical sciences, could be applied to population biology was an important stimulus to the development of genetic theory. However, just as the behavior of a single molecule defied prediction even when the aggregate behavior of a population of millions conformed to expectations, the fate of an individual usually cannot be predicted strictly on the basis of population statistics. Because the understanding of biological events demands the study of populations, variation within as well as between populations must be taken into account. General acceptance of the importance of variation in the biology of populations has had the salutary effect of reducing the tendency to expect individuals to be identical or to conform to a type.

The study of human populations is the science of **demography.** From the standpoint of both the human biologist and the social scientist, the age and sex distributions in human populations are important. Age distributions tell us a great deal about the health and life expectancies of the population under investigation. The demographic profile of a population living in an industrialized and relatively affluent country will differ markedly from the profile of a population in a country that is less developed and less affluent. The age distributions seen in Figure 23-1 illustrate the contrasting patterns seen in the United States and in India.

Why do the demographic profiles of these two populations look so different? The answer lies in the differences in the vital statistics affecting population numbers. The population's size at any time is a function of its size at an earlier

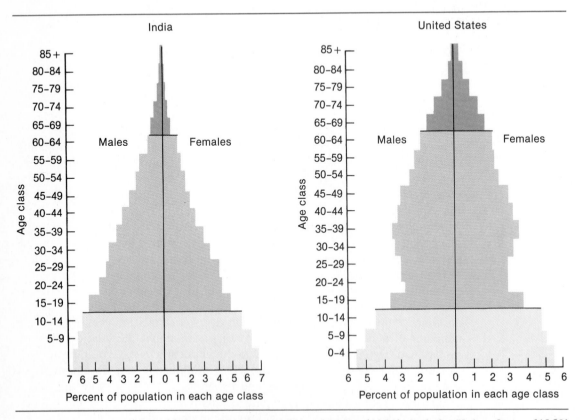

Figure 23-1 Demographic profiles of India (1951) and the Unites States (1960) SOURCE: *Levine, N.D.* Human Ecology, *North Scituate, MA: Duxbury Press, 1975, pp. 290-91.*

time, plus the number of individuals born, minus the number of individuals who die. If we are interested in the population of the world, the vital statistics of interest are those for births and deaths. If we focus on some subset of the world's population, however, it is necessary to account for the effects of people moving into the population as well as people moving out of it. As the size of the population being studied decreases, the impact of a drastic change in birth and death rates and in immigration and emigration increases. This is why small-population phenomena have been of such interest to population biologists whose major concern is evolutionary change. (See the discussion in Chapter 7).

When a population is in equilibrium (that is, of stable size), we can assume that the number of individuals being added through birth and immigration is matched by the number being lost to death and emigration. If we ignore for the moment the effects of migration both into and out of the population, we can make an estimate of the natural rate of increase. Throughout most of human history, growth of the world's population was very gradual (Coale, 1974; Deevey, 1960). At times, such as during the great plagues of the fourteenth to the eighteenth centuries in Europe, populations declined (Langer, 1964). During the past two centuries, however, there has been a sustained period of population growth. Because such periods tend to increase the number of young people who are entering their own reproductive years, the kind of growth that the world's population has been experiencing has the potential to accelerate rapidly with succeeding generations. This acceleration is the basis for the "population explosion" that has created such concern, since continuous rapid growth of the world's human population will inevitably lead to the depletion of life-sustaining resources, with the concomitant decline in the quality of life and, ultimately, increased mortality.

While many factors help to limit the growth of human populations, there is a theoretical potential for exponential growth when birth rates are high and mortality rates are low (Wilson and Bossert, 1971). If, for instance, every woman in a population were to achieve her full reproductive potential over a 30-year period (roughly between the ages of 15 and 45), each could bear 30 children even in the absence of multiple births. If children of each generation began having children at age 15, each woman would have her last child at about the time her first grandchild was born. The explosive potential of the possible increase in the size of succeeding generations under such circumstances is obvious. The fact is, however, that human populations have never attained this level of reproductive success. The reasons for the theoretical and actual rates of population increase being so different are of considerable interest to human biologists and will be discussed in some detail later.

To quantify the analysis of human population growth, the vital statistics underlying increase or decrease can be arranged in the form of an equation. For instance, when population size is stable,

$$B + I = D + E$$ where B = Births   I = Immigrants
D = Deaths   E = Emigrants

If we ignore migration for the time being, then the equation is reduced to B =D. On a worldwide basis, such an equality of births and deaths would mean *zero population growth* (ZPG). Many demographers and ecologists are convinced that ZPG must be achieved soon if we are to avoid irreversible degradation of the environment. But, although population size may be stable when the number of deaths is equal to the number of births, this equality can be attained in several ways. For instance, it is likely that for most of the history of our species, high birth rates were offset by high death rates, with a high rate of mortality occurring within the first year of life. The current trend, especially in the industrialized countries, is toward lower birth rates and increased life expectancies. Table 23-1 presents populations, birth rates, and death rates of major segments of the world's population, along with their rates of increase.

When birth rates are high and life expectancies short, the result is a younger population. The current "graying of America" is the result of a trend that has been at work for about 100 years, during which birth rates have declined while average life expectancies have increased. Today one of the major differences between "third-world" or less-developed countries (LDCs) and the industrialized nations is that the LDCs' populations are substantially younger. One result of the relative youth of these populations is their higher proportion of people of reproductive age. Thus, even if family size is limited, the number of families having children is large, and the potential for explosive population growth is high.

POPULATION STRUCTURE AND GROWTH

Population growth, loss, or stability are closely related to factors influencing birth and death rates. Depending upon the interplay of birth rates and death rates, the age distribution of a population can vary substantially. Factors that

Table 23-1 Populations, Birth and Death Rates, and Annual Rate of Increase of Selected Populations, 1985

	Population (in millions)	Birth Rate (per 1000)	Death Rate (per 1000)	Annual Rate of Increase (%)[*]
Europe	492	14	11	0.3
Asia	2,818	27	10	1.7
Africa	555	46	17	2.9
North America	264	16	9	0.9
Latin America	405	32	8	2.3
World	4,837	27	11	1.7

SOURCE: [*]Data from *The United Nations Yearbook*, 1985 New York; United Nations, 1987. The annual rate of increase experienced by the world's population in 1985 will, if continued, result in a doubling of the population in 41 years. This would result in a population of 9,674,000,000 in the year 2026.

increase life expectancy will tend to increase the average age of a population unless the survival of a greater number of newborns offsets their effect. Examination of a population's age distribution can be very informative in the attempt to ascertain the impact of birth and death rates on the survivorship curve. If sufficient data are available, the impact of past epidemics affecting specific age groups, such as young children, can be seen in the perturbations they cause in the curve. Short-term increases or decreases in the birth rate can be detected as a "ripple" in the curve that will progress through the age categories as the affected cohort ages. Large-scale phenomena, such as the post-World War II "baby boom" which lasted for 20 years in the United States, provide interesting examples of such a ripple. When the cohort is large enough, it can have major effects on the socioeconomic system itself, with sociopolitical attitudes and the demand for certain goods and services, such as education and medical care, reflecting the passage of an unusually large cohort through the population.

Population biologists have conventionally applied a set of basic concepts to assess the relationships between the ages of individuals within a population and its growth. The first of these concepts is that an **age distribution** can be determined for each population. To do this, it is necessary to divide the population into age categories, usually 5-year intervals (as seen in Figure 23-1), and then to count the number of individuals in each category and calculate the percentage of the total population they represent (Roughgarden, 1979). Figure 23-2 illustrates the fact that age distributions can be very different in present-day populations.

The age structure of a population has an important influence on disease experience and mortality statistics. For instance, the incidence of cardiovascular disease rises steadily with increasing age. Most (but not all) cancers are more prevalent in older age groups. Even when epidemics of infectious disease occur, their impact can be expected to be greater in some age groups than in others. For instance, in the great influenza epidemic of 1919, the mortality rate among the very young and the very old was much higher than that among young and middle-aged adults. Because of these and other factors, the age distribution of a population is an important determinant of the way in which natural selection influences gene frequencies. Viewed from another perspective, the age distribution of a population reveals a great deal about the kinds of selection already at work. For instance, comparisons of the demographic profiles of Tunisia and France (Figure 23-3) show a much more pronounced drop in the percentage of survivors of the first year of life in Tunisia. As a matter of fact, survivorship levels throughout the age categories are distinctly different in the two populations. From this comparison, it can be seen that inferences about natural selection can be drawn from careful analysis of population structure, and that the link between demographic and evolutionary dynamics is in the area of population genetics, where changes in gene frequency associated with age distributions are translated into their evolutionary consequences.

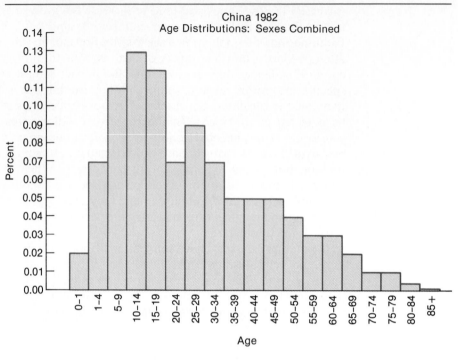

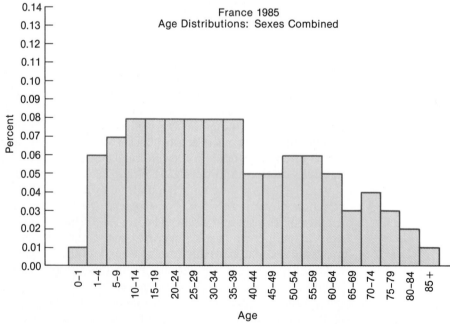

Figure 23-2 Age distribution of Chinese and French populations

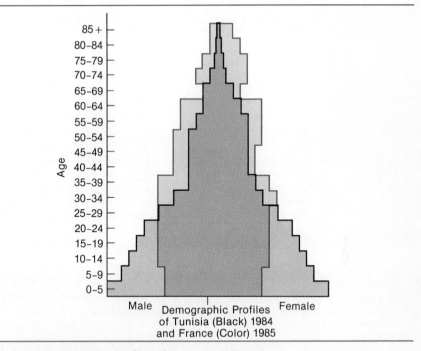

Figure 23-3 Demographic profiles of France and Tunisia

The structure of the population seen in the demographic profile is shaped in part by the previously mentioned factor: **age-specific mortality.** The demographic profile demonstrates that the first year of life is the most hazardous year in the lives of most humans. There are a number of reasons for this, including birth defects, but the difference in infant mortalities (deaths occurring between birth and the age of 1 year) in developed and less-developed countries indicates a strong environmental component in these early mortalities. Statistics on infant mortality rates are often interpreted as indicators of the quality of a country's medical and social services. Table 23-2 summarizes recent figures on infant mortality in a number of developed and less-developed countries.

Although a relatively small proportion of the human population survives to age 100, the probability of death after the first year of life is generally quite small up to about age 40. Table 23-3 gives examples of death rates for specific ages in several developed and less-developed countries. The death rate in Japanese males, for example, drops from 6.6 per thousand during the first year of life to 0.6 per thousand in the age group from 1 through 4 years, 0.3 per thousand for ages 5 through 9, and 0.2 per thousand for ages 10 through 14. In the age group from 50 through 54 years, the rate climbs to 6.4 per thousand, and from the age of 70 to 74, it rises sharply to 37.3 per thousand. In the ages beyond 85 years, the death rate among Japanese males is 192.5. Significantly,

Table 23-2 Infant Mortality Rates (deaths per 1,000 live births)

Japan (1984)	6.0 (male 6.6, female 5.3)
Canada (1983)	8.5 (male 9.3, female 7.7)
Australia (1984)	9.2 (male 10.5, female 7.9)
United Kingdom (1984)	9.5 (male 10.6, female 8.3)
France (1982)	9.5 (male 10.7, female 8.1)
West Germany (1984)	9.6 (male 10.7, female 8.6)
United States (1982)	11.5 (male 12.8, female 10.2)
Italy (1980)	14.6 (male 16.4, female 12.5)
Czechoslovakia (1984)	15.3 (male 17.4, female 13.1)
Cuba (1983)	16.8 (male 19.3, female 14.1)
Pakistan (1979)	94.5 (male 100.7, female 88.1)

SOURCE: Data from *the United Nations Yearbook, 1985.* New York: United Nations, 1987.

the death rate for Japanese females over age 85 is 156.4 per thousand, a sex difference that is consistently seen in all developed countries but is less pronounced in the less-developed ones. The high mortality rate associated with pregnancy, childbirth, and lactation in impoverished rural populations is a major factor in LDC demographics.

Overall death rates are, of course, the result of the death rates of all age groups and, as such, determine differences in life expectancies when populations are compared. Table 23-4 shows the death rates for seven countries since 1976.

Another way of viewing the mortality rate in a population is the calculation of the probability of survival from one age category to another. This is done simply by determining the probability of surviving from year X to year X+1. This probability is calculated conditionally in that it assumes that the population for which the probability is being estimated is only that which has survived to year X. Like the estimates of the probability of surviving from year X+1 to year X+2, succeeding estimates are conditional. The advantage of using the conditional probability is that it permits age categories to be directly compared with each other without obscuring the result by the effects of cumulative reductions in survivorship since birth.

Figure 23-4, which shows the age-specific conditional probabilities of survival among Japanese males in 1984, provides a visual illustration of how death rates vary among 5-year age categories in this long-lived population. Figure 23-4 shows that the probability of surviving from birth to age 5 is lower than the probability of surviving from age 5 to age 10. The probability of surviving from age 10 to age 15 is virtually identical to that for ages 5 to 10 and for ages 15 to 20. Notable declines in the probability of survival are evident at ages 55 to 60 and thereafter, with the probability approximating 56 percent for 80-year-old Japanese men surviving to age 85.

As the groups approach the age of 100, probabilities decline to near 0. However, it is important to note that the probability of surviving to a given age is much higher for individuals who have lived up to the preceding age than it is

Table 23-3 Death Rates for Specific Age Groups (per 1000)

		0-1	1-4	5-9	10-14	15-19	20-24	24-29	30-34	35-39	40-44	45-49	50-54	55-59	60-64	65-69	70-74	75-79	80-84	85+
CANADA	M	9.0	0.5	0.3	0.3	1.1	1.4	1.2	1.2	1.6	2.4	4.0	6.9	11.4	18.8	29.1	44.7	69.3	104.1	186.3
	F	7.2	0.4	0.2	0.2	0.3	0.4	0.4	0.6	0.8	1.4	2.2	3.7	6.0	9.1	14.7	23.0	38.4	63.9	138.7
JAPAN	M	6.6	0.6	0.3	0.2	0.7	0.8	0.8	1.0	1.4	2.3	3.8	6.4	9.1	13.4	22.2	37.3	65.4	111.4	192.5
	F	5.3	0.5	0.2	0.1	0.2	0.3	0.4	0.6	0.8	1.2	1.9	2.9	4.2	6.6	11.7	20.6	39.1	74.8	156.4
FRANCE	M	9.7	0.6	0.3	0.3	1.0	1.8	1.6	1.7	2.4	3.4	5.7	9.3	13.8	21.3	27.2	45.9	77.2	130.4	244.9
	F	7.4	0.5	0.2	0.2	0.4	0.6	0.6	0.8	1.2	1.6	2.4	3.6	5.2	8.4	11.0	21.1	41.3	81.1	191.5
UNITED KINGDOM	M	10.8	0.5	0.2	0.3	0.7	0.8	0.8	0.9	1.3	2.1	4.0	7.0	12.7	21.6	35.0	54.5	84.6	129.9	211.3
	F	8.5	0.4	0.2	0.2	0.3	0.3	0.4	0.6	0.9	1.4	2.5	4.3	7.3	11.5	18.4	29.1	48.3	82.1	169.0

SOURCE: Data from the *United Nations Yearbook, 1985*. New York: United Nations, 1987.

Table 23-4 **Death Rates (deaths per 1,000 population)**

	1976	1977	1978	1979	1980	1981	1982	1983	1984	1985
Australia	8.0	7.7	7.5	7.3	7.4	7.3	7.6	7.2	7.1	NA
United States	8.5	8.6	8.7	8.5	8.7	8.8	8.5	8.6	8.6	8.7
France	10.5	10.1	10.2	10.1	10.2	10.2	10.0	10.2	9.8	10.1
United Kingdom	12.1	11.6	11.8	12.0	11.7	11.6	11.7	11.7	11.4	NA
West Germany	11.9	11.5	11.8	11.6	11.6	11.7	11.6	11.7	11.4	11.5
India	15.0	14.7	14.2	13.0	12.6	12.5	11.9	11.9	NA	NA
Czechoslovakia	11.4	11.5	11.6	11.5	12.2	11.8	11.8	12.1	11.9	11.8

SOURCE: Data from *United Nations Yearbook, 1985,* New York: United Nations, 1987.

for individuals at birth, since life expectancies at birth are skewed by neonatal and infant mortalities. Therefore, when the life expectancies at birth are cited, it is important to keep in mind that it is not justified to subtract an individual's present age from that figure to estimate remaining years of life.

The demographic characteristics of a population reflect the degree of success that that population has experienced in coping with its environment. "Young" populations usually result from the occurrence of high birth rates and short life expectancies. The more effective a population's adaptations to

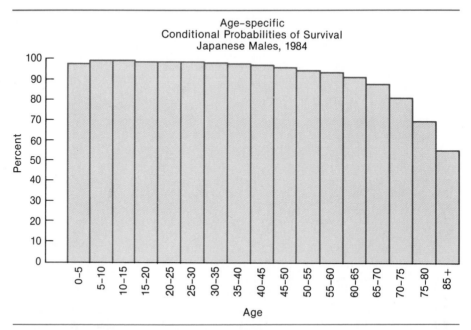

Figure 23-4 Age specific conditional probabilities of survival, Japanese Males, 1984
SOURCE: *Data from* United Nations Yearbook, 1985, *New York: United Nations, 1987.*

the demands created by its environment, the less dependent it will be on high birth rates to sustain itself. Some of the adaptations employed by human populations appear to reflect evolutionary responses to specific climatic stresses. It is therefore of interest to examine some of the elements of human climatic adaptation.

HUMAN VARIATION

Climatic Adaptations

Human populations can be found in virtually every climate on earth. Members of our species live in tropical rain forests, the high altitudes of the Andes and Himalayas, and the Arctic regions of the far north. Very few other species exploit a range of habitats as broad as that inhabited by humans, and those that do, such as rats, dogs, and cats, do so because of their association with humans.

The wide range of habitats we now occupy is the product of a great deal of adaptation, some of it at the genetic level, but most of it physiological and behavioral—that is, through sociocultural devices that help us modify and control our habitat. It is quite certain that the origin of our species was in the tropics of the Old World. Survival without technology would still be unlikely in the temperate and arctic zones. Other primate species have not ventured far from the tropics. Although macaques can be found in the far north of Japan and in the foothills of the Himalayas, our closest living relatives, the chimpanzees, gorillas, and orangutans, all live near the equator.

Observation of climatic adaptations in other species has stimulated curiosity about the degree to which humans have been shaped by their environment. Certain so-called ecological rules that appear to explain regional variations in other mammals have been tested to ascertain their validity in humans. For the most part, the results have been disappointing, although total rejection of all hypotheses linking climatic conditions to morphological and physiological variations has not been generally accepted. Whether or not human climatic adaptations have been incorporated into the hereditary material of specific human populations, the question of the role of human adaptability in the evolution of the species is a valid one. Some knowledge of the ways in which the organism can adjust to environmental challenges is essential if only to permit well-defined experiments focusing on the processes of adjustment.

THE ECOLOGICAL RULES

It has long been known that there is a tendency for **homeothermic** (temperature-regulating) animals that live in a cold habitat to be larger. A number of species have been shown to exhibit a size gradient, with the largest specimens being found in the coldest parts of the species' range. In addition to being larger in colder regions, many animals will have proportionally shorter appendages. These characteristics are thought to be advantageous where heat conservation is important to survival. Heat is produced as a by-product of energy metabolism. As simple sugars are broken down and metabolized to supply energy for muscle contractions, cellular functions, and biochemical reactions, some energy is given off in the form of heat, which, in warmer climates, must be dissipated. When activity levels are high, breakdown of energy-storing molecules, primarily adenosine triphosphate (ATP), increases the amount of heat released. This can be easily demonstrated if one notes the level of discomfort experienced when quietly resting following a brisk run at a moderate outdoor temperature of, say, 20°C (68°F). After one runs or rapidly walks for 20 minutes, sufficient energy release will have occurred to cause the sensation of continued heat buildup during the subsequent resting period. This *delayed heat* is really an external indicator of the replacement of ATP molecules consumed during exercise. When the exercised muscles have regained their normal compliment of ATP, metabolic rate will slow and body temperature will gradually return to normal. Since the production of heat by metabolic activity is directly related to the level of muscular activity attained, more heat will be produced by larger animals, who must recruit more muscles to perform each function. Even at rest, greater muscle mass will require more energy to support the cost of cellular maintenance.

Increased muscle metabolism is not the only factor that yields an advantage to large mammals in cold climates, however. This is because as animals increase in size, their mass increases more rapidly than their surface area. This is reflected in the units used to measure the various aspects of body size. When length increases, we measure the increase in centimeters (or inches), but when the body's length increases in centimeters, its surface areas must increase in square centimeters and its volume in cubic centimeters. Since the calculations are made using exponents of the linear dimension (cm^1, cm^2, cm^3), we can easily see that the increase in volume is an order of magnitude greater than that of surface areas. Since most heat escapes from the body at its surface, the increase in mass or volume with respect to surface area will result in an increased proportion of heat being retained by a larger animal. Observations of the aforementioned gradients in body size of homeotherms have led to the conclusion that the increased body size seen in colder areas of the species range is adaptive and that it reflects conformation to one of the "ecological rules" governing body size. In this instance, the ecological rule is *Bergmann's rule,* which deals with body mass. Theoretically, the colder the climate, the heavier the individual, and vice-versa.

A related rule, *Allen's rule,* was formulated to accommodate the observation of the tendency to reduce the length of appendages, such as ears or limbs, in colder areas. Again, a decrease in surface-to-volume ratio is the benefit gained from such reduction, since appendages have a higher surface-to-volume ratio than the head or trunk. The lowest ratio of surface to volume is that of a sphere. The closer the shape of the animal can come to a spherical shape, the less heat it will lose. Reduction in the length of appendages will, of course, serve to bring the organism closer to the ideal spherical shape.

DO HUMANS CONFORM TO ECOLOGICAL RULES?

Bergmann's and Allen's rules provide the opportunity to seek evidence for climatic adaptations in humans. Since humans are homeotherms with a worldwide distribution, it would be of interest to identify modifications in human anatomy consistent with those seen in other mammals that occupy ranges spanning large temperature gradients. However, the evidence for such anatomical adaptations in humans is ambiguous. It is generally true that the Eskimo and some other inhabitants of Arctic regions are of short stature and have a high sitting height ratio (meaning that the head and trunk make up a greater proportion of total body length than in most other human populations). It is also true that the fingers of the Eskimo hand are relatively short and that the nose is relatively flat. These observations are consistent with the forms we would anticipate if Bergmann's and Allen's rules were applied to human anatomy. However, these traits can be found in populations living in tropical habitats as well as in the Arctic. Moreover, the length of time that human populations have inhabited the severe climates of the far north has been quite brief (in evolutionary terms) and may have been insufficient for the process of natural selection to have produced truly adapted populations.

Other factors that make it difficult to test hypotheses of human adaptation to cold habitats include the highly developed tendency of human populations to modify the environment. If the major stressors of a habitat are eliminated or modified, natural selection will not operate to change gene frequencies in classical Darwinian fashion. Human populations could not have penetrated the hostile climates of the Arctic without a well-developed technology. Their entry into the most challenging regions was unlikely to have been abrupt and may well have been tentative at first. Commitment to a challenging existence in the Arctic would have been unlikely in the absence of a technology sufficiently well-developed to promise some chance of survival. Once the major stressors of the Arctic environment, cold and starvation, were brought under control by technological means, the likelihood of major anatomical changes would have been diminished. In many respects, human populations living in the far North carry a subtropical habitat with them. Their ability to survive and reproduce derives more from the benefits of nongenetic adjustments than to any anatomical adaptations they may possess.

TECHNOLOGY AND PHYSIOLOGY
AS ADAPTIVE STRATEGIES IN THE ARCTIC

The technology developed by the Eskimo to survive in the Arctic is truly impressive. The skins of animals are used to break the force of the wind and to trap layers of dead air between the skin and the outside air. Footwear insulates against the penetration of cold during hours of standing at a seal hole. The parka is designed to permit the venting of heat during heavy exercise, thereby avoiding moisture buildup that would compromise the insulative properties of the dead air space. Snow goggles carved out of bone protect against the glare of sunlight reflected from ice and snow. Fish hooks and harpoon points are also carved from fish and animal bones. Huts and igloos are built with an entrance lower than the living quarters to trap cold air before it chills the sleeping area. Whale-oil lamps give light and heat.

Despite the effectiveness of these technological devices for coping with the Arctic environment, fishing and seal hunting require exposure of the face and hands to severe cold. The threat of frostbite is ever-present, as the hands must be plunged into icy water and exposed to high winds in temperatures as low as −50°F. (−46°C). Physiological mechanisms to reduce the risk of frostbite are therefore still important to the Eskimo. The mechanisms of vasoconstriction (the reduction of blood flow by contraction of smooth muscle in the walls of the arteries and arterioles) and vasodilation (the increase in blood flow arising from relaxation in the smooth muscle of arteries and arterioles, permitting them to expand to a greater diameter), which alternate to reduce and increase blood flow to the surface of the fingers, keep heat loss to a minimum while ensuring that the important structures in the dermis do not freeze. The Eskimo differs from people who experience less severe cold exposure, such as the Australian Aborigine, in that permitting skin temperature to fall to the level of the surrounding area would severely damage tissue. Therefore, while the Australian Aborigine's physiology allows vasoconstriction to reduce the blood flow to the skin of the extremities in order to maintain the core temperature of the body, the Eskimo dilates the vessels of the arms and hands at intervals in order to keep skin temperature above freezing. This means that the Eskimo permits more body heat to escape from the skin's surface and must therefore produce more heat to maintain the core temperature of 37°C. The demand for heat is met in the Eskimo by maintaining a high basal metabolic rate (BMR). It is not known whether the high BMR of the Eskimo is a hereditary trait or merely the result of their high-fat, high-protein diet. Whether genetic or dietary or both, the high BMR of the Eskimo is an essential part of their survival strategy in the hostile environment of the Arctic (Frisancho, 1985).

ADAPTABILITY

One of the characteristics of living organisms is their ability to react to the environment. While there is a wide range of variation in the degree to which this ability is expressed, it is present even in the simplest of organisms. Because the environment is seldom constant in all of its aspects, the ability to make minor adjustments at relatively little cost is a valuable asset. In a simple single-celled organism, the adjustment may be as modest as the closing of a channel in the cell membrane in order to bar the entry of an ion or molecule. In more complex organisms, adjustments involve large numbers of cells, tissues, organs, and organ systems, and, ultimately, the whole organism in the form of altered behavior. Behavioral alterations can be reflexive, or automatic, such as the knee-jerk response to the tap of a rubber hammer. Other behavioral responses can be preprogrammed, or stereotypic, and can be comprised of a series of interrelated movements initiated by the appropriate stimulus. Some of the mating patterns of fish and birds belong in this category.

In most organisms, individual activities are sometimes linked with activities of others. Such linkages can become increasingly subtle and complex as the information-processing capacity of the organism increases. Humans have achieved a very high capacity for processing information and have thereby gained the capacity to behave in a highly complex and subtle manner in coping with the demands of their environment. Whereas many other species rely upon stereotypic behavior patterns to ensure successful performance of such biologically significant functions as mating and care of the young, humans exploit a wide array of options.

The availability of choice is partially the result of the assurance of success in the interaction with the environment that comes with the support of other individuals in a social system. As social systems have become increasingly successful in gaining control over the environment, humans have been freed from many constraints on individual behavior. In this sense, modern cultures, which permit many aspects of the environment to be adjusted to suit individual needs, maximize the ability to experiment without the risk of extinction. This perspective on the biological significance of human culture has led to the development of the concept of **"buffered evolution."**

Buffered evolution may best be viewed as a system of defenses that permit the organism to adjust to environmental stresses with the least biological cost. From the perspective of the individual, the lowest biological cost would be incurred if a stress were anticipated and dealt with by some facet of the culture without necessitating any response by the individual. It is possible, for example, to survive very cold winter weather simply by staying in heated buildings and cars, and by wearing specially designed insulated clothing. By staying within the buffer zone provided by these culturally derived defenses, it is possible to live through the most severe winter while experiencing little or no discomfort and no threat to survival or reproductive success. However, the cultural buffer may not always be available or effective. A power outage or vehicle breakdown may necessitate individual or group responses to compensate for the buffer that has been removed or penetrated. Intelligent, cooperative responses to such emergencies may be viewed as another buffer zone that may be sufficient to ameliorate the environmental stress. Using emergency heating units or extra blankets, huddling together to conserve heat, and seeking help all constitute active responses invoked by individuals to compensate for the loss of protection against cold that is usually afforded by cultural buffers.

When such buffers prove insufficient, other individual behaviors may be used to cope with the threat that severe cold represents. Moving about and stomping the feet to stimulate circulation to the extremities are conscious actions that will provide some measure of protection against frostbite. Such behavior may be considered another buffer. When such conscious actions are insufficient to maintain body temperature, an involuntary response, shivering, will use the heat generated by repeated small muscular contractions to supplement that generated by other metabolic activity in an effort to compensate for heat loss. This can be considered another buffer, as well as a clear sign that cold stress is no longer being dealt with by cultural or behavioral buffers, but has penetrated to the level at which a physiological response may be necessary for survival.

At this level of buffering there are also adjustments to be made at the cardiovascular level, with constriction and dilation of blood vessels occurring as a part of an overall heat-conservation effort. Some buffering may occur at the level of the cell in certain tissues where the breakdown of glucose may accelerate heat production.

When all of these protective mechanisms prove inadequate and exposure to extreme cold persists, death is inevitable. Since death before the end of reproductive capability has potential genetic consequences, penetration of all of these buffer systems may be a mechanism of natural selection. Populations that are exposed to cold stress without an elaborate system of buffers at the cultural, behavioral, and physiological levels would be expected to adapt through selection of the most-fit alleles at loci that mediate cell-level responses.

Those lacking effective buffers at the cultural and behavioral level can be expected to experience allelic selection favoring the most effective adjustments of the physiological mechanisms maintaining homeostasis. While all aspects of adaptation are ultimately under genetic control, adaptation through gene loss and replacement indicates failure of the buffer system that literally and figuratively surrounds and protects the vital genetic core of the population. A successful buffer system permits the retention of variation that may become the margin of survival when some future event significantly changes the environment. Thus it may be inferred that the more effective the species' buffering system is, the more variation it will be able to maintain. Since the human buffer system is the most elaborate and most effective to emerge so far on earth, students of human biology are inevitably drawn to discussions of human variability since it is indeed one of our most "human" attributes (Stini, 1975).

MECHANISMS UNDERLYING HUMAN VARIATION: GROWTH AND DEVELOPMENT

The phenotype is the product of the interaction of the genotype and the environment. In a well-buffered species, such as our own, the expression of the genotype should be less subject to modification by intrusion of the environment than in species lacking elaborate cultural buffers. It can be shown, however, that humans are sensitive to certain environmental influences, and that some differences between human populations can be at least partly explained on the basis of environmental factors. This observation may at first seem to contradict the argument that humans have developed the most effective and most elaborate buffer system known. The apparent contradiction can be resolved by taking a closer look at the way in which the genotype and the environment combine to produce the adult phenotype.

When this interaction is examined in greater detail, it can be seen that the mechanisms that produce variation in the expression of traits in the individual are actually a part of the buffer system. However, the most visible aspects of variation, such as body size, can be altered by environmental factors only if they are experienced while the individual is growing. Since humans remain in an immature state longer than other mammals, they remain capable of being shaped by their environment for a longer period of time. The lengthy delay experienced by humans in the attainment of sexual maturity and the cessation of growth is an important element of the human adaptive strategy. It allows each individual to be shaped physically and intellectually to optimize its "fit" to its environment.

Since most of the environment surrounding the immature human consists of other humans and the products of human culture, much of the shaping is in terms of fitting into a cultural niche. Most of the benefit derived from the lengthy deferment of maturity characterizing human growth and development is therefore in terms of learning and socialization. Humans rely more heavily than other animals on learning and on the support of their social and cultural systems. Therefore, lengthening of the period during which these attributes can develop is adaptive and is evolutionarily significant. It is not known whether delayed maturation preceded or followed such important evolutionary events as the development of language or the manufacture of stone tools. However, once the human adaptive strategy became committed to the transmission of learned behavior to gain control over the environment, delayed maturation conferred an important advantage that could provide a focus for natural selection. (The importance of learning and delayed maturation is discussed in several other chapters; see, for example, Chapter 22.)

The delay of sexual maturation characterizing human growth and development would, pursuing the foregoing argument, facilitate learning, the acquisition of language, and the elaboration of culture. It would, perhaps incidentally, also increase the period during which the phenotype could be altered in other ways. However, the evidence for major evolutionary trends attributable to climatic factors within our species is exceedingly sparse. With certain minor exceptions (to be discussed in a later section), human growth and development is effectively channeled to minimize the impact of all but the most profound environmental stressors. The complex interactions necessary to allow the adult organism to function do not permit gross deviations from the normal pattern of development. Severely deviant individuals have little chance of survival and therefore do not usually reproduce. The genetic basis for deviant developmental patterns is subject to continual selective pressure, and it should be expected that processes as critical as normal growth and development will be highly buffered. Closer examination of the processes of human growth and development will be helpful in understanding how they shape the human phenotype. It will also help to clarify the environmental factors that influence the growth process and therefore alter the phenotype.

HUMAN EVOLUTION: AN UNCONVENTIONAL EXAMPLE

A highly successful buffer system such as that of humans reduces the intensity of selection on many traits, in effect rendering many of them selectively neutral. Under such circumstances, mutations and duplications can be tolerated, enhancing the pool of new variation. The importance of selective neutrality as an evolutionary force has been convincingly argued by Crow and Kimura (1970). The significance of gene duplication in evolution has been summarized by Ohno (1970) and Kimura and Ohta (1971). The modern view of evolution has been strongly influenced by the monumental work of Wright, who, more than any other individual, led the movement away from the position that all evolution could be explained strictly on the basis of natural selection (Wright, 1968, 1969). It is of special interest to biological anthropologists that evolutionary theory is increasingly concerned with the factors that modify or obviate the effect of natural selection on the process of evolution. Because of the highly developed system of cultural buffers that surround human populations, our species is the prime candidate for evolutionary change in response to factors other than natural selection in the strict Darwinian sense. Population size and structure in this view of evolution are extremely important, since small populations provide a setting well suited to the occurrence of evolutionary significant chance events.

The success that humans have had in modifying and controlling their environment has had the effect of reducing the influence of the climate in the shaping of human phenotypes. The relaxation of selective pressure on a number of traits increases the tolerance for variation in those traits. The effective neutrality of such traits enhances the trend toward a non-Darwinian evolutionary process in humans. This has led to the de-emphasis of conventional natural selection as the major force of evolution in our species.

BIBLIOGRAPHY

COALE, A. J. 1974. The history of the human population. *Scientific American* 231: 40–51.

CROW, J. F., and M. KIMURA. 1970. *An Introduction to Population Genetic Theory.* New York: Harper & Row, Pub.

DEEVEY, E. S., JR. 1960. The human population. *Scientific American* 203: 195–203.

FRISANCHO, A. R. 1985. *Human Adaptation.* Ann Arbor: University of Michigan Press.

KIMURA, M., and T. OHTA. 1971. *Theoretical Aspects of Population Genetics.* Princeton, N. J.: Princeton University Press.

LANGER, W. L. 1964. The Black Death. *Scientific American* 210: 214–21.

LEVINE, N. D. 1975. *Human Ecology,* pp. 290–91. North Scituate, Mass.: Duxbury Press.

OHNO, S. 1970. *Evolution by Gene Duplication.* New York: Springer Verlag.

ROUGHGARDEN, J. 1979. *Theory of Population Genetics and Evolutionary Ecology: An Introduction.* New York: Macmillan.

STINI, W. A. 1975. *Ecology and Human Adaptation.* Dubuque, Iowa: Wm. C. Brown.

UNITED NATIONS. 1987. *United Nations Yearbook: 1985.* New York: United Nations.

WILSON, E. O., and W. H. BOSSERT. 1971. *A Primer of Population Biology.* Stamford, Conn.: Sinauer.

WRIGHT, S. 1968. *Evolution and the Genetics of Populations (vol. 1): Genetic and Biometric Foundations.* Chicago: University of Chicago Press.

WRIGHT, S. 1969. *Evolution and the Genetics of Populations (vol. 2): The Theory of Gene Frequencies.* Chicago: University of Chicago Press.

How Biological Anthropologists Measure Human Variation

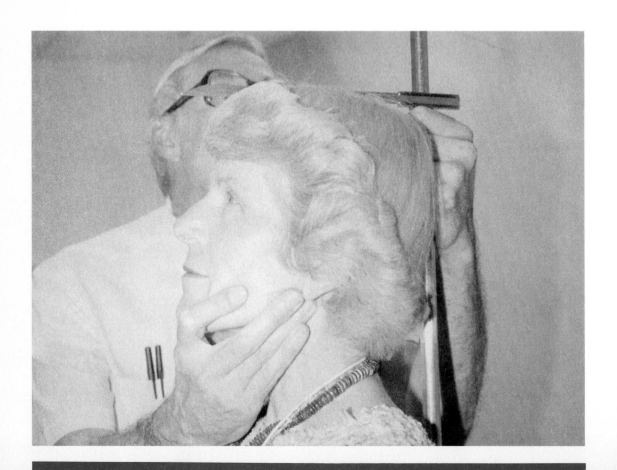

Measurement of the human body has a long and noble history. The anatomical drawings of Leonardo da Vinci were in large part the result of the desire to assess the proportions and relationships of body segments. Physical anthropologists have extended the scope of their investigations beyond the taking of anatomical measurements. The determination of body composition, the physiological processes involved in work, and the biochemical characteristics of the blood all are important in the analysis of human variation. Inspection of chromosomes and chromosome sets has permitted the identification of the specific location of elements of genetic variability in the nucleus of the cell. Use of immunological techniques allows exploitation of the capacity to differentiate self from nonself to identify discrete traits that can be used to compare and contrast individuals and populations. The sampling of methods that follows has been chosen to illustrate the range of techniques that can be used to generate the data that biological anthropologists use as descriptors of human variation. In recent years, laboratory techniques have become increasingly complex and sophisticated. The result has been an increasing tendency for the biological anthropologist to seek collaborators whose interests are complementary and whose laboratories are equipped to analyze samples collected in the field. The combination of field and laboratory methods that characterizes much of contemporary human biological research has been highly productive, allowing the biological anthropologist to take advantage of the anthropological perspective in the field while addressing questions that can be answered only under controlled laboratory conditions. As a result of this combination, biological anthropologists can often be found working in teams with biomedical researchers.

METHODS USED BY BIOLOGICAL ANTHROPOLOGISTS

Anthropometry, the measurement of the human body, is an essential component of the study of growth, development, and variation. A number of instruments have been developed that allow relatively precise measurement in field situations—an essential condition for many anthropological research projects. Other instruments permit more sophisticated measurements but require the more controlled environment of the laboratory. A brief summary of the major methods and instruments used in studies of human variability will help to clarify the nature as well as the limitations of the data that physical anthropologists generate, analyze, and debate.

FIELD ANTHROPOMETRY

Although the number of measurements that can be taken on the human body is limited only by the imagination of the measurer, the list of those most often taken is usually determined by practical concerns as well as by the purpose of

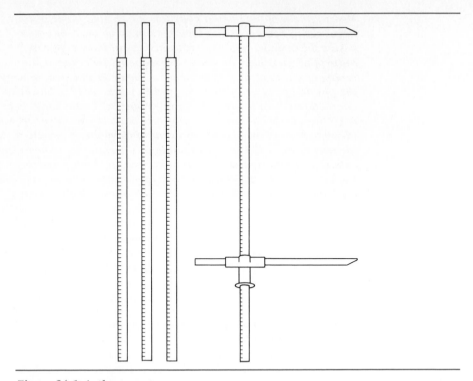

Figure 24-1 Anthropometer

the study. The International Biological Program (IBP) developed a basic list of 21 measurements that can be expanded to a full list of 38 when the situation demands. The basic list and the full list are shown in Table 24-1 (Weiner and Laurie, 1969). All of these measurements can be taken using a total of 6 instruments, the use of which has been standardized over many thousands of measurements. These instruments are the anthropometer, the spreading caliper, the sliding caliper, the tape measure, the skinfold caliper, and the scale (Figures 24-1, 24-2, and 24-3). Although the use of these anthropometric instruments is intrinsically simple, a substantial amount of practice and frequent monitoring of technique to avoid systematic errors is essential. Most anthropometric surveys are done by teams, often working in pairs with one member measuring and the other recording. Subsamples are remeasured at intervals to ensure the reliability of the measurements. In large projects, a criterion anthropometrist may also sample from the measured population to determine the accuracy of the measurement team's recorded values. Because of the potential for distorted results arising from even small measurement errors, the demands of a **longitudinal study,** wherein the same individuals are measured repeatedly over time to monitor growth or aging, are especially rigorous. **Cross-sectional studies,** wherein a population is measured once, with

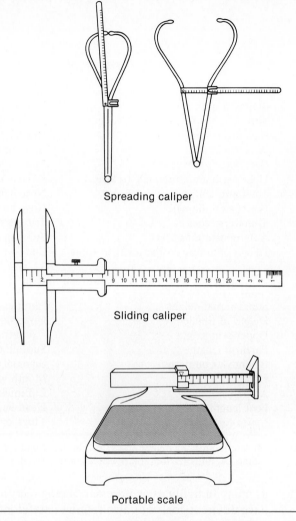

Spreading caliper

Sliding caliper

Portable scale

Figure 24-2 A spreading caliper, a sliding caliper and a scale

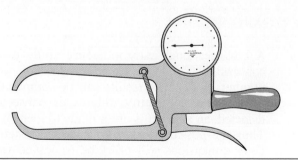

Figure 24-3 A Harpenden skinfold caliper

Table 24-1 Anthropometric Measurements

IBP Measurements
Basic List (21 measurements)

Stature/Supine length	Biiliocristal diameter
Sitting height/Crown–rump length	Head length
Bicondylar femur	Head breadth
Wrist breadth	Bizygomatic diameter
Calf circumference	Morphological face height
Upper-arm circumference (relaxed)	(nasion-gnathion)
Total arm length	Nose height
Biacromial diameter	Nose breadth
Transverse chest	Triceps skinfold
Anteroposterior chest	Subscapular skinfold
Height of anterior superior iliac spine	Body weight

Full List (17 additional measurements)

Suprasternal height	Chest circumference
Height of tibiale	Upper-arm circumference
Upper-arm length	(contracted)
Forearm length	Suprailiac skinfold
Bicondylar humerus	Bigonial diameter
Hand breadth	Mouth width
Ankle breadth	Lip thickness
Foot length	Head height
Lower-leg length	Thigh circumference

SOURCE: From J. S. Weiner and J. A. Laurie, *Human Biology: A Guide to Field Methods,* IBP Handbook, no. 9 (Oxford: Blackwell Scientific, 1969), p.5.

as many individuals as necessary being recruited to attain statistical validity, have different goals but also require careful attention to technique (Johnston, 1974).

CROSS-SECTIONAL STUDIES

A cross-sectional anthropometric study can yield important information concerning population characteristics of size, shape, and proportionality (Tanner, 1968). The results can be compared to those obtained from other populations to identify differences between them. When differences are detected, an attempt is often made to identify the reasons for the differences. Thus the possible environmental and genetic determinants of growth and body dimensions will often be examined when significant anthropometric differences are detected. In most cases, a limited number of variables will be drawn from the list for intensive scrutiny. Single variables, often stature, weight, or sitting height, are used to construct a composite growth curve. This procedure requires a substantial number of individuals because it is necessary to have ample numbers in each age category to permit statistical analysis of the results (Sinclair, 1985). Although longitudinal analyses of growth and development are preferred, practical concerns may make it necessary to rely on cross-sectional data. This is often the case when remote and difficult-to-recruit populations are of interest and assurance of repeat measurements is not possible (Tanner, 1979).

LONGITUDINAL STUDIES

Longitudinal anthropometric studies can provide a true description of the rate of growth as well as the values attained in a population. While adequate sample size is more difficult to maintain in a longitudinal study, repeat measurements allow assessment of growth velocity and acceleration (Goldstein, 1979). These important aspects of the growth process cannot be obtained from even the best-constructed cross-sectional study because the inter-individual variations in the timing and rate of growth obscure intra-individual changes in velocity when population data are combined and averaged.

Because anthropometry yields important information about growth, it has long been a valuable tool in biomedical research and in health surveys. Nutritional scientists use many of the same techniques that physical anthropologists use to assess the nutritional status of communities. Considerable attention has recently been directed toward a better understanding of the changes associated with human aging. Anthropometric techniques are increasingly being used in this context (Ross, Martin, and Ward, 1987).

INDEXES

Certain relationships between anthropometric values have been used to assess aspects of body composition indirectly. Although the subject of considerable criticism (Garn, Leonard, and Hawthorn, 1982; Ross et al., 1988), indexes such as the body mass index (BMI) and Ponderal index have been used as simple non-invasive estimates of the fat-to-lean tissue ratio. The BMI is calculated by dividing the weight in kilograms by the height in meters squared. Thus, an individual with a weight of 80 kilograms and a stature of 190 centimeters has a BMI of 22.16. The generally accepted desirable range for BMI is from 21 to 25. A BMI over 25 is associated with overweight.

$$BMI = \frac{Weight \ (kg)}{Height \ (m)^2}$$

SKINFOLDS AND SUBCUTANEOUS FAT

When there is a need to gain additional information about the body composition of a subject, the use of the skinfold measurements becomes important (Ross et al., 1988). The skinfold caliper measures a pinch of skin and subcutaneous tissue while exerting a constant pressure. Since the epidermis and dermis combined are, on the average, only 1 millimeter thick, most of the skinfold measured will represent subcutaneous fat. If a sufficient number of skinfolds are measured at the appropriate sites, an estimate of total body fat can be made. From this estimate, an estimation of body composition is derived. Most population surveys limit the skinfolds measured to two—one at the back of the arm at the **triceps** site and the other on the back at the **subscapular** site. These two sites are chosen most often because they are fairly accessible and provide a sample of fat located in the trunk and a sample of fat located in the extremities. Additional skinfold sites are sometimes used to increase the precision of subcutaneous fat measurement.

BODY COMPOSITION

When an accurate determination of body composition is sought, the preferred method is through underwater weighing. The principle involved (Archimedes principle) is that the weight of the individual when immersed in water will reflect the degree to which the mass of the body exceeds that of the water it displaces. Since muscle is much heavier than fat, a muscular person will sink farther and therefore weigh more in water than will a fat one of the same weight (Brozek et al., 1963). Comparison of weight when measured in air to weight measured in water allows a calculation of the body's density. The amount of air remaining in the lungs must be calculated as well. Equations have been developed to convert the calculation of density to calculations of percent fat and percent lean body mass. Underwater (hydrostatic) weighing is frequently called the "gold standard" of body composition analysis (Lohman, Roche, and Martorell, 1988).

BIOELECTRIC RESISTANCE

A recently developed technique for estimating body composition by means other than underwater weighing is by the use of *bioelectric resistance.* The principle involved in this method is that the resistance of the body to the flow of a low-energy, high-frequency electrical signal is a function of body size and composition. At a specific body size, a leaner body will conduct an electrical signal better than a fatter one. This is because the lean tissues have a higher percentage of water and electrolytes than the fat tissue. The current is allowed to pass through the body from electrodes attached at the wrists and ankles and the amount of resistance the current encounters is measured (Valhalla Scientific, 1988). Using the stature and weight of the subject, the percentage of fat is calculated from the resistance recorded. The percentage of fat is then subtracted from the total body weight to calculate the percentage of lean tissue. Although there is the potential for inaccuracy in the results obtained from this technique, it yields a reasonably accurate estimate of body composition without the elaborate and demanding procedures of underwater weighing. As bioelectric-resistance instrumentation becomes more sophisticated and widely used, it promises to yield increasingly accurate estimates.

RADIOLOGY

Radiographic methods have been used to determine the extent of skeletal maturation for many years. The most frequently used site for these determinations is the hand and wrist. Methods of reading the radiographic plate have been modified considerably over the years. The Greulich-Pyle atlas (Greulich and Pyle, 1959) is still a frequently used reference, but refinements of the atlas method have been developed by several investigators, among them Tanner and Whitehouse, whose TW-2 method is widely used (Tanner, Whitehouse, and Marshall, 1975). The RWT method, a method for assessing skeletal maturity with radiographs of the knee, was developed by Roche, Wainer, and Thissen (1975). It is sometimes used in combination with hand-wrist radiographs to assess the level of skeletal maturation with evidence from two widely separated anatomical sites.

PHOTON ABSORPTIOMETRY

Photon absorptiometry, a technique using the low-risk gamma radiation of such isotopes as iodine-125, permits the assessment of bone mineral content. Since the loss of bone density is part of the aging process, this technique has been used in both clinical studies and surveys. The method can be either *single-photon,* which is limited to such sites as the forearm or leg, or *dual photon* which has been widely used to detect changes in the spine and in the neck of the femur. Although essentially clinical instruments, they are quite useful for monitoring bone-density changes on a longitudinal basis (Mazess, 1987).

BLOOD SAMPLES AND THEIR ANALYSIS

Studies aimed at the identification of genetic relationships within and among populations will inevitably require the collection of blood samples. This will sometimes require the participation of a licensed physician, nurse, or medical technician. Small blood samples can be drawn from a fingertip or earlobe. This technique is often used when blood-group typing is all that is to be done. When more extensive analysis of blood is contemplated, larger samples of 5 to 10 milliliters are needed. These are drawn into sterile vials and transported to the laboratory as promptly as possible. Some preparation, such as freezing, may be necessary if the samples must be shipped long distances (Weiner and Lourie, 1969).

In the laboratory, blood-group determinations are carried out by treating red cells with appropriate antisera. More intensive analysis of blood to determine the nature of serum proteins such as haptoglobin and transferrin requires such techniques as electrophoresis or chromatography. Blood-chemistry values, such as serum calcium, total protein, protein fractions, trace minerals, and the by-products of liver function, can be determined in conventional clinical laboratory facilities. The biological anthropologist whose interests require extensive biochemical laboratory testing will usually work with collaborators who are interested in researching problems that require both field work and laboratory facilities.

KARYOTYPING

Karyotyping is a laboratory technique that has been applied by biological anthropologists in their own laboratories. This technique, which allows the inspection of the chromosomes and chromosome sets of human subjects, requires a modest amount of laboratory equipment but is labor intensive. It involves the culture of human cells, usually peripheral white blood cells, for several days in an artificial medium (Sutton, 1980). The cells are then treated with **colchicine,** a plant alkaloid that arrests cell division at the metaphase stage. The cells that are in the process of division are thus held in a relatively stable state of suspended cell division at a point where the chromosomes are in their most visible form. The cells are then immersed in a **hypotonic** solution. In such a solution, the salt concentration is lower than that of body fluids, including the intracellular fluid; therefore, water moves into the cells, inflating them and spreading out the structures they contain. The chromosomes are spread out sufficiently to prevent them from clumping or stacking in the preparation to be examined. The cells are then transferred to a microscope slide and air-dried. As the surrounding fluid evaporates, the cells flatten out on the slide surface, spreading the chromosomes farther apart. A fixative is then applied along with a stain that is specifically attracted to the **chromatin** that makes up the chromosomes. The slides are then photographed and the photos enlarged. The photographs of the individual chromosomes are then cut out and arranged into the categories making up the total human karyotype. Figure 24-4 shows a spread made from a lymphocyte culture and the subsequent arrangement of the photographs of the individual chromosomes into a complete human karyotype.

There are a number of fluorescent stains that are attracted to specific areas of the chromosome. When a chromosome preparation is treated with one or more of these stains, a fluorescent **banding** pattern can be seen on the chromosomes. The bands, called **Q bands,** form patterns that permit chromosomes to be distinguished from one another with a high degree of certainty. (A Q-banded karyotype is shown in Figure 24-5.) It is also possible to treat the preparation with heat, acid, or alkali in order to alter or break down proteins and prevent the usual staining. By holding cells thus treated at a normal body temperature of 37°C and at neutral pH for a time, it is possible to preferentially stain the regions alongside the **centromeres** and the secondary constrictions

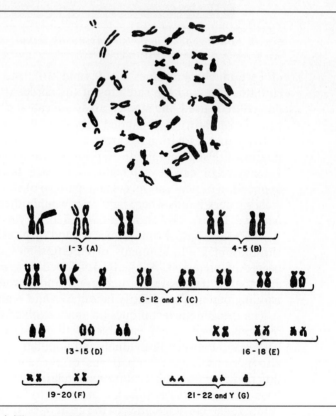

Figure 24-4 The typical human chromosome complement

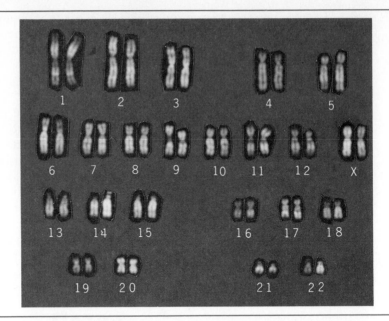

Figure 24-5 A human male karyotype with quinacrine staining showing Q-bands

of certain chromosomes (1, 9, and 16), the distal long arm of the Y chromosome, and the satellites of the acrocentric chromosomes. When this procedure is used, the stained areas are called *C bands* (*C* is for constituative heterochromatin). A C-banded karyotype is shown in Figure 24-6.

Even finer resolution of chromosomes can be accomplished by variations in treatment of slide preparations prior to staining. For example, use of modified Giemsa stain can reveal bands that have been designated *G bands.* The application of heat can reverse the pattern of staining produced in G banding, creating dark bands where light ones would otherwise appear. This is called *R banding.* Figure 24-7 shows a G-banded karyotype.

The analysis of chromosomes treated by a series of such techniques allows chromosomes and segments of chromosomes to be identified with a high degree of precision. A highly developed system of nomenclature has been adopted to designate chromosomes and chromosome segments using the banding patterns to identify landmarks and regions.

The cytogenetic techniques that have evolved through development of these methods have proven valuable in the analysis of chromosomal variation within and between individuals and populations of living humans. They have also permitted the comparisons of the chromosomes and karyotypes of different species. The evolutionary relationships of the living primates have been a major focus of this line of research. The use of banding techniques to compare the chromosomes of the great apes, other primates, and humans has confirmed the close relationship between chimpanzees, gorillas, and humans

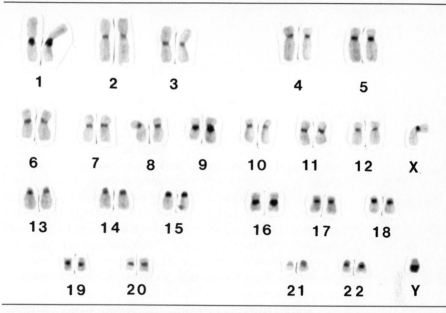

Figure 24-6 Karyotype of a human male showing C-bands

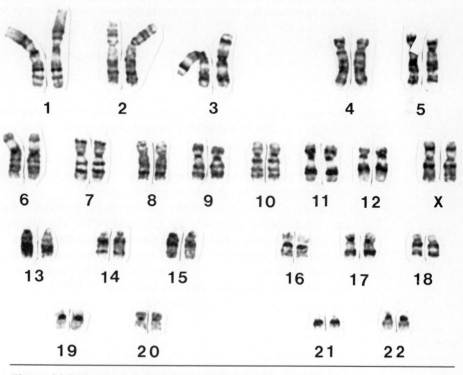

Figure 24-7 Karyotype of a human male showing G-bands

and the greater phyletic distance between orangutans, gibbons, and humans (Sutton, 1980).

WORK PHYSIOLOGY

The cost of activity is energy. Since energy is obtained from food, the ultimate determinant of the nutritional requirements of humans is the amount of energy expended to perform a normal round of activities. Methods have been developed to measure the energy cost of activity indirectly (McGuire, 1979). The principle involved is that cellular activity is fueled by the oxidation of nutrients. Blood glucose is combined with oxygen, releasing energy and carbon dioxide. The measurement of the amount of oxygen consumed and the amount of carbon dioxide released permits estimation of the amount of glucose oxidized. When this is known, food requirements can be determined using conversion values that translate specific food items into specific nutrients. Carbohydrates, proteins, and fats are all normally converted into glucose to be oxidized in the cell. Since the structure of proteins and fats requires alteration to produce glucose, they are less efficient sources of energy than carbohydrates, which are complexes of glucose. The relative efficiencies of foods in producing energy can be stated as the *respiratory quotient* (RQ), which is simply the ratio of the volume of carbon dioxide exhaled to the oxygen inhaled:

$$RQ = \frac{CO_2 \text{ exhaled}}{O_2 \text{ inhaled}}$$

The RQ is measured by having the subject breathe air through a tube that has a flowmeter attached. The flowmeter measures the amount of air passing through the tube in a specified period of time. The volume of air can then be used to calculate the volume of oxygen inhaled by using the percentage of oxygen in the atmosphere (20.95%) and correcting for altitude and temperature. The result is the volume of oxygen that is actually available for cellular metabolism over the period of time monitored.

The exhaled air is collected in a bag, and the mixture of gases in the bag is then analyzed by emptying the contents of the bag through a gas meter. A correction is also made for pressure and temperature, and the volume measurement is adjusted to STP (standard temperature and pressure). The gas is then analyzed in an oxygen analyzer, which can be fitted with a carbon dioxide absorbing agent (Weiner and Lourie, 1969).

WORK

The oxygen consumption and carbon dioxide exhalation can be used to estimate the number of glucose molecules oxidized, and thus the calories of heat energy liberated, during the monitoring period. This result can then be compared with the amount of work being done by the subject. The most common method of measuring work output is through the use of a bicycle ergometer (Bradfield, 1971). Ergometers can be adjusted to require greater or less pedal pressure. The force necessary to turn the wheel of the bicycle one time can be multiplied by the number of rotations of the wheel occurring during the test interval. Thus a measure of the amount of work performed and the amount of energy consumed in the same interval can be calculated.

HEART-RATE MONITORING

While the amount of work is being measured on the bicycle ergometer, the heart rate is also monitored. The oxygen consumption measured at various heart rates can be converted to energy consumed at that heart rate, which can also be converted to the amount of work done. When a subject has been carefully monitored at a number of levels of work output and heart rate on the bicycle ergometer, it is possible to make estimates of work load and energy consumption occurring in other situations simply by monitoring the heart rate. Using this approach, energy consumption in complex activities, such as planting rice in a flooded field, can be estimated through the use of a heart-rate monitor. The monitor is a small electrical device that is worn by the subject throughout the day. Some heart-rate monitors are designed to include a wristwatch and can be worn on the wrist without interfering with normal activity. The accumulated record of heart beats can be read into an analyzer which can produce a record of heart beats occurring throughout the period monitored. This record can then be converted into a record of the energy consumed during the period monitored (Brun, 1984). In order to gain the maximum information from this procedure, it is necessary to observe and record the activities undertaken while the heart rate is being monitored. Although this procedure is indirect and subject to inaccuracy, it has been used to provide useful estimates of the amount of energy consumed in a wide variety of activities and settings. When combined with accurate records of food intake, it can yield reasonable estimates of the **bioenergetics** of humans in natural settings. Although the results are not as accurate as could be obtained under controlled laboratory conditions, they can nonetheless prove useful where the nutritional status of a community must be assessed.

SKIN-COLOR MEASUREMENT

Skin color is measured through a technique called *reflectance spectrophotometry.* The areas chosen for measurement are the middle of the forehead, the back of the left forearm, and the inner aspect of the left arm. The last-mentioned site is subject to the least sun exposure and is therefore less tanned than the other two. Light emitted from a standard source is shined onto the surface of the skin through a series of blue, green, and amber filters. The light that is reflected from the skin is picked up by a photocell. The photocell is hooked to a galvanometer, a device used to detect and measure small electrical currents. The amount of current produced by the photocell as a result of the light reflected from the skin is then compared to that reflected from a pure-white standard, usually a block of magnesium oxide or magnesium carbonate.

Figure 24-8 (from Harrison, et al., 1977) compares the reflectance curves of a fair-skinned European and a black African. The amount of light reflected from the European's skin is greater than that reflected from the African's at all wavelengths. The white skin shows a rapid rise of reflection from the blue (left) end of the spectrum, with a trough in the green wavelengths. This trough is the result of absorption of light at these wavelengths by hemoglobin. The dark skin shows a barely perceptible dip at that point. The more linear plot of reflectance from the skin of the African is the result of the predominance of the pigment melanin present in the epidermis. In fact, the curve obtained from reflectance of highly melanized skin is very similar to that obtained from an aqueous suspension of melanin itself.

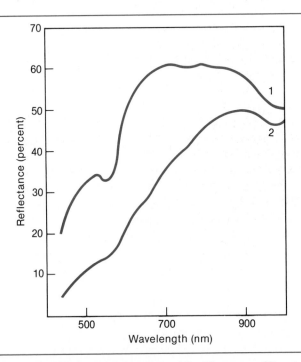

Figure 24-8 Skin reflectance curves of a light-skinned person of European extraction (1) and that of a dark-skinned African (2)

Biological anthropologists have borrowed many of their methods from researchers in other disciplines. Because so much of contemporary research in human variability is concerned with processes as well as structures, some of these methods serve as useful diagnostic procedures to a physician as well as important means of collecting population data for a biological anthropologist. Blood-group serology, body-composition analysis, radiography, karyotyping, and photon absorptiometry all have medical applications. However, because their frequent use by physicians has made them reliable and often economical, it has been possible to apply them as research tools broadening the scope of research into the nature of human variation.

BIBLIOGRAPHY

BRADFIELD, R. B. 1971. Technique for determination of usual energy expenditures in the field. *American Journal of Clinical Nutrition* 24: 1148–54.

BROZEK, J., et al. 1963. Densitometric analysis of body composition: Revisions of some quantitative assumptions. *Annals of the New York Academy of Science* 110: 113–40.

BRUN, T. 1984. Physiological measurement of activity among adults under free-living conditions. In *Energy Intake and Activity,* E. Pollitt and P. Amante, eds. New York: Alan R. Liss.

GARN, S. M., W. R. LEONARD, and V. M. HAWTHORN. 1982. Three limitations of the body mass index. *American Journal of Clinical Nutrition* 36: 573–75.

GOLDSTEIN, H. 1979. *The Design and Analysis of Longitudinal Studies.* London: Academic Press.

GREULICH, W. W., and S. I. PYLE. 1959. *Radiographic Atlas of Skeletal Development of the Hand and Wrist.* Stanford: Stanford University Press.

HARRISON, G.A., J.S. WEINER, J.M. TANNER and N.A. BARNICOT 1977. Human Biology (2nd Edition) Oxford: Oxford University Press.

JOHNSTON, F. E. 1974. Cross-sectional versus longitudinal studies. In *Nutrition and Malnutrition,* A. F. Roche and F. Falkner, eds., pp. 287–307. New York: Pleunum Press.

LOHMAN, T., A. S. ROCHE, and R. MARTORELL (eds.). 1988. *Anthropometric Standardization Reference Manual.* Champaign: Human Kinetics Press.

MAZESS, R. B. 1987. Bone density in diagnosis of osteoporosis: thresholds and breakpoints. *Calcified Tissue International* 41: 117–18.

McGUIRE, J. S. 1979. Seasonal changes in rural energy expenditure and work patterns in rural Guatamalan women. PhD thesis. Massachusetts Institute of Technology.

ROCHE, A. F., H. WAINER, and D. THISSEN. 1975. *Skeletal Maturity: The Knee Joints as a Biological Indicator.* New York: Plenum Press.

ROSS, W. D., A. D. MARTIN, and R. WARD. 1987. Body composition and aging: Theoretical and methodological implications. *Colleguim Anthropologicum* 11: 15–44.

ROSS, W. D., et al. 1988. The relationship of the BMI with skinfolds, girths, and bone breadths in Canadian men and women age 20 to 70 years. *American Journal of Physical Anthropology.*

SINCLAIR, D. 1985. *Human Growth After Birth.* Oxford: Oxford University Press.

SUTTON, H. E. 1980. *An Introduction to Human Genetics,* 3d ed., pp. 62–80. Philadelphia: Saunders College.

TANNER, J. M. 1968. Normal growth and techniques in growth assessment. *Clinical Endocrinology and Metabolism* 15: 411–51.

TANNER, J. M. 1979. *A History of the Study of Human Growth.* Cambridge: Cambridge University Press.

TANNER, J. M., R. M. WHITEHOUSE, and W. A. MARSHALL. 1975. *Assessment of Skeletal Maturity and Prediction of Adult Height: TW2 Method.* London: Academic Press.

VALHALLA SCIENTIFIC. 1988. Body composition analysis through bioimpedance: Fact or fiction? San Diego: Valhalla Scientific.

WEINER, J. S., and J. A. LOURIE. 1969. *Human Biology: A Guide to Field Methods,* IBP Handbook, no. 9. Oxford: Blackwell Scientific.

Chapter
25
Human Skin: The First
Line of Defense

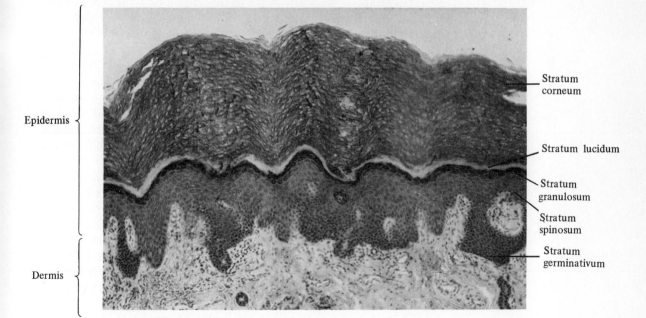

Epidermis

Dermis

Stratum corneum

Stratum lucidum

Stratum granulosum

Stratum spinosum

Stratum germinativum

The skin is the boundary between the individual and the environment. As such, it is subject to insults and injuries not normally experienced by other tissues. Human skin is strikingly naked compared to that of any other primate. The lack of protection from a thick coat of hair or fur has made it necessary to protect the vital structures in the skin by other mechanisms. Human skin is covered by an outer layer of dead cells that are continually being shed. This inert layer of the outer epidermis absorbs most of the punishment inflicted by the environment. In addition, the skin protects its vital deeper layers by darkening when excessive solar radiation is experienced. Variations in skin color in different populations probably reflect differences in the need to shield the deeper skin layers from ultraviolet radiation. The skin has a remarkable capacity to heal when damaged. It also participates in physiological functions, such as the synthesis of vitamin D and the maturation of certain cells of the immune system, that influence the entire body. The ability to sweat is highly developed in humans. The use of evaporative cooling to dissipate heat is a major component of the human thermoregulatory system. The mechanisms that make evaporative cooling possible involve specialized glands located in the skin. The distribution of sweat glands in humans is unique, even among primates and, combined with behavior and cultural adaptations, allows humans to survive in the world's hottest and driest habitats.

SKIN COLOR, CLIMATE, AND DISEASE

The skin has been called the largest organ of the human body. It is not only a large organ, but it performs a wide variety of functions, some of which have only recently been discovered. Human skin, although not hairless, is relatively so when compared with that of most other mammals. Thus it is continually exposed to solar radiation and other environmental conditions. Skin is a constantly renewing tissue. The outer surface, being composed of dead cells, is always being sloughed and replaced by cells beneath it. The layer of dead cells is an effective barrier to water. Consequently, one can be immersed in water without becoming waterlogged. Despite its water resistant properties, a small amount of water in the form of **insensible perspiration** leaves the surface of the skin even when the sweat glands are inactive.

Skin ages and undergoes many changes in appearance through life. It is one of our most visible features and is therefore important in individual identification. Skin pigmentation has also been used as a marker for group identification and at many times and in many places has had important social and economic connotations. The question of why there are differences in the color of the skin in different human populations still awaits a definitive answer. However, some knowledge of the functions of the skin will permit a critical evaluation of the hypotheses that have been offered to explain this most visible aspect of human variation.

The ability of most humans to change skin color during the course of a year and over a lifetime presents another example of seasonal acclimatization, which lends strength to the argument that the most effective human adaptation is the retention of multiple options through adaptability. As the interface between the organism and the environment, the skin should be expected to exhibit important components of the human capacity to adjust to environmental challenges. The importance of the skin's integrity becomes evident when it is damaged, as it is, for instance, by extensive burns. Burns affecting 40 percent or more of the skin's surface are life threatening, with the entire body's fluid balance being disrupted.

CHARACTERISTICS OF THE SKIN

Skin is elastic. If a piece is cut out of it, the wound will gape. It does heal, however, through the rapid proliferation of cells in the deeper layers. Many structures in the skin perform specific functions. Hair follicles, sweat glands, sebaceous glands, and sensory end organs to monitor heat, cold, pressure, and pain are all located in the skin (Harrison and Montagna, 1969). Specialized or encapsulated nerve end organs are found beneath the hairless surfaces of the fingers, palms, soles, and borders of the lips. These nerve end organs are very sensitive. Pigment-producing cells (melanocytes) function to alter the color of the skin in response to solar radiation. It has also been shown that certain cells in the skin (keratinocytes) have an important role in the maturation and enhancement of specific immunologic responses of T cells of the immune system (Edelson and Fink, 1985). In addition, the skin produces 7-dehydrocholesterol, which, when irradiated by ultraviolet light, is transformed to cholecalciferol (Vitamin D_3). After additional processing in the liver and kidney, Vitamin D_3 plays a major role in the absorption and metabolism of calcium (Omdahl and DeLuca, 1973).

THE LAYERS OF HUMAN SKIN

Human skin is made up of the outer layers, the *epidermis,* and the deeper layers, the *dermis.* These components of the skin have different embryological origins and are functionally distinct (see Figure 25-1).

The epidermis has no blood supply. Its outer layer, the **stratum corneum** is made up of flattened, dead cells. Beneath the stratum corneum is the **stratum lucidum,** the cells of which contain a translucent compound from which keratin forms. This layer is present only in the thick skins of the palm and sole. Under the stratum lucidum is the **stratum granulosum,** which contains cells that are in transition as they lose their nuclei and accumulate granules of **keratin** (the horny substance that makes the skin waterproof), and the **stratum spinosum,** which contains a special category of "prickly" cells.

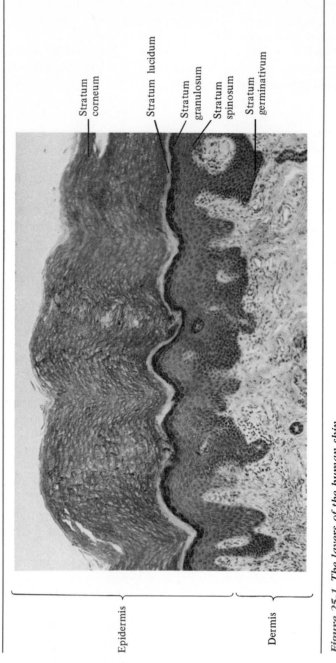

Stratum
corneum

Stratum lucidum

Stratum
granulosum

Stratum
spinosum

Stratum
germinativum

Epidermis

Dermis

Figure 25-1 The layers of the human skin

The deepest and most important layer of the epidermis is the **stratum germinativum,** which contains the only cells in the epidermis that can still divide. The ability of the epidermis to regenerate by replacing the cells sloughed off the external surface is dependent upon the activity of the stratum germinativum.

MELANOCYTES

Besides the cells that will lose their nuclei and migrate to the horny layer (taking approximately 4 weeks to get there), the stratum germinativum (also called the *malpighian layer*) also contains the **melanocytes.** These are the cells that produce melanin, the dark pigment that gives the skin a tan, brown, or black color (Fitzpatrick et al., 1971). The melanocytes are stimulated by sunlight to produce the pigment melanin. The process involves oxidation of the amino acid tyrosine and the action of tyrosinase on tyrosine. Differences in the amount of melanin in the skin are the basis for different skin colors. Although people with darker skins do not necessarily have more melanocytes, they do have more *active* melanocytes (Garcia et al., 1977). When a melanocyte produces melanin, it deposits it in an organelle called a *melanosome.* The melanosomes are then transferred through a cellular extension called a **dendritic process** to the surrounding keratinocytes. Each melanocyte "services" about 36 keratinocytes. In the young keratinocyte, the melanin then disperses into smaller particles that form a cap over the cell nucleus. Melanin absorbs the ultraviolet radiation in sunlight that would otherwise penetrate the nuclei of the dividing cells of the skin. Damage to the DNA by ultraviolet radiation is a major cause of skin cancer. Therefore, persons who synthesize less melanin and have skin that is less pigmented are more susceptible to damage from ultraviolet radiation.

THE BASAL LAYER

In addition to the melanocytes, the stratum germinativum also contains **basal cells,** which are anchored to a **basement membrane.** Also present are Langerhans cells, which have been shown to synthesize interleukin-I. Interleukin-I is critical in the initiation of T cell–mediated immunity. Langerhans cells also capture and present foreign antigens to induce helper T cells to respond (Edelson and Fink, 1985). Excessive ultra violet exposure has been shown to suppress Langerhans cell activity and thereby diminish the effectiveness of the immune response. Thus, the ability to darken the skin and thereby reduce the level of exposure of the stratum germinativum to ultraviolet light has important implications for the immune response.

THE DERMIS

The dermal layer of the skin is the site of the hair follicles, nerves, sweat and sebaceous glands, and blood and lymph vessels. It also has, on its outer surface and adjacent to the basement membrane of the epidermis, the ridges and valleys that determine the shape of the dermatoglyphics (finger, palm, toe, and sole prints). The dermis is well supplied with blood and is of different embryological origin than the epidermis, being derived from mesoderm while the epidermis derives from ectoderm. The outer layer of the dermis is the papillary layer. Underneath it is the coarse structure called the **reticular layer,** which is attached to the underlying muscles by a sheet of areolar tissue usually containing subcutaneous fat. When a skinfold measurement is taken, it is this layer of subcutaneous fat that makes up the bulk of the tissue. The skin itself, dermis and epidermis combined, is only about 1 millimeter thick. Because a skinfold measurement is taken by picking up a pinch of skin and measuring it in a caliper, the skin accounts for 2 millimeters of the total measurement. The rest is considered to be subcutaneous fat, although a small amount of connective tissue will always be present.

APPENDAGES OF THE SKIN

The appendages of the skin have a variety of functions and, in the case of hair, provide much individual variation. Hair color, texture, and distribution all combine to give a person a distinctive appearance, and the uniqueness of the finger and palm prints has been used to identify individuals when all other descriptors are in doubt.

The hair follicles first appear on the scalp and face at about the third month of gestation. The appearance of follicles on the trunk comes later by a month or two. The sweat glands of the hairy skin develop first, and a human infant at birth has all of the sweat pores that it will ever have. Full development of the sweat glands will not be complete until after puberty, when the **apocrine** glands become fully functional. Children under 2 years of age sweat poorly and irregularly and are therefore not able to cope with heat stress with all of the mechanisms available to the adult. In the early years of postnatal life, the sebaceous glands, which secrete an oily substance in the vicinity of the hair follicles, are also poorly developed. These also will become much more active at the time of pubescence, since their function is under the control of the endocrine system.

Fingernails and toenails are a modified version of the horny outer layer of the epidermis. They undergo a process of renewal similar to that of the skin itself and, unless damaged or diseased, grow at the rate of about 1 millimeter a week. A lost fingernail will usually be regenerated in less than 6 months, but a lost toenail will take up to 8 months to be replaced.

WOUND HEALING

Because of its role as the first line of defense against environmentally induced injury, the skin is often damaged. Its ability to heal is therefore an important aspect of its function. The secretions of the glands of the skin maintain an acidic environment on its surface. This acidic environment protects it against irritants and bacteria. When a skin disease or external conditions destroy its ability to maintain an acidic state, it becomes vulnerable to bacterial invasion. Under these conditions, an injury is especially prone to infections, which can spread into the deeper layers of the skin.

In the absence of a serious infection, the healing of a wound follows a well-defined course. First, local bleeding eventually leads to the formation of a clot. Dilation of the vessels in the area of the wound permits circulating cells, nutrients, and oxygen to be delivered to the damaged area. Phagocytes, or specialized white cells, move into the area and begin to remove debris. Buds of the capillary system, which begin to develop within a day of the damage, will form the basis of the renewed circulatory supply to the area. The clot is made up of fibrin threads which form a network that traps red cells.

Fibroblasts in the area surrounding the wound divide and invade the clot. Eventually they start to produce collagen fibers. During the second week of healing, a considerable amount of collagen is laid down, greatly increasing the strength of the replacement tissue. Epithelial cells migrate from all sides of the wound until they finally meet one another. For a while the layer of epithelial cells overlying the wound and the collagen repair material is only one cell-layer thick. It later increases in thickness and ultimately approximates normal. For a while, and sometimes permanently, the new tissue will lack the normal patterning of the skin surface and will have a shiny appearance. In more extensive wounds, **granulation tissue** may be produced. This is the result of the accumulation of fluid and cells from damaged blood vessels.

Newly formed collagen has a tendency to contract. Such contraction pulls the edges of the wound together. This is important in finally closing the wound completely (Sinclair, 1985).

SHORT-TERM ADJUSTMENTS TO HIGH LEVELS OF SOLAR RADIATION

With the abundance of sensitive and vital functions performed in the skin, protection against the most threatening kinds of environmental damage is essential. One kind of damage that is regularly encountered, especially in the tropical latitudes, is solar radiation. The most damaging wavelengths of solar radiation are those in the ultraviolet range.

It was mentioned earlier that ultraviolet radiation can cause suppression of helper T cell activity and consequently can reduce the capacity of the immune system to deal with a variety of pathogens and perhaps neoplasms. There is a very high correlation between the amount of solar radiation exposure experienced in an area and the incidence of skin cancer there. The European-derived populations of Australia and the southwestern United States have an exceptionally high incidence of both basal cell carcinoma and malignant melanoma. The latter is an extremely invasive and therefore dangerous form of cancer. The individuals most vulnerable to the threat of skin cancer are those who have light skin. Albinos are the most affected since they are incapable of producing the enzyme tyrosinase that is needed to make melanin. Red-haired people and those with very fair complexions can produce some melanin, but not enough to protect the germinative layer of the epidermis; they are therefore susceptible to severe damage with relatively little exposure. Darker-haired, darker-skinned people are less susceptible, and the incidence of skin cancer in populations where extremely dark skin is the norm, as in parts of Africa, Melanesia, and among the Australian Aborigines, is very low.

TANNING

The short-term defense against solar radiation damage is tanning. It has long been known that some people tan more quickly and more deeply than others (Quevedo et al., 1975). It is often not realized that tanning, or more properly, increased darkening of the skin, occurs even in dark-skinned people. It is simply not as obvious when the skin is already dark. Unprotected exposure to the sun can result in sunburn, a painful and potentially dangerous condition the symptoms of which are familiar. The heat, reddening, and peeling associated with sunburn are often considered mild discomforts that are the necessary price of acquiring a healthy tan. However, sunburn is a genuine burn, and severe and lasting tissue damage can result from allowing the skin to absorb ultraviolet radiation at a rate exceeding the capacity to produce an effective defense. Such damage can result in deterioration of the thermoregulatory capacity as well as skin cancer.

The defense is staged, in that there is a rapid darkening of the skin soon after exposure begins. This immediate darkening occurs within 5 to 10 minutes and may last up to 4 hours. It is the result of rapid darkening of preformed melanin and the rapid transfer and distribution of melanosomes which are subjected to photo-oxidation, a light-induced chemical reaction which produces dark pigment (Frisancho, 1979). Exposure for 90 to 120 minutes may produce a residual hyperpigmentation lasting up to 36 hours. Although this darkening fades rather quickly, it is followed by the phenomenon of **delayed tanning,** which takes 48 to 72 hours. This form of tanning involves the formation of a number of new melanosomes which will be transferred to keratinocytes. These keratinocytes will be present in a more pigmented form as they move outward to the stratum corneum, where they are eventually shed. Since this process takes an average of 27 days, the protection conferred by delayed tanning lasts nearly a month. Repeated exposure at nonburning levels will reinforce the delayed tanning process and darken the skin further until the individual's tanning limit is reached. Long-term exposure appears to produce permanent darkening, although an extended period without exposure will generally lead to some fading.

It will be recalled that the melanized keratinocytes distribute the melanin they receive from the melanocytes in an arc that shields their nuclei from the incoming radiation. This process is most pronounced in individuals who inherit dark skin. When many such keratinocytes are arranged in layers from the stratum germinativum to the surface of the stratum corneum, their combined melanin shielding provides considerable protection for the cells in the sensitive germinativum layer. Since these are the cells that may still divide, their shielding from the potential effects of ionizing radiation such as ultraviolet will reduce the probability of DNA damage as they divide. Overexposure that leads to burning and peeling of the skin will interfere with melanization. Repeated burning raises the probability of DNA damage and skin cancer.

VITAMIN D

The protection afforded by highly melanized skin comes at the cost of reducing the amount of vitamin D_3 formation taking place in the skin (Loomis, 1967). Under most circumstances this is not a major problem, since the exposure necessary is quite low. In certain circumstances, however, the amount of vitamin D_3 available may fall to levels low enough to have an impact on calcium absorption and bone formation. In the extreme, low calcium availability can lead to insufficient mineralization of the bones of growing children and their deformation in the condition called **rickets** (Loomis, 1970). The bones remain soft in this condition because the collagen (protein) framework is laid down at about the normal rate, but bone mineral crystallization, which gives the bones their structural rigidity, does not keep pace in the absence of sufficient calcium. The softer bones bend and distort under stress and may ultimately harden in their deformed state. One of the most frequent signs of childhood rickets is permanently bowed legs. The maturation of the pelvis is also subject to distortion, and the size and shape of the birth canal of the female pelvis can be sufficiently altered to make normal births impossible. The removal of rickets-prone females from the reproducing segment of a population would have powerful selective implications and would act directly against genotypes unable to adjust to reduced availability of ultraviolet light in sufficient amounts to maintain physiological levels of vitamin D_3 (Neer, 1975).

THE EFFECT OF LATITUDE ON SOLAR RADIATION

The amount of daylight reaching the earth during the course of a year is identical at all latitudes. However, the distribution of daylight hours varies widely from the equator to the poles. Day and night are of equal length at the equator, and in the absence of heavy cloud cover, the midday sun will irradiate the exposed skin with equal intensity throughout the year. The situation is quite different at the higher latitudes. At the poles, the day is 24 hours long at the summer solstice, and the night is 24 hours long at the winter solstice. Thus the midnight sun is a genuine phenomenon on or about June 21st at the North Pole and December 21st at the South Pole. Continual darkness occurs on or about December 21st at the North Pole and June 21st at the South Pole.

Since there are very few humans at either pole, the extreme day lengths there have had little if any influence on human populations. However, the extremely long winter nights of northern Europe have had the potential to affect human populations in relatively large numbers. Most of Europe and the Soviet Union lie north of the 45th parallel, half the distance from the equator to the North Pole. Almost all of Ireland and the United Kingdom are north of the 50th parallel, and most of Norway, Sweden, and Finland are north of the 60th parallel, extending north of the Arctic Circle. During the winter months, these populations receive very little daylight; just as important, the light they do receive reaches the earth at a low angle. This factor is even important during the summer at high latitudes. The intensity of the solar radiation received at an angle low to the horizon is drastically reduced by its extended passage through the atmosphere.

Human populations living in these northerly regions experience extended periods of low ultraviolet exposure and are at risk for **hypovitaminosis D.** Rickets was common in European populations until measures to ensure adequate vitamin intake, either through artificial sources of ultraviolet light or through supplementation of a vitamin D precursor in such foods as milk or bread, were developed. The problem of rickets in the northern hemisphere was not matched in the southern hemisphere because the distribution of the world's land mass greatly favors the north. Africa extends southward only to the 35th parallel, Australia to the 40th, and New Zealand to the 46th, only as far from the equator as Portland, Oregon; Bordeaux, France; or Venice, Italy. The southernmost tip of South America does extend to the 56th parallel at Tierra del Fuego, but its population is quite sparse and quite recent.

RICKETS AND SKIN COLOR

When rickets occurred in Europe it was most prevalent among immigrants from sunnier, more southerly regions, although it was not unknown among the blue-eyed, blond-haired natives of the far north. However, in addition to the advantage attached to low skin pigmentation levels where daylight is weak and of short duration for an extended period each year, much of the population of northern Europe were members of maritime cultures who consumed substantial amounts of seafood. Since certain organs of marine species are rich in vitamin D, the risk of rickets was probably modified to some extent by dietary factors once successful methods of supplying marine foods were widespread. However, dietary supplementation of vitamin D was unlikely to have been widely and consistently available from the beginnings of human habitation of northern Europe, and there was ample time for selection in favor of lightly pigmented genotypes to influence gene frequencies.

The retention of the ability to tan during the months when solar radiation is high would, in these populations, provide an acclimatization to summer conditions that would be necessary to lower the risk of skin cancer and immune suppression that would otherwise accompany reduced melanization of the skin. It should be remembered that even in northern European populations, there is considerable variation in the level of pigmentation and the ability to tan. Not all Swedes are blue-eyed blonds.

CLINAL VARIATION IN SKIN COLOR

As is the case for most human characteristics, **clinal variation**—the expression of traits at varying levels, creating a gradient along geographical distance—seems to be the pattern for human skin color. In areas where solar radiation is a constant throughout the year, the advantage of dark skin is not offset by reduced vitamin D synthesis. In these populations, intensity of pigmentation sufficient to avoid the risk of damage to the deeper layers of the epidermis and the dermis is an unqualified advantage, and selection of the normalizing or stabilizing category would work to maintain it.

It should be remembered that even African blacks can tan and, to some extent, fade, but they maintain their pigmentation at a high level that may well be that which characterized the ancestors of all humans. Since there is little doubt that the earliest stages of human evolution took place in the tropical regions of the Old World, the appropriate pigmentation for those regions would have been dark. The advantages of reduced pigmentation to sustain adequate vitamin D levels would not have been a factor until human populations moved far enough north to experience hypovitaminosis D as an effect of low solar radiation. We may never know when or where this happened. The most convincing evidence of its occurrence would be the presence of osteological signs of rickets in sufficient quantity to justify the inference that natural selection was at work to produce lighter-skinned population.

SKIN COLOR AND COLD STRESS

When darker skin is exposed to sunlight, it absorbs more energy in the form of ultraviolet and infrared radiation. Much of the absorbed energy is converted to heat, producing a higher skin temperature and an enhanced tendency for the skin to radiate heat toward anything that is cooler. Thus, darker skin will radiate more heat and receive less heat in a cold environment than lighter skin does. Pigmented skin, whether that of humans or of experimental animals, appears to be more susceptible to frostbite than lighter skin. Injury due to frostbite was more common among darker-skinned soldiers than among lighter-skinned ones in the U.S. Army in both World Wars and in the Korean War. Post and colleagues (1975) argue that lighter skin conveyed a selective advantage as humans moved farther from their original tropical habitat toward the higher latitudes. Thus the existence of a gradient in pigmentation, with darkest skin occurring in equatorial regions and lightest in such areas as northern Europe, could be the result of synergistic effects of higher production of vitamin D and lower susceptibility to frostbite associated with lighter pigmentation.

OTHER FACTORS INFLUENCING SKIN COLOR

Skin color is not solely the product of melanin formation. The amount of carotene in the skin, the thickness of the keratin in the epidermis, and, to a certain extent, the oxygenation of the blood flowing through the cutaneous circulation will all influence the color of the skin. Blushing and flushing transiently change the color of the skin, while a shock that reduces blood flow to the skin will quickly produce a pallor. Factors that produce a high percentage of **carboxyhemoglobin** (red cells carrying carbon dioxide instead of oxygen) will lend a blue tint to the skin. An extreme example of the effect of high carboxyhemoglobin levels can be seen among Monge's disease victims—high-altitude dwellers who have lost their adaptation to hypoxia (see the discussion of high-altitude stress in Chapter 27). The thickness of the skin also affects its color, because a thicker layer of keratin reduces the degree to which the blood of the cutaneous circulation will influence color. Carotene, which has an orange-yellow color, gives the skin a yellow tint; on occasion, the overconsumption of carotene will lead to a bright-yellow pigmentation often limited to the stratum lucidum of the thickened skin of the palms and soles.

EYE AND HAIR COLOR

The color of the eyes and the hair are also affected by the level of melanin produced—an example of pleiotropy, in which a single gene affects the expression of several traits. As a rule, very dark skin is accompanied by very dark hair and light skin by blond hair. The melanocytes of blond individuals inject less melanin into the shaft of the growing hair, leaving it more influenced by the keratin than is the case with darker individuals. Red hair is the result of very small amounts of melanin being present, with the result that the predominant color is that of keratin. Red-haired individuals often have green eyes, also the result of very low melanin levels. Blue eyes lack melanin entirely, and the blue color is the result of refraction of light being reflected by the blood passing through the eyeball. Hazel and brown eyes have increasing amounts of melanin.

SKIN COLOR AND HEAT STRESS

Dark skin in areas of high solar radiation is disadvantageous in certain respects when heat stress is also a factor. This is because a dark surface absorbs more heat than a light one, and buildup of the heat load is therefore more rapid. It has been shown that the internal temperature of blacks working in the midday sun is higher than that of whites working under the same circumstances (Baker, 1958). However, the increased heat load is compensated for by the production of more sweat.

Evaporative Cooling: Sweat

Darkly pigmented people have, on the average, the same number of or slightly more sweat glands than lightly pigmented people. However, the sweat glands of darkly pigmented people are more active (Weiner, 1976). This allows the surface of the skin to be cooled by evaporation. Evaporative cooling is a very effective way of dissipating heat. Sweat glands maximize the effectiveness of evaporative cooling by secreting a thin film of sweat over a large area of skin. An increase in the activity of sweat glands increases the area capable of dissipating heat and therefore more effectively reduces the heat load. This process is most effective in dry heat, where evaporation is most rapid. In exceedingly humid conditions, the ability to evaporate sweat is greatly diminished, and sweating becomes a very inefficient means of dissipating heat.

THE ACTIVITY OF SWEAT GLANDS

The sweat glands produce sweat by filtering serum from the blood. The capacity to produce sweat appears to be limited primarily by the body's ability to maintain fluid and electrolyte balance. Sweat rates of a liter an hour have been measured. The loss of fluid caused by such sweating can become life threatening if rehydration is not possible and may lead to heat prostration, or heat stroke, accompanied by a breakdown in the thermoregulatory system, very high body temperature, and convulsions. Although the possibility of heat stroke and death is a real one when severe heat conditions are experienced and adequate fluid intake does not compensate for sweat loss, the sweat glands are remarkably effective under all but the most extreme conditions (Mitchell et al., 1976). Their wide distribution and high capacity for continuous cooling is an adaptation unique to humans. It is a capacity that is most valuable in warm climates, presumably in the parts of the world where human evolution occurred. The reduction in hair coverage of the body that distinguishes humans from other primates has been combined with an increase in the number of one category of sweat glands (the eccrine glands) to cover most of the body's surface.

APOCRINE GLANDS

The sweat glands in human skin are of two major categories (see Figure 25-2): **eccrine** and apocrine. The apocrine glands secrete a pale fluid that seems to have no other function than to produce a characteristic odor. This odor may function, perhaps unconsciously, as a sexual attractant. They develop close to hair follicles and empty into the follicle rather than directly onto the surface of the skin. An interesting feature of the human apocrine glands is that they begin to appear nearly everywhere on the body of the human fetus during the fifth month of gestation. A few weeks after their appearance, most of them disappear, leaving only those in the axilla (armpit), the anogenital surfaces, the nipples, the navel, and the external canal of the ear. It is in these areas that apocrine gland activity is most important in the adult. The concentration of apocrine glands and their development is greatest in the axillae. In contrast to the eccrine glands, which function to produce sweat to cool the body's surface as it evaporates, and which respond primarily to a rise in body temperature, the apocrine glands respond to stress and sexual stimulation. In humans, the combination of apocrine and eccrine glands in the axillae allows the apocrine secretions to be spread over a larger area and aerated. This facilitates their breakdown by bacterial action, producing a characteristic odor. Humans share this combination of apocrine and eccrine glands (called the axillary organ) only with the gorilla and the chimpanzee.

ECCRINE SWEAT GLANDS

The eccrine sweat glands are not unique to humans but are unique in their wide distribution over the surface of the human body. Cats and dogs and some other animals have eccrine sweat glands on their digital pads. Their activity

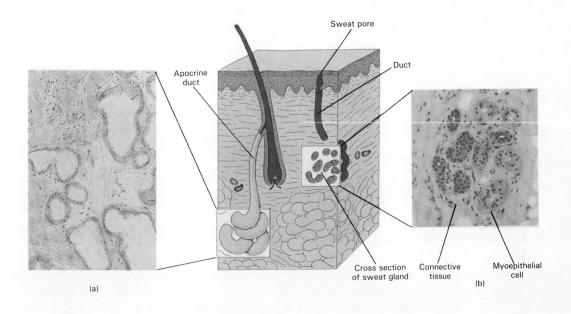

Labels on figure: Sweat pore; Apocrine duct; Duct; Cross section of sweat gland; Connective tissue; Myoepithelial cell; (a); (b)

Figure 25-2 Human sweat glands; a = apocrine; b = eccrine

can be detected by observing the footprints appearing on the veterinarian's stainless steel table as a nervous pet is examined. This form of eccrine gland has its human equivalent on the palms of the hands and the soles of the feet. It is believed that the thin film of eccrine secretion present on the friction, or gripping, surfaces of the hands and feet enhance both their sensitivity and their nonskid properties. These friction-related eccrine glands are located along the ridges of the dermatoglyphic patterns of ridges and valleys. They can be found in the same areas on all other primates. However, in South American monkeys with prehensile tails, they are also found on the gripping surface of the tail. In gorillas and chimpanzees, such friction surfaces, complete with ridges and valleys and their eccrine glands, are found on the backs of the fingers. In this location, their antiskid properties are apparently valuable as a part of the knuckle-walking mode of locomotion. Gorillas and chimpanzees also have a higher percentage of eccrine glands as opposed to apocrine glands than other primates, about half of the total sweat gland population being of the eccrine category.

However, humans have by far the greatest proportion, with virtually all of the sweat glands on the skin being eccrine glands. The human skin has anywhere from 2 to 5 million eccrine glands spread over its surface. Their density of distribution ranges from 150 to 340 per square centimeter of skin.

They are most heavily distributed on the palms and soles. The head, trunk, and extremities have lower densities. Men and women have proportionally the same number of eccrine glands, but there is considerable individual variability. While human variability includes differences in the amount of sweat produced, heavy sweating capacity does not necessarily indicate the presence of more sweat glands since some of them are functionless even though of normal appearance. All of the sweat glands, both apocrine and eccrine, are under the control and regulation of the autonomic nervous system.

THE SKIN AS AN ADAPTIVE ORGAN

The combination of functions performed by the skin in conditions of heat and high levels of solar radiation presents an informative example of the capacity for short-term and long-term adaptation. The sensitive lower layers of the epidermis and the important organs located in the dermis are vulnerable to damage arising from ultraviolet radiation, abrasions, and heat damage.

The mechanisms of adaptation include short-term tanning upon short exposure to solar radiation. This process involves the oxidation and darkening of existing melanin and provides enhanced protection for only about 4 hours. An extended version of this process may occur if exposure time is increased to an hour or more. This form of darkening may persist for 2 or 3 days—long enough for long-term tanning to have its effect through the production of more melanin and its transfer to large numbers of keratinocytes. This protection will last up to a month after a single exposure. With repeated exposures, the tanning process will be reinforced as additional layers of melanized keratinocytes are needed.

The evaporative cooling system made possible by the generous supply of eccrine sweat glands on the human body reduces the heat load and, by providing a thin film of fluid over the surface of the body, enhances reflectivity. As in the case of the tanning response, the effectiveness of the sweating response increases with repeated exposure. This is an example of acclimitization. As acclimatization to heat stress is achieved, the tendency to produce sweat at a rate too rapid to maximize evaporative efficiency is reduced. Well-acclimatized individuals sweat at a more economic level in terms of fluid loss and still achieve the benefits of evaporative cooling since very little benefit is gained when sweat drips rather than evaporates.

NONPHYSIOLOGICAL ADAPTATIONS TO THE STRESS OF A HOT, DRY ENVIRONMENT

The physiological responses to exposure to the heat and solar radiation in the tropics throughout the year and much of the temperate zone during the summer months can properly be viewed as seasonal acclimatization. In the temperate zones, the skin grows paler and sweating becomes less efficient in the winter months. In the hot, dry regions of the world's tropics, however, conditions are such that seasonal loss of acclimatization does not occur. It is in these regions that long-term and persistent stress has had the opportunity to evoke a more permanent response, in the form of either a developmental acclimatization or a true genetic adaptation. The maintenance of dark pigmentation and widespread distribution of active eccrine sweat glands seems to be genetically determined in the native populations of the tropics. However, customs and practices have been adopted in the arid tropics that add another dimension to the adaptive response. These practices transcend the physiological capacity to modify the stress through the deployment of behaviors that modify the environment at several levels. The concept of a graded response is useful in evaluating the degree to which such behaviors either supplement or supplant the physiological mechanisms of adjustment.

DESERT ADAPTATION

In the arid tropics, in such areas as the Sahara or the Arabian deserts, human populations have long been exposed to the hazards of heat, solar radiation, and dehydration. In an extremely arid region, where atmospheric moisture is effectively absent and where intense heat and drying winds remove sweat from the body as rapidly as it can be produced, the advantages of evaporative cooling can be quite quickly offset by the danger of dehydration.

It was mentioned earlier that humans can lose sweat at a rate of a liter an hour or perhaps even more. Human thirst does not keep up with the demand created by such losses. In many cases, sufficient drinking water is not available to support such losses on a regular basis. In addition, the loss of sweat also involves the loss of salts, mainly sodium chloride. The depletion of fluids and electrolytes constitutes a severe threat to survival. The methods employed to minimize this depletion are largely focused on the use of garments and dwellings that minimize the loss of fluid while simultaneously lowering the exposure of the skin to the damage of solar radiation.

ACTIVITY PATTERNS IN DESERT ENVIRONMENTS

A frequent practice in desert environments is to restrict activity to the nighttime hours. This is particularly true of caravan travel, which follows a schedule of movement through the night and rest under cover during the day. This pattern serves to reduce both the level of solar radiation experienced and the increase in the sweat rate associated with work at high temperatures. The desert environment is one in which wide ranges of temperature occur over the course of the day. Nights may be quite cool despite high temperatures during the day. Desert-adapted human populations resemble other desert dwellers, such as rodents and reptiles, in favoring nocturnal activity.

CLOTHING

Another behavioral adjustment to the demands of the desert habitat is the use of clothing that modifies the environment. A nude human achieves a maximum sweat rate at a temperature of about 43°C (109°F). But when one is clothed in the traditional garments of the desert dweller, maximum sweat rate occurs at a temperature of 52°C (126°F). Ideal clothing for the desert environment is light in weight, loosely woven, and light in color to maximize reflectivity. It should cover the body well, but be loose enough to maintain a layer of air between the cloth and the skin's surface. This description applies to the garments worn by most desert-adapted people. While reducing the amount of sweat loss, such garments also allow evaporation of sweat through the porous weave of the cloth. This loss cools the cloth itself and avoids the buildup of moisture inside the garment. Such buildup would increase discomfort at the same time that it reduced the insulative efficiency of the dead air space surrounding the body. The use of tents to create shade is essentially an extension of this concept.

With the employment of these behavioral and technological devices, desert populations have achieved an adjustment to the major stressors of their habitat that reduces the demand on their physiological responses. Although the linear body build that facilitates heat loss is seen in some desert-adapted populations, the absence of obvious genetic adaptations to the desert environment after thousands of years of exposure by many native populations is an indication of the effectiveness of their cultural and behavioral adaptations.

The human skin is a remarkable organ that performs a wide variety of functions above and beyond that of protecting the rest of the body from damage. One of the skin's special adaptations is the ability to sweat and cool the body, permitting heat dissipation even when the air temperature exceeds that of the interior of the body. Variations in human skin color and sweat rate appear to be responses to the various demands created by the habitat. However, the differences among human populations are modest when the magnitude of the differences in environmental conditions is taken into account. The human capacity to employ behavioral and cultural means to cope with and modify the environment has allowed the retention of similar structural and physiological features in human skin in hot, cold, wet, or dry parts of the world.

BIBLIOGRAPHY

BAKER, P. T. 1958. The biological adaptation of man to hot deserts. *American Naturalist* 92: 337–57.

EDELSON, E. L., and J. M. FINK. 1985. The immunologic function of skin. *Scientific American* 252: 46–53.

FITZPATRICK, T. B., et al. 1971. The melanocyte system. In *Dermatology in General Medicine,* T. B. Fitzpatrick, ed. New York: McGraw-Hill.

FRISANCHO, A. R. 1979. *Human Adaptation.* St. Louis: C. V. Mosby.

GARCIA, R. D., et al. 1977. Number of epidermal melanocytes, hair follicles, and sweat ducts in the skin of Solomon Islanders. *American Journal of Physical Anthropology* 47: 427–34.

HARRISON, R. J., and W. MONTAGNA. 1969. *Man,* pp. 141–68. New York: Appleton-Century-Crofts.

LOOMIS, W. F. 1967. Skin pigment regulation of vitamin D biosynthesis in man. *Science* 157: 501–6.

LOOMIS, W. F. 1970. Rickets. *Scientific American* 223: 409–16.

MITCHELL, D., et al. 1976. Acclimatization in a hot, humid environment: Energy exchange, body temperature, and sweating. *Journal of Applied Physiology* 40: 768–78.

NEER, R. M. 1975. The evolutionary significance of vitamin D, skin pigment, and ultraviolet light. *American Journal of Physical Anthropology* 43: 409–16.

OMDAHL, J. L., and H. F. DeLUCA. 1973. Regulation of vitamin D metabolism and function. *Physiological Reviews* 53: 327–72.

POST, P. W., F. DANIELS, JR., and R. T. BINFORD. 1975. Cold injury and the evolution of "white" skin. *Human Biology* 47: 65–80.

QUEVEDO, W. C., JR., et al. 1975. Role of light in human skin color variation. *American Journal of Physical Anthropology* 43: 393–408.

SINCLAIR, D. 1985. *Human Growth After Birth.* Oxford: Oxford University Press.

WEINER, J. S. 1976. *Physiological Variability and Its Genetic Basis.* London: Taylor and Francis.

Chapter
26
Ancient Enemies:
Disease and the Immune
System

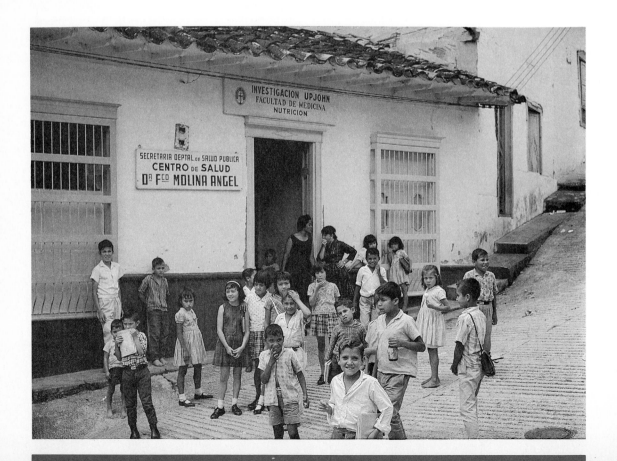

Since the time when human populations became successful in ensuring themselves a supply of food, the tendency to settle down and build homes, villages, and cities has become an important aspect of human sociocultural behavior. Along with the advantages of a steady food supply and increasingly elaborate shelter came an increase in the exposure to disease. When hunting and gathering people spent a large proportion of their time moving from place to place in pursuit of food, opportunities for contagion were limited. It is thought that the earliest humans probably carried endoparasites similar to those that infest living nonhuman primates, but these parasites have a relatively minor effect on the health of their hosts. Many biologists believe that lengthy exposure to a pathogen will lead to mutual adaptations that permit both host and parasite to survive. When humans became sedentary and kept domesticated animals close to their dwellings, they greatly increased the variety of pathogenic organisms to which they were exposed. The disposal of wastes became a problem, as did the frequent exposure to air exhaled by other, possibly infected, individuals. The larger the community, the greater the likelihood of disease transmission. Humans have lived in villages and small towns for many thousands of years, and large cities have existed for at least 2,000 years. With the reduction in the impact of the climate that these communities have provided has come the increase in the importance of disease as an agent of natural selection. The challenge that frequent disease exposure has presented to the human immune system has been met with remarkable success. However, the mechanisms that permit the immune system to limit and prevent diseases have been countered by some disease organisms. Therefore, other defenses, some of which involve genetic change, have evolved. The variety of these defenses is a measure of the magnitude of the challenge presented by certain diseases. Malaria is one of the most instructive examples of the ongoing battle between disease and human populations.

COEXISTENCE VS. LETHALITY: MEASURES OF VIRULENCE

As human populations became increasingly successful in ensuring food supplies through horticulture and animal husbandry, they became more sedentary. Villages, towns, and cities eventually arose, and human existence was never the same. With all the benefits that accompany complex cultural systems came some equally significant problems. Sedentary populations, densely concentrated in villages and towns without the benefit of sewage systems, water treatment plants, and public health systems that are taken for granted today, were vulnerable to the spread of disease (Armelagos and Dewey, 1970). Epidemics became one of the hazards of life. When an increased number of deaths were the result of infectious disease, the immune system became the focus of human adaptation. Many diseases have become epidemic over the centuries, and a few—notably bubonic plague and influenza—have been widespread and deadly enough to be called **pandemic.**

Certain **pathogens,** or infectious organisms, are more tolerable than others. Some can be tolerated without serious effects on the health of the infected individual. Some produce the symptoms of disease only when their host has suffered a decline in health for some other reason. Some are likely to produce symptoms that may be only annoying; others are lethal. The degree to which a pathogen affects the health and survival of its host is a measure of its **virulence.** Some pathogens, such as *Clostridium botulinum,* the organism that causes botulism, are so highly virulent that they are usually fatal in the absence of prompt and effective treatment. Others, like the viruses that cause influenza, will produce a serious and acute illness that the victim usually survives. Others, among them the herpes virus, become chronic, producing symptoms only occasionally but persisting in the host for long periods. Some infections are essentially beneficial, as in the case of certain **Lactobacilli** that actually contribute nutrients to their host while inhabiting its intestinal tract. Some parasites, such as roundworm, hookworm, tapeworm, and certain flukes, can be tolerated for an entire lifetime but exact a toll in terms of blood loss and stolen nutrients that has an impact on the health and vitality of their human hosts.

The diseases that affect humans are often variants of diseases that affect other species. It is thought that periodic epidemics of influenza are the result of the passage of a strain of the virus through another host species, where it produces a mutation that makes it temporarily invisible to the human immune system. It is the change in *antigenicity,* the property of producing recognition by the immune system, that made the influenza epidemic that swept much of the world in 1918 and 1919 so deadly. It is believed that the new strain of the virus first appeared in the population of domestic hogs that passed through the Kansas City stockyards. When the virus found its way into the densely packed population at the military base at Fort Riley, Kansas, it swept through the population rapidly, killing many of the young recruits who were being prepared to go to Europe to fight in World War I. The disease spread rapidly beyond the military population and swept through the civilian populations of much of the world (Kaplan and Webster, 1977).

THE GREAT PLAGUES

The plagues that swept Europe between the fourteenth and the eighteenth centuries killed up to half of the citizens of several major cities and wreaked havoc on the socioeconomic system of much of Europe. The pathogen in this case, *Yersinia pestis,* was a bacterium that was transmitted to the human host by fleas that had been carried into human dwellings by rats. It was the movement of rats from city to city, often on sailing ships, that spread the disease (Langer, 1964). The question of what caused the end of the great plagues is still a perplexing one. There are still reservoirs of the disease in Asia and in the southwestern United States, but human fatalities in the United States rarely exceed 6 to 10 persons per year.

The list of diseases that have had a major impact on human populations is a long one. A disease that is relatively mild in a population that has been infected with it for an extended period will often become extremely virulent in a population exposed to it for the first time. Populations of American Indians were decimated on initial exposure to measles, smallpox, and chicken pox (Black, 1975). Eskimo and Pacific Island populations were similarly affected. Their susceptibility was not the result of racial differences. Rather, their naive immune systems, which lacked a memory of these pathogens, permitted them to multiply and invade the cells of the host without resistance. By the time an immune response began, the damage was often fatal. But it must be pointed out that, just as in Europe during the great plagues and throughout the world during the influenza pandemic, there were usually survivors. In most cases, the survivors outnumbered the fatalities and future generations were more resistant to the disease. Of course, what these diseases and many others are doing is testing the immune system of the humans who are infected.

THE IMMUNE SYSTEM AS AN ADAPTATION

The remarkable fact is that the immune system has been able to keep up with the continual onslaught of new and potentially lethal pathogens. It would not be an overstatement to say that the immune response is one of our species' most impressive adaptations. With centuries of regular exposure to contagious diseases in densely populated communities, the human immune system has been subjected to frequent challenges that it has generally met. The opportunity for selection arising from continual exposure to infectious diseases would qualify disease as one of the major evolutionary factors affecting our species. The truth of the matter, however, is that we know very little about how disease has restructured human gene frequencies.

One reason for this is that the immune system itself creates the opportunity for copying errors to produce mutant genotypes continually. Mistakes in DNA replication are exploited to produce proteins that recognize previously unknown antigens. The incessant shuffling of the DNA determining the structures of receptor sites on antibodies and immune cells produces an almost infinite array of configurations to match those of new pathogenic invaders.

MAXIMIZATION OF GENETIC DIVERSITY: THE IMMUNE SYSTEM

The immune system in humans is a complex system responsible for distinguishing self from nonself, recognizing foreign intruders, such as bacteria and viruses, and either disabling or destroying them. The immune system is actually composed of two separate systems which interact to protect the organism from invaders. The two types of immune function involve different types of cells and are referred to as **cell-mediated immunity** and **humoral immunity.**

Cell-mediated immunity involves the activity of a class of cells called **phagocytes.** Phagocytes directly attack and destroy invading organisms and the cells that are infected with them. Phagocytic cells either engulf and digest the foreign invader or release chemicals that destroy it. Some phagocytes specifically attack parasites; others are specific to bacteria, fungi, or viruses. Other phagocytes are responsible for removing dead and damaged cells from the tissues and bloodstream.

Humoral immunity refers to the portion of the immune system that consists of circulating immune cells. The cells of the humoral system are present in the blood and lymph tissue and are largely responsible for recognizing foreign invaders and marking them for destruction. Many of the cells in the humoral system work cooperatively with the phagocytes in effecting an immune response.

A class of cells called **lymphocytes** plays a crucial role in the function of both humoral and cell-mediated immunity. These cells originate in the bone marrow and migrate to the liver, thymus, or lymph tissue, where they mature into **T cells, B cells,** or **macrophages.**

B cells are found in the bone marrow, lymph nodes, spleen, liver, and bloodstream. These circulating cells, when activated by the presence of a foreign intruder, mature into **plasma cells.** The plasma cells secrete proteins called **antibodies,** which recognize substances on the surfaces of foreign cells called **antigens.** An antigen may be a protein or any other substance that elicits an antibody response. The surface of a cell may exhibit a number of different antigens, and it is up to the immune system to determine whether the surface antigen is foreign or not. How this determination is made is not well understood, but it is clear that the immune system distinguishes self from nonself on the basis of its ability to recognize antigens.

Other immune cells also originate in the bone marrow but migrate to the thymus gland, where they mature into T cells. There are three distinct types of T cells, each performing a different but related role in the immune system. The three types of T cells are the **killers,** the **helpers,** and the **suppressors.**

The killer T cells are actually part of the cell-mediated immune response. When activated by an antigen, the killer T cell releases a substance called a **lymphotoxin,** which destroys the antigen-bearing cell. While the precise way in which the helper T cells function is unclear, they are crucial to the operation of the immune system. Both the cell-mediated and humoral immune responses are activated by the helper T cells. If helper T cells are damaged or destroyed, the other components of the immune system are unable to respond to antigens. The third type of T cell, the suppressor T cell, seems to play an important role in immune regulation. It is the suppressor T cell which turns off the immune response when it is no longer needed.

In addition to B cells and T cells, there is the **macrophage,** a third important type of cell involved in the immune response. Macrophages have receptors on the cell surface which recognize and bind to antigens. Once macrophages have accumulated enough antigen on their surfaces, they interact with the helper T cells to stimulate the killer T cells and B cells to respond.

When the human body is invaded by a foreign organism, such as a bacteria or a virus, the immune system is alerted. The foreign invader will have some type of identifying antigen on its surface. This antigen will be recognized as foreign by one of the circulating helper T cells. The helper T cells apparently are involved in capturing the antigen and transferring it to the receptors on the surface of the circulating macrophages. Once the macrophages have accumulated a certain concentration of antigen on their surfaces, they present themselves to the B cells.

Meanwhile, the helper T cells begin releasing substances called **lymphokines,** which seem to play a major role in activating other cells. These lymphokines include such substances as **interferon** and **interleukins 1** and **2.** Interferon apparently stimulates the activity of the macrophages, while interleukin-1 causes the B cells to mature into plasma cells and begin producing antibodies. Interleukin-2 seems to activate the killer T cells and to enhance the activities of the phagocytes.

It might be noted here that interferon and interleukin-2 are currently used experimentally in the treatment of some cancers and of acquired immune deficiency syndrome (AIDS). One of the reasons that AIDS is such a devastating disease is that it directly attacks the immune system at its most crucial point, the helper T cells. The virus that causes the destruction of the immune system, the human immunodeficiency virus (HIV), preferentially attacks helper T cells. The virus not only takes over the cell, using its resources to replicate itself, but in the process it disables the T cell. AIDS victims have greatly reduced numbers of helper T cells. Even though the rest of the immune system is relatively unaffected (there are still plenty of killer T cells, and normal quantities of antibodies are produced), the healthy portions of the immune system cannot be activated because the helper T cells have been destroyed. Treatments involving interferon and the interleukins are based on the hope that, by replacing the helper T cell products, T cell function can be simulated and immune system function restored. Unfortunately, such experimental treatments have not been as successful as hoped.

Once the T cells and macrophages have recognized the foreign antigen, the B cells are activated. Some of the B cells mature into plasma cells and begin to secrete **antibodies.** Antibodies are proteins whose individual structure is specific to particular antigens. Since there are an essentially infinite number of different possible antigens, B cells must be capable of producing an infinite number of different types of antibodies. In order to understand how this occurs, it is necessary to understand something about the genetics of antibody formation.

An antibody is composed of four polypeptide chains: two heavy chains, each about 440 amino acids long, and two light chains, each about 214 amino acids long. There are, in addition, two different types of light chains: kappa and lambda. Either type of light chain may combine with the heavy chain, although an antibody will contain either kappa or lambda chains, but never both at once. The heavy and light chains each have both constant and variable portions. In both cases the first 110 amino acids constitute the variable portion of the molecule. It is this portion of the antibody which is specific to a particular antigen (Figure 26-1).

The immune system has the capacity to produce millions of different proteins (antibodies), yet there are clearly not millions of different genes involved. How and why this occurs is an important issue in antibody genetics research. Since there are considerably fewer genes than there are antibodies, some genes must be capable of producing more than one kind of antibody. In fact, it appears that all of the heavy chains, both constant and variable portions, are made by a single gene. Likewise, each of the two types of light chains appears to result from a single gene. We are then faced with the problem

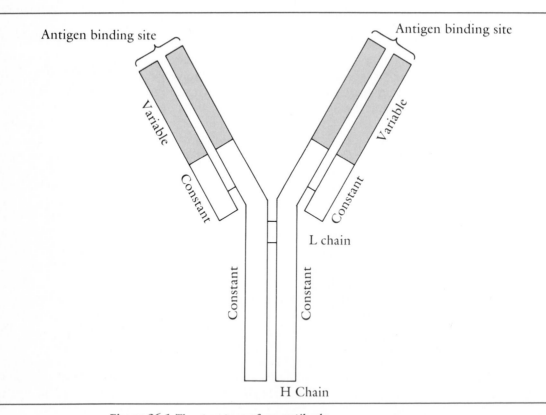

Figure 26-1 The structure of an antibody

of how millions of different antibodies can be produced by only two or three genes.

In Chapter 4, we discussed the role that differential processing can play in producing a variety of different mRNAs from a single primary transcript. It appears that a similar process occurs during the production of antibodies. The main difference is that the splicing appears to occur at the level of the DNA rather than at the RNA level. Figure 26-2 schematically represents the structure of one of the light-chain genes. The kappa light-chain gene is believed to have a few hundred variable-region exons, followed by four or five joining-region exons and a constant-region exon. It is thought that when B cells are produced, one of the variable regions is randomly selected and paired with one of the randomly selected joining regions. The remaining variable and joining regions are thought to be spliced out, so that each B cell is capable of making only one type of light chain. Since a similar splicing process occurs at the heavy-chain gene, the B cell is capable of producing a unique antibody.

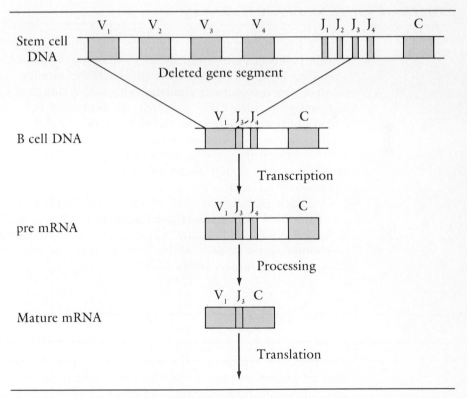

Figure 26-2 A schematic representation of the structures of an immunoglobulin light chain gene and the steps involved in its translation into a functional protein

While any one B cell is capable of producing only a single type of antibody, it is highly unlikely that two different B cells will produce the same antibody.

As mentioned earlier, activated B cells undergo mitosis. Some of the B cells mature into plasma cells while others remain dormant, existing as **memory cells.** The mature plasma cells begin to secrete antibodies, which bind to the antigens. It is this antigen–antibody complex which appears to stimulate the activities of the phagocytes, which attack and destroy the intruder. An antibody-producing plasma cell can secrete antibodies at the rate of more than a thousand per minute, yet the plasma cell itself lives for only a few days. The memory cells, by contrast, live for months or even years. When an antigen is introduced a second time, the memory cells recognize it and are able to respond quickly, bypassing some of the early stages of the immune response. The use of vaccines to reduce the effects of exposure to certain viruses is possible because of this ability of B cells to remember previous exposure to an antigen and respond appropriately.

LIMITS OF IMMUNE EFFECTIVENESS

With all of its remarkable properties, the immune system has limits, and certain pathogens are extremely effective in testing those limits. The strategy employed by these pathogens is to match the immune system's ability to produce new receptor-site configurations with a similar system for producing new antigenic identities. Although the host may deal effectively with 95 percent of the pathogens, the remaining 5 percent are invisible and multiply rapidly before the immune system learns the combination. By that time, another new antigenicity has been produced. By this system, some pathogens manage to stay a step ahead of the immune response and are therefore dangerously virulent.

One such pathogen is that which causes sleeping sickness, a protozoan parasite called *Trypanosoma gambiense;* this parasite has proven extremely difficult to eradicate. The human immune response has thus far been incapable of countering its strategy of beating the immune system at its own game (Donelson and Turner, 1985).

MALARIA

The pathogen responsible for malaria is capable of similar tricks. This is another protozoan parasite that probably affects more human victims than any other infectious disease. While some immunity can be acquired, a comparatively brief cessation in exposure to the pathogen leaves the infected person relatively defenseless. The inference that can be drawn from this apparent loss of immunity in the absence of exposure to the parasite is that the parasite is accumulating changes in its antigenic profile that eventually make it invisible to the immune system. Thus, intermittent exposure to malaria can actually be more dangerous than continuous exposure.

MOSQUITOES AND MALARIA

In many parts of the world, malaria is **endemic.** That is, exposure to the disease is likely at any time since the pathogen is always present. However, the parasite, *Plasmodium ssp,* can infect a new host only if transmitted by a mosquito, generally the genus *Anopheles.* Even in areas where malaria is endemic, there are often seasonal variations in the number of mosquitoes present and, as a result, exposure is more intermittent than continuous.

Since malaria is an exceedingly debilitating and, in the very young, an often fatal disease, other modes of defense to supplement the immune system are of great value. These supplementary mechanisms provide an interesting example of a multiple-backup system where a challenge to survival is widespread, severe, and capable of circumventing the immune system. A brief description of the etiology of malaria will be useful in the consideration of its role in the generation of certain elements of human phenotypic variability.

The malarial parasite is widely distributed throughout the tropical and subtropical regions of the world. Malaria has extended well into the temperate zone, however, especially in the area around the Mediterranean Sea. Occasional outbreaks have also occurred in the United States in such unlikely places as Washington, D.C., and, during the late nineteenth century, Tucson, Arizona. The presence of the appropriate mosquito and a body of standing water in which it can breed are essential conditions for the transmission of malaria.

ENDEMIC MALARIA IN WEST AFRICA

The parasite responsible for malaria in humans may also infect pongid primates. It is thought that malarial infections were endemic among pongids living in West Africa before human populations displaced them. As the development of agriculture allowed human populations to grow and become more sedentary, the pongid populations declined and the *Anopheles* mosquitoes that fed on them increasingly turned to human hosts. Thus, possibly for the first time, malaria began to affect large numbers of humans. Livingstone (1958) argues that the need to clear land to expand areas of cultivation changed the habitat in ways that made malarial infection virtually inevitable. The collection of standing water in the vicinity of expanding agricultural villages created ideal breeding conditions for mosquitoes, which must spend the larval stage of their development in still water. Therefore, malaria became an endemic disease in a large area of West Africa.

THE ETIOLOGY OF MALARIA

There are at least four species of *Plasmodium* known to cause some form of malaria in humans: *Plasmodium vivax, P. falciparum, P. malariae,* and *P. ovale.* Of these, *P. falciparum* is the most virulent. When transmitted by the female mosquito's bite, the parasite has already undergone the sexual phase of its life cycle in the mosquito. The first stage of the parasite's development in a human host takes place in the liver. Between 5 and 11 days after infection, large numbers of parasites enter the bloodstream from the liver and seek out red blood cells. The parasites then invade the red blood cells and begin to multiply rapidly. After about 48 hours, the invaded red blood cells rupture and a massive number of parasites are freed (see Figure 26-3). As the red blood cells are being ruptured in large numbers, the victim begins to feel chills that last from 15 minutes to an hour. The chills may be accompanied by nausea, vomiting, and headache, and are followed by a fever that may last several hours and may go as high as 104°F (40°C). It is thought that during the fever, parasites are invading more red blood cells. The fever is followed by profuse sweating, a period during which the victim usually falls asleep and feels somewhat better.

The cycle is irregular in the early stages of the disease, but it eventually repeats itself every 48 hours in infections of *P. falciparum;* falciparum malaria has been called *malignant tertian malaria* in reference to the recurrent 3-day cycles. The cycle of *P. vivax* infections is less severe; hence the name *benign tertian malaria.*

DAMAGE TO THE VICTIM OF MALARIA

Because of the recurrent loss of red blood cells, the victim becomes increasingly weak. The spleen, which must capture the breakdown products of the ruptured red blood cells, is often overwhelmed by the volume of material entering it and becomes enlarged (splenomegaly) and finally ceases to function. The liver may also become enlarged (hepatomegaly), and its function may be impaired due to congestion of its blood vessels with the products of red blood cell breakdown. If the infection is severe and prolonged enough, the continual loss of red cells leads to the loss of breakdown products in the urine, a serious condition that was once called **black water fever** due to the darkening of the urine. In severe *P. falciparum* infection, 20 to 30 percent of the red blood cells can be infected at any given time, and the blood-forming tissues are not

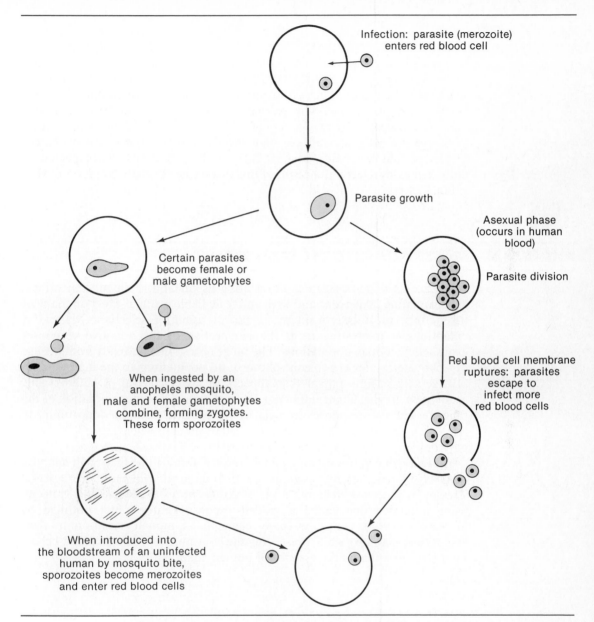

Figure 26-3 The life cycle of Plasmodium *parasites, the organism responsible for malaria in humans and some other primates*

able to replace the losses as rapidly as they occur. Consequently, prolonged malarial infection results in severe anemia, often accompanied by a low white cell count. The liver and kidney both suffer impaired function, and many patients become jaundiced.

COMPLICATIONS

Complications in severe and prolonged malaria may involve the central nervous system (cerebral malaria), as high fevers produce headaches, convulsions, delirium, and coma. Gastrointestinal symptoms resembling those of cholera may also occur. The reduced white cell count is associated with increased susceptibility to a variety of other infections. With the constellation of symptoms and side effects that severe malaria presents, it is hardly surprising that mortality rates as high as 30 percent can be expected in untreated cases. Death as a result of this disease is especially common in very young victims.

MALARIA AS AN AGENT OF NATURAL SELECTION

A disease as widespread and devastating as malaria, with mortality rates approximating 30 percent and with an incalculable residual effect on many of its victims, must be considered a potent agent of selection. Malaria is exceptionally interesting from the perspective of the adaptive responses exhibited by human populations. The range of responses extends from the use of technological devices to control mosquito populations to the maintenance of a genetic polymorphism that appears to favor survival of heterozygous genotypes carrying abnormal hemoglobin alleles. A closer examination of the range of adaptive responses to malaria will provide a unique opportunity to appreciate the levels of adaptation invoked by humans when a specific form of environmental stress is strong and persistent.

A useful concept for organizing this information will be that of an *adaptive buffering system,* whereby human populations deal with an environmental stressor by the most efficient and least costly means available. This concept, using a related one called a graded-response strategy, first outlined by Slobodkin (1968), considers many elements of human variation in their evolutionary context while preserving the continuity of biological and behavioral strategies that is the essence of human adaptability.

ENVIRONMENTAL CONTROL OF MALARIA

Soon after the discovery of the pesticide dichloro-diphenyl-trichloroethane (DDT), the mosquito populations of tropical areas were thought to have been brought under control. The incidence of malaria in parts of India was sharply reduced, and there were many optimistic predictions that malaria would someday be totally eradicated. Subsequent events have led to a far less optimistic prognosis. Realization of the undesirable side effects of heavy DDT use and the appearance of DDT-resistant strains of mosquitoes have combined to reverse the decline in mosquito populations and in malaria incidence. More people are affected today than before the discovery of DDT, but technological means for controlling mosquito populations are still being explored. In some areas, reasonable success has been won through careful monitoring of all potential breeding sites and judicious use of insecticides. If successful, these technological means would constitute the least-disruptive and preferred method of eradicating malaria.

MEDICAL CONTROL OF MALARIA

Unless or until success in controlling mosquito populations is attained, the next line of defense (or buffer) available to human populations exposed to the transmission of malaria by mosquitos is the use of medication that protects against the symptoms of the disease even though infection occurs. Quinine has been a successful prophylactic medication for many years. However, the malaria parasite, being a resourceful pathogen, has produced resistant strains for which quinine is not an effective preventive measure. Travel to some parts of the world today requires the use of quinine and one or more other medications to protect against the possible combination of resistant strains that might be encountered. It is clear that the battle has not yet been won. When malaria exposure is intermittent or only occasional, however, there is no chance to develop an effective immune response and the use of medication is essential.

DIETARY FACTORS AND MALARIA

Populations living in malarial areas have developed a different, but in some ways similar, strategy of preventive medication. Certain foods, notably manioc *(Manihot esculenta),* a tuber that is widely consumed in many tropical areas, contain compounds called cyanates. These cyanide-bearing compounds are potentially highly toxic, as cyanide is one of the more potent poisons known. In manioc root, cyanates are bound to a glycoside (a carbohydrate synthesized by plants) and are not toxic in their bound form. If the root is bruised, however, cyanide is released. Native consumers of manioc prepare it using methods that free most, but not all, of the cyanide into the air. The remaining cyanates are probably absorbed in the digestive tract. The absorbed cyanates have been shown to inhibit the activity of glucose-6-phosphate dehydrogenase (G-6-PD) (Jackson, Chandler, and Jackson, 1979; Katz, 1987). When this important enzyme is inhibited, the red cells become very vulnerable to damage caused by an invading malarial parasite. The red cell under these circumstances will usually be killed, and the parasite will thus be prevented from multiplying.

OTHER DEFENSE MECHANISMS

Although control of mosquito populations and the use of medications and foods that reduce the virulence of malarial infection have yielded unquestionable benefits in reducing the overall impact of malaria on human populations, these buffers are far from total successes. The most vulnerable segment of the human population, the young child residing in areas of endemic malaria exposure, often experiences a first infection without benefit of medication. In addition, first exposure also usually occurs before the immune system has had the opportunity to develop an effective response. It is in these individuals that some form of intrinsic, genetically transmitted defense is of major importance. That such defenses exist is not surprising in view of the frequency, intensity, and persistence of the selection taking place. What is surprising is the number of traits that appears to have evolved in response to the same agent of selection. The biological cost of these responses varies, but there is a cost in each instance, and in the context of a graded response system, each represents a more significant commitment to the resolution of the problem of malaria than the technological and behavioral ones discussed earlier.

GENETIC TRAITS: G-6-PD DEFICIENCY

Several genetically transmitted traits appear to confer resistance to malaria or reduce the severity of the symptoms when infection occurs. One such trait involves a deficiency of the enzyme G-6-PD. This enzyme, which is involved in the metabolism of glucose, is produced in lower-than-normal quantities in individuals inheriting the G-6-PD deficiency allele. (The G-6-PD locus is located on the X chromosome and is thus an example of X-linked inheritance.) People with a G-6-PD deficiency are normal in most respects but are sensitive to antimalarial drugs and to substances contained in *Vicia faba,* the fava bean. When exposed to these substances, the individual with a G-6-PD deficiency will suffer **hemolysis,** a breakdown of the red blood cells, which can range from very mild to life-threatening. However, the disadvantage of this condition appears to be offset by enhanced resistance to malaria. It is believed that *Plasmodium* requires access to the G-6-PD of its host cell in order to reproduce. When the enzyme is deficient, the parasite is incapable of establishing its cycle of reproduction in the red blood cells and the characteristic symptoms of malaria are absent.

Except in the unfortunate instance of the consumption of fava beans or quinine, the price paid for malaria resistance seems to be a modest one. The high frequencies of the G-6-PD-deficient allele in a number of Mediterranean populations have been interpreted by most geneticists as evidence of natural selection favoring it. Frequencies as high as 60 percent in some Middle Eastern

Jewish populations and 35 percent in Sardinian villages would argue for a relatively strong selective pressure on this allele (Bodmer and Cavalli-Sforza, 1976).

THALASSEMIA

A second genetically transmitted trait that appears to confer resistance to malaria is that for thalassemia. Thalassemia is a defect in the synthesis of one of the pairs of chains that make up hemoglobin. Normal hemoglobin (hemoglobin A) is a protein consisting of two α chains and two β chains. These two pairs of chains interact in a way that places their **heme groups** (the iron-bearing component of the molecule) either closer together or farther apart. The repositioning of the heme groups permits the oxygen-attracting iron atom to attach to an oxygen molecule or to release it. This mechanism for attracting and releasing oxygen is the underlying basis for oxygen transport. Red blood cells passing through the lungs pick up oxygen and then release it in the oxygen-poor environment of the tissues. Hemoglobin also attracts carbon dioxide that is released from the tissues and then releases it on return to the lungs. Since the oxidation of glucose is the major source of energy for metabolism, any interruption of the supply of oxygen or the removal of carbon dioxide can be life-threatening. Therefore, a defect in the formation of hemoglobin is potentially lethal.

The most common form of thalassemia involves a defect in the production of β chains. This form is called β thalassemia. If it is inherited from both parents, the homozygote suffers a serious form of anemia that is almost certain to lead to an early death. If the trait is inherited from only one parent, however, the heterozygote offspring has no serious disability.

There is also a form of thalassemia in which the defect affects the synthesis of the α chains. This is called α thalassemia and is also virtually always fatal to those who inherit it from both parents, but has no serious effects in heterozygotes. It is therefore appropriate to consider both the α- and β-thalassemia alleles to be recessive lethals. In both forms, the defect is thought to be in the production of messenger RNA produced by the respective genes. Although homozygotes die early whether the defect is in α- or β-chain synthesis, α-thalassemia homozygotes die much earlier. This is thought to be because the α chain is part of all of the variants of normal hemoglobin from fetal life onward but there are several alternatives that can substitute for the β chain. The α chain is made up of 141 amino acids, while the β chain is made up of 146. The α chain pairs with the β chain and the other forms, such as δ and γ chains, with little loss of effectiveness. When the synthesis of α chains is defective, however, the hemoglobin produced is made up of either four β chains, called hemoglobin H (β_4), or four γ chains, called hemoglobin Barts (γ_4). Individuals producing these types of hemoglobin are severely anemic.

During gestation, the production of hemoglobin goes through several distinct phases. The first hemoglobin chains produced are called *embryonic* and are given the designation ϵ (epsilon). The production of ϵ chains then ceases, and the production of γ chains begins. Finally, production of γ^* chains is phased out and β-chain production, which will continue through adulthood, begins to predominate. At around the sixth month of gestation, a small amount of the δ chain is produced. This minor fraction of the total hemoglobin, which will pair with α chains to produce hemoglobin A_2, will be present throughout adulthood but the concentration will remain low.

By about the age of two months, almost all of the hemoglobin being produced in the normal individual is hemoglobin A, which has the molecular structure $\alpha_2^A\beta_2^A$. The remainder (about 5 percent) is hemoglobin A_2, with the molecular structure $\alpha_2^A\delta_2^A$. When a defect in one of the hemoglobin chains is inherited, there can be a variety of phenotypic expressions that will be identifiable as forms of thalassemia. In some cases, there will be higher-than-normal percentages of fetal hemoglobin ($\alpha_2^A\gamma_2^F$). In other cases, there will be a higher-than-normal percentage of fetal hemoglobin and hemoglobin A_2 ($\alpha_2^A\delta_2^A$).

As more has been learned about the variations in hemoglobin content subsumed under the classification "thalassemia," it has become apparent that the genetic basis for the condition is more subtle and complex than had earlier been thought. The common element of all of the variations is the low proportion of normal hemoglobin A. It is thought either that the scarcity of normal hemoglobin retards the reproduction of the malarial parasite or that the continued production of fetal hemoglobin is associated with greater fragility of the red blood cell, predisposing to early death when invaded by a parasite. The evidence that thalassemia confers resistance to malaria is circumstantial. The distribution of thalassemia and endemic malaria as seen in Figure 26-4 appears to support the assumption that thalassemia enhances survival. More evidence bearing on the mechanisms by which survival is enhanced is needed to complete the picture.

ABNORMAL HEMOGLOBINS

Another genetically transmitted hemoglobin abnormality that is believed to confer resistance to malaria involves amino acid substitutions in the β chain. While there are a number of such substitutions, two of them are believed to enhance resistance to malaria. One of them, hemoglobin S, causes a peculiar form of anemia when inherited from both parents. This anemia is called **sickle-cell anemia** because of distortion of the red blood cells arising from crystallization of the hemoglobin under certain circumstances (see Figures 26-5 and 26-6).

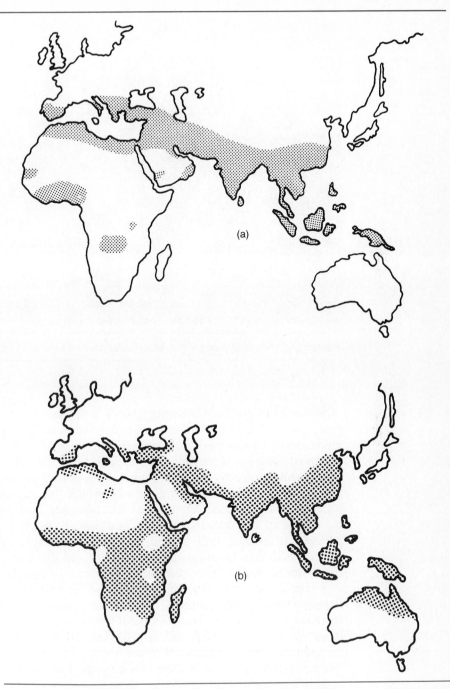

Figure 26-4 Distribution of (A) Mediterranean thalassemia and (B) falciparum malaria

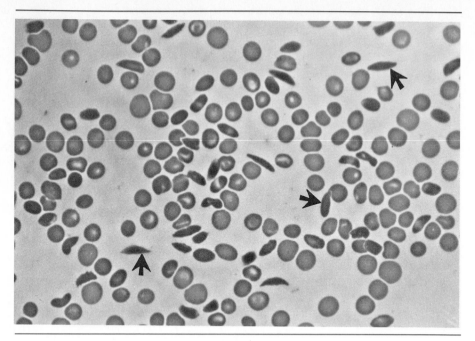

Figure 26-5 Normal human red blood cells and sickled red cells (arrows)

While homozygotes for hemoglobin S suffer severe anemia, heterozygotes experience sickling of their red cells only when the oxygen supply is inadequate. Most of the time their oxygen supply is adequate and their oxygen transport function is entirely normal. The heterozygotes do, however, differ from normal homozygotes for hemoglobin A in that they possess resistance to falciparum malaria. The mechanism by which this resistance is obtained is uncertain. It has been argued that the presence of hemoglobin S on the membrane of red cells makes them resistant to penetration by the malarial parasite. It has also been argued that the heterozygote's red blood cells are more sensitive to invasions by the parasite and die prematurely, preventing successful reproduction by the parasite (Friedman and Trager, 1981).

A similar advantage has been postulated for another hemoglobin variant, hemoglobin C. Hemoglobin C is also the product of an amino acid substitution in the β chain. The position of the substitution (the sixth amino acid) is the same in both HbS and HbC. While HbA has glutamic acid at that position, HbS has valine and HbC has lysine. Only one of the 146 amino acids in the β chain is changed in these two variants. The significant alteration of the protein's properties exhibited by these two hemoglobins can therefore be attributed to the structural differences produced by this substitution. The homozygote for hemoglobin C has a much milder form of anemia than the

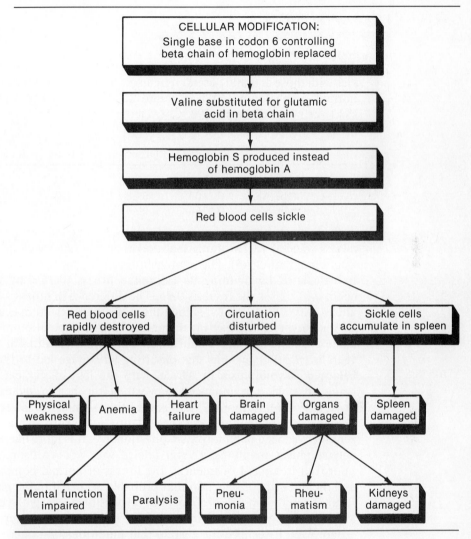

Figure 26-6 A simplified sequence of events in sickle-cell anemia

homozygote for hemoglobin S, and both homozygotes and heterozygotes appear to have malaria resistance.

There has been considerable interest in the superior fitness of the AS heterozygotes. It appears that the fitness of the heterozygote is sufficiently improved to offset the loss of the homozygote to sickle-cell anemia. In order to maintain the gene for hemoglobin S in the population at a level higher than that which could be maintained by recurrent mutation, the heterozygotes must have fitness superior to that of the normal homozygote. In order to test the hypothesis of fitness, the concept of Hardy-Weinberg equilibrium as discussed in chapter 7 can be usefully employed.

CALCULATION OF FITNESS

Using the observations of Allison, who collected data on gene frequencies in African populations, it is possible to compare the expected genotype frequencies with those actually observed (Allison, 1964). The frequency of the gene for normal hemoglobin (A) was found to be 0.808. The frequency for the sickle-cell gene (S) was 0.192. Converting to Hardy-Weinberg notation, $A=p$, $S=q$, and $p+q = 1$.

	Expected	Observed	Fitness	Relative Fitness
Genotype AA	0.6529	0.616	0.943	0.76
Genotype AS	0.3103	0.384	1.238	1.00
Genotype SS	0.0368	0	0	0.00

Since the most fit genotype can be seen to be AS, we assign it a relative fitness value of 1.0 (meaning that the other genotypes will have a fitness some fraction of that of AS). The relative fitness value for the AA genotype can then be calculated by dividing its estimated fitness (0.943) by that of the A/S genotype (1.238); the result is 0.76. The difference in fitness values for the two alleles, $1.0 - 0.76 = 0.24$, is then the measure of selection against the normal A/A genotype. The offsetting advantage for the population maintaining the S allele is substantial but would disappear if malaria did not exist. For some years it was thought that this offsetting advantage led to the existence of a **balanced polymorphism** in Africa, with the loss of sickle-cell homozygotes being offset by the enhanced survival of the heterozygotes. However, the existence of hemoglobin C (and some other variants in lower frequencies) in these populations complicates the situation sufficiently to make assertions of a genuine balanced polymorphism questionable. It is more likely that a **transient polymorphism** involving several alleles was what Allison observed. With improved treatment of malaria, the fitness of normal homozygotes is rising and the intensity of selection that probably occurred in the past is unlikely to recur. Therefore, it will probably not be possible to say with certainty whether a balanced polymorphism involving the sickle-cell gene ever existed.

However, it seems quite certain that mutations that altered the β chain of the hemoglobin molecule conferred some advantage on their possessors in the presence of malaria. Although a great deal remains to be learned about the mechanisms involved in the disease resistance associated with the abnormal hemoglobins as well as with the various forms of thalassemia, the distribution of these traits match the distribution of malaria well enough to justify the conclusion that natural selection has occurred (Figure 26-7).

THE GRADED RESPONSE TO MALARIA

From the perspective of the adaptive buffer system outlined earlier, these genetic responses to the persistent threat to survival represented by malaria

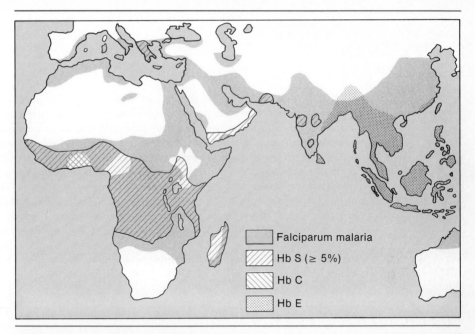

Figure 26-7 Distribution of falciparum malaria and abnormal hemoglobin

might be regarded as the last line of defense. Their benefits must be gained through payment of the cost exacted by natural selection in terms of reduced reproductive success on the part of a sizeable portion of the population. As long as the sickle-cell allele persists in high frequencies in the population, a portion of every generation will be born with sickle-cell anemia and will die young. The cost is similar but probably more severe than that associated with resistance through the maintenance of thalassemia. The cost of G-6-PD deficiency is probably lower than that associated with the hemoglobin defects, and that of using cyanate-containing foods such as manioc are lower yet. Prevention of the disease by prophylaxis, such as through the use of chloroquine and sulfa drugs, has an even lower cost and can make all of the other defenses unnecessary. And of course, the eradication of the parasite-bearing mosquitoes would be the least intrusive strategy of all.

As the least intrusive and least costly defenses fail, the more costly ones must be invoked, and the graded-response system progresses toward the last resort: the loss of genes. This defense may be permanent and has the potential to produce evolutionary change. For species other than primates that pursue a strategy of rapid reproduction and short life spans, the so-called r-strategists, the price of natural selection is offset by the advantages of access to new resources as new niches are filled by newly evolved genotypes. This has not been the strategy of our species, however, and elaborate devices for the preservation of the individual are more in keeping with the human tendency to survive through adaptability. Further evidence of that tendency will be encountered in the discussion of high-altitude adaptations.

When the immune system is capable of responding effectively to infection, lifetime resistance to that particular disease frequently results. However, some diseases have developed mechanisms that allow them to circumvent the immune response. Before the development of technological means of preventing disease, humans were effectively defenseless when a disease evolved such mechanisms. The continued exposure of large human populations to one such disease, malaria, has resulted in a variety of biological responses that appear to be the result of genetic adaptations. They share the characteristic of paying a price, often in the form of loss of some percentage of the offspring of each generation, to maintain a defense where the immune system alone has been inadequate. In recent times, human populations have added technological defenses to supplement, and sometimes supplant, those that were evoked biologically.

BIBLIOGRAPHY

ALLISON, A. C. 1964. Protection afforded by the sickle-cell trait against subtertian malarial infection. *British Medical Journal* 1: 290–94.

ARMELAGOS, G., and J. R. DEWEY. 1970. Evolutionary response to human infectious disease. *Bioscience* 157: 638–44.

BLACK, F. L. 1975. Infectious disease in primitive societies. *Science* 187: 515–18.

BODMER, W. F., and L. L. CAVALLI-SFORZA. 1976. *Genetics, Evolution, and Man,* pp. 321–23. San Francisco: W. H. Freeman.

DONELSON, J. E., and M. J. TURNER. 1985. How the trypanosome changes its coat. *Scientific American* 252/2: 44–51.

FRIEDMAN, M. J., and W. TRAGER. 1981. The biochemistry of resistance to malaria. *Scientific American* 244/3: 154–64.

JACKSON, L. C., J. P. CHANDLER, and R. T. JACKSON. 1986. Inhibition and adaptation of red cell glucose-6-phosphate dehydrogenase (G-6-PD) in vivo to chronic sublethal cyanide in an animal model. *Human Biology* 58/1: 67–77.

KAPLAN, M. M., and R. G. WEBSTER. 1977. The epidemiology of influenza. *Scientific American* 237/6: 88–106.

KATZ, S. H. 1987. Food and biocultural evolution: A model for the investigation of modern nutritional problems. In *Nutritional Anthropology,* F. E. Johnston, ed. New York: Alan R. Liss.

LANGER, W. L. 1964. The Black Death. *Scientific American* 210: 214–21.

LIVINGSTONE, F. B. 1958. Anthropological implications of sickle-cell gene distribution in West Africa. *American Anthropologist* 60: 533–62.

SLOBODKIN, L. B. 1968. Toward a predictive theory of evolution. In *Population Biology and Evolution,* R. C. Lewontin, ed. Syracuse: Syracuse University Press.

High-Altitude Adaptation: An Example of Human Response to Severe and Persistent Stress

Human adaptability has produced a variety of cultural, behavioral, and physiological responses to environmental stressors. Much of the environment currently inhabited by most human populations has been sufficiently modified to reduce most aspects of climatic stress to negligible levels. The cultural buffers that have permitted human populations to penetrate virtually all of the world's habitats have done so by using technology to compensate for the deficiencies of the habitat. If the climate is cold, technological devices for supplying and retaining heat are employed. If the climate is hot, methods of reducing the impact of solar radiation and of dissipating heat have been developed. One stressor that is extremely difficult to modify on a population-wide basis is the lack of sufficient oxygen. Because humans have high metabolic requirements, it is essential to maintain a sufficient supply of oxygen to the tissues at all times. This is particularly important in the case of the brain, which cannot tolerate oxygen starvation for more than a few minutes. Because oxygen starvation is a major threat to survival, it is not surprising that the high-altitude environment is one of the most challenging on earth. Our admiration for the handful of mountaineers who challenge Mt. Everest every few years is enhanced by a full appreciation of the magnitude of the challenge they experience at 8,900 meters above sea level. Perhaps just as impressive is the fact that whole populations live above 3,000 meters, and some above 4,500 meters. Their adaptations are more physiological than cultural and give us some idea of the limits of human adaptability.

POPULATIONS AT HIGH ALTITUDES

It is generally agreed that altitudes in excess of 3,200 meters (10,000 feet) create some degree of stress for the non-native. Nevertheless, over 20 million people live at altitudes equalling or surpassing 4,000 meters (Baker, 1969). The largest concentrations of human populations living at high altitude are in the Andes of South America and in the Himalayas of Asia. It is quite certain that some of these populations have several millennia of history in these high-altitude environments (Pawson and Jest, 1978). After 100 or more generations of high-altitude exposure, there has been ample opportunity for gene frequencies to reflect the effects of persistent environmental stress. Despite the opportunity these populations have had for genetic adaptations, there is surprisingly little evidence of major genetic differences between high-altitude populations and those dwelling close to sea level. More sophisticated methods may eventually lead to the identification of differences thus far undetected, but the effectiveness of the nongenetic adaptations occurring in these populations makes it unlikely that such differences will be of major significance.

A MULTISTRESS HABITAT

The mountainous habitat is a multistress environment (Thomas and Winterhalder, 1976). At the higher elevations, low temperatures and high

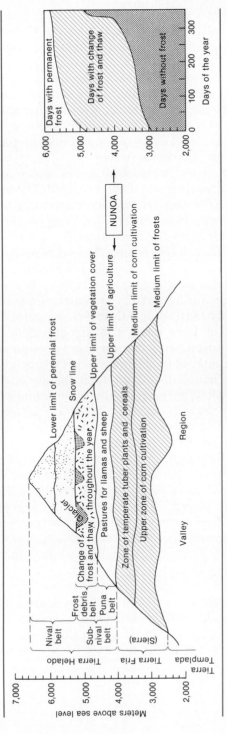

Figure 27-1 The zones of agriculture and frost lines in the Andes of Southern Peru

winds are a frequent problem. Solar radiation is intense and the terrain is rough. Poor soils and the general absence of flat surfaces for cultivation make food production difficult. Each of these conditions could make the high-altitude environment challenging. In their aggregate, and combined with the low barometric pressures that characterize high elevations, they create a formidable challenge to the human capacity to adapt. Because low barometric pressure is the element of the multistress environment that is unique to high altitudes, we will focus on the levels of response to that element in order to gain a fuller understanding of the limits of human adaptability to a major, inescapable, and persistent stress.

Because oxidative metabolism is our major source of energy, supply of oxygen to the tissues is essential for survival. The pulmonary and cardiovascular systems are, at sea-level barometric pressures, highly effective at extracting oxygen from the atmosphere and delivering it to all parts of the body. Certain tissues, among them the neurons of the central nervous system, are very intolerant of oxygen deprivation. Serious brain damage can be anticipated if respiration is suspended for as little as 6 minutes. The risk to survival created by even a brief interruption of breathing is a strong indication that the cardiovascular and respiratory systems must perform reliably at all times. Thus it would be surprising if there were not substantial capacity for adjusting the function of these systems to accommodate to reduced availability of oxygen. The adjustments that are made provide instructive examples of the limits of tolerance of human physiological function.

Oxygen is harder to extract from the air at high altitudes because the molecules of all of the gases making up the atmosphere move farther apart as distance from sea level increases. The air is therefore "less dense" even though the mixture of gases present contains the same proportions as at sea level. Table 27-1 shows the decrease in barometric pressures at levels above sea level. The major component of our atmosphere is nitrogen, which makes up 78 percent of its total volume. Oxygen is second most abundant, making up 20.95 percent of the volume. Small amounts of carbon dioxide (0.03 percent), trace elements (0.01 percent), and water vapor are also present. The percentages of nitrogen, oxygen, carbon dioxide, and trace elements do not change as barometric pressure decreases. Therefore, the amount of oxygen present in each liter of air inhaled will decline as altitude increases. This decline is also shown in Table 27-1.

As a result of these decreases in partial pressure of oxygen, each liter of air inhaled will yield fewer molecules of oxygen at each higher altitude. Because of the increasing difficulty in obtaining the amount of oxygen needed to sustain activity, the stress experienced at high altitudes may begin to be felt at levels as low as 2,000 meters if it is necessary to exercise upon arrival.

Table 27-1 Barometric Pressure and Partial Pressure of Oxygen at Selected Altitudes

Altitude Feet	Meters	Total Pressure	Partial Pressure of Oxygen
0	0	760 mm	159 mm
5,000	1,524	632 mm	132 mm
10,000	3,048	523 mm	110 mm
12,000	3,658	483 mm	101 mm
15,000	4,575	429 mm	90 mm
18,000	5,486	379 mm	79 mm
20,000	6,069	349 mm	73 mm
29,000	8,839	236 mm	49 mm

OXYGEN GRADIENT BETWEEN TISSUES

The dimensions of the problem can be better appreciated when the gradient of oxygen concentrations from inhaled air down to the tissues is taken into account. Table 27-2 shows the decline in oxygen pressure at several points in the delivery system. When the declines in partial pressure of oxygen shown in Table 27-1 are considered, it can readily be seen that the tissues are severely deprived of essential oxygen unless the volume of oxygen delivered to the arterial blood is maintained at normal levels by increasing the volume of gas delivered to the alveoli. The alveoli are the ultimate branches of the system, which starts with the **trachea,** giving rise to the **bronchi,** the **alveolar duct,** and, finally, the alveoli. The system is shown in Figure 27-2.

INSPIRATION AND EXPIRATION

The process of breathing involves **inspiration** (inhaling) and **expiration** (exhaling). The method by which air is brought into the lungs in humans is quite

Table 27-2 Declines in Gaseous Pressure of Inhaled Air to Venous Blood

	Inhaled Air	Trachea	Alveoli	Arterial Blood	Venous
pO_2	159.1	149.2	104.0	100.0	40.0
pCO_2	0.3	0.3	40.0	40.0	46.0
pH_2O	0.0	47.0	47.0	47.0	47.0
pN_2	600.6	563.5	569.0	573.0	573.0
Total	760.0	760.0	760.0	760.0	706.0

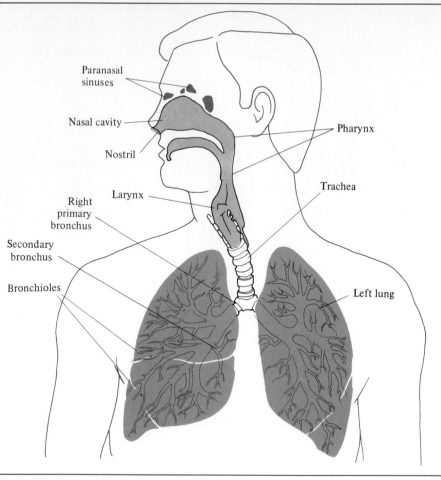

Paranasal
sinuses

Nasal cavity

Nostril

Right
primary
bronchus

Secondary
bronchus

Bronchioles

Larynx

Pharynx

Trachea

Left lung

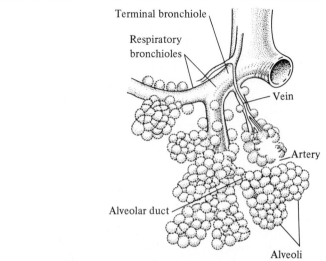

Terminal bronchiole

Respiratory
bronchioles

Vein

Artery

Alveolar duct

Alveoli

Figure 27-2 The pharynx, trachea lungs, and the alveoli

different than that seen in quadrupeds, although certain aspects of it are similar. Because we are erect bipeds, the rib cage is located in front of, and not below, the spinal column. Because of the angle of attachment of the ribs to the spine and the elliptical shape of the chest in cross-section, it is possible to expand the volume of the chest cavity by pulling the entire rib cage upward. This is the act of **forced inspiration.** During and after strenuous exercise, forced inspiration is used to bring a larger volume of air into the lungs and thus more oxygen into the alveoli. Figure 27-3 illustrates the effect of this reorientation of the rib cage.

Inspiration also involves contraction of the muscles of the **diaphragm,** which separates the **thoracic cavity** (which contains the heart and lungs) from the abdominal cavity (which contains the liver, stomach, intestines, and other organs). When the muscles of the diaphragm contract, the organs beneath it

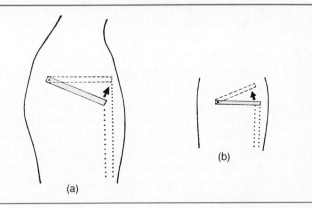

Figure 27-3 The mechanics of forced inspiration. In the adult (a), raising the ribcage increases the distance between the ends of the ribs, consequently the diameter of the entire rib cage. In a baby (b) this effect does not yet occur.

are pushed farther down into the abdominal cavity. The result is an increase in the size of the thoracic cavity, which results in lowered air pressure within the lungs. The combined effect of contracting the diaphragm and raising the rib cage expands the thoracic cavity substantially and creates a partial vacuum within the lungs. Air rushes into the lungs through the air passages to equalize the pressure. Thus, the amount of air that can be inhaled in a given breath (the **tidal volume**) is determined by the amount of space that can be made available to permit the lungs to expand.

Expiration is largely a passive process. The rib cage is allowed to fall back to its resting position and the relaxed diaphragm permits the organs beneath it to push it farther up into the thorax. By decreasing the size of the thoracic space and lungs, the air pressure inside the lungs is increased and some of it is forced out through the air passages. It is not possible to expire all of the air in the lungs. A residual amount of air, called **dead space,** is always retained. In certain illnesses, notably emphysema, the proportion of dead space to tidal volume becomes quite large, and it is impossible to exchange air effectively.

OXYGENATION OF THE BLOOD

When the inspired air enters the alveoli, oxygen diffuses across the alveolar membranes to the capillaries that surround them. At the same time, carbon dioxide diffuses from the blood in the capillaries across the alveolar membranes into the alveoli to be expelled at the next expiration. Very little oxygen is dissolved in the blood in the capillaries. Almost all of it is immediately attracted to the hemoglobin on the red blood cells. In the oxygen-rich environment of the alveolar capillary bed, the hemoglobin chains open up to expose their points of attachment for oxygen. If the normal number of red cells is circulating in the blood (4.7 to 5.0 million per milliliter of blood), all of the oxygen entering the capillaries will be picked up and will soon become available to the tissues. The oxygenated blood returns to the heart through the **pulmonary vein** and is collected in the **left atrium.** When the left atrium is filled with oxygen-rich blood, the **mitral valve** opens, permitting its contents to flow into the **left ventricle.** The ventricle is a muscular pump that will drive the blood out through the **aorta** and into the systemic circulation. Some will be directed to the head and upper portions of the body, and the rest will supply the remainder of the body (Figure 27-4).

In the oxygen-poor environment of the tissues, blood again enters the capillaries, where oxygen is released by **hemoglobin** which has reoriented its **heme groups** in response to the changed gaseous pressure. After releasing its oxygen, the cell may pick up molecules of carbon dioxide for the return trip to the lungs. From the capillaries of the tissues, the red blood cells and their carbon dioxide enter the **venules** and then the **veins** and finally return to the

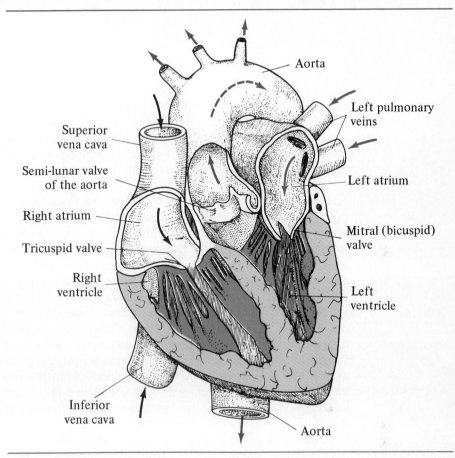

Figure 27-4 Frontal section of the human heart. Arrows indicate direction of blood flow.

heart through large veins called the **superior** and **inferior vena cava.** The oxygen-poor, carbon dioxide-rich blood then enters the **right atrium.** When the right atrium has filled, its contents are emptied into the **right ventricle,** from which it is pumped through the pulmonary arteries to the lungs, where it will pass once again through the alveolar capillary bed to give up its carbon dioxide and pick up more oxygen.

Many factors influence the rate at which oxygen is picked up and released by the hemoglobin of the red blood cells. The acidity or alkalinity of the blood will alter the affinity of hemoglobin for oxygen. Thus under more acidic conditions, oxygen will be more quickly released to the tissues than at normal pH. Temperature variations will also affect the oxygen transport system in a variety of ways.

SHORT-TERM ADJUSTMENT TO HIGH ALTITUDE

Exposure to a high-altitude environment for the first time sets off a series of reactions that represent an attempt to reestablish equilibrium levels of oxygen and carbon dioxide in the blood. If, for example, a sea-level resident travels to a mountain resort at an altitude of 4,000 meters (13,000 feet), the a mount of oxygen available in each liter of air inhaled will be nearly 39 percent less than it had been back home. The lower concentration of oxygen in the alveoli will, as can be seen in Table 27-2, lead to even lower oxygen concentration in the arterial blood and thus to less oxygen available for energy metabolism.

The lowered availability of oxygen at the tissue level will quite quickly produce a sensation of breathlessness, which stimulates an altered breathing pattern. The first response is to breathe more deeply, filling the lungs more completely with the thinner air. At sea level, the average person inhales about 14.5 times a minute. Each breath draws about 500 milliliters **(tidal volume)** of air into the lungs. Therefore, about 7.25 liters of air is exchanged each minute. This is called the **minute volume.** At 4,000 meters, tidal volume will increase to about 700 milliliters. Respiratory rate increases slightly to 15 breaths per minute. As a result, the minute volume rises to about 10.5 liters per minute, thereby effecting a 45 percent increase in the amount of air entering the alveoli. This increase effectively compensates for the 39 percent decrease in oxygen available to enter the capillary blood from the alveoli. If exercise is undertaken, the adjustment will be much more difficult, and both respiratory rate and tidal volume will increase in an attempt to compensate for the oxygen deficit. These changes in respiratory pattern are, for the most part, involuntary, being triggered by stimuli received in **chemoreceptors** (sensing devices that monitor changes in the chemical properties of the blood) located at several points in the circulatory system (Frisancho, 1979).

HYPERVENTILATION AND BLOOD CHEMISTRY

Although the increase in minute volume can compensate for the reduced amount of oxygen present in the air, prolonged **hyperventilation** will lead to a change in blood chemistry associated with the loss of more carbon dioxide than normal. The loss of carbon dioxide leads to a lowered capacity to maintain the normal blood pH of 7.2, allowing the blood to become more alkaline, with a pH of 7.4 or above. Since the maintenance of normal pH is necessary for many important biochemical reactions, including the release of oxygen from red blood cells to the tissues, this is tolerable for only a short time, and eventually a correction must be made.

HEART RATE

The increase in minute volume of respiration is accompanied by an increase in resting heart rate from an average of 70 beats per minute at sea level to about 100 beats at high altitude. However, the heart rate achieved during maximal exercise at high altitude is lower than at sea level, with the result that less blood can be delivered to the tissues in the high-altitude environment.

RED BLOOD CELL INCREASE

One of the most impressive aspects of short-term high-altitude adaptations is the increased release of red blood cells into the circulation. Under normal circumstances, red blood cells live an average of 120 days. They are then destroyed, usually in the spleen, and their structural components, including iron, are recycled. Cells are released and destroyed in numbers that balance each other so that a sea-level red blood cell count of 4.7 to 5 million per milliliter is maintained.

Shortly after arrival at high altitude, however, production of red cells starts to exceed destruction, thereby creating a net increase in the number of circulating red cells. The number may climb as high as 6.5 million per milliliter at 4,000 meters and 7 million at 5,000 meters. The increase in red blood cell number is directly associated with an increase in the amount of hemoglobin available to bring oxygen to the tissues and organs and remove carbon dioxide. The increase in hemoglobin concentration peaks between 1 and 2 weeks after arrival but may continue for up to 6 months and then stabilize. The increase in red cell volume, called **polycythemia,** may be as much as 25 percent above normal. Since the total volume of blood increases only slightly, the increase in cellular components is at the expense of the liquid component **(plasma)** of the blood. Thicker blood has higher viscosity and therefore the heart must work harder to pump it through the circulatory system.

OTHER ASPECTS OF HYPOXIC STRESS

The experience of high-altitude adaptation has many unpleasant aspects. Light sensitivity and visual acuity are usually impaired. Memory and learning are also adversely affected, as is coordination of neuromuscular activities. The sense of taste is altered and the appetite declines. Fatty foods become especially unappealing. As a result of the loss of interest in food as well as some fluid loss, there is generally a loss of body weight. It is difficult to sleep, and a number of changes in the endocrine system take place. While the adrenal cortex becomes more active in producing stress hormones, the thyroid and testes both experience decreased activity. While virtually everyone experiences some or all of these symptoms at high altitude, it appears that men are more affected than women (although women often experience menstrual problems); older people are more affected than young people; and physically fit people seem to fare better than the average.

ACCLIMATIZATION

If the stay at high altitude is extended, **acclimatization** will usually occur. The increased number of red blood cells improves the delivery of oxygen to the tissues, and blood alkalinity levels begin to return to normal. If the individual is in reasonably good health, normal performance of most tasks is possible. But if the altitude is above 4,500 meters, it is unlikely that a non-native will achieve functional levels approximating those of the native-born. The physiological adjustments that are made ensure delivery of oxygen to the tissues and removal of waste products. Prolonged activity at high altitude remains fatiguing, but work capacity may eventually improve to a point exceeding sea-level performance. Many native Andeans believe that the chewing of coca leaves reduces the fatigue associated with high-altitude exercise. A preference for carbohydrates will probably persist since the use of carbohydrates is more efficient than that of proteins and especially fats. If blood pressure had risen early in the stay at high altitude, it will probably return to normal.

PULMONARY EDEMA

It is unfortunate that sea-level dwellers who manage an effective acclimatization to high altitude are at risk for pulmonary edema if they return to sea level for a week or two and then go back to the high-altitude environment. It is thought that a return to the normal sea-level proportion of fluid (plasma) in the blood when at sea level leads to the leakage of fluid into the lungs upon return to high altitude. This potentially dangerous condition is not experienced by everyone undergoing the sequence of moves to and from low altitude, and those who stay at high altitude seem to have no serious difficulty maintaining their acclimatized state.

DEVELOPMENTAL ACCLIMATIZATION

Low-altitude natives who acclimatize to the high-altitude environment as adults do not achieve the level of performance that characterizes the high-altitude native. Having been born at high altitude, and having experienced the challenges of hypoxia throughout growth and development, high-altitude natives exhibit more deep-seated physiological and anatomical adjustments to the demands of their environment. Because these adjustments are largely irreversible, they have been called **developmental acclimatization.** A high-altitude native who moved to sea level would retain most of the characteristics that differentiate the native from the acclimatized non-native. Since high-altitude populations have had a long history of living in their challenging environment, it is not possible to rule out the existence of some genetic differences from their low-altitude neighbors (Cruz-Coke, 1978).

CHARACTERISTICS OF HIGH-ALTITUDE NATIVES

The traits that most clearly distinguish high-altitude natives from all others are associated with the oxygen-delivery system. They are both physiological and anatomical. A brief description of the traits that are generally seen in high-altitude natives reveals much about the nature of the stresses that affected their growth and development. It also reveals much about the degree to which the environment can shape the growing organism.

THE ALTITUDE THORAX

The most striking anatomical feature of the high-altitude native is the **altitude thorax.** It gives the appearance of a barrel-shaped chest, which, when combined with relatively short stature, is unique among human populations. The barrel chest is the product of an expanded rib cage. The expansion is in all directions, greatly expanding the lung capacity. In many respects the altitude thorax resembles an anatomical fixation of the configuration assumed by the chest during forced inspiration. It is expanded in the anterior-posterior dimension as well as at the lower end of the rib cage, and is thus more circular in cross-section than the low-altitude thorax. It also exhibits a longer breast-bone (sternum). These externally visible traits are closely related to internal ones that are of major functional significance: The lungs are large and are endowed with an extremely large capillary bed, and the diaphragm is powerful and of large diameter.

The combination of large lungs and a large, powerful diaphragm permits large volumes of air to be exchanged through a large tidal volume. Ascertainments of **forced expiratory volume** (the amount of air that can be expelled from the lungs in a single breath) indicate that the high-altitude native has an extraordinary capacity for air exchange. The volume of air that the lungs can hold is called the **vital capacity** and is generally considered a reliable indicator of physical fitness. Judged on that basis, high-altitude natives are virtually all extremely fit.

THE HEART AND BLOOD VESSELS

Associated with the increased work load created by the greatly enlarged capillary bed of the lungs and the more viscous blood of the high-altitude dweller are anatomical changes in the heart and major blood vessels. During the normal course of growth and development at sea level, the left ventricle grows more rapidly than the right. Because the function of the left ventricle involves propelling blood through the entire body, the demands made on it are far greater than those made on the right ventricle, which supplies only the lungs. By the time a sea-level dweller reaches adulthood, the left ventricle is substantially larger than the right.

RIGHT VENTRICULAR HYPERTROPHY

Since the ventricles are essentially specialized muscles, each has the capacity to enlarge through hypertrophy (increase in cell size) as its function requires. The high-altitude dweller, experiencing a greatly increased workload on the right ventricle, responds by hypertrophy of the right ventricle. This enlargement of the right ventricle is usually accompanied by increased muscularization of the large blood vessels leaving the heart, making the entire system a more sturdy one. These anatomical changes become a permanent feature of high-altitude anatomy and are susceptible to very little alteration if the high-altitude dweller moves to a lower altitude. **Right ventricular hypertrophy** must be considered another aspect of the developmental acclimatization to high altitude. It can be compared to the enlargement of the heart experienced by some endurance athletes, except that in such cases the enlargement favors the left ventricle.

POLYCYTHEMIA AND OXYGEN AVAILABILITY

High-altitude Andean natives maintain physiological characteristics that are gradually established in newcomers. These include large numbers of red blood cells and the associated increase in total hemoglobin to transport oxygen and carbon dioxide. The pH of the high-altitude native's blood is more acidic than that of the normal sea-level dweller. The lower pH is associated with easier release of oxygen from the red blood cells, even though the saturation level (percentage of red blood cells carrying oxygen) is low. This is generally referred to as a shift in the oxygen dissociation curve. Figure 27-5 shows the curves representing the percent saturation of red blood cells at various partial pressures of oxygen. It can be seen that at pH 7.2, the maximum percent saturation of the red blood cells is 5 percent lower than at pH 7.4, and 8 percent to 10 percent lower than at pH 7.6. The physiological significance of

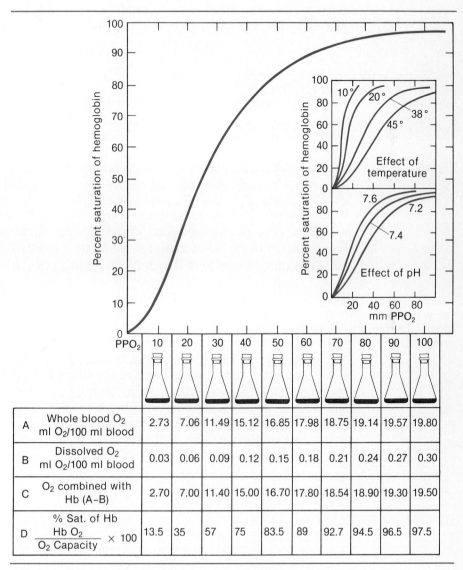

		PPO₂ 10	20	30	40	50	60	70	80	90	100
A	Whole blood O₂ ml O₂/100 ml blood	2.73	7.06	11.49	15.12	16.85	17.98	18.75	19.14	19.57	19.80
B	Dissolved O₂ ml O₂/100 ml blood	0.03	0.06	0.09	0.12	0.15	0.18	0.21	0.24	0.27	0.30
C	O₂ combined with Hb (A–B)	2.70	7.00	11.40	15.00	16.70	17.80	18.54	18.90	19.30	19.50
D	% Sat. of Hb $\dfrac{Hb\ O_2}{O_2\ Capacity} \times 100$	13.5	35	57	75	83.5	89	92.7	94.5	96.5	97.5

Figure 27-5 Shifts in the oxygen dissociation curve as affected by temperature and pH

these curves is simply that the oxygen attached to the red blood cells is more available to the tissues in a more acidic environment. Since Andean high-altitude dwellers tend to maintain a more acidic environment, they can unload oxygen from their red blood cells and supply their tissues more effectively than lowlanders when oxygen partial pressures are low (Buskirk, 1978). This ability, combined with the greater cardiac output, increased pulmonary circulation, and greater number of red blood cells, provides the high-altitude native with maximum capacity to extract oxygen from the thin air, diffuse it into the blood, and transport it to the tissues.

POPULATION DIFFERENCES

It is possible that the high-altitude natives of the New World and the Old World have developed somewhat different adaptations to hypoxic stress. At least some investigators report that the Sherpa of the Himalayas have lower red blood cell counts than those reported for the Quechua of the Andes. If this is true, it is possible that superior efficiency in oxygen utilization at the cell level has evolved in the Himalayan population (Lahiri et al., 1969). The altitude thorax is present in both populations, but the degree of right ventricular hypertrophy seen in the Quechua is not found in the Sherpa. The lower viscosity of the blood of the Sherpa in the absence of the high red blood cell count (polycythemia) of the Quechua could account for this difference.

MIGRATIONS

The intriguing possibility of a genetically determined difference between these widely separated high-altitude populations guarantees continued interest in their physiology and anatomy. As a result of recent migrations of some high-altitude populations to lower altitudes, the next generation will grow up without the stress of hypoxia. The degree to which their phenotypes differ from those of their parents will provide a measure of the environmental impact on the growth process.

BIRTH WEIGHTS

What evidence is now available to assess the environmental component of the high-altitude phenotype? Comparisons of the growth rate of high-altitude and low-altitude children have been quite informative. One observation of considerable interest is that birth weights in Andean high-altitude populations are very similar to those of sea-level populations, whereas high-altitude populations of fairly recent origin, such as that at Leadville, Colorado, have far more low birthweight babies (McClung, 1969). It is generally agreed that the placenta of the Andean baby undergoes considerable modification to increase its diffusing capacity. Although the examination of many placentas has confirmed this mechanism of adaptation, it is not known whether the ability to adapt in this way is inherited in populations of long residence at high altitude or whether it is a capability that is present everywhere but only expressed at high altitude.

POSTNATAL GROWTH

Postnatal growth at high altitude is, in most respects, slower than at sea level. Weight increases are slower, as is epiphyseal growth of the long bones. However, growth of the chest is more rapid at high altitude, as is growth of the lungs. The oxygen-diffusing capacity of children growing up at high altitude is superior to that of their low-altitude age mates throughout childhood. The enlarged right ventricle of the high-altitude Andean native can be discerned early in childhood.

Skeletal growth retardation is an important feature of the high-altitude growth pattern. Epiphyses grow slowly, and compared with standards for the ossification of the hand, wrist, and knee that were developed in the United States, Andean children are significantly delayed (about 20 percent). The delay is not as great after age 16 (about 10 percent). Adult stature is usually attained by about age 20 in females and 22 in males. Because of the prolonged delay in the epiphyseal growth of the long bones, the total length attained is probably less than its genetic potential. Thus it is thought that the short stature of the high-altitude native is environmentally determined (Frisancho, 1978).

SEXUAL MATURATION

Sexual maturation is delayed in high-altitude natives, with menarche occurring at an average age of 13.6 years for Quechua girls, about a year later than in most low-altitude populations. The age of menarche is much later for Sherpa girls, about 18 years. It is of interest that the age of menarche for highland Ethiopian girls is almost identical to that of low-altitude populations.

LOSS OF ADAPTATION

Even among native high-altitude populations there are individuals who appear to lose their adaptation in adulthood. This condition, which has been termed **Monge's disease,** occurs in young and middle-aged males and has symptoms that could be viewed as an overexpression of adaptive mechanisms. The red blood cell count is astronomically high in the victim of Monge's disease. Arterial blood pressure is twice the normal value, with the result that hemorrhages occur under the fingernails. The right ventricular hypertrophy that characterizes the high-altitude native is pronounced, and in most cases both ventricles are enlarged. The oxygen saturation of the arterial blood is low and the partial pressure of carbon dioxide is high, indicating that despite the presence of the mechanisms that permit successful oxygen transport in high-altitude dwellers, these individuals suffer from poor ventilation. A blue color (cyanosis) of the lips, tongue, and sclera of the eye is a diagnostic characteristic of this condition, which seems to be associated with infections such as tuberculosis as well as with neuromuscular disorders affecting the thoracic cage, deformities of the spine, and emphysema (Monge, 1948).

ATHLETIC COMPETITIONS AT HIGH ALTITUDE

The 1968 Olympic Games were held in Mexico City at an altitude of 2,380 meters. During the preparation for the track and field events, there was considerable concern about the effect the altitude would have on performances. It was predicted that times in the sprints (100 meters up to 400 meters) would be better than at lower altitudes but that the longer endurance events would produce poorer times. These predictions proved accurate. In addition, the longest long jump ever, along with exceptionally good javelin, discus, and hammer throws, were recorded in the thin air of Mexico City. The times in the 10,000 meter run were slower than in previous games, and the first five places were won by either high-altitude natives or acclimatized residents. The longer the run, the slower the times recorded in comparison to previous performances. Sea-level natives were slower by 6 to 8 percent than their times at sea level. However, an attention-getting fact was that runners who were adapted to higher altitudes improved their times by from 2 to 4 percent when running in Mexico City. This led to experimentation with new training procedures in which periods of work at altitudes higher than those anticipated at the competition were an important element. It was concluded that altitude training leads to improved anaerobic glycolysis (the breakdown of blood sugar for energy in the absence of oxygen) in the heart muscle. This could permit continued metabolism of glucose for energy even in the presence of a reduced supply of oxygen. The improvements in oxygen transport that accompany high-altitude acclimatization could also translate into improved performance in endurance events at low altitude. Since one of the characteristic features of the physiology of both high-altitude natives and acclimatized non-natives is an increase in the number of red blood cells, some trainers were convinced that training at high altitude could be simulated simply by increasing the red blood cell count of their athletes. This can be accomplished by drawing off blood periodically and storing the cells until shortly before the competition, when they can be reintroduced into the athlete's circulation. The ethical propriety of this procedure, commonly called "blood doping," has been widely questioned. There may be sound medical reasons for objecting to it as well, since there is often a rapid loss of the reintroduced cells. The potential damage that could result from the presence of breakdown products in the blood, kidney, liver, and spleen is ample cause for concern.

The adjustments made by visitors to high-altitude areas resemble, but do not replicate, those seen in high altitude natives. While the low-altitude native visiting a high-altitude area compensates by the release of additional red blood cells and adjustments of blood chemistry, the anatomical characteristics that mark the high-altitude native can be acquired only through prolonged exposure throughout the process of growth and development. Because the combination of anatomical and physiological traits seen in high-altitude natives has proven so effective in maintaining work capacity under demanding circumstances, sports physiologists and athletic trainers have taken considerable interest in the biology of high-altitude natives. As more has been learned about their capabilities and limitations, it has been shown that many of them are indeed living very close to the limits of human adaptability.

BIBLIOGRAPHY

BAKER, P. T. 1969. Human adaptation to high altitude. *Science* 163: 1149–56.

BUSKIRK, E. R. 1978. Work capacity of high-altitude natives. In *The Biology of High-Altitude Peoples,* International Biological Program Publication no. 14, P. T. Baker, ed., pp. 173–87. Cambridge: Cambridge University Press.

CRUZ-COKE, R. 1978. A genetic description of high-altitude populations. In *The Biology of High-Altitude Peoples,* International Biological Program Publications no. 14, P. T. Baker, ed., pp. 47–63. Cambridge: Cambridge University Press.

FRISANCHO, A. R. 1978. Human growth and development among high-altitude populations. In *The Biology of High-Altitude Peoples,* International Biological Program Publications no. 14, P. T. Baker, ed., pp. 117–71. Cambridge: Cambridge University Press.

FRISANCHO, A. R. 1979. *Human Adaptation.* St. Louis: C. V. Mosby.

LAHIRI, S., et al. 1969. Blunted hypoxic drive to ventilation in subjects with life-long hypoxemia. *Federation Proceedings* 28: 289.

McCLUNG, J. 1969. *Effects of High Altitude on Human Birth.* Cambridge, Mass.: Harvard University Press.

MONGE, M. C. 1948. *Acclimatization in the Andes.* Baltimore: Johns Hopkins Press.

PAWSON, I. G., and C. JEST. 1978. The high-altitude areas of the world and their cultures. In *The Biology of High-Altitude Peoples,* International Biological Program Publications no. 14, P. T. Baker, ed., Cambridge: Cambridge University Press.

THOMAS, R. B., and B. P. WINTERHALDER. 1976. Physical and biotic environment of Southern Highland Peru. In *Man in the Andes: A Multidisciplinary Study of High-Altitude Quechua,* P. T. Baker and M. A. Little, eds. Stroudsburg, Penn.: Dowden, Hutchinson & Ross.

Glossary

Acclimatization A physiological adjustment to accommodate to an environmental stressor.

Acheulian Lower Paleolithic Old World handaxe tool tradition; usually associated with *Homo erectus.*

Acrocentric A term describing the shape of a chromosome. In an acrocentric chromosome, the centromere is near one end of the chromosome, resulting in two arms of different lengths.

Actin A protein present in all cells and possessing the property of contractility.

Adaptation The adjustment (can be genetic, behavioral, physiological, or cultural) that is made to environmental change.

Adaptive radiation Branching out from a basic form to meet diversified ecological niches; a basic feature in the early evolutionary stages of new life forms.

Adenine A purine base found in DNA and RNA; it always bonds to thymine in DNA and to uracil in RNA.

Adolescent growth spurt The period of accelerated growth that occurs in both sexes prior to the attainment of sexual maturity.

Age distribution The distribution of individuals in a population with respect to age categories.

Age-specific mortality The likelihood of death at any specific age in a population.

Agglutination reaction The clumping of red cells in a serological test indicating an antigen–antibody reaction.

Allele One of the alternative forms of a gene.

Allelic variation The existence of alternative forms of expression at a specific locus.

Allometry Referring to the fact that growth in some parts of the body is disproportionately related to growth in other parts.

Alpha chain One of several types of polypeptide chains that appear in hemoglobin molecules. Two copies of the alpha chain always appear in combination with two copies of either beta, delta, gamma, or epsilon chains.

Altitude thorax The expanded thorax and barrel-shaped chest characteristic of high-altitude natives.

Alveolar ducts The passages that connect the respiratory bronchioles and the alveolar sacs in the lungs.

Amino acid The basic unit of which proteins are composed. There are 20 different amino acids found in biological compounds, which, in varying numbers and combinations, result in the wide variety of proteins found in all organisms.

Amniotic egg Reptilian adaptation to life on land whereby the embryo is surrounded by three different sacs and the structures are encased by a shell.

Anabolism The building of tissue.

Anagenesis Evolutionary origin of one species from another of the same lineage; phyletic evolution.

Anaphase The third stage of mitosis, in which the chromatids separate with one copy being pulled to each side of the cell.

Anaphase I The third stage of meiosis, in which the homologous members of each pair separate and are pulled along spindle fibers to opposite poles.

Anaphase II The seventh stage of meiosis, identical to anaphase in mitosis except that the cell is haploid.

Ancestral traits Adaptations inherited from a species' ancestors.

Androgenic hormones Male sex hormones. Some are produced in the cortex of the adrenal gland in both sexes. These are called the adrenal androgens. In males, testosterone is produced in the Leydig's cells of the testes. Consequently males maintain higher concentrations of male sex hormones.

Annular epiphyses The epiphyses located on the superior and inferior surfaces of the vertebrae which permit increase in the length of the spine.

Anopheles A genus of mosquito that is the vector of malarial parasites of the genus *Plasmodium.*

Anthropoid The suborder of Primates, including all living and fossil New and Old World monkeys, apes, and humans.

Anthropometry Measurement of the human body.

Antibody a protein produced by the immune system in response to the presence of a foreign substance (antigen) in the body.

Anticodon The sequence of three bases on one arm of a transfer RNA that corresponds to a codon found on the DNA strand and which is complementary to a codon found in messenger RNA.

Antigen Any substance that is capable of evoking an antibody response.

Aortas The large blood vessels that transport oxygenated blood to the upper portion of the body (the ascending aorta) and to the lower portion of the body (the descending aorta).

Apocrine Specialized sweat glands producing a substance having a characteristic odor when acted on by bacteria.

Appendicular skeleton The bones making up the limbs, as opposed to the axial skeleton which is made up of the head and trunk.

Arboreal Tree-dwelling.

Artifacts Cultural remains, including tools.

Assortative mating Selection of mates that either resemble oneself (positive assortative mating) or that differ in some respect (negative assortative mating).

Atria The chambers of the heart that collect blood returning from the lungs or systemic circulation before it enters the ventricles to be pumped to the rest of the body.

Autosome Any chromosome other than the sex chromosomes. Humans have 44 autosomes, occurring in 22 pairs.

B cells Lymphocytes which, when stimulated by the presence of a foreign antigen, proliferate and mature into either antibody-producing plasma cells or memory cells.

Babinski reflex A reflex present in the normal newborn that leads to dorsiflexion of the big toe when the sole of the foot is stroked.

Balanced polymorphism A balance of alleles in a population that is maintained by superior fitness of the heterozygote.

Banding The staining of chromosomes to reveal patterns that distinguish chromosomes and chromosome segments from each other.

Barr body The inactivated X chromosome seen in human females and in males with Klinefelter syndrome.

Basal cells Cells of the epidermis that anchor it to the basement membrane immediately overlying the dermis.

Base A chemical, attached to a sugar and phosphate group, which forms a nucleotide. The DNA bases are adenine, thymine, guanine, and cytosine. In RNA, uracil is substituted for thymine. The sequence of bases on a strand of DNA determines the protein that will ultimately be produced.

Base substitution A type of point mutation in which one base is substituted for another, resulting in a variant codon, and ultimately in altered instructions for the production of a protein.

Basement membrane The juncture of the epidermis and the dermis of the skin.

Beta chain One of several types of polypeptide chains found in hemoglobin. Two copies of beta chains are generally found in combination with two alpha chains in normal adult hemoglobin.

Bicuspid Having two cusps; a trait of the first lower premolar in humans, distinguishing it from the unicuspid (sectorial) lower premolar of monkeys and apes.

Bifacial flaking Removing flakes from both sides of a stone tool.

Bilophodont molars A configuration of elevations on the molar teeth of Old World monkeys.

Binomial Assignment of two Latin names, the genus and species, to an organism.

Bioenergetics The study of energy transformations in cells and tissues.

Biological distance A measure of the genetic differences that accumulate when two populations are separated.

Bipedal Walking erect on the hind legs.

Black water fever Severe malaria marked by darkening of the urine due to loss of large numbers of red blood cells and impaired kidney function.

Blood group One of a number of inherited substances possessing characteristic antigenic properties frequently used as a genetic marker.

Brachiation Locomotor behavior involving swinging beneath branches by the arms.

Bronchi The larger air passages within the lungs.

Brush border The presence of extensions, or microvilli, on the surface of cells involved in absorption. Such extensions increase the surface area and therefore the absorptive capacity.

"Buffered evolution" The softening of the pressure of natural selection by the use of adaptive strategies, including physiological, behavioral, and cultural adjustments, to cope with an environmental stressor.

Burin Chisel-edged stone tool for incising and cutting wood, bone, and ivory; found in the upper Paleolithic.

Canine diastema Gap between the canine and first premolar or lateral incisor to accommodate the projecting canine from the opposing jaw. In the mandible, the diastema is between the canine and first premolar. On the maxilla, the diastema is between the lateral incisor and the canine.

Carboxyhemoglobin Hemoglobin to which carbon dioxide is attached.

Carrier An individual who carries a recessive allele in a heterozygous genotype.

Carriers do not express the allele in their own genotype, but have the potential to pass it on to offspring.

Cartilage models The first stages of formation of bone. Cartilage-forming cells (chondrocytes) produce cartilage structures that precede the formation of true bone. These structures are subsequently destroyed and replaced by bone. Some bone, such as that making up the vault of the skull, is formed without a cartilage model, arising instead from membraneous tissue.

Catarrhines The primate group including humans, apes, and Old World monkeys.

Catastrophism A belief that the earth's history consists of a series of great catastrophes. After each catastrophe, new and more advanced species appear. Popularized by G. Cuvier in the nineteenth century.

Caudal The tail end of an organism. The term is used to describe location on the embryo in terms of distance from the head. This means of describing location is used even when the tail is absent as in the case of the human embryo, where the feet are caudal to the hip joint which is in turn caudal to the rib cage.

Ceboidea Superfamily of New World monkeys.

Cell-mediated immunity The portion of the immune system concerned with the destruction of foreign intruders by various types of phagocytic cells.

Centrioles Small particles in the cytoplasm which are involved in producing spindle fibers during cell division.

Centromere A constricted area on the chromosome where the spindle fibers attach during mitosis and meiosis. When duplicated, the two sister chromatids are joined at the centromere.

Cephalic The head end of the organism.

Cercopithecoidea Superfamily of Old World monkeys.

Cerebellum Section of the hindbrain that functions in the maintenance of equilibrium and the unconscious control of skeletal muscles.

Cerebrum Section of the forebrain responsible for reasoning and learned hand movements.

Cerebrospinal fluid An ultrafiltrate of the serum of the blood which surrounds the structures of the central nervous system, the brain, and the spinal cord.

Cervical Referring to the neck.

Chemo receptors Receptors located in the body that monitor changes in body chemistry such as oxygen saturation or carbon dioxide level of the blood.

Chopper Large, unifacially or bifacially flaked general-purpose stone tool; one of the earliest types of stone tools.

Chromatid One copy of a duplicated chromosome, attached to its counterpart at the centromere.

Chromatin The substance made up of nucleoproteins and nucleic acids that constitutes the genetic material within the nucleus.

Chromosomes Structures found within the nucleus which carry the hereditary material. Chromosomes are composed of DNA and proteins.

Chronometric dating A technique for determining the age, in years, of a specimen or geological formation.

Clade Group of a species sharing a single common ancestor.

Cladogenesis Splitting of one evolutionary lineage into two or more lineages.

Clavicle Bone connecting the sternum, or breast bone, with the scapula, or shoulder bone; functions to stabilize the shoulder.

Clinal variation Variation of a trait characterized by gradual transitions occurring over geographical distance, as opposed to a sharp disjuncture.

Clostridium botulinum An especially virulent bacterium whose powerful exotoxin causes the often-fatal disease botulism in humans and some other organisms.

Clovis Earliest Paleo-Indian fluted-point tradition in the New World.

Codominant The full expression of both alleles in a heterozygous genotype.

Codon A sequence of three bases in DNA or RNA which represents a single amino acid.

Colchicine A plant alkaloid that arrests cell division at the metaphase stage.

Complement A substance present in the serum of the blood which combines with an antigen-antibody complex to lyse, or destroy, the cell membrane of a pathogen.

Continuous trait A trait that may be expressed over a range of values and is therefore measured rather than counted.

Convergence Process whereby dissimilar and unrelated lineages evolve superficially similar structures.

Cranial–caudal gradient The difference in maturity seen in most organisms, including humans, the head being more mature than the tail throughout development.

Cranial capacity Brain size. The measurement is given in cubic centimeters (cc).

Cranium Part of the skull enclosing the brain; also referred to as the *brain case.*

Cretinism A form of growth retardation which includes mental retardation and is associated with iodine deficiency in fetal and early neonatal life.

Cross-sectional studies A study which focuses on measurements in a population taken during a single survey. Cross-sectional studies can be used to construct a composite growth curve.

Crossing-over The phenomenon, occurring only in meiosis, where genetic material is exchanged between two homologous chromosomes.

Crypt cells Cells located at the base of the villi of the intestinal wall. Certain enzymes that facilitate breakdown and absorption of nutrients are produced in the crypt cells.

Cusp Elevation on the crowns of the premolars and molars, the shape, disposition, and number of which are important taxonomic diagnostic traits.

Cytokinesis The division of a cell into two cells by the gradual invagination of the cell wall.

Cytoplasm The portion of the cell which surrounds the nucleus and contains a number of organelles involved in cell function.

Cytosine A pyrimidine base found in DNA and RNA; it always bonds to guanine.

Dead space The residual air remaining in the lungs after expiration.

Deciduous Refers to the first set of, or temporary, teeth; the so-called milk teeth.

Delayed tanning Darkening of the skin that takes place 48 to 72 hours after exposure to the sun.

Deletion A chromosomal-level mutation in which a portion of a chromosome is broken off and lost. Deletions most commonly occur as the result of errors during crossing-over in meiosis.

Delta chain A variant form of a polypeptide chain, found in small amounts in the hemoglobin of adults.

Demography The study of populations, their characteristics, and the factors associated with changes in population size and structure.

Dendritic process Cellular extensions that facilitate communication and exchange with other cells.

Dental formula The number and types of teeth present in each quadrant of the dentition. In most Old World primates the dental formula is 2-1-2-3: 2 incisors, 1 canine, 2 premolars, and 3 molars on each side of the upper and lower jaw.

Deoxyribonucleic acid (DNA) A double-stranded molecule composed of bases (adenine, guanine, cytosine, and thymine), phosphate groups, and sugars arranged in a helical, ladder-like structure. DNA is the carrier of the genetic information.

Deoxyribose A type of sugar, found in DNA. This sugar alternates with phosphate groups to form the "backbone" of the molecule.

Derived trait Characteristic resulting from recent adaptations.

Developmental acclimatization An acclimatization that occurs during the growth and developmental process and that is irreversible in the adult.

Diaphragm The large, circular muscle that contracts to enlarge the thoracic cavity during inspiration.

Dietary hypothesis Hypothesis proposed by J. Robinson to explain differences between gracile and robust australopithecines.

Differential reproduction Differing numbers of surviving offspring. Can result from differential fertility and differential survivorship.

Diploid Possessing the full set of chromosomes: in humans this consists of 22 pairs of autosomes plus one pair of sex chromosomes for a total of 46 chromosomes.

Directional selection Selection that will produce changes in the population average for a continuous trait through favoring individuals expressing the trait at one or the other end of the range of values.

Discrete (discontinuous) trait A trait that is expressed in alternative forms without intermediate values; usually the product of a single gene.

Diurnal Day-living life-style, in contrast to nocturnal, or night-living, life-style.

DNA hybridization A laboratory technique in which the DNA of two different species is fused, forming a hybrid strand, with each half of the molecule contributed by a different species. By measuring the number of matches and mismatches of bases along the strand, the number of accumulated mutations between the species can be estimated.

DNA ligase An enzyme involved in the replication of a DNA molecule. DNA ligase is responsible for joining together the discontinuous segments (Okazaki fragments) of DNA formed along one side of the template strand.

DNA polymerase An enzyme involved in the replication of a DNA molecule. DNA polymerase is responsible for adding nucleotides to the DNA strands forming along the template strands.

Dominance hierarchy A system in which individuals are ranked relative to other individuals.

Dominant An allele that is expressed in the phenotype whether it is present in a homozygote or a heterozygote.

Down syndrome A condition resulting from the possession of an extra copy of chromosome 21. Down syndrome is characterized by a series of physical and mental abnormalities.

Ductus arteriosis A fetal blood vessel that connects the pulmonary artery to the descending aorta. Eccrine sweatglands distributed over the body surface which play a major role in thermoregulation through evaporative cooling.

Eccrine Sweat glands distributed over the body surface which play a major role in thermoregulation through evaporative cooling.

Econiche The life-style of a species in its habitat.

Ectoderm The first of the primordial tissues to appear; primordial to the epidermal layers of the skin, the nervous system, and parts of many organs.

Ectodermal cells Cells whose origin can be traced to an ectodermal precursor.

Effectance motivation Behavior, such as investigatory and play behavior, not serving an immediate end; an important mammalian trait.

Effective population size The segment of a population that has the capability and the opportunity to reproduce.

Electrophoresis The separation of molecules in a solution through the application of an electric field to the surrounding medium. Molecular weight and electrical charge of the molecules will determine the rate and direction of their movement in the medium.

Embryo The earliest stage of growth and development constituting the first eight weeks of human intrauterine life.

Embryogenesis The development of the embryo by cell division and tissue differentiation.

Endemic A disease that is continually present but not necessarily responsible for a high rate of mortality.

Endocranial cast Fossil cast of the interior of the skull. The cast represents the shape and size of the brain.

Endoderm The inside layer of the early stages of blastocyst formation which will ultimately give rise to much of the digestive system and associated organs.

Endoplasmic reticulum A network of membrane-like material in the cytoplasm of the cell. It is involved in the transport of gene products out of the cell and many other functions.

Enzyme A substance composed of a protein, and in some cases other molecules, which functions as biological catalyst.

Eocene Second Cenozoic geological epoch.

Epiphyseal growth Growth of bones characterized by the presence of an epiphyseal cartilage alongside the zone of hypertrophic growth. Epiphyseal growth is seen at the ends of the long bones and at the superior and inferior borders of the vertebrae.

Epsilon chain A variant form of a polypeptide chain found in hemoglobins early in fetal development. They occur in very small amounts in the hemoglobin of some adults.

Estrus The time when a female nonhuman primate is ovulating and is receptive to copulation.

Ethnoarchaeology Gathering data on living populations to help reconstruct the past.

Ethogram Behavioral profile of an animal group.

Ethologist An individual who studies behavior.

Ethology Scientific study of animal behavior.

Evaginating An outpocketing of the outer membrane.

Evolution Refers to a change in gene frequencies of a population through time.

Exon The sequence of bases in a strand of DNA which will eventually be translated into a protein. These coding sequences are interrupted by numerous, noncoding introns which are spliced out before the protein is translated.

Expiration The exhalation of air from the lungs.

Extinct Refers to a taxon of which no living members remain.

F_1 The first filial generation; the first generation of offspring in a genetic breeding experiment.

F_2 The second filial generation; the second generation of offspring in a genetic breeding experiment.

Fallopian tube The tube leading from the proximity of the ovary to the uterus. The place where fertilization of the egg by the sperm usually occurs in humans.

Femur Bone of the thigh.

Fetus The stage of human development lasting from the eighth week of intrauterine life until birth.

Fibula Smaller of the two bones forming the leg, the distal segment of the lower limb.

Fission-track dating Method of dating volcanic substances.

Fist-walking Method of locomotion common to orangutans; walking on clenched fists.

Fitness The degree to which a specific allele is favored in comparison with other alleles at the same locus. The most-favored allele possesses a fitness of 1.0. The concept of fitness may also be applied to genotypes.

Fixation The attainment of a frequency of 100 percent by one allele at a locus resulting from the loss of all other less-fit alleles.

Fixity of species Pre-evolutionary idea stating that once species are created they do not change.

Flagellum A whiplike tail used by many single-celled organisms, including human sperm, to propel themselves through a fluid medium.

Folsom Second Paleo-Indian fluted-point tradition in the New World.

Foramen magnum Opening at the base of the skull through which the spinal cord passes.

Foramen ovale An opening in the wall between the two atria of the fetal heart. When not entirely closed after birth, this opening permits mixture of oxygenated and deoxygenated blood to be pumped to the tissues, leading to the cyanosis that gave rise to the term "blue baby."

Forced expiratory volume The amount of air that can be forced out of the lungs in a single exhalation.

Forced inspiration The increase intake of air associated with the raising of the rib cage by muscular contractions.

Fossil Remains or imprints of plants or animals that once existed.

Fossiliferous Containing fossil materials.

Frameshift mutation A type of point mutation in which a base is either added or deleted from the DNA sequence. Since the mutation affects all of the codons downstream from the error, this type of mutation nearly always renders the gene nonfunctional.

Frontal bone Bone forming the forehead.

Frugivorous Refers to feeding on fruit.

Galvanometer An instrument used to detect minute electrical currents.

Gamete An egg or a sperm bearing a haploid set of chromosomes.

Gamma chain A variant form of a polypeptide chain appearing in fetal hemoglobin and in smaller quantities in adult hemoglobin.

Gene The unit of inheritance, carried on chromosomes. The gene is the segment of DNA responsible for determining a single trait.

Gene cluster A group of genes which produce different gene products (proteins), but which have enough similarities to suggest that they have been ultimately derived from a single ancestral gene through duplication; also known as a *gene family*.

Gene family A group of genes which produce different gene products (proteins), but which have enough similarities to suggest that they have been ultimately derived from a single ancestral gene through duplication; also known as a *gene cluster*.

Generalized Refers to animal or organ not specifically adapted to any given environment or task; the ability to function in a number of ways or in a number of environments.

Genetic code This term refers to the relationship between the sequence of codons found in the DNA and RNA and the sequence of amino acids appearing in the protein product.

Genotype The genetic constitution of an individual.

Genus Taxonomic category larger than the species and smaller than the family. A genus may include a number of species; a number of genera form a family.

Glaciation Period of cold weather characterized by large ice sheets.

Glucose A simple monosaccharide that is the chief energy source in cellular metabolism.

Glucose-6 phosphate dehydrogenase (G-6 PD) A red cell enzyme important in the cell's energy metabolism.

Glycoprotein A compound of a protein and a carbohydrate, often possessing antigenic properties.

Graded response A response that exacts the lowest biological cost to cope with a stressor by exhausting the least demanding options, such as behavioral modifications before invoking physiological changes, anatomical alterations, morbidity, or mortality.

Granulation tissue A tissue that appears during the healing of a deep wound and containing the leakage from damaged blood vessels.

Grooming Behavioral pattern in which an animal picks through the hair of another animal with either or both hands and teeth (*social grooming*) or picks through its own hair (*allogrooming*).

Guanine A purine base found in DNA and RNA; it always bonds to cytosine.

Habitat The geographical and ecological areas where a species lives.

Handaxe Bifacially flaked core tool; one of the first formal stone implements.

Haploid Possessing a single set of chromosomes, as found in the gametes. When two gametes join in the act of fertilization, their haploid sets combine to form the diploid set of chromosomes characteristic of all somatic cells.

Haptoglobin A four-chain protein found in the blood. Its function is to attach to free hemoglobin and prevent its loss through the kidneys.

Helper T cell A type of T cell which mediates the immune response through the release of substances known as *lymphokines,* which activate the other immune cells.

Heme groups The portion of the hemoglobin molecule that bears an iron atom which attracts oxygen. One heme group is attached to each of the four chains of a hemoglobin molecule.

Hemoglobin A protein molecule found in the blood which is responsible for the transport of oxygen to the tissue.

Hemolysis The lysis, or rupture, of the membrane of the red blood cell, releasing the hemoglobin and other constituents of the cell into the bloodstream.

Hepatomegaly Enlargement of the liver which can be caused by a number of infections and is sometimes seen in advanced cases of malaria.

Herbivorous Refers to a dietary pattern in which vegetable matter predominates.

Heterodontism Differentiation of the teeth for different functions.

Heterozygous Possessing different alleles on each chromosome in a homologous pair.

HLA A group of inherited glycoproteins that confer specific antigenic properties to certain human cells. HLA is important in the body's ability to differentiate self from nonself.

Homeothermy Maintenance of a constant body temperature; "warm-bloodedness."

Home range Area in which an animal lives; the total geographic area normally covered.

Hominid Any living or fossil member of the family Hominidae.

Hominoid Referring to members of the human and ape families. Pertains to the taxonomic superfamily Hominoidea.

Homolog One member of a chromosomal pair.

Homologous Refers to each member of a pair of chromosomes. Homologous chromosomes share the same genes and often exchange genetic material during meiosis.

Homologous structures Functionally and ancestrally equivalent structures.

Homozygote An individual who has inherited the same allele of a gene from both parents.

Homozygous Possessing the same allele on both copies of an individual's chromosome.

Hormone Any of a number of circulating proteins produced in various organs which regulate specific cellular activities.

Humerus The long bone of the arm which links the forearm to the shoulder joint.

Humoral immunity The portion of the immune system concerned with identifying and disabling foreign invaders. Humoral immunity involves the production of antibodies.

Hunter-gatherer People living a way of life characteristic of most of human evolutionary history prior to agriculture. Foods consist of hunted and gathered items.

Hydrolysis The breakdown of a substance by the addition of water. The hydroxyl group is incorporated in one fragment and the hydrogen atom in the other.

Hyperplasia Increase in cell number by repeated division.

Hypertrophy Increase in cell size by uptake of proteins and other nutrients.

Hyperventilation Increased amount of air exchange.

Hypotonic A solution that contains a lower concentration of salt than that found in tissue fluids.

Hypovitaminosis D Insufficient synthesis or dietary intake of vitamin D.

Ilium The large, flat bone forming part of the pelvis.

Implantation The imbedding of the trophoblast in the highly vascularized uterine wall, where it will develop a placenta and establish communication with the maternal vascular system.

Incest taboo Sexual or marriage prohibition between individuals considered to be related.

Inclusive fitness Concept of fitness extended to include not only one's own reproductive fitness, but the reproductive success of one's relatives.

Independent assortment The random shuffling and recombination of chromosomes during gamete formation. The result is the production of new combinations of traits.

Insectivorous Feeding on insects.

Insensible perspiration The perspiration that passes through the skin even when the individual is at rest and not in need of thermal regulation through evaporation.

Inspiration The inhalation of air into the lungs.

Interferon A lymphokine produced by helper T cells which appears to stimulate the activity of macrophages.

Interleukin 1 A lymphokine produced by helper T cells which stimulates B cells to mature into antibody-producing plasma cells.

Interleukin 2 A lymphokine produced by helper T cells which appears to activate the killer T cells and to stimulate the activity of phagocytes.

Interphase The stage preceding mitosis in which the chromosomes duplicate. The cell is metabolically active during this stage.

Interstitial wear Wear between adjacent teeth.

Introgression Gene flow involving the movement of genes from one population into and through the gene pool of another population.

Introns Noncoding sequences found interspersed among the coding sequences in a strand of DNA or RNA.

Inversion A chromosomal alteration, occurring during meiotic crossing-over, in which a segment of a chromosome is broken off and rotated 180° before reattaching to the rest of the chromosome.

Invertebrates Animals without backbones.

In vitro Outside the living organism, as in a test tube or other laboratory-testing conditions.

In vivo In the living organism, as opposed to *in vitro,* or under artificial conditions in a laboratory setting.

Ischial callosities Calloused regions on the rumps of many monkeys and some apes which are adaptations to sitting.

Ischium Lowermost portion of the pelvis.

Karyotype A graphic representation of all of the chromosomes in a cell, arranged according to size and banding pattern.

Karyotyping Analysis of the chromosome set of an individual.

Keratin An insoluble protein which contains sulfer, tyrosine, and leucine and is contained in all of the cells of the outer epidermis.

Killer T cell A type of T cell which directly attacks and destroys cells bearing foreign antigens. Killer T cells produce substances called *lymphotoxins* which destroy the antigen-bearing cells.

Kin selection A theory stating that an individual can help its kin and thereby promote the maximal replication of its genes through its relatives.

Klinefelter syndrome A condition found in males who possess an extra copy of the X chromosome.

Knuckle-walking Walking by placing some of the weight on the knuckles, as is done by modern chimpanzees and gorillas.

Lactase An enzyme produced in the small intestine that breaks down lactose to glucose and galactose.

Lactobacillus A genus of bacteria thought to be beneficial in the human intestine.

Lactose Milk sugar; present in varying quantities in all mammals except sea mammals.

Left atrium The collecting chamber of the heart that receives oxygenated blood from the lungs via the pulmonary veins.

Left ventricle The muscular chamber of the heart that pumps oxygenated blood to the systemic circulation.

Levallois technique Method of tool manufacture in which a core is percussion-flaked to a desired shape. A large flake of predetermined form is struck from the core. Associated with the Mousterian.

Linkage The occurrence of two loci close together on the same chromosome, with the result that the traits they determine do not segregate independently.

Living floor Area of cultural activity within a hominid fossil site.

Locus The location of a gene on a chromosome.

Longitudinal study A study that follows the same individuals over a period of time. Longitudinal studies are important in the assessment of growth, development and aging.

Lumbar The lower portion of the spine between the thorax and the sacrum.

Lymphocytes Circulating cells found in the blood and lymph system that are responsible for identifying and disabling foreign intruders; they include the T cells, B cells, and macrophages.

Lymphokines Substances produced by helper T cells that activate other cells and mediate the immune response.

Lymphotoxin A substance produced by killer T cells that destroys cells bearing foreign antigens on their surfaces.

Lysozymes Cellular organelles responsible for breaking down and digesting cellular debris.

Macroevolution Evolutionary changes leading to the rise of new species and genera.

Macrophage A lymphocyte that interacts with the T cells and B cells to produce an immune response. Some macrophages are also phagocytic.

Mandible Lower jaw.

Manioc A tuber grown in many tropical areas and consumed after cooking to release cyanates.

Manuport Material carried into a human occupation site; often refers to unworked stones.

Masseter muscle Large chewing muscle originating on the cranium and inserting on the mandible.

Maxilla Upper jaw.

Megaevolution A state of rapid evolutionary change.

Meiosis A cell division process that produces haploid cells (gametes). Meiosis is a reduction division, in which a diploid cell undergoes two divisions, resulting in the production of gametes containing one-half the genetic material.

Melanocytes Cells located in the *stratum germinativum* which produce the dark pigment melanin.

Memory cells B cells that do not mature into plasma cells and produce antibodies, but that remember the foreign antigen and maintain the ability to respond quickly if the antigen is ever reintroduced.

Menarche The occurrence of the first menstrual period.

Messenger RNA An RNA molecule responsible for copying the sequence of codons found in a segment of DNA and carrying the message to the cytoplasm, where it can be used to produce a protein.

Metabolism The transformation and use of energy to develop and maintain tissue and to perform work at the cellular level.

Metacentric A term describing the shape of a chromosome. In a metacentric chromosome, the centromere is near the center, producing two arms of approximately equal length.

Metaphase The second stage of mitosis, in which the duplicated chromosomes migrate toward the center of the cell and align themselves along the equatorial plane.

Metaphase I The second stage of meiosis, where the paired chromosomes align along the equatorial plane.

Metaphase II The sixth stage of meiosis, identical to metaphase in mitosis except that the cell is haploid.

Microevolution Genetic changes within potentially continuous populations; changes below the species level.

Minute volume The amount of air that is exchanged by the lungs in one minute.

Miocene Fourth geological epoch of the Cenozoic Era.

Missense mutation A type of point mutation in which the substituted base ultimately results in a different amino acid appearing in a polypeptide chain, producing a different protein from that originally coded in the DNA.

Mitochondria Cellular organelles found in the cytoplasm and involved in the energy metabolism of the cell.

Mitosis A cell-division process occurring in somatic cells. Mitosis begins with a single diploid cell, which replicates and then divides, resulting in two new cells identical to the original.

Mitral valve The valve that opens to permit oxygenated blood from the left atrium to enter the left ventricle of the heart.

Molecular clock A technique for estimating the divergence times of two species. The molecular clock uses data derived from DNA hybridization studies and, by assuming a constant mutation rate, attempts to estimate when the divergence of the species occurred.

Monge's disease The loss of acclimatization to high altitude that occasionally occurs in high-altitude natives.

Moro reflex An embracelike movement of the newborn in response to a loud noise.

Morphology The structure or form of an object.

Mosaic evolution Evolution of different features at different rates.

Mousterian Cultural assemblage commonly associated with the Neanderthals.

Musculoskeletal system The muscles, tendons, ligaments, and bones that permit movement of the body.

Mutation An error occurring during replication which interferes with the structural integrity of the DNA and which may result in an altered gene product.

Myelin A fatty substance produced by specialized cells in the nervous system (Schwann cells) which covers nerve tracts and increases the speed of transmission of signals.

Natural selection The mechanism of evolutionary change whereby the most-fit genotypes are represented by proportionally larger numbers of offspring in succeeding generations.

Naturalism Viewing humans as part of the natural world and as being governed by natural laws. A concept characterizing eighteenth-century scientific thought.

Neonate A newborn infant.

Neurohypophysis The posterior lobe of the pituitary gland.

Neurons Nerve cells.

Neutral mutation A point mutation in which the substituted base results in a different codon that represents the same amino acid. A neutral mutation has no measurable effect on the phenotype.

Nondisjunction Any of several types of errors that can occur during meiosis, resulting in the improper allocation of chromosomes into gametes.

Nonsense mutation A type of point mutation in which the substituted base results in the conversion of a normal codon into a termination codon. This type of mutation will produce a nonfunctional protein.

Notochord A mesoderm-derived rod that forms beneath the ectoderm and induces the formation of the neural tube in early embryogenesis.

Nuchal Referring to the nape of the neck.

Nuchal crest Crest, or ridge, of bone on the occipital bone to which neck muscles attach.

Nuclear membrane A structure which surrounds the nucleus of a cell, separating its contents from the cytoplasm.

Nucleotide pair Refers to two DNA nucleotides joined by hydrogen bonds which form between complementary bases.

Nucleotide A structure composed of a single base, phosphate, and sugar. Both DNA and RNA are composed of strings of nucleotides.

Nucleus The portion of the cell that contains the chromosomes.

Occipital bone Rearmost bone in the skull; forms base of the skull.

Occipital bun Exaggerated rearward protrusion of the occipital bone.

Occipital condyle Projection at the base of the occipital bone with which the first cervical vertebra articulates.

Occlusion Anatomical term referring to the meeting of the tooth cusps when the upper and lower jaws are closed.

Okazaki fragments The discontinuous segments of DNA that form along the 3′ to 5′ strand of DNA during replication. They are joined by DNA ligase to form a continuous strand.

Oldowan Tool-making tradition in which pebbles are flaked to form an irregular cutting surface on one side. The modified tools are a general, all-purpose tool. The oldest tool tradition, first developed in Africa.

Olfactory Referring to the sense of smell.

Oligocene Third geological epoch of the Cenozoic Era.

Omnivorous A diet not specialized for one food source.

Opposable Ability to rotate a digit out of the plane of others, allowing it to be opposed.

Organelles Small structures found within the cytoplasm of a cell. Organelles are involved in various cellular activities.

Organogenesis The formation of organs from differentiating primordial tissues.

Ossification The formation of bone or the transformation of cartilage into bone.

Osteodontokeratic culture Dart's name for a bone, tooth, and antler culture of the australopithecines. A pre-stone tool culture in which tools are used but not made.

Osteogenic layer The inner layer of the periosteum that is involved in bone formation, resorption, and remodelling.

Osteological Referring to bone material

Osteometry Techniques for measuring bone.

Ovum The egg or female gamete.

Oxytocin A hormone produced in the hypothalamus and stored in the posterior lobe of the pituitary gland. When released from the pituitary gland, oxytocin stimulates uterine contractions that initiate parturition.

P_1 The parental generation in a genetic breeding experiment.

Paleocene First geological epoch of the Cenozoic Era.

Paleomagnetism One of several forms of relative dating. Based on shifts in the earth's magnetic poles.

Palynology Analysis of fossil pollens and spores. Very helpful in reconstructing paleoecological conditions.

Pandemic An especially widespread epidemic of a disease.

Parallelism Evolution of similar adaptations in forms that were once related but then diverged, developing along similar lines.

Parietals The bones on each side of the top of the skull.

Pathogen Any substance or organism capable of producing a disease.

Peak height velocity The short period during the adolescent growth spurt when the rate of increase in height is at its maximum.

Pebble tools Stone tools associated with early hominids.

Pentadactyly Having five fingers and five toes on each hand and foot.

Peptide bonds Chemical bonds that occur between two amino acids, forming polypeptide chains.

Percussion flaking Use of a stone as a hammer to chip off flakes on one or two sides of another stone.

Periosteum The membrane surrounding bones. The osteogenic layer of the periosteum contains cells that form and destroy the bone adjacent to them.

Phagocyte A cell with the ability to surround, engulf, and destroy viruses, bacteria, and other foreign particles.

Phenocopy An environmentally modified expression of a trait that causes the phenotype to resemble the expression of a different genotype.

Phenotype An expressed trait. The phenotype is the product of the genotype and any environmental influences that may have occurred during growth and development of the individual.

Phosphate group Alternates with sugars to form the "backbone" of a DNA molecule.

Phyletic evolution The evolution of one species from another of the same lineage; anagenesis.

Phylogenetic tree Branching diagram representing evolutionary relationships of a group of species.

Pisum sativum The common garden pea, used by Mendel in his breeding experiments.

Pituitary gland The two-lobed gland located beneath the hypothalamus of the brain and often called the "master gland" of the endocrine system because of its widespread influence on other glands and end organs.

Placentation The formation of a placenta, which will permit exchange of nutrients and metabolic by-products between the embryo or fetus and the mother.

Plano Late Paleo-Indian tradition in the New World.

Plasma The fluid portion of the blood.

Plasma cell A mature, antibody-producing B cell.

Plasmodium A genus of parasites transmitted to human hosts by the bite of a mosquito. Four species, each responsible for one type of malaria, are of clinical significance.

Platycephaly Flattening of the top of the skull, characteristic of many *Homo erectus* fossils.

Platyrrhine Infraorder which includes all New World primates.

Pleistocene Sixth geological epoch of the Cenozoic Era.

Pliocene Fifth geological epoch of the Cenozoic Era.

Pluvial Period of increased rainfall.

Point mutation An error occurring during replication of a strand of DNA, resulting in the addition, deletion, or substitution of one base for another.

Polar body One of the products of cell division occurring in oocytes and the fertilized egg. Polar bodies have little cytoplasm and are seldom fertilized.

Polycythemia The condition of having more than the normal number of circulating red blood cells.

Polygenic trait A trait that is determined by the combined action of a number of loci.

Polymorphism The existence in a population of two or more common alleles at a locus.

Polypeptide A chain of amino acids, held together by peptide bonds. A protein consists of one or more polypeptide chains.

Pongid Referring to the great apes.

Pongidae The taxonomic family that includes the great apes.

Postcranial skeleton The skeleton below the head.

Postorbital bar Bone enclosure at the rear of the eye orbit; diagnostic trait of most living and fossil primates.

Postorbital constriction Constriction of the skull behind the brow ridges.

Potassium-argon dating (K/Ar dating) Method of chronometrically dating volcanically derived material.

Power grip Grip involving all the fingers of the hand; the thumb and forefingers are not opposed.

Preadaptation An adaptation that forms the basis for successive adaptations; an adaptation that is potentially advantageous in a new set of circumstances.

Precision grip Grip used in holding small objects, such as a pen, by opposing the thumb and forefingers.

Prehensile Refers to the ability to grasp.

Premessenger RNA The initial copy of the messenger RNA, before it is processed to remove the introns; also called the *primary transcript.*

Prepared core The shape of a stone is obtained by removal of small flakes from the entire surface. This allows more cutting surface in less time from less stone, as well as the manufacture of a more standardized tool.

Primary transcript The initial copy of messenger RNA, before it is processed to remove the introns; also called *premessenger RNA.*

Probabilistic Using the laws of probability to predict the outcome of an event.

Procumbant Jutting forward of the incisors.

Prognathism Forward protrusion of the lower face and jaw.

Prophase The first stage of mitosis, in which the chromosomes begin to condense.

Prophase I The first stage of meiosis, when the duplicated chromosomes condense and pair with their homologs.

Prophase II The fifth stage of meiosis, identical to prophase in mitosis except that the cell is haploid.

Prosimian Refers to the lower primates. A member of the taxonomic suborder Prosimii, which includes all fossil and living lemurs, lorises, and galagos, as well as other fossil forms.

Protein Any of a large number of different molecules formed from one or more polypeptide chains.

Protein synthesis The multistep process by which a message, encoded in the DNA, is transported to the cytoplasm and used to construct a protein from component amino acids.

Provisioned colony A colony of animals fed by humans.

Pseudogene A segment of DNA that does not code for a functional protein, but which has too many similarities to a functional gene to exist merely by chance. It is believed that most pseudogenes are the product of either gene duplication or reverse transcription.

Pubis Foremost of the three pelvic bones.

Pulmonary vein The vein that returns oxygenated blood from the lungs to the left atrium of the heart.

Punctuated equilibrium Model of evolutionary change in which long periods of stasis alternate with briefer periods of rapid speciation.

Purine Refers to bases that have a double-ringed structure; adenine and guanine.

Pyrimidine Refers to bases that have a single-ringed structure; cytosine, thymine, and uracil.

Q bands Patterns revealed on chromosomes treated with certain fluorescent stains.

Quadrupedalism Locomotion using all four limbs.

Quinine An alkaloid obtained from cinchona bark that is used as a prophylaxis against malaria.

Radiocarbon (C_{14}) dating Chronometric dating technique; dates the time when an organism died by measuring the amount of radioactive C_{14} that has disappeared.

Radius One of the two forearm bones.

Recessive An allele that is not expressed in the phenotype when paired with a dominant allele.

Reciprocal altruism A form of altruistic behavior that can occur between related or unrelated individuals enhancing the genetic fitness of both.

Recombination The reassortment of alleles that occurs during meiosis.

Regulatory genes Segments of DNA that are responsible for regulating the activity of structural genes.

Relative dating Dating methods that establish a chronological sequence from youngest to oldest.

Replication The process by which a strand of DNA is duplicated, producing two copies identical to each other and to the original.

Reticular layer The deep layer of the dermis which attaches to the underlying cutaneous musculature.

Reverse transcriptase An enzyme which facilitates the transcription of DNA on an RNA template.

Reverse transcription A process by which DNA can be transcribed from messenger RNA.

Ribonucleic acid (RNA) A single-stranded molecule, composed of sugars (ribose), phosphate groups, and bases (adenine, guanine, cytosine, and uracil). There are several types of RNAs, all involved in the transport and translation of the DNA-encoded message into a protein.

Ribosomal RNA A type of RNA, which together with several types of proteins form the structure known as a *ribosome.*

Ribosomes Particles, formed from ribosomal RNA and proteins, that are involved in protein synthesis. The messenger RNA (carrying the DNA message) and the transfer RNAs (carrying the amino acids) are brought together at the ribosome, where the protein is constructed.

Rickets A condition characterized by poorly mineralized bones that are soft and easily distorted. Often associated with vitamin D deficiency.

Right atrium The collecting chamber of the heart that receives deoxygenated blood returning from the tissues.

Right ventricle The muscular chamber of the heart that pumps blood to the lungs through the pulmonary arteries.

Right ventricular hypertrophy The enlarged right ventricle seen in the heart of some high-altitude natives.

RNA polymerase An enzyme responsible for producing a messenger RNA transcript which contains a sequence of bases complementary to the sequence on the DNA template on which it forms.

Rooting reflex A reflex by which the newborn orients its head to permit it to find the nipple preparatory to suckling.

Scapula The shoulder blade: The large bone which articulates with the humerus to form the shoulder joint.

Sectorial premolar A unicuspid premolar; characteristic of the premolar of most primates except humans. Associated with the presence of a large maxillary canine.

Segregation The separation of the two alleles inherited by an individual, resulting in each gamete having only one.

Serology The study of antigen–antibody reactions under laboratory conditions; usually involves determination of blood group antigens.

Sex cells Gametes; eggs and sperm.

Sex chromosome The X or Y chromosome.

Sexual dimorphism Marked differences in certain traits of males and females.

Sickle-cell anemia A condition usually associated with the inheritance of the abnormal hemoglobin S from both parents. It is characterized by the distortion and destruction of red blood cells when the oxygen concentration in the blood is low.

Sister chromatids The pair of chromatids in a duplicated chromosome.

Site A location where traces of occupation or activity are found.

Skewness The tendency for a continuous trait to be expressed more often at one end of its range of values than at the other, producing a distribution curve with many outlyers at one end.

Socionomic sex ratio Ratio of females to males in primate groups.

Sociobiology Application of natural selection theory to the study of behavior. The theory is especially concerned with the behavioral aspects affecting reproductive success.

Soft-hammer technique Wood, bone, or antler used instead of rock to chip flakes from a core; allows more control over length, width, and thickness of the flake removed.

Somatic cells Body cells. Somatic cells replicate through mitosis.

Somites Aggregations of mesoderm that appear alongside the notochord in early embryogenesis and ultimately give rise to muscle, bone, and kidneys.

Specialization Adaptation of an organism to a way of life or function; may limit evolutionary possibilities.

Speciation Process through which a species evolves into one or more different species.

Species A group of organisms capable of interbreeding and producing viable offspring.

Spermatid An immature sperm.

Spermatozoon A mature sperm.

Spinal column Bony structure which protects the spinal cord and provides stability and strength to the back; characteristic of vertebrates.

Spindle fibers Elastic fibers, produced by the centrioles, involved in the movement of chromosomes during cell division.

Splenomegaly Enlargement of the spleen, sometimes caused by the breakdown of large numbers of red blood cells, as in malaria.

Stereoscopic vision Ability to merge visual images from both eyes; allows depth perception.

Stratigraphy Sequence of geological strata and/or the study of a sequence.

Stratum corneum The outer layer of the epidermis, made up of dead cells.

Stratum germinativum The deepest layer of the epidermis; contains the active and dividing cells.

Stratum granulosum One of the deeper layers of the epidermis; contains cells in the process of losing their nuclei while accumulating keratin.

Stratum lucidum The layer of the epidermis beneath the stratum corneum. This layer is present only in thickened areas of the skin, such as the palms and soles.

Stratum spinosum One of the deeper layers of the epidermis; contains a special category of prickly cells.

Structural gene A segment of DNA whose base sequence represents the sequence of amino acids in a protein.

Subscapular The region on the back immediately beneath the scapula; a point where subcutaneous fat is often measured.

Subspecies A subdivision of a species; consists of individuals in a given geographic area and differs slightly from, but can interbreed with, other subspecies of the same species.

Sucking reflex The reflex, present at birth of the human infant, that permits it to suckle at the breast.

Supraorbital torus (brow ridges) Bony ridges above the eyes.

Superior and inferior vena cava The large vessels that receive deoxygenated blood from the veins and transport it to the right atrium of the heart.

Suppressor T cell A type of T cell which is responsible for regulating the immune response by shutting it down when it is no longer needed.

Synapses Points at which nerve cells communicate with each other.

Synapsis The physical joining of two homologous chromosomes during meiosis. Crossing over occurs at the points where the chromosomes are joined.

Systematics Scientific study of the types and diversity of living organisms and of the relationships between them.

T cells Lymphocytes responsible for cellular component of the immune response; the types of T cells include helper T cells, killer T cells, and suppressor T cells.

T complex Dental traits which Jolly attributed to adaptations of seed-eating diets.

Taphonomy Study of the fossilization process.

Taurodont Referring to an enlarged molar root cavity and perhaps fusion of molar roots.

Taxon (pl., taxa) A group of organisms whose members are evolutionarily related and distinct from other such groups.

Taxonomy Science of the rules for classification of living forms in a manner best suited to show their relationship to one another.

Telophase The final stage of mitosis, when nuclear membranes form around each set of chromosomes and the cell begins to physically divide.

Telophase I The fourth stage of meiosis, in which the cells divide, resulting in two haploid cells, each still containing duplicated chromosomes.

Telophase II The final stage of meiosis, identical to telophase in mitosis except that the cells are haploid. At the end of telophase, males have produced four haploid gametes and females have produced a single haploid gamete and either two or three polar bodies.

Temporal bones Lateral bones of the skull, composing the side of the head.

Temporal lobe Part of the cerebral hemisphere; important for memory.

Teleologist One who accepts the idea that there is intelligent design in the universe and that nature's processes are directed to certain ends.

Territory That part of the home range defended against others.

Thalassemia A defect in the synthesis of one of the pairs of chains making up hemoglobin. It has been called Cooley's anemia and occurs in high frequency in populations living around the Mediterranean Sea.

Thoracic cavity The space enclosed by the rib cage and containing the heart, lungs, and great vessels.

Thymine A pyrimidine base found in DNA; it always bonds to adenine.

Tibia Larger of the two bones forming the leg, or distal segment of the lower limb.

Tidal volume The amount of air inhaled in a single breath.

Trachea The "windpipe." The tube that connects the larynx and the bronchi through which inhaled and exhaled air must pass.

Tracts Collections of nerve fibers that have the same origin, termination, and function.

Transcription The first step in protein synthesis, in which messenger RNA is produced on a DNA template.

Transfer RNA An RNA molecule involved in protein synthesis; responsible for bringing the appropriate amino acid to the ribosome, where it can be added to the growing polypeptide chain.

Transferrin A protein found in the serum of the blood; functions to complex with free iron in the blood and return it to the bone marrow.

Translation The second step in protein synthesis, in which the message encoded in the messenger RNA is used to assemble a protein. This step involves transfer RNA and the ribosomes.

Translocation A chromosome-level mutation, occurring as the result of an error during meiotic crossing-over, in which a portion of a chromosome is exchanged with a segment of a nonhomologous chromosome.

Transient polymorphism The presence of two or more alleles in a population, preceding the loss or fixation of one of the alleles.

Triceps An area on the back of the arm at the insertion of the triceps muscle where a frequently used skinfold measurement is taken.

Trisomy-21 A condition in which an individual possesses three copies of chromosome 21. This condition results from nondisjunction in meiosis, in which either a sperm or an egg has two copies of the 21st chromosome. When fused with a normal gamete upon fertilization, the zygote will have three copies of this chromosome and exhibit the traits characteristic of Down syndrome.

Trypanosoma gambiense A parasite that causes sleeping sickness in a human host. It is transmitted by the bite of the tsetse fly common to many parts of equatorial Africa.

Turner syndrome A condition found in females who possess only a single copy of the X chromosome.

Type specimen The specimen to which all subsequent finds are compared. The first recovered specimen on which a taxonomic designation is based.

Ulna The forearm bone which terminates at the wrist on the little-finger side of the hand.

Unequal crossing over A phenomenon which can occur during meiotic crossing-over in which the homologous chromosomes break in different places and exchange unequal amounts of genetic material. Unequal crossing-over can result in two copies of the same gene appearing in tandem on the same chromosome.

Upper Paleolithic The tool industry associated with early *Homo sapiens sapiens.*

Uniformitarianism The doctrine that geological strata can be interpreted by assuming that they were formed by agencies operating in a uniform way and at a rate comparable with the action of contemporary agencies. Formulated by C. Lyell.

Uracil A pyrimidine base found in RNA; it always bonds to adenine.

Veins The blood vessels that return deoxygenated blood from the tissues to the heart.

Venules The small veins that collect deoxygenated blood emerging from the capillaries.

Vertebrate Animal possessing a spinal column.

Villafranchian fauna Faunal assemblage marking the beginning of the Pleistocene era. Includes representatives of the modern genera of horse, elephant, and cattle, among others.

Villi Finger-like projections on the inner or absorptive surface of an organ. In the intestine, the presence of villi increases the surface area and capacity to absorb nutrients.

Virulence The level of pathogenicity of a disease-producing substance or organism as measured by its clinical effects or lethality.

Vital capacity The total amount of air that the lungs can hold.

Viviparous Giving birth to live young rather than laying eggs.

Yersinia pestis The pathogen responsible for bubonic plague. It is a small Gram-negative bacterium transmitted to humans by fleas (formerly designated *Pasteurella pestis*).

Zygote The diploid cell which results from the fusion of an egg and a sperm.

Zygomatic arches An arch of bone made up of the zygomatic process of the temporal bone and part of the malar (cheek bone).

FIGURE CREDITS

Chapter 1: Chapter opening photos courtesy Nancy Staley, Columbus Zoo, Columbus, Ohio; W.E.L. Clarke, *The Fossil Evidence for Human Evolution,* 2/e (1964), skull of male gorilla © 1955, 1964 by the University of Chicago, all rights reserved; M. Leakey, *Olduvai Gorge Vol. I, Excavations in Beds I and II* (Cambridge University Press), 1971. Copyrighted by and used with the permission of Cambridge University Press; and B. Albers et al., *Molecular Biology of the Cell* (New York: Garland, 1983).

Chapter 2: Chapter opening photo and Figure 2-1 Fred A. Racle, *Introduction to Evolution,* © 1979, p. 28. Reprinted by permission of Prentice-Hall, Inc. Englewood Cliffs, N.J.; Figure 2-2, ibid, p. 27.

Chapter 3: Chapter opening photo and Figure 3-8 after B. Albers et al., *Molecular Biology of the Cell* (New York: Garland, 1983).

Chapter 4: Figure 4-3 A. J. Kelso/Wanda R. Trevalthan, *Physical Anthropology,* 3/e © 1984. Reprinted by permission of Prentice-Hall, Englewood Cliffs, N.J.; Figure 4-5 Barrett/Abramoff/ Kuraman/Millington, *Biology,* © 1986, p. 643. Reprinted by permission of Prentice Hall, Inc., Englewood Cliffs, N.J.; Figure 4-7 reprinted by permission from page 186 of *Human Heredity* by M.R. Cummings, copyright © 1988 by West Publishing Company, all rights reserved.

Chapter 5: Chapter opening photo same as Figure 5-6; Figure 5-1 from "Catholic Churchmen in Science"; Figures 5-6, 5-7, and 5-8 reprinted by permission from pages 298 and 299 from *Human Heredity: Principles and Issues* by M.R. Cummings, copyright © 1988 by West Publishing Company, all rights reserved; Figure 5-9 after J. E. Crouch, *Functional Human Anatomy,* 3rd ed. (Philadelphia: Lea and Febiger, 1978). Figure 5-10 D. Walcher and N. Kretchmer, *Food Nutrition and Evolution* (New York: Masson Publishing, 1981), p. 5.

Chapter 6: Chapter opening photo same as Figure 6-3; Figures 6-1, 6-2, and 6-3 Fred A. Racle, *Introduction to Evolution,* © 1979. Reprinted by permission of Prentice-Hall, Inc., Englewood Cliffs, New Jersey; Figure 6-4 L. Stebbins, *Processes of Organic Evolution,* 1977, p. 5. Reprinted by permission of Prentice-Hall, Inc., Englewood Cliffs, New Jersey.

Chapter 7: Chapter opening photo courtesy Gregory Acciaioli.

Chapter 8: Chapter opening photo same as Figure 8-17A; Figure 8-1 courtesy Frank E. Poirier; Figure 8-2 courtesy Warren G. Kinzey; Figures 8-3 and 8-4 courtesy Pat Asher, Columbus Zoo, Columbus, Ohio; Figures 8-5, 8-6, and 8-7 courtesy Warren G. Kinzey; Figure 8-8 A.J. Kelso and W.R. Trevathan, *Physical Anthropology,* 3/e, © 1984, p. 179. Reprinted by permission of Prentice-Hall, Inc., Englewood Cliffs, N.J.; Figures 8-9, 8-10, 8-11, 8-12, 8-13, 8-14 courtesy Frank E. Poirier; Figure 8-15(a) courtesy Frank E. Poirier; (b) courtesy Alyson Poirier; Figures 8-16 and 8-17 courtesy Frank E. Poirier.

Chapter 9: Chapter opening photo and Figures 9-1, 9-2, and 9-3 courtesy C.E.G. Tutin; Figure 9-4 courtesy Nancy Staley, Columbus Zoo, Columbus, Ohio; Figure 9-5 courtesy Andrea Gorzitze.

Chapter 10: Chapter opening photo courtesy Frank E. Poirier.

Chapter 11: Chapter opening photo and Figure 11-1, Negative #334421, courtesy Department of Library Services American Museum of Natural History; Figure 11-2 courtesy R. Prebeg, Columbus Zoo, Columbus, Ohio; Figure 11-3 A.J. Kelso and W.R. Trevathan, *Physical Anthropology,* 3/e, © 1984, p. 70. Reprinted by permission of Prentice-Hall, Inc., Englewood Cliffs, New Jersey.

Chapter 12: Chapter opening photo courtesy C.E.G. Tutin; Figure 12-1 Neg. No. 321683, photo by Rota, courtesy Department of Library Services, American Museum of Natural History; Figures 12-2, 12-3, 12-4 Fred A. Racle, *Introduction to Evolution,* © 1979, pages 102 and 108, reprinted by permission of Prentice-Hall, Inc., Englewood Cliffs, N.J.; Figure 12-5 A.J. Kelso and W.R.

Trevathan, *Physical Anthropology,* 3/e, © 1984, p. 152. Reprinted by permission of Prentice-Hall, Inc., Englewood Cliffs, N.J.; Figure 12-6 courtesy R. Prebeg, Columbus Zoo, Columbus, Ohio.

Chapter 13: Chapter opening photo W. Bishop and J.D. Clark, eds., *Background to Evolution in Africa* (Chicago: University of Chicago Press), 1967; Figure 13-1 R. Flint, *Glacial and Quartenary Geology,* 1971. Reprinted by permission of John Wiley and Sons.

Chapter 14: Chapter opening photo neg. no. 37373, photo by A.E. Anderson, courtesy Department of Library Services American Museum of Natural History, Figures 14-1 and 14-2 A.J. Kelso and W.R. Trevathan, *Physical Anthropology,* 3/e, p. 173. Reprinted by permission of Prentice-Hall, Inc., Englewood Cliffs, N.J.; Figure 14-3 neg. n. 37373, photo by A.E. Anderson, courtesy Department of Library Services American Museum of Natural History; Figure 14-4 M. Cartmill, *Primate Origins* (Minneapolis: Burgess Publishing Co.), reprinted by permission of Burgess Publishing Co.

Chapter 15: Chapter opening photo courtesy R. L. Ciochon and S. Nash; Figures 15-1 and 15-2 courtesy R. L. Ciochon; Figure 15-3 courtesy R. L. Ciochon and S. Nash; Figure 15-4 courtesy Dr. A. Bellisari; Figure 15-5 I. Tattersall, *The Evolutionary Significance of Ramapithecus* (Minneapolis: Burgess Publishing Co.), 1975; Figures 15-6 and 15-7 courtesy Wu Rukang, Institute of Vertebrate Palentology and Paleoanthropology, Beijing, P.R.C.; Figure 15-8 courtesy Professor Zuo Guoxing, Beijing Natural History Museum, Beijing, P.R.C.; Figure 15-9 reproduced with permission from M.H. Day, *The Fossil History of Man,* 3/e, 1984, Carolina Biology Readers Series No. 32. Copyright Carolina Biological Supply Co., Burlington, N.C.; Figure 15-10 cast provided by Prof. Wu Xinzhi, photo by Frank E. Poirier; Figure 15-11 neg. no. 298869, photo by Bierwert & Rota, courtesy Department of Library Services, American Museum of Natural History.

Chapter 16: Chapter opening photo courtesy C.E.G. Tutin; Figure 16-1 Joseph B. Birdsell, *Human Evolution,* copyright © 1975, 1981 by Harper and Row, Publishers, Inc. Reprinted by permission of the publisher; Figure 16-2 courtesy Georgette Goldberg Haydu; Figure 16-3 G. Tunnell, *Culture and Biology* (Minneapolis: Burgess Publishing), 1973; Figure 16-4 courtesy C.E.G. Tutin; Figure 16-5 model by Dr. L.H. Briesemeister.

Chapter 17: Chapter opening photo courtesy R. Prebeg; Figure 17-1 courtesy Georgette Goldberg Haydu; Figure 17-2 courtesy F.E. Poirier; Figure 17-3 W. Bishop and J.D. Clark, eds., *Background to Evolution in Africa* (Chicago: University of Chicago Press), 1967; Figure 17-4 courtesy R. Prebeg; Figure 17-5 reproduced with permission from M.H. Day, *The Fossil History of Man,* 3/e, Carolina Biology Readers Series No. 32 (1984), copyright Carolina Biological Supply Company, Burlington, N.C.; Figure 17-6 courtesy R. Prebeg; Figure 17-7 courtesy Frank E. Poirier; Figure 17-8 courtesy Dr. John T. Robinson; Figure 17-9 W.E.L. Clarke, The Fossil Evidence for Human Evolution, 2/e (1964), skull of male gorilla © 1955, 1964 by the University of Chicago, all rights reserved; Figure 17-10 Negative # 3k9573, photo by Leon Botin, courtesy Department of Library Services, American Museum of Natural History; Figure 17-11 reproduced with permission of M.H. Day, *The Fossil History of Man,* 3/e, 1984, Carolina Biological Supply Co., Burlington, N.C.; Figure 17-12 courtesy R. Prebeg; Figure 17-13 courtesy Georgette Goldberg Haydu; Figure 17-14 courtesy Dr. John T. Robinson; Figure 17-15 courtesy Wenner-Gren Foundation for Anthropological Research, Inc. and with permission of the owner of the original specimen; Figures 17-16, 17-17, and 17-18 courtesy Dr. John T. Robinson; Figure 17-21 A.J. Kelso and W.R. Trevathan, *Physical Anthropology,* 3/e, © 1984, p. 235. Reprinted with permission of Prentice-Hall, Inc., Englewood Cliffs, N.J.; Figure 17-22 from *American Journal of Physical Anthropology* 57: 1982, used by permission of Alan R. Liss, Inc.

Chapter 18: Chapter opening photo Negative # 333193, courtesy Department of Library Services, American Museum of Natural History; Figures 18-1 and 18-2 A.J. Kelso and W.R. Trevathan, *Physical Anthropology,* 3/e, © 1984, pp. 237 and 239. Reprinted by permission of Prentice-Hall, Inc., Englewood Cliffs, N.J.; Figure 18-3 courtesy Georgette Goldberg Haydu; Figure 18-4 courtesy Frank E. Poirier; Figure 18-5 reproduced with permission from M.H. Day, *The Fossil History of Man,* 3/e, Carolina Biology Readers Series, No. 32 (1984). Copyright Carolina Biological Supply Co., Burlington, N.C.; Figure 18-6 courtesy Dr. John T. Robinson; Figure 18-7 courtesy Frank E. Poirier; Figure 18-8 photos A-C Frank E. Poirier, photos D-E Alyson Poirier; Figure 18-9 courtesy Zhou Guoxing, Beijing Natural History Museum; Figure 18-10 courtesy

Frank E. Poirier; Figure 18-11 M. Leakey, *Olduvai Gorge, Vol. 3: Excavations in Beds I and II* (Cambridge University Press), 1971. Copyrighted by and used with the permission of Cambridge University Press.

Chapter 19: Chapter opening photo, Figures 19-1 and 19-2 courtesy Wenner-Gren Foundation for Anthropological Research, Inc., and owner of original specimen; Figures 19-3 and 19-4 reproduced with permission from M.H. Day, *The Fossil History of Man*, 3/e, 1984. Carolina Biology Readers Series, no. 32. Copyright Carolina Biological Supply Co., Burlington, N.C.

Chapter 20: Chapter opening photo courtesy Wenner-Gren Foundation for Anthropological Research, Inc., and owners of original specimen; Figures 20-1 and 20-2 courtesy The Croation Natural History Museum, photos by Dr. F.H. Smith; Figure 20-3 courtesy Georgette Goldberg Haydu; Figure 20-4 Negative # 27935, photo by J. Kirschner, courtesy Department of Library Services, American Museum of Natural History; Figures 20-5 and 20-6 courtesy The Yugoslavian Academy of Sciences and the Arts, photos by Dr. F.H. Smith; Figure 20-7 courtesy Wenner-Gren Foundation for Anthropological Research, Inc., and owners of original specimen; Figure 20-8 courtesy Wu Xinzhi, Institute of Vertebrate Paleontology and Paleoanthropology, Beijing, People's Republic of China.

Chapter 21: Chapter opening photo and Figure 21-1 Negative # 39686, photo by Kirschner, courtesy Department of Library Services, American Museum of Natural History; Figure 21-2 Negative # 322602, courtesy Department of Library Services, American Museum of Natural History; Figure 21-3 Negative # 329853, photo by Logan, courtesy Department of Library Services, American Museum of Natural History; Figure 21-4 Negative # 624832, courtesy Department of Library Services, American Museum of Natural History; Figure 21-5 Negative # 122527, courtesy Department of Library Services, American Museum of Natural History; Figure 21-6 A.J. Kelso and W.R. Trevathan, *Physical Anthropology*, 3/e, © 1984, p. 230. Reprinted by permission of Prentice-Hall, Inc., Englewood Cliffs, N.J.; Figure 21-7 Negative # 323737, photo by Rota, courtesy Department of Library Services, American Museum of Natural History; Figure 21-8 reproduced with permission from M.H. Day, *The Fossil History of Man*, 3/e, 1984. Carolina Biology Readers Series, no. 32, copyright Carolina Biological Supply Co., Burlington, N.C.; Figure 21-9 Negative # 109229, photo by Kirschner, courtesy Department of Library Services, American Museum of Natural History; Figure 21-10 courtesy Dr. J.M. Adovasio, Dept. of Anthropology, University of Pittsburgh.

Chapter 22: Chapter opening photo same as Figure 22-8; Figure 22-1 Barrett/Abrahamoff/Kuraman/Millington, *Biology,* © 1986, p. 671. Reprinted by permission of Prentice Hall, Inc., Englewood Cliffs, New Jersey; Figure 22-2 Dr. Landrum B. Shettles; Figures 22-4, 22-5, 22-8, 22-9 D. Sinclair, *Human Growth After Birth,* 4/e, Oxford University Press, pp. 19, 27, 29, 30.

Chapter 23: Chapter opening photo same as Figure 23-4; Figure 23-1 N.D. Levine, *Human Ecology* (North Scituate, MA: Duxbury Press), 1975, pp. 290-91.

Chapter 24: Chapter opening photo courtesy Alison Galloway; Figure 24-4 Photo Researchers, Inc.; Figures 24-5, 24-6, 24-7 courtesy Dr. Oscar Ward.

Chapter 25: Chapter opening photo and Figure 25-1 Eric Gravé, Photo Researchers, Inc.; Figure 25-2 Barrett/Abrahamoff/Kumaran/Millington, *Biology,* © 1986, p. 321. Reprinted by permission of Prentice Hall, Inc., Englewood Cliffs, New Jersey.

Chapter 26: Chapter opening photo courtesy William Stini; Figure 26-5 Robert Knauft/ © Biology Media 1979/Photo Researchers.

Chapter 27: Chapter opening photo courtesy R. Brooke Thomas; Figure 27-1 I.G. Pawson, C. Jest, in P.T. Baker, ed., *The Biology of High Altitude* (Cambridge: Cambridge University Press, 1978), p. 33. Figures 27-2 and 27-4 Barrett/Abrahamoff/Kuraman/Millington, *Biology,* © 1986, pp. 328 and 300. Reprinted by permission of Prentice Hall, Inc., Englewood Cliffs, New Jersey. Figure 27-5 J.H. Comroe, *Physiology of Respiration* (Chicago: Year Book Medical Publishers, Inc., 1965), p. 161.

Index